# 18th SIGMORPHON Workshop on Computational Research in Phonetics Phonology, and Morphology (SIGMORPHON 2021)

Held online due to COVID-19



Bangkok, Thailand
5 August 2021

ISBN: 978-1-7138-3385-7

**Printed from e-media with permission by:**

Curran Associates, Inc.
57 Morehouse Lane
Red Hook, NY 12571

CURRAN ASSOCIATES INC. proceedings .com

**Some format issues inherent in the e-media version may also appear in this print version.**



Association for Computational Linguistics
209 N. Eighth Street
Stroudsburg, Pennsylvania 18360

Phone: 1-570-476-8006
Fax: 1-570-476-0860

acl@aclweb.org

**Additional copies of this publication are available from:**

Curran Associates, Inc.
57 Morehouse Lane
Red Hook, NY 12571 USA
Phone: 845-758-0400
Fax: 845-758-2633
Email: curran@proceedings.com
Web: www.proceedings.com

SIGMORPHON 2021

# 18th SIGMORPHON Workshop on Computational Research in Phonetics, Phonology, and Morphology

**Proceedings of the Workshop**

August 5, 2021
Bangkok, Thailand (online)

## Preface

Welcome to the 18th SIGMORPHON Workshop on Computational Research in Phonetics, Phonology, and Morphology, to be held on August 5, 2021 as part of a virtual ACL. The workshop aims to bring together researchers interested in applying computational techniques to problems in morphology, phonology, and phonetics. Our program this year highlights the ongoing investigations into how neural models process phonology and morphology, as well as the development of finite-state models for low-resource languages with complex morphology. .

We received 25 submissions, and after a competitive reviewing process, we accepted 14.

The workshop is privileged to present four invited talks this year, all from very respected members of the SIGMORPHON community. Reut Tsarfaty, Kenny Smith, Kristine Yu, and Ekaterina Vylomova all presented talks at this year's workshop.

This year also marks the sixth iteration of the SIGMORPHON Shared Task. Following upon the success of last year's multiple tasks, we again hosted 3 shared tasks:

**Task 0**:

SIGMORPHON's sixth installment of its inflection generation shared task is divided into two parts: Generalization, and cognitive plausibility.

In the first part, participants designed a model that learned to generate morphological inflections from a lemma and a set of morphosyntactic features of the target form, similar to previous year's tasks. This year, participants learned morphological tendencies on a set of development languages, and then generalized these findings to new languages - without much time to adapt their models to new phenomena.

The second part asks participants to inflect nonce words in the past tense, which are then judged for plausibility by native speakers. This task aims to investigate whether state-of-the-art inflectors are learning in a way that mimics human learners.

**Task 1**:

The second SIGMORPHON shared task on grapheme-to-phoneme conversion expands on the task from last year, recategorizing data as belonging to one of three different classes: low-resource, medium-resource, and high-resource.

The task saw 23 submissions from 9 participants.

**Task 2**:

Task 2 continues the effort from the 2020 shared task in unsupervised morphology. Unlike last year's task, which asked participants to implement a complete unsupervised morphology induction pipeline, this year's task concentrates on a single aspect of morphology discovery: paradigm induction. This task asks participants to cluster words into inflectional paradigms, given no more than raw text.

The task saw 14 submissions from 4 teams.

We are grateful to the program committee for their careful and thoughtful reviews of the papers submitted this year. Likewise, we are thankful to the shared task organizers for their hard work in preparing the shared tasks. We are looking forward to a workshop covering a wide range of topics, and we hope for lively discussions.

Garrett Nicolai
Kyle Gorman

Ryan Cotterell

## Organizing Committee

Garrett Nicolai (University of British Columbia, Canada)
Kyle Gorman (City University of New York, USA)
Ryan Cotterell (ETH Zürich, Switzerland)

## Program Committee

Damián Blasi (Harvard University)
Grzegorz Chrupała (Tilburg University)
Jane Chandlee (Haverford College)
Çağrı Çöltekin (University of Tübingen)
Daniel Dakota (Indiana University)
Colin de la Higuera (University of Nantes)
Micha Elsner (The Ohio State University)
Nizar Habash (NYU Abu Dhabi)
Jeffrey Heinz (University of Delaware)
Mans Hulden (University of Colorado)
Adam Jardine (Rutgers University)
Christo Kirov (Google AI)
Greg Kobele (Universität Leipzig)
Grzegorz Kondrak (University of Alberta)
Sandra Kübler (Indiana University)
Adam Lamont (University of Massachusetts Amherst)
Kevin McMullin (University of Ottawa)
Kemal Oflazer (CMU Qatar)
Jeff Parker (Brigham Young University)
Gerald Penn (University of Toronto)
Jelena Prokic (Universiteit Leiden)
Miikka Silfverberg (University of British Columbia)
Kairit Sirts (University of Tartu)
Kenneth Steimel (Indiana University)
Reut Tsarfaty (Bar-Ilan University)
Francis Tyers (Indiana University)
Ekaterina Vylomova (University of Melbourne)
Adina Williams (Facebook AI Research)
Anssi Yli-Jyrä (University of Helsinki)
Kristine Yu (University of Massachusetts)

## Task 0 Organizing Committee

Tiago Pimentel (University of Cambridge)
Brian Leonard (Brian Leonard Consulting)
Maria Ryskina (Carnegie Mellon University)
Sabrina Mielke (Johns Hopkins University)
Coleman Haley (Johns Hopkins University)
Eleanor Chodroff (University of York)
Johann-Mattis List (Max Planck Institute)
Adina Williams (Facebook AI Research)
Ryan Cotterell (ETH Zürich)
Ekaterina Vylomova (University of Melbourne)
Ben Ambridge (University of Liverpool)

## Task 1 Organizing Committee

To come

## Task 2 Organizing Committee

Adam Wiemerslage( University of Colorado Boulder)
Arya McCarthy (Johns Hopkins University)
Alexander Erdmann (Ohio State University)
Manex Agirrezabal (University of Copenhagen)
Garrett Nicolai (University of British Columbia)
Miikka Silfverberg (University of British Columbia)
Mans Hulden (University of Colorado Boulder)
Katharina Kann (University of Colorado Boulder)

# Table of Contents

## Workshop Program

Due to the ongoing pandemic, and the virtual nature of the workshop, the papers will be presented asynchronously, with designated question periods.

*Towards Detection and Remediation of Phonemic Confusion*
Francois Roewer-Despres, Arnold Yeung and Ilan Kogan

*Recursive prosody is not finite-state*
Hossep Dolatian, Aniello De Santo and Thomas Graf

*The Match-Extend serialization algorithm in Multiprecedence*
Maxime Papillon

*What transfers in morphological inflection? Experiments with analogical models*
Micha Elsner

*Simple induction of (deterministic) probabilistic finite-state automata for phonotactics by stochastic gradient descent*
Huteng Dai and Richard Futrell

*Incorporating tone in the calculation of phonotactic probability*
James Kirby

*Recognizing Reduplicated Forms: Finite-State Buffered Machines*
Yang Wang

*An FST morphological analyzer for the Gitksan language*
Clarissa Forbes, Garrett Nicolai and Miikka Silfverberg

*MorphyNet: a Large Multilingual Database of Derivational and Inflectional Morphology*
Khuyagbaatar Batsuren, Gábor Bella and Fausto Giunchiglia

*Comparative Error Analysis in Neural and Finite-state Models for Unsupervised Character-level Transduction*
Maria Ryskina, Eduard Hovy, Taylor Berg-Kirkpatrick and Matthew R. Gormley

*Finite-state Model of Shupamem Reduplication*
Magdalena Markowska, Jeffrey Heinz and Owen Rambow

*A Study of Morphological Robustness of Neural Machine Translation*
Sai Muralidhar Jayanthi and Adithya Pratapa

**No Day Set (continued)**

# Towards Detection and Remediation of Phonemic Confusion

**Francois Roewer-Despres**[1*] **Arnold YS Yeung**[1*] **Ilan Kogan**[2*]
[1]Department of Computer Science [2]Department of Statistics
University of Toronto
{francoisrd, arnoldyeung}@cs.toronto.edu
mail@ilankogan.ca

## Abstract

Reducing communication breakdown is critical to success in interactive NLP applications, such as dialogue systems. To this end, we propose a confusion-mitigation framework for the detection and remediation of communication breakdown. In this work, as a first step towards implementing this framework, we focus on detecting phonemic sources of confusion. As a proof-of-concept, we evaluate two neural architectures in predicting the probability that a listener will misunderstand phonemes in an utterance. We show that both neural models outperform a weighted $n$-gram baseline, showing early promise for the broader framework.

## 1 Introduction

Ensuring that interactive NLP applications, such as dialogue systems, communicate clearly and effectively is critical to their long-term success and viability, especially in high-stakes domains, such as healthcare. Successful systems should thus seek to reduce communication breakdown. One aspect of successful communication is the degree to which each party understands the other. For example, properly diagnosing a patient may necessitate asking logically complex questions, but these questions should be phrased as clearly as possible to promote understanding and mitigate confusion.

To reduce confusion-related communication breakdown, we propose that generative NLP systems integrate a novel confusion-mitigation framework into their natural language generation (NLG) processes. In brief, this framework ensures that such systems avoid transmitting utterances with high predicted probabilities of confusion. In the simplest and most decoupled formulation, an existing NLG component simply produces alternatives to any rejected utterances without additional guiding information. In more advanced and coupled formulations, the NLG and confusion prediction components can be closely integrated to better determine precisely how to avoid confusion. This process can also be conditioned on models of the current listener or task to achieve personalized or context-dependent results. Figure 1 shows the simplest variant of the framework.

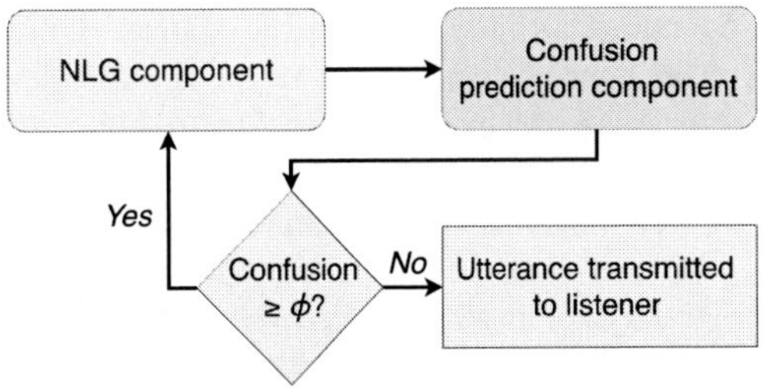


Figure 1: A simplified variant of our proposed confusion-mitigation framework, which enables generative NLP systems to detect and remediate confusion-related communication breakdown. The confusion prediction component predicts the confusion probability of candidate utterances, which are rejected if this probability is above a decision threshold, $\phi$.

As a first step towards implementing this framework, we work towards developing its central confusion prediction component, which predicts the confusion probability of an utterance. In this work, we specifically target phonemic confusion, that is, the misidentification of heard phonemes by a listener. We consider two potential neural architectures for this purpose: a fixed-context, feed-forward network and a residual, bidirectional LSTM network. We train these models using a novel proxy data set derived from audiobook recordings, and compare their performance to that of a weighted $n$-gram baseline.

[*] Equal contribution.



*Proceedings of the Seventeenth SIGMORPHON Workshop on Computational Research in Phonetics, Phonology, and Morphology*, pages 1–10

## 2 Background and Related Work

Prior work focused on identifying confusion in natural language, rather than proactively altering it to help reduce communication breakdown, as our framework proposes. For example, Batliner et al. (2003) showed that certain features of recorded speech (e.g., repetition, hyperarticulation, strong emphasis) can be used to identify communication breakdown. The authors relied primarily on prosodic properties of recorded phrases, rather than the underlying phonemes, words, or semantics, for identifying communication breakdown. On the other hand, conversational repair is a turn-level process in which conversational partners first identify and then remediate communication breakdown as part of a trouble-source repair (TSR) sequence (Sacks et al., 1974). Using this approach, Orange et al. (1996) identified differences in TSR patterns amongst people with no, early-stage, and middle-stage Alzheimer's, highlighting the usefulness of communication breakdown detection. However, such work does not directly address the issue of proactive confusion mitigation and remediation, which the more advanced formulation of our framework aims to address through listener and task conditioning. Our focus is on the simpler formulation in this preliminary work.

Rothwell (2010) identified four types of noise that may cause confusion: physical noise (e.g., a loud highway), physiological noise (e.g., hearing impairment), psychological noise (e.g., attentiveness of listener), and semantic noise (e.g., word choice). We postulate that mitigating confusion resulting from each type of noise may be possible, at least to some extent, given sufficient context to make an informed compensatory decision. For example, given a particularly physically noisy environment, speaking loudly would seem appropriate. Unfortunately, such contextual information is often lacking from existing data sets. In particular, the physiological and psychological states of listeners is rarely recorded. Even when such information is recorded (e.g., in Alzheimer's speech studies Orange et al., 1996), the information is very coarse (e.g, broad Alzheimer's categories such as `none`, `early-stage`, and `middle-stage`).

We leave these non-trivial data gathering challenges as future work, instead focusing on phonemic confusion, which is significantly easier to operationalize. In practice, confusion at the phoneme-level may arise from any category of Rothwell noise. It may also arise from the natural similarities between phonemes (discussed next). While many of these will not be represented in the text-based phonemic transcriptions data set used in this preliminary work, our approach can be extended to include them.

Researchers in speech processing have studied the prediction of phonemic confusion but, to our knowledge, this work has not been adapted to utterance generation. Instead, tasks such as preventing of sound-alike medication errors (i.e., naming medications so that two medications do not sound identical) are common (Lambert, 1997). Zgank and Kacic (2012) showed that the potential confusability of a word can be estimated by calculating the Levenshtein distance (Levenshtein, 1966) of its phonemic transcription to that of all others in the vocabulary. We take inspiration from Zgank and Kacic (2012) and employ a phoneme-level Levenshtein distance approach in this work.

In the basic definition of the Levenshtein distance, all errors are equally weighted. In practice, however, words that share many similar or identical phonemes are more likely to be confused for one another. Given this, Sabourin and Fabiani (2000) developed a *weighted* phoneme-level Levenshtein distance, where weights are determined by a human expert or a learned model, such as a hidden Markov model. Unfortunately, while these weights are meant to represent phonemic similarity, selecting an appropriate distance metric in phoneme space is non-trivial. The classical results of Miller (1954) and Miller and Nicely (1955) group phonemes experimentally based on the noise level at which they become indiscernible. The authors identify voicing, nasality, affrication, duration, and place of articulation as sub-phoneme features that predict a phoneme's sensitivity to distortion, and therefore measure its proximity to others. Unfortunately, later work showed that these controlled conditions do not map cleanly to the real world (Batliner et al., 2003). In addition, Wickelgren (1965) found alternative phonemic distance features that could be adapted into a distance metric.

While this prior research sought to directly define a distance metric between phonemes based on sub-phoneme features, since no method has emerged as clearly superior, researchers now favour direct, empirical measures of confusability (Bailey and Hahn, 2005). Likewise, our work assumes that these classical feature-engineering approaches to predicting phoneme confusability can be improved upon with neural approaches, just as automatic speech recognition (ASR) systems have been improved through the use of similar methods (e.g., Seide et al., 2011; Zeyer et al., 2019; Kumar et al., 2020). In addition, these classical approaches do not account for context (i.e., other phonemes surrounding the phoneme of interest), whereas our approach conditions on such context to refine the confusion estimate.

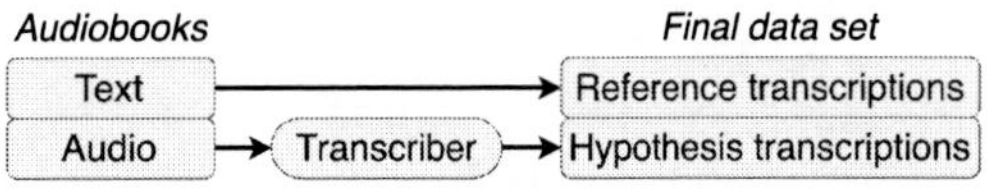


Figure 2: We create a new data set with parallel reference and hypothesis transcriptions from audiobook data with parallel text and audio recordings. The text simply becomes the reference transcriptions. A transcriber converts the audio recordings into hypothesis transcriptions. In this preliminary work, we use an ASR system as a proxy for human transcribers.

## 3 Data

### 3.1 Data Gathering Process

To predict the phonemic confusability of utterances, we would ideally use a data set in which each utterance is annotated with speaker phonemic transcription (the reference transcription), as well as listener perceived phonemic transcription (the hypothesis transcription). We could then compare these transcriptions to identify phonemic confusion.

To the best of our knowledge, a data set of this type does not exist. The English Consistent Confusion Corpus contains a collection of individual words spoken against a noisy background, with human listener transcriptions (Marxer et al., 2016). This is similar to our ideal data set, however the words are spoken in isolation, and thus without any utterance context. This same issue arises in the Diagnostic Rhyme Test and its derivative data sets (Voiers et al., 1975; Greenspan et al., 1998). Other corpora, such as the BioScope Corpus (Vincze et al., 2008) and the AMI Corpus (Carletta et al., 2005), contain annotations of dialogue acts, which represent the intention of the speaker in producing each utterance (e.g., asking a question is labeled with the dialogue act `elicit_information`). However, dialogue acts relating to confusion only appear when a listener explicitly requests clarification from the speaker. This does not provide fine-grained information regarding which phonemes caused the confusion, nor does it capture any instances of confusion in which the listener does not explicitly vocalize their confusion.

We thus create a new data set for this work (Figure 2). The Parallel Audiobook Corpus contains 121 hours of recorded speech data across 59 speakers (Ribeiro, 2018). We use four of its audiobooks: *Adventures of Huckleberry Finn*, *Emma*, *Treasure Island*, and *The Adventures of Sherlock Holmes*. Crucially, the audio recordings in this corpus are aligned with the text being read, which allows us to create aligned reference and hypothesis transcriptions. For each text-audio pair, the text simply becomes the reference transcriptions, while a transcriber converts the audio into hypothesis transcriptions. Given the preliminary nature of this work, we create a proxy data set in which we use Google Cloud's publicly-available ASR system as a proxy for human transcribers (Cloud, 2019). We then process these transcriptions to identify phonemic confusion events (as described in Section 3.2). The final data set contains 84,253 parallel transcriptions. We split these into 63,189 training, 10,532 validation, and 10,532 test transcriptions (a 75%-12.5%-12.5% split). The average reference and hypothesis transcription lengths are 65.2 and 62.3 phonemes, respectively. The transcription error rate (i.e., the proportion of phonemes that are mis-transcribed) is only 8%, so there is significant imbalance in the data set.

For the purposes of this preliminary work, the Google Cloud ASR system (Cloud, 2019) is an acceptable proxy for human transcription ability under the reasonable assumption that, for any particular transcriber, the distribution of error rates across different phoneme sequences is nonuniform (i.e., within-transcriber variation is present). This assumption holds in all practical cases, and is reasonable since the confusion-mitigation framework we propose can be conditioned on different transcribers to control for inter-transcriber variation as future work.

### 3.2 Transcription Error Labeling

We post-process our aligned reference-hypothesis transcription data set in two steps. First, each transcription must be converted from the word-level to the phoneme-level. For this, we use the CMU Pronouncing Dictionary (Weide, 1998), which is based on the ARPAbet symbol set. For any words with multiple phonemic conversions, we simply

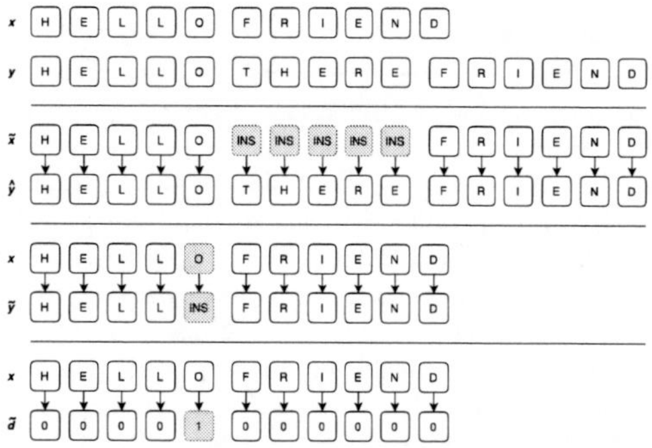


Figure 3: Illustration of our transcription error labeling process (using letters instead of phonemes for readability). Given aligned reference ($\boldsymbol{x}$) and hypothesis ($\boldsymbol{y}$) vectors, we use the Levenshtein algorithm to ensure they have the same length. Because $\boldsymbol{y}$ is not available at test time, we then "collapse" consecutive insertion tokens to force the vectors to have the original length of $\boldsymbol{x}$. Finally, we replace $\tilde{\boldsymbol{y}}$ with the binary vector $\tilde{\boldsymbol{d}}$, which has 1's wherever $\boldsymbol{x}$ and $\tilde{\boldsymbol{y}}$ don't match.

default to the first conversion returned by the API.

Second, we label each resulting phoneme in each reference transcription as either correctly or incorrectly transcribed. This is nontrivial, because the number of phonemes in the reference and hypothesis transcriptions are rarely equal, and thus require phoneme-level alignment. For this purpose, we use a variant of the phoneme-level Levenshtein distance that returns the actual alignment, rather than the final distance score (Figure 3).

Formally, let $\boldsymbol{x} \in \mathbb{K}^a$ be a vector of reference phonemes and $\boldsymbol{y} \in \mathbb{K}^b$ be a vector of hypothesis phonemes from the data set. $\mathbb{K}$ refers to the set $\{1, 2, 3, \ldots, k, \texttt{<INS>}, \texttt{<DEL>}, \texttt{<SOS>}, \texttt{<EOS>}\}$, where $k$ is the number of unique phonemes in the language being considered (e.g., in English, $k \approx 40$ depending on the dialect). In general, $a \neq b$, but we can manipulate the vectors by incorporating insertion, deletion, and substitution tokens (as done in the Levenshtein distance algorithm). In general, this yields two vectors of the same length, $\tilde{\boldsymbol{x}}, \tilde{\boldsymbol{y}} \in \mathbb{K}^c, c = \max(a, b)$. While this manipulation can be performed at training time because $\boldsymbol{y}$ and $b$ are known, such information is unavailable at test time. Therefore, we modify the alignment at training time to ensure $\tilde{\boldsymbol{x}} \equiv \boldsymbol{x}$ and $c \equiv a$. To achieve this, we "collapse" consecutive insertion tokens into a single instance of the insertion token, which ensures that $|\tilde{\boldsymbol{y}}| = a$.

Additionally, we assume that each hypothesis phoneme, $\tilde{y}_i \in \tilde{\boldsymbol{y}}$, is conditionally independent of the others. That is, $P(\tilde{y}_i = x_i \mid \boldsymbol{x}, \tilde{y}_{\neq i}) = P(\tilde{y}_i = x_i \mid \boldsymbol{x})$.[1] We hypothesize that this assumption, similar to the conditional independence assumption of Naïve Bayes (Zhang, 2004), will still yield directionally-correct results, while drastically increasing the tractability of the computation.

This assumption also allows us to simplify the output space of the problem. Specifically, since we only care to predict $P(\tilde{\boldsymbol{y}} \neq \boldsymbol{x})$, with this assumption, we now only need to consider, for each $i$, whether $\tilde{y}_i = x_i$, rather than dealing with the much harder problem of predicting the exact value of $\tilde{y}_i$. To achieve this, we use an element-wise Kronecker delta function to replace $\tilde{\boldsymbol{y}}$ with a binary vector, $\tilde{\boldsymbol{d}}$, such that $\tilde{d}_i \leftarrow \tilde{y}_i \neq x_i$. Thus, the binary vector $\tilde{\boldsymbol{d}}$ records the position of each transcription error, that is, the position of each phoneme in $\boldsymbol{x}$ that was confused.

With the $\boldsymbol{x}$'s as inputs and the $\tilde{\boldsymbol{d}}$'s as ground truth labels, we can train models to predict $P(\tilde{d}_i \mid \boldsymbol{x})$ for each $i$. As a post-processing step, we can then combine these individual probabilities to estimate the utterance-level probability of phonemic confusion, $P(\tilde{\boldsymbol{y}} \neq \boldsymbol{x})$, which is the output of the central confusion prediction component in Figure 1.

This formulation is general in the sense that any $x_i$ can affect the predicted probability of any $\tilde{d}_i$. In practice, however, and especially for long utterances, this is overly conservative, as only nearby phonemes are likely to have a significant effect. In Section 4, we describe any additional conditional independence assumptions that each architecture makes to further simplify its probability estimate.

## 4 Model Architectures and Baseline

With recent advances, various neural architectures have been applied to NLP tasks. Early work includes $n$-gram-based, fully-connected architectures for language modeling tasks (Bengio et al., 2003; Mikolov et al., 2013). Recurrent neural network (RNN) architectures were then shown to be successful for applications such as language modeling, speech recognition, and phoneme recognition (Graves and Schmidhuber, 2005; Mikolov et al., 2011). RNN architectures such as the LSTM (Hochreiter and Schmidhuber, 1997) and GRU (Chung et al., 2015) variants had been successful in many NLP applications, such as machine language translation and phoneme classification (Sundermeyer et al., 2012; Graves et al., 2013; Graves

[1] $\tilde{y}_{\neq i}$ is every element in $\tilde{\boldsymbol{y}}$ except the one at position $i$.

and Schmidhuber, 2005). Recently, the transformer architecture (Vaswani et al., 2017), which uses attention instead of recurrence to form dependencies between inputs, has shown state-of-the-art results in many areas of NLP, including syllable-based tasks (e.g., Zhou et al., 2018).

In this work, we propose a fixed-context-window architecture and a residual bi-LSTM architecture for the central component of our confusion-mitigation framework. While similar architectures have already been applied to phoneme-based applications, such as phoneme recognition and classification (Graves and Schmidhuber, 2005; Weninger et al., 2015; Graves et al., 2013; Li et al., 2017), to our knowledge, our study is the first to apply these architectures to identify phonemes related to confusion for listeners. In our opinion, these architectures strike an acceptable balance between compute and capability for this current work, unlike the more advanced transformer architectures, which require significantly more resources to train.[2]

Since the data set is imbalanced (see Section 3.1), without sample weighting, early experiments showed that both architectures never identified any phonemes as likely to be mis-transcribed (i.e., high specificity, low sensitivity). Accordingly, since the imbalance ratio is approximately 1:10, transcription errors are given 10-times more weight than properly-transcribed phonemes in our binary cross-entropy loss function.

### 4.1 Fixed-Context Network

The fixed-context network takes as input the current phoneme, $x_i$, and the 4 phonemes before and after it as a fixed window of context (Figure 4a). This results in the additional conditional independence assumption that $P(\tilde{d}_i \mid \boldsymbol{x}) = P(\tilde{d}_i \mid x_{i-4:i+4})$. That is, only phonemes within the fixed context window of size 4 can affect the predicted probability of $\tilde{d}_i$.

These 9 phonemes are first embedded in a 15-dimensional embedding space. The embedding layer is followed by a sequence of seven fully-connected hidden layers with 512, 256, 256, 128, 128, 64, and 64 neurons respectively. Each layer is separated by Rectified Linear Unit (ReLU) non-linearities (Nair and Hinton, 2010; He et al., 2016). Finally, an output with a sigmoid activation function predicts the probability of a transcription error. We train with minibatches of size 32, using the Adam optimizer with parameters $\alpha = 0.001$, $\beta_1 = 0.9$, and $\beta_2 = 0.999$ (Kingma and Ba, 2014) to optimize a 1:10 weighted binary cross-entropy loss function. We explored alternative parameter settings, and in particular a larger number of neurons, but found this architecture to be the most stable and highest performing of all variants tested, given the nature and relatively small size of the data set.

### 4.2 LSTM Network

The LSTM network receives the entire reference transcription, $\boldsymbol{x}$, as input and predicts the entire binarized hypothesis transcription, $\tilde{\boldsymbol{d}}$, as output (Figure 4b). Since the LSTM is bidirectional, we do not introduce any additional conditional independence assumptions. Each input phoneme is passed through an embedding layer of dimension 42 (equal to $|\mathbb{K}|$) followed by a bidirectional LSTM layer and two residual linear blocks with ReLU activations (He et al., 2016). An output residual linear block with a sigmoid activation predicts the probability of a transcription error. These skip connections are added since residual layers tend to outperform simpler alternatives (He et al., 2016). Passing the embedded input via skip connections ensures that the original input is accessible at all depths of the network, and also helps mitigate against any vanishing gradients that may arise in the LSTM.

We use the following output dimensions for each layer: 50 for LSTM hidden and cell states, 40 for the first residual linear block, and 10 for the second. We train with minibatches of size 256, using the Adam optimizer with parameters $\alpha = 0.00005$, $\beta_1 = 0.9$, and $\beta_2 = 0.999$ (Kingma and Ba, 2014) to optimize a 1:10 weighted binary cross-entropy loss function.

### 4.3 Weighted $n$-Gram Baseline

We compare our neural models to a weighted $n$-gram baseline model. That is, $\tilde{d}_i$ depends only on the $n$ previous phonemes in $\boldsymbol{x}$ (an order-$n$ Markov assumption). Formally, we make the conditional independence assumption that $P(\tilde{d}_i \mid \boldsymbol{x}) = p(\tilde{d}_i \mid x_{i-n+1:i})$. Extending this baseline model to include future phonemes would violate the order-$n$ Markov assumption that is standard in $n$-gram approaches. In this preliminary work, we opt to keep the baseline as standard as possible.

A weighted $n$-gram model is computed using an algorithm similar to the standard maximum likelihood estimation (MLE) $n$-gram counting algo-

[2]Link to code: https://github.com/francois-rd/phonemic-confusion

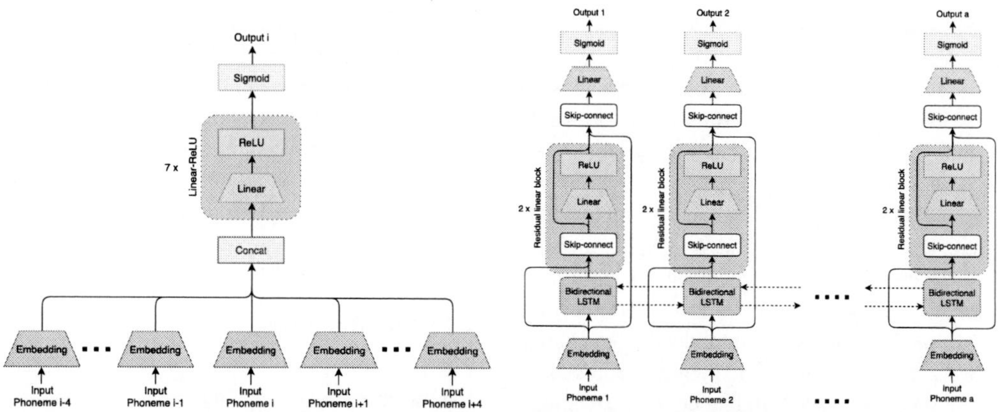


(a) The fixed-context network uses a fixed window of context of size 4. These 9 phonemes are embedded using a shared embedding layer, concatenated, and then passed through 7 linear layers with ReLU activations, followed by an output layer with a sigmoid activation.

(b) Unrolled architecture of the LSTM network. The architecture consists of one bidirectional LSTM layer, two residual linear blocks with ReLU activations, and an output residual linear block with a sigmoid activation. Additional skip connections are added throughout.

Figure 4: Architectural variants of the confusion prediction component of our confusion-mitigation framework.

rithm, but with the introduction of a weighting scheme to deal with the class imbalance issue. The weighting is necessary for a fair comparison to the weighted loss function used in the neural network models. This approaches generalizes the standard MLE $n$-gram counting algorithm, which implicitly uses a weight of 1.

Formally, let $W > 0$ be the selected weight, and define $c_i \equiv x_{i-n+1:i}$ to simplify the notation. Also, let $C(\tilde{d}_i \mid c_i)$ be the *count* of all incorrect phoneme transcriptions in the context $c_i$ in the entire data set, and similarly, $C(1 - \tilde{d}_i \mid c_i)$ for correct transcriptions.[3] The weighted $n$-gram is then computed as follows:

$$P(\tilde{d}_i \mid c_i) = \frac{W \times C(\tilde{d}_i \mid c_i)}{C(1 - \tilde{d}_i \mid c_i) + W \times C(\tilde{d}_i \mid c_i)}$$

Empirically, we find that a weighted 3-gram model works best; larger contexts are too sparse given the size of the data set and smaller contexts lack expressive capacity. We do not use any $n$-gram smoothing methods. Instead, any missing contexts encountered at test time are simply marked as incorrect predictions. For this particular data set, such missing contexts are vanishingly rare (occurring only 0.003% of the time), which justifies our approach.

[3]We slightly abuse the notation here. Recall that $\tilde{d}_i \leftarrow \tilde{y}_i \neq x_i$, so we notate $\tilde{y}_i = x_i$ as $1 - \tilde{d}_i$.

## 5 Results and Discussion

### 5.1 Quantitative Analysis

We report receiver operating characteristic (ROC) curves for all models (Figure 5). To facilitate fair comparison, all models are trained with the same random ordering of training data in each epoch. Both neural network architectures outperform the weighted $n$-gram baseline by a small margin, with the fixed-context network appearing to perform slightly better overall. While no individual model exhibits any significant performance gain over the others, all models perform significantly better than random chance. This shows the promise of our framework, which is precisely the objective of this work. We next speculate as to the causes of the slight gaps that are observed.

The neural network models likely outperform the weighted $n$-gram baseline for multiple reasons. First, both neural network models condition on a context that includes both past and future phonemes (i.e., bidirectional), whereas the baseline only conditions on past phonemes (i.e., unidirectional). Utilizing future phonemes as context is useful since both humans and most state-of-the-art ASR systems use this information to revise their predictions. Second, the neural networks can learn subcontextual patterns that the baseline cannot. For example, the contexts `A B C` and `A B D` have the sub-context `A B` in common. Whereas the weighted $n$-gram treats these as completely dif-

| Ground Truth Phrase | Transcription of Audio Recording |
|---|---|
| ... for they say **every body** is in love once ... | ... for they say **everybody** is in love once ... |
| ... his grave **looks shewed** that she was not ... | ... his grave **look showed** that she was not ... |
| ... shall use the carriage **to night** ... | ... shall use the carriage **tonight** ... |
| ... making him understand I **warn't** dead ... | ... making him understand I **warrant** dead ... |
| ... **shore** at that place so we **warn't** afraid ... | ... **sure** at that place so we **weren't** afraid ... |
| ... read Elton's **letter as** I was **shewn** in ... | ... read Elton's **letters** I was **shown** in ... |
| ... sacrifice my poor **hair to night** and ... | ... sacrifice my poor **head tonight** and ... |
| ... we **warn't** feeling just right ... | ... we **weren't** feeling just right ... |
| ... that there was no **want of taste** ... | ... that there was no **on toothpaste** ... |
| ... knew **that Arthur had** discovered ... | ... knew **was it also have** discovered ... |

Table 1: Randomly selected phrases from amongst the top 100 phonemes predicted to be *incorrectly* transcribed by the fixed-context model (transcription error probability $> 0.999$). Bold text denotes ASR transcription errors.

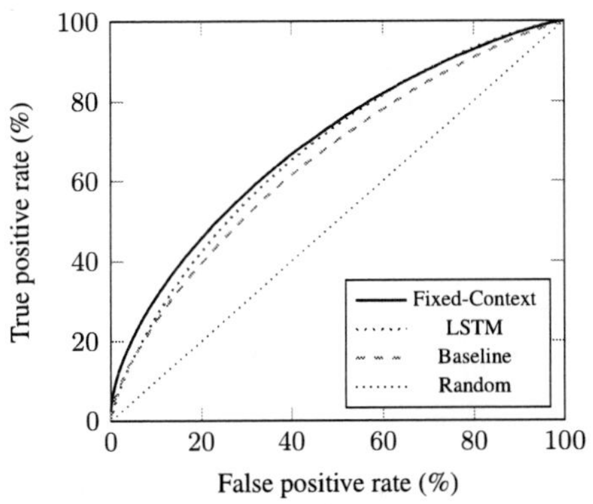


Figure 5: ROC curves for our model variants.

ferent contexts, the neural networks may be able to exploit the similarity between them. This kind of parameter sharing is more data efficient, which can lead to lower variance estimates (less overfitting) in the small data set setting we are considering.

The simpler fixed-context network slightly outperforms the more complex LSTM alternative. While RNN architectures have been shown to outperform feed-forward networks in language processing tasks (Sundermeyer et al., 2012), other research has shown that simpler architectures are still able to process phonemic data effectively (Ba and Caruana, 2014). The lack of an additional conditional independence assumption for the LSTM model may have resulted in worse data efficiency, since the model needs to expend parameters on all reference phonemes, even those very far away that may have little impact on the current one. In addition, the smaller number of parameters to estimate may have lead to lower variance in the fixed-context model. Given this, our avoidance of more advanced or deeper model, such as transformers, seems justified for this preliminary work. We hypothesize that such models could outperform all the models considered here given a significantly larger data set.

## 5.2 Qualitative Analysis

### 5.2.1 Description

We perform qualitative error analysis on randomly selected phonemes from amongst those that are most (Table 1) and least (Table 2) likely to contain transcription errors according to the fixed-context model. This offers some qualitative insights regarding phonemic confusion. We sample from the fixed-context model due to its slightly superior performance, and show small phrases centered around the phoneme most (least) likely to cause confusion, rather than full transcriptions, for clarity.

In addition, to improve readability, we show words rather than the underlying phonemes. As a result, some of the errors appear to be orthographic in nature even if they are not. For example, "every body" becomes "everybody" in the first example of Table 1. However, the phonemes that constitute "every body" and "everybody" are indeed different: "`EH V` **`ER`** `IY B AA D IY`" versus "`EH V` **`R`** `IY B AA D IY`". As per our definitions in Section 3.2, these cases do represent transcription errors. However, it may be argued that such errors introduce unwanted noise in the data set, which we hope to correct in future work.

### 5.2.2 Analysis

First, we note that every sample in Table 1 does indeed have a transcription error, while few sam-

| Ground Truth Phrase | Transcription of Audio Recording |
|---|---|
| ... the exquisite feelings of delight and ... | ... the exquisite feelings of delight and ... |
| ... gone Mister Knightley called ... | ... gone Mister Knightley called ... |
| ... has been exceptionally ... | ... has been exceptionally ... |
| ... not afraid **of your** seeing ... | ... not afraid **if you're** saying ... |
| ... the sale of Randalls was long ... | ... the sale of Randalls was long ... |
| ... her very kind reception **of** himself ... | ... her very kind reception **to** himself ... |
| ... for the purpose of preparatory inspection ... | ... for the purpose of preparatory inspection ... |
| ... you would not be happy until you ... | ... you would not be happy until you ... |
| ... with the exception of this little blot ... | ... with the exception of this little blot ... |
| ... night we were in a great bustle getting ... | ... night we were in a great bustle getting ... |

Table 2: Randomly selected phrases from amongst the top 100 phonemes predicted to be *correctly* transcribed by the fixed-context model (transcription error probability $< 0.03$). Bold text denotes ASR transcription errors.

ples have errors in Table 2. It therefore seems as though, when the fixed-context model is very certain about the presence or absence of errors, it is usually correct.

Second, many of the transcription errors in Table 1 are seemingly caused by the archaic or idiosyncratic writing present in the books used to create the data set. While this can be seen as a source of unwanted noise (we used an ASR system trained on standard modern English), we argue that, as per Rothwell's model of communication (Section 2), familiarity with the vocabulary is, in fact, a very legitimate source of semantic noise. Indeed, phrases using more modern and standard vernacular are seemingly less likely to be confusing, according to the fixed-context model.

Third, many of the errors not related to archaism involve stop words, homonyms, or near-homophones, which intuitively makes sense. Additionally, hard consonant sounds between words (and stress at the beginning rather than at the end of words) appears more common in the set of correctly-transcribed phrases as compared to the set of incorrectly-transcribed ones. These findings suggest the fixed-context model has picked up on some underlying patterns governing phonemic confusion, which is promising for our confusion-mitigation framework as a whole.

### 5.3 Future Work

This work uses a relatively small data set. Creating and using a significantly larger corpus using human subjects rather than an ASR proxy would likely yield more directly relevant results. We postulate that, with a larger and higher quality data set, a deeper and more advanced neural network architecture, such as the transformer, may produce stronger results. Future work can also investigate the differences in human phonemic confusability on 'natural' versus semantically-unpredictable sentences.

A major aspect of our confusion-mitigation framework, which we have not explored in this work, is the generation of alternative, clearer utterances that retain the initial meaning. Constructively enumerating these alternatives is non-trivial, as is identifying the neighbourhood beyond which their meaning differs too significantly from the original. Conditioning on a specific listener's priors as an additional mechanism to reduce communication breakdown is another major aspect we leave to future work.

Perhaps most significantly, we have limited the scope of our confusion assessment drastically in this preliminary work, primarily to simplify the data gathering process. While our results are promising, communication breakdown is a nuanced and multi-faceted phenomenon of which phonemic confusion is but one small component. Modeling these larger and more complex processes remains an important open challenge.

## 6 Conclusion

Reducing communication breakdown is critical to successful interaction in dialogue systems and other generative NLP systems. In this work, we proposed a novel confusion-mitigation framework that such systems could employ to help minimize the probability of human confusion during an interaction. As a first step towards implementing this framework, we evaluated two potential neural architectures—a fixed-context network and an LSTM network—for its central component, which predicts the confusion probability of a candidate utterance. These neural architectures outperformed a weighted $n$-gram baseline (with the fixed-context network performing best overall) when trained using a proxy data set derived from audiobook recordings. In addition, qualitative analyses suggest that the fixed-context model has uncovered some of the more intuitive causes of phonemic confusion, including stop words, homonyms, near-homophones, and familiarity with the vocabulary. These preliminary results show the promise of our confusion-mitigation framework. Given this early success, further investigation and refinement is warranted.

## Acknowledgments

Resources used in preparing this research were provided, in part, by the Province of Ontario, the Government of Canada through CIFAR, and companies sponsoring the Vector Institute (www.vectorinstitute.ai/partners).

## References

Jimmy Ba and Rich Caruana. 2014. Do Deep Nets Really Need to be Deep? In Z. Ghahramani, M. Welling, C. Cortes, N. D. Lawrence, and K. Q. Weinberger, editors, *Advances in Neural Information Processing Systems 27*, pages 2654–2662. Curran Associates, Inc.

Todd M. Bailey and Ulrike Hahn. 2005. Phoneme similarity and confusability. *Journal of Memory and Language*, 52(3):339–362.

Anton Batliner, Kerstin Fischer, Richard Huber, Jörg Spilker, and Elmar Nöth. 2003. How to find trouble in communication. *Speech Communication*, 40(1-2):117–143.

Yoshua Bengio, Réjean Ducharme, Pascal Vincent, and Christian Jauvin. 2003. A neural probabilistic language model. *Journal of Machine Learning Research*, 3(Feb):1137–1155.

Jean Carletta, Simone Ashby, Sebastien Bourban, Mike Flynn, Mael Guillemot, Thomas Hain, Jaroslav Kadlec, Vasilis Karaiskos, Wessel Kraaij, Melissa Kronenthal, et al. 2005. The AMI Meeting Corpus: A Pre-Announcement. In *International Workshop on Machine Learning for Multimodal Interaction*, pages 28–39. Springer.

Junyoung Chung, Caglar Gulcehre, Kyunghyun Cho, and Yoshua Bengio. 2015. Gated Feedback Recurrent Neural Networks. In *International Conference on Machine Learning*, pages 2067–2075.

Google Cloud. 2019. Speech-to-Text Client Libraries.

Alex Graves, Abdel-rahman Mohamed, and Geoffrey Hinton. 2013. Speech recognition with deep recurrent neural networks. In *2013 IEEE International Conference on Acoustics, Speech and Signal Processing*, pages 6645–6649. IEEE.

Alex Graves and Jürgen Schmidhuber. 2005. Framewise phoneme classification with bidirectional LSTM and other neural network architectures. *Neural Networks*, 18(5-6):602–610.

Steven L Greenspan, Raymond W Bennett, and Ann K Syrdal. 1998. An evaluation of the diagnostic rhyme test. *International Journal of Speech Technology*, 2(3):201–214.

Kaiming He, Xiangyu Zhang, Shaoqing Ren, and Jian Sun. 2016. Deep Residual Learning for Image Recognition. In *2016 IEEE Conference on Computer Vision and Pattern Recognition (CVPR)*, pages 770–778. ISSN: 1063-6919.

Sepp Hochreiter and Jürgen Schmidhuber. 1997. Long Short-Term Memory. *Neural Computation*, 9(8):1735–1780.

Diederik P Kingma and Jimmy Ba. 2014. Adam: A method for stochastic optimization. *arXiv preprint arXiv:1412.6980*.

Kshitiz Kumar, Chaojun Liu, Yifan Gong, and Jian Wu. 2020. 1-D Row-Convolution LSTM: Fast Streaming ASR at Accuracy Parity with LC-BLSTM. *Proc. Interspeech 2020*, pages 2107–2111.

Bruce L. Lambert. 1997. Predicting look-alike and sound-alike medication errors. *American Journal of Health-System Pharmacy*, 54(10):1161–1171.

Vladimir I Levenshtein. 1966. Binary codes capable of correcting deletions, insertions, and reversals. In *Soviet Physics Doklady*, volume 10, pages 707–710.

Kun Li, Xiaojun Qian, and Helen Meng. 2017. Mispronunciation Detection and Diagnosis in L2 English Speech Using Multidistribution Deep Neural Networks. *IEEE/ACM Transactions on Audio, Speech, and Language Processing*, 25(1):193–207.

Ricard Marxer, Jon Barker, Martin Cooke, and Maria Luisa Garcia Lecumberri. 2016. A corpus of noise-induced word misperceptions for English. *The Journal of the Acoustical Society of America*, 140(5):EL458–EL463.

Tomáš Mikolov, Stefan Kombrink, Lukáš Burget, Jan Černocký, and Sanjeev Khudanpur. 2011. Extensions of recurrent neural network language model. In *2011 IEEE International Conference on Acoustics, Speech and Signal Processing (ICASSP)*, pages 5528–5531. IEEE.

Tomas Mikolov, Ilya Sutskever, Kai Chen, Greg S. Corrado, and Jeff Dean. 2013. Distributed Representations of Words and Phrases and their Compositionality. In *Advances in neural information processing systems*, pages 3111–3119.

George A. Miller. 1954. An Analysis of the Confusion among English Consonants Heard in the Presence of Random Noise. *Journal of The Acoustical Society of America*, 26.

George A. Miller and Patricia E. Nicely. 1955. An analysis of perceptual confusions among some English consonants. *The Journal of the Acoustical Society of America*, 27(2):338–352.

Vinod Nair and Geoffrey E Hinton. 2010. Rectified linear units improve restricted boltzmann machines. In *Icml*.

John B. Orange, Rosemary B. Lubinski, and D. Jeffery Higginbotham. 1996. Conversational Repair by Individuals with Dementia of the Alzheimer's Type. *Journal of Speech, Language, and Hearing Research*, 39(4):881–895.

Manuel Sam Ribeiro. 2018. Parallel Audiobook Corpus. University of Edinburgh School of Informatics.

J. Dan Rothwell. 2010. *In the Company of Others: An Introduction to Communication*. New York: Oxford University Press.

Michael Sabourin and Marc Fabiani. 2000. Predicting auditory confusions using a weighted Levinstein distance. US Patent 6,073,099.

Harvey Sacks, Emanuel Schegloff, and Gail Jefferson. 1974. A Simple Systematic for the Organisation of Turn-Taking in Conversation. *Language*, 50:696–735.

Frank Seide, Gang Li, and Dong Yu. 2011. Conversational Speech Transcription Using Context-Dependent Deep Neural Networks. In *Twelfth Annual Conference of the International Speech Communication Association*.

Martin Sundermeyer, Ralf Schlüter, and Hermann Ney. 2012. LSTM Neural Networks for Language Modeling. In *Thirteenth Annual Conference of the International Speech Communication Association*.

Ashish Vaswani, Noam Shazeer, Niki Parmar, Jakob Uszkoreit, Llion Jones, Aidan N Gomez, Łukasz Kaiser, and Illia Polosukhin. 2017. Attention is all you need. *arXiv preprint arXiv:1706.03762*.

Veronika Vincze, György Szarvas, Richárd Farkas, György Móra, and János Csirik. 2008. The BioScope corpus: biomedical texts annotated for uncertainty, negation and their scopes. *BMC Bioinformatics*, 9(11):S9.

William D Voiers, Alan D Sharpley, and Carl J Hehmsoth. 1975. *Research on Diagnostic Evaluation of Speech Intelligibility*. Research Report AFCRL-72-0694, Air Force Cambridge Research Laboratories, Bedford, Massachusetts.

Robert L. Weide. 1998. The CMU pronouncing dictionary. *The Speech Group*.

Felix Weninger, Hakan Erdogan, Shinji Watanabe, Emmanuel Vincent, Jonathan Le Roux, John R Hershey, and Björn Schuller. 2015. Speech Enhancement with LSTM Recurrent Neural Networks and its Application to Noise-Robust ASR. In *International Conference on Latent Variable Analysis and Signal Separation*, pages 91–99. Springer.

Wayne A. Wickelgren. 1965. Acoustic similarity and intrusion errors in short-term memory. *Journal of Experimental Psychology*, 70(1):102.

Albert Zeyer, Parnia Bahar, Kazuki Irie, Ralf Schlüter, and Hermann Ney. 2019. A Comparison of Transformer and LSTM Encoder Decoder Models for ASR. In *2019 IEEE Automatic Speech Recognition and Understanding Workshop (ASRU)*, pages 8–15. IEEE.

Andrej Zgank and Zdravko Kacic. 2012. Predicting the Acoustic Confusability between Words for a Speech Recognition System using Levenshtein Distance. *Elektronika ir Elektrotechnika*, 18(8):81–84.

Harry Zhang. 2004. The optimality of naive Bayes. *American Association for Artificial Intelligence*, 1(2):3.

Shiyu Zhou, Linhao Dong, Shuang Xu, and Bo Xu. 2018. Syllable-Based Sequence-to-Sequence Speech Recognition with the Transformer in Mandarin Chinese. *arXiv preprint arXiv:1804.10752*.

# Recursive prosody is not finite-state

**Hossep Dolatian**
Department of Linguistics
Stony Brook University
Stony Brook, NY, USA
hossep.dolatian@stonybrook.edu

**Aniello De Santo**
Department of Linguistics
University of Utah
Salt Lake City, Utah, USA
aniello.desanto@utah.edu

**Thomas Graf**
Department of Linguistics
Stony Brook University
Stony Brook, NY, USA
mail@thomasgraf.net

## Abstract

This paper investigates bounds on the generative capacity of prosodic processes, by focusing on the complexity of recursive prosody in coordination contexts in English (Wagner, 2010). Although all phonological processes and most prosodic processes are computationally regular string languages, we show that recursive prosody is not. The output string language is instead parallel multiple context-free (Seki et al., 1991). We evaluate the complexity of the pattern over strings, and then move on to a characterization over trees that requires the expressivity of multi bottom-up tree transducers. In doing so, we provide a foundation for future mathematically grounded investigations of the syntax-prosody interface.

## 1 Introduction

At the level of words, all attested processes in phonology form regular string languages and can be generated via finite-state acceptors (FSAs) and transducers (FSTs) (Johnson, 1972; Kaplan and Kay, 1994; Heinz, 2018). However, not much attention has been given to the generative capacity of prosodic processes at the phrasal or sentential level (but see Yu, 2019). The little work that exists in this respect has shown that many attested intonational processes are finite-state and regular (Pierrehumbert, 1980). It is thus a common hypothesis in the literature that the cross-linguistic typology of prosodic phonology should also be regular.

In this paper, we falsify this hypothesis by providing a mathematically grounded characterization of a pattern of recursive prosody in English coordination, as empirically documented by Wagner (2010). Specifically, we show that when converting a syntactic representation into a prosodic representation, the string language that is generated by this prosodic process is neither a regular nor context-free language, and thus cannot be generated by string-based FSAs. As a tree-to-tree function, the pattern can be captured by a class of bottom-up tree transducers whose outputs correspond to parallel multiple context-free string languages.

This paper is organized as follows. In §2, we provide a literature review of phonology and prosodic phonology, with emphasis on the general tendency for regular computation. In §3, we describe the recursive prosody of coordination structures, and why it cannot be generated with an FST over string inputs. In §4, we show how a multi bottom-up tree transducer can generate the prosodic patterns. We discuss our results in §5, and conclude in §6.

## 2 Computation of prosody

Within computational prosody, there are two strands of work. One focuses on the generation of prosodic structure at or below the word level. The other operates above the word-level.

At the word level, there is a plethora of work on generating prosodic constituents, all of which require finite-state or regular computation, whether for syllables (Kiraz and Möbius, 1998; Yap, 2006; Hulden, 2006; Idsardi, 2009), feet (van Oostendorp, 1993; Idsardi, 2009; Yu, 2017), or prosodic words (Coleman, 1995; Chew, 2003).[1] In fact, most word-level prosody seems to require at most *subregular* computation (Strother-Garcia, 2018, 2019; Hao, 2020; Dolatian, 2020; Dolatian et al., 2021; Koser, in prep).

However, there is a dearth of formal results for phrasal or intonational prosody. Early work in generative phonology treated the prosodic representations as directly generated from the syntax, with any deviations caused by readjustment rules (Chomsky and Halle, 1968). Notoriously, syntactic representations are at

[1] For syllables and feet, there is a large literature of formalization within Declarative Phonology (Scobbie et al., 1996). This work tends to employ formal representations that are similar to context-free grammars (Klein, 1991; Walther, 1993, 1995; Dirksen, 1993; Coleman, 1991, 1992, 1993, 1996, 2000, 1998; Coleman and Pierrehumbert, 1997; Chew, 2003). But these representations can be restricted enough to be equivalent to regular languages (see earlier such restrictions in Church, 1983).



*Proceedings of the Seventeenth SIGMORPHON Workshop on Computational Research in Phonetics, Phonology, and Morphology*, pages 11–22

least context-free (Chomsky, 1956; Chomsky and Schützenberger, 1959). Because sentential prosody interacts with the syntactic level in non-trivial ways, it might seem sensible to assume that 1) the transformation from syntax to prosody is not finite-state definable (= definable with finite-state transducers), and that 2) the string language of prosodic representations is a supra-regular language, not a regular language. Importantly though, this assumption is not trivially true. In fact, early work has shown that even if syntax is context-free, the corresponding prosodic structures can be a regular string language. For instance, Reich (1969) argued that the prosodic structures in SPE can be generated via finite-state devices (see also Langendoen, 1975), while Pierrehumbert (1980) modeled English intonation using a simple finite-state acceptor.

When analyzed over string languages, this mismatch between supra-regular syntax and regular prosody was not explored much in the subsequent literature. In fact, it seems that current research on computational prosody uses the premise that prosodic structures are at most regular (Gibbon, 2001). Crucially, this premise is confounded by the general lack of explicit mathematical formalizations of prosodic systems. For example, there are algorithms for Dutch intonation that capture surface intonational contours and other acoustic cues (t'Hart and Cohen, 1973; t'Hart and Collier, 1975). These algorithms however do not themselves provide sufficient mathematical detail to show that the prosodic phenomenon in question is a regular string language. Instead, one has to deduce that Dutch intonation is regular because the algorithm does not utilize counting or unbounded look-ahead (t'Hart et al., 2006, pg. 114).

As a reflection of this mismatch, early work in prosodic phonology assumed something known as the strict layer hypothesis (SLH; Nespor and Vogel, 1986; Selkirk, 1986). The SLH assumed that prosodic trees cannot be recursive — i.e. a prosodic phrase cannot dominate another prosodic phrase — thus ensuring that a prosodic tree will have fixed depth. Subsequent work in prosodic phonology weakened the SLH: prosodic recursion at the phrase or sentence level is now accepted as empirically robust (Ladd 1986, 2008, ch8; Selkirk 2011; Ito and Mester 2012, 2013). But empirically, it is difficult to find cases of unbounded prosodic recursion (Van der Hulst, 2010). Consider a language that uses only bounded prosodic recursion — e.g. there can be at most two recursive levels of prosodic phrases. The prosodic tree will have fixed depth; and the computation of the corresponding string language is regular. It is then possible to create a computational network that uses a supra-regular grammar for the syntax which interacts with a finite-state grammar for the prosody (Yu and Stabler, 2017; Yu, 2019). To summarize, it seems that the implicit consensus in computational prosody is that 1) syntax can be supra-regular, but the corresponding prosody is regular; 2) prosodic recursion is bounded.

However, as we elaborate in the next section, coordination data from Wagner (2005) is a case where syntactic recursion generates potentially unbounded-recursive prosodic structure. The rest of the paper is then dedicated to exploring the consequences of this construction for the expressivity of sentential prosody.

## 3 Prosodic recursion in coordination

To our knowledge, Wagner (2005, 2010) is the clearest case where syntactic recursion gets mapped to recursive prosody, such that the recursion is unboundedly deep for the prosody. In this section, we go over the data and generalizations (§3.1), we sketch Wagner's cyclic analysis (§3.2), and we discuss issues with finiteness (§3.3). Finally, we show that that this construction does not correspond to a regular string language (§3.4).

### 3.1 Unbounded recursive prosody

Wagner documents unbounded prosodic recursion in the coordination of nouns, in contrast to earlier results which reported flat non-recursive prosody (Langendoen, 1987, 1998). Based on experimental and acoustic studies, Wagner reports that recursive coordination creates recursively strong prosodic boundaries. Syntactic edges have a prosodic strength that incrementally depends on their distance from the bottom-most constituents.

When three items are coordinated with two non-identical operators, then two syntactic parses are possible. Each syntactic parse has an analogous prosodic parse. The prosodic parse is based on the relative strength of a prosodic boundary, with | being weaker than ||. The boundary is placed before the operator.

Table 1: Prosody of three items with non-identical operators

| Syntactic grouping | Prosodic grouping |
|---|---|
| [A and [B or C]] | A ‖ and B \| or C |
| [[A and B] or C] | A \| and B ‖ or C |

When the two operators are identical, then three syntactic and prosodic parses are possible. The difference between the parses is determined by semantic associativity. For example, a sentence like *I saw [[A and B] and C]* means that I saw A and B together, and I saw C separately.

Table 2: Prosody of three items with identical operators

| Syntactic grouping | Prosodic grouping |
|---|---|
| [A and [B and C]] | A \|\| and B \| and C |
| [[A and B] and C] | A \| and B \|\| and C |
| [[A and B and C] | A \| and B \| and C |

When four items are coordinated, then at most 11 parses are possible. The maximum is reached when the three operators are identical. We can have three levels of prosodic boundaries, ranging from the weakest | to the strongest |||.

Table 3: Prosody of four items with identical operators

| Syntactic grouping | Prosodic grouping |
|---|---|
| [A and B and C and D] | A \| and B \| and C \| and D |
| [A and B and [C and D]] | A \|\| and B \|\| and C \| and D |
| [A and [B and C] and D] | A \|\| and B \| and C \|\| and D |
| [[A and B] and C and D] | A \| and B \|\| and C \|\| and D |
| [A and [B and C and D]] | A \|\| and B \| and C \| and D |
| [[A and B and C] and D] | A \| and B \| and C \|\| and D |
| [[A and B] and [C and D]] | A \| and B \|\| and C \| and D |
| [A and [B and [C and D]] | A \|\|\| and B \|\| and C \| and D |
| [A and [[B and C] and D]] | A \|\|\| and B \| and C \|\| and D |
| [[A and [B and C]] and D] | A \|\| and B \| and C \|\|\| and D |
| [[[A and B] and C] and D] | A \| and B \|\| and C \|\|\| and D |

We can extract the following generalizations from the data above. First, the depth of a constituent directly affects the prosodic strength of its edges. At a syntactic edge, the strength of the prosodic boundary depends on the distance between that edge and the most embedded element: for instance, in (1a) the left-bracket between A-B is mapped to a prosodic boundary of strength three |||, because A is above two layers of coordination. The deepest constituent C-D gets the weakest boundary |. Second, when there is associativity, the prosodic strength percolates to other positions within this associative span. For example, in (1b) the boundary of strength || is percolated to A-B from B-C.

1. *Generalizations on coordination*
   (a) *Strength is long-distantly calculated*
   [A and [B and [C and D]]] *is mapped to*
   A ||| and B || and C | and D
   (b) *Strength percolates when associative*
   [A and B and [C and D]] *is mapped to*
   A || and B || and C | and D

### 3.2 Wagner's cyclic analysis

In order to generate the above forms, Wagner devised a cyclic procedure which we summarize with the algorithm below.

2. *Wagner's cyclic algorithm*
   (a) **Base case**: Let X be a constituent that contains a set of unprosodified nouns (terminal nodes) that are in an associative coordination. Place a boundary of strength | between each noun.
   (b) **Recursive case**: Consider a constituent Y. Let S be a set of constituents S (terminals or non-terminals) that is properly contained in Y, such that at least one constituent in S be prosodified. Let $|^k$ be the strongest prosodic boundary inside Y. Place the boundary $|^{k+1}$ between each constituent in Y.

The algorithm is generalized to coordination of any depth. It takes as input a syntactic tree, and the output is prosodically marked strings. We illustrate this below, with the input tree represented as a bracketed string.

3. *Illustrating Wagner's algorithm*

| | |
|---|---|
| Input | [A and B and [C and D]] |
| Base case | C \| and D |
| Recursive case | A \|\| and B \|\| and C \| and D |

### 3.3 Issues of finiteness

Because Wagner's study used noun phrases with at most three or four items, the resulting language of prosodic parses is a finite language. Thus, the relevant syntax-to-prosody function is bounded. It is difficult to elicit coordination of 5 items, likely due to processing reasons (Wagner, 2010, 194).

If the primary culprit is performance, though, then syntactic competence may in fact allow for coordination constructions of unbounded depth with any number of items. Wagner's algorithm generates a prosodic structure for any such sentence, such as for (4). For the rest of this paper, we abstract away the finite bounds on coordination size in order to analyze the generative capacity of the underlying system (see Savitch, 1993, for mathematical arguments in support of factoring out finite bounds).

4. *Hypothetical prosody for large coordination*
   [A and B and [C and [D and E]]] *is mapped to*
   A ||| and B ||| and C || and D | and E

### 3.4 Computing recursive prosody over strings

The choice of representation plays an important role in determining the generative capacity of the prosodic mapping. We first start by treating the mapping as a string-to-string function. We show that the mapping is not regular.

Let the input language be a bracketed string language, such that the input alphabet is a set of nouns{A, ..., Z}, coordinators, and brackets. The output language replaces the brackets with substrings of $|^*$. For illustration, assume that the input language is guaranteed to be a well-bracketed string. At a syntactic boundary, we have to calculate the number of intervening boundaries between it and deepest node. But this requires unbounded memory. For instance, to parse the example below, we incrementally increase the prosodic strength of each boundary as we read the input left-to-right.

5. *Linearly parsing the prosody*:
   [[[A and B] and C] and D] *is mapped to*
   A | and B || and C ||| and D, *where*
   *Input alphabet* $\Sigma$ ={ A, ... , Z, and, or, [, ]}
   *Output alphabet* $\Delta$ ={ A, ... , Z, and, or, |}
   *Input language is* $\Sigma^*$ *and well-bracketed*

Given the above string with only left-branching syntax, the leftmost prosodic boundary will have a juncture of strength |. Every subsequent prosodic boundary will have incrementally larger strength. Over a string, this means we have to memorize the number $x$ of prosodic junctures that were generated at any point in order to then generate $x+1$ junctures at the next point. A 1-way FST cannot memorize an unbounded amount of information. Thus, this function is not rational function and cannot be defined by a 1-way FST. To prove this, we can look at this function in terms of the size of the input and output strings.

6. *Illustrating growth size of recursive prosody*
   $[^n$ $A_0$ and $A_1$ ] and $A_2$] and ... and $A_n$]
   *is mapped to*
   $A_0$ | and $A_1$ || and $A_2$ ||| and ... $|^n$ and $A_n$

Abstractly, for a left-branching input string with $n$ number of left-brackets [, the output string has a monotonically increasing number of prosodic junctures: | ··· || ··· ||| ··· $|n$. The total number of prosodic junctures is a triangular number $n(n+1)/2$. We thus derive the following lemma.

**Lemma 1.** *For generating coordination prosody as a string-to-string function, the size of the output string grows at a rate of at least $O(n^2)$ where $n$ is the size of the input string.*

Such a function is neither rational nor regular. Rational functions are computed by 1-way FSTs, and regular functions by 2-way FSTs (Engelfriet and Hoogeboom, 2001).[2] They share the following property in terms of growth rates (Lhote, 2020).

**Theorem 1.** *Given an input string of size $n$, the size of the output string of a regular function grows at most linearly as $c{\cdot}n$, where c is a constant.*

Thus, this string-to-string function is not regular. It could be a more expressive polyregular function (Engelfriet and Maneth, 2002; Engelfriet, 2015; Bojańczyk, 2018; Bojańczyk et al., 2019), a question that we leave for future work.

The discussion in this section focused on generating the output prosodic string when the input syntax is a *bracketed string*. Importantly though, Lemma 1 entails that no matter how one chooses their string encoding of syntactic structure, prosody cannot be modeled as a rational transduction unless there is an upper bound on the minimum number of output symbols that a single syntactic boundary must be rewritten as. To the best of our knowledge, there is no syntactic string encoding that guarantees such a bound. In the next section, we will discuss how to compute prosodic strength starting from a *tree*.

## 4 Computing recursive prosody over trees

Wagner (2010)'s treatment of recursive prosody assumes an algorithm that maps a syntactic tree to a prosodic string. It is thus valuable to understand the complexity of processes at the syntax-prosody interface starting from the tree representation of a sentence. Assuming we start from trees, there is one more choice to be made, namely whether the prosodic information (in the output) is present within a string or a tree. Notably, every tree-to-string transduction can be regarded as a tree-to-tree transduction plus a string yield mapping. As the tree-to-tree case subsumes the tree-to-string one, it makes sense to consider only the former. For a tree-to-tree mapping, the goal is to obtain a tree representation that already contains the correct prosodic information (Ladd, 1986; Selkirk, 2011). This is the focus of the rest of this paper.

### 4.1 Dependency trees

When working over syntactic structures explicitly, it is important to commit to a specific tree representation.

[2]This equivalence only holds for functions and deterministic FSTs. Non-deterministic FSTs can also compute relations.

In what follows, we adopt a type of *dependency trees*, where the head of a phrase is treated as the mother of the subtree that contains its arguments. For example, the coordinated noun phrase *Pearl and Garnet* is represented as the following dependency tree.

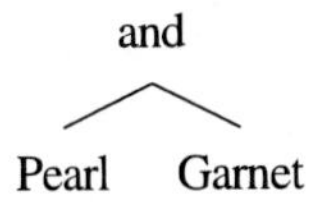


Dependency trees have a rich tradition in descriptive, theoretical, and computational approaches to language, and their properties have been defined across a variety of grammar formalisms (Tesnière, 1965; Nivre, 2005; Boston et al., 2009; Kuhlmann, 2013; Debusmann and Kuhlmann, 2010; De Marneffe and Nivre, 2019; Graf and De Santo, 2019; Shafiei and Graf, 2020, a.o.). Dependency trees keep the relation between heads and arguments local, and they maximally simplify the readability of our mapping rules. Hence, they allow us to focus our discussion on issues that are directly related to the connection of coordinated embeddings and prosodic strength, without having to commit to a particular analysis of coordinate structure.

Importantly, this choice does not impact the generalizability of the solution. It is fairly straightforward to convert basic dependency trees into phrase structure trees. Similarly, although it is possible to adopt $n$-ary branching structures, we chose to limit ourselves to binary trees (in the input). This turns out to be the most conservative assumption, as it forces us to explicitly deal with associativity and flat prosody.

## 4.2 Encoding prosodic strength over trees

We are interested in the complexity of mapping a "plain" syntactic tree to a tree representation which contains the correct prosodic information. Because of this, we encode prosodic strength over trees in the form of strength boundaries at each level of embedding. Each embedding level in our final tree representation will thus have a prosodic strength branch. The tree below shows how the syntactic tree for *Pearl and Garnet* is enriched with prosodic information, according to our encoding choices. For readability, we use \$ to mark prosodic boundaries in trees instead of |, since the latter could be confused with a unary tree branch.

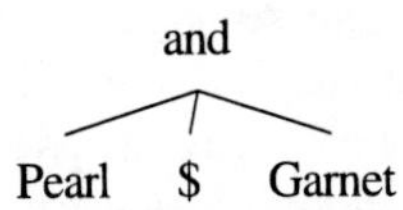


As the tree below shows, the depth of the prosody branch at each embedding level corresponds to the number of prosodic boundaries needed at that level.

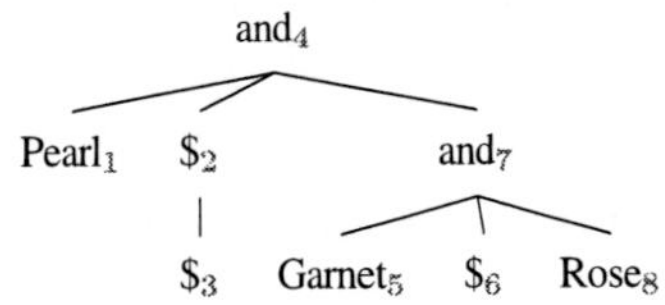


Finally, the prosodic tree is fed to a *yield function* to generate an output prosodified string. In particular, the correct tree-to-string mapping can be obtained by a modified version of a recursive-descent yield, which enumerates nodes left-to-right, depth first, and only enumerates the mother node of each level *after* the boundary branch. This strategy is depicted by the numerical subscripts in the tree above, which reconstruct how the yield of the prosodically annotated tree produces the string: *Pearl || and Garnet | and Rose*. The rest of this section will focus on how to obtain the correct tree encoding of prosodic information, starting from a plain dependency tree.

## 4.3 Mathematical preliminaries

For a natural number $n$, we let $[n] = \{1,...,n\}$. A *ranked alphabet* $\Sigma$ is a finite set of symbols, each one of which has a *rank* assigned by the function $r:\Sigma\rightarrow\mathbb{N}$. We write $\Sigma^{(n)}$ to denote $\{\sigma\in\Sigma\,|\,r(\sigma)=n\}$, and $\sigma^{(n)}$ indicates that $\sigma$ has rank $n$.

Given a ranked alphabet $\Sigma$ and a set $A$, $T_\Sigma(A)$ is the set of all trees over $\Sigma$ indexed by $A$. The symbols in $\Sigma$ are possible labels for nodes in the tree, indexed by elements in $A$. The set $T_\Sigma$ of $\Sigma$-*trees* contains all $\sigma\in\Sigma^{(0)}$ and all terms $\sigma^{(n)}(t_1,...,t_n)$ $(n\geq 0)$ such that $t_1,\ldots,t_n \in T_\Sigma$. Given a term $m^{(n)}(s_1,\ldots,s_n)$ where each $s_i$ is a subtree with root $d_i$, we call $m$ the *mother* of the *daughters* $d_1,...,d_n$ $(1\leq i\leq n)$. If two distinct nodes have the same mother, they are *siblings*. Essentially, the rank of a symbol denotes the finite number of daughters that it can take. Elements of $A$ are considered as additional symbols of rank 0.

*Example 1.* Given $\Sigma := \{a^{(0)},b^{(0)},c^{(2)},d^{(2)}\}$, $T_\Sigma$ is an infinite set. The symbol $a^{(0)}$ means that $a$ is a terminal node without daughters, while $c^{(2)}$ is a non-terminal node with two daughters. For example, consider the tree below.

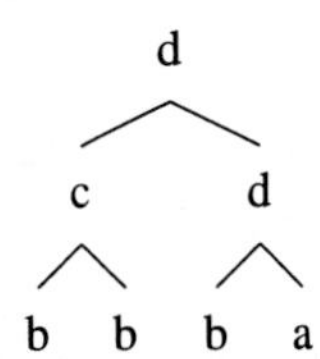


This tree corresponds to the term $d(c(b,b),d(b,a))$, contained in $T_\Sigma$. ⌟

As is standard in defining meta-rules, we introduce $X$ as a countably infinite set of variable symbols ($X \cap \Sigma = X$) to be used as place-holders in the definitions of transduction rules over trees.

### 4.4 Multi bottom-up tree transducers

We assume that the starting point of the prosodic process is a plain syntactic tree. Thus, in order to derive the correct prosodic encoding, we need to propagate information about levels of coordination embedding and about associativity. We adopt a bottom-up approach, and characterize this process in terms of *multi bottom-up tree transducers* (MBOT; Engelfriet et al., 1980; Lilin, 1981; Maletti, 2011). Essentially, MBOTs generalize traditional bottom–up tree transducers in that they allow states to pass more than one output subtree up to subsequent transducer operations (Gildea, 2012). In other words, each MBOT rule potentially specifies several parts of the output tree. This is highlighted by the fact that the transducer states ($q \in Q$) can have rank greater than one — i.e. they can have more than one daughter, where the additional daughters are used to hold subtrees in *memory*. We follow Fülöp et al. (2004) in presenting the semantics of MBOTs.

**Definition 1** (MBOT). A multi bottom-up tree transducer (MBOT) is a tuple $M = (Q,\Sigma,\Delta,root,q_f,R)$, where $Q$, $\Sigma \cup \Delta$, $\{root\}$, $\{q_f\}$ are pairwise disjoint, such that:

- $Q$ is a ranked alphabet with $Q^{(0)} = \emptyset$, called the set of states
- $\Sigma$ and $\Delta$ are ranked input and output alphabets, respectively
- *root* is a unary symbol, called the root symbol
- $q_f$ is a unary symbol called the final state

$R$ is a finite set of rules of two forms:

- $\sigma(q_1(x_{1,1},\ldots,x_{1,n_1}),\ldots,q_k(x_{k,1},\ldots,x_{k,n_k})) \rightarrow q_0(t_1,\ldots,t_{n_0})$

where $k \geq 0$, $\sigma \in \Sigma^{(k)}$, for every $i \in [k] \cup \{0\}$, $q_i \in Q^{(n_i)}$ for some $n_i \geq 1$, for every $j \in [n_0]$, $t_j \in T_\Delta(\{x_{i,j} | i \in [k], j \in [n_i]\})$.

- $root(q(x_1,\ldots,x_n)) \rightarrow q_f(t)$

where $n \geq 1, q \in Q^{(n)}$, and $t \in T_\Delta(X_n)$. ⌟

The derivational relation induced by $M$ is a binary relation $\Rightarrow_M$ over the set $T_{\Sigma\cup\Delta\cup Q\cup\{root,q_f\}}$ defined as follows. For every $\varphi,\psi \in T_{\Sigma\cup\Delta\cup Q\cup\{root,q_f\}}$, $\varphi \Rightarrow_M \psi$ iff there is a tree $\beta \in T_{\Sigma\cup\Delta\cup Q\cup\{root,q_f\}}(X_1)$ s.t. $x_1$ occurs exactly once in $\beta$ and either there is a rule

- $\sigma(q_1(x_{1,1},\ldots,x_{1,n_1}),\ldots,q_k(x_{k,1},\ldots,x_{k,n_k})) \rightarrow r$ in $R$

and there are trees $T_{i,j} \in T_\Sigma$ for every $i \in [k]$ and $j \in [n_i]$, s.t. $\varphi = \beta[\sigma(q_1(t_{1,1}, \ldots, t_{1,n_1}), \ldots, q_k(t_{k,1}, \ldots, t_{k,n_k}))]$, and $\psi = \beta[r[x_{i,j} \leftarrow t_{i,j} | i \in [k], j \in [n_i]]]$; or there is a rule

- $root(q(x_1,\ldots,x_n)) \rightarrow q_f(t)$ in $R$

and there are trees $t_i \in T_\Delta$ for every $i \in [n]$ s.t. $\varphi = \beta[root(q(t_1,\ldots,t_n))]$, and $\psi = \beta[q_f(t[t_1,\ldots,t_n])]$. The tree transformation computed by $M$ is the relation:

$$\tau_M = \{(s,t) \in T_\Sigma \times T_\Delta \mid root(s) \Rightarrow^*_M q_f(t)\}$$

Intuitively, tree transductions are performed by rewriting a local tree fragment as specified by one of the rules in $R$. For instance, a rule can replace a subtree, or copy it to a different position. Rules apply bottom–up from the leaves of the input tree, and terminate in an accepting state $q_f$.

### 4.5 MBOT for recursive prosody

We want a transducer which captures Wagner (2010)'s bottom-up cyclic procedure. Consider now the MBOT $M_{pros} = (Q, \Sigma, \Delta, root, q_f, R)$, with $Q = \{q_*, q_c\}$, $\sigma_c \in \{and,or\} \subsetneq \Sigma$, $\sigma \in \Sigma - \{and,or\}$, and $\Sigma = \Delta$. We use $q_c$ to indicate that $M_{pros}$ has verified that a branch contains a coordination (so $\sigma_c$), with $q_*$ assigned to any other branch. As mentioned, we use \$ to mark prosodic boundaries in the trees instead of |. The set of rules $R$ is as follows.

Rule 1 rewrites a terminal symbol $\sigma$ as itself. The MBOT for that branch transitions to $q_*(\sigma)$.

$$\sigma \rightarrow q_*(\sigma) \qquad (1)$$

Rule 2 applies to a subtree headed by $\sigma_c \in \{and,or\}$, with only terminal symbols as daughters: $\sigma_c(q_*(x),q_*(y))$. It inserts a prosodic boundary \$ between the daughters $x,y$. The boundary \$ is also copied as a daughter of the mother $q_c$, as record of the fact that we have seen one coordination level.

$$\sigma_c(q_*(x),q_*(y)) \rightarrow q_c(\sigma_c(x,\$,y),\$) \qquad (2)$$

We illustrate this in Figure 1 with a coordination of two items, representing the mapping: [B and A] $\rightarrow$ *B* | *and A*. We also assume that sentence-initial boundaries are vacuously interpreted.

We now consider cases where a coordination is the mother not just of terminal nodes, but of other coordinated phrases. Rule 3 handles the case in which

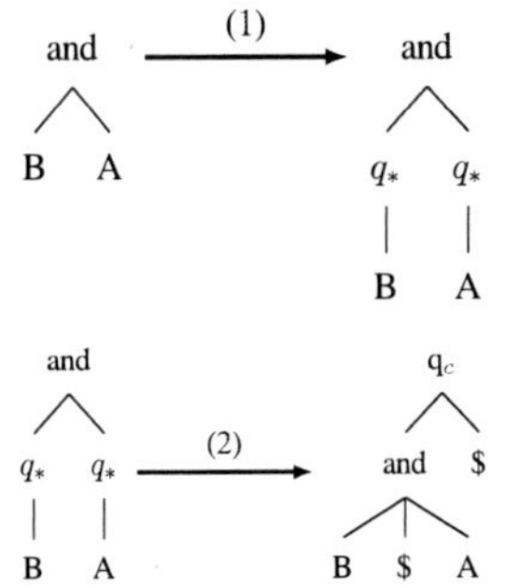


Figure 1: Example of the application of rules (1) and (2). The numerical label on the arrow indicates which rule was applied in order to rewrite the tree on the left as the tree on the right.

the right sibling of the mother was also headed by a coordination (as encoded by $\sigma_c$ having $q_c$ as one of its daughters). Here, $q_c$ is the result of a previous rule application (e.g. rule 2) and it has two subtrees itself: $q_c(w,y)$. Although we do not have access to the internal labels of $x$, $y$, and $w$, by the format of the previous rules we know that the right daughter of $q_c$ (i.e. $y$) is the one that contains the strength information. Then, rule 3 has three things to do. It increments $y$ by one boundary: $\$(y)$. It places $\$(y)$ in between the two subtrees $x$ and $w$. And, it copies $\$(y)$ as the daughter of the new $q_c$ state in order to propagate $\$(y)$ to the next embedding level (see Figure 2).

$$\sigma_c(q_*(x),q_c(w,y)) \rightarrow q_c(\sigma_c(x,\$(y),w),\$(y)) \quad (3)$$

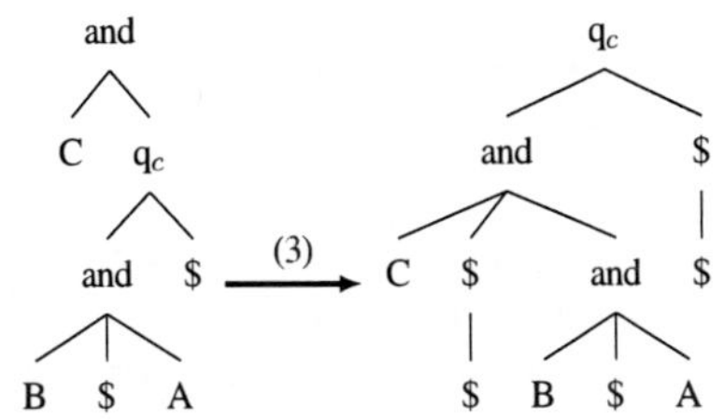


Figure 2: Example of the application of rule (3). For ease of readability, we omit $q_*$ states over terminal nodes.

Rule 4 applies once all coordinate phrases up to the root have been rewritten. It simply rewrites the root as the final accepting state. It gets rid of the daughter of $q_c$ that contains the strength markers, since there is no need to propagate them any further.

$$root(q_c(x,y)) \rightarrow q_f(x) \quad (4)$$

As the examples so far should have clarified, $M_{pros}$ as currently defined readily handles cases where the embedding of the coordination is strictly right branching, with the bulk of the work done via rule 3. However, while these rules work well for instances in which a coordination is always the right daughter of a node, they cannot deal with cases in which the coordination branches left, or alternates between the two. This is easily fixed by introducing variants to rule 3, which consider the position of the coordination as marked by $q_c$. Importantly, the position of the copy of the boundary branch is not altered, and it is always kept as the rightmost sibling of $q_c$. What changes is the relative position of the $w$ and $x$ subbranches in the output (see Figure 3).

$$\sigma_c(q_c(w,y),q_*(x)) \rightarrow q_c(\sigma_c(w,\$(y),x),\$(y)) \quad (5)$$

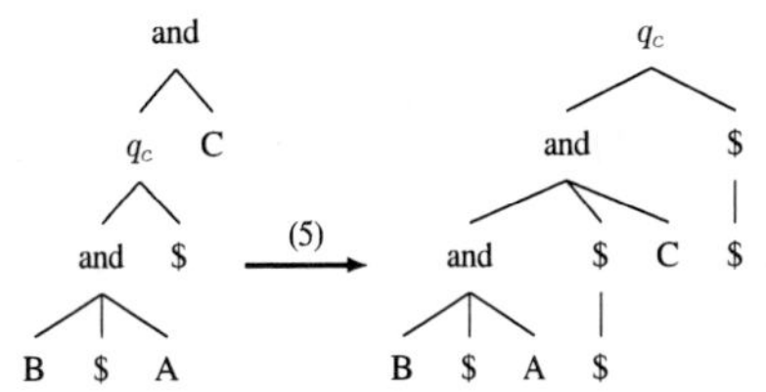


Figure 3: Left branching example as in rule (5).

Following the same logic, rule 6 handles cases like *[[A and B] and [C and D]]*, in which both daughters of a coordination are headed by a coordination themselves (see Figure 4).

$$\sigma_c(q_c(x,z),q_c(y,w)) \rightarrow q_c(\$(x),\sigma_c(z,\$(x),w)) \quad (6)$$

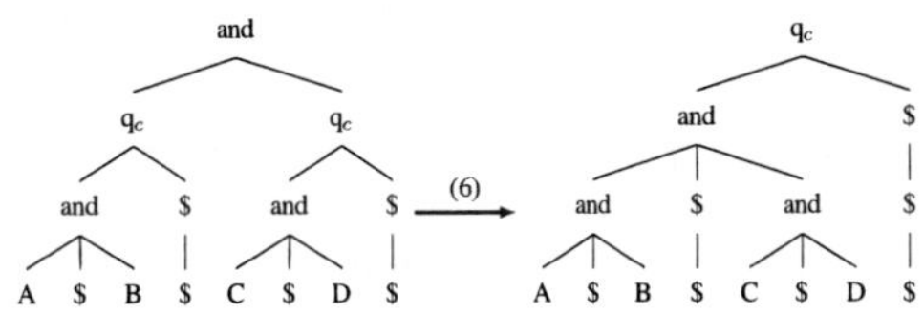


Figure 4: Example of the application of rule (6).

Finally, we need to take care of the flat prosody or associativity issue. The MBOT $M_{pros}$ as outlined so far increases the depth of the boundary branch at each level of embedding. Because we are adopting binary branching trees, the current set of rules is trivially unable to encode cases like *[A and B and C]*. We follow Wagner's assumption that semantic information on the syntactic tree guides the prosody cycles. Representationally, we mark this by using specific labels on the internal nodes of the tree. We assume that the flat constituent interpretation is

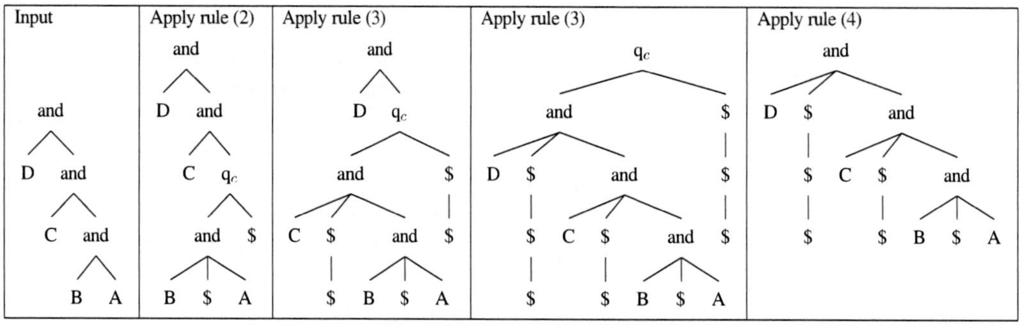


Figure 5: Walk-through of the transduction defined by $M_{pros}$. For ease of readability, and to highlight how $q_c$ propagates embedding information about the coordination, $q_*$ and $q_f$ states are omitted.

obtained by marking internal nodes as non-cyclic, introducing the alphabet symbol $\sigma_n$:

$$\sigma_n(q_*(x),q_c(w,y)) \rightarrow q_c(\sigma_c(x,y,w),y) \quad (7)$$

Essentially, rule 7 tells us that when a coordination node is marked as $\sigma_n$, $M_{pros}$ just propagates the level of prosodic strength that it currently has registered (in $y$), without increments (see Figure 6). This rule can be trivially adjusted to deal with branching differences, as done for rules 3 and 5.

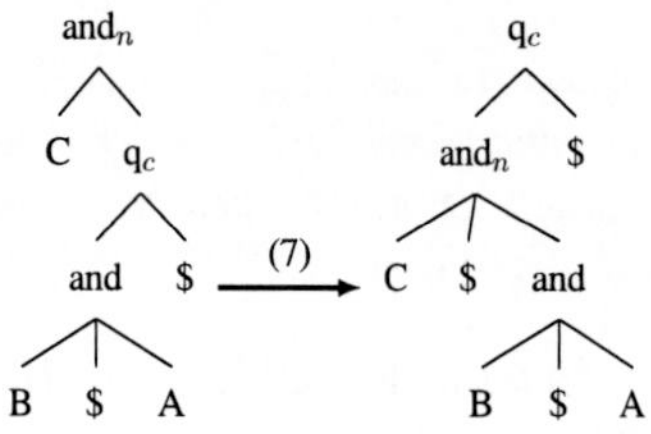

Figure 6: Application of rule (7) for flat prosody.

A full, step by step $M_{pros}$ transduction is shown in Figure 5. Taken together, the recursive prosodic patterns are fully characterized by $M_{pros}$ when it is adjusted with a set of rules to deal with alternating branching and flat associativity. The tree transducer generates tree representations where each level of embedding is marked by a branch, which carries information about the prosodic strength for that level. As outlined in Section 4.2, this final representation may then be fed to a modified string yield function for dependency tree languages.

Dependency trees allowed us to present a transducer with rules that are relatively easy to read. But, as mentioned before, this choice does not affect our general result. Under the standard assumption that the distance between the head of a phrase and its maximal projection is bounded, $M_{pros}$ can be extended to phrase structure trees, by virtue of the bottom-up strategy being intrinsically equipped with finite look-ahead. A switch to phrase structure trees may prove useful for future work on the interaction of prosody and movement.

## 5 Generating recursive prosody

The previous section characterized recursive prosody over trees with a non-linear, deterministic MBOT. This is a nice result, as MBOTs are generally well-understood in terms of their algorithmic properties. Moreover, this result is in line with past work exploring the connections of MBOTs, tree languages, and the complexity of movement and copying operations in syntax (Kobele, 2006; Kobele et al., 2007, a.o.).

We can now ask what the complexity of this approach is. MBOTs generate output string languages that are potentially parallel multiple context-free languages (PMCFL; Seki et al., 1991, 1993; Gildea, 2012; Maletti, 2014; Fülöp et al., 2005). Since this class of string languages is more powerful than context-free, the corresponding tree language is not a regular tree language (Gécseg and Steinby, 1997). This is not surprising, as MBOTs can be understood as an extension of synchronous tree substitution grammars (Maletti, 2014).

Notably, independently of our specific MBOT solution, prosody as defined in this paper generates at least some output string languages that lack the constant growth property — hence, that are PMCFLs. Consider as input a regular tree language of left-branching coordinationate phrases, where each level is simply of the form *and(X, Mary)*. The $n-th$ level of embedding from the top extends the string yield by $n+2$ symbols. This immediately implies no constant growth, and thus no semi-linearity (Weir, 1988; Joshi et al., 1990).

Interestingly though, the prosody MBOT developed here is fairly limited in its expressivity as the transducer states themselves do almost no work, and most of the transduction rules in $M_{pros}$ rely on the ability to store the prosody strength branch. Hence, the specific MBOT in this paper might turn out to belong to a relatively weak subclass of tree transductions with copying, perhaps a variant of input strictly local tree transductions (cf. Ikawa et al., 2020; Ji and Heinz, 2020), or a transducer variant of sensing tree automata (cf. Fülöp et al., 2004; Kobele et al., 2007; Maletti, 2011, 2014; Graf and De Santo, 2019). Since all of those have recently been used in the formal study of syntax, they are natural candidates for a computational model of prosody, and their sensitivity to minor representational difference might also illuminate what aspects of syntactic representation affect the complexity of prosodic processes.

Finally, one might worry that the mathematical complexity is a confound of the representation we use, rather than a genuine property of the phenomenon. However, a representation of prosodic strength is necessary and cannot be reduced further for two reasons. First, strength cannot be reduced to syntactic boundaries because a single prosodic edge ( may correspond to $|^k$ for any $k \geq 1$. As discussed in depth by Wagner (2005, 2010), one cannot simply convert a syntactic tree into a prosodic tree by replacing the labels of nonterminal nodes. Second, strength also cannot be reduced to different categories of prosodic constituents — e.g. assuming that | is a prosodic phrase while || is an intonational phrase. As argued in depth in (Wagner, 2005, 2010), these different constituent types do not map neatly to prosodic strength. Instead, these boundaries all encode relative strengths of prosodic phrase boundaries.

## 6 Conclusion

This paper formalizes the computation of unbounded recursive prosodic structures in coordination. Their computation cannot be done by string-based finite-state transducers. They instead need more expressive grammars. To our knowledge, this paper is one of the few (if only) formal results on how prosodic phonology at the sentence-level is computationally more expressive than phonology at the word-level.

As discussed above, recent work in prosodic phonology relies on the assumption that prosodic structure can be recursive. However, because such work usually uses bounded-recursion, such phenomena are computationally regular. Departing from this stance, this paper focused on the prosodic phenomena reported in Wagner (2005) as a core case study, because of the following fundamental properties:

- The syntax has unbounded recursion.
- The prosody has unbounded recursion.
- All recursive prosodic constituents have the same prosodic label (= a prosodic phrase).
- The recursive prosodic constituents have acoustic cues marking different strengths.
- There is an algorithm which explicitly assigns the recursive prosodic constituents to these different strengths.

In this paper, we focused on explicitly generating the prosodic strengths at each recursive prosodic levels, putting aside the mathematically simpler task of converting a recursive syntactic tree into a recursive prosodic tree (Elfner, 2015; Bennett and Elfner, 2019) — which is a process essentially analogous to a relabeling of the nonterminal nodes of the syntactic tree, without care for the prosodic strength. The mapping studied in this paper has been conjectured in the past to be computationally more expressive than regular languages or functions (Yu and Stabler, 2017). Here, we formally verified that hypothesis.

An open question then is to find other empirical phenomena which also have the above properties. One potential area of investigation is the assignment of relative prominence relations in English compound prosody (Chomsky and Halle, 1968). However, English compound prosody is a highly controversial area. It is unclear what is the current consensus on an *exact* algorithm for these compounds, especially one that utilizes recursion and is not based on impressionistic judgments (Liberman and Prince, 1977; Gussenhoven, 2011). In this sense, the mathematical results in this paper highlight the importance of representational commitments and of explicit assumptions in the study of prosodic expressivity. Our paper might then help identify crucial issues in future theoretical and empirical investigations of the syntax-prosody interface.

## Acknowledgements

We are grateful to our anonymous reviewers, Jon Rawski, and Kristine Yu. Thomas Graf is supported by the National Science Foundation under Grant No. BCS-1845344.

## References

Ryan Bennett and Emily Elfner. 2019. The syntax–prosody interface. *Annual Review of Linguistics*, 5:151–171.

Mikołaj Bojańczyk. 2018. Polyregular functions. *arXiv preprint arXiv:1810.08760*.

Mikołaj Bojańczyk, Sandra Kiefer, and Nathan Lhote. 2019. String-to-string interpretations with polynomial-size output. In *46th International Colloquium on Automata, Languages, and Programming, ICALP 2019, July 9-12, Patras, Greece. (LIPIcs)*, volume 132, page 106:1–106:14, Schloss Dagstuhl - Leibniz-Zentrum fuer Informatik.

Marisa Ferrara Boston, John T. Hale, and Marco Kuhlmann. 2009. Dependency structures derived from minimalist grammars. In *The Mathematics of Language*, pages 1–12. Springer.

Peter Chew. 2003. *A computational phonology of Russian.* Universal-Publishers, Parkland, FL.

Noam Chomsky. 1956. Three models for the description of language. *IRE Transactions on information theory*, 2(3):113–124.

Noam Chomsky and Morris Halle. 1968. *The sound pattern of English.* MIT Press, Cambridge, MA.

Noam Chomsky and Marcel P Schützenberger. 1959. The algebraic theory of context-free languages. In *Studies in Logic and the Foundations of Mathematics*, volume 26, pages 118–161. Elsevier.

Kenneth Ward Church. 1983. *Phrase-structure parsing: A method for taking advantage of allophonic constraints.* Ph.D. thesis, Massachusetts Institute of Technology.

John Coleman. 1992. The phonetic interpretation of headed phonological structures containing overlapping constituents. *Phonology*, 9(1):1–44.

John Coleman. 1993. English word-stress in unification-based grammar. In T. Mark Ellison and James Scobbie, editors, *Computational Phonology*, page 97–106. Centre for Cognitive Science, University of Edinburgh.

John Coleman. 1995. Declarative lexical phonology. In Jacques Durand and Francsis Katamba, editors, *Frontiers of phonology: Atoms, structures, derivations*, pages 333–383. Longman, London.

John Coleman. 1996. Declarative syllabification in Tashlhit Berber. In Jacques Durand and Bernard Laks, editors, *Current trends in phonology: Models and methods*, volume 1, pages 175–216. European Studies Research Institute, University of Salford, Salford.

John Coleman. 1998. *Phonological representations: Their names, forms and powers.* Cambridge University Press, Cambridge.

John Coleman. 2000. Candidate selection. *The Linguistic Review*, 17(2-4):167–180.

John Coleman and Janet Pierrehumbert. 1997. Stochastic phonological grammars and acceptability. In *Third meeting of the ACL special interest group in computational phonology: Proceedings of the workshop*, pages 49–56, East Stroudsburg, PA. Association for computational linguistics.

John S Coleman. 1991. Prosodic structure, parameter-setting and ID/LP grammar. In Steven Bird, editor, *Declarative perspectives on phonology*, pages 65–78. Centre for Cognitive Science, University of Edinburgh.

Marie-Catherine De Marneffe and Joakim Nivre. 2019. Dependency grammar. *Annual Review of Linguistics*, 5:197–218.

Ralph Debusmann and Marco Kuhlmann. 2010. Dependency grammar: Classification and exploration. In *Resource-adaptive cognitive processes*, pages 365–388. Springer.

Arthur Dirksen. 1993. Phrase structure phonology. In T. Mark Ellison and James Scobbie, editors, *Computational Phonology*, page 81–96. Centre for Cognitive Science, University of Edinburgh.

Hossep Dolatian. 2020. *Computational locality of cyclic phonology in Armenian.* Ph.D. thesis, Stony Brook University.

Hossep Dolatian, Nate Koser, Kristina Strother-Garcia, and Jonathan Rawski. 2021. Computational restrictions on iterative prosodic processes. In *Proceedings of the 2019 Annual Meeting on Phonology*. Linguistic Society of America.

Emily Elfner. 2015. Recursion in prosodic phrasing: Evidence from Connemara Irish. *Natural Language & Linguistic Theory*, 33(4):1169–1208.

Joost Engelfriet. 2015. Two-way pebble transducers for partial functions and their composition. *Acta Informatica*, 52(7-8):559–571.

Joost Engelfriet and Hendrik Jan Hoogeboom. 2001. MSO definable string transductions and two-way finite-state transducers. *Transactions of the Association for Computational Linguistics*, 2(2):216–254.

Joost Engelfriet and Sebastian Maneth. 2002. Two-way finite state transducers with nested pebbles. In *International Symposium on Mathematical Foundations of Computer Science*, pages 234–244. Springer.

Joost Engelfriet, Grzegorz Rozenberg, and Giora Slutzki. 1980. Tree transducers, l systems, and two-way machines. *Journal of Computer and System Sciences*, 20(2):150–202.

Zoltán Fülöp, Armin Kühnemann, and Heiko Vogler. 2004. A bottom-up characterization of deterministic top-down tree transducers with regular look-ahead. *Information Processing Letters*, 91(2):57–67.

Zoltán Fülöp, Armin Kühnemann, and Heiko Vogler. 2005. Linear deterministic multi bottom-up tree transducers. *Theoretical computer science*, 347(1-2):276–287.

Ferenc Gécseg and Magnus Steinby. 1997. Tree languages. In *Handbook of formal languages*, pages 1–68. Springer.

Dafydd Gibbon. 2001. Finite state prosodic analysis of African corpus resources. In *EUROSPEECH 2001 Scandinavia, $7^{th}$ European Conference on Speech Communication and Technology, $2^{nd}$ INTERSPEECH Event, Aalborg, Denmark, September 3-7, 2001*, pages 83–86. ISCA.

Daniel Gildea. 2012. On the string translations produced by multi bottom–up tree transducers. *Computational Linguistics*, 38(3):673–693.

Thomas Graf and Aniello De Santo. 2019. Sensing tree automata as a model of syntactic dependencies. In *Proceedings of the $16^{th}$ Meeting on the Mathematics of Language*, pages 12–26, Toronto, Canada. Association for Computational Linguistics.

Carlos Gussenhoven. 2011. Sentential prominence in English. In Marc van Oostendorp, Colin Ewen, Elizabeth Hume, and Keren Rice, editors, *The Blackwell companion to phonology*, volume 5, pages 1–29. Wiley-Blackwell, Malden, MA.

Yiding Hao. 2020. Metrical grids and generalized tier projection. In *Proceedings of the Society for Computation in Linguistics*, volume 3.

Jeffrey Heinz. 2018. The computational nature of phonological generalizations. In Larry Hyman and Frans Plank, editors, *Phonological Typology*, Phonetics and Phonology, chapter 5, pages 126–195. Mouton de Gruyter, Berlin.

Mans Hulden. 2006. Finite-state syllabification. In Anssi Yli-Jyrä, Lauri Karttunen, and Juhani Karhumäki, editors, *Finite-State Methods and Natural Language Processing. FSMNLP 2005. Lecture Notes in Computer Science*, volume 4002. Springer, Berlin/Heidelberg.

Harry Van der Hulst. 2010. A note on recursion in phonology recursion. In Harry Van der Hulst, editor, *Recursion and human language*, pages 301–342. Mouton de Gruyter, Berlin & New York.

William J Idsardi. 2009. Calculating metrical structure. In Eric Raimy and Charles E. Cairns, editors, *Contemporary views on architecture and representations in phonology*, number 48 in Current Studies in Linguistics, pages 191–211. MIT Press, Cambridge, MA.

Shiori Ikawa, Akane Ohtaka, and Adam Jardine. 2020. Quantifier-free tree transductions. *Proceedings of the Society for Computation in Linguistics*, 3(1):455–458.

Junko Ito and Armin Mester. 2012. Recursive prosodic phrasing in Japanese. In Toni Borowsky, Shigeto Kawahara, Shinya Takahito, and Mariko Sugahara, editors, *Prosody matters: Essays in honor of Elisabeth Selkirk*, pages 280–303. Equinox Publishing, London.

Junko Ito and Armin Mester. 2013. Prosodic subcategories in Japanese. *Lingua*, 124:20–40.

Jing Ji and Jeffrey Heinz. 2020. Input strictly local tree transducers. In *International Conference on Language and Automata Theory and Applications*, pages 369–381. Springer.

C Douglas Johnson. 1972. *Formal aspects of phonological description*. Mouton, The Hague.

Aravind K Joshi, K Vijay Shanker, and David Weir. 1990. The convergence of mildly context-sensitive grammar formalisms. *Technical Reports (CIS)*, page 539.

Ronald M. Kaplan and Martin Kay. 1994. Regular models of phonological rule systems. *Computational linguistics*, 20(3):331–378.

George Anton Kiraz and Bernd Möbius. 1998. Multilingual syllabification using weighted finite-state transducers. In *The third ESCA/COCOSDA workshop (ETRW) on speech synthesis*.

Ewan Klein. 1991. Phonological data types. In Steven Bird, editor, *Declarative perspectives on phonology*, pages 127–138. Centre for Cognitive Science, University of Edinburgh.

Gregory M. Kobele, Christian Retoré, and Sylvain Salvati. 2007. An automata-theoretic approach to minimalism. *Model theoretic syntax at 10*, pages 71–80.

Gregory Michael Kobele. 2006. *Generating Copies: An investigation into structural identity in language and grammar*. Ph.D. thesis, University of California, Los Angeles.

Nate Koser. in prep. *The computational nature of stress assignment*. Ph.D. thesis, Rutgers University.

Marco Kuhlmann. 2013. Mildly non-projective dependency grammar. *Computational Linguistics*, 39(2):355–387.

D. Robert Ladd. 1986. Intonational phrasing: The case for recursive prosodic structure. *Phonology*, 3:311–340.

D. Robert Ladd. 2008. *Intonational phonology*. Cambridge University Press, Cambridge.

D. Terence Langendoen. 1975. Finite-state parsing of phrase-structure languages and the status of readjustment rules in grammar. *Linguistic Inquiry*, 6(4):533–554.

D. Terence Langendoen. 1987. On the phrasing of coordinate compound structures. In Brian Joseph and Arnold Zwicky, editors, *A festschrift for Ilse Lehiste*, page 186–196. Ohio State University, Ohio.

D. Terence Langendoen. 1998. Limitations on embedding in coordinate structures. *Journal of Psycholinguistic Research*, 27(2):235–259.

Nathan Lhote. 2020. Pebble minimization of polyregular functions. In *Proceedings of the 35th Annual ACM/IEEE Symposium on Logic in Computer Science*, pages 703–712.

Mark Liberman and Alan Prince. 1977. On stress and linguistic rhythm. *Linguistic inquiry*, 8(2):249–336.

Eric Lilin. 1981. Propriétés de clôture d'une extension de transducteurs d'arbres déterministes. In *Colloquium on Trees in Algebra and Programming*, pages 280–289. Springer.

Andreas Maletti. 2011. How to train your multi bottom-up tree transducer. In *Proceedings of the 49th Annual Meeting of the Association for Computational Linguistics: Human Language Technologies*, pages 825–834.

Andreas Maletti. 2014. The power of regularity-preserving multi bottom-up tree transducers. In *International Conference on Implementation and Application of Automata*, pages 278–289. Springer.

Marina Nespor and Irene Vogel. 1986. *Prosodic phonology*. Foris, Dordrecht.

Joakim Nivre. 2005. Dependency grammar and dependency parsing. *MSI report*, 5133.1959:1–32.

Marc van Oostendorp. 1993. Formal properties of metrical structure. In *Sixth Conference of the European Chapter of the Association for Computational Linguistics*, pages 322–331, Utrecht. ACL.

Janet Breckenridge Pierrehumbert. 1980. *The phonology and phonetics of English intonation*. Ph.D. thesis, Massachusetts Institute of Technology.

Peter. A. Reich. 1969. The finiteness of natural language. *Language*, 45:831–843.

Walter J Savitch. 1993. Why it might pay to assume that languages are infinite. *Annals of Mathematics and Artificial Intelligence*, 8(1-2):17–25.

James M. Scobbie, John S. Coleman, and Steven Bird. 1996. Key aspects of declarative phonology. In Jacques Durand and Bernard Laks, editors, *Current Trends in Phonology: Models and Methods*, volume 2. European Studies Research Institute, Salford, Manchester.

Hiroyuki Seki, Takashi Matsumura, Mamoru Fujii, and Tadao Kasami. 1991. On multiple context-free grammars. *Theoretical Computer Science*, 88(2):191–229.

Hiroyuki Seki, Ryuichi Nakanishi, Yuichi Kaji, Sachiko Ando, and Tadao Kasami. 1993. Parallel multiple context-free grammars, finite-state translation systems, and polynomial-time recognizable subclasses of lexical-functional grammars. In *Proceedings of the 31st annual meeting on Association for Computational Linguistics*, pages 130–139. Association for Computational Linguistics.

Elisabeth Selkirk. 1986. On derived domains in sentence phonology. *Phonology Yearbook*, 3(1):371–405.

Elisabeth Selkirk. 2011. The syntax-phonology interface. In John Goldsmith, Jason Riggle, and Alan C. L. Yu, editors, *The Handbook of Phonological Theory*, 2 edition, pages 435–483. Blackwell, Oxford.

Nazila Shafiei and Thomas Graf. 2020. The subregular complexity of syntactic islands. In *Proceedings of the Society for Computation in Linguistics*, volume 3.

Kristina Strother-Garcia. 2018. Imdlawn Tashlhiyt Berber syllabification is quantifier-free. In *Proceedings of the Society for Computation in Linguistics*, volume 1, pages 145–153.

Kristina Strother-Garcia. 2019. *Using model theory in phonology: a novel characterization of syllable structure and syllabification*. Ph.D. thesis, University of Delaware.

Lucien Tesnière. 1965. Eléments de syntaxe structurale, 1959. *Paris, Klincksieck*.

Johan t'Hart and Antonie Cohen. 1973. Intonation by rule: a perceptual quest. *Journal of Phonetics*, 1(4):309–327.

Johan t'Hart and René Collier. 1975. Integrating different levels of intonation analysis. *Journal of Phonetics*, 3(4):235–255.

Johan t'Hart, René Collier, and Antonie Cohen. 2006. *A perceptual study of intonation: An experimental-phonetic approach to speech melody*. Cambridge University Press.

Michael Wagner. 2005. *Prosody and recursion*. Ph.D. thesis, Massachusetts Institute of Technology.

Michael Wagner. 2010. Prosody and recursion in coordinate structures and beyond. *Natural Language & Linguistic Theory*, 28(1):183–237.

Markus Walther. 1993. Declarative syllabification with applications to German. In T. Mark Ellison and James Scobbie, editors, *Computational Phonology*, pages 55–79. Centre for Cognitive Science, University of Edinburgh.

Markus Walther. 1995. A strictly lexicalized approach to phonology. In *Proceedings of DGfS/CL'95*, page 108–113, Düsseldorf. Deutsche Gesellschaft für Sprachwissenschaft, Sektion Computerlinguistik.

David Jeremy Weir. 1988. *Characterizing mildly context-sensitive grammar formalisms*. Ph.D. thesis, University of Pennsylvania.

Ngee Thai Yap. 2006. *Modeling syllable theory with finite-state transducers*. Ph.D. thesis, University of Delaware.

Kristine M. Yu. 2017. Advantages of constituency: Computational perspectives on Samoan word prosody. In *International Conference on Formal Grammar 2017*, page 105–124, Berlin. Spring.

Kristine M. Yu. 2019. Parsing with minimalist grammars and prosodic trees. In Robert C. Berwick and Edward P. Stabler, editors, *Minimalist Parsing*, pages 69–109. Oxford University Press, London.

Kristine M. Yu and Edward P. Stabler. 2017. (In) variability in the Samoan syntax/prosody interface and consequences for syntactic parsing. *Laboratory Phonology: Journal of the Association for Laboratory Phonology*, 8(1):1–44.

# The Match-Extend Serialization Algorithm in Multiprecedence

**Maxime Papillon**
Classic, Modern Languages and Linguistics, Concordia University
papillonmaxime@gmail.com

## Abstract

Raimy (1999; 2000a; 2000b) proposed a graphical formalism for modeling reduplication, originallymostly focused on phonological overapplication in a derivational framework. This framework is now known as Precedence-based phonology or Multiprecedence phonology. Raimy's idea is that the segments at the input to the phonology are not totally ordered by precedence. This paper tackles a challenge that arose with Raimy's work, the development of a deterministic serialization algorithm as part of the derivation of surface forms. The Match-Extend algorithm introduced here requires fewer assumptions and sticks tighter to the attested typology. The algorithm also contains no parameter or constraint specific to individual graphs or topologies, unlike previous proposals. Match-Extend requires nothing except knowing the last added set of links.

## 1 Introduction

This paper provides a general serialization algorithm for all morphological structures in all languages. The challenge of converting non-linear structures of linguistic representation into a format ready to be handled in production is one that matters to both morphosyntax and morphophonology. Reduplication is a phenomenon at the frontier of morphology and phonology that has drawn a lot of attention in the last few decades. Reduplication's non-concatenative nature and the fact that it manifests long-distance dependencies among segments set it apart from the 'standard' word-formation that most theories are designed to handle. These properties have often pushed theoreticians to propose expansive systems such as copying procedures on top of traditional linear segmental phonology to make the system powerful enough to handle these dependencies. The multiprecedence model expanded upon here builds on properties that are already implicit in all approaches to phonological representation, and actually gets rid of some standard assumptions. It accounts for attested patterns and predicts an unattested reduplication pattern to be impossible.

## 2 Multiprecedence

The theory of Multiprecedence seeks to account for reduplication representationally via loops in a graph. Eschewing correspondence statements and copying procedures, Multiprecedence treats reduplication as fundamentally a structural property created by the addition of an affix, whose serialization has the effect of pronouncing all or part of the form twice.

Consider a string like Fig. 1a, the standard way of representing the segments that constitute a phonological representation. An alternative way to encode that same information is in the form of a set of immediate precedence statements like Fig. 1b. For legibility the set of pairs in Fig. 1b can be represented in the form of a graph. Adding the convention that of using # and % for the START and END symbols respectively we get the picture in Fig. 1c. In general I will refer to this as the graph representation.

a.kæt
b. { ⟨ START, k ⟩, ⟨ k,æ ⟩,⟨ æ,t ⟩,⟨ t,END ⟩}
c. # $\rightarrow$ k $\rightarrow$ æ$\rightarrow$ t $\rightarrow$ %

Figure 1: Phonological representations of the word *cat* as a string (a), ordered pairs (b), and a graph (c).

The graph representation should highlight an important detail. There is no a priori logical reason in this representation why forms should be linear, with one segment following another in a chain. This is only an assumption that we impose on the



*Proceedings of the Seventeenth SIGMORPHON Workshop on Computational Research in Phonetics, Phonology, and Morphology*,pages 23–31

structure when assuming strings. This assumption is what Multiprecedence abandons. Multiprecedence proposes that asymmetry and irreflexivity are not relevant to phonology. A segment can precede or follow multiple segment, two segments can transitively precede each other, and a segment can precede itself. A valid multiprecedence graph is not restricted by topology, a term a will use for the pattern of the graph independent from the content of the nodes.

Using this view of precedence, affixation is the process of combining the graph representations of different morphemes. A word is a graph consisting of the edges and vertices (precedence relations and segments) of one or more morphemes. An example of the suffixation of the English plural is shown in Fig. 2a, and the infixation of the Atayal animate focus morpheme is given in Fig. 2b. Full root reduplication, which expresses the plural of nouns in Indonesian is shown in Fig. 2c. There are two things to notice in Fig. 2c. First, that a precedence arrow is added, without any segmental material: the reduplicative morpheme consists of just that arrow. Second, although Fig. 2a and Fig. 2b each offer two paths from the START to the END of the graph, Fig. 2c contains a loop that offers an infinite number of paths from START to End. The representation itself does not enforce how many times the arrow added by the plural morpheme should be traversed. All three of these structures have to be handled by a *serialization* algorithm in order to be actualized by the phonetic motor system, which selects a path through the graph to be sent to the articulators. A correct serialization algorithm must be able to select the correct of the two paths in Fig. 2a and Fig. 2b and the path going through the back loop only once in Fig. 2c.

I will assume here that these forms are constructed by the attachment of an affix morpheme onto a stem as in Fig. 3. English speakers have a graph as a lexical item for the plural as in Fig. 3a and a lexical item for CAT as in Fig. 3b, which combine as in Fig. 3c. The moniker "last segment" is an informal way to refer to that part of the affix that is responsible for attaching it to the stem in the right location. This piece of the plural affix will attach onto the last segment, the one preceding the end of the word %, of what it combined with, and onto %, yielding Fig 3c. Similarly the Atayal form in Fig. 2 is built from a root *#hŋuʔ%* 'soak' and an infix *-m-* marking the animate actor focus and attaching between the first and the second segment. For details on the mechanics of attachment see Raimy (2000a, §3.2), Samuels (2009, p.177-87), and Papillon (2020, §2.2). It suffices here to say that at vocabulary insertion an affix can target certain segments of the stem for attachment. Raimy (2000a) shows how this representation can generate the reduplicative patterns from numerous languages as well as account for such phenomena as over- and under-application of phonological processes in reduplication.

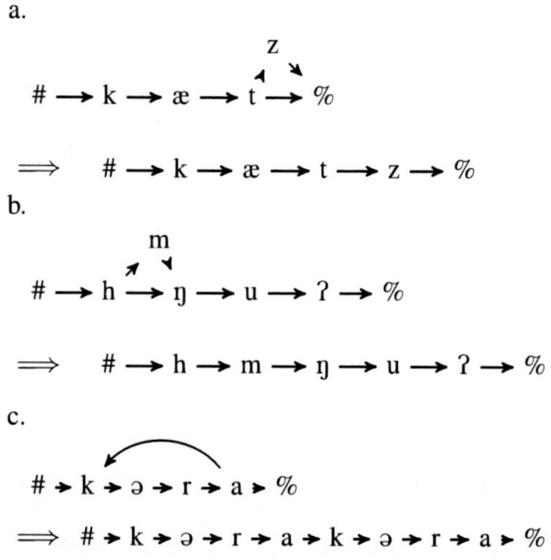


Figure 2: Affixation in Multiprecedence. Suffixation (a), infixation (b), reduplication (c).

a. [last segment] → z → %
b. # → k → æ→ t → %
c.

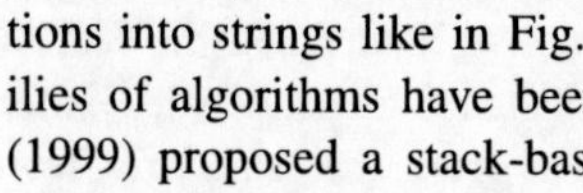


Figure 3: Affix (a) and root (b) combined in (c).

Given the assumption that a non-linear graph cannot be pronounced, phonology requires an algorithm capable of converting graph representations into strings like in Fig. 2. Two main families of algorithms have been proposed. Raimy (1999) proposed a stack-based algorithm which was expanded upon by Idsardi and Shorey (2007) and McClory and Raimy (2007). This algorithm traverses the graph from # to % by accessing the stack. This idea suffers the problem of requiring parameters on individual arcs. Every morphologically-added precedence link must be parametrized as to its priority determining whether it goes to the top or the bottom of the stack. This is necessary in this system because when a given arc is traversed is not predictable on the basis of when it is encountered in a traversal. This parametrization radically explodes the range of patterns predicted to be possible much beyond what is attested. Fitzpatrick and Nevins (2002; 2004) proposed a different constraint-base algorithm which globally compares paths through the graph for completeness and economy but suffers the problem of requiring ad hoc constraints targeting individual types of graphs, lacking generality. In the rest of this article I will present a new algorithm which lacks any parameter and whose two operations are generic and not geared towards any specific configuration.

## 3 The Match-Extend algorithm

This section will present the Match-Extend algorithm and follow up with a demonstration of its operation on various attested Multiprecedence topologies.

The input to the algorithm is the set of pairs of segments corresponding to the pairs of segments in immediate precedence relation without the affix, e.g. {#k,kæ,æt,t%} for the English stem *kæt*, and the set of pair of segments corresponding to the precedence links added by the affix, e.g. {tz,z%} when the plural is added.

Intuitively the algorithm starts from the morphologically added links and extends outwards by following the precedence links in the StemSet, the set of all precedence links in the stem to which the morpheme is being added. If there is more than one morphologically added link, they all extend in parallel and collapse together if one string ends in one or more segment and the other begins with the same segment or segments. A working version of this algorithm coded in Python will be included as supplementary material.

### 3.1 Match-Extend in action

Consider first total reduplication as in Fig. 2c above. Fig. 3.1 shows the full derivation of *kəra-kəra* with total reduplication. As there is only one morphologically-added link, no Match step will happen.

Let us turn to more complex graphs discussed in the literature. Raimy discusses a process of CV

1 .The precedence links of the stem begin in a set StemSet.
2. The morphologically added links begin in a set WorkSpace.
3. Whenever two strings in the WorkSpace match such that the end of one string is identical to the end of the other, the operation Match collapses the two into one string such that the shared part appears once. E.g. `abcd` and `cdef` to `abcdef`. A Match along multiple characters is done first.
4. When there is no match within the WorkSpace, the operation Extend simultaneously lengthens all strings in the WorkSpace to the right and left using matching precedence links of the stem. StemSet remains unchanged.
5.Steps 3 and 4 are repeated until # and % have been reached by Extend and there is a single string in the WorkSpace.

**Algorithm 1:** The Match-Extend Algorithm (informal version).

| StemSet | { #k , kə , ər , ra , a% } |
|---|---|
| WorkSpace | ak |
| Extend | rakə |
| Extend | ərakər |
| Extend | kərakəra |
| Extend | #kərakəra% |

Figure 4: Match-Extend derivation of *kəra-kəra*.

reduplication in Tohono O'odham involving reduplicated pattern such as *babað* to *ba-b-bað*, and *čipkan* to *či-čpkan* requiring graphs as in Raimy (2000a, p.114). Although there are multiple plausible paths through this graph, only one is attested and this path requires traversing the graph by following the backlink before the front-link, even though the front-link would be encountered first in a traversal.

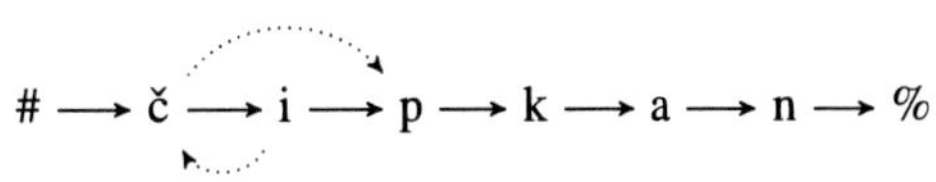


Figure 5: Tohono O'odham *či-čpkan*.

The match-Extend algorithm will correctly derive the correct form as shown in . Right away the strings `ič` and `čp` match, as one starts with the node `c` and the other ends with the same node. The two are collapsed as `ičp` and then keep extending.

| StemSet | {#č, či, ip, pk, ka, an, n%} |
|---|---|
| WorkSpace | čp<br>ič |
| Match | ič̲p |
| Extend | čičpk |
| Extend | #čičpka |
| Extend | #čičpkan |
| Extend | #čičpkan% |

Figure 6: Match-extend derivation of Tohono O'odham *čičpkan*.

A similarly complex graph is needed in Nancowry. Raimy (2000a, p.81) discusses examples like Nancowry reduplication of the last consonant toward the beginning of the word, e.g. *sut* 'to rub' to *ʔit-sut* which requires a graph as in Fig. 7. However here the opposite order of traversal must be followed, not skipping the first forward link. I assume here, like Raimy, that the glottal stop is epenthetic and added after serialization. Here, not taking the first link would also result in the wrong output [*sutsut]. So this form requires the first morphologically-added link to be taken to produce the correct form.

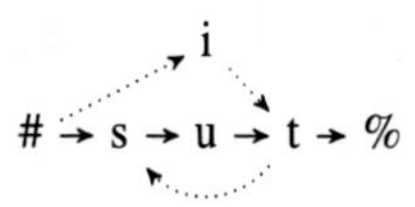


Figure 7: Nancowry *ʔit-sut*.

Again Match-Extend will serialize Fig. 7 without any further parameter as in Fig. 8. The three strings `#i`, `it`, and `ts` can match right away into a single string `#its` which will keep extending.

As these examples illustrate, Match-Extend does not need to be specified with look-ahead, global considerations, or graph-by-graph specifications of serialization to derive the attested serialization of graphs like Fig. 5 or Fig. 7. The serialization starts in parallel from two added links that extend until they reach each other in the middle, and this will work regardless of the order in which 'backward' and 'forward' arcs are located. They will meet in one direction and serialize in this order.

Another interesting topology is found in the analysis of Lushotseed. Fitzpatrick & Nevins

| StemSet | {#s, su, ut, t%} |
|---|---|
| WorkSpace | #i<br>it<br>ts |
| Match | #i̲t<br>ts |
| Match | #it̲s |
| Extend | #itsu |
| Extend | #itsut |
| Extend | #itsut% |

Figure 8: Derivation of Nancowry *ʔitsut*.

(2002; 2004) observed that in cases where multiple reduplication processes of different size happen to the same form, with multiple morphologically added arrows forking away from the same segment, these graphs are seemingly universally serialized such that they follow the shorter arc first. They discuss Lushotseed forms with both distributive and Out-Of-Control (OOC) reduplication. They argue on the basis of the fact that in either scope order the form is serialized in the same way, suggesting that they are serialized simultaneously. This implies forms like $g^{w}ad$, 'talk', surfacing in the distributive OOC or the OOC distributive as $g^{w}ad\text{-}ad\text{-}g^{w}ad$, requiring a graphs like Fig. 9.

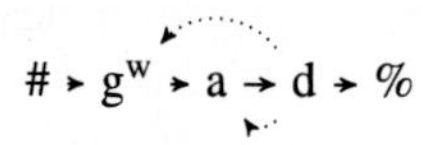


Figure 9: Lushotseed $g^{w}ad\text{-}ad\text{-}g^{w}ad$.

Fitzpatrick & Nevins (2002; 2004) proposed an ad hoc constraint to handle this type of scenario, the constraint SHORTEST, enforcing serializations that follow the shorter arrow first. But Match-Extend derives the attested pattern without any further assumptions. Consider the derivation of the Lushotseed form in Fig. 9. After one Extend step, the two strings adg$^w$a and `adad` match along the nodes `ad`. You might notice that the two strings also match in the other order with the node `a`, so we must assume the reasonable principle that in case of multiple matches, the best match, meaning the match along more nodes, is chosen. From that point on adadg$^w$a extends into the desired form.

It is somewhat intuitive to see why this works: because Match-Extend applies one step of Extend at a time and must Match and collapse separate

| StemSet | { #g$^w$, g$^w$a, ad, d%} |
|---|---|
| WorkSpace | dg$^w$<br>da |
| Extend | adg$^w$a<br>adad |
| Match | adadg$^w$a |
| Extend | g$^w$adadg$^w$ad |
| Extend | #g$^w$adadg$^w$ad% |

Figure 10: Derivation of Lushotseed *g$^w$adadg$^w$ad*.

strings from the WorkSpace immediately when a Match is found, two arcs added by the morphology will necessarily match in the direction in which they are the closest. The end of the d→a arc is closer to the beginning of the d→g$^w$ one than vice-versa, and hence the two will join in this direction and therefore surface in this order. This can be generalized as Fig. 11.

- If the graph contains two morphologically added links $\alpha \rightarrow \beta$ and $\gamma \rightarrow \delta$, and
  - ▶ There is a unique path X from $\beta$ to $\gamma$ not going through $\alpha \rightarrow \beta$ or $\gamma \rightarrow \delta$, and
  - ▶ There is a unique path Y from $\delta$ to $\alpha$ not going through $\alpha \rightarrow \beta$ or $\gamma \rightarrow \delta$,
- Then the Match-Extend algorithm will output a string containing:
  - ▶ ...$\alpha\beta$...$\gamma\delta$... if X is shorter than Y
  - ▶ ...$\gamma\delta$...$\alpha\beta$... if Y is shorter than X

Figure 11: Closest Attachment in Match-Extend.

Note that this is not a new assumption: this is a theorem of the model derivable from the way Match and Extend interact with multiple morphologically added arcs. This can allow us to work out some serializations without having to do the whole derivation.

Consider for instance the Nlaka'pamuctsin distributive+diminutive double reduplication, e.g. *sil*, 'calico', to *sil-si-sil*, (Broselow, 1983). This pattern requires the Multiprecedence graph to look as in Fig. 12.

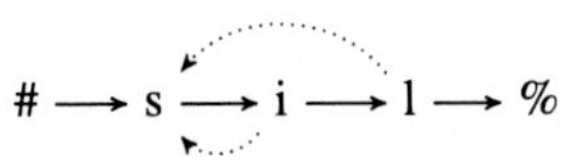

Figure 12: Nlaka'pamuctsin *sil-si-sil*.

The graph in Fig. 12 is simply the transpose graph of a graph where SHORTEST would apply like Fig. 9, but it does not actually fit the pattern of SHORTEST as its two 'backward' arrows do not start from the same node. In fact if anything SHORTEST would predict the wrong surface form, as **si-sil-sil* would be the form if the shorter path were taken first. In Match-Extend and Closest Attachment Fig. 11 the prediction is clear: it is predicted to serialize as *sil-si-sil* because the path from l→s to i→s is shorter than the path from i→s to l→s, thus deriving the correct string.

Fitzpatrick and Nevins (2002) report some forms with graphs like Fig. 12 which must be linearized in ways that would contradict Match-Extend, such as *sax$^w$* to *sa-sax$^w$-sax$^w$* in Lusotsheed Diminutive+Distributive forms. But contrary to the Distributive+OOC forms discussed earlier there is no independent evidence here for the two reduplications being serialized together. I therefore assume that those instances consist of two separate cycles, serialized one at a time: *sax$^w$* to *sax$^w$-sax$^w$* to *sa-sax$^w$-sax$^w$*. Match-Extend therefore relies on cyclicity, with the graph built up through affixation and serialized multiple times over the course of the derivation.

### 3.2 Non-Edge Fixed Segmentism

Fixed segmentism refers to cases of reduplication where a segment of one copy is overridden by one or more fixed segments. A well known English example is *schm*-reduplication like *table* to *table-schmable* where *schm*-replaces the initial onset. I will call Non-Edge Fixed Segmentism (NEFS) the special case of fixed segmentism where the fixed segment is not at the edge of one of the copies. These are the examples where the graph needed is like Fig. 13 or Fig. 14.

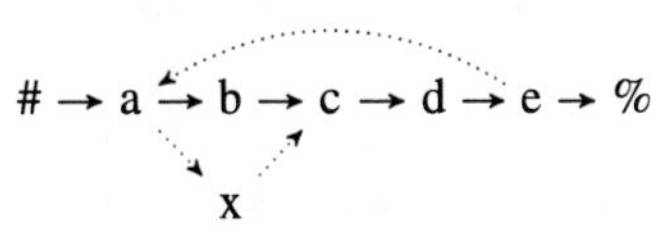

Figure 13: NEFS 'early' in the copy.

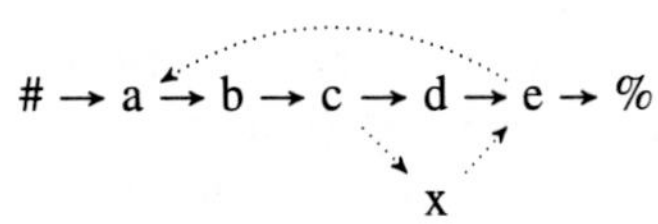

Figure 14: NEFS 'late' in the copy.

Closest Attachment in Match-Extend predicts that if a fixed-segment is added towards the beginning of the form, it should surface in the second copy, and if it is added toward the end of the form, it should surface in the first copy. Or in other words the fixed segment will always occur in the copy such that the fixed segment is closer to the juncture of the two copies. The graph in Fig. 13 will serialize as `abcde-a`**`x`**`cde` and the graph in Fig. 14 will serialize as `abc`**`x`**`e-abcde`. This follows from the properties of Match and Extend: as the precedence pairs of the overwriting segment and the precedence pair of the backward link extend outward, it will either reach the left or right side first and this will determine the order in which they appear in the final serialized form.

This prediction is borne out by many examples of productive patterns of reduplication with NEFS such as Marathi *saman-**suman*** (Alderete et al., 1999, citing Apte 1968), Bengali sajɹa-**s**u**j**ɹa (Khan, 2006, p.14), Kinnauri migo-**m**ə**g**o (Chang, 2007).

Apparent counterexamples exist, but have other plausible analyses. A major one worth discussing briefly is the previous multiprecedence analysis of the Javanese Habitual-Repetitive as described by Yip (1995; 1998). Most forms surface with a fixed /a/ in the first copy as in *el**a**ŋ-eliŋ* 'remember'. This requires a graph such as Fig. 15 which serializes in comformity with Match-Extend.

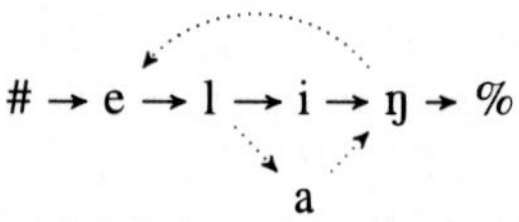


Figure 15: Javanese *elaŋ-eliŋ*.

However when the first copy already contains /a/ as the second vowel the form is realized with /e/ in the second copy as *udan-uden* 'rain'. Idsardi and Shorey (2007) and McClory and Raimy (2007) have analyzed this as a phonologically-conditioned allomorph with fixed segment /e/ that must be serialized differently from the /a/ allomorph, with the overwriting vowel in the second copy, i.e. a graph such as Fig. 16 that does not serialize in comformity with Match-Extend. Idsardi and Shorey (2007) and McClory and Raimy (2007) use this example to argue for a system of stacks that serialization must read from the top-down. Precedence arcs in turn can be lexically parametrized as to whether they are added on top or at the bottom of the stack upon affixation, thus deriving *elaŋeliŋ* from the /a/ allomorph being on top of the stack and traversed early and *udanuden* from the /e/ allomorph being at the bottom of the stack and traversed late. This freedom of lexical specification grants their system the power to enforce any order needed, including the capacity to handle the 'look-ahead' and 'shortest' cases above in terms of full lexical specification. They could also easily handle languages with the equivalent of a LONGEST constraint. This model is less predictive while also being more complex.

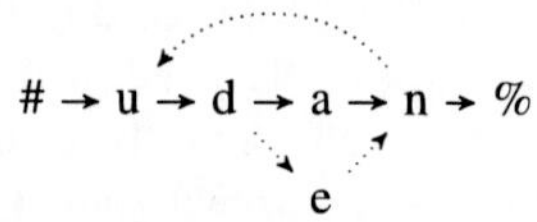


Figure 16: Javanese *udan-uden* according to Idsardi and Shorey (2007) and McClory and Raimy (2007).

But this complexity is unneeded if we instead adopt dissimilation analysis closer in spirit to Yip's original Optimality-Theory analysis. We can say that the /a/ of the first copy is an overwritten /a/ in both *elaŋ-eliŋ* and in *udan-uden* and a phonological process causes dissimilation of the root /a/ in the presence of the added /a/. In Optimality-Theory this requires an appeal to the Obligatory Contour Principle operating between the two copies, but in Multiprecedence the dissimilation is even simpler to state because the two /a/'s are very local in the graph. We simply need a rule to the effect of raising a stem /a/ in the context of a morphologically-added /a/ that precedes the same segment as in Fig.17.

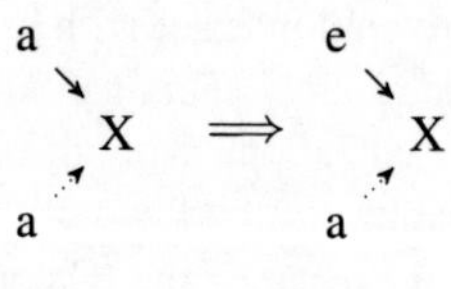


Figure 17: Dissimilation Rule

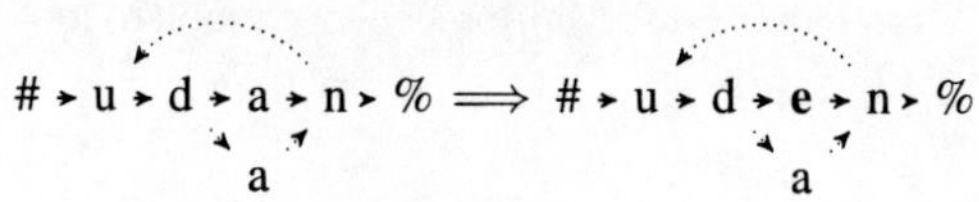


Figure 18: Derivation of *udan-uden*.

There is therefore no need to abandon Match-

Extend on the basis of Javanese.

Consider another apparent counterexample to the prediction: the Palauan root /rɛbət$^{h}$/ forms its distributive with CVCV reduplication and the verbal prefix *mə-* forming *mə-rəbə-rɛbət$^{h}$* (Zuraw, 2003). At first blush, one may be tempted to see the first schwa of the first copy as overwriting the root's /ɛ/. But the presence of this schwa actually follows from the independently-motivated phonology of Palauan in which all non-stressed vowels go to [ə]. This thus is the result of a phonological rule applying after serialization about which Match-Extend has nothing to say.

Relatedly, other apparent issues may be caused by interactions with phonology. D'souza (1991, p.294) describes how echo-formation in some Munda languages is accomplished by replacing all the vowels in the second copy with a fixed vowel, e.g. Gorum *bubuʔ* 'snake' > *bubuʔ-bibiʔ*. Fixed segmentism of each vowel individually may not be the best analysis of these forms, there may instead be a single fixed segment and a separate process of vowel harmony or something along those lines. This type of complex interaction of non-local phonology with reduplication has been investigated before in Multiprecedence, e.g. the analyses of Tuvan vowel harmony in reduplicated forms in Harrison and Raimy (2004) and Papillon (2020, §7.1), but these analyses make extra assumptions about possible Multiprecedence structures that go far beyond the basics explored here. The subject requires further exploration, but appears to be more of an issue of phonology and representation than of serialization per se.

Apparent counterexamples will have to be approached on a case-by case basis, but I have not identified many problematic examples so far that did not turn out to be errors of analysis.[1]

We have therefore seen that Match-Extend can straightforwardly account for a number of attested complex reduplicative patterns without any special stipulations. More interestingly Match-Extend makes strong novel predictions about the location of fixed segments. I have not been able to locate many examples of NEFS in the literature. For example the typology of fixed segmentism in Alderete et al. (1999) does not contain any example of NEFS. This will require further empirical research.

## 4 One limitation of Match-Extend: overly symmetrical graphs

There is a gap in the predictions of Fig. 11: Closest Attachment predicts that morphologically-added edges will attach in the order they are the closest, which relies on an asymmetry in the form such that morphologically-added links are closer in one order than the other. This leaves the problem of symmetrical forms like Fig. 19. The former of there was posited in the analysis of Semai continuative reduplication by Raimy (2000a, p.146-47) for forms like *dŋɔh* 'appearance of nodding' to *dh-dŋɔh*; the latter would be needed in various languages reduplicating CVC forms with vowel changes such as the Takelma aorist described in Sapir (1922, p.58) like *t'eu* 'play shinny' to *t'eut'au*.

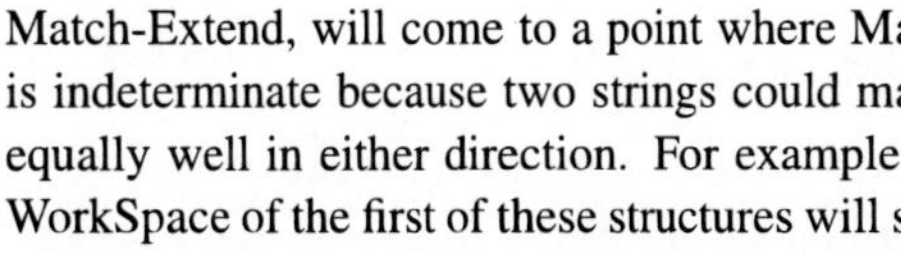


Figure 19: Two structures overly symmetrical for Match-Extend.

These are the forms which, in the course of Match-Extend, will come to a point where Match is indeterminate because two strings could match equally well in either direction. For example the WorkSpace of the first of these structures will start with `ac` and `ca`, which can match either as `a`**`c`**`a` or `c`**`a`**`c`. The former would extend into `#acabc%` and the latter into `#abcac%`. Match-Extend as stated so far is therefore indeterminate with regard to these symmetrical forms.

This is not an insurmountable problem for Match-Extend. To the contrary this is a problem

[1] One such apparent counter-example is worth briefly commenting on here due to its being mentioned in well-known surveys of reduplication. This alleged reduplication is from in Macdonald and Darjowidjojo (1967, p.54) and repeated in Rubino (2005, p.16): Indonesian *belat* 'screen' to *belat-belit* 'underhanded'. If correct this example would be a counterexample to Match-Extend, as a fixed /i/ must surface in the second copy. However this pair seems to be misidentified. The English-Indonesian bilingual dictionary by (Stevens and Schmidgall-Tellings, 2004) lists a word *belit* meaning 'crooked, cunning, deceitful, dishonest, underhanded', which semantically seems like a more plausible source for the reduplicated form *belat-belit* and fits the predictions of Match-Extend. The same dictionary's entry under *belat* lists some screen-related entries and then *belat-belit* as meaning 'crooked, devious, artful, cunning, insincere' cross-referencing to *belit* as the base. I conclude that this example was misidentified by previous authors and is unproblematic for Match-Extend.

of having too many solutions without a way to decide between them, none of which require adding parametrization to Match-Extend. Maybe symmetrical forms crash the derivation and all apparent instances in the literature must contain some hidden asymmetry. It is worth noting that the pattern in Fig. 19 attested in Semai has a close cognate in Temiar, but in this language the symmetrical structure is only obtained for simple onsets, *kɔw* 'call' to *kw-kɔw*, but *slɔg* 'sleep with' to *s-g-lɔg* (Raimy, 2000a, p.146). This asymmetry resolves the Match-Extend derivation. It may simply be the case that the forms that look symmetrical have a hidden asymmetry in the form of silent segments. For example if the root has an X at the start as in Fig. 21. This is obviously very ad hoc and powerful so minimally we should seek language-internal evidence for such a segment before jumping to conclusions.

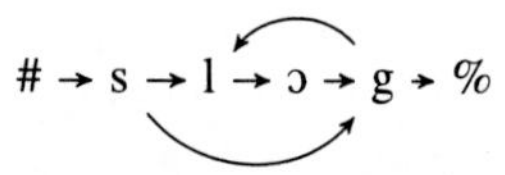


Figure 20: Temiar *sglog*.

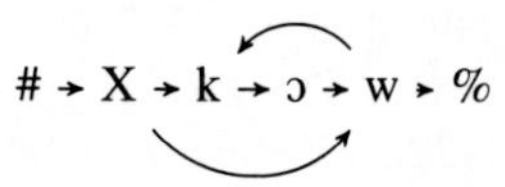


Figure 21: Semai *kw-kɔw* with hidden asymmetry in the form of a segment X without a phonetic correlate, which breaks the symmetry.

Alternatively it could be that symmetrical forms lead to both options being constructed and this optionality is resolved in extra-grammatical ways. I will leave this hole in the theory open, as a problem to be resolved through further research.

## 5 Conclusion

This article presents an invariant serialization algorithm for all morphological patterns in Multiprecedence.

The Multiprecedence research program has been fruitful in bringing various non-concatenative phenomena other than reduplication within the scope of a derivational item-and-arrangement model of morphology, including e.g. subtractive morphology (Gagnon and Piché, 2007), Semitic templatic morphology (Raimy, 2007), and vowel harmony, word tone, and allomorphy (Papillon, 2020). A serialization algorithm capable of handling these structures is crucial for the completeness of the theory.

As pointed out by a reviewer, it is crucial to develop a a typology of the possible attested graphical input structures to the algorithm so as to properly characterize and formalize the algorithm needed. In every form discussed here the roots is implicitly assumed to be underlyingly linear and affixes alone add some topological variety to the graphs, as is mostly the case in all the forms from (Raimy, 1999; Raimy, 2000a). Elsewhere I have challenged this idea by positing parallel structures both underlyingly and in the output of phonology (Papillon, 2020). If these structures are allowed in Multiprecedence Phonology then Match-Extend will need to be amended or enhanced to handle more varied structures.

In this paper I proposed a model that departs from the previous ones in being framed as patching a path from the morphology-added links towards # and % from the inside-out, as opposed to the existing models seeking to give a set of instructions to correctly traverse the graph from # to % from beginning to the end.

## References


John Alderete, Jill Beckman, Laura Benua, Amalia Gnanadesikan, John McCarthy, and Suzanne Urbanczyk. 1999. Reduplication with fixed segmentism. *Linguistic inquiry*, 30(3):327–364.

Ellen I Broselow. 1983. Salish double reduplications: subjacency in morphology. *Natural Language & Linguistic Theory*, 1(3):317–346.

Charles B Chang. 2007. Accounting for the phonology of reduplication. Presentation at LASSO XXXVI. Available on `https://cbchang.com/curriculum-vitae/presentations/`.

Jean D'souza. 1991. Echos in a sociolinguistic area. *Language sciences*, 13(2):289–299.

Justin Fitzpatrick and Andrew Nevins. 2002. Phonological occurrences: Relations and copying. In *Second North American Phonology Conference, Montreal*.

Justin Fitzpatrick and Andrew Nevins. 2004. Linearization of nested and overlapping precedence in multiple reduplication.

Michaël Gagnon and Maxime Piché. 2007. Principles of linearization & subtractive morphology. In *CUNY Phonology Forum Conference on Precedence Relations*.

K. David Harrison and Eric Raimy. 2004. Reduplication in Tuvan: Exponence, readjustment and phonology. In *Proceedings of Workshop in Altaic Formal Linguistics*, volume 1. Citeseer.

William Idsardi and Rachel Shorey. 2007. Unwinding morphology. In *CUNY Phonology Forum Workshop on Precedence Relations*.

SD Khan. 2006. *Similarity Avoidance in Bengali Fixed-Segment Reduplication*. Ph.D. thesis, University of California.

Roderick Ross Macdonald and Soenjono Darjowidjojo. 1967. *A student's reference grammar of modern formal Indonesian*. Georgetown University Press.

Daniel McClory and Eric Raimy. 2007. Enhanced edges: morphological influence on linearization. In *Poster presented at The 81st Annual Meeting of the Linguistics Society of America. Anaheim, CA*.

Maxime Papillon. 2020. *Precedence and the Lack Thereof: Precedence-Relation-Oriented Phonology*. Ph.D. thesis. https://drum.lib.umd.edu/handle/1903/26391.

Eric Raimy. 1999. *Representing reduplication*. Ph.D. thesis, University of Delaware.

Eric Raimy. 2000a. *The phonology and morphology of reduplication*, volume 52. Walter de Gruyter.

Eric Raimy. 2000b. Remarks on backcopying. *Linguistic Inquiry*, 31(3):541–552.

Eric Raimy. 2007. Precedence theory, root and template morphology, priming effects and the structure of the lexicon. CUNY Phonology Symposium Precedence Conference, January.

Carl Rubino. 2005. Reduplication: Form, function and distribution. *Studies on reduplication*, pages 11–29.

Bridget Samuels. 2009. *The structure of phonological theory*. Harvard University.

Edward Sapir. 1922. Takelma. In Franz Boas, editor, *Handbook of American Indian Languages,*. Smithsonian Institution. Bureau of American Ethnology.

Alan M. Stevens and A. Ed. Schmidgall-Tellings. 2004. *A comprehensive Indonesian-English dictionary*. PT Mizan Publika.

Moira Yip. 1995. Repetition and its avoidance: The case in Javanese.

Moira Yip. 1998. Identity avoidance in phonology and morphology. In *Morphology and its Relation to Phonology and Syntax*, pages 216–246. CSLI Publications.

Kie Zuraw. 2003. Vowel reduction in Palauan reduplicants. In *Proceedings of the 8th Annual Meeting of the Austronesian Formal Linguistics Association [AFLA 8]*, pages 385–398.

# Incorporating tone in the calculation of phonotactic probability

**James P. Kirby**
University of Edinburgh
School of Philosophy, Psychology, and Language Sciences
j.kirby@ed.ac.uk

## Abstract

This paper investigates how the ordering of tone relative to the segmental string influences the calculation of phonotactic probability. Trigram and recurrent neural network models were trained on syllable lexicons of four Asian syllable-tone languages (Mandarin, Thai, Vietnamese, and Cantonese) in which tone was treated as a segment occurring in different positions in the string. For trigram models, the optimal permutation interacted with language, while neural network models were relatively unaffected by tone position in all languages. In addition to providing a baseline for future evaluation, these results suggest that phonotactic probability is robust to choices of how tone is ordered with respect to other elements in the syllable.

## 1 Introduction

The phonotactic probability of a string is an important quantity in several areas of linguistic research, including language acquisition, wordlikeness, word segmentation, and speech production and perception (Bailey and Hahn, 2001; Daland and Pierrehumbert, 2011; Storkel and Lee, 2011; Vitevitch and Luce, 1999). When the language of interest is a tone language, the question arises of how tone should be incorporated into the probability calculation. As phonotactic probability is frequently computed based on some type of $n$-gram model, this means deciding on which segment(s) the probability of a tone should be conditioned. For instance, using a bigram model, one might compute the probability of the Mandarin syllable *fāng* as $P(\text{a}|\text{f}) \times P(\text{ŋ}|\text{a}) \times P(\text{tone 1}|\text{ŋ})$, but could just as well consider $P(\text{tone 1}|\text{f}) \times P(\text{a}|1) \times P(\text{ŋ}|\text{a})$, or any other conceivable permutation of tone and segments.

While this issue is occasionally remarked on (e.g. Newman et al., 2011: 246), there remains no widespread consensus in practice. Choice of ordering is sometimes justified based on segment-tone co-occurrence restrictions in the language under study (Myers and Tsay, 2005), but is often presented without justification (Kirby and Yu, 2007; Yang et al., 2018), and in some cases tone is simply ignored (Gong, 2017). When the space of possibilities is considered, researchers generally select the permutation which maximizes model fit to some external data, such as participant judgments of phonological distance (Do and Lai, 2021a) or wordlikeness (Do and Lai, 2021b).

Although extrinsic evaluation is in some sense a gold standard, intrinsic metrics of model fit can also be informative, in part because extrinsic metrics are not always robust across data sets. For instance, participant wordlikeness judgments can vary considerably based on the particulars of the experimental design (Myers and Tsay, 2005; Shademan, 2006; Vitevitch and Luce, 1999), so the treatment of tone that produces a best-fit model for one dataset may not do so for another. The lexicon of a given language is much more internally stable in terms of how segments and tones are distributed, so intrinsic evaluation may provide a useful baseline for reasoning about the treatment of tone relative to segments both within and across languages.

This short paper considers a simple information-theoretic motivation for selecting a permutation: all else being equal, we should prefer a model that maximizes the probability of the lexicon (i.e., minimizes the cross-entropy loss), because this will be the model that by definition does the best job of capturing the phonotactic regularities of the lexicon (Cherry



*Proceedings of the Seventeenth SIGMORPHON Workshop on Computational Research in Phonetics, Phonology, and Morphology*, pages 32–38

et al., 1953; Goldsmith, 2002; Pimentel et al., 2020). By treating tone as another phone in the segmental string, we can see whether and to what degree this choice has an effect on the overall entropy of the lexicon.

Intuitively, *any* model that can take into account phonotactic constraints will result in a reduction in entropy. Thus, even an $n$-gram model with a sufficiently large context window should in principle be able model segment-tone co-occurrences at the syllable level. However, tone languages differ with respect to tone-segment co-occurrence restrictions (see Sec. 2). If a relevant constraint primarily targets syllable onsets, for instance, placing the tonal "segment" in immediate proximity to the onset will increase the probability of the string, even relative to a model capable of capturing the dependency at a longer distance.

## 2 Languages

Four syllable-tone languages were selected for this study: Mandarin Chinese, Cantonese, Vietnamese and Thai. They are partially a convenience sample in that the necessary lexical resources were readily available, but also have some useful similarities: all share a similar syllable structure template and have five or six tones. However, the four languages vary in terms of their segment-tone co-occurrence restrictions, as detailed below.

In all cases, the lexicon was defined as the set of unique syllable shapes in each language. For consistency, the syllable template in all four languages is considered to be $(C_1)(C_2)V(C)T$, with variable positioning of T. Offglides were treated as codas in all languages. The syllable lexicons for all four languages are provided in the supplementary materials (`http://doi.org/10.17605/OSF.IO/NA5FB`).

**Mandarin (`cmn`)** The Mandarin syllabary consists of 1,226 syllables based on list of attested readings of the 13,060 BIG5 characters from Tsai (2000), phonetized using the phonological system of Duanmu (2007). This representation encodes 22 onsets, 3 medials (/j ɥ w/), 6 nuclei, 4 codas and 5 tones (including the neutral tone). In Mandarin, unaspirated obstruent onsets rarely appear with mid-rising tone (MC *yang ping*), and sonorant onsets rarely occur with the high-level tone (MC *yin ping*). Obstruents never occur as codas.

**Thai (`tha`)** A Thai lexicon of 4,133 unique syllables was created based on the dictionary of Haas (1964) which contains around 19,000 entries and 47,000 syllables. The phonemic representation encodes 20 onsets, 3 medials /w l r/, 21 nuclei (vowel length being contrastive in Thai), 8 codas and 5 tones. In Thai, high tone is rare/unattested following unaspirated and voiced onsets, but there is also statistical evidence for a restriction on rising tones with these onsets (Perkins, 2013). In syllables with an obstruent coda (/p t k/), only high, low, or falling tones occur, depending on length of the nuclear vowel (Morén and Zsiga, 2006).

**Vietnamese (`vie`)** The Vietnamese lexicon of 8,128 syllables was derived from a freely available dictionary of around 74,000 words (Đức, 2004), phonetized using a spelling pronunciation (Kirby, 2008). The resulting representation encodes 24 onsets, 1 medial (/w/), 14 nuclei, 8 codas and 6 tones. Vietnamese syllables ending in obstruents /p t k/ are restricted to just one of two tones.

**Cantonese (`yue`)** The Cantonese syllabary consists of the 1,884 unique syllables in the Chinese Character Database (Kwan et al., 2003), encoded using the *jyutping* system. This representation distinguishes 22 onsets, 1 medial (/w/), 11 nuclei, 5 codas and 6 tones. In Cantonese, unaspirated initials do not occur in syllables with low-falling tones, and aspirated initials do not occur with the low tone. Syllables ending with /p t k/ are restricted to one of the three "entering" tones (Yue-Hashimoto, 1972).

## 3 Methods

Two classes of character-level language models (LMs) were considered: simple $n$-gram models and recurrent neural networks (Mikolov et al., 2010). In an $n$-gram model, the probability of a string is proportional to the conditional probabilities of the component $n$-grams:

$$P(x_i|x_1^{i-1}) \approx P(x_i|x_{i-n+1}^{i-1}) \tag{1}$$

The degree of context taken into account is thus determined by the value chosen for $n$.

In a recurrent neural network (RNN), the next character in a sequence is predicting using the current character and the previous hidden state. At each step $t$, the network retrieves an embedding for the current input $x_t$ and combines it with the hidden layer from the previous step to compute a new hidden layer $h_t$:

$$h_t = g(Uh_{t-1} + Wx_t) \tag{2}$$

where $W$ is the weight matrix for the current time step, $U$ the weight matrix for the previous time step, and $g$ is an appropriate non-linear activation function. This hidden layer $h_t$ is then used to generate an output layer $y_t$, which is passed through a softmax layer to generate a probability distribution over the entire vocabulary. The probability of a sequence $x_1, x_2 \ldots x_z$ is then just the product of the probabilities of each character in the sequence:

$$P(x_1, x_2 \ldots x_z) = \prod_{i=1}^{z} y_i \tag{3}$$

The incorporation of the recurrent connection as part of the hidden layer allows RNNs to avoid the problem of limited context inherent in $n$-gram models, because the hidden state embodies (some type of) information about *all* of the preceding characters in the string. Although RNNs cannot capture arbitrarily long-distance dependencies, this is unlikely to make a difference for the relatively short distances involved in phonotactic modeling.

Trigram models were built using the SRILM toolkit (Stolcke, 2002), with maximum likelihood estimates smoothed using interpolated Witten-Bell discounting (Witten and Bell, 1991). RNN LMs were built using PyTorch (Paszke et al., 2019), based on an implementation by Mayer and Nelson (2020). The results reported here make use of simple recurrent networks (Elman, 1990), but similar results were obtained using an LSTM layer (Hochreiter and Schmidhuber, 1997).

### 3.1 Procedure

The syllables in each lexicon were arranged in 5 distinct permutations: tone following the coda (T|C), nucleus (T|N), medial (T|M), onset (T|O) and with tone as the initial segment in the syllable (T|#). As many syllables in these languages lack onsets, medials, and/or codas, a sizable number of the resulting strings were identical across permutations. Both smoothed trigram and simple RNN LMs were then fit to each permuted lexicon 10 times, with random 80/20 train/dev splits (other splits produced similar results). For each run, the perplexity of the language model on the dev set $D = x_1 x_2 \ldots x_N$ (i.e., the exponentiated cross-entropy[1]) was recorded:

$$PPL(D) = b^{H(D)} \tag{4}$$

$$= b^{-\frac{1}{N} log_b P(x_1 x_2 \ldots x_N)} \tag{5}$$

## 4 Results

For brevity, only the main findings are summarized here; the full results are available as part of the online supplementary materials (`http://doi.org/10.17605/OSF.IO/NA5FB`).

Table 1 show the orderings which minimized perplexity for each method and language, averaged over 10 runs. Table 2 shows the average perplexity over all permutations for a given language and method.

| method | lexicon | order | PPL |
|---|---|---|---|
| 3-gram | cmn | T\|C | 4.91 (0.06) |
| | tha | T\|M | 7.34 (0.12) |
| | vie | T\|C | 7.35 (0.03) |
| | yue | T\|M | 5.84 (0.09) |
| RNN | cmn | T\|M | 4.01 (0.08) |
| | tha | T\|M | 5.20 (0.04) |
| | vie | T\|M | 5.16 (0.02) |
| | yue | T\|# | 4.37 (0.05) |

Table 1: Orders which produced the lowest perplexities averaged over 10 runs (means and standard deviations).

Differences between orderings were then assessed visually, aided by simple analyses of variance. For the trigram LMs, perplexity was lowest in Mandarin when tones followed codas, while differences in perplexity between other orderings were negligible. For Thai, Vietnamese, and Cantonese, all orderings were roughly comparable except for when tone was ordered as the first segment in the syllable (T|#), which increased perplexity by up to 1 over the mean of the other orderings. For Thai, the ordering T|M resulted in significantly lower perplexities compared to all other

[1]Equivalently, we may think of $PPL(D)$ as the inverse probability of the set of syllables $D$, normalized for the number of phonemes.

| | cmn | tha | vie | yue |
|---|---|---|---|---|
| 3-gram | 5.15 (0.17) | 7.76 (0.4) | 7.49 (0.27) | 5.98 (0.18) |
| RNN | 4.01 (0.07) | 5.28 (0.05) | 5.18 (0.03) | 4.42 (0.07) |

Table 2: Mean and standard deviation of perplexity across all permutations by lexicon and language model.

permutations. For the RNN LMs, although T|M was the numerically optimal ordering for three out of the four languages, in practical terms permutation had no effect on perplexity, with numerical differences of no greater than 0.1 (see Table 2).

## 5 Discussion

Consistent with other recent work in computational phonotactics (e.g. Mayer and Nelson, 2020; Mirea and Bicknell, 2019; Pimentel et al., 2020), the neural network models outperformed the trigram baselines by a considerable margin (a reduction in average perplexity of up to 2.5, depending on language). Neural network models were also much less sensitive to the linear position of tone relative to other elements in the segmental string (cf. Do and Lai, 2021b), no doubt due to the fact that the ability of the RNNs to model co-occurrence tendencies within the syllable is not constrained by context in the way that $n$-gram models are.

Perhaps as a result, however, the RNN models reveal little about the nature of segment-tone co-occurrence restrictions in any of the languages investigated. In this regard, the trigram models, while clearly less optimal in a global sense, are still informative. The fact that the ordering T|# was significantly worse under the trigram model for Cantonese, Vietnamese and Thai but not Mandarin can be explained (or predicted) by the fact that of the four languages, only Mandarin does not permit obstruent codas, and consequently has no coda-tone co-occurrence restrictions (indeed, the four primary tones of Mandarin occur with more or less equal type frequency). In the other three languages, syllables with obstruent codas can only bear a restricted set of tones, and in a trigram model, this dependency is not modeled when tone is prepended to the syllable, since this means it will frequently, though not always, fall outside the window visible to the language model. Even a model with a large enough context window to capture such dependencies will assign the lexicon a higher perplexity when structured in this way.

The finding that the T|M ordering is always optimal in Thai (and by a larger margin than in the other languages) is presumably due to the fact that the distribution of the medials /w l r/ is severely restricted in this language, occurring only after /p $p^h$ t $t^h$ k $k^h$ f/. The distribution of tones after onset-medial clusters is inherently more constrained and therefore more predictable. A similar restriction holds in Cantonese, albeit to a lesser degree (the medial /w/ only occurs with onsets /k/ and /$k^h$/).

### 5.1 Shortcomings and extensions

This work did not explore representations based on phonological features, given that their incorporation has failed to provide evaluative improvements in other studies of computational phonotactics (Mayer and Nelson, 2020; Mirea and Bicknell, 2019; Pimentel et al., 2020). However, feature-based approaches can be both theoretically insightful and may even prove necessary for other quantifications, such as the measure of phonological distance where tone is involved (Do and Lai, 2021a).

The present study has focused on a small sample of structurally and typologically similar languages. All have relatively simple syllable structures in which one and only one tone is associated with each syllable. Not all tone languages share these properties, however. In so-called "word-tone" languages, such as Japanese or Shanghainese, the surface tone with which a given syllable is realized is frequently not lexically specified. In other languages, such as Yoloxóchitl Mixtec (DiCanio et al., 2014), tonal specification may be tied to sub-syllabic units, such as the mora. Finally, data from many other languages, such as Kukuya (Hyman, 1987), make it clear that in at least in some cases tones can only be treated in terms of abstract melodies, which do not have a consistent association to syllables, moras, or vowels (Goldsmith, 1976). In these and many other cases, careful consideration of the theoretical motivations justifying a particular representation are required before it makes sense to consider ordering effects.

However, to the extent that it is possible to generate a segmental representation of a tone language in which surface tones are indicated, what the present work suggests is that the precise ordering of the tonal symbols with respect to other symbols in the string is unlikely to have a significant impact on phonotactic probability. This follows from two assumption (or constraints): first, that the set of symbols used to indicate tones is distinct from those used to indicate the vowels and consonants; and second, that one and only one such tone symbol appears per string domain (here, the syllable). If these two constraints hold, the complexity of the syllable template should in general have a greater impact on the entropy of the string set than the position of the tone symbol, although the number of unique tone symbols relative to the number of segmental symbols may also have an effect. According to Maddieson (2013) and Easterday (2019), languages with complex syllable structures (defined as those permitting fairly free combinations of two or more consonants in the position before a vowel, and/or two or more consonants in the position after the vowel) rarely have complex tone systems, or indeed tone systems at all, so this is unlikely to be an issue for most tone languages.

One possibility the present work did not address is whether it is even necessary, or desirable, to include tone in phonotactic probability calculations in the first place. The probability of the lexicon of a tonal language would surely change if tone is ignored, but whether listeners' judgments of a sequence as well- or ill-formed is better predicted by a model that takes tone into account vs. one that does not is an empirical question (but see Kirby and Yu, 2007; Do and Lai, 2021b for some evidence that it may not). Similarly, for research questions focused on tone sandhis, or on the distributions of the tonal sequences themselves (tonotactics), the relevant computations will be restricted to the tonal tier in the first instance, and ordering with respect to segments may simply not be relevant (but see Goldsmith and Riggle, 2012).

Finally, the present study has focused on the lexical representation of tone, but in many languages tone primarily serves a morphological function. The SIGMORPHON 2020 Task 0 shared challenge (Vylomova et al., 2020) included inflection data from several tonal Oto-Manguean languages in which tone was orthographically encoded in different ways via string diacritics. While the authors noted the existence these differences, it is unclear whether and to what extent the different representations of tones affected system performance. Similarly, the potential impact of tone ordering relative to other elements in the string has yet to be systematically investigated in this setting.

## 6 Conclusion

This paper has assessed how different permutations of tone and segments affects the perplexity of the lexicon in four syllable-tone languages using two types of phonotactic language models, an interpolated trigram model and a simple recurrent neural network. The perplexities assigned by the neural network models were essentially unaffected by different choices of ordering; while the trigram model was more sensitive to permutations of tone and segments, the effects on perplexity remained minimal. In addition to providing a baseline for future evaluation, these results suggest that the phonotactic probability of a syllable is relatively robust to choice of how tone is ordered with respect to other elements in the string, especially when using a model capable of encoding dependencies across the entire syllable.


## Acknowledgments

This work was supported in part by the ERC EVOTONE project (grant no. 758605).


## References


Todd Bailey and Ulrike Hahn. 2001. Determinants of wordlikeness: phonotactics or lexical neighborhoods? *Journal of Memory and Language*, 44:568–591.

E. Colin Cherry, Morris Halle, and Roman Jakobson. 1953. Toward the logical description of languages in their phonemic aspect. *Language*, 29(1):34–46.

Robert Daland and Janet B. Pierrehumbert. 2011. Learning diphone-based segmentation. *Cognitive Science*, 35(1):119–155.

Christian DiCanio, Jonathan D Amith, and Rey Castillo García. 2014. The phonetics of moraic alignment in yoloxóchitl mixtec. In *Proceedings of the 4th International Symposium on Tonal Aspects of Languages (TAL-2014)*, pages 203–210.

Youngah Do and Ryan Ka Yau Lai. 2021a. Accounting for lexical tones when modeling phonological distance. *Language*, 97(1):e39–e67.

Youngah Do and Ryan Ka Yau Lai. 2021b. Incorporating tone in the modelling of wordlikeness judgements. *Phonology*, 37:577–615.

San Duanmu. 2007. *The phonology of standard Chinese*, 2nd edition. Oxford University Press, Oxford.

Shelece Easterday. 2019. *Highly complex syllable structure: A typological and diachronic study*. Studies in Laboratory Phonology. Language Science Press.

Jeffrey L. Elman. 1990. Finding structure in time. *Cognitive Science*, 14(2):179–211.

John Goldsmith. 1976. *Autosegmental Phonology*. Ph.D. thesis, MIT. [Published by Garland Press, New York, 1979.].

John Goldsmith. 2002. Phonology as information minimization. *Phonological Studies*, 5:21–46.

John Goldsmith and Jason Riggle. 2012. Information theoretic approaches to phonological structure: the case of Finnish vowel harmony. *Natural Language and Linguistic Theory*, 30:859–896.

Donald Shuxiao Gong. 2017. Grammaticality and lexical statistics in Chinese unnatural phonotactics. *UCL Working Papers in Linguistics*, 17:1–23.

Mary R. Haas. 1964. *Thai-English student's dictionary*. Stanford University Press, Stanford.

Sepp Hochreiter and Jürgen Schmidhuber. 1997. Long short-term memory. *Neural Computation*, 9(8):1735–1780.

Larry M. Hyman. 1987. Prosodic domains in Kukuya. *Natural Language & Linguistic Theory*, 5(3):311–333.

James P. Kirby. 2008. vPhon: a Vietnamese phonetizer (version 2.1.1) [computer program]. https://github.com/kirbyj/vPhon.

James P. Kirby and Alan C. L. Yu. 2007. Lexical and phonotactic effects on wordlikeness judgments in Cantonese. In *Proceedings of the 16th International Conference of the Phonetic Sciences*, pages 1389–1392, Saarbrücken.

Tze-Wan Kwan, Wai-Sang Tang, Tze-Ming Chiu, Lei-Yin Wong, Denise Wong, and Li Zhong. 2003. Chinese character database with word-formations phonologically disambiguated according to the Cantonese dialect. http://humanum.arts.cuhk.edu.hk/Lexis/lexican/. Accessed 9 February 2007.

Ian Maddieson. 2013. Tone. In Matthew S. Dryer and Martin Haspelmath, editors, *The World Atlas of Language Structures Online*. Max Planck Institute for Evolutionary Anthropology.

Connor Mayer and Max Nelson. 2020. Phonotactic learning with neural language models. *Proceedings of the Society for Computation in Linguistics*, 3:16.

Tomáš Mikolov, Martin Karafiát, Lukáš Burget, Jan Černocký, and Sanjeev Khudanpur. 2010. Recurrent neural network based language model. In *Proc. INTERSPEECH 2010*, page 1045–1048.

Nicole Mirea and Klinton Bicknell. 2019. Using LSTMs to assess the obligatoriness of phonological distinctive features for phonotactic learning. In *Proceedings of the 57th Annual Meeting of the Association for Computational Linguistics*, pages 1595–1605. Association for Computational Linguistics.

Bruce Morén and Elizabeth Zsiga. 2006. The lexical and post-lexical phonology of Thai tones. *Natural Language and Linguistic Theory*, 24(1):113–178.

James Myers and Jane Tsay. 2005. The processing of phonological acceptability judgements. In *Proc. Symposium on 90-92 NSC Projects*, Taipei.

Ellen Hamilton Newman, Twila Tardif, Jingyuan Huang, and Hua Shu. 2011. Phonemes matter: The role of phoneme-level awareness in emergent Chinese readers. *Journal of Experimental Child Psychology*, 108(2):242–259.

Adam Paszke, Sam Gross, Francisco Massa, Adam Lerer, James Bradbury, Gregory Chanan, Trevor Killeen, Zeming Lin, Natalia Gimelshein, Luca Antiga, Alban Desmaison, Andreas Kopf, Edward Yang, Zachary DeVito, Martin Raison, Alykhan Tejani, Sasank Chilamkurthy, Benoit Steiner, Lu Fang, Junjie Bai, and Soumith Chintala. 2019. Pytorch: An imperative style, high-performance deep learning library. In H. Wallach, H. Larochelle, A. Beygelzimer, F. d'Alché-Buc, E. Fox, and R. Garnett, editors, *Advances in Neural Information Processing Systems 32*, pages 8024–8035. Curran Associates, Inc.

Jeremy Perkins. 2013. *Consonant-tone interaction in Thai.* Ph.D. thesis, Rutgers, The State University of New Jersey.

Tiago Pimentel, Brian Roark, and Ryan Cotterell. 2020. Phonotactic complexity and its trade-offs. *Transactions of the Association for Computational Linguistics*, 8:1–18.

Shabnam Shademan. 2006. Is phonotactic knowledge grammatical knowledge? In *Proceedings of the 25th West Coast Conference on Formal Linguistics*, pages 371–379. Cascadilla Proceedings Project.

Andreas Stolcke. 2002. SRILM – an extensible language modeling toolkit. In *Proc. Intl. Conf. on Spoken Language Processing Vol. 2*, pages 901–904, Denver.

Holly L. Storkel and Su-Yeon Lee. 2011. The independent effects of phonotactic probability and neighbourhood density on lexical acquisition by preschool children. *Language and Cognitive Processes*, 26(2):191–211.

Chih-Hao Tsai. 2000. Mandarin syllable frequency counts for Chinese characters. http://technology.chtsai.org/syllable/. Accessed 10 March 2021.

Michael S. Vitevitch and Paul A. Luce. 1999. Probabilistic phonotactics and neighborhood activation in spoken word recognition. *Journal of Memory and Language*, 40:374–408.

Ekaterina Vylomova, Jennifer White, Elizabeth Salesky, Sabrina J. Mielke, Shijie Wu, Edoardo Maria Ponti, Rowan Hall Maudslay, Ran Zmigrod, Josef Valvoda, Svetlana Toldova, and et al. 2020. Sigmorphon 2020 shared task 0: Typologically diverse morphological inflection. In *Proceedings of the 17th SIGMORPHON Workshop on Computational Research in Phonetics, Phonology, and Morphology*, page 1–39. Association for Computational Linguistics.

Ian H. Witten and Timothy C. Bell. 1991. The zero-frequency problem: estimating the probabilities of novel events in adaptive text compression. *IEEE Transactions on Information Theory*, 37(4):1085–1094.

Shiying Yang, Chelsea Sanker, and Uriel Cohen Priva. 2018. The organization of lexicons: a cross-linguistic analysis of monosyllabic words. In *Proceedings of the Society for Computation in Linguistics (SCiL) 2018*, page 164–173.

Anne O. Yue-Hashimoto. 1972. *Studies in Yue Dialects 1: Phonology of Cantonese.* Cambridge University Press.

Hồ Ngọc Đức. 2004. Vietnamese word list. http://www.informatik.uni-leipzig.de/~duc/software/misc/wordlist.html. Accessed 24 February 2021.

# MorphyNet: a Large Multilingual Database of Derivational and Inflectional Morphology

**Khuyagbaatar Batsuren**[1], **Gábor Bella**[2], **and Fausto Giunchiglia**[2,3]
[1]National University of Mongolia, Mongolia
[2]DISI, University of Trento, Italy
[3]College of Computer Science and Technology, Jilin University, China
khuyagbaatar@num.edu.mn;{gabor.bella,fausto.giunchiglia}@unitn.it

## Abstract

Large-scale morphological databases provide essential input to a wide range of NLP applications. Inflectional data is of particular importance for morphologically rich (agglutinative and highly inflecting) languages, and derivations can be used, e.g. to infer the semantics of out-of-vocabulary words. Extending the scope of state-of-the-art multilingual morphological databases, we announce the release of MorphyNet, a high-quality resource with 15 languages, 519k derivational and 10.1M inflectional entries, and a rich set of morphological features. MorphyNet was extracted from Wiktionary using both hand-crafted and automated methods, and was manually evaluated to be of a precision higher than 98%. Both the resource generation logic and the resulting database are made freely available[1][2] and are reusable as stand-alone tools or in combination with existing resources.

## 1 Introduction

Despite repeated paradigm shifts in computational linguistics and natural language processing, morphological analysis and its related tasks, such as lemmatization, stemming, or compound splitting, have always remained essential components within language processing systems. Recently, in the context of language models based on subword embeddings, a morphologically meaningful splitting of words has been shown to improve the efficiency of downstream tasks (Devlin et al., 2019; Sennrich et al., 2016; Bojanowski et al., 2017; Provilkov et al., 2020). In particular, the reintroduction of linguistically motivated approaches and high-quality linguistic resources into deep learning architectures has been crucial for dealing with morphologically rich—highly inflecting, agglutinative—languages more efficiently (Pinnis et al., 2017; Vylomova et al., 2017; Ataman and Federico, 2018; Gerz et al., 2018).

In response to such needs, and as simple and convenient substitutes for monolingual morphological analyzers, multilingual *morphological databases* have been developed, indicating for each word form entry one or more corresponding root or dictionary entries, as well as analysis (features) (Kirov et al., 2018; Metheniti and Neumann, 2020; Vidra et al., 2019). The precision and recall of these resources vary wildly, and there is still a lot of ground to cover with respect to the support of new languages, the modelling of the inflectional and derivational complexity of each language, as well as the richness of the information (features, affixes, parts of speech, etc.) provided.

As a further step towards extending online morphological data, we introduce *MorphyNet*, a new database that addresses both derivational and inflectional morphology. Its current version covers 15 languages and has 519k derivational and 10.1M inflectional entries, as well as a rich set of features (lemma, parts of speech, morphological tags, affixes, etc.). Similarly to certain existing databases, MorphyNet was built from *Wiktionary* data; however, our extraction logic allows for a more exhaustive coverage of both derivational and inflectional cases.

The contributions of this paper are the freely available MorphyNet resource, the description of the data extraction logic and tool, also made freely accessible, as well as its evaluation and comparison to state-of-the-art multilingual morphological databases. Due to the limited overlap between the contents of these resources and MorphyNet, we consider it as complementary and therefore usable in combination with them.

Section 2 of the paper presents the state of the art. Section 3 gives details on our method for generat-

[1]http://ukc.disi.unitn.it/index.php/MorphyNet
[2]http://github.com/kbatsuren/MorphyNet



*Proceedings of the Seventeenth SIGMORPHON Workshop on Computational Research in Phonetics, Phonology, and Morphology*, pages 39–48

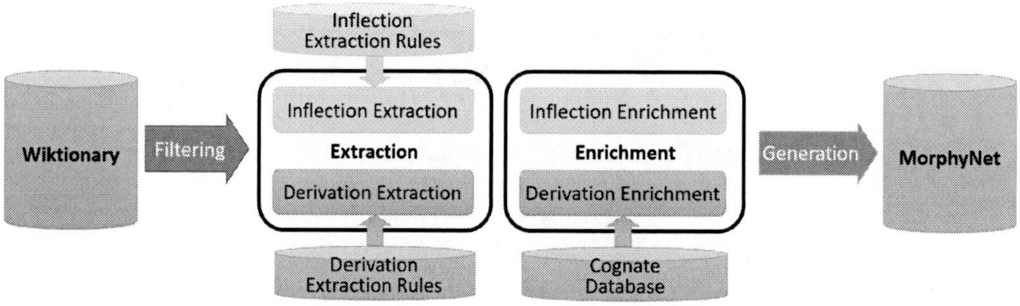


Figure 1: The MorphyNet generation process and the input datasets used.

ing MorphyNet data. Section 4 presents the resulting resource, and Section 5 evaluates it. Section 6 concludes the paper.

## 2 State of the Art

Ever since the early days of computational linguistics, morphological analysis and its related tasks—such as stemming and lemmatization—have been part of NLP systems. Earlier grammar-based systems used finite-state transducers or affix stripping techniques, and certain of them were already multilingual and were capable of tackling morphologically complex languages (Beesley and Karttunen, 2003; Trón et al., 2005; Inxight, 2005). However, due to the costliness of producing the grammar rules that drove them, many of these systems were only commercially available.

More recently, several projects have followed the approach of formalizing and/or integrating existing morphological data for multiple languages. *UDer (Universal Derivations)* (Kyjánek et al., 2020) integrates 27 derivational morphology resources in 20 languages. *UniMorph* (Kirov et al., 2016, 2018) and the *Wikinflection Corpus* (Metheniti and Neumann, 2020) rely mostly on *Wiktionary* from which they extract inflectional information. Beyond the data source, however, the two last projects have little in common: UniMorph is by far more precise and complete, and being used as gold standard for NLP community (Cotterell et al., 2017, 2018) (recently covering 133 languages (McCarthy et al., 2020)), while Wikinflection follows a naïve, linguistically uninformed approach of merely concatenating affixes, generating an abundance of ungrammatical word forms (e.g. for Hungarian or Finnish).

MorphyNet is also based on extracting morphological information from Wiktionary, extending the scope of UniMorph by new extraction rules and logic. The first version of MorphyNet covers 15 languages, and it is distinct from other resources in three aspects: (1) it includes both inflectional and derivational data; (2) it extracts a significantly higher number of inflections from Wiktionary; and (3) it provides a wider range of morphological information. While for the languages it covers MorphyNet can be considered a superset of UniMorph, the latter supports more languages. With UDer, as we show in section 4, the overlap is minor on all languages. For these reasons, we consider MorphyNet as complementary to these databases, considerably enriching their coverage on the 15 supported languages but not replacing them.

## 3 MorphyNet Generation

MorphyNet is generated mainly from Wiktionary, through the following steps.

1. *Filtering* returns XML-based Wiktionary content from specific sections of relevant lexical entries: headword lines, etymology sections, and inflectional tables are returned for nouns, verbs, and adjectives.

2. *Extraction* obtains raw morphological data by parsing the sections above.

3. *Enrichment* algorithmically extends the coverage of derivations and inflections obtained from Wiktionary, through entirely distinct methods for inflection and derivation.

4. *Resource generation*, finally, outputs MorphyNet data.

Below we explain the non-trivial Wiktionary extraction and enrichment steps, while Section 4 provides details on the generated resource itself.

### 3.1 Wiktionary Extraction

We extract inflectional and derivational data through hand-crafted extraction rules that target recurrent patterns in Wiktionary content both in source markdown and in HTML-rendered form. With respect to UniMorph that takes a similar approach and scrapes tables that provide inflectional paradigms, the scope of extraction is considerably extended, also including headword lines and etymology sections. This allows us to obtain new derivations, inflections, and features not covered by UniMorph, such as gender information or noun and adjective declensions for Catalan, French, Italian, Spanish, Russian, English, or Serbo-Croatian. Our rules target nouns, adjectives, and verbs in all languages covered.

*Inflection extraction rules* target two types of Wiktionary content: *inflectional tables* and *headword lines*. Inflectional tables provide conjugation and declension paradigms for a subset of verbs, nouns, and adjectives in Wiktionary. On tables, our extraction method was similar to that of UniMorph as described in (Kirov et al., 2016, 2018), with one major difference. UniMorph also extracted a large number of separate entries with modifier and auxiliary words, such as Spanish negative imperatives (*no comas*, *no coma*, *no comamos* etc.) or Finnish negative indicatives (*en puhu*, *et puhu*, *eivät puhu* etc.). MorphyNet, on the other hand, has a single entry for each distinct word form, regardless of the modifier word used. This policy had a particular impact on the size of the Finnish vocabulary.

As inflectional tables are only provided by Wiktionary for 62.5%[3] of nouns, verbs, and adjectives, we extended the scope of extraction to headword lines, such as

**banca** *f* (*plural* **banche**)

From this headword line, we extract two entries: one for *banca* is feminine singular and second for *banche* is feminine plural. We created specific parsing rules for nouns, verbs, and adjectives because each part of speech is described through a different set of morphological features. For example, valency (*transitive* or *reflexive*) and aspect (*perfective* or *imperfective*) are essential for verbs, while gender (*masculine* or *feminine*) and number (*singular* or *plural*) pertain to nouns and adjectives.

*Derivation extraction rules* were applied to the

[3] Computed over the 15 languages covered by MorphyNet.

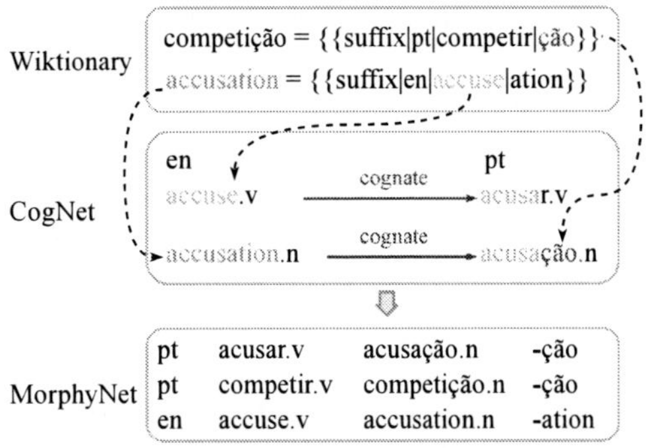


Figure 2: Derivation enrichment example: inference of the derivation of the Portuguese word *acusação*.

etymology sections of Wiktionary entries to collect the Morphology template usages, such as for the English *accusation*:

Equivalent to **accuse** + **-ation**.

where we have a morphology entry {{suffix|en|accuse|-ation}} from the Wiktionary XML dump. After collecting all morphology entries, we applied the enrichment method to increase its coverage.

### 3.2 Derivation Enrichment

Derivation enrichment is based on a linguistically informed cross-lingual generalization of derivational patterns observed in Wiktionary data, in order to extend the coverage of derivational data.

In the example shown in Figure 2, Wiktionary contains the Portuguese derivation *competir* (*to compete*) → *competição* (*competition*) but not *acusar* (*to accuse*) → *acusação* (*accusation*). An indiscriminate application of the suffix *-ção* to all verbs would, of course, generate lots of false positives, such as *chegar* (*to arrive*) ↛ **chegação*. Even when the target word does exist, the inferred derivation is often false, as in the case of *corar* (*to blush*) ↛ *coração* (*heart*). A counter-example from English could be *jewel* + *-ery* → *jewellery* but *gal* + *-ery* ↛ *gallery*.

For this reason, we use stronger cross-lingual derivational evidence to induce the applicability of the affix. In the example above, the existence of the English derivation *accuse* → *accusation*, where the meanings of the English and the corresponding Portuguese words are the same, serves as a strong hint for the applicability of the Portuguese pattern.

This intuition is formalized in MorphyNet as fol-

Table 1: Structure of MorphyNet inflectional data and its comparison to UniMorph. Data provided only by MorphyNet is highlighted in bold. The rest is provided by both resources in a nearly identical format.

| Language | base_word | trg_word | features | **src_word** | **morpheme** |
|---|---|---|---|---|---|
| Hungarian | ház | házak | N;NOM;PL | **ház** | **-ak** |
| Hungarian | ház | házat | N;ACC;SG | **ház** | **-at** |
| Hungarian | ház | házakat | N;ACC;PL | **házak** | **-at** |
| Russian | играть | играть | V;NFIN;**IPFV;ACT** | **играть** | |
| Russian | играть | играют | V;**IND**;PRS;3;PL;**IPFV;ACT;FIN** | **играть** | **-ают** |
| Russian | играть | играющий | V;V.PTCP;ACT;PRS | **играют** | **-щий** |

Table 2: Structure of MorphyNet derivational data and its comparison to UDer. Data only provided by MorphyNet is highlighted in bold. The rest is provided by both resources in a nearly identical format.

| Language | src_word | trg_word | src_pos | trg_pos | **morpheme** |
|---|---|---|---|---|---|
| English | time | timeless | noun | adjective | **-less** |
| English | soda | sodium | noun | **substance.**noun | **-ium** |
| English | zoo | zoophobia | noun | **state.**noun | **-phobia** |
| Finnish | kirjoittaa | kirjoittaminen | verb | noun | **-minen** |
| Finnish | lyödä | lyöjä | verb | **person.**noun | **-jä** |

lows: if in language $A$ a derivation from source word $w_s^A$ to target word $w_t^A$ through the affix $a^A$ is not explicitly asserted (e.g. by Wiktionary) but it is asserted for the corresponding *cognates* in at least one language $B$, then we infer its existence:

$$\text{cog}(w_s^A, w_s^B) \wedge \text{cog}(w_t^A, w_t^B) \wedge \text{cog}(a^A, a^B)$$

$$\wedge\ \text{der}(w_s^B, a^B) = w_t^B \Rightarrow \text{der}(w_s^A, a^A) = w_t^A$$

where $\text{cog}(x, y)$ means that the words $x$ and $y$ are cognates and $\text{der}(b, a) = d$ that word $d$ is derived from base word $b$ and affix $a$. In our example, $A = Portuguese$, $B = English$, $w_s^A = acusar$, $w_s^B = accuse$, $w_t^A = acusação$, $w_t^B = accusation$, $a^A = \text{-}ção$, and $a^B = \text{-}tion$.

As shown in Figure 1, we exploited a cognate database, *CogNet*[4] (Batsuren et al., 2019, 2021), that has 8.1M cognate pairs, for evidence on cognacy: $\text{cog}(w^A, w^B) = True$ is asserted by the presence of the word pair in CogNet.

The result of enrichment was a total increase of 25.6% of the number of derivations in MorphyNet. Efficiency varies among languages, essentially depending on the completeness of the Wiktionary coverage: it was the lowest for English with 3% and the highest for Spanish with 57%.

### 3.3 Inflection Enrichment

The enrichment of inflectional data is based on the simple observation that Wiktionary does not provide the root word for all inflected forms. For example, for the Hungarian *múltjával* (*with his/her/its past*), Wiktionary provides the inflection *múltja* → *múltjával* (*his/her/its past* + instrumental). For *múltja*, in turn, it provides *múlt* → *múltja* (*past* + possessive). It does not, however, directly provide the combination of the two inflections: *múlt* → *múltjával* (*past* + possessive + instrumental). Inflection enrichment consists of inferring such missing rules from the existing data.

The case above is formalized as follows: if, after the Wiktionary extraction phase, the MorphyNet data contains the inflections $w_r \rightarrow w_1$ (with feature set $F_1$) as well as $w_1 \rightarrow w_2$ (with feature set $F_2$), then we create the new inflection $w_r \rightarrow w_2$ with feature set $F_1 \cup F_2$.

The application of this logic increased the inflectional coverage of MorphyNet by 10.8% and its recall (with respect to ground truth data presented in section 5) by 8.2% on average.

## 4 The MorphyNet Resource

Morphynet is freely available for download, both as text files containing the data and as the source code of the Wiktionary extractor.[5] Two text files are provided per language: one for inflections and one for derivations. The structure of the two types of files is illustrated in Tables 1 and 2, respectively. As shown, MorphyNet covers all data fields provided by UniMorph for inflections and by UDer for derivations. In addition, it extends UniMorph by indicating the affix and the immediate source word that produced the inflection. Such information is useful, for example, to NLP applications that rely on subword information for understand-

[4] http://github.com/kbatsuren/CogNet

[5] http://github.com/kbatsuren/WiktConv

Table 3: MorphyNet dataset statistics

| # | Languages | Inflectional morphology words | entries | morphemes | Derivational morphology words | entries | morphemes | Total |
|---|---|---|---|---|---|---|---|---|
| 1 | Finnish | 65,402 | 1,617,751 | 1,139 | 18,142 | 37,199 | 446 | 1,654,950 |
| 2 | Serbo-Croatian | 68,757 | 1,760,095 | 263 | 8,553 | 20,008 | 429 | 1,780,103 |
| 3 | Italian | 75,089 | 748,321 | 104 | 22,650 | 42,149 | 749 | 790,470 |
| 4 | Hungarian | 38,067 | 1,034,317 | 428 | 14,566 | 37,940 | 832 | 1,072,257 |
| 5 | Russian | 67,695 | 1,343,760 | 252 | 21,922 | 36,922 | 575 | 1,380,682 |
| 6 | Spanish | 67,796 | 677,423 | 145 | 16,268 | 27,633 | 490 | 705,056 |
| 7 | French | 44,729 | 453,229 | 98 | 15,473 | 37,203 | 636 | 490,432 |
| 8 | Portuguese | 30,969 | 329,861 | 161 | 10,504 | 15,974 | 387 | 345,835 |
| 9 | Polish | 36,940 | 663,545 | 251 | 9,518 | 18,404 | 405 | 681,949 |
| 10 | German | 35,086 | 214,401 | 243 | 13,070 | 23,867 | 465 | 238,268 |
| 11 | Czech | 9,781 | 298,888 | 112 | 4,875 | 9,660 | 318 | 307,935 |
| 12 | English | 149,265 | 652,487 | 8 | 67,412 | 200,365 | 2,445 | 852,852 |
| 13 | Catalan | 16,404 | 168,462 | 91 | 3,244 | 4,083 | 220 | 172,545 |
| 14 | Swedish | 14,485 | 131,693 | 32 | 3,190 | 5,810 | 217 | 137,503 |
| 15 | Mongolian | 2,085 | 14,592 | 35 | 1,410 | 1,940 | 229 | 16,532 |
| | Total | 722,550 | 10,108,825 | 3,362 | 230,797 | 519,157 | 8,843 | 10,627,369 |

Table 4: UniMorph and MorphyNet data sizes compared to Universal Dependencies content.

| Language | UniMorph | MorphyNet | Univ. Dep. |
|---|---|---|---|
| Catalan | 81,576 | 168,462 | 25,443 |
| Czech | 134,528 | 298,888 | 151,838 |
| English | 115,523 | 652,487 | 17,296 |
| French | 367,733 | 453,229 | 28,921 |
| Finnish | 2,490,377 | 1,617,751 | 47,813 |
| Hungarian | 552,950 | 1,034,317 | 3,685 |
| Italian | 509,575 | 748,321 | 24,002 |
| Serbo-Croatian | 840,799 | 1,760,095 | 35,936 |
| Spanish | 382,955 | 677,423 | 32,571 |
| Swedish | 78,411 | 131,693 | 15,030 |
| Russian | 473,482 | 1,343,760 | 18,774 |
| Total | 5,893,381 | 8,886,426 | 401,309 |

ing out-of-vocabulary words. MorphyNet also extends the UDer structure by indicating the affix and the semantic category for the target word when it can be inferred from the morpheme. Such information is again useful for subword regularization of derivationally rich languages, such as English.

Table 4 provides per-language statistics on MorphyNet data. The present version of the resource contains 10.6 million entries, of which 95% are inflections. Highly inflecting and agglutinative languages are dominating the resource as 55% of all entries belong to Finnish, Hungarian, Russian, and Serbo-Croatian. Language coverage above all depends on the completeness of Wiktionary, the main source of our data.

## 5 Evaluation

We evaluated MorphyNet through two different methods: (1) through *comparison to ground truth* and (2) through *manual validation* by experts.

**Comparison to ground truth.** The quality evaluation of morphology database is a challenging task due to many weird morphology aspects of languages evaluated (Gorman et al., 2019). As ground truth on inflections we used the *Universal Dependencies*[6] dataset (Nivre et al., 2016, 2017), which (among others) provides morphological analysis of inflected words over a multilingual corpus of hand-annotated sentences. McCarthy et al. (2018) built a Python tool[7] to convert these treebanks into UniMorph schema (Sylak-Glassman, 2016). We evaluated both UniMorph 2.0 and MorphyNet against this data (performing the necessary mapping of feature tags beforehand) over the 11 languages in the intersection of the two resources: Hungarian (Vincze et al., 2010), Catalan, Spanish (Taulé et al., 2008), Czech (Bejček et al., 2013), Finnish (Pyysalo et al., 2015), Russian (Lyashevskaya et al., 2016), Serbo-Croatian (De Melo, 2014), French (Guillaume et al., 2019), Italian (Bosco et al., 2013), Swedish (Nivre and Megyesi, 2007), and English (Silveira et al., 2014). Table 5 contains evaluation results over nouns, verbs, and adjectives separately, as well as totals per language. Missing data points (e.g. for Catalan nouns) indicate that UniMorph did not have any corresponding inflections. For languages and parts of speech where both resources provide data, MorphyNet always provides higher recall. The exception is Finnish because of our policy of not extracting conjugations with auxiliary and modifier words as separate entries (see Section 3.1). Overall, as

[6]`https://universaldependencies.org/`
[7]`https://github.com/unimorph/ud-compatibility`

Table 5: Inflectional morphology evaluation of MorphyNet against UniMorph on Universal Dependencies

| Language | Resource | Noun | | | Verb | | | Adjective | | | Total | | |
|---|---|---|---|---|---|---|---|---|---|---|---|---|---|
| | | R | P | $F_1$ | R | P | $F_1$ | R | P | $F_1$ | R | P | $F_1$ |
| Catalan | UniMorph | - | - | - | 71.9 | 99.3 | 83.4 | - | - | - | 21.3 | 99.3 | 35.1 |
| | MorphyNet | 66.0 | 98.4 | 79.0 | 73.8 | 99.1 | 84.6 | 48.2 | 99.6 | 65.0 | 64.3 | 98.8 | 77.9 |
| Czech | UniMorph | 28.2 | 99.1 | 43.9 | 9.5 | 18.1 | 12.5 | 17.6 | 44.8 | 25.3 | 21.0 | 72.7 | 32.6 |
| | MorphyNet | 33.2 | 98.9 | 49.7 | 28.2 | 93.8 | 43.4 | 36.1 | 98.1 | 52.8 | 34.2 | 98.0 | 50.7 |
| English | UniMorph | - | - | - | 96.1 | 90.9 | 93.4 | - | - | - | 28.3 | 90.9 | 43.2 |
| | MorphyNet | 81.5 | 99.1 | 89.4 | 97.1 | 96.8 | 96.9 | 85.3 | 99.7 | 91.9 | 83.2 | 98.8 | 90.3 |
| French | UniMorph | - | - | - | 70.6 | 98.5 | 82.2 | - | - | - | 20.6 | 98.5 | 34.1 |
| | MorphyNet | 80.2 | 98.6 | 88.5 | 94.4 | 98.5 | 96.4 | 60.1 | 94.6 | 73.5 | 79.7 | 97.9 | 87.9 |
| Finnish | UniMorph | 45.5 | 99.5 | 62.4 | 50.5 | 88.4 | 64.3 | 61.4 | 81.7 | 70.1 | 49.1 | 93.5 | 64.4 |
| | MorphyNet | 49.8 | 99.4 | 66.4 | 53.8 | 89.5 | 67.2 | 67.2 | 98.1 | 79.8 | 54.5 | 96.7 | 69.7 |
| Hungarian | UniMorph | 45.3 | 99.0 | 62.2 | 31.9 | 97.8 | 48.1 | - | - | - | 30.8 | 98.8 | 47.0 |
| | MorphyNet | 55.2 | 99.1 | 70.9 | 77.2 | 96.9 | 85.9 | 43.1 | 95.9 | 59.5 | 56.3 | 97.9 | 71.5 |
| Italian | UniMorph | - | - | - | 66.1 | 91.6 | 76.8 | - | - | - | 22.8 | 91.6 | 36.5 |
| | MorphyNet | 86.7 | 99.0 | 92.4 | 88.8 | 96.9 | 92.7 | 84.9 | 98.9 | 91.4 | 87.0 | 98.2 | 92.3 |
| Serbo-Croatian | UniMorph | 0.0 | 0.0 | 0.0 | 0.0 | 0.0 | 0.0 | 49.4 | 47.4 | 48.4 | 18.5 | 47.4 | 26.6 |
| | MorphyNet | 69.5 | 88.4 | 77.8 | 69.1 | 98.1 | 81.1 | 54.9 | 98.6 | 70.5 | 63.9 | 93.3 | 75.9 |
| Spanish | UniMorph | - | - | - | 93.0 | 99.8 | 96.3 | - | - | - | 32.1 | 99.8 | 48.6 |
| | MorphyNet | 88.3 | 99.2 | 93.4 | 97.0 | 99.5 | 98.2 | 81.9 | 99.2 | 89.7 | 89.7 | 99.3 | 94.3 |
| Swedish | UniMorph | 15.1 | 98.4 | 26.2 | 59.7 | 84.8 | 70.1 | 34.1 | 94.8 | 50.2 | 27.1 | 92.0 | 41.9 |
| | MorphyNet | 36.8 | 99.4 | 53.7 | 78.0 | 98.1 | 86.9 | 38.1 | 99.6 | 55.1 | 44.6 | 99.1 | 61.5 |
| Russian | UniMorph | 0.0 | 0.0 | 0.0 | 0.0 | 0.0 | 0.0 | 52.8 | 97.4 | 68.5 | 10.8 | 97.4 | 19.4 |
| | MorphyNet | 56.5 | 95.1 | 70.9 | 67.7 | 92.9 | 78.3 | 64.5 | 99.0 | 78.1 | 61.5 | 95.2 | 74.7 |

seen from Table 4, MorphyNet contains about 47% more entries over the 11 languages where it overlaps with UniMorph. In terms of precision, the two resources are comparable, except for Finnish (adjectives) and Swedish (adjectives and verbs) where MorphyNet appears to be significantly more precise.

UDer (Kyjánek et al., 2020) is a collection of individual monolingual resources of derivational morphology. Most of them have been carefully evaluated against their own datasets and offer high quality. We evaluated MorphyNet derivational data against UDer over the nine languages covered by both resources: French (Hathout and Namer, 2014), Portuguese (de Paiva et al., 2014), Czech (Vidra et al., 2019), German (Zeller et al., 2013), Russian (Vodolazsky, 2020), Italian (Talamo et al., 2016), Finnish (Lindén and Carlson, 2010; Lindén et al., 2012), Latin (Litta et al., 2016), and English (Habash and Dorr, 2003). Statistics and results are shown in Table 6. First of all, the overlap between MorphyNet and UDer is small, which is visible from our recall values relative to UDer that vary between 0.6% (Czech) and 59.5% (Italian). Among the languages evaluated, six were better covered by MorphyNet and the remaining three (Czech, German, and Russian) by UDer. The agreement between the two resources, computed as Cohen's Kappa, was 0.85 overall, varying between 0.74 (Finnish) and 0.97 (Portuguese). If we consider UDer as gold standard, we obtain precision figures between 87% and 99%.

**Manual evaluation** was carried out by language experts over sample data from five languages: English, Italian, French, Hungarian, and Mongolian. The sample consisted of 1,000 randomly selected entries per language, half of them inflectional and the other half derivational. The experts were asked to validate the correctness of source–target word pairs, of morphemes, as well as inflectional features and parts of speech (the latter for derivations). Table 7 shows detailed results. The overall precision is 98.9%, per-language values varying between 98.2% (Hungarian) and 99.5% (English). The good results are proof both of the high quality of Wiktionary data and of the general correctness of the data extraction and enrichment logic of MorphyNet. A manual checking of the incorrect entries revealed that most of them were due to the failure of extraction rules due to occasional deviations in Wiktionary from its own conventions.

## 6 Conclusions and Future Work

We consider the resource released and described here as an initial work-in-progress version that we plan to extend and improve. We are currently

Table 6: Derivational morphology evaluation of MorphyNet against Universal Derivations (UDer)

| # | Language | MorphyNet | Univeral Derivations (UDer) | | UDer ∩ MorphyNet | Recall | Precision | Kappa |
|---|---|---|---|---|---|---|---|---|
| 1 | French | 37,203 | Démonette | 13,272 | 2,558 | 18.5 | 95.5 | 0.91 |
| 2 | Portuguese | 15,974 | NomLex-PT | 3,420 | 1,235 | 35.8 | 98.9 | 0.97 |
| 3 | Czech | 9,660 | Derinet | 804,011 | 5,347 | 0.6 | 94.1 | 0.88 |
| 4 | German | 23,867 | DerivBase | 35,528 | 5,878 | 15.6 | 93.5 | 0.87 |
| 5 | Russian | 36,922 | DerivBase.RU | 118,374 | 6,370 | 12.3 | 88.1 | 0.76 |
| 6 | Italian | 42,149 | DerIvaTario | 1,548 | 958 | 59.5 | 90.7 | 0.81 |
| 7 | Finnish | 37,199 | FinnWordnet | 8,337 | 2,664 | 30.6 | 87.0 | 0.74 |
| 8 | Latin | 9,191 | WFL | 2,792 | 4,037 | 14.0 | 93.7 | 0.87 |
| 9 | English | 200,365 | CatVar | 16,185 | 7,397 | 45.7 | 91.9 | 0.83 |
| | Total | 412,530 | | 1,003,467 | 36,444 | 25.8 | 92.6 | 0.85 |

Table 7: Manual validation of language experts on MorphyNet

| | | Inflectional morphology | | | Derivational morphology | | | |
|---|---|---|---|---|---|---|---|---|
| # | Language | word pair | features | morphemes | trg words | POS | morphemes | Total |
| 1 | English | 99.2 | 100.0 | 99.0 | 100.0 | 99.0 | 100.0 | 99.5 |
| 2 | French | 99.8 | 98.0 | 100.0 | 100.0 | 96.8 | 100.0 | 99.1 |
| 3 | Hungarian | 97.0 | 95.0 | 100.0 | 98.6 | 99.1 | 99.2 | 98.2 |
| 4 | Italian | 100.0 | 100.0 | 99.4 | 98.0 | 97.4 | 99.0 | 99.0 |
| 5 | Mongolian | 98.2 | 100.0 | 99.2 | 98.4 | 98.1 | 98.6 | 98.8 |
| | Average. | 98.8 | 98.6 | 99.5 | 99.0 | 98.1 | 99.4 | 98.9 |

working on increasing the coverage to 20 languages. We also plan to extend MorphyNet data with additional features and the semantic categories of words (e.g. animate or inanimate object, action) inferred from derivations. We are planning to conduct a more in-depth study of our evaluation results, especially with respect to UDer where it is not yet clear whether the occasional lower precision figures (87% for Finnish, 88% for Russian) are due to mistakes in MorphyNet, in the UDer resources, or are caused by other factors.

A major piece of ongoing work concerns the representation of MorphyNet derivational data as a lexico-semantic graph, as it is done in wordnets (Miller, 1998; Giunchiglia et al., 2017) where derivationally related word senses are interconnected by associative relationships. This effort, justifying the *-Net* in the name of our resource, will allow us to address completeness issues in existing wordnets by extending them by morphological relations and derived words.

We are happy to offer the MorphyNet extraction logic to be reused on a community basis. As extending the tool with new Wiktionary extraction rules is straightforward, we hope that the availability of the tool will allow language coverage to grow even further. We also hope that the MorphyNet data and the extraction logic can serve existing high-quality projects such as UniMorph and UDer.

## References


Duygu Ataman and Marcello Federico. 2018. Compositional representation of morphologically-rich input for neural machine translation. In *Proceedings of the 56th Annual Meeting of the Association for Computational Linguistics (Volume 2: Short Papers)*, pages 305–311.

Khuyagbaatar Batsuren, Gábor Bella, and Fausto Giunchiglia. 2021. A large and evolving cognate database. *Language Resources and Evaluation.*

Khuyagbaatar Batsuren, Gábor Bella, and Fausto Giunchiglia. 2019. Cognet: a large-scale cognate database. In *Proceedings of ACL 2019, Florence, Italy.*

Kenneth R Beesley and Lauri Karttunen. 2003. Finite-state morphology: Xerox tools and techniques. *CSLI, Stanford.*

Eduard Bejček, Eva Hajičová, Jan Hajič, Pavlína Jínová, Václava Kettnerová, Veronika Kolářová, Marie Mikulová, Jiří Mírovský, Anna Nedoluzhko, Jarmila Panevová, et al. 2013. Prague dependency treebank 3.0.

Piotr Bojanowski, Edouard Grave, Armand Joulin, and Tomas Mikolov. 2017. Enriching word vectors with subword information. *Transactions of the Association for Computational Linguistics*, 5:135–146.

Cristina Bosco, Montemagni Simonetta, and Simi Maria. 2013. Converting italian treebanks: Towards an italian stanford dependency treebank. In *7th Linguistic Annotation Workshop and Interoperability with Discourse*, pages 61–69. The Association for Computational Linguistics.

Ryan Cotterell, Christo Kirov, John Sylak-Glassman, Géraldine Walther, Ekaterina Vylomova, Arya D McCarthy, Katharina Kann, Sebastian J Mielke, Garrett Nicolai, Miikka Silfverberg, et al. 2018. The conll–sigmorphon 2018 shared task: Universal morphological reinflection. In *Proceedings of the CoNLL–SIGMORPHON 2018 Shared Task: Universal Morphological Reinflection*, pages 1–27.

Ryan Cotterell, Christo Kirov, John Sylak-Glassman, Géraldine Walther, Ekaterina Vylomova, Patrick Xia, Manaal Faruqui, Sandra Kübler, David Yarowsky, Jason Eisner, et al. 2017. Conll-sigmorphon 2017 shared task: Universal morphological reinflection in 52 languages. In *Proceedings of the CoNLL SIGMORPHON 2017 Shared Task: Universal Morphological Reinflection*, pages 1–30.

Gerard De Melo. 2014. Etymological wordnet: Tracing the history of words. In *LREC*, pages 1148–1154. Citeseer.

Valeria de Paiva, Livy Real, Alexandre Rademaker, and Gerard de Melo. 2014. Nomlex-pt: A lexicon of portuguese nominalizations. In *Proceedings of the Ninth International Conference on Language Resources and Evaluation (LREC'14)*, pages 2851–2858.

Jacob Devlin, Ming-Wei Chang, Kenton Lee, and Kristina Toutanova. 2019. Bert: Pre-training of deep bidirectional transformers for language understanding. In *Proceedings of the 2019 Conference of the North American Chapter of the Association for Computational Linguistics: Human Language Technologies, Volume 1 (Long and Short Papers)*, pages 4171–4186.

Daniela Gerz, Ivan Vulić, Edoardo Ponti, Jason Naradowsky, Roi Reichart, and Anna Korhonen. 2018. Language modeling for morphologically rich languages: Character-aware modeling for word-level prediction. *Transactions of the Association for Computational Linguistics*, 6:451–465.

Fausto Giunchiglia, Khuyagbaatar Batsuren, and Gabor Bella. 2017. Understanding and exploiting language diversity. In *IJCAI*, pages 4009–4017.

Kyle Gorman, Arya D McCarthy, Ryan Cotterell, Ekaterina Vylomova, Miikka Silfverberg, and Magdalena Markowska. 2019. Weird inflects but ok: Making sense of morphological generation errors. In *Proceedings of the 23rd Conference on Computational Natural Language Learning (CoNLL)*, pages 140–151.

Bruno Guillaume, Marie-Catherine de Marneffe, and Guy Perrier. 2019. Conversion et améliorations de corpus du français annotés en universal dependencies. *Traitement Automatique des Langues*, 60(2):71–95.

Nizar Habash and Bonnie Dorr. 2003. Catvar: A database of categorial variations for english. In *Proceedings of the MT Summit*, pages 471–474. Citeseer.

Nabil Hathout and Fiammetta Namer. 2014. Démonette, a french derivational morpho-semantic network. In *Linguistic Issues in Language Technology, Volume 11, 2014-Theoretical and Computational Morphology: New Trends and Synergies*.

Inxight. 2005. Linguistx natural language processing platform.

Christo Kirov, Ryan Cotterell, John Sylak-Glassman, Géraldine Walther, Ekaterina Vylomova, Patrick Xia, Manaal Faruqui, Sabrina J Mielke, Arya D McCarthy, Sandra Kübler, et al. 2018. Unimorph 2.0: Universal morphology. In *Proceedings of the Eleventh International Conference on Language Resources and Evaluation (LREC 2018)*.

Christo Kirov, John Sylak-Glassman, Roger Que, and David Yarowsky. 2016. Very-large scale parsing and normalization of wiktionary morphological paradigms. In *Proceedings of the Tenth International Conference on Language Resources and Evaluation (LREC'16)*, pages 3121–3126.

Lukáš Kyjánek, Zdeněk Žabokrtský, Magda Ševčíková, and Jonáš Vidra. 2020. Universal derivations 1.0, a growing collection of harmonised word-formation resources. *The Prague Bulletin of Mathematical Linguistics*, (115):5–30.

Krister Lindén and Lauri Carlson. 2010. Finnwordnet–finnish wordnet by translation. *LexicoNordica–Nordic Journal of Lexicography*, 17:119–140.

Krister Lindén, Jyrki Niemi, and Mirka Hyvärinen. 2012. Extending and updating the finnish wordnet. In *Shall We Play the Festschrift Game?*, pages 67–98. Springer.

Eleonora Litta, Marco Passarotti, and Chris Culy. 2016. Formatio formosa est. Building a Word Formation Lexicon for Latin. In *Proceedings of the Third Italian Conference on Computational Linguistics (CLIC–IT 2016)*, pages 185–189.

Olga Lyashevskaya, Kira Droganova, Daniel Zeman, Maria Alexeeva, Tatiana Gavrilova, Nina Mustafina, Elena Shakurova, et al. 2016. Universal dependencies for russian: A new syntactic dependencies tagset. *Lyashevkaya, K. Droganova, D. Zeman, M. Alexeeva, T. Gavrilova, N. Mustafina, E. Shakurova//Higher School of Economics Research Paper No. WP BRP*, 44.

Arya D McCarthy, Christo Kirov, Matteo Grella, Amrit Nidhi, Patrick Xia, Kyle Gorman, Ekaterina Vylomova, Sabrina J Mielke, Garrett Nicolai, Miikka Silfverberg, et al. 2020. Unimorph 3.0: Universal morphology. In *Proceedings of The 12th Language Resources and Evaluation Conference*, pages 3922–3931.

Arya D McCarthy, Miikka Silfverberg, Ryan Cotterell, Mans Hulden, and David Yarowsky. 2018. Marrying universal dependencies and universal morphology. In *Proceedings of the Second Workshop on Universal Dependencies (UDW 2018)*, pages 91–101.

Eleni Metheniti and Günter Neumann. 2020. Wikinflection corpus: A (better) multilingual, morpheme-annotated inflectional corpus. In *Proceedings of The 12th Language Resources and Evaluation Conference*, pages 3905–3912.

George A Miller. 1998. *WordNet: An electronic lexical database*. MIT press.

Joakim Nivre, Željko Agić, Lars Ahrenberg, Lene Antonsen, Maria Jesus Aranzabe, Masayuki Asahara, Luma Ateyah, Mohammed Attia, Aitziber Atutxa, Liesbeth Augustinus, et al. 2017. Universal dependencies 2.1.

Joakim Nivre, Marie-Catherine De Marneffe, Filip Ginter, Yoav Goldberg, Jan Hajic, Christopher D Manning, Ryan McDonald, Slav Petrov, Sampo Pyysalo, Natalia Silveira, et al. 2016. Universal dependencies v1: A multilingual treebank collection. In *Proceedings of the Tenth International Conference on Language Resources and Evaluation (LREC'16)*, pages 1659–1666.

Joakim Nivre and Beata Megyesi. 2007. Bootstrapping a swedish treebank using cross-corpus harmonization and annotation projection. In *Proceedings of the 6th international workshop on treebanks and linguistic theories*, pages 97–102. Citeseer.

Mārcis Pinnis, Rihards Krišlauks, Daiga Deksne, and Toms Miks. 2017. Neural machine translation for morphologically rich languages with improved sub-word units and synthetic data. In *International Conference on Text, Speech, and Dialogue*, pages 237–245. Springer.

Ivan Provilkov, Dmitrii Emelianenko, and Elena Voita. 2020. Bpe-dropout: Simple and effective subword regularization. In *Proceedings of the 58th Annual Meeting of the Association for Computational Linguistics*, pages 1882–1892.

Sampo Pyysalo, Jenna Kanerva, Anna Missilä, Veronika Laippala, and Filip Ginter. 2015. Universal dependencies for finnish. In *Proceedings of the 20th Nordic Conference of Computational Linguistics (Nodalida 2015)*, pages 163–172.

Rico Sennrich, Barry Haddow, and Alexandra Birch. 2016. Neural machine translation of rare words with subword units. In *Proceedings of the 54th Annual Meeting of the Association for Computational Linguistics (Volume 1: Long Papers)*, pages 1715–1725.

Natalia Silveira, Timothy Dozat, Marie-Catherine de Marneffe, Samuel Bowman, Miriam Connor, John Bauer, and Christopher D. Manning. 2014.

A gold standard dependency corpus for English. In *Proceedings of the Ninth International Conference on Language Resources and Evaluation (LREC-2014)*.

John Sylak-Glassman. 2016. The composition and use of the universal morphological feature schema (unimorph schema). *Johns Hopkins University*.

Luigi Talamo, Chiara Celata, and Pier Marco Bertinetto. 2016. Derivatario: An annotated lexicon of italian derivatives. *Word Structure*, 9(1):72–102.

Mariona Taulé, Maria Antònia Martí, and Marta Recasens. 2008. Ancora: Multilevel annotated corpora for catalan and spanish. In *Lrec*.

Viktor Trón, Gyögy Gyepesi, Péter Halácsy, András Kornai, László Németh, and Dániel Varga. 2005. Hunmorph: open source word analysis. In *Proceedings of Workshop on Software*, pages 77–85.

Jonáš Vidra, Zdeněk Žabokrtský, Magda Ševčíková, and Lukáš Kyjánek. 2019. Derinet 2.0: towards an all-in-one word-formation resource. In *Proceedings of the Second International Workshop on Resources and Tools for Derivational Morphology*, pages 81–89.

Veronika Vincze, Dóra Szauter, Attila Almási, György Móra, Zoltán Alexin, and János Csirik. 2010. Hungarian dependency treebank.

Daniil Vodolazsky. 2020. Derivbase. ru: A derivational morphology resource for russian. In *Proceedings of The 12th Language Resources and Evaluation Conference*, pages 3937–3943.

Ekaterina Vylomova, Trevor Cohn, Xuanli He, and Gholamreza Haffari. 2017. Word representation models for morphologically rich languages in neural machine translation. In *Proceedings of the First Workshop on Subword and Character Level Models in NLP*, pages 103–108.

Britta Zeller, Jan Šnajder, and Sebastian Padó. 2013. Derivbase: Inducing and evaluating a derivational morphology resource for german. In *Proceedings of the 51st Annual Meeting of the Association for Computational Linguistics (Volume 1: Long Papers)*, pages 1201–1211.

# A Study of Morphological Robustness of Neural Machine Translation

**Sai Muralidhar Jayanthi,*  Adithya Pratapa***
Language Technologies Institute
Carnegie Mellon University
{sjayanth,vpratapa}@cs.cmu.edu

## Abstract

In this work, we analyze the robustness of neural machine translation systems towards grammatical perturbations in the source. In particular, we focus on morphological inflection related perturbations. While this has been recently studied for English→French translation (MORPHEUS) (Tan et al., 2020), it is unclear how this extends to Any→English translation systems. We propose MORPHEUS-MULTILINGUAL that utilizes UniMorph dictionaries to identify morphological perturbations to source that adversely affect the translation models. Along with an analysis of state-of-the-art pretrained MT systems, we train and analyze systems for 11 language pairs using the multilingual TED corpus (Qi et al., 2018). We also compare this to actual errors of non-native speakers using Grammatical Error Correction datasets. Finally, we present a qualitative and quantitative analysis of the robustness of Any→English translation systems. Code for our work is publicly available.[1]

## 1 Introduction

Multilingual machine translation is commonplace, with high-quality commercial systems available in over 100 languages (Johnson et al., 2017). However, translation from and into low-resource languages remains a challenge (Arivazhagan et al., 2019). Additionally, translation from morphologically-rich languages to English (and vice-versa) presents new challenges due to the wide differences in morphosyntactic phenomenon of the source and target languages. In this work, we study the effect of noisy inputs to neural machine translation (NMT) systems. A concrete practical application for this is the translation of text from non-native speakers. While the brittleness of NMT systems to input noise is well-studied (Belinkov and Bisk, 2018), most prior work has focused on translation from English (English→X) (Anastasopoulos et al., 2019; Alam and Anastasopoulos, 2020).

With over 800 million second-language (L2) speakers for English, it is imperative that the translation models should be robust to any potential errors in the source English text. A recent work (Tan et al., 2020) has shown that English→X translation systems are not robust to inflectional perturbations in the source. Inspired by this work, we aim to quantify the impact of inflectional perturbations for X→English translation systems. We hypothesize that inflectional perturbations to source tokens shouldn't adversely affect the translation quality. However, morphologically-rich languages tend to have free word order as compared to English, and small perturbations in the word inflections can lead to significant changes to the overall meaning of the sentence. This is a challenge to our analysis.

We build upon Tan et al. (2020) to induce inflectional perturbations to source tokens using the `unimorph_inflect` tool (Anastasopoulos and Neubig, 2019) along with UniMorph dictionaries (McCarthy et al., 2020) (§2). We then present a comprehensive evaluation of the robustness of MT systems for languages from different language families (§3). To understand the impact of size of parallel corpora available for training, we experiment on a spectrum of high, medium and low-resource languages. Furthermore, to understand the impact in real settings, we run our adversarial perturbation algorithm on learners' text from Grammatical Error Correction datasets for German and Russian (§3.3).

## 2 Methodology

To evaluate the robustness of X→English NMT systems, we generate inflectional perturbations to the tokens in source language text. In our methodology,

* Equal contribution.

[1] https://github.com/murali1996/morpheus_multilingual



*Proceedings of the Seventeenth SIGMORPHON Workshop on Computational Research in Phonetics, Phonology, and Morphology*, pages 49–59

we aim to identify adversarial examples that lead to maximum degradation in the translation quality. We build upon the recently proposed MORPHEUS toolkit (Tan et al., 2020), that evaluated the robustness of NMT systems translating from English→X. For a given source English text, MORPHEUS works by greedily looking for inflectional perturbations by sequentially iterating through the tokens in input text. For each token, it identifies inflectional edits that lead to maximum drop in BLEU score.

We extend this approach to test X→English translation systems. Since their toolkit[2] is limited to perturbations in English only, in this work we develop our own inflectional methodology that relies on UniMorph (McCarthy et al., 2020).

### 2.1 Reinflection

UniMorph project[3] provides morphological data for numerous languages under a universal schema. The project supports over 100 languages and provides morphological inflection dictionaries for upto three part-of-speech tags, nouns (N), adjectives (ADJ) and verbs (V). While some UniMorph dictionaries include a large number of types (or paradigms) (German (≈15k), Russian (≈28k)), many dictionaries are relatively small (Turkish (≈3.5k), Estonian (<1k)). This puts a limit on the number of tokens we can perturb via UniMorph dictionary look-up. To overcome this limitation, we use the `unimorph_inflect` toolkit[4] that takes as input the lemma and the morphosyntactic description (MSD) and returns a reinflected word form. This tool was trained using UniMorph dictionaries and generalizes to unseen types. An illustration of our inflectional perturbation methodology is described in Table 1.

### 2.2 MORPHEUS-MULTILINGUAL

Given an input sentence, our proposed method, MORPHEUS-MULTILINGUAL, identifies adversarial inflectional perturbations to the input tokens that leads to maximum degradation in performance of the machine translation system. We first iterate through the sentence to extract all possible inflectional forms for each of the constituent tokens. Since, we are relying on UniMorph dictionaries, we are limited to perturbing only nouns, adjectives and verbs.[5] Now, to construct a perturbed sentence, we iterate through each token and uniformly sample one inflectional form from the candidate inflections. We repeat this process $N$ (=50) times and compile our pool of perturbed sentences.[6]

To identify the adversarial sentence, we compute the chrF score (Popović, 2017) using the sacrebleu toolkit (Post, 2018) and select the sentence that results in the maximum drop in chrF score (if any). In our preliminary experiments, we found chrF to be more reliable than BLEU (Papineni et al., 2002) for identifying adversarial candidates. While BLEU uses word $n$-grams to compare the translation output with the reference, chrF uses character $n$-grams instead; which helps with matching morphological variants of words.

The original MORPHEUS toolkit follows a slightly different algorithm to identify adversaries. Similar to our approach, they first extract all possible inflectional forms for each of the constituent tokens. Then, they sequentially iterate through the tokens in the sentence, and for each token, they select an inflectional form that results in the worst BLEU score. Once an adversarial form is identified, they directly replace the form in the original sentence and continue to the next token. While a similar approach is possible in our setup, we found their algorithm to be computationally expensive as it prevents from performing efficient batching.

It is important to note that neither MORPHEUS-MULTILINGUAL nor the original MORPHEUS exhaustively searches over all possible sentences, due to memory and time constraints. However, our approach in MORPHEUS-MULTILINGUAL can be efficiently implemented and reduces the inference time by almost a factor of 20. We experiment on 11 different language pairs, therefore, the run time and computational costs are critical to our experiments.

## 3 Experiments

In this section, we present a comprehensive evaluation of the robustness of X→English machine translation systems. Since it is natural for NMT models to be more robust when trained on large amounts of parallel data, we experiment with two

[2]https://github.com/salesforce/morpheus

[3]https://unimorph.github.io/

[4]https://github.com/antonisa/unimorph_inflect

[5]Some dictionaries might contain fewer POS tags, for example, in German we are restricted to just nouns and verbs.

[6]$N$ is a hyperparameter, and in our preliminary experiments, we find $N = 50$ to be sufficiently high to generate many uniquely perturbed sentences and also keep the process computationally tractable.

| PRON | VERB | PART | PUNCT | ADV | NOUN | VERB | AUX |
|---|---|---|---|---|---|---|---|
| Sie | wissen | nicht | , | wann | Räuber | kommen | können |
| you-NOM.3PL | knowledge-PRS.3PL | not-NEG | , | when | robber-NOM.PL | come-NFIN | can-PRS.3PL |
| (*) Sie | wissten | nicht | , | wann | Räuber | kommen | können |
| (*) Sie | wissen | nicht | , | wann | Räuber | kommen | könne |
| (*) Sie | wisse | nicht | , | wann | Räuber | kommen | könnte |

Table 1: Example inflectional perturbations on a German text.

sets of translation systems. First, we use state-of-the-art pre-trained models for Russian→English and German→English from `fairseq` (Ott et al., 2019).[7] Secondly, we use the multilingual TED corpus (Qi et al., 2018) to train transformer-based translation systems from scratch.[8] Using the TED corpus allows us to expand our evaluation to a larger pool of language pairs.

### 3.1 WMT19 Pretrained Models

We evaluate the robustness of best-performing systems from WMT19 news translation shared task (Barrault et al., 2019), specifically for Russian→English and German→English (Ott et al., 2019). We follow the original work and use *newstest2018* as our test set for adversarial evaluation. Using the procedure described in §2.2, we create adversarial versions of *newstest2018* for both the language pairs. In Table 2, we present the baseline and adversarial results using BLEU and chrF metrics. For both the language pairs, we notice significant drops on both metrics. Before diving further into the qualitative analysis of these MT systems, we first present a broader evaluation on MT systems trained on multilingual TED corpus.

| lg | Baseline | | Adversarial | | |
|---|---|---|---|---|---|
| | BLEU | chrF | BLEU | chrF | NR |
| `rus` | 38.33 | 0.63 | 18.50 | 0.47 | 0.81 |
| `deu` | 48.40 | 0.70 | 33.43 | 0.59 | 1.00 |

Table 2: Baseline & Adversarial results on *newstest2018* using `fairseq`'s pre-trained models. NR denotes Target-Source Noise Ratio (2).

[7]Due to resource constraints, we only experiment with the single models and leave the evaluation of ensemble models for future work.

[8]For the selected languages, we train an MT model with *'transformer_iwslt_de_en'* architecture from `fairseq`. We use a sentence-piece vocab size of 8000, and train up to 80 epochs with Adam optimizer (see A.2 in Appendix for more details)

### 3.2 TED corpus

The multilingual TED corpus (Qi et al., 2018) provides parallel data for over 50 language pairs, but in our experiments we only use a subset of these language pairs. We selected our test language pairs (X→English) to maximize the diversity in language families, as well as the resources available for training MT systems. Since we rely on UniMorph and `unimorph_inflect` for generating perturbations, we only select languages that have reasonably high accuracy in `unimorph_inflect` (>80%). Table 3 presents an overview of the chosen source languages, along with the information on language family and training resources.

We also quantify the morphological richness for the languages listed in Table 3. As we are not aware of any standard metric to gauge morphological richness of a language, we use the reinflection dictionaries to define this metric. We compute the morphological richness using the Type-Token Ratio (TTR) as follows,

$$\text{TTR}_{lg} = \frac{N_{\text{types}}(lg)}{N_{\text{tokens}}(lg)} = \frac{N_{\text{paradigms}}(lg)}{N_{\text{forms}}(lg)} \qquad (1)$$

In Table 3, we report the $\text{TTR}_{lg}$ scores measured on UniMorph dictionaries as well as on the UniMorph-style dictionaries constructed from TED dev splits using `unimorph_inflect` tool. Note that, $\text{TTR}_{lg}$, as defined here, slightly differs from the widely known Type-Token ration used for measuring lexical diversity (or richness) of a corpus.

We run MORPHEUS-MULTILINGUAL to generate adversarial sentences for the validation splits of the TED corpus. We term a sentence adversarial if it leads to the maximum drop in chrF score. Note that, it is possible to have perturbed sentences that may not lead to any drop in chrF scores. In Figure 1, we plot the fraction of perturbed sentences along with adversarial fraction for each of the source languages. We see considerable perturbations for most languages, with the exception of Swedish, Lithuanian, Ukrainian, and Estonian.

| lg | Family | Resource | TTR |
|---|---|---|---|
| heb | Semetic | High | (0.044, 0.191) |
| rus | Slavic | High | (0.080, 0.107) |
| tur | Turkic | High | (0.016, 0.048) |
| deu | Germanic | High | (0.210, 0.321) |
| ukr | Slavic | High | (0.103, 0.143) |
| ces | Slavic | High | (0.071, 0.082) |
| swe | Germanic | Medium | (0.156, 0.281) |
| lit | Baltic | Medium | (0.051, 0.084) |
| slv | Slavic | Low | (0.109, 0.087) |
| kat | Kartvelian | Low | (0.057, ——) |
| est | Uralic | Low | (0.026, 0.056) |

Table 3: List of language chosen from multilingual TED corpus. For each language, the table presents the language family, resource level as the Type-Token ratio ($TTR_{lg}$). We measure the ratio using the types and tokens present in the reinflection dictionaries (UniMorph, lexicon from TED *dev*)

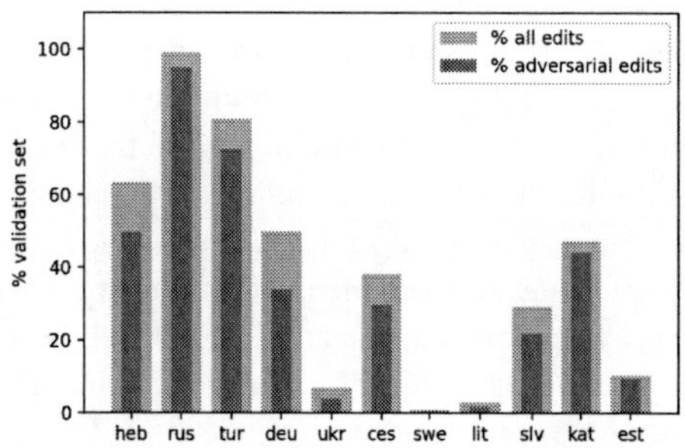


Figure 1: Perturbation statistics for selected TED languages

In preparing our adversarial set, we retain the original source sentence if we fail to create any perturbation or if none of the identified perturbations lead to a drop in chrF score. This is to make sure the adversarial set has the same number of sentences as the original validation set. In Table 4, we present the baseline and adversarial MT results. We notice a considerable drop in performance for Hebrew, Russian, Turkish and Georgian. As expected, the % drops are correlated to the perturbations statistics from Figure 1.

### 3.3 Translating Learner's Text

In the previous sections (§3.1, §3.2), we have seen the impact of noisy inputs to MT systems. While, these results indicate a need for improving the robustness of MT systems, the above-constructed ad-

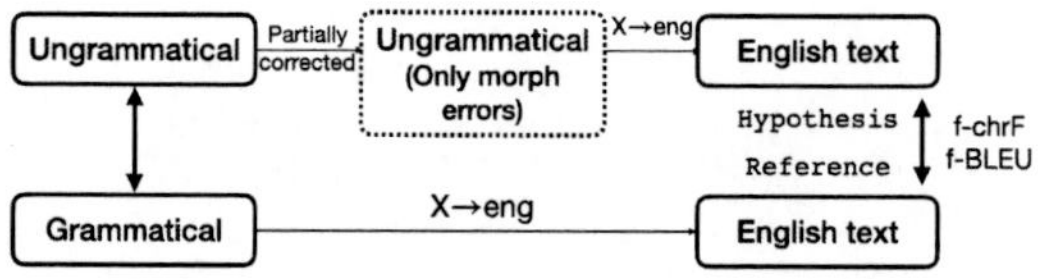


Figure 2: Schematic for preliminary evaluation on learners' language text. This is similar to the methodology used in Anastasopoulos (2019).

versarial sets are however synthetic. In this section, we evaluate the impact of morphological inflection related errors directly on learners' text.

To this end, we utilize two grammatical error correction (GEC) datasets, German Falko-MERLIN-GEC (Boyd, 2018), Russian RULEC-GEC (Rozovskaya and Roth, 2019). Both of these datasets contain labeled error types relating to word morphology. Evaluating the robustness on these datasets will give us a better understanding of the performance on actual text produced by second language (L2) speakers.

Unfortunately, we don't have gold English translations for the grammatically incorrect (or corrected) text from GEC datasets. While there is a related prior work (Anastasopoulos et al., 2019) that annotated Spanish translations for English GEC data, we are not aware of any prior work that provide gold English translations for grammatically incorrect data in non-English languages. Therefore, we propose a pseudo-evaluation methodology that allows for measuring robustness of MT systems. A schematic overview of our methodology is presented in Figure 2. We take the ungrammatical text and use the gold GEC annotations to correct all errors except for the morphology related errors. We now have ungrammatical text that only contains morphology related errors and it is similar to the perturbed outputs from MORPHEUS-MULTILINGUAL. Since, we don't have gold translations for the input Russian/German sentences, we use the machine translation output of the fully grammatical text as reference and the translation output of partially-corrected text as hypothesis. In Table 5, we present the results on both Russian and German learners' text.

Overall, we find that the pre-trained MT models from `fairseq` are quite robust to noise in learners' text. We manually inspected some examples, and found the MT systems to sufficiently robust to morphological perturbations and changes in the output translation (if any) are mostly warranted.

| X→English | Code | # train | Baseline | | Adversarial | | |
|---|---|---|---|---|---|---|---|
| | | | BLEU | chrF | BLEU | chrF | NR |
| Hebrew | heb | 211K | 40.06 | 0.5898 | 33.94 (-15%) | 0.5354 (-9%) | 1.56 |
| Russian | rus | 208K | 25.64 | 0.4784 | 11.70 (-54%) | 0.3475 (-27%) | 1.03 |
| Turkish | tur | 182K | 27.77 | 0.5006 | 18.90 (-32%) | 0.4087 (-18%) | 1.43 |
| German | deu | 168K | 34.15 | 0.5606 | 31.29 (-8%) | 0.5373 (-4%) | 1.82 |
| Ukrainian | ukr | 108K | 25.83 | 0.4726 | 25.66 (-1%) | 0.4702 (-1%) | 2.96 |
| Czech | ces | 103K | 29.35 | 0.5147 | 26.58 (-9%) | 0.4889 (-5%) | 2.11 |
| Swedish | swe | 56K | 36.93 | 0.5654 | 36.84 (-0%) | 0.5646 (-0%) | 3.48 |
| Lithuanian | lit | 41K | 18.88 | 0.3959 | 18.82 (-0%) | 0.3948 (-0%) | 3.42 |
| Slovenian | slv | 19K | 11.53 | 0.3259 | 10.48 (-9%) | 0.3100 (-5%) | 3.23 |
| Georgian | kat | 13K | 5.83 | 0.2462 | 4.92 (-16%) | 0.2146 (-13%) | 2.49 |
| Estonian | est | 10K | 6.68 | 0.2606 | 6.53 (-2%) | 0.2546 (-2%) | 4.72 |

Table 4: Results on multilingual TED corpus (Qi et al., 2018)

| Dataset | f-BLEU | f-chrF |
|---|---|---|
| Russian GEC | 85.77 | 91.56 |
| German GEC | 89.60 | 93.95 |

Table 5: Translation results on Russian and German GEC corpora. An oracle (aka. fully robust) MT system would give a perfect score. We adopt the *faux*-BLEU terminology from Anastasopoulos (2019). f-BLEU is identical to BLEU, except that it is computed against a pseudo-reference instead of true reference.

Viewing these results in combination with results on TED corpus, we believe that X→English are robust to morphological perturbations at source as long as they are trained on sufficiently large parallel corpus.

## 4 Analysis

To better understand what makes a given MT system to be robust to morphology related grammatical perturbations in source, we present a thorough analysis of our results and also highlight a few limitations of our adversarial methodology.

**Adversarial Dimensions:** To quantify the impact of each inflectional perturbation, we perform a fine-grained analysis on the adversarial sentences obtained from multilingual TED corpus. For each perturbed token in the adversarial sentence, we identify the part-of-speech (POS) and the feature dimension(s) (dim) perturbed in the token. We uniformly distribute the % drop in sentence-level chrF score to each (POS, dim) perturbation in the adversarial sentence. This allows us to quantitatively compare the impact of each perturbation type (POS, dim) on the overall performance of MT model. Additionally, as seen in Figure 1, all inflectional perturbations need not cause a drop in chrF (or BLEU) scores. The adversarial sentences only capture the worst case drop in chrF. Therefore, to analyze the overall impact of the each perturbation (POS, dim), we also compute the impact score on the entire set of perturbed sentences explored by MORPHEUS-MULTILINGUAL.

Table 8 (in Appendix) presents the results for all the TED languages. First, the trends for adversarial perturbations is quite similar to all explored perturbations. This indicates that the adversarial impact of a perturbation is not determined by just the perturbation type (POS, dim) but is lexically dependent.

**Evaluation Metrics:** In the results presented in §3, we reported the performance using BLEU and chrF metrics (following prior work (Tan et al., 2020)). We noticed significant drops on these metrics, even for high-resource languages like Russian, Turkish and Hebrew, including the state-of-the-art `fairseq` models. To better understand these drops, we inspected the output translations of adversarial source sentences. We found a number of cases where the new translation is semantically valid but both the metrics incorrectly score them low (see S2 in Table 6). This is a limitation of using surface level metrics like BLEU/chrF.

Additionally, we require the new translation to be as close as possible to the original translation, but this can be a strict requirement on many occasions. For instance, if we changed a noun in the

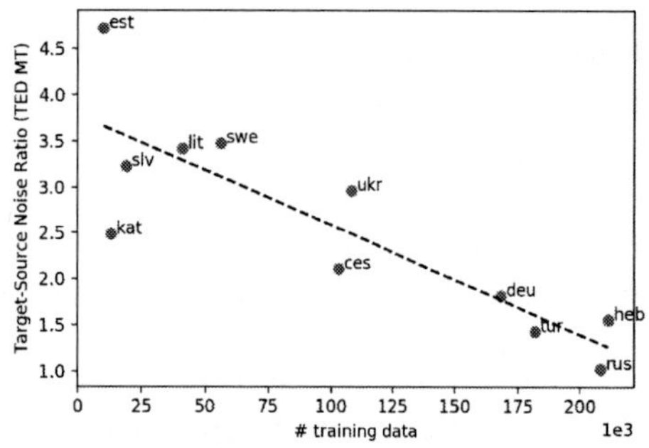


Figure 3: Correlation between Noise Ratio (NR) and # train. The results indicate that, larger the training data, the models are more robust towards source perturbations (NR≈1).

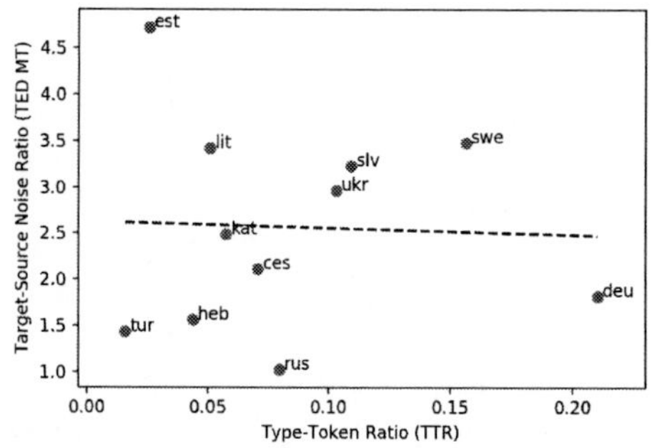


Figure 4: Correlation between Target-Source Noise Ratio (NR) on TED machine translation and Type-Token Ratio ($TTR_{lg}$) of the source language (from UniMorph). The results indicate that the morphological richness of the source language doesn't necessarily correlate to NMT robustness.

source from its singular to plural form, it is natural to expect a robust translation system to reflect that change in the output translation. To account for this behavior, we compute Target-Source Noise Ratio (NR) metric from Anastasopoulos (2019). NR is computed as follows,

$$\mathrm{NR}(s,t,\tilde{s},\tilde{t}) = \frac{100 - \mathrm{BLEU}(t,\tilde{t})}{100 - \mathrm{BLEU}(s,\tilde{s})} \quad (2)$$

The ideal NR is ∼1, where a change in the source ($s \rightarrow \tilde{s}$) results in a proportional change in the target ($t \rightarrow \tilde{t}$). For the adversarial experiments on TED corpus, we compute the NR metric for each language pair and the results are presented in Table 4. Interestingly, while Russian sees a major drop in BLEU/chrF score, the noise ratio is close to 1. This indicates that the Russian MT is actually quite robust to morphological perturbations. Furthermore, in Figure 3, we present a correlation analysis between the size of parallel corpus available for training *vs* noise ratio metric. We see a very strong negative correlation, indicating that high-resource MT systems (e.g., heb, rus, tur) are quite robust to inflectional perturbations, inspite of the large drops in BLEU/chrF scores. Additionally, we noticed that morphological richness of the source language (measured via TTR in Table 3) doesn't play any significant role in the MT performance under adversarial settings (e.g., rus, tur *vs* deu). The scatter plot between TTR and NR for TED translation task is presented in Figure 4.

**Morphological Richness:** To analyze the impact of morphological richness of source, we look deeper into the Slavic language family. We experimented with four languages within the Slavic family, Czech, Ukranian, Russian and Slovenian. All except Slovenian are high-resource. These languages differ significantly in their morphological richness (TTR) with, $\mathrm{TTR}_{\mathtt{ces}} < \mathrm{TTR}_{\mathtt{slv}} << \mathrm{TTR}_{\mathtt{rus}} << \mathrm{TTR}_{\mathtt{ukr}}$.[9] As we have already seen in above analysis (see Figure 4), morphological richness isn't indicative of the noise ratio (NR), and this behavior is also true for Slavic languages. We now check if morphological richness determines the drop in BLEU/chrF scores? In fact, we find that this is also not the case. We see larger % drop for rus as compared to slv or ukr. We instead notice that the % drop in BLEU/chrF is dependent on the % edits we make to the validation set. The % edits we were able to make follows the order, $\delta_{\mathtt{rus}} >> \delta_{\mathtt{ces}} > \delta_{\mathtt{slv}} >> \delta_{\mathtt{ukr}}$ (see Figure 1).

While NR is driven by size of training set, and % drop in BLEU is driven by % edits to the validation set. The % edits in turn depends on the size of UniMorph dictionaries and not on morphological richness of the language. Therefore, we conclude that both the metrics, % drop in BLEU/chrF and NR are *dependent on the resource size* (parallel data and UniMorph dictionaries) and *not on the morphological richness of the language*.

**Semantic Change:** In our adversarial attacks, we aim to create a ungrammatical source via inflectional edits and evaluate the robustness of systems for these edits. While these adversarial attacks can help us discover any significant biases in the transla-

[9] $\mathrm{TTR}_{lg}$ measured on lexicons from TED dev splits.

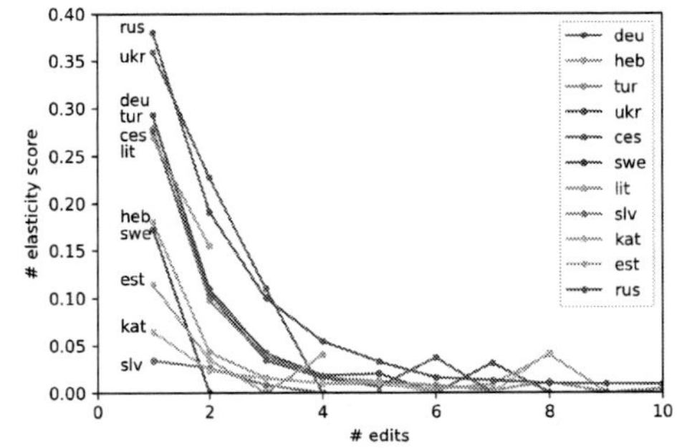


Figure 5: Elasticity score for TED languages

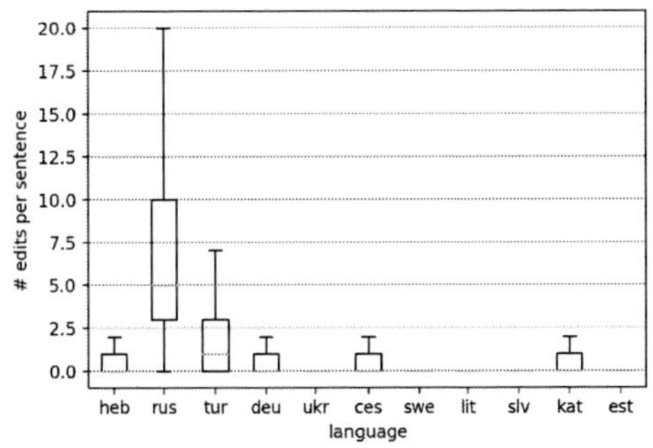


Figure 6: Boxplots for the distribution of # edits per sentence in the adversarial TED validation set.

tion systems, they can often lead to unintended consequences. Consider the example Russian sentence S1 ($s$) from Table 6. The sentence is grammatically correct, with the subject Тренер ('Coach') and object игрока ('player') in NOM and ACC cases respectively. If were perturb this sentence to A-S1 ($\tilde{s}$), the new words Тренера ('Coach'), and игрок ('player') are now in ACC and NOM cases respectively. Due to case assignment phenomenon in Russian, this perturbation ($s \to \tilde{s}$) has essentially swapped the subject and object roles in the Russian sentence. As we can see in the example, the English translation, $\tilde{t}$ (A-T1) does in fact correctly capture this change. This indicates that our attacks can sometimes lead to significant change in the semantics of the source sentence. Handling such cases would require deeper understanding of each language grammar and we leave this for future work.

**Elasticity:** As we have seen in discussion on noise ratio, it is natural for MT systems to transfer changes in source to the target. However, inspired by (Anastasopoulos, 2019), we wanted to understand how this behavior changes as we increase the number of edits in the source sentence. For this purpose, we first bucket all the explored perturbed sentences based on the number of edits (or perturbations) from the original source. Within each bucket, we compute the fraction of perturbed source sentences that result in same translation as the original source. We define this fraction as the *elasticity* score, i.e. whether the translation remains the same under changes in source. Figure 5 presents the results and we find the elasticity score dropping quickly to zero as the # edits increase. Notably, `ukr` drops quickly to zero, while `rus` retains reasonable elasticity score for higher number of edits.

**Aggressive edits:** Our algorithm doesn't put any restrictions on the number of tokens that can be perturbed in a given sentence. This can lead to aggressive edits, especially in languages like Russian that are morphologically-rich and the reinflection lexicons are sufficiently large. As we illustrate in Figure 6, median edits per sentence in `rus` is 5, significantly higher than the next language (`tur` at 1). Such aggressive edits in Russian can lead to unrealistic sentences, and far from our intended simulation of learners' text. We leave the idea of thresholding # edits to future work.

**Adversarial Training:** In an attempt to improve robustness of NMT systems against morphological perturbations, we propose training NMT models with augmenting adversarially perturbed sentences. Due to computational constraints, we evaluate this setting only for `slv`. We follow the strategy outlined in Section 2 to obtain adversarial perturbations for TED corpus training data. We observe that the adversarially trained model performs marginally poorer (BLEU 10.30 from 10.48 when trained without data augmentation). We hypothesize that this could possibly due to small training data, and believe that this training setting can better benefit models with already high BLEU scores. We leave extensive evaluation and further analysis on adversarial training to future work.

## 5 Conclusion

In this work, we propose MORPHEUS-MULTILINGUAL, a tool to analyze the robustness of X→English NMT systems under morphological perturbations. Using this tool, we experiment with 11 different languages selected from diverse language families with varied training resources.

| | | | |
|---|---|---|---|
| rus | S1 | Source ($s$) | Тренер полностью поддержал игрока. |
| | T1 | Target ($t$) | The coach fully supported the player. |
| | A-S1 | Source ($\tilde{s}$) | Тренера полностью поддержал игрок. |
| | A-T1 | Target ($\tilde{t}$) | The coach was fully supported by the player. |
| deu | S2 | Source ($s$) | Dinosaurier benutzte Tarnung, um seinen Feinden auszuweichen |
| | T2 | Target ($t$) | Dinosaur used camouflage to evade its enemies (1.000) |
| | A-S2 | Source ($\tilde{s}$) | Dinosaurier benutze Tarnung, um seinen Feindes auszuweichen |
| | A-T2 | Target ($\tilde{t}$) | Dinosaur Use camouflage to dodge his enemy (0.512) |
| rus | S3 | Source ($s$) | У нас вообще телесные наказания не редкость. |
| | T3 | Target ($t$) | In general, corporal punishment is not uncommon. (0.885) |
| | A-S3 | Source ($\tilde{s}$) | У нас вообще телесных наказании не редкостях. |
| | A-T3 | Target ($\tilde{t}$) | We don't have corporal punishment at all. (0.405) |
| rus | S4 | Source ($s$) | Вот телесные наказания - спасибо, не надо. |
| | T4 | Target ($t$) | That's corporal punishment - thank you, you don't have to. (0.458) |
| | A-S4 | Source ($\tilde{s}$) | Вот телесных наказаний - спасибах, не надо. |
| | A-T4 | Target ($\tilde{t}$) | That's why I'm here. (0.047) |
| deu | S5 | Source ($s$) | Die Schießereien haben nicht aufgehört. |
| | T5 | Target ($t$) | The shootings have not stopped. (0.852) |
| | A-S5 | Source ($\tilde{s}$) | Die Schießereien habe nicht aufgehört. |
| | A-T5 | Target ($\tilde{t}$) | The shootings did not stop, he said. (0.513) |
| rus | S6 | Source ($s$) | Всякое бывает. |
| | T6 | Target ($t$) | Anything happens. (0.587) |
| | A-S6 | Source ($\tilde{s}$) | Всякое будете бывать. |
| | A-T6 | Target ($\tilde{t}$) | You'll be everywhere. (0.037) |
| kat | S7 | Source ($s$) | ნამდვილი სკოლა. |
| | T7 | Target ($t$) | It 's a real school. (0.821) |
| | A-S7 | Source ($\tilde{s}$) | ნამდვილნი სკოლები. |
| | A-T7 | Target ($\tilde{t}$) | There 's a man who 's friend. (0.107) |
| est | S8 | Source ($s$) | Ning meie laste tuleviku varastamine saab ühel päeval kuriteoks. |
| | T8 | Target ($t$) | And our children 's going to be the future of our own day. (0.446) |
| | A-S8 | Source ($\tilde{s}$) | Ning meie laptegs tuleviku varastamine saab ühel päeval kuriteoks. |
| | A-T8 | Target ($\tilde{t}$) | And our future is about the future of the future. (0.227) |
| est | S9 | Source ($s$) | Nad pagevad üle piiride nagu see. |
| | T9 | Target ($t$) | They like that overdights like this. (0.318) |
| | A-S9 | Source ($\tilde{s}$) | Nad pagevad üle piirete nagu see. |
| | A-T9 | Target ($\tilde{t}$) | They dress it as well as well. (0.141) |
| rus | S10 | Source ($s$) | Мой дедушка был необычайным человеком того времени. |
| | T10 | Target ($t$) | My grandfather was an extraordinary man at that time. (0.802) |
| | A-S10 | Source ($\tilde{s}$) | Мой дедушка будё необычайна человеков того времи. |
| | A-T10 | Target ($\tilde{t}$) | My grandfather is incredibly harmful. (0.335) |

Table 6: Qualitative analysis. (1) semantic change, (2) issues with evaluation metrics, (3,4,5,6,7,10) good examples for attacks, (8) poor attacks, (9) poor translation quality ($s \rightarrow t$)

We evaluate NMT models trained on TED corpus as well as pretrained models readily available as part of `fairseq` library. We observe a wide range of 0-50% drop in performances under adversarial setting. We further supplement our experiments with an analysis on GEC-learners corpus for Russian and German. We qualitatively and quantitatively analyze the perturbations created by our methodology and presented its strengths as well as limitations, outlining some avenues for future research towards building more robust NMT systems.

## References


Md Mahfuz Ibn Alam and Antonios Anastasopoulos. 2020. Fine-tuning MT systems for robustness to second-language speaker variations. In *Proceedings of the Sixth Workshop on Noisy User-generated Text (W-NUT 2020)*, pages 149–158, Online. Association for Computational Linguistics.

Antonios Anastasopoulos. 2019. An analysis of source-side grammatical errors in NMT. In *Proceedings of the 2019 ACL Workshop BlackboxNLP: Analyzing and Interpreting Neural Networks for NLP*, pages 213–223, Florence, Italy. Association for Computational Linguistics.

Antonios Anastasopoulos, Alison Lui, Toan Q. Nguyen, and David Chiang. 2019. Neural machine translation of text from non-native speakers. In *Proceedings of the 2019 Conference of the North American Chapter of the Association for Computational Linguistics: Human Language Technologies, Volume 1 (Long and Short Papers)*, pages 3070–3080, Minneapolis, Minnesota. Association for Computational Linguistics.

Antonios Anastasopoulos and Graham Neubig. 2019. Pushing the limits of low-resource morphological inflection. In *Proceedings of the 2019 Conference on Empirical Methods in Natural Language Processing and the 9th International Joint Conference on Natural Language Processing (EMNLP-IJCNLP)*, pages 984–996, Hong Kong, China. Association for Computational Linguistics.

Naveen Arivazhagan, Ankur Bapna, Orhan Firat, Dmitry Lepikhin, Melvin Johnson, Maxim Krikun, Mia Xu Chen, Yuan Cao, George Foster, Colin Cherry, et al. 2019. Massively multilingual neural machine translation in the wild: Findings and challenges. *arXiv preprint arXiv:1907.05019*.

Loïc Barrault, Ondřej Bojar, Marta R. Costa-jussà, Christian Federmann, Mark Fishel, Yvette Graham, Barry Haddow, Matthias Huck, Philipp Koehn, Shervin Malmasi, Christof Monz, Mathias Müller, Santanu Pal, Matt Post, and Marcos Zampieri. 2019. Findings of the 2019 conference on machine translation (WMT19). In *Proceedings of the Fourth Conference on Machine Translation (Volume 2: Shared Task Papers, Day 1)*, pages 1–61, Florence, Italy. Association for Computational Linguistics.

Yonatan Belinkov and Yonatan Bisk. 2018. Synthetic and natural noise both break neural machine translation. In *International Conference on Learning Representations*.

Adriane Boyd. 2018. Using Wikipedia edits in low resource grammatical error correction. In *Proceedings of the 2018 EMNLP Workshop W-NUT: The 4th Workshop on Noisy User-generated Text*, pages 79–84, Brussels, Belgium. Association for Computational Linguistics.

Melvin Johnson, Mike Schuster, Quoc V. Le, Maxim Krikun, Yonghui Wu, Zhifeng Chen, Nikhil Thorat, Fernanda Viégas, Martin Wattenberg, Greg Corrado, Macduff Hughes, and Jeffrey Dean. 2017. Google's multilingual neural machine translation system: Enabling zero-shot translation. *Transactions of the Association for Computational Linguistics*, 5:339–351.

Arya D. McCarthy, Christo Kirov, Matteo Grella, Amrit Nidhi, Patrick Xia, Kyle Gorman, Ekaterina Vylomova, Sabrina J. Mielke, Garrett Nicolai, Miikka Silfverberg, Timofey Arkhangelskiy, Nataly Krizhanovsky, Andrew Krizhanovsky, Elena Klyachko, Alexey Sorokin, John Mansfield, Valts Ernštreits, Yuval Pinter, Cassandra L. Jacobs, Ryan Cotterell, Mans Hulden, and David Yarowsky. 2020. UniMorph 3.0: Universal Morphology. In *Proceedings of the 12th Language Resources and Evaluation Conference*, pages 3922–3931, Marseille, France. European Language Resources Association.

Myle Ott, Sergey Edunov, Alexei Baevski, Angela Fan, Sam Gross, Nathan Ng, David Grangier, and Michael Auli. 2019. fairseq: A fast, extensible toolkit for sequence modeling. In *Proceedings of the 2019 Conference of the North American Chapter of the Association for Computational Linguistics (Demonstrations)*, pages 48–53, Minneapolis, Minnesota. Association for Computational Linguistics.

Kishore Papineni, Salim Roukos, Todd Ward, and Wei-Jing Zhu. 2002. Bleu: a method for automatic evaluation of machine translation. In *Proceedings of the 40th Annual Meeting of the Association for Computational Linguistics*, pages 311–318, Philadelphia, Pennsylvania, USA. Association for Computational Linguistics.

Maja Popović. 2017. chrF++: words helping character n-grams. In *Proceedings of the Second Conference on Machine Translation*, pages 612–618, Copenhagen, Denmark. Association for Computational Linguistics.

Matt Post. 2018. A call for clarity in reporting BLEU scores. In *Proceedings of the Third Conference on*

*Machine Translation: Research Papers*, pages 186–191, Brussels, Belgium. Association for Computational Linguistics.

Ye Qi, Devendra Sachan, Matthieu Felix, Sarguna Padmanabhan, and Graham Neubig. 2018. When and why are pre-trained word embeddings useful for neural machine translation? In *Proceedings of the 2018 Conference of the North American Chapter of the Association for Computational Linguistics: Human Language Technologies, Volume 2 (Short Papers)*, pages 529–535, New Orleans, Louisiana. Association for Computational Linguistics.

Alla Rozovskaya and Dan Roth. 2019. Grammar error correction in morphologically rich languages: The case of Russian. *Transactions of the Association for Computational Linguistics*, 7:1–17.

Samson Tan, Shafiq Joty, Min-Yen Kan, and Richard Socher. 2020. It's morphin' time! Combating linguistic discrimination with inflectional perturbations. In *Proceedings of the 58th Annual Meeting of the Association for Computational Linguistics*, pages 2920–2935, Online. Association for Computational Linguistics.

# A Appendix

## A.1 UniMorph Example

An example from German UniMorph dictionary is presented in Table 7.

| Paradigm | Form | MSD |
|---|---|---|
| abspielen ('play') | abgespielt ('played') | V.PTCP;PST |
| abspielen ('play') | abspielend ('playing') | V.PTCP;PRS |
| abspielen ('play') | abspielen ('play') | V;NFIN |

Table 7: Example inflections for German verb *abspielen* ('play') from the UniMorph dictionary.

## A.2 MT training

For all the languages in TED corpus, we train Any→English using the `fairseq` toolkit. Specifically, we use the 'transformer_iwslt_de_en' architecture, and train the model using Adam optimizer. We use an inverse square root learning rate scheduler with warm-up update steps of 4000. In the linear warm-up phase, we use an initial learning rate of 1e-7 until a configured rate of 2e-4. We use cross entropy criterion with label smoothing of 0.1.

## A.3 Dimension Analysis

| Dimension | ces | deu | est | heb | kat | lit | rus | slv | swe | tur | ukr |
|---|---|---|---|---|---|---|---|---|---|---|---|
| ADJ.Animacy | - | - | - | - | - | - | $3.51_{(0.89)}$ | - | - | - | - |
| ADJ.Case | $4.31_{(0.81)}$ | - | - | - | $10.67_{(2.59)}$ | - | $4.78_{(0.91)}$ | - | $5.05_{(5.05)}$ | - | $6.04_{(1.10)}$ |
| ADJ.Comparison | - | - | - | - | - | $7.99_{(0.46)}$ | - | - | - | - | - |
| ADJ.Gender | $3.83_{(0.78)}$ | - | - | - | - | $6.81_{(-1.35)}$ | $5.30_{(1.00)}$ | - | - | - | - |
| ADJ.Number | $4.07_{(0.78)}$ | - | - | - | $13.90_{(1.52)}$ | $6.31_{(-2.26)}$ | $4.67_{(0.94)}$ | - | $5.05_{(5.05)}$ | $7.92_{(2.23)}$ | $6.25_{(1.29)}$ |
| ADJ.Person | - | - | - | - | - | - | - | - | - | $8.89_{(2.43)}$ | - |
| N.Animacy | - | - | - | - | - | - | $6.53_{(1.19)}$ | - | - | - | - |
| N.Case | $6.94_{(0.81)}$ | $6.39_{(1.26)}$ | $12.35_{(1.50)}$ | - | $15.38_{(0.98)}$ | - | $6.65_{(1.20)}$ | - | $4.29_{(1.05)}$ | $14.39_{(2.37)}$ | $10.28_{(7.66)}$ |
| N.Definiteness | - | - | - | - | - | - | - | - | $8.36_{(1.61)}$ | - | - |
| N.Number | $5.44_{(0.77)}$ | $5.70_{(1.27)}$ | $8.10_{(1.33)}$ | $16.22_{(5.92)}$ | $14.46_{(0.66)}$ | - | $6.12_{(1.22)}$ | - | $4.30_{(1.52)}$ | $13.08_{(2.31)}$ | $21.20_{(15.96)}$ |
| N.Possession | - | - | - | $12.63_{(4.31)}$ | - | - | - | - | - | - | - |
| V.Aspect | - | - | - | - | $14.17_{(-0.38)}$ | - | - | - | - | - | - |
| V.Gender | - | - | - | - | - | - | $6.52_{(1.51)}$ | - | - | - | - |
| V.Mood | $13.17_{(2.78)}$ | $15.89_{(2.77)}$ | - | - | $11.11_{(0.58)}$ | - | - | $21.49_{(3.73)}$ | - | - | - |
| V.Number | $8.23_{(2.72)}$ | $32.86_{(8.12)}$ | - | $13.78_{(4.60)}$ | $9.02_{(1.33)}$ | - | $6.23_{(1.44)}$ | $21.47_{(-9.47)}$ | - | - | - |
| V.Person | $6.58_{(2.69)}$ | $6.22_{(1.50)}$ | - | $10.86_{(4.99)}$ | $12.37_{(1.33)}$ | - | $6.10_{(1.29)}$ | - | - | - | - |
| V.Tense | - | - | - | $17.52_{(7.13)}$ | $13.09_{(1.05)}$ | - | $6.59_{(1.61)}$ | - | - | - | - |
| V.CVB.Tense | - | - | - | - | - | - | $6.70_{(0.87)}$ | - | - | - | $9.09_{(2.62)}$ |
| V.MSDR.Aspect | - | - | - | - | $14.39_{(4.68)}$ | - | - | - | - | - | - |
| V.PTCP.Gender | $10.28_{(2.75)}$ | - | - | - | - | - | - | - | - | - | - |
| V.PTCP.Number | $9.31_{(2.51)}$ | - | - | - | - | - | - | - | - | - | - |

Table 8: Fine-grained analysis of X→English translation performance w.r.t the perturbation type (POS, Morphological feature dimension). The number reported in this table indicate the average *% drop* in sentence level chrF for an adversarial pertubation on a token with POS on the dimension (dim). The numbers in the parentheses indicate average *% drop* for all the tested perturbations including the adversarial perturbations.

# Sample-efficient Linguistic Generalizations through Program Synthesis: Experiments with Phonology Problems

**Saujas Vaduguru**[1] **Aalok Sathe**[2] **Monojit Choudhury**[3] **Dipti Misra Sharma**[1]
[1] IIIT Hyderabad [2] MIT BCS*
[3] Microsoft Research India
[1] {saujas.vaduguru@research.,dipti@}iiit.ac.in
[2] aalok.sathe@{mit.edu, richmond.edu}
[3] monojitc@microsoft.com

## Abstract

Neural models excel at extracting statistical patterns from large amounts of data, but struggle to learn patterns or reason about language from only a few examples. In this paper, we ask: Can we learn explicit rules that generalize well from only a few examples? We explore this question using program synthesis. We develop a synthesis model to learn phonology rules as programs in a domain-specific language. We test the ability of our models to generalize from few training examples using our new dataset of problems from the Linguistics Olympiad, a challenging set of tasks that require strong linguistic reasoning ability. In addition to being highly sample-efficient, our approach generates human-readable programs, and allows control over the generalizability of the learnt programs.

## 1 Introduction

In the last few years, the application of deep neural models has allowed rapid progress in NLP. Tasks in phonology and morphology have been no exception to this, with neural encoder-decoder models achieving strong results in recent shared tasks in phonology (Gorman et al., 2020) and morphology (Vylomova et al., 2020). However, the neural models that perform well on these tasks make use of hundreds, if not thousands of training examples for each language. Additionally, the patterns that neural models identify are not interpretable. In this paper, we explore the problem of learning interpretable phonological and morphological rules from only a small number of examples, a task that humans are able to perform.

Consider the example of verb forms in the language Mandar presented in Table 1. How would a neural model tasked with filling the two blank cells do? The data comes from a language that is not represented in large-scale text datasets that could allow the model to harness pretraining, and the number of samples presented here is likely not sufficient for the neural model to learn the task.

| **to *V*** | **to be *V*ed** |
|---|---|
| mappasuŋ | dipasuŋ |
| mattunu | ditunu |
| ? | ditimbe |
| ? | dipande |

Table 1: Verb forms in Mandar (McCoy, 2018)

However, a human would fare much better at this task even if they didn't know Mandar. Identifying rules and patterns in a different language is a principal concern of a descriptive linguist (Brown and Ogilvie, 2010). Even people who aren't trained in linguistics would be able to solve such a task, as evidenced by contestants in the Linguistics Olympiads[1], and general-audience puzzle books (Bellos, 2020). In addition to being able to solve the task, humans would be able to express their solution explicitly in terms of rules, that is to say, a *program* that maps inputs to outputs.

*Program synthesis* (Gulwani et al., 2017) is a method that can be used to learn programs that map an input to an output in a *domain-specific language* (DSL). It has been shown to be a highly sample-efficient technique to learn interpretable rules by specifying the assumptions of the task in the DSL (Gulwani, 2011).

This raises the questions (i) Can program synthesis be used to learn linguistic rules from only a few examples? (ii) If so, what kind of rules can be learnt? (iii) What kind of operations need to explicitly be defined in the DSL to allow it to model linguistic rules? (iv) What knowledge must be im-

*Work done while at the University of Richmond

[1] https://www.ioling.org/



*Proceedings of the Seventeenth SIGMORPHON Workshop on Computational Research in Phonetics, Phonology, and Morphology*, pages 60–71

plicitly provided with these operations to allow the model to choose rules that generalize well?

In this work, we use program synthesis to learn phonological rules for solving Linguistics Olympiad problems, where only the minimal number of examples necessary to generalize are given (Şahin et al., 2020). We present a program synthesis model and a DSL for learning phonological rules, and curate a set of Linguistics Olympiad problems for evaluation.

We perform experiments and comparisons to baselines, and find that program synthesis does significantly better than our baseline approaches. We also present some observations about the ability of our system to find rules that generalize well, and discuss examples of where it fails.

## 2 Program synthesis

Program synthesis is "the task of automatically finding programs from the underlying programming language that satisfy (user) intent expressed in some form of constraints" (Gulwani et al., 2017). This method allows us to specify domain-specific assumptions as a language, and use generic synthesis approches like FlashMeta (Polozov and Gulwani, 2015) to synthesize programs.

The ability to explicitly encode domain-specific assumptions gives program synthesis broad applicability to various tasks. In this paper, we explore applying it to the task of learning phonological rules. Whereas previous work on rule-learning has focused on learning rules of a specific type (Brill, 1992; Johnson, 1984), the DSL in program synthesis allows learning rules of different types, and in different rule formalisms.

In this work, we explore learning rules similar to rewrite rules (Chomsky and Halle, 1968) that are used extensively to describe phonology. Sequences of rules are learnt using a noisy disjunctive synthesis algorithm NDSyn (Iyer et al., 2019) extended to learn *stateful multi-pass rules* (Sarthi et al., 2021).

### 2.1 Phonological rules as programs

The synthesis task we solve is to learn a program in a domain-specific language (DSL) for string transduction, that is, to transform a given sequence of input tokens $i \in \mathcal{I}^*$ to a sequence of output tokens $o \in \mathcal{O}^*$, where $\mathcal{I}$ is the set of input tokens, and $\mathcal{O}$ is the set of output tokens. Each token is a symbol accompanied by a feature set, a set of key-value pairs that maps feature names to boolean values.

We learn programs for token-level examples, which transform an input token in its context to output tokens. The program is a sequence of rules which are applied to each token in an input string to produce the output string. The rules learnt are similar to rewrite rules, of the form

$$\phi_{-l} \cdots \phi_{-2}\phi_{-1} X \phi_1\phi_2 \cdots \phi_r \rightarrow T$$

where (i) $X : \mathcal{I} \rightarrow \mathbb{B}$ is a boolean predicate that determines input tokens to which the rule is applied (ii) $\phi_i : \mathcal{I} \rightarrow \mathbb{B}$ is a boolean predicate applied to the $i^{\text{th}}$ character relative to $X$, and the predicates $\phi$ collectively determine the context in which the rule is applied (iii) $T : \mathcal{I} \rightarrow \mathcal{O}^*$ is a function that maps an input token to a sequence of output tokens.

$X$ and $\phi$ belong to a set of predicates $\mathcal{P}$, and $T$ is a function belonging to a set of transformation functions $\mathcal{T}$. $\mathcal{P}$ and $\mathcal{T}$ are specified by the DSL.

We allow the model to synthesize programs that apply multiple rules to a single token by synthesizing rules in passes and maintaining state from one pass to the next. This allows the system to learn stateful multi-pass rules (Sarthi et al., 2021).

### 2.2 Domain-specific language

The domain-specific language (DSL) is the declarative language which defines the allowable string transformation operations. The DSL is defined by a set of operators, a grammar which determines how they can be combined, and a semantics which determines what each operator does. By defining operators to capture domain-specific phenomena, we can reduce the space of programs to be searched to include those programs that capture distinctions relevant to the domain. This allows us to explicitly encode knowledge of the domain into the system.

Operators in the DSL also have a score associated with each operator that allows for setting domain-specific preferences for certain kinds of programs. We can combine scores for each operator in a program to compute a ranking score that we can use to identify the most preferred program among candidates. The ranking score can capture implicit preferences like shorter programs, more/-less general programs, certain classes of transformations, etc.

The DSL defines the predicates $\mathcal{P}$ and set of transformations $\mathcal{T}$ that can be applied to a particular token. The predicates and transformations in the DSL we use, along with the description of their semantics, can be found in Tables 2 and 3.

| Predicate | |
|---|---|
| IsToken($w, s, i$) | Is $x$ equal to the token $s$? This allows us to evaluate matches with specific tokens. |
| Is($w, f, i$) | Is $f$ true for $x$? This allows us to generalize beyond single tokens and use features that apply to multiple tokens. |
| TransformationApplied($w, t, i$) | Has the transformation $t$ has been applied to $x$ in a previous pass? This allows us to reference previous passes in learning rules for the current pass. |
| Not($p$) | Negates the predicate $p$. |

Table 2: Predicates that are used for synthesis. The predicates are applied to a token $x$ that is at an offset $i$ from the current token in the word $w$. The offset may be positive to refer to tokens after the current token, zero to refer to the current token, or negative to refer to tokens before the current token.

| Transformation | |
|---|---|
| ReplaceBy($x, s_1, s_2$) | If $x$ is $s_1$, it is replaced with $s_2$. This allows the system to learn conditional substitutions. |
| ReplaceAnyBy($x, s$) | $x$ is replaced with $s$. This allows the system to learn unconditional substitutions. |
| Insert($x, S$) | This inserts a sequence of tokens $S$ after $x$ at the end of the pass. It allows for the insertion of variable-length affixes. |
| Delete($x$) | This deletes $x$ from the word at the end of the pass. |
| CopyReplace($x, i$)<br>CopyInsert($x, i$) | These are analogues of the ReplaceBy and Insert transformations where the token which is added is the same as the token at an offset $i$ from $x$. They allow the system to learn phonological transformations such as assimilation and gemination. |
| Identity($x$) | This returns $x$ unchanged. It allows the system where a transformation applies under certain conditions, but does not under others. |

Table 3: Transformations that are used for synthesis. The transformations are applied to a token $x$ in the word $w$. The offset $i$ for the Copy transformations may be positive to refer to tokens after the current token, zero to refer to the current token, or negative to refer to tokens before the current token.

```
output := Map(disjunction, input_tokens)
disjunction := Else(rule, disjunction)
rule := transformation
      | IfThen(predicate, rule);
```

Figure 1: IfThen-Else statements in the DSL

Sequences of rules are learnt as disjunctions of IfThen operators, and are applied to each token of the input using a Map operator (Figure 1). The conjunction of predicates $X$ and $\phi$ that define the context are learnt by nesting IfThen operators.

A transformation produces an token that is tagged with the transformation that is applied. This allows for maintaining state across passes.

The operators in our DSL are quite generic and can be applied to other string transformations as well. In addition to designing our DSL for string transformation tasks, we allow for phonological information to be specified as features, which are a set of key-value pairs that map attributes to boolean values. While we restrict our investigation to features based only on the symbols in the input, more complex features based on meaning and linguistic categories can be provided to a system that works on learning rules for more complex domains like morphology or syntax. We leave this investigation for future work.

## 2.3 Synthesis algorithm

We use an extension (Sarthi et al., 2021) of the NDSyn algorithm (Iyer et al., 2019) that can synthesize stateful multi-pass rules. Iyer et al. (2019) describe an algorithm for selecting disjunctions of rules, and use the FlashMeta algorithm as the rule synthesis component. Sarthi et al. (2021) extend the approach proposed by Iyer et al. (2019) for disjunctive synthesis to the task of grapheme-to-phoneme (G2P) conversion in Hindi and Tamil. They propose the idea of learning transformations on token aligned examples, and use language-specific predicates and transformations to learn rules for G2P conversion. We use a similar approach, and use a different set of predicates and

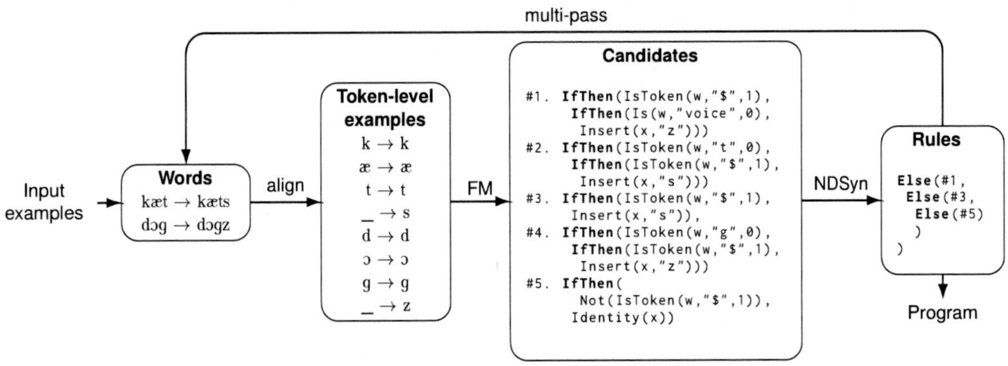


Figure 2: An illustration of the synthesis algorithm. FM is FlashMeta, which synthesizes rules which are combined into a disjunction of rules by NDSyn. Here, rule #1 is chosen over #4 since it uses the more general concept of the `voice` feature as opposed to a specific token, and thus has a higher ranking score.

transformations that are language-agnostic. Figure 2 sketches the working of the algorithm.

The NDSyn algorithm is an algorithm for learning disjunctions of rules, of the form shown in Figure 1. Given a set of examples, it first generates a set of candidate rules using the FlashMeta synthesis algorithm (Polozov and Gulwani, 2015). This algorithm searches for a program in the DSL that satisfies a set of examples by recursively breaking down the search problem into smaller subproblems. Given an operator, and the input-output constraints it must satisfy, it infers constraints on each of the arguments to the operator, allowing it to recursively search for programs that satisfy these constraints on each of the arguments. For example, given the `Is` predicate and a set of examples where the predicate is true or false, the algorithm infers constraints on the arguments the token $s$ and offset $i$ such that the set of examples is satisfied. The working of FlashMeta is illustrated with an example in Figure 3. We use the implementation of the FlashMeta algorithm available as part of the PROSE[2] framework.

From the set of candidate rules, NDSyn selects a subset of rules with a high ranking score that correctly answers the most examples as well incorrectly answers the least[3]. Additional details about the algorithm are provided in Appendix A.

The synthesis of multi-pass rules proceeds in passes. In each pass, a set of token-aligned examples is provided as input to the NDSyn algorithm. The resulting rules are then applied to all the examples, and those that are not solved are passed as the set of examples to NDSyn in the next pass. This proceeds until all the examples are solved, or for a maximum number of passes.

## 3 Dataset

To test the ability of our program synthesis system to learn linguistic rules from only a few examples, we require a task with a small number of training examples, and a number of test examples which measure how well the model generalises to unseen data. Additionally, to ensure a fair evaluation, the test examples should be chosen such that the samples in the training data provide sufficient evidence to correctly solve the test examples.

To this end, we use problems from the Linguistics Olympiad. The Linguistics Olympiad is an umbrella term describing contests for high school students across the globe. Students are tasked with solving linguistics problems—a genre of composition that presents linguistic facts and phenomena in enigmatic form (Derzhanski and Payne, 2010). These problems typically have 2 parts: the *data* and the *assignments*.

The data consists of examples where the solver is presented with the application rules to some linguistic forms (words, phrases, sentences) and the forms derived by applying the rules to these forms. The data typically consists of 20-50 forms, the minimal number of examples required to infer the correct rules is presented (Şahin et al., 2020).

The assignments provide other linguistic forms, and the solver is tasked with applying the rules inferred from the data to these forms. The forms in the assignments are carefully selected by the

[2] `https://www.microsoft.com/en-us/research/group/prose/`

[3] A rule will not produce any answer to examples that don't satisfy the context constraints of the rule.

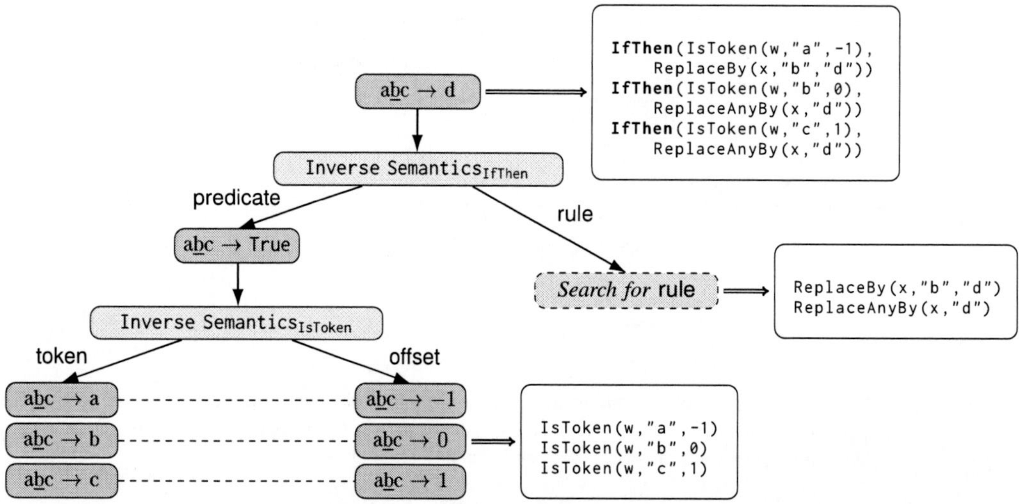


Figure 3: An illustration of the search performed by the FlashMeta algorithm. The blue boxes show the specification that an operator must satisfy in terms of input-output examples, with the input token underlined in the context of the word. The Inverse Semantics of an operator is a function that is used to infer the specification for each argument of the operator based on the semantics of the operator. This may be a single specification (as for predicate) or a disjunction of specifications (as for token and offset). The algorithm then recursively searches for programs to satisfy the specification for each argument, and combines the results of the search to obtain a program. The search for the rule in an IfThen statement proceeds similarly to the search for a predicate. Examples of programs that are inferred from a specification are indicated with $\Longrightarrow$. A dashed line between inferred specifications indicates that the specifications are inferred jointly.

designer to test whether the solver has correctly inferred the rules, including making generalizations to unseen data. This allows us to see how much of the intended solution has been learnt by the solver by examining responses to the assignments.

The small number of training examples (data) tests the generalization ability and sample efficiency of the system, and presents a challenging learning problem for the system. The careful selection of test examples (assignment) lets us use them to measure how well the model learns these generalizations.

We present a dataset of 34 linguistics problems, collected from various publicly accessible sources. These problems are based on phonology, and some aspects of the morphology of languages, as well as the orthographic properties of languages. These problems are chosen such that the underlying rules depend only on the given word forms, and not on inherent properties of the word like grammatical gender or animacy. The problems involve (1) inferring phonological rules in morphological inflection (Table 4a) (2) inferring phonological changes between multiple related languages (Table 4b) (3) converting between the orthographic form of a language and the corresponding phonological form (Table 4c) (4) marking the phonological stress on a given word (Table 4d). We refer to each of these categories of problems as morphophonology, multilingual, transliteration, and stress respectively. We further describe the dataset in Appendix B[4].

### 3.1 Structure of the problems

Each problem is presented in the form of a matrix $M$. Each row of the matrix contains data pertaining to a single word/linguistic form, and each column contains the same form of different words, i.e., an inflectional or derivational paradigm, the word form in a particular language, the word in a particular script, or the stress values for each phoneme in a word. A test sample in this case is presented as a particular cell $M_{ij}$ in the table that has to be filled. The model has to use the data from other words in the same row ($M_{i:}$) and the words in the column ($M_{:j}$) to predict the form of the word in $M_{ij}$.

In addition to the data in the table, each problem contains some additional information about the symbols used to represent the words. This addi-

[4]The dataset is available here.

| base form | negative form |
|---|---|
| joy | kas joya:ya’ |
| bi:law | kas bika’law |
| tipoysu:da | ? |
| ? | kas wurula:la’ |

(a) Movima negation

| Turkish | Tatar |
|---|---|
| bandır | mandır |
| yelken | cilkän |
| ? | osta |
| bilezik | ? |

(b) Turkish and Tatar

| Listuguj | Pronunciation |
|---|---|
| *g’p’ta’q* | gəbəda:x |
| *epsaqtejg* | epsaxteck |
| *emtoqwatg* | ? |
| ? | əmteskəm |

(c) Micmac orthography

| Aleut | Stress |
|---|---|
| tatul | `01000` |
| nətɣəlqin | `000010000` |
| sawat | ? |
| qalpuqal | `00001000` |

(d) Aleut stress

Table 4: A few examples from different types of Linguistics Olympiad problems. ‘?’ represents a cell in the table that is part of the test set.

tional information is meant to aid the solver understand the meaning of a symbol they may not have seen before. We manually encode this information in the feature set associated with each token for synthesis. Where applicable, we also add consonant/vowel distinctions in the given features, since this is a basic distinction assumed in the solutions to many Olympiad problems.

We use the assignments that accompany every problem as the test set, ensuring that the correct answer can be inferred based on the given data.

### 3.2 Dataset statistics

The dataset we present is highly multilingual. The 34 problems contain samples from 38 languages, drawn from across 19 language families. There are 15 morphophonology problems, 7 multilingual problems, 6 stress, and 6 transliteration problems. The set contains 1452 training words with an average of 43 words per problem, and 319 test words with an average of 9 per problem. Each problem has a matrix that has between 7 and 43 rows, with an average of 23. The number of columns ranges from 2 to 6, with most problems having 2.

## 4 Experiments

### 4.1 Baselines

Given that we model our task as string transduction, we compare with the following transduction models used as baselines in shared tasks on G2P conversion (Gorman et al., 2020) and morphological reinflection (Vylomova et al., 2020).

**Neural:** We use LSTM-based sequence-to-sequence models with attention as well as Transformer models as implemented by Wu (2020). For each problem, we train a single neural model that takes the source and target column numbers, and the source word, and predicts the target word.

**WFST:** We use models similar to the pair $n$-gram models (Novak et al., 2016), with the implementation similar to that used by Lee et al. (2020). We train a model for each pair of columns in a problem. For each test example $M_{ij}$, we find the column with the smallest index $j'$ such that $M_{ij'}$ is non-empty and use $M_{ij'}$ as the source string to infer $M_{ij}$.

Additional details of baselines are provided in Appendix C.

### 4.2 Program synthesis experiments

As discussed in Section 3.1, the examples in a problem are in a matrix, and we synthesize programs to transform entries in one column to entries in another. Given a problem matrix $M$, we refer to a program to transform an entry in column $i$ to an entry in column $j$ as $M_{:i} \rightarrow M_{:j}$. To obtain token-level examples, we use the Smith-Waterman alignment algorithm (Smith et al., 1981), which favours contiguous sequences in aligned strings.

We train three variants of our synthesis system with different scores for the `Is` and `IsToken` operators. The first one, NoFeature, does not use features, or the `Is` predicate. The second one, Token, assigns a higher score to `IsToken` and prefers more specific rules that reference tokens. The third one, Feature, assigns a higher score to `Is` and prefers more general rules that reference features instead of tokens. All other aspects of the model remain the same across variants.

**Morphophonology and multilingual problems:** For every pair of columns $(s, t)$ in the problem matrix $M$, we synthesize the program $M_{:s} \rightarrow M_{:t}$. To predict the form of a test sample $M_{ij}$, we find a column $k$ such that the program $M_{:k} \rightarrow M_{:j}$ has the best ranking score, and evaluate it on $M_{ik}$.

**Transliteration problems:** Given a problem matrix $M$, we construct a new matrix $M'$ for each pair of columns $(s, t)$ such that all entries in $M'$ are in the same script. We align word pairs $(M_{is}, M_{it})$ using the Phonetisaurus many-to-many alignment tool (Jiampojamarn et al., 2007), and build a simple mapping $f$ for each source token to the target token with which it is most frequently aligned. We fill in $M'_{is}$ by applying $f$ to each token of $M_{is}$ and

| Model | All | | Morphophonology | | Multilingual | | Transliteration | | Stress |
|---|---|---|---|---|---|---|---|---|---|
| | EXACT | CHRF | EXACT | CHRF | EXACT | CHRF | EXACT | CHRF | EXACT |
| NOFEATURE | 26.8% | 0.64 | 30.1% | 0.72 | 42.1% | 0.59 | 12.0% | 0.51 | 15.4% |
| TOKEN | **32.7%** | 0.63 | 37.5% | 0.68 | **45.3%** | 0.60 | 16.4% | 0.52 | 22.2% |
| FEATURE | 30.9% | 0.51 | **38.6%** | 0.56 | 39.9% | 0.42 | 9.5% | 0.49 | **23.0%** |
| LSTM | 8.2% | 0.44 | 9.2% | 0.49 | 5.7% | 0.45 | 2.1% | 0.31 | 15.0% |
| Transformer | 5.4% | 0.42 | 2.3% | 0.39 | 9.2% | 0.50 | 1.7% | 0.42 | 12.6% |
| WFST | 20.9% | 0.56 | 16.3% | 0.47 | 38.7% | 0.63 | **29.7%** | 0.71 | 2.8% |

Table 5: Metrics for all problems, and for problems of each type. The CHFF score for stress problems is not calculated, and not used to determine the overall CHRF score.

$M'_{it} = M_{it}$. We then find a program $M'_{:s} \to M'_{:t}$.
**Stress problems:** For these problems, we do not perform any alignment, since the training pairs are already token aligned. The synthesis system learns to transform the source string to the sequence of stress values.

### 4.3 Metrics

We calculate two metrics: exact match accuracy, and CHRF score (Popović, 2015). The exact match accuracy measures the fraction of examples the synthesis system gets fully correct.

$$\text{EXACT} = \frac{\#\{\text{correctly predicted test samples}\}}{\#\{\text{test samples}\}}$$

The CHRF score is calculated only at the token level, and measures the $n$-gram overlaps between the predicted answer and the true answer, and allows us to measure partially correct answers. We do not calculate the CHRF score for stress problems as $n$-gram overlap is not a meaningful measure of performance for these problems.

### 4.4 Results

Table 5 summarizes the results of our experiments. We report the average of each metric across problems for all problems and by category.

We find that neural models that don't have specific inductive biases for the kind of tasks we present here are not able to perform well with this amount of data. The synthesis models do better than the WFST baseline overall, and on all types of problems except transliteration. This could be due to the simple map computed from alignments before program synthesis causing errors that the rule learning process cannot correct.

## 5 Analysis

We examine two aspects of the program synthesis models we propose. The first is the way it uses the explicit knowledge in the DSL and implicit knowledge provided as the ranking score to generalize. We then consider specific examples of problems, and show examples of where our models succeed and fail in learning different types of patterns.

| Model | 100% | $\geq 75\%$ | $\geq 50\%$ |
|---|---|---|---|
| NOFEATURE | 3 | 5 | 7 |
| TOKEN | 3 | 6 | 10 |
| FEATURE | **3** | **6** | **11** |
| WFST | 1 | 2 | 7 |

Table 6: Number of problems where the model achieves different thresholds of the EXACT score.

### 5.1 Features aid generalization

Since the test examples are chosen to test specific rules, solving more test examples correctly is indicative of the number of rules inferred correctly. In Table 6, we see that providing the model with features allows it to infer more general rules, solving a greater fraction of more problems. We see that allowing the model to use features increases its performance, and having it prefer more general rules involving features lets it do even better.

### 5.2 Correct programs are short

In Figure 4 we see that the number of rules in a problem[5] tends to be higher when the model gets the problem wrong, than when it gets it right. This indicates that when the model finds many specific rules, it overfits to the training data, and fails to generalize well. This holds true for all the variants, as seen in the downward slope of the lines.

We also find that allowing and encouraging a model to use features leads to shorter programs. The average length of a program synthesized by

[5]To account for some problems having more columns than others (and hence more rules), we find the average number of rules for each pair of columns.

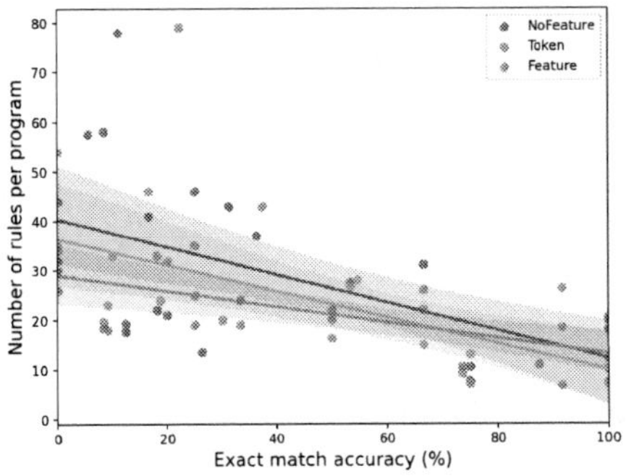


Figure 4: Number of rules plotted against EXACT score

NOFEATURES is 30.5 rules, while it is 25.8 for TOKEN, and 20.7 for FEATURE. This suggests that explicit access to features, and implicit preference for them leads to fewer, more general rules.

### 5.3 Using features

Some problems provide additional information about certain sounds. For example, a problem based on the alternation retroflexes in Warlpiri words (Laughren, 2011) explicitly identifies retroflex sounds in the problem statement. In this case, a program produced by our FEATURE system is able to use these features, and isolate the focus of the problem by learning rules such as

```
IfThen(Not(Is(w, "retroflex", 0)),
    Identity(x))
```

The system learns a concise solution, and is able to generalize using features rather than learning separate rules for individual sounds.

In the case of inflecting a Mandar verb (McCoy, 2018), the FEATURE system uses a feature to find a more general rule than is the case. To capture the rule that the prefix *di-* changes to *mas-* when the root starts with *s*, the model synthesizes

```
IfThen(Is(w, "fricative", 1),
    ReplaceBy(x, "i", "s"))
```

However, since *s* is the only fricative in the data, this rule is equivalent to a rule specific to *s*. This rule also covers examples where the root starts with *s*, and causes the model to miss the more general rule of a voiceless sound at the beginning of the root to be copied to the end of the prefix. It identifies this rule only for roots starting with *p* as

```
IfThen(IsToken(w, "p", 1),
    CopyReplace(x, w, 1))
```

The TOKEN system does not synthesize these rules based on features, and instead chooses rules specific to each initial character in the root.

Since the DSL allows for substituting one token with one other, or inserting multiple tokens, the system has to use multiple rules to substitute one token with multiple tokens. In the case of Mandar, we see one way it does this, by performing multiple substitutions (to transform *di-* to *mas-* it replaces *d* and *i* with *a* and *s* respectively, and then inserts *m*).

### 5.4 Multi-pass rules

In a problem on Somali verb forms (Somers, 2016), we see a different way of handling multi-token substitutions by using multi-pass rules to create a complex rule using simpler elements. The problem requires being able to convert verbs from 1st person to 3rd person singular. The solution includes a rule where a single token (*l*) is replaced with (*sh*). The learned program uses two passes to capture this rule through sequential application of two rules: first `ReplaceBy(x, "l", "h")`, followed by

```
IfThen(TransformationApplied(w,
        "{ReplaceBy, h}", 1),
    Insert(x, "s"))
```

### 5.5 Selecting spans of the input

In a problem involving reduplication in Tarangan (Warner, 2019), all variants fail to capture any synthesis rules. Reduplication in Tarangan involves copying one or two syllables in the source word to produce the target word. However, the DSL we use does not have any predicates or transformations that allow the system to reference a span of multiple tokens (which would form a syllable) in the input. Therefore, it fails to model reduplication.

### 5.6 Global constraints

Since we provide the synthesis model with token-level examples, it does not have access to word-level information. This results in poor performance on stress problems, as stress depends on the entire word. Consider the example of Chickasaw stress (Vaduguru, 2019). It correctly learns the rule

```
IfThen(Is(w, "long", 0),
    ReplaceAnyBy(x, "1"))
```

that stresses any long vowel in the word. However, since it cannot check if the word has a long vowel that has already been stressed, it is not able to correctly model the case when the word doesn't have a long vowel. This results in some samples being marked with stress at two locations, one where the rule for long vowels applies, and one where the rule for words without long vowels applies.

## 6 Related work

Gildea and Jurafsky (1996) also study the problem of learning phonological rules from data, and explicitly controlling generalization behaviour. We pursue a similar goal, but in a few-shot setting.

Barke et al. (2019) and Ellis et al. (2015) study program synthesis applied to linguistic rule learning. They make much stronger assumptions about the data (the existence of an underlying form, and the availability of additional information like IPA features). We take a different approach, and study program synthesis models that can work only on the tokens in the word (like NOFEATURE), and also explore the effect of providing features in these cases. We also test our approach on a more varied set of problems that involves aspects of morphology, transliteration, multilinguality, and stress.

Şahin et al. (2020) also present a set of Linguistics Olympiad problems as a test of the metalinguistic reasoning abilities of NLP models. While problems in their set involve finding phonological rules, they also require the knowledge of syntax and semantics that are out of the scope of our study. We present a set of problems that only requires reasoning about surface word forms, and without requiring the meanings.

## 7 Conclusion

In this paper, we explore the problem of learning linguistic rules from only a few training examples. We approach this using program synthesis, and demonstrate that it is a powerful and flexible technique for learning phonology rules in Olympiad problems. These problems are designed to be challenging tasks that require learning rules from a minimal number of examples. These problems also allow us to specifically test for generalization.

We compare our approach to various baselines, and find that it is capable of learning phonological rules that generalize much better than existing approaches. We show that using the DSL, we can explicitly control the structure of rules, and using the ranking score, we can provide the model with implicit preferences for certain kinds of rules.

Having demonstrated the potential of program synthesis as a learning technique that can work with very little data and provide human-readable models, we hope to apply it to learning more complex types of lingusitic rules in the future.

In addition to being a way to learn rules from data, the ability to explicity control the generalization behaviour of the model allows for the use of program synthesis to understand the kinds of learning biases and operations that are required to model various linguistic processes. We leave this exploration to future work.

## Acknowledgements

We would like to thank Partho Sarthi for invaluable help with PROSE and NDSyn. We would also like to thank the authors of the ProLinguist paper for their assistance. Finally, we would like to thank the anonymous reviewers for their feedback.

## References

Shraddha Barke, Rose Kunkel, Nadia Polikarpova, Eric Meinhardt, Eric Bakovic, and Leon Bergen. 2019. Constraint-based learning of phonological processes. In *Proceedings of the 2019 Conference on Empirical Methods in Natural Language Processing and the 9th International Joint Conference on Natural Language Processing (EMNLP-IJCNLP)*, pages 6176–6186, Hong Kong, China. Association for Computational Linguistics.

A. Bellos. 2020. *The Language Lover's Puzzle Book: Lexical perplexities and cracking conundrums from across the globe.* Guardian Faber Publishing.

Eric Brill. 1992. A simple rule-based part of speech tagger. In *Speech and Natural Language: Proceedings of a Workshop Held at Harriman, New York, February 23-26, 1992.*

Keith Brown and Sarah Ogilvie. 2010. *Concise encyclopedia of languages of the world.* Elsevier.

Noam Chomsky and Morris Halle. 1968. The sound pattern of english.

Ivan Derzhanski and Thomas Payne. 2010. *The Linguistic Olympiads: academic competitions in linguistics for secondary school students*, page 213–226. Cambridge University Press.

Kevin Ellis, Armando Solar-Lezama, and Josh Tenenbaum. 2015. Unsupervised learning by program synthesis. In C. Cortes, N. D. Lawrence, D. D. Lee, M. Sugiyama, and R. Garnett, editors, *Advances in Neural Information Processing Systems 28*, pages 973–981. Curran Associates, Inc.

Daniel Gildea and Daniel Jurafsky. 1996. Learning bias and phonological-rule induction. *Computational Linguistics*, 22(4):497–530.

Kyle Gorman, Lucas F.E. Ashby, Aaron Goyzueta, Arya McCarthy, Shijie Wu, and Daniel You. 2020. The SIGMORPHON 2020 shared task on multilingual grapheme-to-phoneme conversion. In *Proceedings of the 17th SIGMORPHON Workshop on Computational Research in Phonetics, Phonology, and Morphology*, pages 40–50, Online. Association for Computational Linguistics.

Sumit Gulwani. 2011. Automating string processing in spreadsheets using input-output examples. *SIGPLAN Not.*, 46(1):317–330.

Sumit Gulwani, Oleksandr Polozov, and Rishabh Singh. 2017. Program synthesis. *Foundations and Trends® in Programming Languages*, 4(1-2):1–119.

Arun Iyer, Manohar Jonnalagedda, Suresh Parthasarathy, Arjun Radhakrishna, and Sriram K Rajamani. 2019. Synthesis and machine learning for heterogeneous extraction. In *Proceedings of the 40th ACM SIGPLAN Conference on Programming Language Design and Implementation*, pages 301–315.

Sittichai Jiampojamarn, Grzegorz Kondrak, and Tarek Sherif. 2007. Applying many-to-many alignments and hidden Markov models to letter-to-phoneme conversion. In *Human Language Technologies 2007: The Conference of the North American Chapter of the Association for Computational Linguistics; Proceedings of the Main Conference*, pages 372–379, Rochester, New York. Association for Computational Linguistics.

Mark Johnson. 1984. A discovery procedure for certain phonological rules. In *10th International Conference on Computational Linguistics and 22nd Annual Meeting of the Association for Computational Linguistics*, pages 344–347, Stanford, California, USA. Association for Computational Linguistics.

Mary Laughren. 2011. Stopping and flapping in warlpiri. In Dragomir Radev and Patrick Littell, editors, *North American Computational Linguistics Olympiad 2011: Invitational Round*. North American Computational Linguistics Olympiad.

Jackson L. Lee, Lucas F.E. Ashby, M. Elizabeth Garza, Yeonju Lee-Sikka, Sean Miller, Alan Wong, Arya D. McCarthy, and Kyle Gorman. 2020. Massively multilingual pronunciation modeling with WikiPron. In *Proceedings of the 12th Language Resources and Evaluation Conference*, pages 4223–4228, Marseille, France. European Language Resources Association.

Minh-Thang Luong, Hieu Pham, and Christopher D Manning. 2015. Effective approaches to attention-based neural machine translation. *arXiv preprint arXiv:1508.04025*.

Tom McCoy. 2018. Better left unsaid. In Patrick Littell, Tom McCoy, Dragomir Radev, and Ali Sharman, editors, *North American Computational Linguistics Olympiad 2018: Invitational Round*. North American Computational Linguistics Olympiad.

Josef Robert Novak, Nobuaki Minematsu, and Keikichi Hirose. 2016. Phonetisaurus: Exploring grapheme-to-phoneme conversion with joint n-gram models in the wfst framework. *Natural Language Engineering*, 22(6):907–938.

Oleksandr Polozov and Sumit Gulwani. 2015. Flashmeta: A framework for inductive program synthesis. *SIGPLAN Not.*, 50(10):107–126.

Maja Popović. 2015. chrF: character n-gram F-score for automatic MT evaluation. In *Proceedings of the Tenth Workshop on Statistical Machine Translation*, pages 392–395, Lisbon, Portugal. Association for Computational Linguistics.

Gözde Gül Şahin, Yova Kementchedjhieva, Phillip Rust, and Iryna Gurevych. 2020. PuzzLing Machines: A Challenge on Learning From Small Data. In *Proceedings of the 58th Annual Meeting of the Association for Computational Linguistics*, pages 1241–1254, Online. Association for Computational Linguistics.

Partho Sarthi, Monojit Choudhury, Arun Iyer, Suresh Parthasarathy, Arjun Radhakrishna, and Sriram Rajamani. 2021. ProLinguist: Program Synthesis for Linguistics and NLP. *IJCAI Workshop on Neuro-Symbolic Natural Language Inference*.

Temple F Smith, Michael S Waterman, et al. 1981. Identification of common molecular subsequences. *Journal of molecular biology*, 147(1):195–197.

Harold Somers. 2016. Changing the subject. In Andrew Lamont and Dragomir Radev, editors, *North American Computational Linguistics Olympiad 2016: Invitational Round*. North American Computational Linguistics Olympiad.

Saujas Vaduguru. 2019. Chickasaw stress. In Shardul Chiplunkar and Saujas Vaduguru, editors, *Panini Linguistics Olympiad 2019*. Panini Linguistics Olympiad.

Ashish Vaswani, Noam Shazeer, Niki Parmar, Jakob Uszkoreit, Llion Jones, Aidan N Gomez, Ł ukasz Kaiser, and Illia Polosukhin. 2017. Attention is all you need. In *Advances in Neural Information Processing Systems*, volume 30. Curran Associates, Inc.

Ekaterina Vylomova, Jennifer White, Elizabeth Salesky, Sabrina J. Mielke, Shijie Wu, Edoardo Maria Ponti, Rowan Hall Maudslay, Ran Zmigrod, Josef Valvoda, Svetlana Toldova, Francis Tyers, Elena Klyachko, Ilya Yegorov, Natalia Krizhanovsky, Paula Czarnowska, Irene Nikkarinen, Andrew Krizhanovsky, Tiago Pimentel, Lucas Torroba Hennigen, Christo Kirov, Garrett Nicolai, Adina Williams, Antonios Anastasopoulos, Hilaria Cruz, Eleanor Chodroff, Ryan Cotterell, Miikka Silfverberg, and Mans Hulden. 2020. SIGMORPHON 2020 shared task 0: Typologically diverse morphological inflection. In *Proceedings of the 17th SIGMORPHON Workshop on Computational*

*Research in Phonetics, Phonology, and Morphology*, pages 1–39, Online. Association for Computational Linguistics.

Elysia Warner. 2019. Tarangan. In Samuel Ahmed, Bozhidar Bozhanov, Ivan Derzhanski (technical editor), Hugh Dobbs, Dmitry Gerasimov, Shinjini Ghosh, Ksenia Gilyarova, Stanislav Gurevich, Gabrijela Hladnik, Boris Iomdin, Bruno L'Astorina, Tae Hun Lee (editor-in chief), Tom McCoy, André Nikulin, Miina Norvik, Tung-Le Pan, Aleksejs Peguševs, Alexander Piperski, Maria Rubinstein, Daniel Rucki, Artūrs Semeņuks, Nathan Somers, Milena Veneva, and Elysia Warner, editors, *International Linguistics Olympiad 2019*. International Linguistics Olympiad.

Shijie Wu. 2020. Neural transducer. `https://github.com/shijie-wu/neural-transducer/`.

## A NDSyn algorithm

We use the NDSyn algorithm to learn disjunctions of rules. We apply NDSyn in multiple passes to allow the model to learn multi-pass rules.

At each pass, the algorithm learns rules to perform token-level transformations that are applied to each element of the input sequence. The token-level examples are passed to NDSyn, which learns the if-then-else statements that constitute a set of rules. This is done by first generating a set of candidate rules by randomly sampling a token-level example and synthesizing a set of rules that satisfy the example. Then, rules are selected to cover the token-level examples.

Rules that satisfy a randomly sampled example are learnt using the FlashMeta program synthesis algorithm (Polozov and Gulwani, 2015). The synthesis task is given by the DSL operator $P$ and the specification of constraints $\mathcal{X}$ that the synthesized program must satisfy. In our application, this specification is in the form of token-level examples, and the DSL operators are the predicates and transformations defined in the paper. The algorithm recursively decomposes the synthesis problem $(P, \mathcal{X})$ into smaller tasks $(P_i, \mathcal{X}_i)$ for each argument $P_i$ to the operator. $\mathcal{X}_i$ is inferred using the inverse semantics of the operator $P_i$, which is encoded as a *witness function*. The inverse semantics provides the possible values for the arguments of an operator, given the output of the operator. We refer the reader to the paper by Polozov and Gulwani (2015) for a full description of the synthesis algorithm.

After the candidates are generated, they are ranked according to a ranking score of each program. The ranking score for an operator in a program is computed as a function of the scores of its arguments. The arguments may be other operators, offsets, or other constants (like tokens or features). The score for an operator in the argument is computed recursively. The score for an offset favours smaller numbers and local rules by decreasing the score for larger offsets. The score for other constants is chosen to be a small negative constant. The scores for the arguments are added up, along with a small negative penalty to favour shorter programs, to obtain the final score for the operator.

This ranking score selects for programs that are shorter, and favours either choosing more general by giving the `Is` predicate a higher score (FEATURE) or more specific rules by giving the `IsToken` predicate a higher score (TOKEN). The top $k$ programs according to the ranking function are chosen as candidates for the next step.

To choose the final set of rules from the candidates generated using the FlashMeta algorithm, we use a *set covering* algorithm that chooses the rules that correctly answer the most number of examples while also incorrectly answering the least. These rules are applied to each example, and the output tokens are tagged with the transformation that is applied. These outputs are then the input to the next pass of the algorithm.

## B Dataset

We select problems from various Linguistics Olympiads to create our dataset. We include publicly available problems that have appeared in Olympiads before. We choose problems that only involve rules based on the symbols in the data, and not based on knowledge of notions such as gender, tense, case, or semantic role. These problems are based on the phonology of a particular language, and include aspects of morphology and orthography, and maybe also the phonology of a different language. In some cases where a single Olympiad problem involves multiple components that can be solved independent of each other, we include them as separate problems in our dataset.

We put the data and assignments in a matrix, as described in Section 3.1 . We separate tokens in a word by a space while transcribing the problems from their source PDFs. We do not separate diacritics as different tokens, and include them as part of the same token. For each token in the Roman script, we add the boolean features `vowel` and `consonant`, and manually tag the tokens according to whether they are a vowel or consonant.

We store the problems in JSON files with details about the languages, the families to which the languages belong, the data matrix, the notes used to create the features, and the feature sets for each token.

## C Baselines

### C.1 Neural

Following Şahin et al. (2020), we use small neural models for sequence-to-sequence tasks. We train a single neural model for each task, and provide the column numbers as tags in addition to the source sequence. We find that the single model approach works better than training a model for each pair of columns.

**LSTM:** We use LSTM models with soft attention (Luong et al., 2015), with embeddings of size 64, hidden layers of size 128, a 2-layer encoder and a single layer decoder. We apply a dropout of 0.3 for all layers. We train the model for 100 epochs using the Adam optimizer with a learning rate of $10^{-3}$, learning rate reduction on plateau, and a batch size of 2. We clip the gradient norm to 5.

**Transformer:** We use Transformer models (Vaswani et al., 2017) with embeddings of size 128, hidden layers of size 256, a 2-layer encoder and a 2-layer decoder. We apply a dropout of 0.3 for all layers. We train the model for 2000 steps using the Adam optimizer with a learning rate of $10^{-3}$, warmup of 400 steps, learning rate reduction on plateau, and a batch size of 2. We use a label smoothing value of 0.1, and clip the gradient norm to 1.

We use the implementations provided at `https://github.com/shijie-wu/neural-transducer/` for all neural models.

### C.2 WFST

We use the implementation the WFST models available at `https://github.com/sigmorphon/2020/tree/master/task1/baselines/fst` for the WFST models. We train a model for each pair of columns. We report the results for models of order 5, which were found to perform the best on the test data (highest EXACT score) among models of order 3 to 9.

# Findings of the SIGMORPHON 2021 Shared Task on Unsupervised Morphological Paradigm Clustering

**Adam Wiemerslage**[†] **Arya McCarthy**[‡] **Alexander Erdmann**[∇]
**Garrett Nicolai**[ψ] **Manex Agirrezabal**[ϕ] **Miikka Silfverberg**[ψ]
**Mans Hulden**[†] **Katharina Kann**[†]
[†]University of Colorado Boulder [‡]Johns Hopkins University [∇]Ohio State University
[ϕ]University of Copenhagen [ψ]University of British Columbia
{adam.wiemerslage,katharina.kann}@colorado.edu

## Abstract

We describe the second SIGMORPHON shared task on unsupervised morphology: the goal of the SIGMORPHON 2021 Shared Task on Unsupervised Morphological Paradigm Clustering is to cluster word types from a raw text corpus into paradigms. To this end, we release corpora for 5 development and 9 test languages, as well as gold partial paradigms for evaluation. We receive 14 submissions from 4 teams that follow different strategies, and the best performing system is based on adaptor grammars. Results vary significantly across languages. However, all systems are outperformed by a supervised lemmatizer, implying that there is still room for improvement.

## 1 Introduction

In recent years, most research in the area of computational morphology has focused on the application of supervised machine learning methods to word inflection: generating the inflected forms of a word, often a lemma, in order to express certain grammatical properties. For example, a supervised inflection system for Spanish might be provided with a lemma *disfrutar* (English: *to enjoy*) and morphological features such as *indicative*, *present tense* & *1st person singular*, and generate the corresponding inflected form *disfruto* as output.

However, a supervised machine learning setup is quite different from a human first language (L1) acquisition setting. Young children must learn to segment a continuous speech signal into discrete words and perform unsupervised classification, decoding, and eventually, inference with incomplete feedback on this noisy input. The task of unsupervised paradigm clustering aims to replicate one of the steps in this process—namely, the grouping of word forms belonging to the same lexeme into inflectional paradigms. In this unsupervised task, a system does not know about lemmas. Furthermore,

Figure 1: Unsupervised morphological paradigm clustering consists of clustering word forms from raw text into paradigms.

neither does it know (a) the features for which a lemma typically inflects, nor (b) the number of distinct inflected forms which constitute the paradigm.

A successful unsupervised paradigm clustering system leverages common patterns in the language's inflectional morphology while simultaneously ignoring regular circumstantial similarities along with derivational patterns. For example, an accurate unsupervised system must recognize that *disfrutamos* (English: *we enjoy*) and *disfruta* (English: *he/she/it enjoys*) are inflected variants of the same paradigm, but that the orthographically similar *disparamos* (English: *we shoot*), belongs to a separate paradigm. Likewise, a successful system for English will recognize that *walk* and *walked* belong to the same verbal paradigm but *walker* is a derived form belonging to a distinct nominal paradigm. Such fine-grained distinctions are difficult to learn in an unsupervised manner.

This paper describes the SIGMORPHON 2021 Shared Task on Unsupervised Morphological Paradigm Clustering. Participants are asked to submit systems which cluster words from the Bible into inflectional paradigms.[1] Participants are not allowed to use any external resources. Four teams submit at least one system for the shared task and

[1]Bible translations for five development and nine test languages were obtained from the Johns Hopkins University Bible Corpus introduced by McCarthy et al. (2020b).



*Proceedings of the Seventeenth SIGMORPHON Workshop on Computational Research in Phonetics, Phonology, and Morphology*, pages 72–81

all teams also submit a system description paper.

The shared task systems can be grouped into two broad categories: *similarity-based* systems experiment with different combinations of orthographic and embedding-based similarity metrics for word forms combined with clustering methods like $k$-means or agglomerative clustering. *Grammar-based* methods instead learn grammars or rules from the data and either apply these to clustering directly, or first segment words into stems and affixes and then cluster forms which share a stem into paradigms. Our official baseline, described in Section 2.3, is based on grouping together word forms sharing a common substring of length $\geq k$, where $k$ is a hyperparameter. Grammar-based systems obtain higher average F1 scores (see Section 2.2 for details on evaluation) across the nine test languages than the baseline. The **Edinburgh** system has the best overall performance: it outperforms the baseline by 34.61% F1 and the second best system by 1.84% F1.

The rest of the paper is organized as follows: Section 2 describes the task of unsupervised morphological paradigm clustering in detail, including the official baseline and all provided datasets. Section 3 gives an overview of the participating systems. Section 4 describes the official results, and 5 presents an analysis. Finally, Section 6 contains a discussion of where the task can move in future iterations and concludes the paper.

## 2 Task Description

Unsupervised morphological paradigm clustering consists of, given a raw text corpus, grouping words from that corpus into their paradigms without any additional information. Recent work in unsupervised morphology has attempted to induce full paradigms from corpora with only a subset of all types. Kann et al. (2020) and Erdmann et al. (2020) explore initial approaches to this task, which is called unsupervised morphological paradigm *completion*, but find it to be challenging. Building upon the SIGMORPHON 2020 Shared Task on Unsupervised Morphological Paradigm Completion (Kann et al., 2020), our shared task is focused on a subset of the overall problem: sorting words into paradigms. This can be seen as an initial step to paradigm completion, as unobserved types do not need to be induced, and the inflectional categories of paradigm slots do not need to be considered.

### 2.1 Data

**Languages** The SIGMORPHON 2021 Shared Task on Unsupervised Morphological Paradigm Clustering features 5 development languages: Maltese, Persian, Portuguese, Russian, and Swedish. The final evaluation is done on 9 test languages: Basque, Bulgarian, English, Finnish, German, Kannada, Navajo, Spanish, and Turkish.

Our languages span 4 writing systems, and represent fusional, agglutinative, templatic, and polysynthetic morphologies. The languages in the development set are mostly suffixing, except for Maltese, which is a templatic language. And while most of the test languages are also predominantly suffixing, Navajo employs prefixes and Basque uses both prefixes and suffixes.

**Text Corpora** We provide corpora from the Johns Hopkins University Bible Corpus (JHUBC) (McCarthy et al., 2020b) for all development and test languages. This is the only resource that systems are allowed to use.

**Gold Partial Paradigms** Along with the Bibles, we also release a set of gold partial paradigms for the development languages to be used for system development. Gold data sets are also compiled for the test languages, but these test sets are withheld until the completion of the shared task.

In order to produce gold partial paradigms, we first take the set of all paradigms $\Pi$ for each language from UniMorph (McCarthy et al., 2020a). We then obtain gold partial paradigms $\Pi_{\hat{G}} = \Pi \bigcap \Sigma$, where $\Sigma$ is the set of types attested in the Bible corpus. Finally, we sample up to 1000 of the resulting gold partial paradigms for each language, resulting in the set $\Pi_G$ according to the following steps:

1. Group gold paradigms in $\Pi_{\hat{G}}$ by size, resulting in the set $G$, where $g_k \in G$ is the group of paradigms with $k$ forms in it.

2. Continually loop over all $g_k \in G$ and randomly sample one paradigm from $g_k$ until we have 1000 paradigms.

Because not every token in the Bible corpora is in UniMorph, we can only evaluate on the subset of paradigms that exist in the UniMorph database. In practice, this means that for several languages, we are not able to sample 1000 paradigms, cf. Tables 1 and 2. Notably, for Basque, we can only provide 12 paradigms.

| | Maltese | Persian | Portuguese | Russian | Swedish |
|---|---|---|---|---|---|
| **# Lines** | 7761 | 7931 | 31167 | 31102 | 31168 |
| **# Tokens** | 193257 | 227584 | 828861 | 727630 | 871707 |
| **# Types** | 16017 | 11877 | 31446 | 46202 | 25913 |
| **TTR** | .083 | .052 | .038 | .063 | .03 |
| **# Paradigms** | 76 | 64 | 1000 | 1000 | 1000 |
| **# Forms in paradigms** | 572 | 446 | 11430 | 6216 | 3596 |
| **Largest paradigm size** | 14 | 20 | 47 | 17 | 9 |

Table 1: Statistics for the development Bible corpora and the dev gold partial paradigms. TTR is the type-token ratio in the corpus. The statistics for the paradigms reflect only those words in our partial paradigms, not the full paradigms from Unimorph.

| | English | Navajo | Spanish | Finnish | Bulgarian | Basque | Kannada | German | Turkish |
|---|---|---|---|---|---|---|---|---|---|
| **# Lines** | 7728 | 5058 | 7337 | 31087 | 31101 | 7958 | 7863 | 31102 | 30182 |
| **# Tokens** | 236465 | 104631 | 251581 | 685699 | 801657 | 195459 | 193213 | 826119 | 616418 |
| **# Types** | 7144 | 18799 | 9755 | 54635 | 37048 | 18376 | 28561 | 22584 | 59458 |
| **TTR** | .03 | .18 | .039 | .08 | .046 | .094 | .148 | .027 | .096 |
| **# Paradigms** | 1000 | 88 | 990 | 1000 | 1000 | 12 | 92 | 1000 | 1000 |
| **# Forms in paradigms** | 2475 | 214 | 5154 | 8509 | 5086 | 63 | 933 | 3628 | 9204 |
| **Largest paradigm size** | 7 | 13 | 34 | 31 | 27 | 25 | 44 | 15 | 49 |

Table 2: Statistics for the test Bible corpora and the test gold partial paradigms.

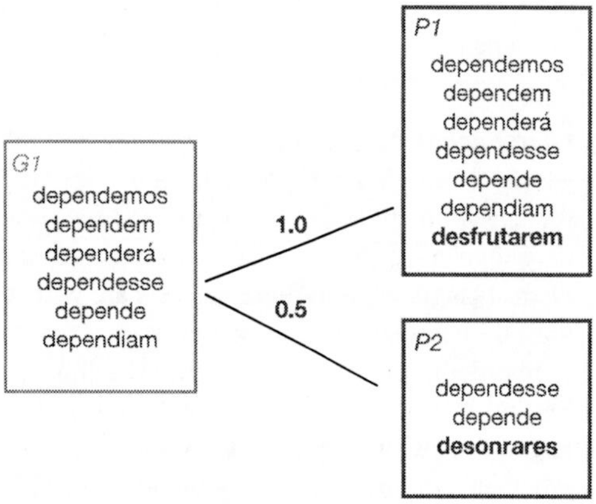


Figure 2: An example matching of predicted paradigms in blue, and a gold paradigm in green. Words in red do not exist in the gold set, and thus cannot be evaluated.

## 2.2 Evaluation

As our task is entirely unsupervised, evaluation is not straightforward: as in Kann et al. (2020), our evaluation requires a mapping from predicted paradigms to gold paradigms. Because our set of gold partial paradigms does not cover all words in the corpus, in practice we only evaluate against a subset of the clusters predicted by systems.

For these reasons, we want an evaluation that assesses the best matching paradigms, ignoring predicted forms that do not occur in the gold set, but still punishing for spurious predictions that *are* in the gold set. For example, Figure 2 shows two candidate matches for a gold partial paradigm. Each one contains a word that does not exist in the set of gold paradigms, and thus cannot be judged – these words are ignored and do not affect evaluation. In this example, the predicted P1 is a better match, resulting in a perfect F1 score. However, our evaluation punishes systems for predicting a second paradigm, P2, with words from G1, reducing the overall precision score of this submission.

Building upon BMAcc (Jin et al., 2020), we use best-match F1 score for evaluation. We define a paradigm as a set of word forms $f \in \pi$. Duplicate forms within $\pi$ (*syncretism*) are discarded. Given a set of gold partial paradigms $\pi^g \in \Pi_G$, a set of predicted paradigms $\pi^p \in \Pi_P$, a gold vocabulary $\Sigma^g = \bigcup \pi^g$, and a predicted vocabulary $\Sigma^p = \bigcup \pi^p$, it works according to the following steps:

1. Redefine each predicted paradigm, removing the words that we cannot evaluate $\pi^{p'} = \pi^p \bigcap \Sigma^g$, to form a set of pruned paradigms $\Pi'_P$.

2. Build a complete Bipartite graph over $\Pi'_P$ and $\Pi_G$, where the edge weight between $\pi^g_i$ and $\pi^{p'}_j$ is the number of true positives $|\pi^g_i \bigcap \pi^{p'}_j|$.

3. Compute the maximum-weight full matching using Karp (1980), in order to find the optimal alignment between $\Pi'_P$ and $\Pi_G$

4. Assign all predicted words $\Sigma^{p'}$ and all gold words $\Sigma^g$ a label corresponding to the gold paradigm, according to the matching found in

3. Any unmatched $w_i^{p'} \in \Sigma^{p'}$ is assigned a label corresponding to a spurious paradigm.

5. Compute the F1 score between the sets of labeled words in $\Sigma^{p'}$ and $\Sigma^g$

### 2.3 Baseline System

We provide a straightforward baseline that constructs paradigms based on substring overlap between words. We construct paradigms out of words that share a substring of length $\geq k$. Since words can share multiple substrings, it is possible that multiple identical, redundant paradigms are created. We reduce these to a single paradigm. Words that do not belong to a cluster are assigned a singleton paradigm, that is, a paradigm that consists of only that word.

We tune $k$ on the development sets and find that $k = 5$ works best on average. This means that a word of less than 5 characters can only ever be in one, singleton, paradigm.

## 3 Submitted Systems

The Boulder-Perkoff-Daniels-Palmer team (**Boulder-PDP**; Perkoff et al., 2021) participates with four submissions, resulting from experiments with two different systems. Both systems apply $k$-means clustering on vector representations of input words. They differ in the type of vector representations used: either orthographic or semantic representations. Semantic skip-gram representations are generated using word2vec (Mikolov et al., 2013). For the orthographic representations, each word is encoded into a vector of fixed dimensionality equaling the word length $|w_{max}|$ for the longest word $w_{max}$ in the input corpus. They associate each character $c \in \Sigma$ in the alphabet of the input corpus with a real number $r \in [0, 1]$ and assign $v_i := r$ if the $i$th character of the input word $w$ is $c$. If $|w| < |w_{max}|$, the remaining entries are assigned to 0.

The number of clusters is a hyperparameter of the $k$-means clustering algorithm. In order to set this hyperparameter, Perkoff et al. (2021) experiment with a graph-based method. The word types in the corpus form the nodes of a graph, where the neighborhood of a word $w$ consists of all words sharing a maximal substring with $w$. The graph is split into highly connected subgraphs (HCS) containing $n$ nodes, where the number of edges that need to be cut in order to split the graph into two disconnected components is $> n/2$ (Hartuv and Shamir, 2000). The number of HCSs is then taken to be the cluster number. In practice, however, the graph-clustering step proves to be prohibitively slow and results for test languages are submitted using fixed numbers of clusters of size 500, 1000, 1500 and 1900. In experiments on the dev languages, they find that the orthographic representations outperform the semantic representations for all languages, and thus submit four systems utilizing orthographic representations.

The Boulder-Gerlach-Wiemerslage-Kann team (**Boulder-GWK**; Gerlach et al., 2021) submits two systems based on an unsupervised lemmatization system originally proposed by Rosa and Zabokrtský (2019). Their approach is based on agglomerative hierarchical clustering of word types, where the distance between word types is computed as a combination of a string distance metric and the cosine distance of fastText embeddings (Bojanowski et al., 2017). Their choice of fastText embeddings is due to the limited size of the shared task datasets. Two variants of edit distance are compared to quantify string distance: (1) Jaro-Winkler edit distance (Winkler, 1990) resembles regular edit distance of strings but emphasizes similarity at the start of strings which is likely to bias the system toward languages expressing inflection via suffixation. (2) A weighted variant of edit distance, where costs for insertions, deletions and substitutions are derived from a character-based language model trained on the shared task data.

The **CU–UBC** (Yang et al., 2021) team provides systems that built upon the official shared task baseline – given the pseudo-paradigms found by the baseline, they extract inflection rules of multiple types. Comparing pairs of words in each paradigm, they learn both continuous and discontinuous character sequences that transform the first word into the second, following work on supervised inflectional morphology, such as Durrett and DeNero (2013); Hulden et al. (2014). Rules are sorted by frequency to separate genuine inflectional patterns from noise. Starting from a random seed word, paradigms are constructed by iteratively applying the most frequent rules. Generated paradigms are further tested for paradigm coherence using metrics such as graph degree calculation and fastText embedding similarity.

The **Edinburgh** team (McCurdy et al., 2021) submits a system based on adaptor grammars (John-

| | | English | Navajo | Spanish | Finnish | Bulgarian | Basque | Kannada | German | Turkish | Average |
|---|---|---|---|---|---|---|---|---|---|---|---|
| | Rec | 28.93 | 32.71 | 23.90 | 18.43 | 20.55 | 28.57 | 25.19 | 25.50 | 15.70 | 24.39 |
| **Boulder-PDP-1** | Prec | 29.27 | 34.15 | 24.68 | 18.81 | 20.75 | 29.51 | 35.18 | 25.64 | 15.90 | 25.99 |
| | F1 | 29.10 | 33.41 | 24.29 | 18.62 | 20.65 | 29.03 | 29.36 | 25.57 | 15.80 | 25.09 |
| | Rec | 36.57 | 36.92 | 28.52 | 23.38 | 26.37 | 30.16 | 25.83 | 33.21 | 19.53 | 28.94 |
| **Boulder-PDP-2** | Prec | 37.00 | 38.54 | 29.45 | 23.86 | 26.63 | 31.15 | 36.08 | 33.40 | 19.79 | 30.65 |
| | F1 | 36.78 | 37.71 | 28.98 | 23.62 | 26.50 | 30.65 | 30.11 | 33.31 | 19.66 | 29.70 |
| | Rec | 42.79 | 37.85 | 29.41 | 26.01 | 28.73 | 26.98 | 25.94 | 38.18 | 21.38 | 30.81 |
| **Boulder-PDP-3** | Prec | 43.30 | 39.51 | 30.37 | 26.55 | 29.01 | 27.87 | 36.23 | 38.39 | 21.66 | 32.54 |
| | F1 | 43.04 | 38.66 | 29.88 | 26.27 | 28.87 | 27.42 | 30.23 | 38.28 | 21.52 | 31.58 |
| | Rec | 45.45 | 40.19 | 30.64 | 26.60 | 29.79 | 28.57 | 24.54 | 39.86 | 21.65 | 31.92 |
| **Boulder-PDP-4** | Prec | 45.99 | 41.95 | 31.63 | 27.15 | 30.08 | 29.51 | 34.28 | 40.08 | 21.93 | 33.62 |
| | F1 | 45.72 | 41.05 | 31.13 | 26.87 | 29.93 | 29.03 | 28.61 | 39.97 | 21.79 | 32.68 |
| | Rec | 28.81 | 10.75 | 19.27 | 22.02 | 30.02 | 19.05 | 18.54 | 31.92 | 20.63 | 22.33 |
| **Boulder-GWK-2** | Prec | 66.33 | 65.71 | 69.93 | 67.36 | 71.69 | 35.29 | 62.45 | 78.56 | 64.09 | 64.60 |
| | F1 | 40.17 | 18.47 | 30.21 | 33.19 | 42.32 | 24.74 | 28.60 | 45.39 | 31.22 | 32.70 |
| | Rec | 24.53 | 11.21 | 18.30 | 22.69 | 31.18 | 25.40 | 16.93 | 30.98 | 21.16 | 22.49 |
| **Boulder-GWK-1** | Prec | 56.47 | 68.57 | 66.41 | 69.41 | 74.46 | 47.06 | 57.04 | 76.26 | 65.74 | 64.60 |
| | F1 | 34.20 | 19.28 | 28.69 | 34.20 | 43.96 | 32.99 | 26.12 | 44.06 | 32.02 | 32.83 |
| | Rec | 76.69 | 59.81 | 72.18 | 76.73 | 73.02 | 25.40 | 38.48 | 77.62 | 65.82 | 62.86 |
| ***Baseline*** | Prec | 38.76 | 23.02 | 26.56 | 17.86 | 26.50 | 18.60 | 17.22 | 25.35 | 15.60 | 23.28 |
| | F1 | 51.49 | 33.25 | 38.83 | 28.97 | 38.89 | 21.48 | 23.79 | 38.22 | 25.23 | 33.35 |
| | Rec | 66.95 | 50.93 | 60.52 | 45.96 | 65.08 | 17.46 | 30.33 | 66.57 | 43.25 | 49.67 |
| **CU–UBC-5** | Prec | 90.40 | 68.55 | 72.70 | 56.47 | 76.85 | 52.38 | 61.26 | 74.40 | 54.05 | 67.45 |
| | F1 | 76.93 | 58.45 | 66.05 | 50.68 | 70.48 | 26.19 | 40.57 | 70.26 | 48.05 | 56.41 |
| | Rec | 63.76 | 51.867 | 63.62 | 48.75 | 63.84 | 17.46 | 33.12 | 65.05 | 45.81 | 50.36 |
| **CU–UBC-6** | Prec | 85.99 | 69.375 | 76.49 | 59.67 | 75.99 | 52.38 | 64.24 | 72.39 | 57.52 | 68.23 |
| | F1 | 73.23 | 59.36 | 69.46 | 53.66 | 69.39 | 26.19 | 43.71 | 68.52 | 51.00 | 57.17 |
| | Rec | 60.36 | 53.74 | 64.05 | 51.51 | 58.18 | 22.22 | 35.37 | 59.32 | 47.74 | 50.28 |
| **CU–UBC-7** | Prec | 81.42 | 72.33 | 76.98 | 62.58 | 69.23 | 66.67 | 69.77 | 66.13 | 60.17 | 69.47 |
| | F1 | 69.33 | **61.66** | 69.92 | 56.51 | 63.23 | **33.33** | 46.94 | 62.54 | 53.24 | 57.41 |
| | Rec | 83.39 | 47.66 | 76.48 | 52.06 | 73.14 | 25.40 | 36.33 | 74.28 | 46.50 | 57.25 |
| **CU–UBC-3** | Prec | 84.38 | 49.76 | 78.97 | 53.14 | 73.87 | 26.23 | 50.75 | 74.70 | 47.10 | 59.88 |
| | F1 | 83.89 | 48.69 | 77.71 | 52.60 | 73.50 | 25.81 | 42.35 | 74.49 | 46.80 | 58.42 |
| | Rec | 80.69 | 47.66 | 78.35 | 57.29 | 73.77 | 28.57 | 40.73 | 74.06 | 50.93 | 59.12 |
| **CU–UBC-4** | Rec | 81.64 | 49.76 | 80.89 | 58.48 | 74.50 | 29.51 | 56.89 | 74.47 | 51.59 | 61.97 |
| | F1 | 81.16 | 48.69 | 79.60 | 57.88 | 74.14 | 29.03 | 47.47 | 74.27 | 51.26 | 60.39 |
| | Rec | 75.96 | 47.66 | 75.73 | 65.35 | 69.07 | 28.57 | 49.52 | 65.08 | 60.58 | 59.73 |
| **CU–UBC-1** | Prec | 76.86 | 49.76 | 78.19 | 66.71 | 69.92 | 29.51 | 69.16 | 65.44 | 61.36 | 62.99 |
| | F1 | 76.41 | 48.69 | 76.94 | 66.03 | 69.50 | 29.03 | 57.71 | 65.26 | 60.97 | 61.17 |
| | Rec | 88.16 | 41.59 | 81.90 | 72.68 | 76.58 | 28.57 | 50.91 | 73.98 | 67.37 | 64.64 |
| **CU–UBC-2** | Prec | 89.21 | 43.41 | 84.56 | 74.18 | 77.34 | 29.51 | 71.11 | 74.39 | 68.24 | 67.99 |
| | F1 | 88.68 | 42.48 | 83.21 | **73.42** | 76.96 | 29.03 | 59.34 | 74.18 | 67.80 | 66.12 |
| | Rec | 89.54 | 41.59 | 82.38 | 59.58 | 80.22 | 31.75 | 58.95 | 78.97 | 72.82 | 66.20 |
| **Edinburgh** | Prec | 90.75 | 43.41 | 85.06 | 60.84 | 83.30 | 32.79 | 82.34 | 79.41 | 73.75 | 70.18 |
| | F1 | **90.14** | 42.48 | **83.70** | 60.20 | **81.73** | 32.26 | **68.71** | **79.19** | **73.28** | **67.96** |
| | Rec | 95.31 | - | 85.49 | 86.21 | 84.74 | 65.08 | - | 79.19 | 86.80 | 83.26 |
| ***stanza*** | Prec | 93.87 | - | 85.84 | 85.91 | 82.79 | 50.62 | - | 71.57 | 86.87 | 79.64 |
| | F1 | 94.59 | - | 85.66 | 86.06 | 83.75 | 56.94 | - | 75.19 | 86.84 | 81.29 |

Table 3: Results on all test languages for all systems in %; the official shared task metric is best-match F1. To provide a more complete picture, we also show precision and recall. *stanza* is a supervised system.

son et al., 2007) modeling word structure. Their work draws on parallels between the unsupervised paradigm clustering task and unsupervised morphological segmentation. Their grammars segment word forms in the shared task corpora into a sequence of zero or more prefixes and a single stem followed by zero or more suffixes.

Based on the segmented words from the raw text data, they then determine whether the language uses prefixes or suffixes for inflection. The final stem for words in a predominantly suffixing language then consists of the prefixes and stem identified by the adaptor grammar. For a predominantly prefixing language, the final stem instead contains all suffixes of the word form. The team notes that this approach is unsuitable for languages which extensively make use of both prefixes and suffixes, such as Basque.

Finally, they group all words which share the same stem into paradigms. However, because sampling from an adaptor grammar is a non-deterministic process – i.e., the system may return multiple possible segmentations for a single word form – they construct preliminary clusters by including all forms which might share a given stem. Then they select the cluster that maximizes a score based on frequency of occurrence of the induced segment in all segmentations.

## 4 Results and Discussion

The official results obtained by all submitted systems on the test sets are shown in Table 3.

The Edinburgh system performs best overall with an average best-match F1 of 67.96%. In general, grammar-based systems attain the best results, with all of the CU–UBC systems and the Edinburgh system outperforming the baseline by at least 23.06% F1. The Boulder-GWK and Boulder-PDP systems, both of which perform clustering over word representations, approach but do not exceed baseline performance. Perkoff et al. (2021) found that clustering over word2vec embeddings performs poorly on the development languages, and their scores on the test set reflect clusters found with vectors based purely on orthography. The Boulder-GWK systems contain incomplete results, and partial evidence suggests that their clustering method, which combines both fastText embeddings trained on the provided bible corpora, and edit distance, *can* indeed outperform the baseline. However, it likely cannot outperform the grammar-based submissions.

For comparison, we also evaluate a supervised lemmatizer from the Stanza toolkit (Qi et al., 2020). The Stanza lemmatizer is a neural network model trained on Universal Dependencies (UD) treebanks (Nivre et al., 2020), which first tags for parts of speech, and then uses these tags to generate lemmas for a given word. Because there is no UD corpus in the current version for Navajo nor Kannada, we do not have scores for those languages. Stanza's accuracy on our task is far lower than that reported for lemmatization on UD data. We note, however, that 1) our data is from a different domain, 2) Biblical language in particular can differ strongly from contemporary text, and 3) we evaluate on only a partial set of types in the corpus, which could represent a particularly challenging set of paradigms for some languages. The Stanza lemmatizer outperforms all systems for all languages, except for German. This is unsurprising as it is a supervised system, though it is interesting that the German score falls short of that of the Edinburgh system.

| | | |
|---|---|---|
| naaghá<br>naashá<br>naayá<br>ninájídaah | neiikai<br>nijighá<br>ninádaah<br>nizhdoogaał | naahkai<br>nideeshaał<br>naniná |

Table 4: A paradigm from our gold set for Navajo.

**Overgeneralization/Underspecification** When acquiring language, children often overgeneralize morphological analogies to new, ungrammatical forms. For example, the past tense of the English verb *to know* might be expressed as *knowed*, rather than the irregular *knew*. The same behavior can also be observed in learning algorithms at some point during the learning process (Kirov and Cotterell, 2018). This is reflected to some extent in Table 3 by trade-offs between precision and recall. A low precision, but high recall indicates that a system is overgeneralizing: some surface forms are erroneously assigned to too many paradigms. In effect, these systems are hypothesizing that a substring is productive, and thus proposing a paradigmatic relationship between two words. For example, the English words *approach* and *approve* share the stem *appro-* with unproductive segments as suffixes. The baseline tends to overgeneralize due to its creation of large paradigms via a naive grouping of words by shared n-grams.

On the other hand, several systems seem to *underspecify*, indicated by their low recall. A low recall, but high precision indicates that a system does not attribute inflected forms to a paradigm that the form does in fact belong to. This can be caused by suppletion in systems based purely on orthography, for example, generating the paradigm with *go* and *goes*, but attributing *went* to a separate paradigm. Underspecification is apparent in the CU–UBC submissions that relied on discontinuous rules (CU–UBC 5, 6, and 7). This is likely because they filtered these systems down to far fewer rules than their prefix/suffix systems, in order to avoid severe overgeneralization that can result from spurious morphemes based on discontinuous substrings. Similarly, the Boulder-GWK systems both have reasonable precision, but very low recalls. They report that this is due to the fact that they ignore any words with less than a certain frequency in the corpus due to time constraints, thus creating small paradigms and ignoring many words completely.

**Language and Typology** In general, we find that Basque and Navajo are the two most difficult test languages. Both languages have relatively small

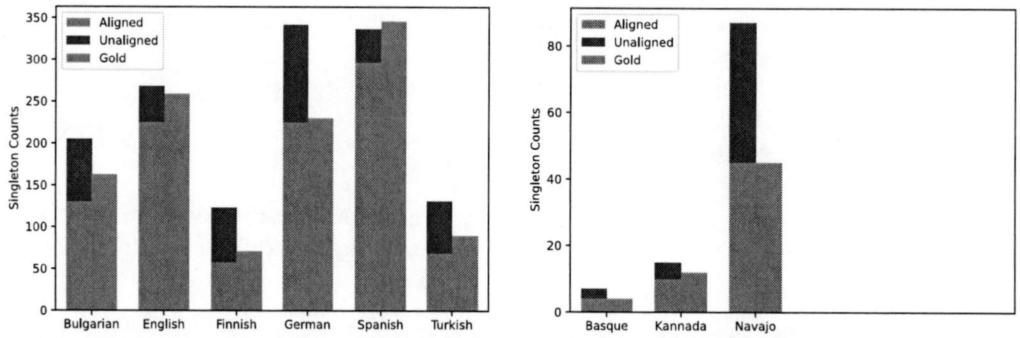


Figure 3: Singleton paradigm counts for the best performing system on all test languages. Languages for which we have more than 100 paradigms on the left, and those for which we have less than 100 paradigms on the right. Predicted singleton paradigms are in red and blue, gold singleton paradigms are in grey.

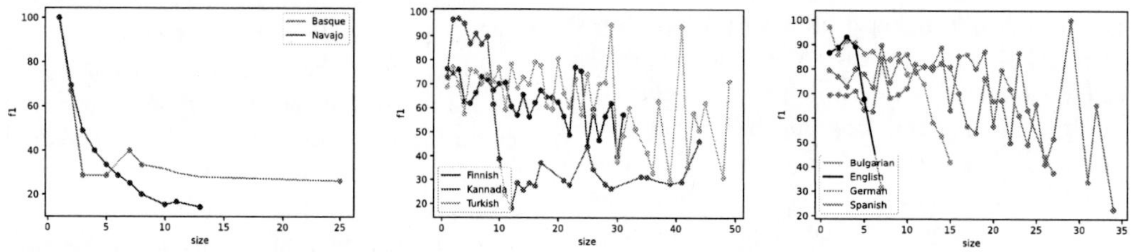


Figure 4: The F1 score across paradigm sizes for the best performing system on all test languages. From left to right, the graphs represent the groups of languages in increasing order of how well systems typically performed on them. F1 scores are interpolated for paradigm sizes that do not exist in a given language.

corpora, and are typlogically agglutinative – that is, they express inflection via the concatenation of potentially many morpheme segments, which can result in a large number of unique surface forms. Both languages thus have relatively high type-token ratios (TTR) – especially Navajo, which has the highest TTR, cf. Table 2. It is also important to note that both Basque and Navajo have comparatively small sets of paradigms against which we evaluate. This leaves the possibility that the subset of paradigms in the gold set are particularly challenging. However, the differences between system scores indicates that these two languages do offer challenges related to their morphology.

Navajo is a predominantly prefixing language – the only one in the development and test sets – and Basque also inflects using prefixes, though to a lesser extent. The top two performing systems both obtain low scores for Navajo. The CU–UBC-2 system considers only suffix rules, which results in it being the lowest performing CU–UBC system on Navajo. The Edinburgh submission *should* be able to identify prefixes and consider the suffix to be part of the stem in Navajo. However, the large number of types, for a relatively small Navajo corpus may cause difficulties for their algorithm that builds clusters based on affix frequency. Notably, the CU-UBC-7 system, which learns discontinuous rules rather than rules that model strictly concatenative morphology, performs best on Navajo by a large margin when compared to the best performing system, which relies on strictly concatenative grammars. It also performs best on Basque, though by a smaller margin. Another difficulty in Navajo morphology is that it exhibits verbal stem alternation for expressing mood, tense, and aspect, which creates challenges for systems that rely on rewrite rules or string similarity, based on continuous substrings. For instance, our evaluation algorithm aligns a singleton predicted paradigm to the gold paradigm in Table 4 for nearly all systems.

On Basque, most systems perform poorly. McCurdy et al. (2021), the best performing system overall, obtains a low score for Basque, which may be due to their system assuming that a language inflects either via prefixation or suffixation, but not both, as Basque does. Other systems, however, attain similarly low scores for Basque.

The next tier of difficulty seems to comprise Finnish, Kannada, and Turkish, on which most systems obtain low scores. All of those languages are suffixing, but also have an agglutinative morphology. The largest paradigm of each of these 3 languages are all in the top 4 largest paradigms in Table 2. This implies that large paradigm sizes and large numbers of distinct inflectional morphemes – two properties often assumed to correlate with agglutinative morphology –, coupled with sparse corpora to learn from, offer challenges for paradigm clustering. Though agglutinative morphology, having relatively unchanged morphemes across words, might be simpler for automatic segmentation systems than morphology characterized as *fusional*, our sparse data sets are likely to complicate this.

Finally, systems obtain the best results for English, followed by Spanish, and then Bulgarian. These three languages are also strongly suffixing, but typically express inflection with a single morpheme. German appears to be a bit of an outlier, generally exhibiting scores that lie somewhere between the highest scoring languages, and the more difficult agglutinative languages. McCurdy et al. (2021) hypothesize that this may be due to non-concatenative morphology from German verbal circumfixes. This hypothesis *could* explain why the Boulder-GWK system performs better on German than other languages: it incorporates semantic information. However, the CU–UBC systems that use discontinuous rules (systems 5, 6, and 7), and thus should better model circumfixation, do not produce higher German scores than the continuous rules, including the suffix-only system.

## 5 Analysis: Partial Paradigm Sizes

The effect of the size of the gold partial paradigms on F1 score for the best system is illustrated in Figure 4. For Basque and Navajo, the F1 score tends to drop as paradigm size increases. We see the same trend for Finnish, Kannada, and German, with a few exceptions, but this trend does not exist for all languages. English resembles something like a bell shape, other than the low scoring outlier for the largest paradigms of size 7. Interestingly, Spanish and Turkish attain both very high and very low scores for larger paradigms.

An artifact of a sparse corpus is that many singleton paradigms arise. For theoretically larger paradigms, only a single inflected form might occur in such a small corpus. Of course, this also happens naturally for certain word classes. However, nouns, verbs, and occasionally adjectives typically form paradigms comprising several inflected forms. Figure 3 demonstrates that the best system tends to overgenerate singleton paradigms. We see this to some extent for all agglutinative languages, which may be due to the high number of typically long, unique forms. This is especially true for Navajo, which has a small corpus and extremely high type–token ratio. On the other hand, for the languages for which the highest scores are obtained, Spanish and English, the system does not overgenerate singleton paradigms. Of the large number of singleton paradigms predicted for both languages, the vast majority are correct. For other systems not pictured in the figure, singleton paradigms are typically *undergenerated* for Spanish and English. In the case of English, this could be due to words that share a derivational relationship. For example, the word *accomplishment* might be assigned to the paradigm for the verb *accomplish*, when, in fact, their relationship is not inflectional.

## 6 Conclusion and Future Shared Tasks

We presented the SIGMORPHON 2021 Shared Task on Unsupervised Morphological Paradigm Clustering. Submissions roughly fell into two categories: similarity-based methods and grammar-based methods, with the latter proving more successful at the task of clustering inflectional paradigms. The best systems significantly improved over the provided $n$-gram baseline, roughly doubling the F1 score – mostly through much improved precision. A comparison against a supervised lemmatizer demonstrated that we have not yet reached the ceiling for paradigm clustering: many words are still either incorrectly left in singleton paradigms or incorrectly clustered with circumstantially (and often derivationally) related words. Regardless of the ground still to be covered, the submitted results were a successful first step in automatically inducing the morphology of a language without access to expert-annotated data.

Unsupervised morphological paradigm clustering is only the first step in a morphological learning process that more closely models human L1 acquisition. We envision future tasks expanding on this task to include other important aspects of morphological acquisition. Paradigm slot categorization is a natural next step. To correctly categorize paradigm slots, cross-paradigmatic similarities must be considered, for example, the German words *liest* and *schreibt* are both 3rd person singular present indicative inflections of two different verbs. This can occasionally be identified via string similarity, but more often requires syntactic information. Syncretism (the collapsing of multiple paradigm slots into a single representation) further complicates the task. A similar subtask involves lemma identification, where a canonical form (Cotterell et al., 2016b) is identified within the paradigm.

Likewise, another important task involves filling unrealized slots in paradigms by generating the correct surface form, which can be approached similarly to previous SIGMORPHON shared tasks on inflection (Cotterell et al., 2016a, 2017, 2018; McCarthy et al., 2019; Vylomova et al., 2020), but will likely be based on noisy information from the slot categorization – all previous tasks have assumed that the morphosyntactic information provided to an inflector is correct. Currently, investigations into the robustness of these systems to noise are sparse.

Another direction for this task is the expansion to more under-resourced languages. The submitted results demonstrate that the task becomes particularly difficult when the provided raw text is small, but under-documented languages are often the ones most in need of morphological corpora. The JHUBC contains Bible data for more than 1500 languages, which can potentially be augmented by other raw text corpora because morphology is relatively stable across domains. Future tasks may enable the construction of inflectional paradigms in languages that require them to construct further computational tools.

## Acknowledgments

We would like to thank all of our shared task participants for their hard work on this difficult task!

## References

Piotr Bojanowski, Edouard Grave, Armand Joulin, and Tomas Mikolov. 2017. Enriching word vectors with subword information. *Transactions of the Association for Computational Linguistics*, 5:135–146.

Ryan Cotterell, Christo Kirov, John Sylak-Glassman, Géraldine Walther, Ekaterina Vylomova, Arya D McCarthy, Katharina Kann, Sabrina J Mielke, Garrett Nicolai, Miikka Silfverberg, et al. 2018. The conll–sigmorphon 2018 shared task: Universal morphological reinflection. *arXiv preprint arXiv:1810.07125*.

Ryan Cotterell, Christo Kirov, John Sylak-Glassman, Géraldine Walther, Ekaterina Vylomova, Patrick Xia, Manaal Faruqui, Sandra Kübler, David Yarowsky, Jason Eisner, et al. 2017. Conll-sigmorphon 2017 shared task: Universal morphological reinflection in 52 languages. In *Proceedings of the CoNLL SIGMORPHON 2017 Shared Task: Universal Morphological Reinflection*, pages 1–30.

Ryan Cotterell, Christo Kirov, John Sylak-Glassman, David Yarowsky, Jason Eisner, and Mans Hulden. 2016a. The sigmorphon 2016 shared task—morphological reinflection. In *Proceedings of the 14th SIGMORPHON Workshop on Computational Research in Phonetics, Phonology, and Morphology*, pages 10–22.

Ryan Cotterell, Tim Vieira, and Hinrich Schütze. 2016b. A joint model of orthography and morphological segmentation. Association for Computational Linguistics.

Greg Durrett and John DeNero. 2013. Supervised learning of complete morphological paradigms. In *Proceedings of the 2013 Conference of the North American Chapter of the Association for Computational Linguistics: Human Language Technologies*, pages 1185–1195.

Alexander Erdmann, Micha Elsner, Shijie Wu, Ryan Cotterell, and Nizar Habash. 2020. The paradigm discovery problem. In *Proceedings of the 58th Annual Meeting of the Association for Computational Linguistics*, pages 7778–7790, Online. Association for Computational Linguistics.

Andrew Gerlach, Adam Wiemerslage, and Katharina Kann. 2021. Paradigm clustering with weighted edit distance. In *Proceedings of the 18th Workshop on Computational Research in Phonetics, Phonology, and Morphology*. Association for Computational Linguistics.

Erez Hartuv and Ron Shamir. 2000. A clustering algorithm based on graph connectivity. *Information processing letters*, 76(4-6):175–181.

Mans Hulden, Markus Forsberg, and Malin Ahlberg. 2014. Semi-supervised learning of morphological paradigms and lexicons. In *Proceedings of the 14th Conference of the European Chapter of the Association for Computational Linguistics*, pages 569–578.

Huiming Jin, Liwei Cai, Yihui Peng, Chen Xia, Arya McCarthy, and Katharina Kann. 2020. Unsupervised morphological paradigm completion. In *Proceedings of the 58th Annual Meeting of the Association for Computational Linguistics*, pages 6696–6707, Online. Association for Computational Linguistics.

Mark Johnson, Thomas L Griffiths, Sharon Goldwater, et al. 2007. Adaptor grammars: A framework for specifying compositional nonparametric bayesian models. *Advances in neural information processing systems*, 19:641.

Katharina Kann, Arya D. McCarthy, Garrett Nicolai, and Mans Hulden. 2020. The SIGMORPHON 2020 shared task on unsupervised morphological paradigm completion. In *Proceedings of the 17th SIGMORPHON Workshop on Computational Research in Phonetics, Phonology, and Morphology*, pages 51–62, Online. Association for Computational Linguistics.

Richard M Karp. 1980. An algorithm to solve the m× n assignment problem in expected time o (mn log n). *Networks*, 10(2):143–152.

Christo Kirov and Ryan Cotterell. 2018. Recurrent neural networks in linguistic theory: Revisiting pinker and prince (1988) and the past tense debate. *Transactions of the Association for Computational Linguistics*, 6:651–665.

Arya D. McCarthy, Christo Kirov, Matteo Grella, Amrit Nidhi, Patrick Xia, Kyle Gorman, Ekaterina Vylomova, Sabrina J. Mielke, Garrett Nicolai, Miikka Silfverberg, Timofey Arkhangelskiy, Nataly Krizhanovsky, Andrew Krizhanovsky, Elena Klyachko, Alexey Sorokin, John Mansfield, Valts Ernštreits, Yuval Pinter, Cassandra L. Jacobs, Ryan Cotterell, Mans Hulden, and David Yarowsky. 2020a. UniMorph 3.0: Universal Morphology. In *Proceedings of the 12th Language Resources and Evaluation Conference*, pages 3922–3931, Marseille, France. European Language Resources Association.

Arya D. McCarthy, Ekaterina Vylomova, Shijie Wu, Chaitanya Malaviya, Lawrence Wolf-Sonkin, Garrett Nicolai, Christo Kirov, Miikka Silfverberg, Sabrina J. Mielke, Jeffrey Heinz, Ryan Cotterell, and Mans Hulden. 2019. The SIGMORPHON 2019 shared task: Morphological analysis in context and cross-lingual transfer for inflection. In *Proceedings of the 16th Workshop on Computational Research in Phonetics, Phonology, and Morphology*, pages 229–244, Florence, Italy. Association for Computational Linguistics.

Arya D. McCarthy, Rachel Wicks, Dylan Lewis, Aaron Mueller, Winston Wu, Oliver Adams, Garrett Nicolai, Matt Post, and David Yarowsky. 2020b. The Johns Hopkins University Bible corpus: 1600+ tongues for typological exploration. In *Proceedings of the 12th Language Resources and Evaluation Conference*, pages 2884–2892, Marseille, France. European Language Resources Association.

Kate McCurdy, Sharon Goldwater, and Adam Lopez. 2021. Adaptor grammars for unsupervised paradigm clustering. In *Proceedings of the 18th Workshop on Computational Research in Phonetics, Phonology, and Morphology*. Association for Computational Linguistics.

Tomas Mikolov, Kai Chen, Greg Corrado, and Jeffrey Dean. 2013. Efficient estimation of word representations in vector space.

Joakim Nivre, Marie-Catherine de Marneffe, Filip Ginter, Jan Hajič, Christopher D. Manning, Sampo Pyysalo, Sebastian Schuster, Francis Tyers, and Daniel Zeman. 2020. Universal Dependencies v2: An evergrowing multilingual treebank collection. In *Proceedings of the 12th Language Resources and Evaluation Conference*, pages 4034–4043, Marseille, France. European Language Resources Association.

E. Margaret Perkoff, Josh Daniels, and Alexis Palmer. 2021. Orthographic vs. semantic representations for unsupervised morphological paradigm clustering. In *Proceedings of the 18th Workshop on Computational Research in Phonetics, Phonology, and Morphology*. Association for Computational Linguistics.

Peng Qi, Yuhao Zhang, Yuhui Zhang, Jason Bolton, and Christopher D. Manning. 2020. Stanza: A python natural language processing toolkit for many human languages. In *Proceedings of the 58th Annual Meeting of the Association for Computational Linguistics: System Demonstrations*, pages 101–108, Online. Association for Computational Linguistics.

Rudolf Rosa and Zdenek Zabokrtský. 2019. Unsupervised lemmatization as embeddings-based word clustering. *CoRR*, abs/1908.08528.

Ekaterina Vylomova, Jennifer White, Elizabeth Salesky, Sabrina J Mielke, Shijie Wu, Edoardo Ponti, Rowan Hall Maudslay, Ran Zmigrod, Josef Valvoda, Svetlana Toldova, et al. 2020. Sigmorphon 2020 shared task 0: Typologically diverse morphological inflection. *arXiv preprint arXiv:2006.11572*.

William E. Winkler. 1990. String comparator metrics and enhanced decision rules in the fellegi-sunter model of record linkage. In *Proceedings of the Section on Survey Research*, pages 354–359.

Changbing Yang, Garrett Nicolai, and Miikka Silfverberg. 2021. Unsupervised paradigm clustering using transformation rules. In *Proceedings of the 18th Workshop on Computational Research in Phonetics, Phonology, and Morphology*. Association for Computational Linguistics.

# Adaptor Grammars for Unsupervised Paradigm Clustering

**Kate McCurdy Sharon Goldwater Adam Lopez**
School of Informatics
University of Edinburgh
kate.mccurdy@ed.ac.uk, {sgwater, alopez}@inf.ed.ac.uk

## Abstract

This work describes the Edinburgh submission to the SIGMORPHON 2021 Shared Task 2 on unsupervised morphological paradigm clustering. Given raw text input, the task was to assign each token to a cluster with other tokens from the same paradigm. We use Adaptor Grammar segmentations combined with frequency-based heuristics to predict paradigm clusters. Our system achieved the highest average F1 score across 9 test languages, placing first out of 15 submissions.

## 1 Introduction

While the task of supervised morphological inflection has seen dramatic gains in accuracy over recent years (e.g. Cotterell et al., 2016, 2017, 2018; Vylomova et al., 2020), unsupervised morphological analysis remains an open challenge. This is evident in the results of the 2020 SIGMORPHON Shared Task 2 on Unsupervised Morphological Paradigm Completion, in which no submission consistently outperformed the baseline (Kann et al., 2020; Jin et al., 2020).

The 2021 Shared Task 2 (Wiemerslage et al., 2021) focuses on a subproblem from the 2020 task: given raw text input, cluster tokens together based on membership in the same *morphological paradigm*. For example, given the sentence "My dog met some other dogs", a successful system would assign "dog" and "dogs" to the same paradigm because they are two inflected forms of the same *lemma* "dog", while each other word would occupy its own cluster. Furthermore, a successful system needs to cluster typologically diverse, morphologically rich languages such as Finnish and Navajo, with inflectional paradigms which are much larger than English paradigms.

## 2 Adaptor Grammars

Our approach is based upon Adaptor Grammars, a framework which achieves state-of-the-art results on the related task of unsupervised morphological segmentation (Eskander et al., 2020).

### 2.1 Model

Adaptor Grammars (AGs; Johnson et al., 2007b) are a class of nonparametric Bayesian probabilistic models which learn structured representations, or parses, of natural language input strings. An AG has two components: a Probabilistic Context-Free Grammar (PCFG) and one or more adaptors. The PCFG is a 5-tuple $(N, W, R, S, \boldsymbol{\theta})$ which specifies a base distribution over parse trees. Parse trees are generated top-down by expanding non-terminals $N$ (including the start symbol $S \in N$) to nonterminals $N$ (excluding $S$) and terminals $W$, using the set of allowed expansion rules $R$ with expansion probability $\theta_r$ for each rule $r \in R$. PCFGs have very strong independence assumptions; the adaptor component relaxes these assumptions by allowing certain nonterminals to *adapt* to a particular corpus, meaning they can cache and re-use subtrees with probabilities conditioned on that corpus.

An AG extends a PCFG by specifying a set of *adapted nonterminals* $A \subseteq N$ and a vector of adaptors $\boldsymbol{C}$. For each adapted nonterminal $X \in A$, the adaptor $C_X$ stores all subtrees previously emitted with the root node $X$. When a new tree rooted in $X$ is sampled, the adaptor $C_X$ either generates a new tree from the PCFG base distribution or returns a previously emitted subtree from its cache. The adaptor distribution is generally based on a Pitman-Yor Process (PYP; Pitman and Yor, 1997), under which the probability of $C_x$ returning a particular subtree $\sigma$ is roughly proportional to the number of times $X$ has previously expanded to $\sigma$. This leads to a "rich-get-richer" effect as more



*Proceedings of the Seventeenth SIGMORPHON Workshop on Computational Research in Phonetics, Phonology, and Morphology*, pages 82–89

Word → Stem Suffix
Word → Stem
Stem → Chars
Suffix → Chars
Chars → Char
Chars → Char Chars

(a) Example grammar. Adapted nonterminals are underlined.

| Word | Segmentation |
|---|---|
| walked | walk-ed |
| jumping | jump-ing |
| walking | walk-ing |
| jump | jump |

(b) Toy corpus with target segmentations

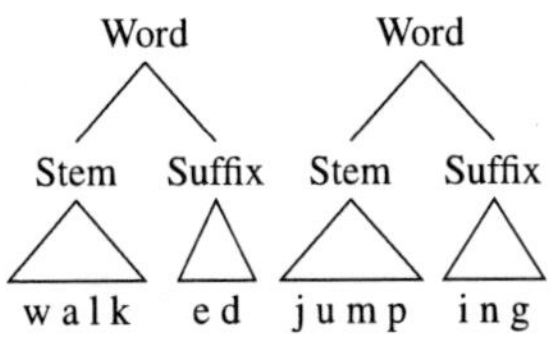


(c) Example target morphological analyses, showing only the top 2 levels of structure

Figure 1: A possible morphological analysis (1c) learned by the grammar in (1a) over the corpus shown in (1b) (from Johnson et al., 2007b)

frequently sampled subtrees gain higher probability within the conditional adapted distribution. Given an AG specification, MCMC sampling can be used to infer values for the PCFG rule probabilities $\theta$ (Johnson et al., 2007a) and PYP hyperparameters (Johnson and Goldwater, 2009).

### 2.2 AGs for Morphological Analysis

The probabilistic parses generated by adaptor grammars can be used to *segment* sequences. In cases where the grammar specifies word structures, the segmentations may reflect morphological analyses. For example, an AG trained with the simple grammar shown in Table 1a may learn to cache "jump" and "walk" as Stem subtrees, and "ing" and "ed" as Suffix subtrees, ideally producing the target segmentations shown in Figure 1c. In practice, researchers have successfully applied AGs to the task of unsupervised morphological segmentation (Sirts and Goldwater, 2013; Eskander et al., 2016). Eskander et al. (2020) found that a language-independent AG framework achieved state-of-the-art results on 12 typologically distinct languages.

## 3 System description

### 3.1 Overview

The task of unsupervised paradigm clustering is closely related to morphological segmentation, but we are not aware of previous applications of AGs to the current task. To use AGs for paradigm clustering, we need a method to group words together based on their AG segmentations. The example segmentations shown in Figure 1 suggest a very simple approach to paradigm clustering: assign all forms with the same *stem* to the same cluster. For example, "walked" and "walking" would correctly cluster together with the shared stem "walk". Our system builds upon this intuition.

As a preliminary step, we **select grammars** to sample from, looking only at the development languages. We build simple clusters and heuristically select grammars which show relatively high performance, as described in Section 3.2. In this case we select two grammars. Once the grammars have been selected, we discard the simple clusters in favor of a more sophisticated strategy.

We implement[1] a procedure to generate clusters for both development and test languages. First, we sample 3 separate AG parses for each corpus and each grammar, resulting in 6 segmentations for each word. We then use frequency-based metrics over the segmentations to identify the language's **adfix direction**, i.e. whether it is predominantly prefixing or suffixing, as described in Section 3.3. Finally, we iterate over the entire vocabulary and apply frequency-based scores to generate paradigm **clusters**, as described in Section 3.4 .

### 3.2 Grammar selection

An adaptor grammar builds upon an initial PCFG specification, and many such grammars can be applied to model word structure. As a first step, we evaluate various grammar specifications on the development languages and select the grammars for our final model.

To train the adaptor grammar representations, we use MorphAGram (Eskander et al., 2020), a framework which extends the adaptor grammar implementation of Johnson et al. (2007b). Eskander et al. (2020) evaluated nine different PCFG grammar specifications on the task of unsupervised word segmentation. Each grammar specifies the range of possible word structures which can be learned under that model. We evaluated six of their nine proposed grammars on the development languages (Maltese, Persian, Portuguese, Russian, and Swedish). Following their procedure, we extracted a vocabulary $V$ of word types as AG inputs.[2]

[1] `https://github.com/kmccurdy/paradigm-clusters`

[2] Although AGs can also model token frequencies (Goldwater et al., 2006), which could conceivably improve perfor-

To evaluate grammar performance, we follow the intuition in Section 3.1 and group by AG-segmented stems. Grouping by stem can be more difficult for complex words. For example, an AG with a more complex grammar might segment the plural noun "actionables" into "action-able-s", with "action" as the stem (see also the example in Figure 2a); however, the target paradigm for clustering includes only "actionable" and "actionables", not "action" and "actions". To address this issue for our clustering task, we make the further simplifying (but linguistically motivated; e.g. Stump, 2005, 56) assumption that inflectional morphology is generally realized on a word's periphery, so a segmentation like "action-able-s" implies the stem "actionable" (in a suffixing language like English, where the prefix is included in the stem). As all of the development languages were predominantly suffixing (with the partial exception of Maltese, which includes root-and-pattern morphology), we simply grouped together words with the same AG-segmented Prefix + Stem.

We selected two grammars with the following desirable attributes: 1) they reliably showed good performance on the development set, relative to other grammars; and 2) they specified very similar structures, making it easier to combine their outputs in later steps. Both grammars model words as a tripartite Prefix-Stem-Suffix sequence. Both grammars also use a SubMorph level of representation, which has been shown to aid word segmentation (Sirts and Goldwater, 2013), although we only consider segments from the level directly above SubMorphs in clustering. The full grammar specifications are included in Appendix A.

- *Simple+SM*: Each word comprises one optional prefix, one stem, and one optional suffix. Each of these levels can comprise one or more SubMorphs.
- *PrStSu+SM* Each word comprises zero or more prefixes, one stem, and zero or more suffixes. Each of these levels can comprise one or more SubMorphs. Eskander et al. (2020) found that this grammar showed the highest performance in unsupervised segmentation across the languages they evaluated.

Sampling from an adaptor grammar is a non-deterministic process, so the same set of initial

mance on this task, we did not explore this option.

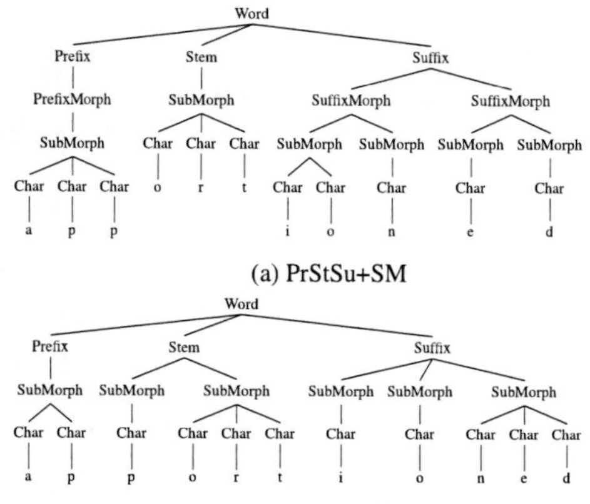


(a) PrStSu+SM

(b) Simple+SM

Figure 2: Two example parses of the word "apportioned" from our two distinct grammar specifications, learned on the English test data.

parameters applied to the same data can predict different segmentation outputs. Given this variability, we run the AG sampler three times for each of our two selected grammars, yielding 6 parses of the lexicon for each language. The number of grammar runs was heuristically selected and not tuned in any way, so adding more runs for each grammar might improve performance (for example, Sirts and Goldwater, 2013, use 5 samples per grammar). We then combine the resulting segmentations using the following procedure.

### 3.3 Adfix direction

The first step is to determine the *adfix direction* for each language, i.e. whether the language uses predominantly prefixing or suffixing inflection. We heuristically select the adfix direction using the following automatic procedure.

First, we count the frequency of each *peripheral segment* across all 6 parses of the lexicon. A peripheral segment is a substring at the start or end of a word, which has been parsed as a segment above the SubMorph level in some AG sample. For instance, in the parse shown in Figure 2a, "app-" would be the initial peripheral segment, and "-ed" would be the final peripheral segment. By contrast, for the parse shown in Figure 2b,"ap-" would be the initial peripheral segment, and "-ioned" would be the final peripheral segment.

Next, we rank the segmented adfixes by their frequency, and select the top $N$ for consideration, where $N$ is some heuristically chosen quantity. In light of the generally Zipfian properties of linguistic distributions, we chose to scale $N$ logarithmically with the vocabulary size, so $N = log(|V|)$.

Finally, we select the majority label (i.e. "prefix" or "suffix") of the $N$ most frequent segments as the adfix direction. This simple approach has obvious limitations — to name just one, it neglects the reality of nonconcatenative morphology, such as the root-and-pattern inflection of many Maltese verbs. Nonetheless, it appears to capture some key distinctions: this method correctly identified Navajo as a prefixing language, and all other development and test languages as predominantly suffixing.

### 3.4 Creating paradigm clusters

Once we have inferred the adfix direction for a language, we use a greedy iterative procedure over words to identify and score potential clusters. Our scoring metric is frequency-based, motivated by the observation that inflectional morphology (such as the "-s" in "actionables") tends to be more frequent across word types relative to derivational morphology (such as the "-able" in "actionables"). Yarowsky and Wicentowski (2000) have demonstrated the value of frequency metrics in aligning inflected forms from the same lemma.

We start with no assigned clusters and iterate through the vocabulary in alphabetical order.[3] For each word $w$ which has not yet been assigned to a cluster, we identify the most likely cluster using the following procedure.

**Find possible stems** Identify each possible stem $s$ from all of the segmentations for $w$, where the "stem" comprises the entire substring up to a peripheral adfix. For example, based on the two parses shown in Figure 2, "apportion" and "apport" would constitute possible stems for the word "apportioned". The word $w$ in its entirety is also considered as a possible stem.

**Find possible cluster members** For each stem $s$, identify other words in the corpus which might share that stem, forming a potential cluster $c_s$. A word potentially shares a stem if it shares the same substring from the non-adfixing-direction — so a stem is a shared prefix substring in a suffixing language like English, and vice-versa for a prefixing language like Navajo. For each word $w_i$ that is identified this way, the rest of the string outside of the possible stem $s$ is a possible adfix $a_i$. In the example from Figure 2, if "apportions" were also in the corpus, it would be added to the cluster for the stem "apportion", with "-s" as the adfix $a_i$. Similarly, it would also be considered in the cluster for the stem "apport", with adfix "-ions".

[3]The method is relatively insensitive to order, except reversed alphabetical order, which is worse for most languages.

**Score cluster members** For each word $w_i$ in $c_s$, calculate a score $x_i$:.

$$x_i = \sqrt{A_i^w} log(A_i) \quad (1)$$

where $A_i$ is the normalized overall frequency of the $i$th adfix $a_i$ (suffix or prefix) per 10,000 types in the corpus of 6 segmentations, and $A_i^w$ is the proportion of segmentations of the $i$th word $w_i$ which contain the adfix $a_i$. For example, if "apportioned" were in consideration for a hypothetical cluster based on the stem "apportion", $A_i$ would be the normalized corpus frequency of "-ed", and $A_i^w$ would be .5 (assuming only the two segmentations shown in Figure 2). For a cluster with the stem "apport", $A_i$ would be the normalized frequency of "-ioned", and $A_i^w$ would still be .5.

Intuitively, when evaluating a single word, Eq. 1 assumes that adfixes which appear frequently in the segmented corpus overall are more likely to be inflectional, so words with more frequent adfixes are more likely paradigm members (the $log(A_i)$ term). For instance, the high frequency of the "-s" suffix in English will increase the score of any word with an "-s" suffix in its segmentation (e.g. "apportion-s"). Eq. 1 also assumes that, for all segmentations of this particular word $w_i$, adfixes which appear in a higher proportion of segmentations are more reliable (the $\sqrt{A_i^w}$ term), so the more times some AG samples the "apportion-s" segmentation, the higher the score for "apportions" membership in the "apportion"-stem paradigm. The square root transform was selected based on development set performance, and has not been tuned extensively.

**Filter and score clusters** For each possible stem cluster $c_s$, filter out words whose score $x_i$ is below the *score threshold* hyperparameter $t$, to create a new cluster $c'_s$. Calculate the cluster score $x_s$ by taking the average of $x_i$ for only those words in $c'_s$, i.e. only words with score $x_i \geq t$. The value for $t$ is selected via grid search on the development set. We found that setting $t = 2$ maximized F1 across the development languages as a whole.

**Select cluster** Select the potential cluster $c'_s$ with the highest score, and assign $w$ to that cluster, along with each word $w_i$ in $c'_s$.

| Language | Precision | Recall | F1 |
|---|---|---|---|
| Maltese | .30 | .30 | .30 |
| Persian | .54 | .52 | .53 |
| Portuguese | .92 | .91 | .91 |
| Russian | .83 | .82 | .82 |
| Swedish | .85 | .81 | .83 |
| Mean | .69 | .67 | .68 |

Table 1: Performance on development languages

| Language | Precision | Recall | F1 |
|---|---|---|---|
| Basque | .33 | .32 | .32 |
| Bulgarian | .83 | .80 | .82 |
| English | .91 | .90 | .90 |
| Finnish | .61 | .60 | .60 |
| German | .79 | .79 | .79 |
| Kannada | .82 | .59 | .69 |
| Navajo | .43 | .42 | .42 |
| Spanish | .85 | .82 | .84 |
| Turkish | .74 | .73 | .73 |
| Mean | .70 | .66 | .68 |

Table 2: Performance on test languages

## 4 Results and Discussion

Performance was evaluated using the script provided by the shared task organizers. Table 1 shows the results for the development languages, and Table 2 shows the results for the test languages. While the average F1 score ends up being quite similar for both development and test languages, it's clear within both groups that there are large differences in performance across different languages.

### 4.1 Error analysis and ways to improve

**Noncontiguous stems** The clustering method described in Section 3.4 makes an unjustifiably strong assumption that stems are contiguous substrings, which effectively eliminates its ability to represent nonconcatenative morphology. This limitation contributes to the low score on Maltese, a Semitic language which includes root-and-pattern morphology for certain verbs. The model further assumes that the left or right edge of a word — the side opposite from the adfix direction — is contiguous with the stem. This leads to errors on German, as most verbs have a circumfixing past participle form "ge- + -t" or "ge- + -en". For example, the model correctly assigns "ändern", "änderten", and "ändert" to the same cluster, but incorrectly assigns "geändert" to a separate cluster. We estimate that roughly 30% of the model's incorrect German predictions stem from this issue. This limitation also contributed to our model's poor performance on Basque, which, like Maltese, uses both prefixing and suffixing inflection to express polypersonal agreement.[4]

One obvious way to improve this issue would be to use an extension of the AG framework which can represent nonconcatenative morphology. Botha and Blunsom (2013) present such an extension, replacing the PCFG with a Probabilistic Simple Range Concatenating Grammar. They report successful results for unsupervised segmentation on Hebrew and Arabic. On the other hand, it's unclear whether such a nonconcatenative-focused approach could also adequately represent concatenative morphology. Fullwood and O'Donnell (2013) explore a similar framework, using Pitman-Yor processes to sample separate lexica of roots, templates, and "residue" segments; they find that their model works well for Arabic, but much less well for English. In addition, Eskander et al. (2020) report state-of-the-art morphological segmentation for Arabic using the *PrStSu+SM* grammar which we also use here. Their findings suggest that, rather than changing the AG framework, we might attempt a more intelligent clustering method based on noncontiguous segmented subsequences rather than contiguous substrings.

**Irregular morphology** The strong assumption of contiguous substrings as stems also hinders accurate clustering of irregular forms of any kind, from predictable stem alternations (such as umlaut in German and Swedish, or theme vowels in Portuguese and Spanish) to more challenging suppletive forms such as English "go"-"went". The latter likely requires additional input from semantic representations, but semiregular alternations in forms could also be handled in principle by a more intelligent clustering process. On this point, we note that some small but significant fraction of AG parses of Portuguese verbs grouped verbal theme vowels and inflections together (e.g. parsing "apresentada" as "apresent-ada" rather than "apresenta-da", "apresentarem" as "apresent-arem" rather than "apresenta-rem", and so on), and these parses were crucial to our model's relatively high performance on Portuguese.

[4]We thank an anonymous reviewer for bringing this to our attention.

**Derivation vs. inflection** Another issue is that the parses sampled by AGs do not distinguish between inflectional and derivational morphology. This is apparent in Figure 2, where both grammars parse "apportioned" with "-ioned" as the suffix. We seek to address this issue with frequency-based metrics in our clustering method, but frequent derivational adfixes often score high enough to be assigned a wrong paradigm cluster. For example, in English our model correctly clusters "allow", "allows", and "allowed" together, but it also incorrectly assigns "allowance" to the same cluster.

A straightforward way to handle this within our existing approach would be to allow language-specific variation of the score threshold $t$. As we had no method for unsupervised estimation of $t$ for unfamiliar languages, we did not pursue this; however, a researcher who had minimal familiarity with the language in question might be able to select a more sensible value for $t$ based on inspecting the clusters. Beyond that, the distinction between inflectional and derivational morphology is an intriguing and contested issue within linguistics (e.g. Stump, 2005), and the question of how to model it computationally requires much more attention.

### 4.2 Things that didn't work

We attempted a number of unsupervised approaches beyond AG segmentations, with the goal of incorporating them during the clustering process; however, we could not consistently improve performance with any of them. It seems likely to us that these methods could still be used to improve AG-segmentation-based clusters, but we could not find immediately obvious ways to do this.

**FastText** As the AG framework only models word structure based on form, we hoped to use the distributional representations learned by FastText (Bojanowski et al., 2017) to incorporate semantic and syntactic information into our model's clusters. We tried several different approaches without success. 1) We trained a skipgram model with a context window of 5 words, a setting often used for semantic applications, in hopes that words from the same paradigm might have similar semantic representations. Agglomerative clustering on these representations alone yielded much worse clusters than the AG method, and we could not find a way to combine them successfully with the AG clusters. 2) Erdmann et al. (2020) trained a skipgram model with a context window of 1 word and a minimum subword length of 2 characters, and used it to cluster words from the same *cell* rather than the same paradigm (e.g. clustering together English verbs in the third person singular such as "walks" and "jumps"). We attempted to follow this procedure, but it proved too difficult, as paradigm cell information was not explicitly included in the development data for this shared task. 3) We used the method described by Bojanowski et al. (2017) to identify important subwords within a word, in hopes of combining them with AG segmentations. However, the identified subwords did not consistently align with stem-adfix segementations as we had hoped, and did not seem to provide any additional benefit.

**Brown clustering** Part of speech tags could provide latent structure as a higher-order grouping for paradigm clusters — for example, verbs would be expected to have paradigms more similar to other verbs than to nouns. Brown clusters (Brown et al., 1992) have been used for unsupervised induction of word classes approximating part of speech tags. We used a spectral clustering algorithm (Stratos et al., 2014) to learn Brown clusters, but they did not reliably correspond to part of speech categories on our development language data.

## 5 Conclusion

The Adaptor Grammar framework has previously been applied to unsupervised morphological segmentation. In this paper, we demonstrate that AG segmentations can be used for the related task of unsupervised paradigm clustering with successful results, as shown by our system's performance in the 2021 SIGMORPHON Shared Task.

We note that there is still considerable room for improvement in our clustering procedure. Two key directions for future development are more sophisticated treatment of nonconcatenative morphology, and incorporation of additional sources of information beyond the word form alone.

## Acknowledgments

This work was supported in part by the EPSRC Centre for Doctoral Training in Data Science, funded by the UK Engineering and Physical Sciences Research Council (grant EP/L016427/1) and the University of Edinburgh, and a James S McDonnell Foundation Scholar Award (#220020374) to the second author.

## References


Piotr Bojanowski, Edouard Grave, Armand Joulin, and Tomas Mikolov. 2017. Enriching Word Vectors with Subword Information. *Transactions of the Association for Computational Linguistics*, 5:135–146.

Jan A Botha and Phil Blunsom. 2013. Adaptor grammars for learning non-concatenative morphology. In *Proceedings of the 2013 conference on empirical methods in natural language processing*, pages 345–356.

Peter F. Brown, Peter V. Desouza, Robert L. Mercer, Vincent J. Della Pietra, and Jenifer C. Lai. 1992. Class-based n-gram models of natural language. *Computational linguistics*, 18(4):467–479.

Ryan Cotterell, Christo Kirov, John Sylak-Glassman, Géraldine Walther, Ekaterina Vylomova, Arya D. McCarthy, Katharina Kann, Sabrina J. Mielke, Garrett Nicolai, Miikka Silfverberg, David Yarowsky, Jason Eisner, and Mans Hulden. 2018. The CoNLL–SIGMORPHON 2018 Shared Task: Universal Morphological Reinflection. In *Proceedings of the CoNLL–SIGMORPHON 2018 Shared Task: Universal Morphological Reinflection*, pages 1–27, Brussels. Association for Computational Linguistics.

Ryan Cotterell, Christo Kirov, John Sylak-Glassman, Gèraldine Walther, Ekaterina Vylomova, Patrick Xia, Manaal Faruqui, Sandra Kübler, David Yarowsky, Jason Eisner, and Mans Hulden. 2017. CoNLL-SIGMORPHON 2017 Shared Task: Universal Morphological Reinflection in 52 Languages. In *Proceedings of the CoNLL SIGMORPHON 2017 Shared Task: Universal Morphological Reinflection*, pages 1–30, Vancouver. Association for Computational Linguistics.

Ryan Cotterell, Christo Kirov, John Sylak-Glassman, David Yarowsky, Jason Eisner, and Mans Hulden. 2016. The SIGMORPHON 2016 Shared Task—Morphological Reinflection. In *Proceedings of the 14th SIGMORPHON Workshop on Computational Research in Phonetics, Phonology, and Morphology*, pages 10–22, Berlin, Germany. Association for Computational Linguistics.

Alexander Erdmann, Micha Elsner, Shijie Wu, Ryan Cotterell, and Nizar Habash. 2020. The Paradigm Discovery Problem. *arXiv:2005.01630 [cs]*. ArXiv: 2005.01630.

Ramy Eskander, Francesca Callejas, Elizabeth Nichols, Judith Klavans, and Smaranda Muresan. 2020. MorphAGram, Evaluation and Framework for Unsupervised Morphological Segmentation. In *Proceedings of the 12th Language Resources and Evaluation Conference*, pages 7112–7122, Marseille, France. European Language Resources Association.

Ramy Eskander, Owen Rambow, and Tianchun Yang. 2016. Extending the Use of Adaptor Grammars for Unsupervised Morphological Segmentation of Unseen Languages. In *Proceedings of COLING 2016, the 26th International Conference on Computational Linguistics: Technical Papers*, pages 900–910, Osaka, Japan. The COLING 2016 Organizing Committee.

Michelle Fullwood and Tim O'Donnell. 2013. Learning non-concatenative morphology. In *Proceedings of the Fourth Annual Workshop on Cognitive Modeling and Computational Linguistics (CMCL)*, pages 21–27, Sofia, Bulgaria. Association for Computational Linguistics.

Sharon Goldwater, Mark Johnson, and Thomas L Griffiths. 2006. Interpolating between types and tokens by estimating power-law generators. In *Advances in neural information processing systems*, pages 459–466.

Huiming Jin, Liwei Cai, Yihui Peng, Chen Xia, Arya D. McCarthy, and Katharina Kann. 2020. Unsupervised Morphological Paradigm Completion. *arXiv:2005.00970 [cs]*. ArXiv: 2005.00970.

Mark Johnson and Sharon Goldwater. 2009. Improving nonparameteric Bayesian inference: experiments on unsupervised word segmentation with adaptor grammars. In *Proceedings of Human Language Technologies: The 2009 Annual Conference of the North American Chapter of the Association for Computational Linguistics*, pages 317–325, Boulder, Colorado. Association for Computational Linguistics.

Mark Johnson, Thomas Griffiths, and Sharon Goldwater. 2007a. Bayesian Inference for PCFGs via Markov Chain Monte Carlo. In *Human Language Technologies 2007: The Conference of the North American Chapter of the Association for Computational Linguistics; Proceedings of the Main Conference*, pages 139–146, Rochester, New York. Association for Computational Linguistics.

Mark Johnson, Thomas L. Griffiths, and Sharon Goldwater. 2007b. Adaptor Grammars:A Framework for Specifying Compositional Nonparametric Bayesian Models. In Bernhard Schölkopf, John Platt, and Thomas Hofmann, editors, *Advances in Neural Information Processing Systems 19*. The MIT Press.

Katharina Kann, Arya D. McCarthy, Garrett Nicolai, and Mans Hulden. 2020. The SIGMORPHON 2020 Shared Task on Unsupervised Morphological Paradigm Completion. In *Proceedings of the 17th SIGMORPHON Workshop on Computational Research in Phonetics, Phonology, and Morphology*, pages 51–62, Online. Association for Computational Linguistics.

Jim Pitman and Marc Yor. 1997. The Two-Parameter Poisson-Dirichlet Distribution Derived from a Stable Subordinator. *The Annals of Probability*, 25(2):855–900. Publisher: Institute of Mathematical Statistics.

Kairit Sirts and Sharon Goldwater. 2013. Minimally-Supervised Morphological Segmentation using Adaptor Grammars. *Transactions of the Association for Computational Linguistics*, 1:255–266.

Karl Stratos, Do-kyum Kim, Michael Collins, and Daniel Hsu. 2014. A spectral algorithm for learning class-based n-gram models of natural language. *Proceedings of the Association for Uncertainty in Artificial Intelligence*.

Gregory T Stump. 2005. Word-formation and inflectional morphology. In *Handbook of word-formation*, volume 64, pages 49–71. Springer, Dordrecht, The Netherlands.

Ekaterina Vylomova, Jennifer White, Elizabeth Salesky, Sabrina J. Mielke, Shijie Wu, Edoardo Maria Ponti, Rowan Hall Maudslay, Ran Zmigrod, Josef Valvoda, Svetlana Toldova, Francis Tyers, Elena Klyachko, Ilya Yegorov, Natalia Krizhanovsky, Paula Czarnowska, Irene Nikkarinen, Andrew Krizhanovsky, Tiago Pimentel, Lucas Torroba Hennigen, Christo Kirov, Garrett Nicolai, Adina Williams, Antonios Anastasopoulos, Hilaria Cruz, Eleanor Chodroff, Ryan Cotterell, Miikka Silfverberg, and Mans Hulden. 2020. SIGMORPHON 2020 Shared Task 0: Typologically Diverse Morphological Inflection. In *Proceedings of the 17th SIGMORPHON Workshop on Computational Research in Phonetics, Phonology, and Morphology*, pages 1–39, Online. Association for Computational Linguistics.

Adam Wiemerslage, Arya McCarthy, Alexander Erdmann, Garrett Nicolai, Manex Agirrezabal, Miikka Silfverberg, Mans Hulden, and Katharina Kann. 2021. The SIGMORPHON 2021 Shared Task on Unsupervised Morphological Paradigm Clustering. In *Proceedings of the 18th SIGMORPHON Workshop on Computational Research in Phonetics, Phonology, and Morphology*. Association for Computational Linguistics.

David Yarowsky and Richard Wicentowski. 2000. Minimally Supervised Morphological Analysis by Multimodal Alignment. pages 207–216.

# A PCFGs

Our system uses the following two grammar specifications, developed by Eskander et al. (2016, 2020). Nonterminals are adapted by default. *Non-adapted* nonterminals are preceded by 1, indicating an expansion probability of 1, i.e. the PCFG always expands this rule and never caches it.

## A.1 Simple+SM

```
1 Word --> Prefix Stem Suffix

Prefix --> ^^^ SubMorphs
Prefix --> ^^^

Stem --> SubMorphs

Suffix --> SubMorphs $$$
Suffix --> $$$

1 SubMorphs --> SubMorph SubMorphs
1 SubMorphs --> SubMorph
SubMorph --> Chars
1 Chars --> Char
1 Chars --> Char Chars
```

## A.2 PrStSu+SM

```
1 Word --> Prefix Stem Suffix

Prefix --> ^^^
Prefix --> ^^^ PrefMorphs
1 PrefMorphs --> PrefMorph PrefMorphs
1 PrefMorphs --> PrefMorph
PrefMorph --> SubMorphs

Stem --> SubMorphs

Suffix --> $$$
Suffix --> SuffMorphs $$$
1 SuffMorphs --> SuffMorph SuffMorphs
1 SuffMorphs --> SuffMorph
SuffMorph --> SubMorphs

1 SubMorphs --> SubMorph SubMorphs
1 SubMorphs --> SubMorph
SubMorph --> Chars
1 Chars --> Char
1 Chars --> Char Chars
```

# Orthographic vs. Semantic Representations for Unsupervised Morphological Paradigm Clustering

**E. Margaret Perkoff**[*] **Josh Daniels**[†] **Alexis Palmer**[†]
[*]Dept. of Computer Science, [†]Dept. of Linguistics
University of Colorado Boulder
{margaret.perkoff, joda4370, alexis.palmer}@colorado.edu

## Abstract

This paper presents two different systems for unsupervised clustering of morphological paradigms, in the context of the SIGMORPHON 2021 Shared Task 2. The goal of this task is to correctly cluster words in a given language by their inflectional paradigm, without any previous knowledge of the language and without supervision from labeled data of any sort. The words in a single morphological paradigm are different inflectional variants of an underlying lemma, meaning that the words share a common core meaning. They also - usually - show a high degree of orthographical similarity. Following these intuitions, we investigate KMeans clustering using two different types of word representations: one focusing on orthographical similarity and the other focusing on semantic similarity. Additionally, we discuss the merits of randomly initialized centroids versus pre-defined centroids for clustering. Pre-defined centroids are identified based on either a standard longest common substring algorithm or a connected graph method built off of longest common substring. For all development languages, the character-based embeddings perform similarly to the baseline, and the semantic embeddings perform well below the baseline. Analysis of the systems' errors suggests that clustering based on orthographic representations is suitable for a wide range of morphological mechanisms, particularly as part of a larger system.

## 1 Introduction

One significant barrier to progress in morphological analysis is the lack of available data for most of the world's languages. As a result, there is a dramatic divide between high and low resource languages when it comes to performance on automated morphological analysis (as well as many other language-related tasks). Even for languages with resources suitable for computational morphological analysis, there is no guarantee that the available data in fact covers all important aspects of the language, leading to significant error rates on unseen data. This uncertainty regarding training data makes unsupervised learning a natural modeling choice for the field of computational morphology. The unsupervised setting takes away the need for large quantities of labeled text in order to detect linguistic phenomena. The SIGMORPHON 2021 shared task aims to leverage the unsupervised setting in order to identify morphological paradigms, at the same time including languages with a wide range of morphological properties.

| Surface Forms | | Morphological Features |
|---|---|---|
| walk | bring | V; 1SG; 2SG; 3PL; 1PL |
| walks | brings | V; 3SG |
| walking | bringing | PRES; PART |
| walked | brought | PAST |

Table 1: Morphological paradigms for the English verbs *walk* and *bring*.

For a given language, the morphological paradigms are the models that relate root forms (or lemmas) of words to their surface forms. The task we tackle is to cluster surface word forms into groups that reflect the application of a morphological paradigm to a single lemma. The lemma of the paradigm is typically the dictionary citation form, and the corresponding surface forms are inflected variations of that lemma, conveying grammatical properties such as tense, gender, or plurality. For example, Table 1 displays partial clusters for two English verbs: *walk* and *bring*.

In developing our system, we consider two types of information that could reasonably play a role in unsupervised paradigm induction. First, the words in a single paradigm cluster are different inflectional variants of an underlying lemma, meaning



*Proceedings of the Seventeenth SIGMORPHON Workshop on Computational Research in Phonetics, Phonology, and Morphology*, pages 90–97

that the words share a common core meaning. They also - usually - show a high degree of orthographical similarity. Following these intuitions, we investigate KMeans clustering using two different types of word representations: one focusing on orthographical similarity and the other focusing on semantic similarity. Intuitively, we would expect the cluster of forms for *walk* to be recognizable largely based on orthographic similarity. The partially irregular cluster for *bring* shows greater orthographical variability in the past-tense form *brought* and so might be expected to require information beyond orthographic similarity.

**System Overview.** The core of our approach is to cluster unlabelled surface word forms using KMeans clustering; a complete architecture diagram can be seen in Figure 1. After reading the input file for a particular language to identify the lexicon and alphabet, we transform each word into two different types of vector representations. To capture semantic information, we train Word2Vec embeddings from the input data. The orthography-based representations we learn are character embeddings, again trained from the input data. Details for both representations appear in section 4.1. For the experiments in this paper, we test each type of representation separately, using randomly initialized centers for the clustering. In later work, we plan to explore the integration of both types of representations. We would also like to explore the use of pre-defined centers for clustering. These pre-defined centers could be provided using either a longest common subsequence method or a graph-based algorithm such as that described in section 4.3. The final output of the system is a set of clusters, each one representing a morphological paradigm.

## 2 Previous Work

The SIGMORPHON 2020 shared task set included an open problem calling for unsupervised systems to complete morphological paradigms. For the 2020 task, participants were provided with the set of lemmas available for each language (Kann, 2020). In contrast, the 2021 SIGMORPHON task 2 outlines that submissions are unsupervised systems that cluster input tokens into the appropriate morphological paradigm (Nicolai et al., 2020). Given the novelty of the task, there is a lack of previous work done to cluster morphological paradigms in an unsupervised manner. However, we have identified key methods from previous work in computational morphology and unsupervised learning that could be combined to approach this problem.

Previous work has identified the benefit of combining rules based on linguistic characteristics with machine learning techniques. Erdmann et al. (2020) established a baseline for the Paradigm Discovery Problem that clusters the unannotated sentences first by a combination of string similarity and lexical semantics and then uses this clustering as input for a neural transducer. Erdmann and Habash (2018) investigated the benefits of different similarity models as they apply to Arabic dialects. Their findings demonstrated that Word2Vec embeddings significantly underperformed in comparison to the Levenshtein distance baseline. The highest performing representation was a combination of FastText and a de-lexicalized morphological analyzer. The FastText embeddings (Bojanowski et al., 2016) have the benefit of including sub-word information by representing words as character n-grams. The de-lexicalized analyzer relies on linguistic expert knowledge of Arabic to identify the morphological closeness of two words. In the context of the paper, it is used to prune out word relations that do not conform to Arabic morphological rules. The approach mentioned greatly benefits from the use of a morphological analyzer, something that is not readily available for low-resource languages. Soricut and Och (2015) focused on the use of morphological transformations as the basis for word representations. Their representation can be quite accurate for affix-based morphology.

Our representations are based entirely off of unlabelled data and do not require linguistic experts to provide morphological transformation rules for the language. Additionally, we hoped to create a system that would be robust for languages that include non-affix based morphology. In this work we compare Word2Vec representations to character-based representations to represent orthography. We have not yet evaluated additional representations or combinations of the two.

## 3 Task overview

The 2021 SIGMORPHON Shared Task 2 created a call for unsupervised systems that would create morphological paradigm clusters. This was intended to build upon the shared task from 2020 that focused on morphological paradigm completion. Participants were provided with tokenized Bible data from the JHU bible corpus (McCarthy et al., 2020) and gold standard paradigm clusters for five development languages: Maltese, Persian, Portuguese, Russian and Swedish. Teams could use this data to train their systems and evaluate against the gold standard files as well as a baseline. The baseline provided groups together words that share a substring of length *n* and then removes any duplicate clusters. The resulting systems were then used to cluster tokenized data from a set of test languages including: Basque, Bulgarian, English, Finnish, German, Kannada, Navajo, Spanish, and Turkish.

## 4 System Architecture

The overall architecture of our system includes several distinct pieces as demonstrated in Figure 1. For a given language, we read the corpus text provided and generate a lexicon of unique words. The lexicon is then fed to an embedding layer and an optional lemma identification layer. The embedding layer generates a vector representation of each word based on either a character level embedding or a Word2Vec embedding. When used, the lemma identification layer generates a set of predefined lemmas from the lexicon based on either the standard longest common substring or a connected graph formed from the longest common substring. Result word embeddings along with the optional set of predefined lemmas are used as input to a KMeans clustering algorithm. In the event predefined lemmas are not provided, the system defaults to using a randomly initialized set of centroids. Otherwise, the initial centroids for the clusters are the result of finding the appropriate word embedding for the lemmas identified. Once a cluster has been created, the output cluster predictions are formatted into a paradigm dictionary which can be written to a file for evaluation.

### 4.1 Word Representations

We create two different types of word representations, aiming to capture information that may reflect the relatedness of words within a paradigm.

**Character Based Embeddings.** To capture orthographic information, we generate a character-based word embedding for the language. For each language we do the following:

1. Generate a lexicon of all the words in the development corpus and an alphabet of unique characters in the language.
2. Identify the maximum word length of the lexicon.
3. Create a dictionary of the alphabet where each character corresponds to a float value between 0 (non-inclusive) and 1 (inclusive).
4. For each word:
   (a) Initialize an array of zeros the same size as the maximum length word.
   (b) Map each character in the word, in order, to its respective float value based on our alphabet dictionary. Leave the remaining values as zero.

This representation focuses purely on the characters of the language. For the time being, it does not take into account the relationship between orthographic characters in any of the languages but future work could attempt to create smarter numerical representations based on these relationships.

**Word Embeddings with Word2Vec.** To incorporate semantic and syntactic information, we use the Word2Vec embeddings. Specifically, we train a Word2Vec model for each language with the Gensim skip-gram representations (Řehůřek and Sojka, 2010).

### 4.2 (Optional) Lemma Identification

**LCS Graph Formation** One of the challenges of using clustering-based methods on this problem is determining the number of morphological paradigms expected to be present and then finding suitable lemmas for each to serve as centers for clustering. One potential approach to find lemmas is to first arrange the words into a network graph based on the longest common substring relationships between them. Specifically, for each attested word W in a language's data, the longest common substring (LCS) is calculated between W and every other attested word in the language. Graph edges are then constructed between W and the word (or words if there are multiple with the same length LCS) that have the longest LCS with W. This process is repeated for every word in the given language's corpus. This results in a large graph that appears to capture many of the morphological dependencies within the language.

Next, we split the graph into highly connected subgraphs (HCSs). HCS are defined as graphs in which the number of edges that would need to be cut to split the graph into two disconnected

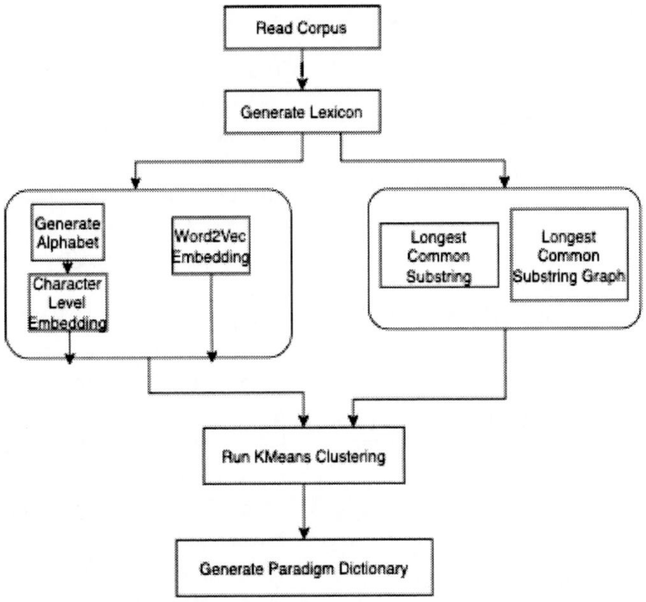


Figure 1: Overall Statistical Clustering Architecture diagram. There are two possible word embedding algorithms represented in the diagram (left side of split). The optional lemma identification layer also includes two possible methods (right side).

subgraphs is greater than one half of the number of nodes. This is helpful because in the LCS graphs generated, morphologically related forms tend to be connected relatively densely to each other and only weakly connect to forms from other paradigms. Additionally, the use of a threshold based algorithm like HCS, unlike other clustering methods, would allow lemmas to be extracted without having to prespecify the expected number of lemmas beforehand. Unfortunately, during testing the HCS graph analysis proved computationally taxing and was unable to be completed in time for evaluation, though qualitative analysis of the generated LCS graphs suggests the technique may still be useful with better computational power. We will explore this method further in future work.

### 4.3 Clustering

The word representations described in section 4.1 are used as input to a clustering algorithm. We use the KMeans algorithm as defined by the sklearn implementation (Pedregosa et al., 2011). The KMeans approach is one of the pioneering algorithms in unsupervised learning (MacQueen et al., 1967). Input values are grouped by continuously shifting clusters and their centers while attempting to minimize the variance of each cluster. This indicates that the cluster that a particular word is assigned to should be as close (as defined by Euclidean distance) to the cluster's center, or the lemma word, as possible.

**Clustering with Randomly Initiated Centers.** For comparison, we evaluate the effectiveness of using randomly initialized centers for our clusters. In the context of this task, this means that the first set of centers fed to the algorithm do not necessarily correspond to any valid word in the given language, or perhaps any language. Another obstacle for this approach in an unsupervised setting is defining the number of clusters to use. Identifying this requires human interference with hyper-parameters that are not going to be cross-linguistically relevant. The size of the input bible corpus and the inflectional morphology of the language both directly impact the number of clusters, or the number of lemmas, that are relevant. We used a range of cluster sizes for the development languages from 100 to 6000 to evaluate which ones provided the highest accuracy. For the test languages, we chose to submit results for clusters of size 500, 1000, 1500, and 1900 to assess performance variability based on number of lemmas.

**Extension: Initializing with Non-Random Centers.** The use of non-random centers would have multiple benefits in the context of this task. This approach would incorporate linguistic information

| Language | BL | KMW2V | KMCE |
|---|---|---|---|
| Maltese | **0.29** | 0.19 | 0.25 |
| Persian | 0.30 | 0.18 | **0.36** |
| Portuguese | **0.34** | 0.06 | 0.24 |
| Russian | **0.36** | 0.11 | 0.34 |
| Swedish | 0.44 | 0.18 | **0.45** |

Table 2: F1 Scores for each of the model types on all development languages. The best F1 scores are in bold. BL is Baseline, KMW2V is KMeans with Word2Vec embeddings, and KMCE is KMeans with Character Embeddings.

| Language | BL | 500 | 1000 | 1500 | 1900 |
|---|---|---|---|---|---|
| Basque | 0.21 | 0.29 | **0.31** | 0.27 | 0.29 |
| Bulgarian | **0.39** | 0.21 | 0.27 | 0.29 | 0.30 |
| English | **0.52** | 0.29 | 0.37 | 0.43 | 0.45 |
| Finnish | **0.29** | 0.19 | 0.24 | 0.26 | 0.27 |
| German | 0.38 | 0.26 | 0.33 | 0.38 | **0.40** |
| Kannada | 0.24 | 0.29 | **0.30** | **0.30** | 0.29 |
| Navajo | 0.33 | 0.33 | 0.38 | 0.39 | **0.41** |
| Spanish | **0.39** | 0.24 | 0.29 | 0.30 | 0.31 |
| Turkish | **0.25** | 0.16 | 0.20 | 0.22 | 0.22 |

Table 3: F1 Scores for the baseline (BL) and the KMCE models on the test languages. The best F1 scores are in bold. Test languages were evaluated on KMCE models with clusters of size 500, 1000, 1500, and 1900.

to inform the initial set of centers. This could lead to quicker convergence of a model due to more intelligently picked centers. It could also prevent the model from being skewed towards less than ideal center values. Additionally, with pre-defined centers we can remove the need to arbitrarily define the number of clusters.

In the scope of this task, we were unable to experiment with pre-defined center values but we have proposed two potential methods for doing so: using longest common substrings and picking highly connected nodes from an LCS graph formation. The longest common substring approach would mimic the lemma identification approach described above (4.2). Both of these systems are represented as an optional lemma identification layer on the right hand side of Figure 1. The output of each one would be a set of words to use as centers. Each word would be converted to the appropriate word representation and then fed as an input to the KMeans clustering.

## 5 Results

Table 2 shows results to date. We compare the two representation methods on the development languages. The KMeans clusterings for the development languages were generated based on optimal cluster values starting with size 100 and increasing to a cluster size of 6000, or until the accuracy no longer improved from an increase in cluster size. For the Word2Vec embeddings we used clusterings of size 110 for Maltese, 130 for Persian, 1490 for Portuguese, 1490 for Russian, and 1490 for Swedish. With the character embeddings, we had 540 clusters for Maltese, 110 clusters for Persian, 2200 clusters for Portuguese, 4000 clusters for Russian, and 5400 clusters for Swedish. The F1 scores provided are based on comparing the appropriate model's predictions to the gold paradigms for this task using the evaluation function defined in the SIGMORPHON 2021 Task 2 github repository. The KMCE models clearly and consistently outperform the KMW2V models, for all development languages.

For test languages, we run clustering only with the better-performing character-based representations. The performance on test languages was evaluated with clusters of size 500, 1000, 1500, and 1900. These results are in Table 3. We found that our algorithm outperformed the baseline for Basque, German, Kannada, and Navajo. For both Basque and Kannada, the largest clustering did not have the highest result suggesting that the corpora provided for these languages contain a smaller number of morphological paradigms. In the case of Bulgarian, English, Spanish, and Finnish, we note that the KMCE model performance increases with each increase in cluster size. This suggests that the model accuracy would continue increasing if we ran the model for these languages with a higher number of clusters. Additional discussion of the error analysis appears in section 6, and fo the results in section 7.

## 6 Error Analysis

We have evaluated the results from the Word2Vec representations and our character-based embedding and compared them to the gold standard paradigms provided by the task organizers. We have found that, overall, the character-based version is more robust on regular verb forms than the Word2Vec version, and that neither is effective on irregular forms. Additionally, we explore some of the nuanced errors with the character based embeddings and how they could be addressed for future work.

### 6.1 Regular Verb Forms

Our results are consistent with our initial expectation that an orthographic word representation would perform better on regular verb forms than the Word2Vec representation, since it weights closeness based on the characters of the word. The character embedding correctly groups many surface forms together based on regular English morphological paradigms, or those that follow the pattern of *-ed* for past tense, *-s* for third person singular present, - $\varnothing$ for first, second and third person plural present. However, there were sometimes words missing from the paradigm. For example, the system generated the paradigm {*stumble, stumbles, stumbling*}. This should have included *stumbled*, but instead that is in a paradigm with *thaddaeus*. In contrast, the Word2Vec representation separates all four surface forms into different morphological paradigms. For Spanish paradigms, we see that the character embeddings perform well for matching some of the regular surface forms together, but cannot handle longer suffixes. For example, *aprendas, aprendan* and *aprenden* are grouped together while leaving out longer surface forms like *aprenderemos*. Similarly, *hablaste, hablaras, hablaran* and *hablara* are grouped in the same morphological paradigm, but *hablar, hablan, hablar, hables* and *hablen* are part of a separate grouping. We discuss the issue of errors related to word length in detail below.

### 6.2 Irregular Verb Forms

Because it focuses on semantic relatedness, we expected the Word2Vec representation to be more accurate in grouping together irregular surface forms from the same paradigm. For example, we have the paradigm for *go*: {*go, goes, going, went*}. In fact, Word2Vec created a morphological paradigm for *go*, one for {*upstairs, carry, goes, favour*}, {*going, reply, robbed, dared, gaius, failed, godless*}, and one for *went*. The orthographical representation also produced some undesired results, with a paradigm for { *eyes, goat, goes, gone, gong, else, eloi, noah, none, sons, long*} and {*gains, noisy, lasea, lysias, gates, lying, fatal, often, notes, loses, latin, latest, going*}. The other surface forms of *went* and *go* also ended up in separate morphological paradigms. These results suggest that neither representation is currently robust enough to handle irregular verb forms.

### 6.3 Character Distance Errors

In some cases, the character representations result in strange cluster formations due to the usage of Euclidean distance in the sklearn KMeans library. Since each character in the language's alphabet was mapped arbitrarily to a numeric value, the closeness of a pair of characters does not reflect a morphological relationship between those symbols. However, characters that are assigned to numerical values that are closer to one another will be classified as closer by the Euclidean distance algorithm. It would be possible to learn more about the language specific character relations by training a recurrent network with a focus on the character sequence alignments. This network could then be used as an encoder to generate character level embeddings.

### 6.4 Non-Affix Based Morphology

For verb forms in English that do not use a regular affixation paradigm, we find that some surface forms are paired together in the correct clusters, but those clusters often contain additional unrelated words. Consider the following group: {*drank, drinks, drink, drunk, breaks, break, branch*}. In this cluster, we see that *drank, drinks, drink* and *drunk* were all correctly identified as being related. The algorithm also matched *break* and *breaks* together. This suggests that character representations have the potential to identify morphological transformations that occur at different points in the word, as opposed to just prefixes or suffixes. However, the result is a combination of what should be three distinct morphological paradigms, including a unique paradigm for *branch*. In Navajo, *jidooleeł* and *dadooleeł* are correctly put in the same paradigm. However, this paradigm also includes *jidooleełgo* and *dadooleełgo*, which are not morphologically related. We also see the tendency of over-grouping in Basque, where *bitzate, nitzan*, and *ditzan* are all grouped together along with over ten other unrelated forms. This could potentially be addressed by increasing the number of clusters to favor smaller clusters. Adding semantic features to the word embeddings such as part of speech or limited context windows may also help filter out words that are not relevant to a particular paradigm.

### 6.5 Word Length

Another type of cluster error has to do with word length. The word representation vectors were sized based on the largest word present in a given language's corpus. If a word is under the maximum length, the remaining vector gets filled in with zeros. This means that words that are similar in length are more likely to be paired together for a cluster. The gold data created the morphological paradigm {*crowd, crowds, crowding*}, while ours created two separate clusterings: {*crowd, crowds*} and {*brawling, proposal, crowding*}. This is also present in the clustering of certain words in Navajo. Our algorithm grouped *nizaad*, and *bizaad* together, but some of the longer forms in this paradigm were excluded such as *danihizaad* and *nihizaad*. In future work, we would attempt to mitigate this by using subword distances or cosine similarity as the basis for distance metrics in a clustering algorithm. This could prevent inaccurate groupings due to large affix lengths.

## 7 Discussion, Conclusions, Future Work

Overall, these results demonstrate an improvement over the baseline in several languages, namely Persian, Swedish, Basque, Germany, Kannada, and Navajo, when using KMeans clustering over character embeddings. This suggests that embedding-based clustering systems merit further exploration as a potential approach to unsupervised problems in morphology. The fact that the character embedding system outperformed the W2V one and the fact that performance was strongest on words with regular inflectional paradigms suggests that this approach might be best suited to synthetic and agglutinating languages in which morphology is encoded fairly simply within the orthography of the word. Languages that rely heavily on more complex morphological processes, particularly non-concatenative morphology, would likely require an extension of this system that integrates more sources of non-orthographic information, or a different approach all together.

One obvious avenue for building on this research is to find more efficient and more effective methods for the initial process of lemma identification. Developing a set of lemmas would allow a pre-defined set of centers to be fed into the clustering algorithm rather than using randomly defined centers, which would likely improve performance. This could be done by leveraging an initial rule based analysis or through the threshold-based graph clustering technique discussed above. Other potential variations on that approach, once the problem of computational limits has been solved, include using longest common sequences rather than longest common substrings, and weighting graph edges by the length of the LCS between the two words. The former would potentially help accommodate forms of non-concatenative morphology, while the latter would potentially include more information about morphological relationships than an unweighted graph does. Future research should also explore how other sources of linguistic information could be leveraged for this task. This could include other forms of semantic information outside of the context-based semantics used by W2V, as well as things like the orthographic-phonetic correspondences in a given language.

Finally, we would like to explore filtering of the output clusters according to language-specific properties in order to improve the overall results.This would involve adding additional layers to our system architecture that take place after a distance-based clustering. One such layer could prune unlikely clusters based off of a morphological transformations, such as the method used by Soricut and Och (2015). Future unsupervised systems for clustering morphological paradigms should consider the benefits of hierarchical models that leverage different algorithm types to gain the most information possible.

## References


Piotr Bojanowski, Edouard Grave, Armand Joulin, and Tomas Mikolov. 2016. Enriching word vectors with subword information.

Alexander Erdmann, Micha Elsner, Shijie Wu, Ryan Cotterell, and Nizar Habash. 2020. The paradigm discovery problem. In *Proceedings of the 58th Annual Meeting of the Association for Computational Linguistics*, pages 7778–7790, Online. Association for Computational Linguistics.

Alexander Erdmann and Nizar Habash. 2018. Complementary strategies for low resourced morphological modeling. In *Proceedings of the Fifteenth Workshop on Computational Research in Phonetics, Phonology, and Morphology*, pages 54–65, Brussels, Belgium. Association for Computational Linguistics.

Katharina Kann. 2020. Acquisition of inflectional morphology in artificial neural networks with prior knowledge. In *Proceedings of the Society for Computation in Linguistics 2020*, pages 144–154, New

York, New York. Association for Computational Linguistics.

MacQueen, J, and author. 1967. Some methods for classification and analysis of multivariate observations. In *Proceedings of the Fifth Berkeley Symposium on Mathematical Statistics and Probability, Volume 1: Statistics*, pages 281–297. University of California Press.

Arya D. McCarthy, Rachel Wicks, Dylan Lewis, Aaron Mueller, Winston Wu, Oliver Adams, Garrett Nicolai, Matt Post, and David Yarowsky. 2020. The Johns Hopkins University Bible corpus: 1600+ tongues for typological exploration. In *Proceedings of the 12th Language Resources and Evaluation Conference*, pages 2884–2892, Marseille, France. European Language Resources Association.

Garrett Nicolai, Kyle Gorman, and Ryan Cotterell, editors. 2020. *Proceedings of the 17th SIGMORPHON Workshop on Computational Research in Phonetics, Phonology, and Morphology*. Association for Computational Linguistics, Online.

F. Pedregosa, G. Varoquaux, A. Gramfort, V. Michel, B. Thirion, O. Grisel, M. Blondel, P. Prettenhofer, R. Weiss, V. Dubourg, J. Vanderplas, A. Passos, D. Cournapeau, M. Brucher, M. Perrot, and E. Duchesnay. 2011. Scikit-learn: Machine learning in Python. *Journal of Machine Learning Research*, 12:2825–2830.

Radu Soricut and Franz Och. 2015. Unsupervised morphology induction using word embeddings. In *Proceedings of the 2015 Conference of the North American Chapter of the Association for Computational Linguistics: Human Language Technologies*, pages 1627–1637, Denver, Colorado. Association for Computational Linguistics.

Radim Řehůřek and Petr Sojka. 2010. Software framework for topic modelling with large corpora. In *Proceedings of LREC 2010 workshop New Challenges for NLP Frameworks*, pages 46–50, Valletta, Malta. University of Malta.

# Unsupervised Paradigm Clustering Using Transformation Rules

Changbing Yang[♣] Garrett Nicolai[♠] Miikka Silfverberg[♠]
[♣]University of Colorado Boulder [♠]University of British Columbia
changbing.yang@colorado.edu first.last@ubc.ca

## Abstract

This paper describes the submission of the CU-UBC team for the SIGMORPHON 2021 Shared Task 2: Unsupervised morphological paradigm clustering. Our system generates paradigms using morphological transformation rules which are discovered from raw data. We experiment with two methods for discovering rules. Our first approach generates prefix and suffix transformations between similar strings. Secondly, we experiment with more general rules which can apply transformations inside the input strings in addition to prefix and suffix transformations. We find that the best overall performance is delivered by prefix and suffix rules but more general transformation rules perform better for languages with templatic morphology and very high morpheme-to-word ratios.

## 1 Introduction

Supervised sequence-to-sequence models for word inflection have delivered impressive results in the past few years and a number of shared tasks on supervised learning of morphology have helped to raise the state of the art of this task (Cotterell et al., 2016, 2017, 2018; McCarthy et al., 2019; Vylomova et al., 2020). In contrast, unsupervised approaches to morphology have received far less attention in recent years. Nevertheless, the question of whether the morphological system of a language can be discovered from raw text data alone is certainly an interesting one.

This paper describes the submission of the CU-UBC team for the SIGMORPHON 2021 Shared Task 2: Unsupervised morphological paradigm clustering (Wiemerslage et al., 2021).[1] The objective of this task is to group the distinct inflected forms of lexemes occurring in a corpus into morphological paradigms. Figure 1 illustrates the task.

Our system generates paradigms using *morphological transformation rules* which are discovered from raw data. As an example, consider the rule **ed** → **ing**, which maps an English past tense verb form like **walked** into the present participle **walking**. In this paper, we use *regular expressions of symbol-pairs* (that is, regular relations) in the well-known Xerox formalism (Beesley and Karttunen, 2003) to denote rules: for example, `?+ e:i d:n 0:g`. These rule can be applied using composition of regular relations:

`[w a l k e d] .o. [?+ e:i d:n 0:g]`

will result in an output form `w a l k i n g`. We cluster forms into the same paradigm if we can find morphological transformation rules which map one of the forms into the other. Our approach is illustrated in Figure 2.

We experiment with two methods for discovering rules, described in Section 3.3. Our first approach is inspired by work on morphology discovery by Soricut and Och (2015), who generate *prefix and suffix transformations* between similar strings. This idea closely parallels our approach for extracting rules. Unlike Soricut and Och (2015), however, we do not utilize word embeddings when extracting rules due to the very small size of the shared task datasets. In addition to prefix and suffix rules, we also experiment with more general *discontinuous transformation rules* which can apply transformations to infixes as well as prefixes and suffixes. For example, the rule

`?+ i:0 ?+ e:i ?+ 0:t`

would transform the input form **gidem** ('to bite' in Maltese) to **gdimt**. Our results

[1]`github.com/changbingY/Sigmorph-2021-task2`



*Proceedings of the Seventeenth SIGMORPHON Workshop on Computational Research in Phonetics, Phonology, and Morphology*, pages 98–106

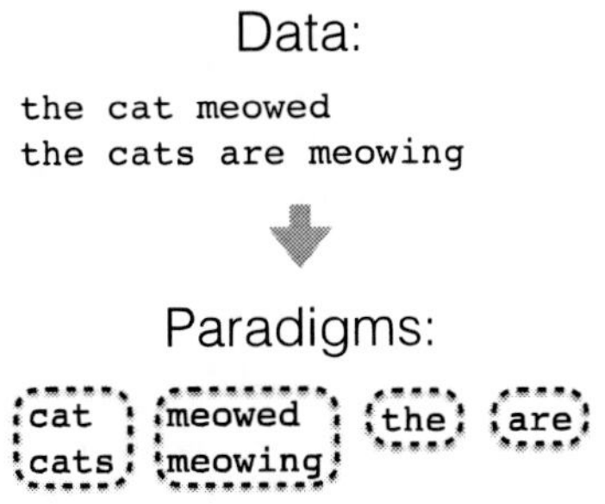


Figure 1: The unsupervised paradigm clustering task.

demonstrate that prefix and suffix rules deliver stronger performance for most languages in the shared task dataset but our more general transformations rules are beneficial for templatic languages like Maltese and languages with a high morpheme-to-word ratio like Basque.

## 2 Related Work

The unsupervised paradigm clustering task is closely related to the 2020 SIGMORPHON shared task on unsupervised morphological paradigm completion (Kann et al., 2020). However, paradigm clustering systems do not infer missing forms in paradigms. Our system resembles the baseline system for the paradigm completion task (Jin et al., 2020) which also extracts transformation rules, however, in the form of edit trees (Chrupala et al., 2008).

Several approaches to unsupervised or minimally supervised morphology learning, which share characteristics with our system, have been proposed. Our rules are essentially identical to the FST rules used by Beemer et al. (2020) for the task of supervised morphological inflection. Likewise, Durrett and DeNero (2013) and Ahlberg et al. (2015) both extract inflectional rules after aligning forms from known paradigms. Yarowsky and Wicentowski (2000) also generate rules for morphological transformations but their system for minimally supervised morphological analysis requires additional information in the form of a list of morphemes as input.

Erdmann et al. (2020) present a task called *the paradigm discovery problem* which is quite similar to the unsupervised paradigm clustering task. In their formulation of the task, inflected forms are clustered into paradigms and corresponding forms in distinct paradigms (like all plural forms of English nouns) are clustered into cells. Their benchmark system is based on splitting every form into a (potentially discontinuous) base and exponent, where the base is the longest common subsequence of the forms in a paradigm and the exponent is the residual of the form. They then maximize the base in each paradigm while minimizing the exponents of individual forms.

## 3 Methods

This section describes how we extract rules from the dataset and apply them to paradigm clustering. We also describe methods for filtering out extraneous forms from generated paradigms.

### 3.1 Baseline

As a baseline, we use the character n-gram clustering method provided by the shared task organizers (Wiemerslage et al., 2021). Here all forms sharing a given substring of length $n$ are clustered into a paradigm. Duplicate paradigms are removed. The hyperparameter $n$ can be tuned on validation data if such data is available (we use $n = 5$ in all our experiments).

### 3.2 Transformation rules

Our approach builds on the baseline paradigms discovered in the previous step. We start by extracting transformation rules between all word forms in a single baseline paradigm. For each pair of strings like **dog** and **dogs** belonging to a paradigm, we generate a rule like `?+ 0:s` which translates the first form into the second one. From a paradigm of size $n$, we can therefore extract $n^2 - n$ rules—one for each ordered pair of distinct word forms. Preliminary experiments showed that large baseline paradigms tended to generate many incorrect rules which did not represent genuine morphological transformations. We, therefore, limited rule-discovery to paradigms spanning maximally 20 forms.

After generating transformation rules, we compute rule-frequency over all baseline paradigms and discard rare rules which are unlikely to represent genuine morphological transformations (the minimum threshold for rule frequency is a hyperparameter). The remaining rules are then applied iteratively to

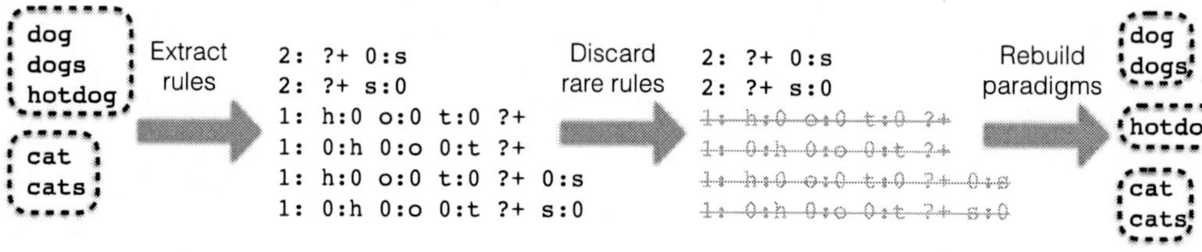


Figure 2: A schematic representation of our approach. We start by generating preliminary paradigms using the baseline method. We then extract transformation rules for each word pair in our paradigms noting how many times each unique rule occurred. For example, here both (**dog**, **dogs**) and (**cat**, **cats**) result in a rule `?* 0:s` which therefore has count 2. Subsequently, we discard rare rules like `h:0 o:0 t:0 ?*` which are unlikely to represent genuine morphological transformations. We then use the remaining rules to reconstruct our morphological paradigms as explained in Section 3.3.

our datasets to construct paradigms. We experiment with two rule types which are described below.

### 3.2.1 Prefix and Suffix Rules

Our first approach to rule-discovery is based on identifying a contiguous word stem shared by both forms. The stem is defined as the longest common substring of the forms. We split both forms into a prefix, stem and suffix. The morphological transformation is then defined as a joint substitution of a prefix and suffix. For example, given the German forms **acker+n** and **ge+acker+t** (German 'to plow'), we would generate a rule:

`0:g 0:e ?+ n:t`

As mentioned above, these rules are extracted from paradigms generated by the baseline system.

We also experiment with a more restricted form of these rules in which only suffix transformations are allowed. While this limits the possible transformations, it will also result in fewer incorrect rules and may, therefore, deliver better performance for languages which are predominantly suffixing.

### 3.2.2 Discontinuous rules

Even though prefix and suffix transformations are adequate for representing morphological transformations in many languages, they fail to derive the appropriate generalizations for languages with templatic morphology like Maltese (which was included among the development languages). For example, it is impossible to identify a contiguous stem-like unit spanning more than a single character for the Maltese forms **gidem** 'to bite' and **gdimt**. We need a rule which can apply transformations inside the input string:

`?+ i:0 ?+ e:i ?+ 0:t`

Like prefix and suffix rules, discontinuous rules are generated from baseline paradigms. Unlike prefix and suffix rules, however, discontinuous rules require a character-level alignment between the input and output string. To this end, we start by generating a dataset consisting of all string pairs like (**dog**, **dogs**) and (**hotdog**, **dog**), where both strings belong to the the same paradigm. We then apply a character-level aligner based on the iterative Markov chain Monte Carlo method to this dataset.[2] Using this method, we can jointly align all string pairs in the baseline paradigms. This is beneficial because the MCMC aligner will prefer common substitutions, deletions and insertions over rare ones.[3] which enforces consistency of the alignment over the entire dataset. This in turn can help us find linguistically motivated transformation rules.

Character-level alignment results in pairs:

| | | | | | | |
|---|---|---|---|---|---|---|
| INPUT: | d | o | g | 0 | | |
| OUTPUT: | d | o | g | s | | |
| INPUT: | h | o | t | d | o | g |
| OUTPUT: | 0 | 0 | 0 | d | o | g |

Each symbol pair in the alignment represents one of the following types: (1) an identity pair `x:x`, (2) an insertion `0:x`, (3) a deletion `x:0`, or (4) a substitution `x:y`. In order to convert a pair of aligned strings into a transformation

[2] This aligner was initially used for the baseline system in the 2016 iteration of the SIGMORPHON shared task (Cotterell et al., 2016).

[3] This is a consequence of the fact that the algorithm iteratively maximizes the likelihood of the alignment for each example given all other examples in the dataset.

rule, we simply replace all contiguous sequences of identity pairs with `?+`. For the alignments above, we get the rules: `?+ 0:s` and `h:0 o:0 t:0 ?+`.

### 3.3 Iterative Application of Rules

After extracting a set of rules from baseline paradigms, we discard the baseline paradigms. We then construct new paradigms using our rules. We start by picking a random word form $w$ from the dataset. We then form the paradigm $P$ for $w$ as the set of all forms in our dataset which can be derived from $w$ by applying our rules iteratively. For example, given the form **eats** and the rules:

`?+ s:0` and `?+ 0:i 0:n 0:g`

the paradigm of **eats** would contain both **eat** (generated by the first rule) and **eating** (generated by the second rule from **eats**) provided that both of these forms are present in our original dataset. All forms in $P$ are removed from the dataset and we then repeat the process for another randomly sampled form in the remaining dataset. This continues until the dataset is exhausted. The procedure is sensitive to the order in which we sample forms from the dataset but exploring the optimal way to sample forms falls beyond the scope of the present work.

For prefix and suffix rules, we limit rule application to a single iteration because this delivered better results in practice. Applying rules iteratively tended to result in very large paradigms. For discontinuous rules, we do apply rules iteratively.

### 3.4 Filtering Paradigms

According to our preliminary experiments, many large paradigms generated by transformation rules contained word forms which were morphologically unrelated to the other forms in the paradigm. To counteract this, we experimented with three strategies for filtering out individual extraneous forms from generated paradigms: the degree test, the rule-frequency test and the embedding-similarity test. Forms which fail all of our three tests are removed from the paradigm.[4]

[4]These filtering strategies are applied to paradigms containing > 20 forms. This threshold was determined based on examining the output clusters for the development languages.

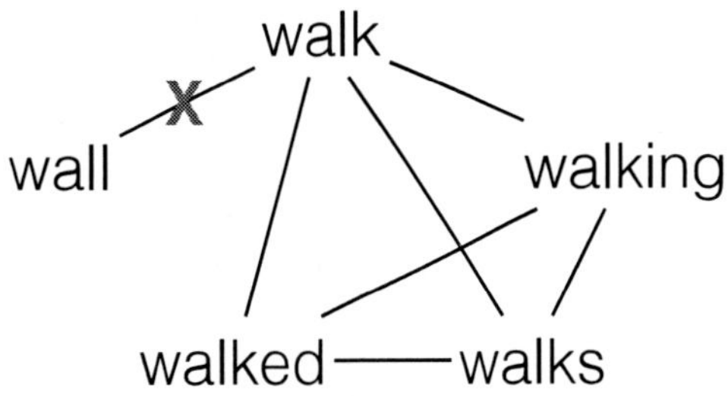


Figure 3: Given the candidate paradigm {**walk**, **wall**, **walking**, **walked**, **walks**}, we can form a graph where two word forms are connected if a rule like `?+ 0:e 0:d` derives one of the forms like **walked** from the other one **walk**. We experiment with filtering out forms which have low degree in this graph since those are more likely to be spurious additions resulting from rules like `?+ l:k` in the example, which do not capture genuine morphological regularities. In this example, **wall** might be filtered out because it has low degree one compared to all other forms which have degree three.

If we first generate all paradigms and then filter out extraneous forms, we will be left with a number of forms which have not been assigned to a paradigm. In order to circumvent this problem, we apply filtering immediately after generating each individual paradigm. Forms which are filtered out from the paradigm are placed back into the original dataset. They can then be included in paradigms which are generated later in the process.

**Degree test** Our morphological transformation rules induce dependencies and therefore a graph structure between the forms in a paradigm as demonstrated in Figure 3. Within each paradigm, we calculate the degree of a word in the following way: For each attested word $w$ in the generated paradigm, its degree is the number of forms $w'$ in the paradigm for which we can find a transformation rule mapping $w \rightarrow w'$. We increment the degree if there is at least one edge between words $w$ and $w'$ in the paradigm (the number of distinct rules mapping form $w$ to $w'$ is irrelevant here as long as there is at least one). *If the degree of a word is less than a third of the paradigm size, the word fails the degree test.*

**Rule-Frequency test** Some rules like `?+ e:i d:n 0:g` for English represent genuine inflectional transformations and will therefore occur often in our datasets. Others, like the rule `?* 1:k` in Figure 3, instead result from coincidence, and will usually have low frequency. We can, therefore, use rule frequency as a criterion when identifying extraneous forms in generated paradigms. We examine the cumulative frequency of all rules applying to the form in our paradigm. *If this frequency is lower than the median cumulative frequency in the paradigm, the form fails the rule-frequency test.*

**Embedding-similarity test** If a word fails to pass the degree and the rule frequency tests, we will measure the semantic similarity of the given form with other forms in the paradigm. To this end, we trained FastText embeddings (Bojanowski et al., 2017) and calculated cosine similarity between embedding vectors as a measure of semantic relatedness.[5] We start by selecting two reference words in the paradigm which have high degree (at least 50% of the maximal degree) and whose cumulative rule frequency is above the paradigm's median value. We then compute their cosine similarity as a reference point $r$. For all other words in the paradigm, we then compare their cosine similarity $r'$ to one of the reference forms. *Forms fail the embedding-similarity test if* $r' < 0.5$ *and* $r - r' > 0.3$.

## 4 Experiments and Results

In this section, we describe experiments on the shared task development and test languages.

### 4.1 Data and Resources

The shared task uses two data resources. Corpus data for the four development languages (Maltese, Persian, Russian and Swedish) and nine test languages (Basque Bulgarian, English, Finnish, German, Kannada, Navajo, Spanish and Turkish) are sourced from the Johns Hopkins Bible Corpus (McCarthy et al., 2020b). For most of the languages, complete Bibles were provided but for some of them, we only had access to a subset (see Wiemerslage et al. (2021) for details). Gold standard paradigms were automatically generated using the Unimorph 3.0 database (McCarthy et al., 2020a).

[5]We train 300-dimensional embeddings with context window 3 and use character $n$-grams of size 3-6.

### 4.2 Experiments on validation languages

Since our transformation rules are generated from paradigms discovered by the baseline system, which contain incorrect items, it is to be expected that some incorrect rules are generated. We filter out infrequent rules, as they are less likely to represent genuine morphological transformations. For prefix and suffix rules (i.e., *PS*), we experimented with including the top 2000 (PS-2000), 5000 (PS-5000), and all rules (PS-all), as measured by rule-frequency. Additionally, we present experiments using a system which relies exclusively on suffix transformations including all of them regardless of frequency (S-all). For discontinuous rules (*D*), we used lower thresholds because our preliminary experiments indicated that incorrect generalizations were a more severe problem for this rule type. We selected the 200 (D-200), 300 (D-300), and 500 (D-500) most frequent rules, respectively. Results with regard to best-match F1 score (see Wiemerslage et al. (2021) for details) are shown in Table 1.

According to the results, all of our systems outperform the baseline system by at least 25.53% as measured using the mean best match F1 score. Plain suffix rules (S-all) provide the best performance with a mean F1 score of 65.41%, followed by other affixal systems (PS-2000, PS-5000 and PS-all). On average, discontinuous rules (D-200, D-300 and D-500) are slightly less-successful, but they deliver the best performance for Maltese. Table 1 demonstrates that simply increasing the number of rules does not always contribute to better performance—the optimal threshold varies between languages.

As explained in Section 3.4, we aim to filter out extraneous forms from overly-large paradigms. We applied this approach to discontinuous rules with a 500 threshold. Results are shown in Table 2. As the table shows, a filtering strategy can offer very limited improvements. Most of the languages do not benefit from this approach and even for languages which do, the gain is miniscule. Due to their very limited effect, we did not apply filtering strategies to test languages.

|  | **Maltese** | **Persian** | **Portuguese** | **Russian** | **Swedish** | **Mean** |
|---|---|---|---|---|---|---|
| Baseline | 29.07 | 30.04 | 34.15 | 36.30 | 43.62 | 34.64 |
| PS-2000 | 35.41 | 50.17 | 65.53 | 81.20 | **81.14** | 62.69 |
| PS-5000 | 36.81 | 50.40 | 71.33 | **81.96** | 79.82 | 64.06 |
| PS-all | 40.67 | 53.15 | 76.63 | 75.39 | 72.46 | 63.66 |
| S-all | 30.32 | 52.69 | **82.67** | 80.65 | 80.74 | **65.41** |
| D-200 | 42.99 | **54.65** | 66.86 | 70.38 | 68.76 | 60.73 |
| D-300 | 42.99 | 53.64 | 69.38 | 72.33 | 67.14 | 61.10 |
| D-500 | **45.05** | 51.82 | 66.37 | 75.26 | 62.30 | 60.16 |

Table 1: F1 Scores for each of the model types on all development languages. The best F1 scores are in bold.

|  | **Maltese** | **Persian** | **Portuguese** | **Russian** | **Swedish** | **Mean** |
|---|---|---|---|---|---|---|
| Baseline | 29.07 | 30.04 | 34.15 | 36.30 | 43.62 | 34.64 |
| D-500 | 45.05 | 51.82 | 66.37 | 75.26 | 62.30 | 60.16 |
| Filter | 45.05 | 51.82 | **66.45** | 75.26 | 62.30 | **60.18** |

Table 2: F1 score for Discontinuous rules systems and Filtering systems across five validation languages.

### 4.3 Experiments on Test Languages

Results for the test languages are presented in Table 3. We find that all of our systems surpassed the baseline results by at least 23.06% in F1 score. The prefix and suffix system using all of the suffix rules displays the best performance with an F1 score of 66.12%. Among the discontinuous systems, the system with a threshold of 500 has the best results. On average, the affixal systems outperform the discontinuous ones. In particular, these methods perform best on languages which are known to be predominantly suffixing, such as English, Spanish, and Finnish. Contrarily, discontinuous rules deliver the best performance for Navajo—a strongly prefixing language. Discontinuous rules also result in the best performance for Basque, which has a very high morpheme-to-word ratio.

In order to better understand the behavior of our systems, we analyzed the distribution of the size of generated paradigms for prefix and suffix systems as well as discontinuous systems. Results for selected systems are shown in Figure 4. We conducted this experiment for the overall best system (S-all), as well as the best discontinuous system (D-500). Both systems follow the same overall pattern: large paradigms are rarer than smaller ones and the frequency drops very rapidly with increasing paradigm size. The majority of generated paradigms have sizes in the range 1-5. Although the tendency is similar for suffix rules and discontinuous rules, discontinuous rules tend to generate more paradigms of size 1. In contrast to the paradigms generated by our systems, the frequency of gold standard paradigms drops far slower as the paradigms grow. For example, for Finnish and Kannada, paradigms containing 10 forms are still very common. The only language where the distribution generated by our systems very closely parallels the gold standard is Spanish. For all other languages, our systems very clearly over-generate small paradigms.

## 5 Discussion and Conclusions

Paradigm construction can suffer from two main difficulties: overgeneralization, and underspecification. In the former, paradigms are too generous when adding new members. Consider, for example, a paradigm headed by "sea". We would want to include the plural "seas", but not the unrelated words "seal", "seals", "undersea", etc. Contrarily, a paradigm selection algorithm that is overly selective will result in a large number of small paradigms - less than ideal in a morphologically-dense language.

Considering the results described in the previous section, we note that our two best models skew towards conservatism - they prefer smaller paradigms. This is likely an artifact of our development cycle - we found that the baseline preferred large paradigms, often capturing derivational features, or even circumstantial

| | English | Navajo | Spanish | Finnish | Bulgarian | Basque | Kannada | German | Turkish | Mean |
|---|---|---|---|---|---|---|---|---|---|---|
| Baseline | 51.49 | 33.25 | 38.83 | 28.97 | 38.89 | 21.48 | 23.79 | 38.22 | 25.23 | 33.35 |
| PS-2000 | 83.89 | 48.69 | 77.71 | 52.60 | 73.50 | 25.81 | 42.35 | **74.49** | 46.80 | 58.42 |
| PS-5000 | 81.16 | 48.69 | 79.60 | 57.88 | 74.14 | 29.03 | 47.47 | 74.27 | 51.26 | 60.39 |
| PS-all | 76.41 | 48.69 | 76.94 | 66.03 | 69.50 | 29.03 | 57.71 | 65.26 | 60.97 | 61.17 |
| S-all | **88.68** | 42.48 | **83.21** | **73.42** | **76.96** | 29.03 | **59.34** | 74.18 | **67.80** | **66.12** |
| D-200 | 76.93 | 58.45 | 66.05 | 50.68 | 70.48 | 26.19 | 40.57 | 70.26 | 48.05 | 56.41 |
| D-300 | 73.23 | 59.36 | 69.46 | 53.66 | 69.39 | 26.19 | 43.71 | 68.52 | 51.00 | 57.17 |
| D-500 | 69.33 | **61.66** | 69.92 | 56.51 | 63.23 | **33.33** | 46.94 | 62.54 | 53.24 | 57.41 |

Table 3: F1 Scores for each of the model types on all test languages. The best F1 scores are in bold.

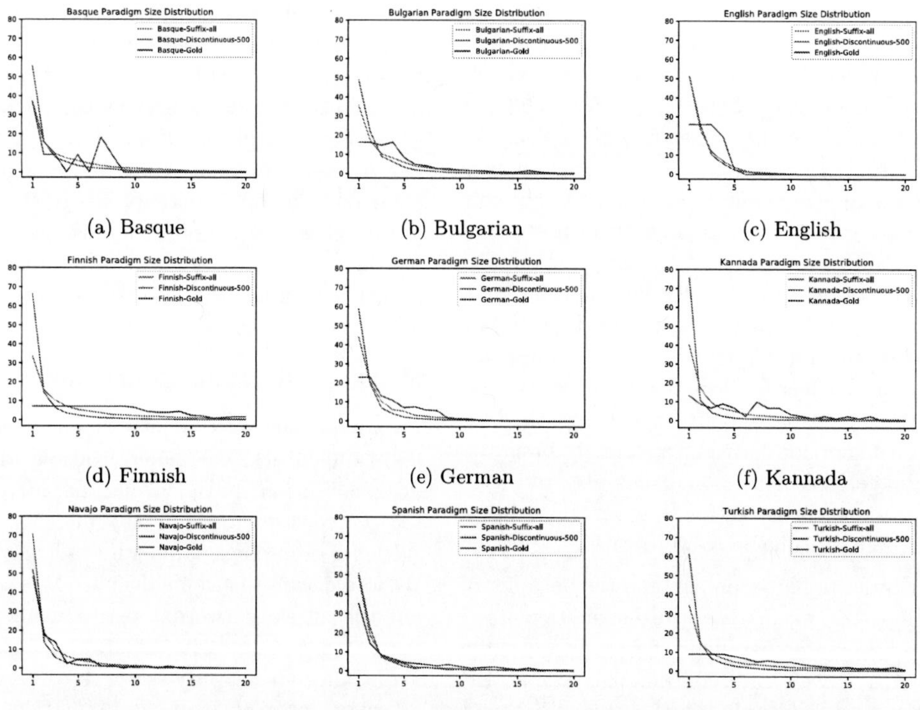


(a) Basque (b) Bulgarian (c) English

(d) Finnish (e) German (f) Kannada

(g) Navajo (h) Spanish (i) Turkish

Figure 4: Paradigm size distribution across nine test languages. The x axis stands for paradigm size ranging from 1 to 20. The y axis shows the percentage of each paradigm size accounts for among all paradigms the system generates.

string similarities, when clustering paradigms. Much of our focus was thus on limiting rule application only to those rules we could be certain were genuine. Unfortunately, this means that many words are excluded, residing in singleton paradigms.

Our methods were also affected by the choice of development languages. Of these languages, only one (Persian) is agglutinating, and none of the authors can read the script, so it had a smaller impact on the evolution of our methods. We believe that several languages —namely, Finnish, Turkish, and Basque— could have benefited from iterative rule application; however, the iterative process was not selected after seeing a degradation (due to overgeneralization) on the development languages.

It is also worth discussing two outliers in our system selection. Our suffix-first model performed very well on all of the development languages except Maltese. This is not surprising, given its templatic morphology. Maltese inspired the creation of our discontinuous rule set, and indeed, these rules outperformed the suffixes for Maltese. Switching to the test languages, we see that this model has higher performance for Navajo and Basque –two languages that are rarely described as templatic. We observe, however, that both languages make heavy use of *prefixing*. Note in Table 2 that including prefixes (PS-All) significantly improves Navajo: the only language to see such a benefit. Likewise, Navajo also has significant stem alternation, which may be benefiting from discontinuous rule sets. Basque is trickier - it does not improve simply from including prefixal rules. Upon closer inspection, we observe that much Basque prefixation more closely resembles *circumfixation*: the stem has a prefixal vowel to indicate tense, which is jointly applied with inflectional suffixes. One round of rule application - even if it includes both suffixes and prefixes, appears to be insufficient.

There is still plenty of ground to be covered, with the mean F1 score below 70%. We believe that the next step lies in re-establishing a bottom-up construction for those paradigms that our methods currently separate into small sub-paradigms. Our methods predict roughly twice to 3 times as many singleton paradigms as exist in the gold data, and there is not significant rule support to combine them. Possible areas for exploration include iterative rule extraction on successively more correct paradigms, or the incorporation of a machine learning element that can predict missing forms.

In this paper, we have presented a method for automatically building inflectional paradigms from raw data. Starting with an $n$-gram baseline, we extract intra-paradigmatic rewrite rules. These rules are then re-applied to the corpus in a discovery process that re-establishes known paradigms. Our methods prove very competitive, with our best model finishing within 2% of the best submitted system.

## References


Malin Ahlberg, Markus Forsberg, and Mans Hulden. 2015. Paradigm classification in supervised learning of morphology. In *Proceedings of the 2015 Conference of the North American Chapter of the Association for Computational Linguistics: Human Language Technologies*, pages 1024–1029.

Sarah Beemer, Zak Boston, April Bukoski, Daniel Chen, Princess Dickens, Andrew Gerlach, Torin Hopkins, Parth Anand Jawale, Chris Koski, Akanksha Malhotra, Piyush Mishra, Saliha Muradoglu, Lan Sang, Tyler Short, Sagarika Shreevastava, Elizabeth Spaulding, Testumichi Umada, Beilei Xiang, Changbing Yang, and Mans Hulden. 2020. Linguist vs. machine: Rapid development of finite-state morphological grammars. In *Proceedings of the 17th SIGMORPHON Workshop on Computational Research in Phonetics, Phonology, and Morphology*, pages 162–170, Online. Association for Computational Linguistics.

Kenneth R Beesley and Lauri Karttunen. 2003. Finite-state morphology: Xerox tools and techniques. *CSLI, Stanford.*

Piotr Bojanowski, Edouard Grave, Armand Joulin, and Tomas Mikolov. 2017. Enriching word vectors with subword information. *Transactions of the Association for Computational Linguistics*, 5:135–146.

Grzegorz Chrupala, Georgiana Dinu, and Josef van Genabith. 2008. Learning morphology with Morfette. In *Proceedings of the Sixth International Conference on Language Resources and Evaluation (LREC'08)*, Marrakech, Morocco. European Language Resources Association (ELRA).

Ryan Cotterell, Christo Kirov, John Sylak-Glassman, Géraldine Walther, Ekaterina Vylomova, Arya D McCarthy, Katharina Kann, Sebastian J Mielke, Garrett Nicolai, Miikka Silfverberg, et al. 2018. The CoNLL–SIGMORPHON 2018 shared task: Universal morphological reinflection. In *Proceedings of the CoNLL–SIGMORPHON 2018 Shared Task: Universal Morphological Reinflection*, pages 1–27.

Ryan Cotterell, Christo Kirov, John Sylak-Glassman, Géraldine Walther, Ekaterina Vylomova, Patrick Xia, Manaal Faruqui, Sandra Kübler, David Yarowsky, Jason Eisner, et al. 2017. Conll-sigmorphon 2017 shared task: Universal morphological reinflection in 52 languages. In *Proceedings of the CoNLL SIGMORPHON 2017 Shared Task: Universal Morphological Reinflection*, pages 1–30.

Ryan Cotterell, Christo Kirov, John Sylak-Glassman, David Yarowsky, Jason Eisner, and Mans Hulden. 2016. The SIGMORPHON 2016 shared task—morphological reinflection. In *Proceedings of the 14th SIGMORPHON Workshop on Computational Research in Phonetics, Phonology, and Morphology*, pages 10–22.

Greg Durrett and John DeNero. 2013. Supervised learning of complete morphological paradigms. In *Proceedings of the 2013 Conference of the North American Chapter of the Association for Computational Linguistics: Human Language Technologies*, pages 1185–1195.

Alexander Erdmann, Micha Elsner, Shijie Wu, Ryan Cotterell, and Nizar Habash. 2020. The paradigm discovery problem. In *Proceedings of the 58th Annual Meeting of the Association for Computational Linguistics*, pages 7778–7790, Online. Association for Computational Linguistics.

Huiming Jin, Liwei Cai, Yihui Peng, Chen Xia, Arya McCarthy, and Katharina Kann. 2020. Unsupervised morphological paradigm completion. In *Proceedings of the 58th Annual Meeting of the Association for Computational Linguistics*, pages 6696–6707, Online. Association for Computational Linguistics.

Katharina Kann, Arya D. McCarthy, Garrett Nicolai, and Mans Hulden. 2020. The SIGMORPHON 2020 shared task on unsupervised morphological paradigm completion. In *Proceedings of the 17th SIGMORPHON Workshop on Computational Research in Phonetics, Phonology, and Morphology*, pages 51–62, Online. Association for Computational Linguistics.

Arya D. McCarthy, Christo Kirov, Matteo Grella, Amrit Nidhi, Patrick Xia, Kyle Gorman, Ekaterina Vylomova, Sabrina J. Mielke, Garrett Nicolai, Miikka Silfverberg, Timofey Arkhangelskiy, Nataly Krizhanovsky, Andrew Krizhanovsky, Elena Klyachko, Alexey Sorokin, John Mansfield, Valts Ernštreits, Yuval Pinter, Cassandra L. Jacobs, Ryan Cotterell, Mans Hulden, and David Yarowsky. 2020a. UniMorph 3.0: Universal Morphology. In *Proceedings of the 12th Language Resources and Evaluation Conference*, pages 3922–3931, Marseille, France. European Language Resources Association.

Arya D McCarthy, Ekaterina Vylomova, Shijie Wu, Chaitanya Malaviya, Lawrence Wolf-Sonkin, Garrett Nicolai, Christo Kirov, Miikka Silfverberg, Sabrina J Mielke, Jeffrey Heinz, et al. 2019. The SIGMORPHON 2019 shared task: Morphological analysis in context and cross-lingual transfer for inflection. In *Proceedings of the 16th Workshop on Computational Research in Phonetics, Phonology, and Morphology*, pages 229–244.

Arya D. McCarthy, Rachel Wicks, Dylan Lewis, Aaron Mueller, Winston Wu, Oliver Adams, Garrett Nicolai, Matt Post, and David Yarowsky. 2020b. The Johns Hopkins University Bible corpus: 1600+ tongues for typological exploration. In *Proceedings of the 12th Language Resources and Evaluation Conference*, pages 2884–2892, Marseille, France. European Language Resources Association.

Radu Soricut and Franz Och. 2015. Unsupervised morphology induction using word embeddings. In *Proceedings of the 2015 Conference of the North American Chapter of the Association for Computational Linguistics: Human Language Technologies*, pages 1627–1637, Denver, Colorado. Association for Computational Linguistics.

Ekaterina Vylomova, Jennifer White, Elizabeth Salesky, Sabrina J Mielke, Shijie Wu, Edoardo Ponti, Rowan Hall Maudslay, Ran Zmigrod, Josef Valvoda, Svetlana Toldova, et al. 2020. SIGMORPHON 2020 shared task 0: Typologically diverse morphological inflection. *SIGMORPHON 2020*.

Adam Wiemerslage, Arya McCarthy, Alexander Erdmann, Garrett Nicolai, Manex Agirrezabal, Miikka Silfverberg, Mans Hulden, and Katharina Kann. 2021. The SIGMORPHON 2021 shared task on unsupervised morphological paradigm clustering. In *Proceedings of the 18th SIGMORPHON Workshop on Computational Research in Phonetics, Phonology, and Morphology*. Association for Computational Linguistics.

David Yarowsky and Richard Wicentowski. 2000. Minimally supervised morphological analysis by multimodal alignment. In *Proceedings of the 38th Annual Meeting of the Association for Computational Linguistics*, pages 207–216, Hong Kong. Association for Computational Linguistics.

# Paradigm Clustering with Weighted Edit Distance

**Andrew Gerlach, Adam Wiemerslage** and **Katharina Kann**
University of Colorado Boulder
first.last@colorado.edu

## Abstract

This paper describes our system for the SIGMORPHON 2021 Shared Task on Unsupervised Morphological Paradigm Clustering, which asks participants to group inflected forms together according their underlying lemma without the aid of annotated training data. We employ agglomerative clustering to group word forms together using a metric that combines an orthographic distance and a semantic distance from word embeddings. We experiment with two variations of an edit distance-based model for quantifying orthographic distance, but, due to time constraints, our systems do not outperform the baseline. However, we also show that, with more time, our results improve strongly.

## 1 Introduction

Most of the world's languages express grammatical properties, such as tense or case, via small changes to a word's surface form. This process is called *morphological inflection*, and the canonical form of a word is known as its *lemma*. A search of the WALS database of linguistic typology shows that 80% of the database's languages mark verb tense and 65% mark grammatical case through morphology (Dryer and Haspelmath, 2013).

The English lemma *do*, for instance, has an inflected form *did* that expresses past tense. Though English verbs inflect to express tense, there are generally only 4 to 5 surface variations for a given English lemma. In contrast, a Russian verb can have up to 30 morphological inflections per lemma, and other languages – such as Basque – have hundreds of forms per lemma, cf. Table 1.

Inflected forms are systematically related to each other: in English, most noun plurals are obtained from the lemma by adding *-s* or *-es* to the end of the noun, e.g., *list/lists* or *kiss/kisses*. However, irregular plurals also exist, such as *ox/oxen* or *mouse/mice*. Although irregular forms are less frequent, they cause challenges for the automatic generation or analysis of the surface forms of English plural nouns.

| **Basque Lemma:** ***egin*** | | |
|---|---|---|
| begi | begiate | begidate |
| begie | begiete | begigu |
| begigute | begik | begin |
| beginate | begio | begiote |
| begit | begite | begitza |
| ... | ... | ... |
| zenegizkigukeen | zenegizkigukete | zenegizkiguketen |
| zenegizkigun | zenegizkigute | zenegizkiguten |
| zenegizkio | zenegizkioke | zenegizkiokeen |
| zenegizkiokete | zenegizkioketen | zenegizkion |
| zenegizkiote | zenegizkioten | zenegizkit |

Table 1: The paradigm of the Basque verb *egin* consists of 674 inflected forms. In contrast, the paradigm of the English verb *do* only consists of 5 inflected forms: *do*, *does*, *doing*, *did*, and *done*.

In this work, we address the SIGMORPHON 2021 Shared Task on Unsupervised Morphological Paradigm Clustering ("Task 2") (Wiemerslage et al., 2021). The goal of this shared task is to group words encountered in naturally occurring text into morphological paradigms. Unsupervised paradigm clustering can be helpful for state-of-the-art natural language processing (NLP) systems, which typically require large amounts of training data. The ability to group words together into paradigms is a useful first step for training a system to induce full paradigms from a limited number of examples, a task known as (supervised) morphological paradigm completion. Building paradigms can help an NLP system



*Proceedings of the Seventeenth SIGMORPHON Workshop on Computational Research in Phonetics, Phonology, and Morphology*, pages 107–114

to induce representations for rare words or to generate words that have not been observed in a given corpus. Lastly, unsupervised systems have the advantage of not needing annotated data, which can be costly in terms of time and money, or, in the case of extinct or endangered languages, entirely impossible.

Since 2016, the Association for Computational Linguistics' Special Interest Group on Computational Morphology and Phonology (SIGMORPHON) has created shared tasks to help spur the development of state-of-the-art systems to explicitly handle morphological processes in a language. These tasks have involved morphological inflection (Cotterell et al., 2016), lemmatization (McCarthy et al., 2019), as well as other, related tasks. SIGMORPHON has increased the level of difficulty of the shared tasks, largely along two dimensions. The first dimension is the amount of data available for models to learn, reflecting the difficulties of analyzing low-resource languages. The second dimension is the amount of structure provided in the input data. Initially, SIGMORPHON shared tasks provided predefined tables of lemmas, morphological tags, and inflected forms. For the SIGMORPHON 2021 Shared Task on Unsupervised Morphological Paradigm Clustering, only raw text is provided as input.

We propose a system that combines orthographic and semantic similarity measures to cluster surface forms found in raw text. We experiment with a character-level language model for weighing substring differences between words. Due to time constraints we are only able to cluster over a subset of each languages' vocabulary. Despite of this, our system's performance is comparable to the baseline.

## 2 Related Work

Unsupervised morphology has attracted a great deal of interest historically, including a large body of work focused on segmentation (Xu et al., 2018; Creutz and Lagus, 2007; Poon et al., 2009; Narasimhan et al., 2015). Recently, the task of unsupervised morphological paradigm completion has been proposed (Kann et al., 2020; Jin et al., 2020; Erdmann et al., 2020), wherein the goal is to induce full paradigms from raw text corpora.

In this year's SIGMORPHON shared task, we are asked to only address part of the unsupervised paradigm completion task: paradigm clustering. Intuitively, the task of segmentation is related to paradigm clustering, but the outputs are different. Goldsmith (2001) produces morphological signatures, which are similar to approximate paradigms, based on an algorithm that uses minimum description length. However, this type of algorithm relies heavily on purely orthographic features of the vocabulary. Schone and Jurafsky (2001) hypothesize that approximating semantic information can help differentiate between hypothesized morphemes, revealing those that are productive. They propose an algorithm that combines orthography, semantics, and syntactic distributions to induce morphological relationships. They used semantic relatedness, quantified by latent semantic analysis, combined with the frequencies of affixes and syntactic context (Schone and Jurafsky, 2000).

More recently, Soricut and Och (2015) have used SkipGram word embeddings (Mikolov et al., 2013) to find meaningful morphemes based on analogies: regularities exhibited by embedding spaces allow for inferences of certain types (e.g., *king* is to *man* what *queen* is to *woman*). Hypothesizing that these regularities also hold for morphological relations, they represent morphemes by vector differences between semantically similar forms, e.g., the vector for the suffix $\vec{s}$ may be represented by the difference between $\overrightarrow{cats}$ and $\overrightarrow{cat}$.

Drawing upon these intuitions, we follow Rosa and Zabokrtský (2019), which combines semantic distance using fastText embeddings (Bojanowski et al., 2017) with an orthographic distance between word pairs. Words are then clustered into paradigms using agglomerative clustering.

## 3 Task Description

Given a raw text corpus, the task is to sort words into clusters that correspond to paradigms. More formally, for the vocabulary $\Sigma$ of all types attested in the corpus and the set of morphological paradigms $\Pi$ for which at least one word is in $\Sigma$, the goal is to output clusters corresponding to $\pi_k \bigcap \Sigma$ for all $\pi_k \in \Pi$.

**Data** As the raw text data for this task, JHU Bible corpora (McCarthy et al., 2020b) are provided by the organizers. This is the only data that systems can use. The organizers further provide development and test sets consisting of gold clusters for a subset of words in the Bible corpora. Each cluster is a list of words representing $\pi_k \bigcap \Sigma$ for $\pi_k \in \Pi_{dev}$ or $\pi_k \in \Pi_{test}$, respectively, and $\Pi_{dev}, \Pi_{test} \subsetneq \Pi$.

The partial morphological paradigms in $\Pi_{dev}$ and $\Pi_{test}$ are taken from the UniMorph database (McCarthy et al., 2020a). Development sets are only available for the development languages, while test sets are only provided for the test languages. All test sets are hidden from the participants until the conclusion of the shared task.

**Languages** The development languages featured in the shared task are Maltese, Persian, Portuguese, Russian, and Swedish. The test languages are Basque, Bulgarian, English, Finnish, German, Kannada, Navajo, Spanish, and Turkish.

## 4 System Descriptions

We submit two systems based on Rosa and Zabokrtský (2019). The first, referred to below as *JW-based clustering*, follows their work very closely. The second, *LM-based clustering*, contains the same main components, but approximates orthographic distances with the help of a language model.

### 4.1 JW-based Clustering

We describe the system of Rosa and Zabokrtský (2019) in more detail here. This system clusters over words whose distance is computed as a combination of orthographic and semantic distances.

**Orthographic Distance** The orthographic distance of two words is computed as their Jaro-Winkler (JW) edit distance (Winkler, 1990). JW distance differs from the more common Levenshtein distance (Levenshtein, 1966) in that JW distance gives more importance to the beginnings of strings than to their ends, which is where characters belonging to the stem are likely to be in suffixing languages.

The JW distance is averaged with the JW distance of a *simplified variant* of the string. The simplified variant is a string that has been lower cased, transliterated to ASCII, and had the non-initial vowels deleted. This is done to soften the impact of characters that are likely to correspond with affixes. Crucially, we believe that this biases the system towards languages that express inflection via suffixation.

**Semantic Distance** We represent words in the corpus by fastText embeddings, similar to Erdmann and Habash (2018), who cluster fastText embeddings for the same task in various Arabic dialects. We expect fastText embeddings to provide better representations than, e.g., Word2Vec (Mikolov et al., 2013), due to the limited size of the Bible corpora. Unfortunately, using fastText may also inadvertently result in higher similarity between words belonging to different lemmas that contain overlapping subwords corresponding to affixes.

**Overall Distance** We compute a pairwise distance matrix for all words in the corpus. The distance between two words $w_1$ and $w_2$ is computed as:

$$d(w_1, w_2) = 1 - \delta(w_1, w_2) \cdot \frac{\cos(\hat{w}_1, \hat{w}_2) + 1}{2}, \quad (1)$$

where $\hat{w}_1$ and $\hat{w}_2$ are the embeddings of $w_1$ and $w_2$, *cos* is the cosine distance, and $\delta$ is the JW edit distance. The cosine distance is mapped to $[0, 1]$ to avoid negative distances.

Finally, agglomerative clustering is performed by first assigning each word form to a unique cluster. At each step, the two clusters with the lowest average distance are merged together. The merging continues while the distance between clusters stays below a threshold. We tune this hyperparameter on the development set, and our final threshold is 0.3.

### 4.2 LM-based Clustering

The JW-based clustering described above relies on heuristics to obtain a good measure of orthographic similarity. These heuristics help to quantify orthographic similarity between two words by relying more on the shared characters in the stem than in the affix: The plural past participles *gravados* and *louvados* in Portuguese have longer substrings in common than the substrings by which they differ. This is due to the affix *-ados*, which indicates that the two words express the same inflectional information, even though their lemmas are different. Similarly, the Portuguese verbs *abafa* and *abafávamos* differ in many characters, though they belong to the same paradigm, as can be observed by the shared stem *abaf.*

However, not all languages express inflection exclusively via suffixation, nor via concatenation. We thus experiment with removing the edit distance heuristics and, instead, utilizing probabilities from a character-level language model (LM) to distinguish between stems and affixes. In doing so, we hope to achieve better results for templatic languages, such as Maltese. We hypothesize that the LM will have a higher confidence for characters that are part of an affix than for those that are part of the stem. We then draw upon this hypothesis and weigh edit operations between two strings based on these confidences.

**LM-weighted Edit Distance** Similar to the intuition behind Silfverberg and Hulden (2018), we train a character-level LM on the entire vocabulary for each Bible corpus. Unlike their work, we do not have inflectional tags for each word. Despite this, we hypothesize that the highly regular and frequent nature of inflectional affixes will lead to higher likelihoods for characters that occur in affixes than for those in stems. We train a two-layer LSTM (Hochreiter and Schmidhuber, 1997) with an embedding size of 128 and a hidden layer size of 128. We train the model until the training loss stops decreasing, for up to 100 epochs, using Adam (Kingma and Ba, 2014) with a learning rate of 0.001 and a batch size of 16.

When calculating the edit distance between two words, the insertion, deletion, or substitution costs are computed as a function of the LM probabilities. We expect this to give more weights to differences in the stem than to those in other parts of the word. Each character is then associated with a cost given by

$$\text{cost}(w_i) = 1 - \frac{p(w_i)}{\sum\limits_{j \in |w|} p(w_j)}, \qquad (2)$$

where $p(w_i)$ is the probability of the $i$th character in word $w$ as given by the LM. We then compute the cost of an insertion or deletion as the cost of the character being inserted or deleted. The cost of a substitution is the average of the costs of the two involved characters. The sum over these operations is the weighted edit distance between two words, $\epsilon(w_1, w_2)$. Finally, we compute pairwise distances using Equation 1, replacing $\delta(w_1, w_2)$ with

$$\frac{\epsilon(w_1, w_2)}{max(|w_1|, |w_2|)}.$$

**Forward vs. Backward LM** We hypothesize that the direction in which the LM is trained affects the probabilities for affixes. Intuitively, an LM is likely to assign higher confidence to characters at the beginning of a word than at the end. Thus, an LM trained on data in the forward direction (LM-F) should be more likely to assign higher probabilities to characters at the beginning of a word, such as prefixes, while a model trained on reversed words (LM-B) should assign higher probabilities to suffixes. In practice, LM-B outperforms LM-F on all development languages, cf. Table 2. Because of that, we employ LM-B to weigh edit operations for all test languages.[1]

[1]This might be caused by none of the development languages being prefixing. However, in order to make a more informed choice, a method to automatically distinguish between prefixing and suffixing languages from raw text alone would be necessary.

| Lang | Baseline | | | LMC-B | | | LMC-F | | | JWC | | |
|---|---|---|---|---|---|---|---|---|---|---|---|---|
| | prec. | rec. | F1 | prec. | rec. | f1 | prec. | rec. | F1 | prec. | rec. | F1 |
| **Maltese** | 0.250 | 0.348 | 0.291 | 0.465 | 0.229 | 0.307 | 0.411 | 0.202 | 0.272 | 0.489 | 0.241 | **0.323** |
| **Persian** | 0.265 | 0.348 | 0.300 | 0.321 | 0.307 | 0.314 | 0.494 | 0.197 | 0.282 | 0.579 | 0.231 | **0.330** |
| **Portuguese** | 0.218 | 0.794 | 0.341 | 0.771 | 0.248 | **0.376** | 0.494 | 0.159 | 0.241 | 0.742 | 0.239 | 0.362 |
| **Russian** | 0.234 | 0.807 | 0.363 | 0.802 | 0.282 | **0.417** | 0.726 | 0.255 | 0.378 | 0.792 | 0.278 | 0.412 |
| **Swedish** | 0.303 | 0.776 | 0.436 | 0.818 | 0.378 | 0.517 | 0.695 | 0.321 | 0.439 | 0.838 | 0.388 | **0.530** |
| **Average** | 0.254 | 0.615 | 0.346 | 0.635 | 0.289 | 0.386 | 0.482 | 0.186 | 0.268 | 0.688 | 0.275 | **0.391** |

Table 2: Precision, recall, and F1 for all development languages. LMC-R is the LM-clustering system for language models trained from left-to-right (reverse). LMC-F are trained from left-to-right, and JWC is the JW-clustering system. The highest F1 for each language is in bold.

| Lang | Baseline | | | LMC | | | JWC | | |
|---|---|---|---|---|---|---|---|---|---|
| | prec. | rec. | F1 | prec. | rec. | F1 | prec. | rec. | F1 |
| **English** | 0.388 | 0.767 | **0.515** | 0.565 | 0.245 | 0.3420 | 0.663 | 0.288 | 0.402 |
| **Navajo** | 0.230 | 0.598 | **0.333** | 0.686 | 0.112 | 0.1928 | 0.657 | 0.108 | 0.185 |
| **Spanish** | 0.266 | 0.722 | **0.388** | 0.664 | 0.183 | 0.2869 | 0.699 | 0.193 | 0.302 |
| **Finnish** | 0.179 | 0.767 | 0.290 | 0.694 | 0.227 | **0.342** | 0.674 | 0.220 | 0.332 |
| **Bulgarian** | 0.265 | 0.730 | 0.390 | 0.745 | 0.312 | **0.440** | 0.717 | 0.300 | 0.423 |
| **Basque** | 0.186 | 0.254 | 0.215 | 0.471 | 0.254 | **0.330** | 0.353 | 0.191 | 0.247 |
| **Kannada** | 0.172 | 0.385 | 0.238 | 0.570 | 0.169 | 0.261 | 0.625 | 0.185 | **0.286** |
| **German** | 0.254 | 0.776 | 0.382 | 0.7626 | 0.310 | 0.441 | 0.787 | 0.319 | **0.454** |
| **Turkish** | 0.156 | 0.658 | 0.252 | 0.6574 | 0.212 | **0.320** | 0.641 | 0.206 | 0.312 |
| **Average** | 0.233 | 0.629 | **0.334** | 0.646 | 0.225 | 0.328 | 0.646 | 0.223 | 0.327 |

Table 3: Precision, recall, and F1 for all test languages. LMC is the LM-clustering system, JWC is the JW-clustering system. The highest F1 for each language is in bold.

## 5 Results and Discussion

The official scores obtained by our systems as well as the baseline are shown in Table 3.

Both of our systems perform minimally worse than the baseline if we consider F1 averaged over languages (0.334 vs. 0.328 and 0.327). However, we believe this to be largely due to our submissions only generating clusters for a subset of the full vocabularies: due to time constraints, we only consider words that appear at least 5 times in the corpus. No other words are included in the predicted clusters. The large gap between precision and recall reflects this constraint: our submissions have a high average precision (0.646 for both systems), indicating that the limited set of words we consider are being clustered more accurately than the F1 scores would suggest. The low recall scores (0.225 and 0.223) are likely at least partially caused by the missing words in our predictions.[2]

Conversely, the baseline system has a high recall (0.629) and a low precision (0.233). This is likely due to it simply clustering words with shared substrings, such that a given word is likely to appear in many predicted clusters.

Interestingly, both of our submissions have the same average precision on the test set, despite varying across languages. Notably, the LM-based clustering system strongly outperforms the JW-based system on Basque with respect to precision. However, the JW-based system outperforms the LM-based one by a large margin on English. One hypothesis for the difference in results is that agglutinating inflection in Basque causes very long affixes, which our LM-based system should downweigh in its measurement of orthographic similarity. Basque is also not a strictly suffixing language, which we expect the JW-based model to be biased towards. On the other hand, English has relatively little inflectional morphology, and is strictly suffixing (in terms of inflection). The assumptions behind the JW-based system are more ideal for a language like English. The JW system performs best on Maltese, which suggests that the heuristics of that system are sufficient for a templatic language, compared to the LM-based system.

[2]We confirm this hypothesis with additional experiments after the shared task's completion. Those results can be found in the appendix.

## 6 Conclusion

We present two systems for the SIGMORPHON 2021 Shared Task on Unsupervised Morphological Paradigm Clustering. Both of our systems perform slighly worse than the official baseline. However, we also show that this is due to our official submissions only making predictions for a subset of the corpus' vocabulary, due to time constraints and that at least one of our systems improves strongly if the time constraints are removed.

## References


Piotr Bojanowski, Edouard Grave, Armand Joulin, and Tomas Mikolov. 2017. Enriching word vectors with subword information. *Transactions of the Association for Computational Linguistics*, 5:135–146.

Ryan Cotterell, Christo Kirov, John Sylak-Glassman, David Yarowsky, Jason Eisner, and Mans Hulden. 2016. The SIGMORPHON 2016 shared task—morphological reinflection. In *Proceedings of the 2016 Meeting of SIGMORPHON*, Berlin, Germany. Association for Computational Linguistics.

Mathias Creutz and Krista Lagus. 2007. Unsupervised models for morpheme segmentation and morphology learning. 4(1).

Matthew S. Dryer and Martin Haspelmath, editors. 2013. *WALS Online*. Max Planck Institute for Evolutionary Anthropology, Leipzig.

Alexander Erdmann, Micha Elsner, Shijie Wu, Ryan Cotterell, and Nizar Habash. 2020. The paradigm discovery problem. In *Proceedings of the 58th Annual Meeting of the Association for Computational Linguistics*, pages 7778–7790, Online. Association for Computational Linguistics.

Alexander Erdmann and Nizar Habash. 2018. Complementary strategies for low resourced morphological modeling. In *Proceedings of the Fifteenth Workshop on Computational Research in Phonetics, Phonology, and Morphology*, pages 54–65, Brussels, Belgium. Association for Computational Linguistics.

John Goldsmith. 2001. Unsupervised learning of the morphology of a natural language. *Computational linguistics*, 27(2):153–198.

Sepp Hochreiter and Jürgen Schmidhuber. 1997. Long short-term memory. *Neural computation*, 9(8):1735–1780.

Huiming Jin, Liwei Cai, Yihui Peng, Chen Xia, Arya McCarthy, and Katharina Kann. 2020. Unsupervised morphological paradigm completion. In *Proceedings of the 58th Annual Meeting of the Association for Computational Linguistics*, pages 6696–6707, Online. Association for Computational Linguistics.

Katharina Kann, Arya D. McCarthy, Garrett Nicolai, and Mans Hulden. 2020. The SIGMORPHON 2020 shared task on unsupervised morphological paradigm completion. In *Proceedings of the 17th SIGMORPHON Workshop on Computational Research in Phonetics, Phonology, and Morphology*, pages 51–62, Online. Association for Computational Linguistics.

Diederik P Kingma and Jimmy Ba. 2014. Adam: A method for stochastic optimization. *arXiv preprint arXiv:1412.6980*.

Vladimir Iosifovich Levenshtein. 1966. Binary codes capable of correcting deletions, insertions and reversals. *Soviet Physics Doklady*, 10(8):707–710. Doklady Akademii Nauk SSSR, V163 No4 845-848 1965.

Arya D. McCarthy, Christo Kirov, Matteo Grella, Amrit Nidhi, Patrick Xia, Kyle Gorman, Ekaterina Vylomova, Sabrina J. Mielke, Garrett Nicolai, Miikka Silfverberg, Timofey Arkhangelskiy, Nataly Krizhanovsky, Andrew Krizhanovsky, Elena Klyachko, Alexey Sorokin, John Mansfield, Valts Ernštreits, Yuval Pinter, Cassandra L. Jacobs, Ryan Cotterell, Mans Hulden, and David Yarowsky. 2020a. UniMorph 3.0: Universal Morphology. In *Proceedings of the 12th Language Resources and Evaluation Conference*, pages 3922–3931, Marseille, France. European Language Resources Association.

Arya D. McCarthy, Ekaterina Vylomova, Shijie Wu, Chaitanya Malaviya, Lawrence Wolf-Sonkin, Garrett Nicolai, Christo Kirov, Miikka Silfverberg, Sabrina J. Mielke, Jeffrey Heinz, Ryan Cotterell, and Mans Hulden. 2019. The SIGMORPHON 2019 shared task: Morphological analysis in context and cross-lingual transfer for inflection. In *Proceedings of the 16th Workshop on Computational Research in Phonetics, Phonology, and Morphology*, pages 229–244, Florence, Italy. Association for Computational Linguistics.

Arya D. McCarthy, Rachel Wicks, Dylan Lewis, Aaron Mueller, Winston Wu, Oliver Adams, Garrett Nicolai, Matt Post, and David Yarowsky. 2020b. The Johns Hopkins University Bible corpus: 1600+ tongues for typological exploration. In *Proceedings of the 12th Language Resources and Evaluation Conference*, pages 2884–2892, Marseille, France. European Language Resources Association.

Tomas Mikolov, Kai Chen, Greg Corrado, and Jeffrey Dean. 2013. Efficient estimation of word representations in vector space.

Karthik Narasimhan, Regina Barzilay, and Tommi Jaakkola. 2015. An unsupervised method for uncovering morphological chains. *Transactions of the Association for Computational Linguistics*, 3:157–167.

Hoifung Poon, Colin Cherry, and Kristina Toutanova. 2009. Unsupervised morphological segmentation with log-linear models. In *Proceedings of Human Language Technologies: The 2009 Annual Conference of the North American Chapter of the Association for Computational Linguistics*, pages 209–217, Boulder, Colorado. Association for Computational Linguistics.

Rudolf Rosa and Zdenek Zabokrtský. 2019. Unsupervised lemmatization as embeddings-based word clustering. *CoRR*, abs/1908.08528.

Patrick Schone and Daniel Jurafsky. 2000. Knowledge-free induction of morphology using latent semantic analysis. In *Fourth Conference on Computational Natural Language Learning and the Second Learning Language in Logic Workshop*.

Patrick Schone and Daniel Jurafsky. 2001. Knowledge-free induction of inflectional morphologies. In *Second Meeting of the North American Chapter of the Association for Computational Linguistics*.

Miikka Silfverberg and Mans Hulden. 2018. An encoder-decoder approach to the paradigm cell filling problem. In *Proceedings of the 2018 Conference on Empirical Methods in Natural Language Processing*, pages 2883–2889, Brussels, Belgium. Association for Computational Linguistics.

Radu Soricut and Franz Och. 2015. Unsupervised morphology induction using word embeddings. In *Proceedings of the 2015 Conference of the North American Chapter of the Association for Computational Linguistics: Human Language Technologies*, pages 1627–1637, Denver, Colorado. Association for Computational Linguistics.

Adam Wiemerslage, Arya McCarthy, Alexander Erdmann, Garrett Nicolai, Manex Agirrezabal, Miikka Silfverberg, Mans Hulden, and Katharina Kann. 2021. The SIGMORPHON 2021 shared task on unsupervised morphological paradigm clustering. In *Proceedings of the 18th SIGMORPHON Workshop on Computational Research in Phonetics, Phonology, and Morphology*. Association for Computational Linguistics.

William E. Winkler. 1990. String comparator metrics and enhanced decision rules in the fellegi-sunter model of record linkage. In *Proceedings of the Section on Survey Research*, pages 354–359.

Ruochen Xu, Yiming Yang, Naoki Otani, and Yuexin Wu. 2018. Unsupervised cross-lingual transfer of word embedding spaces. In *Proceedings of the 2018 Conference on Empirical Methods in Natural Language Processing*, pages 2465–2474, Brussels, Belgium. Association for Computational Linguistics.

## 7 Appendix

Here we present new results which include the entire data set for selected languages. We see an improvement in F1 for each language. This due to the increased recall scores from the paradigms being more complete. Precision scores decrease across the board. This may be due to the languages being sensitive to the threshold value.

| Lang | Subset | | | Full | | |
|---|---|---|---|---|---|---|
| | prec. | rec. | F1 | prec. | rec. | F1 |
| **Basque** | 0.471 | 0.254 | 0.330 | 0.443 | 0.429 | 0.435 |
| **Bulgarian** | 0.745 | 0.312 | 0.440 | 0.638 | 0.631 | 0.634 |
| **English** | 0.565 | 0.245 | 0.342 | 0.430 | 0.425 | 0.428 |
| **German** | 0.763 | 0.310 | 0.441 | 0.703 | 0.699 | 0.701 |
| **Maltese** | 0.465 | 0.229 | 0.307 | 0.402 | 0.400 | 0.401 |
| **Navajo** | 0.686 | 0.112 | 0.193 | 0.449 | 0.430 | 0.435 |
| **Spanish** | 0.664 | 0.183 | 0.287 | 0.579 | 0.560 | 0.569 |
| **Swedish** | 0.818 | 0.378 | 0.517 | 0.783 | 0.737 | 0.759 |
| **Average** | 0.659 | 0.252 | 0.357 | 0.553 | 0.539 | 0.545 |

Table 4: Post-shared task results using the full data set for selected languages. These results use LM-B with a threshold value of 0.3.

# Results of the Second SIGMORPHON Shared Task on Multilingual Grapheme-to-Phoneme Conversion

**Lucas F.E. Ashby**[*], **Travis M. Bartley**[*], **Simon Clematide**[†], **Luca Del Signore**[*], **Cameron Gibson**[*], **Kyle Gorman**[*], **Yeonju Lee-Sikka**[*], **Peter Makarov**[†], **Aidan Malanoski**[*], **Sean Miller**[*], **Omar Ortiz**[*], **Reuben Raff**[*], **Arundhati Sengupta**[*], **Bora Seo**[*], **Yulia Spektor**[*], **Winnie Yan**[*]

[*]Graduate Program in Linguistics, Graduate Center, City University of New York

[†]Department of Computational Linguistics, University of Zurich

## Abstract

Grapheme-to-phoneme conversion is an important component in many speech technologies, but until recently there were no multilingual benchmarks for this task. The second iteration of the SIGMORPHON shared task on multilingual grapheme-to-phoneme conversion features many improvements from the previous year's task (Gorman et al. 2020), including additional languages, a stronger baseline, three subtasks varying the amount of available resources, extensive quality assurance procedures, and automated error analyses. Four teams submitted a total of thirteen systems, at best achieving relative reductions of word error rate of 11% in the high-resource subtask and 4% in the low-resource subtask.

## 1 Introduction

Many speech technologies demand mappings between written words and their pronunciations. In open-vocabulary systems—as well as certain resource-constrained embedded systems—it is insufficient to simply list all possible pronunciations; these mappings must generalize to rare or unseen words as well. Therefore, the mapping must be expressed as a mapping from a sequence of orthographic characters—*graphemes*— to a sequence of sounds—*phones* or *phonemes*.[1]

The earliest work on *grapheme-to-phoneme conversion* (G2P), as this task is known, used ordered rewrite rules. However, such systems are often brittle and the linguistic expertise needed to build, test, and maintain rule-based systems is often in short supply. Furthermore, rule-based systems are outperformed by modern neural sequence-to-sequence models (e.g., Rao et al. 2015, Yao and Zweig 2015, van Esch et al. 2016).

With the possible exception of van Esch et al. (2016), who evaluate against a proprietary database of 20 languages and dialects, virtually all of the prior published research on grapheme-to-phoneme conversion evaluates only on English, for which several free and low-cost pronunciation dictionaries are available. The 2020 SIGMORPHON Shared Task on Multilingual Grapheme-to-Phoneme Conversion (Gorman et al. 2020) represented a first attempt to construct a multilingual benchmark for grapheme-to-phoneme conversion. The 2020 shared task targeted fifteen languages and received 23 submissions from nine teams. The second iteration of this shared task attempts to further refine this benchmark by introducing additional languages, a much stronger baseline model, new quality assurance procedures for the data, and automated error analysis techniques. Furthermore, in response to suggestions from participants in the 2020 shared task, the task has been divided into high-, medium-, and low-resource subtasks.

## 2 Data

As in the previous year's shared task, all data was drawn from WikiPron (Lee et al. 2020), a massively multilingual pronunciation database extracted from the online dictionary Wiktionary. Depending on the language and script, Wiktionary pronunciations are either manually entered by human volunteers working from language-specific pronunciation guidelines and/or generated from the graphemic form via language-specific server-side scripting. WikiPron scrapes these pronunciatons from Wiktionary, optionally applying case-folding to the graphemic form, removing any stress and syllable boundaries, and segmenting the pronunciation—encoded in the Interna-

[1]We note that referring to elements of transcriptions as *phonemes* implies an ontological commitment which may or may not be justified; see Lee et al. 2020 (fn. 4) for discussion. Therefore, we use the term *phone* to refer to symbols used to transcribe pronunciations.



*Proceedings of the Seventeenth SIGMORPHON Workshop on Computational Research in Phonetics, Phonology, and Morphology*, pages 115–125

tional Phonetic Alphabet—using the Python library `segments` (Moran and Cysouw 2018). In all, 21 WikiPron languages were selected for the three subtasks, including seven new languages and fourteen of the fifteen languages used in the 2020 shared task.[2]

In several cases, multiple scripts or dialects are available for a given language. For instance, WikiPron has both Latin and Cyrillic entries for Serbo-Croatian, and three different dialects of Vietnamese. In such case, the largest data set of the available scripts and/or dialects is chosen. Furthermore, WikiPron distinguishes between "broad" transcriptions delimited by forward slash (/) and "narrow" transcriptions delimited by square brackets ( `[` and `]` ).[3] Once again, the larger of the two data sets is the one used for this task.

## 3 Quality assurance

During the previous year's shared task we became aware of several consistency issues with the shared task data. This lead us to develop quality assurance procedures for WikiPron and the "upstream" Wiktionary data. For a few languages, we worked with Wiktionary editors who automatically enforced upstream consistency via "bots", i.e., scripts which automatically edit Wiktionary entries. We also improved WikiPron's routines for extracting pronunciation data from Wiktionary. In some cases (e.g., Vietnamese), this required the creation of language-specific extraction routines.

In early versions of WikiPron, users had limited means to separate out entries for languages written in multiple scripts. We therefore added an automated script detection system which ensures that entries for the many languages written with multiple scripts—including shared task languages Maltese, Japanese, and Serbo-Croatian—are sorted according to script.

We noticed that the WikiPron data includes many hyper-foreign pronunciations with non-native phones. For example, the English data includes a broad pronunciation of *Bach* (the surname of a family of composers) as /bɑːx/ with a velar fricative /x/, a segment which is common in German but absent in modern English. Furthermore, unexpected phones may represent simple human error. Therefore, we wished to exclude pronunciations which include any non-native segments. This was accomplished by creating phonelists which enumerate native phones for a given language. Separate phonelists may be provided for broad and narrow transcriptions of the same language. During data ingestion, if a pronunciation contains any segment not present on the phonelist, the entry was discarded. Phonelist filtration was used for all languages in the medium- and low-resource subtasks, described below.

## 4 Task definition

In this task, participants were provided with a collection of words and their pronunciations, and then scored on their ability to predict the pronunciation of a set of unseen words.

### 4.1 Subtasks

In the previous year's shared task, each language's data consisted of 4,500 examples, sampled from WikiPron, split randomly into 80% training examples, 10% development examples, and 10% test examples. As part of their system development, two teams in the 2020 shared task (Hauer et al. 2020, Yu et al. 2020) down-sampled these data to simulate a lower-resource setting, and one participant expressed concern whether the methods used in the shared task would generalize effectively to high-resource scenarios like the large English data sets traditionally used to evaluate grapheme-to-phoneme systems. This motivated a division of the data into three subtasks, varying the amount of data provided, as described below.[4]

**High-resource subtask** The first subtask consists of a roughly 41,000-word sample of Mainstream American English (`eng_us`). Participating teams were permitted to use any and all external resources to develop their systems except for Wiktionary or WikiPron. It was anticipated participants would exploit other freely available American English pronunciation dictionaries.

**Medium-resource subtask** The second subtask represents a medium-resource task. For each of the ten target languages, a sample of 10,000 words was used. Teams participating in this subtask were

[2] The fifteenth language, Lithuanian, was omitted due to unresolved quality assurance issues.

[3] Sorting by script, dialect, and broad vs. narrow transcription is performed automatically during data ingestion.

[4] Languages were sorted into medium- vs. low-resource subtasks according to data availability. For example, Icelandic was placed in the low-resource shared task simply because it has less than 10,000 pronunciations available.

permitted to use UniMorph paradigms (Kirov et al. 2018) to lemmatize or to look up morphological features, but were not permitted to use any other external resources. The languages for this subtask are listed and exemplified in Table 1.

**Low-resource subtask** The third subtask is designed to simulate a low-resource setting and consists of 1,000 words from ten languages. Teams were were not permitted to use any external resources for this subtask. The languages for this subtask are shown in Table 2.

### 4.2 Data preparation

The procedures for sampling and splitting the data are similar to those used in the previous year's shared task; see Gorman et al. 2020, §3. For each of the three subtasks, the data for each language are first randomly downsampled according to their frequencies in the Wortschatz (Goldhahn et al. 2012) norms. Words containing less than two Unicode characters or less than two phone segments are excluded, as are words with multiple pronunciations. The resulting data are randomly split into 80% training data, 10% development data, and 10% test data. As in the previous year's shared task, these splits are constrained so that inflectional variants of any given lemma—according to the UniMorph (Kirov et al. 2018) paradigms—can occur in at most one of the three shards. Training and development data was made available at the start of the task. The test words were also made available at the start of the task; test pronunciations were withheld until the end of the task. Some additional processing is required for certain languages, as described below.

**English** The Wiktionary American English pronunciations exhibit a large number of inconsistencies. These pronunciations were validated by automatically comparing them with entries in the CALLHOME American English Lexicon (Kingsbury et al. 1997), which provides broad ARPAbet transcriptions of Mainstream American English. Furthermore, a script was used to standardize use of vowel length and enforce consistent use of tie bars with affricates (e.g., /tʃ/ → /t͡ʃ/). However, we note that Gautam et al. (2021:§2.1) report several residual quality issues with this data.

**Bulgarian** Bulgarian Wiktionary transcriptions make inconsistent use of tie bars on affricates; for example, ц is transcribed as both /ts, t͡s/. Furthermore, the broad transcriptions sometimes contain allophones of the consonants /t, d, l/ (Ternes and Vladimirova-Buhtz 1990); e.g., л is transcribed as both /l, ɫ/. A script was used to enforce a consistent broad transcription.

**Maltese** In the Latin-script Maltese data, Wiktionary has multiple transcriptions of digraph *għ*, which in the contemporary language indicates lengthening of an adjacent vowel, except word-finally where it is read as [ħ] (Hoberman 2007:278f.). Rather than excluding multiple pronunciations, a script was used to eliminate pronunciations which contain archaic readings of this digraph, e.g., as pharyngealization or as [ɣ].

**Welsh** WikiPron's transcriptions of the Southern dialect of Welsh include the effects of variable processes of monophthongization and deletion (Hannahs 2013:18–25). Once again, rather than excluding multiple pronunciations, a script was used to select the "longer" pronunciation—naturally, the pronunciation without variable monophthongization or deletion—of Welsh words with multiple pronunciations.

## 5 Evaluation

The primary metric for this task was word error rate (WER), the percentage of words for which the hypothesized transcription sequence is not identical to the gold reference transcription. As the medium- and low-resource subtasks involve multiple languages, macro-averaged WER was used for system ranking. Participants were provided with two evaluation scripts: one which computes WER for a single language, and one which also computes macro-averaged WER across two or more languages. The 2020 shared task also reported another metric, phone error rate (PER), but this was found to be highly correlated with WER and therefore has been omitted here.

## 6 Baseline

The 2020 shared task included three baselines: a WFST-based pair n-gram model, a bidirectional LSTM encoder-decoder network, and a transformer. All models were tuned to minimize per-language development-set WER using a limited-budget grid search. Best results overall were obtained by the bidirectional LSTM. Despite the extensive GPU resources required to execute a

| Armenian (Eastern) | arm_e | համադրություն | h ɑ m ɑ d ə ɾ u tʰ j u n |
|---|---|---|---|
| Bulgarian | bul | обоснованият | o̞ b o̞ s n o v a n i j ə t̪ |
| Dutch | dut | konijn | k oː n ɛ i̯ n |
| French | fre | joindre | ʒ w ɛ̃ d ʁ̃ |
| Georgian | geo | მოუქნელად | m ɔ u kʰ n ɛ l ɑ d |
| Serbo-Croatian (Latin) | hbs_latn | opadati | o p ǎː d a t i |
| Hungarian | hun | lobog | l o b o g |
| Japanese (Hiragana) | jpn_hira | ぜんたいしゅぎ | d͡z ẽ̞ n t a̠ i ɕ ɨᵝ gʲ i |
| Korean | kor | 쇠가마우지 | sʰ w e̞ g a̠ m a̠ u d͡ʑ i |
| Vietnamese (Hanoi) | vie_hanoi | ngừng bắn | ŋ ɨ ŋ ˨˩ ʔ ɓ a n ˧˥ |

Table 1: The ten languages in the medium-resource subtask with language codes and example training data pairs.

| Adyghe | ady | кIэшIыхьан | t͡ʃʼ a ʃʼ ə ħ aː n |
|---|---|---|---|
| Greek | gre | λέγεται | l e ʝ e t e |
| Icelandic | ice | maður | m aː ð ʏ r |
| Italian | ita | marito | m a r i t o |
| Khmer | khm | ប្រហារ | p r ɑ h aː |
| Latvian | lav | mīksts | m îː k s t s |
| Maltese (Latin) | mlt_latn | minna | m ɪ n n a |
| Romanian | rum | ierburi | j e r b u rʲ |
| Slovenian | slv | oprostite | ɔ p r ɔ s t íː t ɛ |
| Welsh (Southwest) | wel_sw | gorff | g ɔ r f |

Table 2: The ten languages in the low-resource subtask with language codes and example training data pairs.

per-language grid search, the best baseline was handily outperformed by nearly all submissions. This led us to seek a simpler, stronger, and less computationally-demanding baseline for this year's shared task.

The baseline for the 2021 shared task is a neural transducer system using an imitation learning paradigm (Makarov and Clematide 2018). A variant of this system (Makarov and Clematide 2020) was the second-best system in the 2020 shared task.[5] Alignments are computed using ten iterations of expectation maximization, and the imitation learning policy is trained for up to sixty epochs (with a patience of twelve) using the Adadelta optimizer. A beam of size of four is used for prediction. Final predictions are produced by a majority-vote ten-component ensemble. Internal processing is performed using the decomposed Unicode normalization form (NFD), but predictions are converted back to the composed form (NFC). An implementation of the baseline was provided during the task and participating teams were encouraged to adapt it for their submissions.

[5]The baseline was implemented using the DyNet neural network toolkit (Neubig et al. 2017). In contrast to the previous year's baseline, the imitation learning system does not require a GPU for efficient training; it runs effectively on CPU and can exploit multiple CPU cores if present. Training, ensembling, and evaluation for all three subtasks took roughly 72 hours of wall-clock time on a commodity desktop PC.

## 7 Submissions

Below we provide brief descriptions of submissions to the shared task; more detailed descriptions—as well as various exploratory analyses and post-submission experiments—can be found in the system papers later in this volume.

**AZ** Hammond (2021) produced a single submission to the low-resource subtask. The model is inspired by the previous year's bidirectional LSTM baseline but also employs several data augmentation strategies. First, much of the development data is used for training rather than for validation. Secondly, new training examples are generated using substrings of other training examples. Finally, the AZ model is trained simultaneously on all languages, a method used in some of the previous year's shared task submissions (e.g., Peters and Martins 2020, Vesik et al. 2020).

**CLUZH** Clematide and Makarov (2021) produced four submissions to the medium-resource subtask and three to the low-resource subtask. All seven submissions are variations on the imitation learning baseline model (section 6). They experiment with processing individual IPA Unicode characters instead of entire IPA "segments" (e.g., CLUZH-1, CLUZH-5, and CLUZH-6), and larger ensembles (e.g., CLUZH-3). They also experiment with input dropout, mogrifier LSTMs, and adaptive batch sizes, among other features.

**Dialpad** Gautam et al. (2021) produced three systems to the high-resource subtask. The Dialpad-1 submission is a large ensemble of seven different sequence models. Dialpad-2 is a smaller ensemble of three models. Dialpad-3 is a single transformer model implemented as part of CMU Sphinx. Gautam et al. also experiment with subword modeling techniques.

**UBC** Lo and Nicolai (2021) submitted two systems for the low-resource subtask, both variations on the baseline model. The UBC-1 submission hypothesizes that, as previously reported by van Esch et al. (2016), inserting explicit syllable boundaries into the phone sequences enhances grapheme-to-phoneme performance. They generate syllable boundaries using an automated onset maximization heuristic. The UBC-2 submission takes a different approach: it assigns additional language-specific penalties for mis-predicted vowels and diacritic characters such as the length mark /ː/.

## 8 Results

Multiple submissions to the high- and low-resource subtasks outperformed the baseline; however, no submission to the medium-resource subtask exceeded the baseline. The best results for each language are shown in Table 3.

### 8.1 Subtasks

**High-resource subtask** The Dialpad team submitted three systems for the high-resource subtask, all of which outperformed the baseline. Results for this subtask are shown in Table 4. The best submission overall, Dialpad-1, a seven-component ensemble, achieved an impressive 4.5% absolute (11% relative) reduction in WER over the baseline.

**Medium-resource subtask** The CLUZH team submitted four systems for the medium-resource subtask. All of of these systems are variants of the baseline model. The results are shown in Table 5; note that the individual language results are expressed as three-digit percentages since there are 1,000 test examples each. While several of the CLUZH systems outperform the baseline on individual languages, including Armenian, French, Hungarian, Japanese, Korean, and Vietnamese, the baseline achieves the best macro-accuracy.

**Low-resource subtask** Three teams—AZ, CLUZH, and UBC—submitted a total of six systems to the low-resource subtask. Results for this subtask are shown in Table 6; note that the results are expressed as two-digit percentages since there are 100 test examples for each language. Three submissions outperformed the baseline. The best-performing submission was UBC-2, an adaptation of the baseline which assigns higher penalties for mis-predicted vowels and diacritic characters. It achieved a 1.0% absolute (4% relative) reduction in WER over the baseline.

### 8.2 Error analysis

Error analysis can help identify strengths and weaknesses of existing models, suggesting future improvements and guiding the construction of ensemble models. Prior experience using gold crowd-sourced data extracted from Wiktionary suggests that a non-trivial portion of errors made by top systems are due to errors in the gold data itself. For example, Gorman et al. (2019) report that a substantial portion of the prediction errors made by the top two systems in the 2017 CoNLL–SIGMORPHON Shared Task on Morphological Reinflection (Cotterell et al. 2017) are due to *target errors*, i.e., errors in the gold data. Therefore we conducted an automatic error analysis for four target languages. It was hoped that this analysis would also help identify (and quantify) target errors in the test data.

Two forms of error analysis were employed here. First, after Makarov and Clematide (2020), the most frequent error types in each language are shown in Table 7. From this table it is clear that many errors can be attributed either to the ambiguity of a language's writing system. For example, in both Serbo-Croatian and Slovenian the most common errors involve the confusion or omission of suprasegmental information such as pitch accent and vowel length, neither of which are represented in the orthography. Likewise, in French and Italian the most frequent errors confuse vowel sounds

| | Baseline WER | Best submission(s) | WER |
|---|---|---|---|
| eng_us | 41.91 | Dialpad-1 | **37.43** |
| arm_e | 7.0 | CLUZH-7 | **6.4** |
| bul | **18.3** | CLUZH-6 | 18.8 |
| dut | **14.7** | CLUZH-7 | **14.7** |
| fre | 8.5 | CLUZH-4, CLUZH-5, CLUHZ-6 | **7.5** |
| geo | **0.0** | CLUZH-4, CLUHZ-5, CLUZH-6, CLUZH-7 | **0.0** |
| hbs_latn | **32.1** | CLUZH-7 | 35.3 |
| hun | 1.8 | CLUZH-6, CLUZH-7 | **1.0** |
| jpn_hira | 5.2 | CLUZH-7 | **5.0** |
| kor | 16.3 | CLUZH-4 | **16.2** |
| vie_hanoi | 2.5 | CLUZH-5, CLUZH-7 | **2.0** |
| ady | **22** | CLUZH-2, CLUZH-3, UBC-2 | **22** |
| gre | 21 | CLUZH-1, CLUZH-3 | **20** |
| ice | 12 | CLUZH-1, CLUZH-3 | **10** |
| ita | **19** | UBC-1 | 20 |
| khm | 34 | UBC-2 | **28** |
| lav | 55 | CLUZH-2, CLUZH-3, UBC-2 | **49** |
| mlt_latn | 19 | CLUZH-1 | **12** |
| rum | **10** | UBC-2 | **10** |
| slv | 49 | UBC-2 | **47** |
| wel_sw | **10** | CLUZH-1 | **10** |

Table 3: Baseline WER, and the best submission(s) and their WER, for each language.

| | Baseline | Dialpad-1 | Dialpad-2 | Dialpad-3 |
|---|---|---|---|---|
| eng_us | 41.94 | **37.43** | 41.72 | 41.58 |

Table 4: Results for the high-resource (US English) subtask.

represented by the same graphemes.

Many errors may also be attributable to problems with the target data. For example, the two most frequent errors for English are predicting [ɪ] instead of [ə], and predicting [ɑ] instead of [ɔ]. Impressionistically, the former is due in part to inconsistent transcription of the *-ed* and *-es* suffixes, whereas the latter may reflect inconsistent transcription of the low back merger.

The second error analysis technique used here is an adaptation of a quality assurance technique proposed by Jansche (2014). For each language targeted by the error analysis, a finite-state covering grammar is constructed by manually listing all pairs of permissible grapheme-phone mappings for that language. Let $C$ be the set of all such $g, p$ pairs. Then, the covering grammar $\gamma$ is the rational relation given by the closure over $C$, thus $\gamma = C^*$. Covering grammars were constructed for three medium-resource languages and four of the low-resource languages. A fragment of the Bulgarian covering grammar, showing readings of the characters б, ф, and ю, is presented in Table 8.[6]

Let $\mathcal{G}$ be the graphemic form of a word and let $\mathcal{P}$ and $\hat{\mathcal{P}}$ be the corresponding gold and hypothesis pronunciations for that word. For error analysis we are naturally interested in cases where $\mathcal{P} \neq \hat{\mathcal{P}}$, i.e., those cases where the gold and hypothesis pronunciations do not match, since these are exactly the cases which contribute to word error rate. Then, $P = \pi_o(\mathcal{G} \circ \gamma)$ is a finite-state lattice representing the set of all "possible" pronunciations of $\mathcal{G}$ admitted by the covering grammar.

When $\mathcal{P} \neq \hat{\mathcal{P}}$ but $\mathcal{P} \in P$—that is, when

[6]Error analysis software was implemented using the Pynini finite-state toolkit (Gorman 2016). See Gorman and Sproat 2021, ch. 3, for definitions of the various finite-state operations used here.

| | Baseline | CLUZH-4 | CLUZH-5 | CLUZH-6 | CLUZH-7 |
|---|---|---|---|---|---|
| arm_e | 7.0 | 7.1 | 6.6 | 6.6 | **6.4** |
| bul | **18.3** | 20.1 | 19.2 | 18.8 | 19.7 |
| dut | **14.7** | 15.0 | 14.9 | 15.6 | **14.7** |
| fre | 8.5 | **7.5** | **7.5** | **7.5** | 7.6 |
| geo | **0.0** | **0.0** | **0.0** | **0.0** | **0.0** |
| hbs_latn | **32.1** | 38.4 | 35.6 | 37.0 | 35.3 |
| hun | 1.8 | 1.5 | 1.2 | **1.0** | **1.0** |
| jpn_hira | 5.2 | 5.9 | 5.3 | 5.5 | **5.0** |
| kor | 16.3 | **16.2** | 16.9 | 17.2 | 16.3 |
| vie_hanoi | 2.5 | 2.3 | **2.0** | 2.1 | **2.0** |
| Macro-average | **10.6** | 11.4 | 10.9 | 11.1 | 10.8 |

Table 5: Results for the medium-resource subtask.

| | Baseline | AZ | CLUZH-1 | CLUZH-2 | CLUZH-3 | UBC-1 | UBC-2 |
|---|---|---|---|---|---|---|---|
| ady | **22** | 30 | 24 | **22** | **22** | 25 | **22** |
| gre | 21 | 23 | **20** | 22 | **20** | 22 | 22 |
| ice | 12 | 22 | **10** | 12 | **10** | 13 | 11 |
| ita | **19** | 25 | 23 | 24 | 21 | 20 | 22 |
| khm | 34 | 42 | 32 | 33 | 32 | 31 | **28** |
| lav | 55 | 53 | 53 | **49** | **49** | 58 | **49** |
| mlt_latn | 19 | 19 | **12** | 16 | 14 | 19 | 18 |
| rum | **10** | 13 | 13 | 13 | 12 | 14 | **10** |
| slv | 49 | 90 | 50 | 59 | 55 | 56 | **47** |
| wel_sw | **10** | 40 | **10** | 13 | 12 | 13 | 12 |
| Macro-average | 25.1 | 35.7 | 24.7 | 26.3 | 24.7 | 27.1 | **24.1** |

Table 6: Results for the low-resource subtask.

the gold pronunciation is one of the possible pronunciations—we refer to such errors as *model deficiencies*, since this condition suggests that the system in question has failed to guess one of several possible pronunciations of the current word. In many cases this reflects genuine ambiguities in the orthography itself. For example, in Italian, *e* is used to write both the phonemes /e, ɛ/ and *o* is similarly read as /o, ɔ/ (Rogers and d'Arcangeli 2004). There are few if any orthographic clues to which mid-vowel phoneme is intended, and all submissions incorrectly predicted that the *o* in *nome* 'name' is read as [ɔ] rather than [o]. Similar issues arise in Icelandic and French. The preceding examples both represent global ambiguities, but model deficiencies may also occur when the system has failed to disambiguate a local ambiguity. One example of this can be found in French: the verbal third-person plural suffix *-ent* is silent whereas the non-suffixal word-final *ent* is normally read as [ɑ̃]. Morphological information was not provided to the covering grammar, but it could easily be exploited by grapheme-to-phoneme models.

Another condition of interest is when $\mathcal{P} \neq \hat{\mathcal{P}}$ but $\mathcal{P} \notin P$. We refer to such errors as *coverage deficiencies*, since they arise when the gold pronunciation is not one permitted by the covering grammar. While coverage deficiencies may result from actual deficiencies in the covering grammar itself, they more often arise when a word does not follow the normal orthographic principles of its language. For instance, Italian has borrowed the English loanword *weekend* [wikɛnd] 'id.' but has not yet adapted it to Italian orthographic principles. Finally, coverage deficiencies may indicate target errors, inconsistencies in the gold data itself. For example, in the Italian data, the tie bars used to indi-

| eng_us | ɪ | ə | 113 | ɑ | ɔ | 112 | _ | ʊ• | 96 | _ | ɪ• | 85 | ɪ | i | 76 |
|---|---|---|---|---|---|---|---|---|---|---|---|---|---|---|---|
| arm_e | _ | ə• | 16 | ə• | _ | 10 | tʰ | d | 6 | d | tʰ | 6 | j• | _ | 3 |
| bul | ɛ• | d͡ | 32 | a | ə | 31 | ə | ɤ | 30 | _ | ◌̥ | 27 | ə | a | 25 |
| dut | ə | eː | 10 | _ | ː | 10 | ə | ɛ | 9 | eː | ə | 8 | z | s | 8 |
| fre | a | ɑ | 6 | _ | •s | 5 | ɔ | o | 5 | e | ɛ•ʁ | 3 | _ | •t | 3 |
| geo | | | | | | | | | | | | | | | |
| hbs_latn | _ | ː | 85 | ː | _ | 76 | _ | ◌̌ | 55 | ◌̌ | ◌̂ | 53 | ◌̌ | _ | 52 |
| hun | _ | ː | 6 | h | ɦ | 3 | ʃ | s | 2 | ː | _ | 2 | | | |
| jpn_hira | _ | ◌̥ | 20 | _ | ◌̊ | 11 | _ | d͡ | 4 | ː | •ɯ̟ᵝ | 3 | h | ɯᵝ | 3 |
| kor | _ | ː | 73 | ː | _ | 28 | ʌ̹ | ɘː | 23 | ʰ | ◌̤ | 9 | ɘː | ʌ̹ | 6 |
| vie_hanoi | _ | w• | 3 | _ | ˧˩ | 3 | _ | w•ŋ͡m• | 2 | ◌͡ɕ | •ɹ | 2 | _ | ʔ• | 2 |
| ady | ’ | _ | 3 | ː | _ | 3 | ʃ | ʂ | 3 | ə• | _ | 2 | a | ə | 2 |
| gre | ɾ | r | 8 | r | ɾ | 3 | i | ʝ | 3 | m• | _ | 2 | ɣ | g | 2 |
| ice | ː | _ | 2 | ◌̥ | _ | 2 | _ | ː | 2 | | | | | | |
| ita | o | ɔ | 6 | e | ɛ | 5 | j | i | 3 | ◌͡ | • | 2 | ɔ | o | 2 |
| khm | aː | i•ə | 3 | _ | ʰ | 3 | _ | •ɑː | 2 | ĕ | ɔ | 2 | ɑ | a | 2 |
| lav | ◌̄ | ◌̂ | 11 | _ | ◌̂ | 10 | ◌̀ | _ | 9 | ◌̄ | _ | 7 | _ | ◌̀ | 4 |
| mlt_latn | _ | ː | 5 | _ | ɪ• | 2 | ɐ | a | 2 | b | p | 2 | a | ɐ | 2 |
| rum | ◌͡ | • | 2 | | | | | | | | | | | | |
| slv | ◌́ | ◌̀ | 7 | ◌̀ː | _ | 6 | ◌́ː | _ | 6 | _ | ◌́ː | 5 | ɛ | éː | 4 |
| wel_sw | ɪ | iː | 3 | ɪ | i̯ | 2 | _ | ɛ• | 2 | | | | | | |

Table 7: The five most frequent error types, represented by the hypothesis string, gold string, and count, for each language; • indicates whitespace and _ the empty string.

| … | |
|---|---|
| б | b |
| б | bʲ |
| б | p |
| … | |
| ф | f |
| ф | fʲ |
| … | |
| ю | ju |
| ю | u |
| … | |

Table 8: Fragment of a covering grammar for Bulgarian; the left column contains graphemes and corresponding phones are given in the right column.

cate affricates are not always present, and many apparent errors are the result of gold pronunciations which omit a tie bar.

WER and model deficiency rate (MDR) is shown for select systems and three languages from the medium-resource subtask in Table 9, and Table 10 shows similar statistics for four low-resource languages. Note that by construction, one can obtain the coverage deficiency rate simply by subtracting MDR from WER. By comparing WER and MDR one can see the overwhelming majority of errors in these seven languages are model deficiencies, most naturally arising from genuine ambiguities in orthography rather than target errors (i.e., data inconsistencies).

To facilitate ensemble construction and further error analysis, we release all submissions' test set predictions to the research community.[7]

## 9 Discussion

We once again see an enormous difference in language difficulty. One of the languages with the highest amount of data, English, also has one of the highest WERs. In contrast, the baseline and all four submissions to the medium-resource subtask achieve perfect performance on Georgian. This is a substantial change from the previous year's shared task: with a sample roughly half the size of this year's task, the best system (Yu et al. 2020) obtained a WER of 24.89 on Georgian (Gorman et al.

[7] https://drive.google.com/drive/folders/1Fer7UfHBnt5k-WFHsVXQO8ac3BvREAyC

|  | Baseline |  | CLUZH-5 |  |
|---|---|---|---|---|
|  | WER | MDR | WER | MDR |
| bul | 18.3 | 17.6 | 19.2 | 19.0 |
| fre | 8.5 | 7.5 | 7.5 | 6.8 |
| jpn_hira | 5.2 | 4.4 | 5.3 | 4.5 |

Table 9: WER and model deficiency rate (MDR) for three languages from the medium-resource subtask.

|  | Baseline |  | AZ |  | CLUZH-1 |  | UBC-2 |  |
|---|---|---|---|---|---|---|---|---|
|  | WER | MDR | WER | MDR | WER | MDR | WER | MDR |
| ady | 22 | 22 | 30 | 23 | 24 | 21 | 22 | 22 |
| gre | 21 | 18 | 23 | 19 | 20 | 17 | 22 | 21 |
| ice | 12 | 9 | 22 | 17 | 10 | 7 | 11 | 5 |
| ita | 19 | 15 | 25 | 19 | 23 | 16 | 22 | 19 |

Table 10: WER and model deficiency rate (MDR) for four languages from the low-resource subtask.

2020:47). This enormous improvement likely reflects quality assurance work on this language,[8] but we did not anticipate reaching ceiling performance. Insofar as the above quality assurance and error analysis techniques prove effective and generalizable, we may soon be able to ask what makes a language hard to pronounce (cf. Gorman et al. 2020:45f.).

As mentioned above, the data here are a mixture of broad and narrow transcriptions. At first glance, this might explain some of the variation in language difficulty; for example, it is easy to imagine that the additional details in narrow transcriptions make them more difficult to predict. However, for many languages, only one of the two levels of transcription is available at scale, and other languages, divergence between broad and narrow transcriptions is impressionistically quite minor. However, this impression ought to be quantified.

While we responded to community demand for lower- and higher-resource subtasks, only one team submitted to the high- and medium-resource subtasks, respectively. It was surprising that none of the medium-resource submissions were able to consistently outperform the baseline model across the ten target languages. Clearly, this year's baseline is much stronger than the previous year's.

Participants in the high- and medium-resource subtasks were permitted to make use of lemmas and morphological tags from UniMorph as additional features. However, no team made use of resources. Some prior work (e.g., Demberg et al. 2007) has found morphological tags highly useful, and error analysis (§8.2) suggests this information would make an impact in French.

There is a large performance gap between the medium-resource and low-resource subtasks. For instance, the baseline achieves a WER of 10.6 in the medium-resource scenario and a WER of 25.1 in the low-resource scenario. It seems that current models are unable to reach peak performance with the 800 training examples provided in the low-resource subtask. Further work is needed to develop more efficient models and data augmentation strategies for low-resource scenarios. In our opinion, this scenario is the most important one for speech technology, since speech resources—including pronunciation data—are scarce for the vast majority of the world's written languages.

## 10 Conclusions

The second iteration of the shared task on multilingual grapheme-to-phoneme conversion features many improvements on the previous year's task, most of all data quality. Four teams submitted thirteen systems, achieving substantial reductions in both absolute and relative error over the baseline in two of three subtasks. We hope the code and data, released under permissive licenses,[9] will be used to benchmark grapheme-to-phoneme conversion and sequence-to-sequence modeling techniques more generally.

[8] https://github.com/CUNY-CL/wikipron/issues/138

[9] https://github.com/sigmorphon/2021-task1/

## Acknowledgements

We thank the Wiktionary contributors, particularly Aryaman Arora, without whom this shared task would be impossible. We also thank contributors to WikiPron, especially Sasha Gutkin, Jackson Lee, and the participants of Hacktoberfest 2020. Finally, thank you to Andrew Kirby for last-minute copy editing assistance.

## References

Simon Clematide and Peter Makarov. 2021. CLUZH at SIGMORPHON 2021 Shared Task on Multilingual Grapheme-to-Phoneme Conversion: variations on a baseline. In *Proceedings of the 18th SIGMORPHON Workshop on Computational Research in Phonetics, Phonology, and Morphology*.

Ryan Cotterell, Christo Kirov, John Sylak-Glassman, Géraldine Walther, Ekaterina Vylomova, Patrick Xia, Manaal Faruqui, Sandra Kübler, David Yarowsky, Jason Eisner, and Mans Hulden. 2017. CoNLL–SIGMORPHON 2017 shared task: universal morphological reinflection in 52 languages. In *Proceedings of the CoNLL SIGMORPHON 2017 Shared Task: Universal Morphological Reinflection*, pages 1–30.

Vera Demberg, Helmut Schmid, and Gregor Möhler. 2007. Phonological constraints and morphological preprocessing for grapheme-to-phoneme conversion. In *Proceedings of the 45th Annual Meeting of the Association of Computational Linguistics*, pages 96–103.

Daan van Esch, Mason Chua, and Kanishka Rao. 2016. Predicting pronunciations with syllabification and stress with recurrent neural networks. In *INTERSPEECH 2016: 17th Annual Conference of the International Speech Communication Association*, pages 2841–2845.

Vasundhara Gautam, Wang Yau Li, Zafarullah Mahmood, Frederic Mailhot, Shreekantha Nadig, Riqiang Wang, and Nathan Zhang. 2021. Avengers, ensemble! Benefits of ensembling in grapheme-to-phoneme prediction. In *Proceedings of the 18th SIGMORPHON Workshop on Computational Research in Phonetics, Phonology, and Morphology*.

Dirk Goldhahn, Thomas Eckart, and Uwe Quasthoff. 2012. Building large monolingual dictionaries at the Leipzig Corpora Collection: from 100 to 200 languages. In *Proceedings of the Eighth International Conference on Language Resources and Evaluation*, pages 759–765.

Kyle Gorman. 2016. Pynini: a Python library for weighted finite-state grammar compilation. In *Proceedings of the SIGFSM Workshop on Statistical NLP and Weighted Automata*, pages 75–80.

Kyle Gorman, Lucas F.E. Ashby, Aaron Goyzueta, Shijie Wu, and Daniel You. 2020. The SIGMORPHON 2020 shared task on multilingual grapheme-to-phoneme conversion. In *Proceedings of the 17th SIGMORPHON Workshop on Computational Research in Phonetics, Phonology, and Morphology*, pages 40–50.

Kyle Gorman, Arya D. McCarthy, Ryan Cotterell, Ekaterina Vylomova, Miikka Silfverberg, and Magdalena Markowska. 2019. Weird inflects but OK: making sense of morphological generation errors. In *Proceedings of the 23rd Conference on Computational Natural Language Learning*, pages 140–151.

Kyle Gorman and Richard Sproat. 2021. *Finite-State Text Processing*. Morgan & Claypool.

Michael Hammond. 2021. Data augmentation for low-resource grapheme-to-phoneme mapping. In *Proceedings of the 18th SIGMORPHON Workshop on Computational Research in Phonetics, Phonology, and Morphology*.

S. J. Hannahs. 2013. *The Phonology of Welsh*. Oxford University Press.

Bradley Hauer, Amir Ahmad Habibi, Yixing Luan, Arnob Mallik, and Grzegorz Kondrak. 2020. Low-resource G2P and P2G conversion with synthetic training data. In *Proceedings of the 17th SIGMORPHON Workshop on Computational Research in Phonetics, Phonology, and Morphology*, pages 117–122.

Robert Hoberman. 2007. Maltese morphology. In Alan S. Kaye, editor, *Morphologies of Asia and Africa*, volume 1, pages 257–282. Eisenbrauns.

Martin Jansche. 2014. Computer-aided quality assurance of an Icelandic pronunciation dictionary. In *Proceedings of the Ninth International Conference on Language Resources and Evaluation*, pages 2111–2114.

Paul Kingsbury, Stephanie Strassel, Cynthia McLemore, and Robert MacIntyre. 1997. CALLHOME American English Lexicon (PRONLEX). LDC97L20.

Christo Kirov, Ryan Cotterell, John Sylak-Glassman, Géraldine Walther, Ekaterina Vylomova, Patrick Xia, Manaal Faruqui, Arya D. McCarthy, Sandra Kübler, David Yarowsky, Jason Eisner, and Mans Hulden. 2018. UniMorph 2.0: universal morphology. In *Proceedings of the 11th Language Resources and Evaluation Conference*, pages 1868–1873.

Jackson L. Lee, Lucas F.E. Ashby, M. Elizabeth Garza, Yeonju Lee-Sikka, Sean Miller, Alan Wong, Arya D. McCarthy, and Kyle Gorman. 2020. Massively multilingual pronunciation mining with WikiPron. In *Proceedings of the 12th Language Resources and Evaluation Conference*, pages 4216–4221.

Roger Yu-Hsiang Lo and Garrett Nicolai. 2021. Linguistic knowledge in multilingual grapheme-to-phoneme conversion. In *Proceedings of the 18th SIGMORPHON Workshop on Computational Research in Phonetics, Phonology, and Morphology*.

Peter Makarov and Simon Clematide. 2018. Imitation learning for neural morphological string transduction. In *Proceedings of the 2018 Conference on Empirical Methods in Natural Language Processing*, pages 2877–2882.

Peter Makarov and Simon Clematide. 2020. CLUZH at SIGMORPHON 2020 shared task on multilingual grapheme-to-phoneme conversion. In *Proceedings of the 17th SIGMORPHON Workshop on Computational Research in Phonetics, Phonology, and Morphology*, pages 171–176.

Steven Moran and Michael Cysouw. 2018. *The Unicode Cookbook for Linguists: Managing Writing Systems using Orthography Profiles*. Language Science Press.

Graham Neubig, Chris Dyer, Yoav Goldberg, Austin Matthews, Waleed Ammar, Antonios Anastasopoulos, and Pengcheng Yin. 2017. DyNet: the dynamic neural network toolkit. arXiv:1701.03980.

Ben Peters and André F.T. Martins. 2020. One-size-fits-all multilingual models. In *Proceedings of the 17th SIGMORPHON Workshop on Computational Research in Phonetics, Phonology, and Morphology*, pages 63–69.

Kanishka Rao, Fuchun Peng, Haşim Sak, and Françoise Beaufays. 2015. Grapheme-to-phoneme conversion using long short-term memory recurrent neural networks. In *2015 IEEE International Conference on Acoustics, Speech and Signal Processing*, pages 4225–4229.

Derek Rogers and Luciana d'Arcangeli. 2004. Italian. *Journal of the International Phonetic Association*, 34(1):117–121.

Elmar Ternes and Tatjana Vladimirova-Buhtz. 1990. Bulgarian. *Journal of the International Phonetic Association*, 20(1):45–47.

Kaili Vesik, Muhammad Abdul-Mageed, and Miikka Silfverberg. 2020. One model to pronounce them all: multilingual grapheme-to-phoneme conversion with a transformer ensemble. In *Proceedings of the 17th SIGMORPHON Workshop on Computational Research in Phonetics, Phonology, and Morphology*, pages 146–152.

Kaisheng Yao and Geoffrey Zweig. 2015. Sequence-to-sequence neural net models for grapheme-to-phoneme conversion. In *INTERSPEECH 2015: 16th Annual Conference of the International Speech Communication Association*, pages 3330–3334.

Xiang Yu, Ngoc Thang Vu, and Jonas Kuhn. 2020. Ensemble self-training for low-resource languages: grapheme-to-phoneme conversion and morphological inflection. In *Proceedings of the 17th SIGMORPHON Workshop on Computational Research in Phonetics, Phonology, and Morphology*, pages 70–78.

# Data augmentation for low-resource grapheme-to-phoneme mapping

**Michael Hammond**
Dept. of Linguistics
U. of Arizona
Tucson, AZ, USA
hammond@u.arizona.edu

## Abstract

In this paper we explore a very simple neural approach to mapping orthography to phonetic transcription in a low-resource context. The basic idea is to start from a baseline system and focus all efforts on data augmentation. We will see that some techniques work, but others do not.

## 1 Introduction

This paper describes a submission by our team to the 2021 edition of the SIGMORPHON Grapheme-to-Phoneme conversion challenge. Here we demonstrate our efforts to improve grapheme-to-phoneme mapping for low-resource languages in a neural context using only data augmentation techniques.

The basic problem in the low-resource condition was to build a system that maps from graphemes to phonemes with very limited data. Specifically, there were 10 languages with 800 training pairs and 100 development pairs. Each pair was a word in its orthographic representation and a phonetic transcription of that word (though some multi-word sequences were also included). Systems were then tested on 100 additional pairs for each language. The 10 languages are given in Table 1.

To focus our efforts, we kept to a single system, intentionally similar to one of the simple baseline systems from the previous year's challenge.

We undertook and tested three data augmentation techniques.

1. move as much development data to training data as possible
2. extract substring pairs from the training data to use as additional training data
3. train all the languages together

In the following, we first provide additional details on our base system and then outline and test each of the moves above separately. We will see that some work and some do not.

| Code | Language |
|---|---|
| ady | Adyghe |
| gre | Modern Greek |
| ice | Icelandic |
| ita | Italian |
| khm | Khmer |
| lav | Latvian |
| mlt(_latn) | Maltese (Latin script) |
| rum | Romanian |
| slv | Slovene |
| wel(_sw) | Welsh (South Wales dialect) |

Table 1: Languages and codes

We acknowledge at the outset that we do not expect a system of this sort to "win". Rather, we were interested in seeing how successful a minimalist approach might be, one that did not require major changes in system architecture or training. This minimalist approach entailed that the system not require a lot of detailed manipulation and so we started with a "canned" system. This approach also entailed that training be something that could be accomplished with modest resources and time. All configurations below were run on a Lambda Labs Tensorbook with a single GPU.[1] No training run took more than 10 minutes.

## 2 General architecture

The general architecture of the model is inspired by one of the 2020 baseline systems (Gorman et al., 2020): a sequence-to-sequence neural net with a two-level LSTM encoder and a two-level LSTM decoder. The system we used is adapted from the OpenNMT base (Klein et al., 2017).

There is a 200-element embedding layer in both

[1] RTX 3080 Max-Q.



*Proceedings of the Seventeenth SIGMORPHON Workshop on Computational Research in Phonetics, Phonology, and Morphology*, pages 126–130

encoder and decoder. Each LSTM layer has 300 nodes. The systems are connected by a 5-head attention mechanism (Luong et al., 2015). Training proceeds in 24,000 steps and the learning rate starts at 1.0 and decays at a rate of 0.8 every 1,000 steps starting at step 10,000. Optimization is stochastic gradient descent, the batch size is 64, the dropout rate is 0.5.

We spent a fair amount of time tuning the system to these settings for optimal performance with this general architecture on these data. We do not detail these efforts as this is just a normal part of working with neural nets and not our focus here.

Precise instructions for building the docker image, full configuration files, and auxiliary code files are available at `https://github.com/hammondm/g2p2021`.

## 3 General results

In this section, we give the general results of the full system with all strategies in place and then in the next sections we strip away each of our augmentation techniques to see what kind of effect each has. In building our system, we did not have access to the correct transcriptions for the test data provided, so we report performance on the development data here.

The system was subject to certain amount of randomness because of randomization of training data and random initial weights in the network. We therefore report mean final accuracy scores over multiple runs.

Our system provides accuracy scores for development data in terms of character-level accuracy. The general task was scored in terms of word-level error rate, but we keep this measure for several reasons. First, it was simply easier as this is what the system provided as a default. Second, this is a more granular measure that enabled us to adjust the system more carefully. Finally, we were able to simulate word-level accuracy in addition as described below.

We use a Monte Carlo simulation to calculate expected word-level accuracy based on character-level accuracy and average transcription length for the training data for the different languages. The simulation works by generating $100,000$ words with a random distribution of a specific character-level accuracy rate and then calculating word-level accuracy from that. Running the full system ten times, we get the results in Table 2. Keep in mind that we are reporting accuracy rather than error rate, so the goal is to maximize these values.

| | Character | Word |
|---|---|---|
| | 94.84 | 75.6 |
| | 94.78 | 75.3 |
| | 94.46 | 74.0 |
| | 94.84 | 75.5 |
| | 94.71 | 75.0 |
| | 94.59 | 74.5 |
| | 94.90 | 75.8 |
| | 94.53 | 74.2 |
| | 94.53 | 74.2 |
| | 94.71 | 75.0 |
| **Mean** | 94.69 | 74.91 |

Table 2: Development accuracy for 10 runs of the full system with all languages grouped together with estimated word-level accuracy

| | Character | Word |
|---|---|---|
| | 94.60 | 74.6 |
| | 94.71 | 75.0 |
| | 94.35 | 73.8 |
| | 94.48 | 74.0 |
| | 94.48 | 74.0 |
| | 94.50 | 74.2 |
| | 94.59 | 74.5 |
| | 94.71 | 75.0 |
| | 94.80 | 75.4 |
| | 94.59 | 74.5 |
| **Mean** | 94.58 | 74.5 |

Table 3: Development accuracy for 10 runs of the reduced system with all languages grouped together with 100 development pairs with estimated word-level accuracy

## 4 Using development data

The default partition for each language is 800 pairs for training and 100 pairs for development. We shifted this to 880 pairs for training and 20 pairs for development. The logic of this choice was to retain what seemed like the minimum number of development items. Running the system ten times without this repartitioning gives the results in Table 3.

There is a small difference in the right direction, but it is not significant for characters ($t = -1.65$, $p = 0.11$, unpaired) or words ($t = -1.56$, $p = 0.13$, unpaired). It may be that with a larger sample of runs, the difference becomes more stable.

| Code | Items added |
|---|---|
| ady | 4 |
| gre | 223 |
| ice | 58 |
| ita | 194 |
| khm | 39 |
| lav | 100 |
| mlt_latn | 62 |
| rum | 119 |
| slv | 127 |
| wel_sw | 7 |

Table 4: Number of substrings added for each language

## 5 Using substrings

This method involves finding peripheral letters that map unambiguously to some symbol and then finding plausible splitting points within words to create partial words that can be added to the training data.

Let's exemplify this with Welsh. First, we identify all word-final letters that always correspond to the same symbol in the transcription. For example, the letter *c* always corresponds to a word-final [k]. Similarly, we identify word-initial characters with the same property. For example, in these data, the word-initial letter *t* always corresponds to [t].[2] We then search for any word in training that has the medial sequence *ct* where the transcription has [kt]. We take each half of the relevant item and add them to the training data if that pair is not already there. For example, the word *actor* [aktɔr] fits the pattern, so we can add the pairs ac-ak and tor-tɔr. to the training data. Table 4 gives the number of items added for each language. This strategy is a more limited version of the "slice-and-shuffle" approach used by Ryan and Hulden (2020) in last year's challenge.

Note that this procedure can make errors. If there are generalizations about the pronunciation of letters that are not local, that involve elements at a distance, this procedure can obscure those. Another example from Welsh makes the point. There are exceptions, but the letter *y* in Welsh is pronounced two ways. In a word-final syllable, it is pronounced [ɨ], e.g. *gwyn* [gwɨn] 'white'. In a non-final syllable, it is pronounced [ə], e.g. *gwynion* [gwənjɔn] 'white ones'. Though it doesn't happen in the training data here, the procedure above could easily result in a *y* in a non-final syllable ending up in a final syllable in a substring generated as above.

[2]This is actually incorrect for the language as a whole. Word-initial *t* in the digraph *th* corresponds to a different sound [θ].

| | Character | Word |
|---|---|---|
| | 95.15 | 76.9 |
| | 94.40 | 73.7 |
| | 95.15 | 76.8 |
| | 94.59 | 74.5 |
| | 94.65 | 74.8 |
| | 95.27 | 77.4 |
| | 94.53 | 74.2 |
| | 94.78 | 75.2 |
| | 95.09 | 76.6 |
| | 94.59 | 74.5 |
| **Mean** | 94.82 | 75.46 |

Table 5: 10 runs with all languages grouped together without substrings added for each language

Table 5 shows the results of 10 runs without these additions and simulated word error rates for each run.

Strikingly, adding the substrings *lowered* performance, but the difference with the full model is not significant for either characters ($t = 1.18$, $p = 0.25$, unpaired) or for words ($t = 1.17$, $p = 0.25$, unpaired). This model without substrings is the best-performing of all the models we tried, so this is what was submitted.

## 6 Training together

The basic idea here was to leverage the entire set of languages. Thus all languages were trained together. To distinguish them, each pair was prefixed by its language code. Thus if we had orthography $O = \langle o_1, o_2, \ldots, o_n \rangle$ and transcription $T = \langle t_1, t_2, \ldots, t_m \rangle$ from language $x$, the net would be trained on the pair $O' = \langle x, o_1, o_2, \ldots, o_n \rangle$ and $T' = \langle x, t_1, t_2, \ldots, t_m \rangle$. The idea is that, while the mappings and orthographies are distinct, there are similarities in what letters encode what sounds and in the possible sequences of sounds that can occur in the transcriptions. This approach is very similar to that of Peters et al. (2017), except that we tag the orthography and the transcription with the same langauge tag. Peters and Martins (2020) took a similar approach in last years challenge, but use embeddings prefixed at each time step.

In Table 6 we give the results for running each language separately 5 times. Since there was a lot less training data for each run, these models settled faster, but we ran them the same number of steps as the full models for comparison purposes.

There's a lot of variation across runs and the means for each language are quite different, presumably based on different levels of orthographic transparency. The general pattern is clear that, overall, training together does better than training separately. Comparing run means with our baseline system is significant ($t = -6.06$, $p < .001$, unpaired).

This is not true in all cases however. For some languages, individual training seems to be better than training together. Our hypothesis is that languages that share similar orthographic systems did better with joint training and that languages with diverging systems suffered.

The final results show that our best system (no substrings included, all languages together, moving development data to training) performed reasonably for some languages, but did quite poorly for others. This suggests a hybrid strategy that would have been more successful. In addition to training the full system here, train individual systems for each language. For test, compare final development results for individual languages for the jointly trained system and the individually trained systems and use whichever does better for each language in testing.

## 7 Conclusion

To conclude, we have augmented a basic sequence-to-sequence LSTM model with several data augmentation moves. Some of these were successful: redistributing data from development to training and training all the languages together. Some techniques were not successful though: the substring strategy resulted in diminished performance.

## Acknowledgments

Thanks to Diane Ohala for useful discussion. Thanks to several anonymous reviewers for very helpful feedback. All errors are my own.

## References

Kyle Gorman, Lucas F.E. Ashby, Aaron Goyzueta, Arya McCarthy, Shijie Wu, and Daniel You. 2020. The SIGMORPHON 2020 shared task on multilingual grapheme-to-phoneme conversion. In *Proceedings of the 17th SIGMORPHON Workshop on Computational Research in Phonetics, Phonology, and Morphology*, pages 40–50. Association for Computational Linguistics.

G. Klein, Y. Kim, Y. Y. Deng, J. Senellart, and A.M. Rush. 2017. OpenNMT: Open-source toolkit for neural machine translation. *ArXiv e-prints*. 1701.02810.

Minh-Thang Luong, Hieu Pham, and Christopher D. Manning. 2015. Effective approaches to attention-based neural machine translation. In *Proceedings of the 2015 Conference on Empirical Methods in Natural Language Processing*, pages 1412–1421.

Ben Peters, Jon Dehdari, and Josef van Genabith. 2017. Massively multilingual neural grapheme-to-phoneme conversion. In *Proceedings of the First Workshop on Building Linguistically Generalizable NLP Systems*, pages 19–26, Copenhagen. Association for Computational Linguistics.

Ben Peters and André F. T. Martins. 2020. DeepSPIN at SIGMORPHON 2020: One-size-fits-all multilingual models. In *Proceedings of the 17th SIGMORPHON Workshop on Computational Research in Phonetics, Phonology, and Morphology*, pages 63–69. Association for Computational Linguistics.

Zach Ryan and Mans Hulden. 2020. Data augmentation for transformer-based G2P. In *Proceedings of the 17th SIGMORPHON Workshop on Computational Research in Phonetics, Phonology, and Morphology*, pages 184–188. Association for Computational Linguistics.

| language | 5 separate runs | | | | | Mean |
|---|---|---|---|---|---|---|
| ady | 95.27 | 91.12 | 93.49 | 94.67 | 93.49 | 93.61 |
| gre | 97.25 | 98.35 | 98.35 | 98.90 | 98.90 | 98.35 |
| ice | 91.16 | 94.56 | 93.88 | 90.48 | 94.56 | 92.93 |
| ita | 93.51 | 94.59 | 94.59 | 94.59 | 94.59 | 94.38 |
| khm | 94.19 | 90.32 | 90.97 | 90.97 | 90.97 | 91.48 |
| lav | 94.00 | 90.67 | 89.33 | 92.00 | 90.67 | 91.33 |
| mlt_latn | 91.89 | 94.59 | 91.89 | 92.57 | 93.24 | 92.84 |
| rum | 95.29 | 96.47 | 94.71 | 95.88 | 95.29 | 95.51 |
| slv | 94.01 | 94.61 | 04.61 | 94.61 | 94.01 | 94.37 |
| wel_sw | 96.30 | 97.04 | 96.30 | 97.04 | 96.30 | 96.59 |
| **Mean** | 94.29 | 94.23 | 93.81 | 94.17 | 94.2 | 94.14 |

Table 6: 5 separate runs for each language

# Linguistic Knowledge in Multilingual Grapheme-to-Phoneme Conversion

**Roger Yu-Hsiang Lo**
Department of Linguistics
The University of British Columbia
roger.lo@ubc.ca

**Garrett Nicolai**
Department of Linguistics
The University of British Columbia
garrett.nicolai@ubc.ca

## Abstract

This paper documents the UBC Linguistics team's approach to the SIGMORPHON 2021 Grapheme-to-Phoneme Shared Task, concentrating on the low-resource setting. Our systems expand the baseline model with simple modifications informed by syllable structure and error analysis. In-depth investigation of test-set predictions shows that our best model rectifies a significant number of mistakes compared to the baseline prediction, besting all other submissions. Our results validate the view that careful error analysis in conjunction with linguistic knowledge can lead to more effective computational modeling.

## 1 Introduction

With speech technologies becoming ever more prevalent, grapheme-to-phoneme (G2P) conversion is an important part of the pipeline. G2P conversion refers to mapping a sequence of orthographic representations in some language to a sequence of phonetic symbols, often transcribed in the International Phonetic Alphabet (IPA). This is often an early step in tasks such as text-to-speech, where the pronunciation must be determined before any speech is produced. An example of such a G2P conversion, in Amharic, is illustrated below:

አማርኛ ↦ [amariɲːa] 'Amharic'

For the second year, one of SIGMORPHON shared tasks concentrates on G2P. This year, the task is further broken into three subtasks of varying data levels: high-resource ( 33K training instances), medium-resource (8K training instances), and low-resource (800 training instances). Our focus is on the low-resource subtask. The language data and associated constraints in the low-resource setting will be summarized in Section 3.1; the reader interested in the other two subtasks is referred to Ashby et al. (this volume) for an overview.

In this paper, we describe our methodology and approaches to the low-resource setting, including insights that informed our methods. We conclude with an extensive error analysis of the effectiveness of our approach.

This paper is structured as follows: Section 2 overviews previous work on G2P conversion. Section 3 gives a description of the data in the low-resource subtask, evaluation metric, and baseline results, along with the baseline model architecture. Section 4 introduces our approaches as well as the motivation behind them. We present our results in Section 5 and associated error analyses in Section 6. Finally, Section 7 concludes our paper.

## 2 Previous Work on G2P conversion

The techniques for performing G2P conversion have long been coupled with contemporary machine learning advances. Early paradigms utilize joint sequence models that rely on the alignment between grapheme and phoneme, usually with variants of the Expectation-Maximization (EM) algorithm (Dempster et al., 1977). The resulting sequences of graphones (i.e., joint grapheme-phoneme tokens) are then modeled with n-gram models or Hidden Markov Models (e.g., Jiampojamarn et al., 2007; Bisani and Ney, 2008; Jiampojamarn and Kondrak, 2010). A variant of this paradigm includes weighted finite-state transducers trained on such graphone sequences (Novak et al., 2012, 2015).

With the rise of various neural network techniques, neural-based methods have dominated the scene ever since. For example, bidirectional long short-term memory-based (LSTM) networks using a connectionist temporal classification layer produce comparable results to earlier n-gram models (Rao et al., 2015). By incorporating alignment information into the model, the ceiling set by n-gram



*Proceedings of the Seventeenth SIGMORPHON Workshop on Computational Research in Phonetics, Phonology, and Morphology*, pages 131–140

models has since been broken (Yao and Zweig, 2015). Attention further improved the performance, as attentional encoder-decoders (Toshniwal and Livescu, 2016) learned to focus on specific input sequences. As attention became "all that was needed" (Vaswani et al., 2017), transformer-based architectures have begun looming large (e.g., Yolchuyeva et al., 2019).

Recent years have also seen works that capitalize on multilingual data to train a single model with grapheme-phoneme pairs from multiple languages. For example, various systems from last year's shared task submissions learned from a multilingual signal (e.g., ElSaadany and Suter, 2020; Peters and Martins, 2020; Vesik et al., 2020).

## 3 The Low-resource Subtask

This section provides relevant information concerning the low-resource subtask.

### 3.1 Task Data

The provided data in the low-resource subtask come from ten languages[1]: Adyghe (`ady`; in the Cyrillic script), Modern Greek (`gre`; in the Greek alphabet), Icelandic (`ice`), Italian (`ita`), Khmer (`khm`; in the Khmer script, which is an alphasyllabary system), Latvian (`lat`), Maltese transliterated into the Latin script (`mlt_latn`), Romanian (`rum`), Slovene (`slv`), and the South Wales dialect of Welsh (`wel_sw`). The data are extracted from Wikitionary[2] using WikiPron (Lee et al., 2020), and filtered and downsampled with proprietary techniques, resulting in each language having 1,000 labeled grapheme-phoneme pairs, split into a training set of 800 pairs, a development set of 100 pairs, and a blind test set of 100 pairs.

### 3.2 The Evaluation Metric

This year, the evaluation metric is the word error rate (WER), which is simply the percentage of words for which the predicted transcription sequence differs from the ground-truth transcription. Different systems are ranked based on the macro-average over all languages, with lower scores indicating better systems. We also adopted this metric when evaluating our models on the development sets.

[1] All output is represented in IPA; unless specified otherwise, the input is written in the Latin alphabet.

[2] `https://www.wiktionary.org/`

### 3.3 Baselines

The official baselines for individual languages are based on an ensembled neural transducer trained with the imitation learning (IL) paradigm (Makarov and Clematide, 2018a). The baseline WERs are tabulated in Table 3. In what follows, we overview this baseline neural-transducer system, as our models are built on top of this system. The detailed formal description of the baseline system can be found in Makarov and Clematide (2018a,b,c, 2020).

The neural transducer in question defines a conditional distribution over edit actions, such as copy, deletion, insertion, and substitution:

$$p_\theta(\boldsymbol{y}, \boldsymbol{a}|x) = \prod_{j=1}^{|\boldsymbol{a}|} p_\theta(a_j|a_{<j}, \boldsymbol{x}),$$

where $\boldsymbol{x}$ denotes an input sequence of graphemes, and $\boldsymbol{a} = a_1 \dots a_{|\boldsymbol{a}|}$ stands for a sequence of edit actions. Note that the ouput sequence $\boldsymbol{y}$ is missing from the conditional probability on the right-hand side as it can be deterministically computed from $\boldsymbol{x}$ and $\boldsymbol{a}$. The model is implemented with an LSTM decoder, coupled with a bidirectional LSTM encoder.

The model is trained with IL and therefore demands an expert policy, which contains demonstrations of how the task can be optimally solved given any configuration. Cast as IL, the mapping from graphemes to phonemes can be understood as following an optimal path dictated by the expert policy that gradually turns input orthographic symbols to output IPA characters. To acquire the expert policy, a Stochastic Edit Distance (Ristad and Yianilos, 1998) model trained with the EM algorithm is employed to find an edit sequence consisting of four types of edits: copy, deletion, insertion, and substitution. During training time, the expert policy is queried to identify the next optimal edit that minimizes the following objective expressed in terms of Levenshtein distance and edit sequence cost:

$$\beta \text{ED}(\hat{\boldsymbol{y}}, \boldsymbol{y}) + \text{ED}(\boldsymbol{x}, \hat{\boldsymbol{y}}), \beta \geq 1,$$

where the first term is the Levenshtein distance between the target sequence $\boldsymbol{y}$ and the predicted sequence $\hat{\boldsymbol{y}}$, and the second term measures the cost of editing $\boldsymbol{x}$ to $\hat{\boldsymbol{y}}$.

The baseline is run with default hyperparameter values, which include ten different initial seeds and a beam of size 4 during inference. The predictions of these individual models are ensembled using a voting majority. Early efforts to modify the ensemble to incorporate system confidence showed that a majority ensemble was sufficient.

This model has proved to be competitive, judging from its performance on the previous year's G2P shared task. We therefore decided to use it as the foundation to construct our systems.

## 4 Our Approaches

This section lays out our attempted approaches. We investigate two alternatives, both linguistic in nature. The first is inspired by a universal linguistic structure—the syllable—and the other by the error patterns discerned from the baseline predictions on the development data.

### 4.1 System 1: Augmenting Data with Unsupervised Syllable Boundaries

Our first approach originates from the observation that, in natural languages, a sequence of sounds does not just assume a flat structure. Neighboring sounds group to form units, such as the onset, nucleus, and coda. In turn, these units can further project to a syllable (see Figure 1 for an example of such projection). Syllables are useful structural units in describing various linguistic phenomena and indeed in predicting the pronunciation of a word in some languages (e.g., Treiman, 1994). For instance, in Dutch, the vowel quality of the nucleus can be reliably inferred from the spelling after proper syllabification: *.dag.* [dɑx] 'day' but *.da.gen.* [daːɣən] 'days', where . marks syllable boundaries. Note that *a* in a closed syllable is pronounced as the short vowel [ɑ], but as the long vowel [aː] in an open syllable. In applying syllabification to G2P conversion, van Esch et al. (2016) find that training RNNs to jointly predict phoneme sequences, syllabification, and stress leads to further performance gains in some languages, compared to models trained without syllabification and stress information.

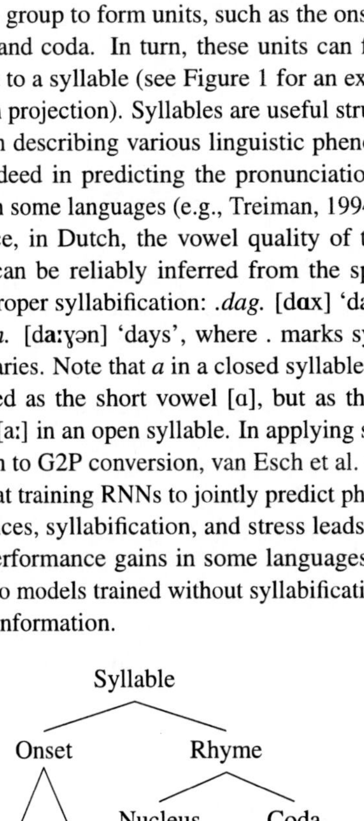


Figure 1: The syllable structure of *twelfth* [twɛɫfθ]

To identify syllable boundaries in the input sequence, we adopted a simple heuristic, the specific steps of which are listed below:[3]

1. **Find vowels in the output:** We first identify the vowels in the phoneme sequence by comparing each segment with the vowel symbols from the IPA chart. For instance, the symbols [ø] and [y] in [tʰrøyst] for Icelandic *traust* are vowels because they match the vowel symbols [ø] and [y] on the IPA chart.

2. **Find vowels in the input:** Next we align the grapheme sequence with the phoneme sequence using an unsupervised many-to-many aligner (Jiampojamarn et al., 2007; Jiampojamarn and Kondrak, 2010). By identifying graphemes that are aligned to phonemic vowels, we can identify vowels in the input. Using the Icelandic example again, the aligner produces a one-to-one mapping: $t \mapsto$ tʰ, $r \mapsto$ r, $a \mapsto$ ø, $u \mapsto$ y, $s \mapsto$ s, and $t \mapsto$ t. We therefore assume that the input characters *a* and *u* represent two vowels. Note that this step is often redundant for input sequences based on the Latin script but is useful in identifying vowel symbols in other scripts.

3. **Find valid onsets and codas:** A key step in syllabification is to identify which sequences of consonants can form an onset or a coda. Without resorting to linguistic knowledge, one way to identify valid onsets and codas is to look at the two ends of a word—consonant sequences appearing word-initially before the first vowel are valid onsets, and consonant sequences after the final vowel are valid codas. Looping through each input sequence in the training data gives us a list of valid onsets and codas. In the Icelandic example *traust*, the initial *tr* sequence must be a valid onset, and the final *st* sequence a valid coda.

4. **Break word-medial consonant sequences into an onset and a coda:** Unfortunately identifying onsets and codas among word-medial consonant sequences is not as straightforward. For example, how do we know the

[3]We are aware that different languages permit distinct syllable constituents (e.g., some languages allow syllabic consonants while others do not), but given the restriction that we are not allowed to use external resources in the low-resource subtask, we simply assume that all syllables must contain a vowel.

sequence in the input V*ngstr*V (V for a vowel character) should be parsed as V*ng.str*V, as V*n.gstr*V, or even as V*.ngstr*V? To tackle this problem, we use the valid onset and coda lists gathered from the previous step: we split the consonant sequence into two parts, and we choose the split where the first part is a valid coda and the second part a valid onset. For instance, suppose we have an onset list {*str*, *tr*} and a coda list {*ng*, *st*}. This implies that we only have a single valid split—V*ng.str*V—so *ng* is treated as the coda for the previous syllable and *str* as the onset for the following syllable. In the case where more than one split is acceptable, we favor the split that produces a more complex onset, based on the linguistic heuristic that natural languages tend to tolerate more complex onsets than codas. For example, V*ng.str*V > V*ngs.tr*V. In the situation where none of the splits produces a concatenation of a valid coda and onset, we adopt the following heuristic:

   - If there is only one medial consonant (such as in the case where the consonant can only occur word-internally but not in the onset or coda position), this consonant is classified as the onset for the following syllable.
   - If there is more than one consonant, the first consonant is classified as the coda and attached to the previous syllable while the rest as the onset of the following syllable.

   Of course, this procedure is not free of errors (e.g., some languages have onsets that are only allowed word-medially, so word-initial onsets will naturally not include them), but overall it gives reasonable results.

5. **Form syllables:** The last step is to put together consonant and vowel characters to form syllables. The simplest approach is to allow each vowel character to be projected as a nucleus and distribute onsets and codas around these nuclei to build syllables. If there are four vowels in the input, there are likewise four syllables. There is one important caveat, however. When there are two or more consecutive vowel characters, some languages prefer to merge them into a single vowel/nucleus in their pronunciation (e.g., Greek χαι ↦ [ce]) while other languages simply default to vowel hiatuses/two side-by-side nuclei (e.g., Italian *badia* ↦ [bad**ia**])—indeed, both are common cross-linguistically. We again rely on the alignment results in the second step to select the vowel segmentation strategy for individual languages.

After we have identified the syllables that compose each word, we augmented the input sequences with syllable boundaries. We identify four labels to distinguish different types of syllable boundaries: `<cc>`, `<cv>`. `<vc>`, and `<vv>`, depending on the classes of sound the segments straddling the syllable boundary belong to. For instance, the input sequence `b í l a v e r k s t æ ð i` in Icelandic will be augmented to be `b í <vc> l a <vc> v e r k <cc> s t æ <vc> ð i`. We applied the same syllabification algorithm to all languages to generate new input sequences, with the exception of Khmer, as the Khmer script does not permit a straightforward linear mapping between input and output sequences, which is crucial for the vowel identification step. We then used these syllabified input sequences, along with their target transcriptions, as the training data for the baseline model.[4]

### 4.2 System 2: Penalizing Vowel and Diacritic Errors

Our second approach focuses on the training objective of the baseline model, and is driven by the errors we observed in the baseline predictions. Specifically, we noticed that the majority of errors for the languages with a high WER—Khmer, Latvian, and Slovene—concerned vowels, some examples of which are given in Table 1. Note the nature of these mistakes: the mismatch can be in the vowel quality (e.g., [ɔ] for [o]), in the vowel length (e.g., [áː] for [á]), in the pitch accent (e.g., [íː] for [ìː]), or a combination thereof.

Based on the above observation, we modified the baseline model to explicitly address this vowel-mismatching issue. We modified the objective such that erroneous vowel or diacritic (e.g., the lengthening marker [ː]) predictions during training incur

[4]The hyperparameters used are the default values provided in the baseline model code: character and action embedding = 100, encoder LSTM state dimension = decoder LSTM state dimension = 200, encoder layer = decoder layer = 1, beam width = 4, roll-in hyperparameter = 1, epochs = 60, patience = 12, batch size = 5, EM iterations = 10, ensemble size = 10.

| Language | Target | Baseline prediction |
|---|---|---|
| khm | n **u** h | n **ŭ** ə h |
| | r **ɔː** j | r **ĕ** ə j |
| | s p **ŏ** ə n | s p **a** n |
| lat | t s **eː** l s | t s **ɛ̂ː** l s |
| | j **u** **ō** k s | j **ù** **o** k s |
| | v **æ̂** l s | v **ǣː** l s |
| slv | j **óː** g **u** r t | j ɔ g **úː** r t |
| | k r **ìː** ʃ | k r **íː** ʃ |
| | z d **á** j | z d **áː** j |

Table 1: Typical errors in the development set that involve vowels from Khmer (khm), Latvian (lat), and Slovene (slv)

additional penalties. Each incorrectly-predicted vowel incurs this penalty. The penalty acts as a regularizer that forces the model to expend more effort on learning vowels. This modification is in the same spirit as the softmax-margin objective of Gimpel and Smith (2010), which penalizes high-cost outputs more heavily, but our approach is even simpler—we merely supplement the loss with additional penalties for vowels and diacritics. We fine-tuned the vowel and diacritic penalties using a grid search on the development data, incrementing each by 0.1, from 0 to 0.5. In the cases of ties, we skewed higher as the penalties generally worked better at higher values. The final values used to generate predictions for the test data are listed in Table 2. We also note that the vowel penalty had significantly more impact than the diacritic penalty.

| | Penalty | |
|---|---|---|
| Language | Vowel | Diacritic |
| ady | 0.5 | 0.3 |
| gre | 0.3 | 0.2 |
| ice | 0.3 | 0.3 |
| ita | 0.5 | 0.5 |
| khm | 0.2 | 0.4 |
| lav | 0.5 | 0.5 |
| mlt_latn | 0.2 | 0.2 |
| rum | 0.5 | 0.2 |
| slv | 0.4 | 0.4 |
| wel_sw | 0.4 | 0.5 |

Table 2: Vowel penalty and diacritic penalty values in the final models

## 5 Results

The performances of our systems, measured in WER, are juxtaposed with the official baseline results in Table 3. We first note that the baseline was particularly strong—gains were difficult to achieve for most languages. Our first system (Syl), which is based on syllabic information, unfortunately does not outperform the baseline. Our second system (VP), which includes additional penalties for vowels and diacritics, however, does outperform the baselines in several languages. Furthermore, the macro WER average not only outperforms the baseline, but all other submitted systems.

| | WER | | |
|---|---|---|---|
| Language | Baseline | Syl | VP |
| ady | 22 | 25 | 22 |
| gre | 21 | 22 | 22 |
| ice | 12 | 13 | **11** |
| ita | 19 | 20 | 22 |
| khm | 34 | **31** | **28** |
| lav | 55 | 58 | **49** |
| mlt_latn | 19 | 19 | **18** |
| rum | 10 | 14 | 10 |
| slv | 49 | 56 | **47** |
| wel_sw | 10 | 13 | 12 |
| Average | 25.1 | 27.1 | **24.1** |

Table 3: Comparison of test-set results based on the word error rates (WERs)

It seems that extra syllable information does not help with predictions in this particular setting. It might be the case that additional syllable boundaries increase input variability without providing much useful information with the current neural-transducer architecture. Alternatively, information about syllable boundary locations might be redundant for this set of languages. Finally, it is possible that the unsupervised nature of our syllable annotation was too noisy to aid the model. We leave these speculations as research questions for future endeavors and restrict the subsequent error analyses and discussion to the results from our vowel-penalty system.[5]

[5]One reviewer raised a question of why only syllable boundaries, as opposed to smaller constituents, such as onsets or codas, are marked. Our hunch is that many phonological alternations happen at syllable boundaries, and that vowel length in some languages depends on whether the nucleus vowel is in a closed or open syllable. Also, given that adding syllable

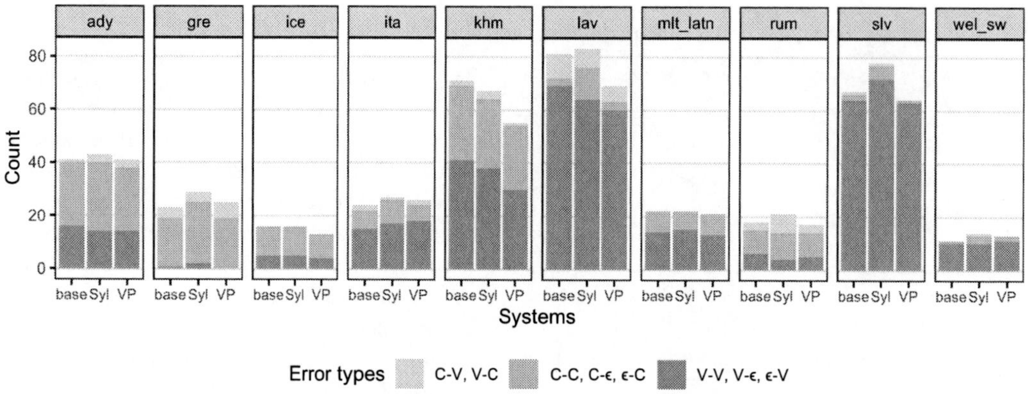


Figure 2: Distributions of error types in test-set predictions across languages. Error types are distinguished based on whether an error involves only consonants, only vowels, or both. For example, C-V means that the error is caused by a ground-truth consonant being replaced by a vowel in the prediction. C-$\epsilon$ means that it is a deletion error where the ground-truth consonant is missing in the prediction while $\epsilon$-C represents an insertion error where a consonant is wrongly added.

## 6 Error Analyses

In this section, we provide detailed error analyses on the test-set predictions from our best system. The goals of these analyses are twofold: (i) to examine the aspects in which this model outperforms the baseline and to what extent, and (ii) to get a better understanding of the nature of errors made by the system—we believe that insights and improvements can be derived from a good grasp of error patterns.

We analyzed the mismatches between predicted sequences and ground-truth sequences at the segmental level. For this purpose, we again utilized many-to-many alignment (Jiampojamarn et al., 2007; Jiampojamarn and Kondrak, 2010), but this time between a predicted sequence and the corresponding ground-truth sequence.[6] For each error along the aligned sequence, we classified it into one of the three kinds:

- Those involving erroneous vowel insertions (e.g., $\epsilon \rightarrow$ [ə]), deletions (e.g., [ə] $\rightarrow \epsilon$), or substitutions (e.g., [ə] $\rightarrow$ [a]).
- In the same vein, those involving erroneous consonant insertions (e.g., $\epsilon \rightarrow$ [ʔ]), deletions (e.g., [ʔ] $\rightarrow \epsilon$), and substitutions (e.g., [d] $\rightarrow$ [t]).
- Those involving exchanges of a vowel and a consonant (e.g., [w] $\rightarrow$ [u]) or vice versa.

The frequency of each error type made by the baseline model and our systems for each individual language is plotted in Figure 2. Some patterns are immediately clear. First, both systems have a similar pattern in terms of the distribution of error types across language, albeit that ours makes fewer errors on average. Second, both systems err on different elements, depending on the language. For instance, while Adyghe (`ady`) and Khmer (`khm`) have a more balanced distribution between consonant and vowel errors, Slovene (`slv`) and Welsh (`wel_sw`) are dominated by vowel errors. Third, the improvements gained in our system seem to come mostly from reduction in vowel errors, as is evident in the case of Khmer, Latvian (`lav`), and, to a lesser extent, Slovene.

The final observation is backed up if we zoom in on the errors in these three languages, which we visualize in Figure 3. Many incorrect vowels generated by the baseline model are now correctly predicted. We note that there are also cases, though less common, where the baseline model gives the right prediction, but ours does not. It should be pointed out that, although our system shows improvement over the baseline, there is still plenty of room for improvement in many languages, and our system still produces incorrect vowels in many

boundaries does not improve the results, it is unlikely that marking constituent boundaries, which adds more variability to the input, will result in better performance, though we did not test this hypothesis.

[6]The parameters used are: allowing deletion of input grapheme strings, maximum length of aligned grapheme and phoneme substring being one, and a training threshold of 0.001.

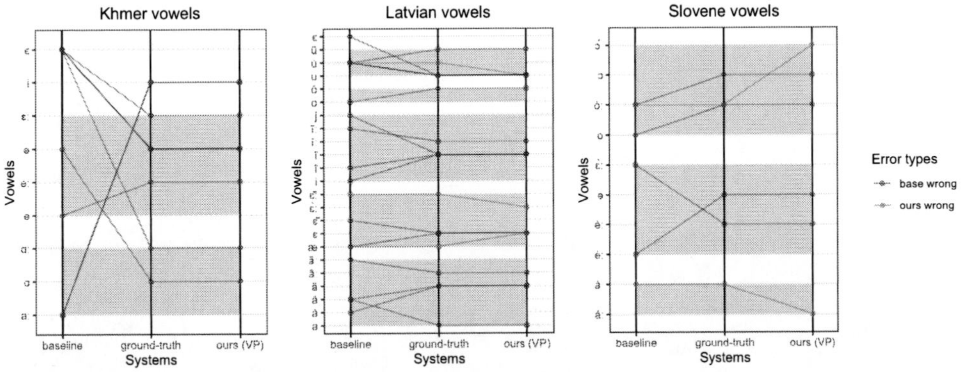


Figure 3: Comparison of vowels predicted by the baseline model and our best system (VP) with the ground-truth vowels. Here we only visualize the cases where either the baseline model gives the right vowel but our system does not, or vice versa. We do not include cases where both the baseline model and our system predict the correct vowel, or both predict an incorrect vowel, to avoid cluttering the view. Each baseline—ground-truth—ours line represents a set of aligned vowels in the same word; the horizontal line segment between a system and the ground-truth means that the prediction from the system agrees with the ground-truth. Color hues are used to distinguish cases where the prediction from the baseline is correct versus those where the prediction from our second system is correct. Shaded areas on the plots enclose vowels of similar vowel quality.

instances.

Finally, we look at several languages which still resulted in high WER on the test set—`ady`, `gre`, `ita`, `khm`, `lav`, and `slv`. We analyze the confusion matrix analysis to identify clusters of commonly-confused phonemes. This analysis again relies on the alignment between the ground-truth sequence and the corresponding predicted sequence to characterize error distributions. The results from this analysis are shown in Figure 4, and some interesting patterns are discussed below. Figure 2 suggests that Khmer has an equal share of consonant and vowel errors, and the heat maps in Figure 4 reveal that these errors do not seem to follow a certain pattern. However, a different picture emerges with Latvian and Slovene. For both languages, Figure 2 indicates the dominance of errors tied to vowels; consonant errors account for a relatively small proportion of errors. This observation is borne out in Figure 4, with the consonant heat maps for the two languages displaying a clear diagonal stripe, and the vowel heat maps showing much more off-diagonal signals. What is more interesting is that the vowel errors in fact form clusters, as highlighted by white squares on the heat maps. The general pattern is that confusion only arises *within* a cluster where vowels are of similar quality but differ in terms of length or pitch accent. For example, while [iː] might be incorrectly-predicted as [i], our model does not confuse it with, say, [u]. The challenges these languages present to the models are therefore largely suprasegmental—vowel length and pitch accent, both of which are lexicalized and not explicitly marked in the orthography. For the other three languages, their errors also show distinct patterns: for Adyghe, consonants differing only in secondary features can get confused; in Greek, many errors can be attributed to the mixing of [r] and [ɾ]; in Italian, front and back mid vowels can trick our model.

We hope that our detailed error analyses show not only that these errors "make linguistic sense"—and therefore attest to the power of the model—but also point out a pathway along which future modeling can be improved.

## 7 Conclusion

This paper presented the approaches adopted by the UBC Linguistics team to tackle the SIGMORPHON 2021 Grapheme-to-Phoneme Conversion challenge in the low-resource setting. Our submissions build upon the baseline model with modifications inspired by syllable structure and vowel error patterns. While the first modification does not result in more accurate predictions, the second modification does lead to sizable improvements over the baseline results. Subsequent error analyses reveal that the modified model indeed reduces erroneous vowel predictions for languages whose errors are dominated by vowel mismatches. Our approaches also demonstrate that patterns uncov-

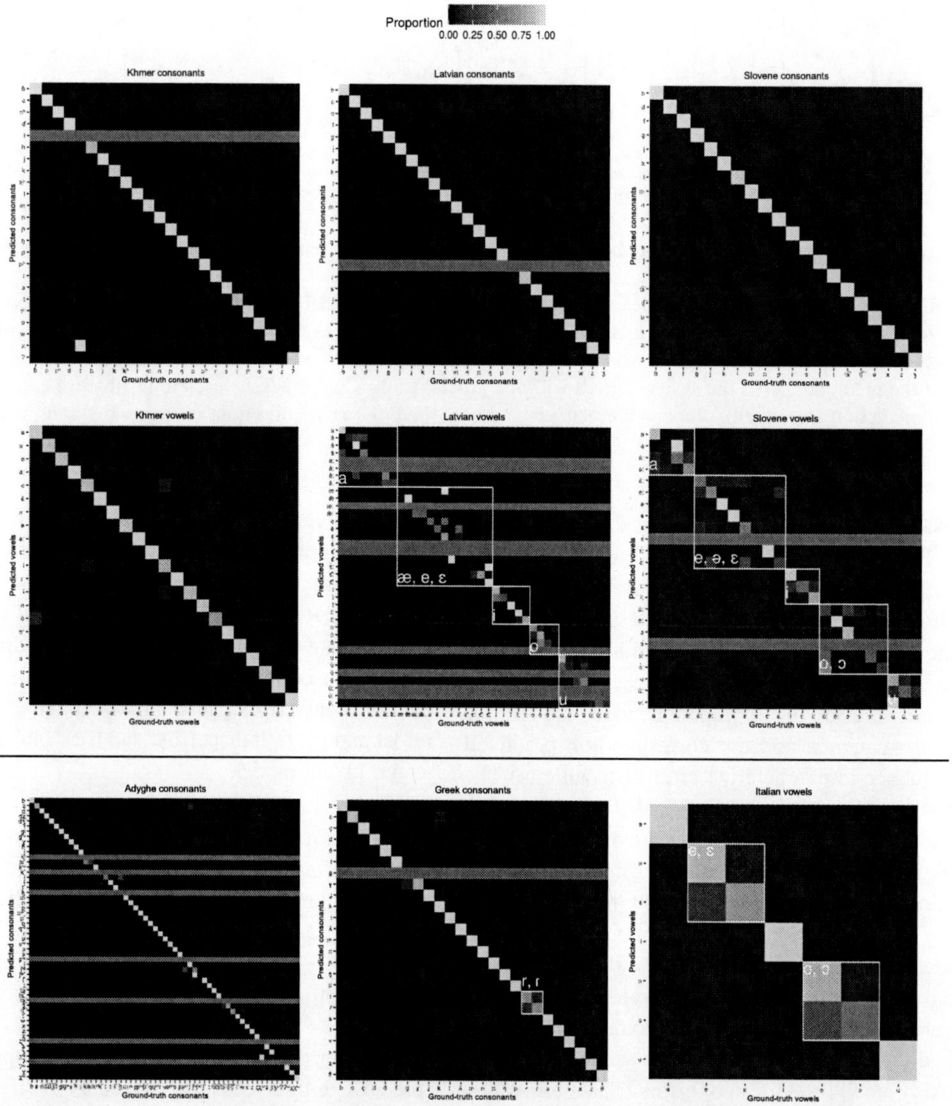

Figure 4: Confusion matrices of vowel and consonant predictions by our second system (VP) for languages with the test WER > 20%. Each row represents a predicted segment, with colors across columns indicating the proportion of times the predicted segment matches individual ground-truth segments. A gray row means the segment in question is absent in any predicted phoneme sequences but is present in at least one ground-truth sequence. The diagonal elements represent the number of times for which the predicted segment matches the target segment, while off-diagonal elements are those that are mis-predicted by the system. White squares are added to highlight segment groups where mismatches are common.

ered from careful error analyses can inform the directions for potential improvements.

## References


Maximilian Bisani and Hermann Ney. 2008. Joint-sequence models for grapheme-to-phoneme conversion. *Speech Communication*, 50:434–451.

A. P. Dempster, N. M. Laird, and D. B. Rubin. 1977. Maximum likelihood from incomplete data via the EM algorithm. *Journal of the Royal Statistical Society. Series B (Methodological)*, 39(1):1–38.

Omnia ElSaadany and Benjamin Suter. 2020. Grapheme-to-phoneme conversion with a multilingual transformer model. In *Proceedings of the Seventeenth SIGMORPHON Workshop on Computational Research in Phonetics, Phonology, and Morphology*, pages 85–89.

Daan van Esch, Mason Chua, and Kanishka Rao. 2016. Predicting pronunciations with syllabification and stress with recurrent neural networks. In *Proceedings of Interspeech 2016*, pages 2841–2845.

Kevin Gimpel and Noah A. Smith. 2010. Softmax-margin CRFs: Training log-linear models with cost functions. In *Human Language Technologies: The 2010 Annual Conference of the North American Chapter of the ACL*, pages 733–736.

Sittichai Jiampojamarn and Grzegorz Kondrak. 2010. Letter-phoneme alignment: An exploration. In *Proceedings of the 48th Annual Meeting of the Association for Computational Linguistics*, pages 780–788.

Sittichai Jiampojamarn, Grzegorz Kondrak, and Tarek Sherif. 2007. Applying many-to-many alignments and Hidden Markov Models to letter-to-phoneme conversion. In *Proceedings of NAACL HLT 2007*, pages 372–379.

Jackson L. Lee, Lucas F. E. Ashby, M. Elizabeth Garza, Yeonju Lee-Sikka, Sean Miller, Alan Wong, Arya D. McCarthy, and Kyle Gorman. 2020. Massively multilingual pronunciation mining with WikiPron. In *Proceedings of the 12th Conference on Language Resources and Evaluation (LREC 2020)*, pages 4223–4228.

Peter Makarov and Simon Clematide. 2018a. Imitation learning for neural morphological string transduction. In *Proceedings of the 2018 Conference on Empirical Methods in Natural Language Processing*, pages 2877–2882.

Peter Makarov and Simon Clematide. 2018b. Neural transition-based string transduction for limited-resource setting in morphology. In *Proceedings of the 27th International Conference on Computational Linguistics*, pages 83–93.

Peter Makarov and Simon Clematide. 2018c. UZH at CoNLL-SIGMORPHON 2018 shared task on universal morphological reinflection. In *Proceedings of the CoNLL-SIGMORPHON 2018 Shared Task: Universal Morphological Reinflection*, pages 69–75.

Peter Makarov and Simon Clematide. 2020. CLUZH at SIGMORPHON 2020 shared task on multilingual grapheme-to-phoneme conversion. In *Proceedings of the Seventeenth SIGMORPHON Workshop on Computational Research in Phonetics, Phonology, and Morphology*, pages 171–176.

Josef R. Novak, Nobuaki Minematsu, and Keikichi Hirose. 2012. WFST-based grapheme-to-phoneme conversion: Open source tools for alignment, model-building and decoding. In *Proceedings of the 10th International Workshop on Finite State Methods and Natural Language Processing*, pages 45–49.

Josef Robert Novak, Nobuaki Minematsu, and Keikichi Hirose. 2015. Phonetisaurus: Exploring garpheme-to-phoneme conversion with joint n-gram models in the WFST framework. *Natural Language Engineering*, 22(6):907–938.

Ben Peters and André F. T. Martins. 2020. DeepSPIN at SIGMORPHON 2020: One-size-fits-all multilingual models. In *Proceedings of the Seventeenth SIGMORPHON Workshop on Computational Research in Phonetics, Phonology, and Morphology*, pages 63–69.

Kanishka Rao, Fuchun Peng, Haşim Sak, and Françoise Beaufays. 2015. Grapheme-to-phoneme conversion using long short-term memory recurrent neural networks. In *IEEE International Conference on Acoustics, Speech and Signal Processing (ICASSP)*, pages 4225–4229.

Eric Sven Ristad and Peter N. Yianilos. 1998. Learning string-edit distance. *IEEE Transactions on Pattern Analysis and Machine Intelligence*, 20(5):522–532.

Shubham Toshniwal and Karen Livescu. 2016. Jointly learning to align and convert graphemes to phonemes with neural attention models. In *2016 IEEE Spoken Language Technology Workshop (SLT)*, pages 76–82.

Rebecca Treiman. 1994. To what extent do orthographic units in print mirror phonological units in speech? *Journal of Psycholinguistic Research*, 23(1):91–110.

Ashish Vaswani, Noam Shazeer, Niki Parmar, Jakob Uszkoreit, Llion Jones, Aidan N. Gomez, Łukaaz Kaiser, and Illia Polosukhin. 2017. Attention is all you need. In *Proceedings of the 31st Conference on Neural Information Processing Systems (NIPS 2017)*, pages 1–11.

Kaili Vesik, Muhammad Abdul-Mageed, and Miikka Silfverberg. 2020. One model to pronounce them all: Multilingual grapheme-to-phoneme conversion with a Transformer ensemble. In *Proceedings of the*

*Seventeenth SIGMORPHON Workshop on Computational Research in Phonetics, Phonology, and Morphology*, pages 146–152.

Kaisheng Yao and Geoffrey Zweig. 2015. Sequence-to-sequence neural net models for grapheme-to-phoneme conversion. In *Proceedings of Interspeech 2015*, pages 3330–3334.

Sevinj Yolchuyeva, Géza Németh, and Bálint Gyires-Tóth. 2019. Transformer based grapheme-to-phoneme conversion. In *Proceedings of Interspeech 2019*, pages 2095–2099.

# Avengers, Ensemble! Benefits of ensembling in grapheme-to-phoneme prediction

**Vasundhara Gautam, Wang Yau Li, Zafarullah Mahmood, Fred Mailhot[*], Shreekantha Nadig[†], Riqiang Wang, Nathan Zhang**

Dialpad Canada [†]Dialpad India
vasundhara,wangyau.li,zafar,fred.mailhot
shree,riqiang.wang,nzhang@dialpad.com

## Abstract

We describe three baseline beating systems for the high-resource English-only sub-task of the SIGMORPHON 2021 Shared Task 1: a small ensemble that Dialpad's[1] speech recognition team uses internally, a well-known off-the-shelf model, and a larger ensemble model comprising these and others. We additionally discuss the challenges related to the provided data, along with the processing steps we took.

## 1 Introduction

The transduction of sequences of *graphemes* to *phones* or *phonemes*,[2] that is from characters used in orthographic representations to characters used to represent minimal units of speech, is a core component of many tasks in speech science & technology. This *grapheme-to-phoneme* conversion (or *g2p*) may be used, e.g., to automate or scale the creation of digital lexicons or pronunciation dictionaries, which are crucial to FST-based approaches to automatic speech recognition (ASR) and synthesis (Mohri et al., 2002).

The SIGMORPHON 2021 Workshop included a Shared Task on g2p conversion, comprising 3 sub-tasks.[3] The low- and medium-resource tasks were multilingual, while the high-resource task was English-only. This paper provides an overview of the three baseline-beating systems submitted by the Dialpad team for the high-resource sub-task, along with discussion of the challenges posed by the data that was provided.

## 2 Sub-task 1: high-resource, English-only

The organizers provided 41,680 lines of data in total; 33,344 for training, and 4,168 each for development and test. The data consists of word/pronunciation pairs (*word-pron pairs*, henceforth), where words are sequences of graphemes and pronunciations are sequences of characters from the International Phonetic Alphabet (International Phonetic Association, 1999). The data was derived from the English portion of the WikiPron database (Lee et al., 2020), a massively multilingual resource of word-pron pairs extracted from Wiktionary[4] and subject to some manual QA and post-processing.[5]

The baseline model provided was the 2nd place finisher from the 2020 g2p shared task (Gorman et al., 2020). It is an ensembled neural transition model that operates over edit actions and is trained via imitation learning (Makarov and Clematide, 2020).

Evaluation scripts were provided to compute *word error rate* (WER), the percentage of words for which the output sequence does not match the gold label.

Notwithstanding the baseline's strong prior performance and the amount of data available, the task proved to be challenging; the baseline system achieved development and test set WERs of **45.13** and **41.94**, respectively. We discuss possible reasons for this below.

[*]Corresponding author. Contributing authors are listed alphabetically.

[1]https://www.dialpad.com/

[2]We use these terms interchangeably here to refer to graphical representations of minimal speech sounds, remaining agnostic as to their theoretical or ontological status.

[3]https://github.com/sigmorphon/2021-task1

[4]https://en.wiktionary.org/

[5]See https://github.com/sigmorphon/2021-task1 for fuller details on data formatting and processing.



*Proceedings of the Seventeenth SIGMORPHON Workshop on Computational Research in Phonetics, Phonology, and Morphology*, pages 141–147

## 2.1 Data-related challenges

Wiktionary is an open, collaborative, public effort to create a free dictionary in multiple languages. Anyone can create an account and add or amend words, pronunciations, etymological information, etc. As with most user-generated content, this is a noisy method of data creation and annotation.

Even setting aside the theory-laden question of when or whether a given word should be counted as English,[6] the open nature of Wiktionary means that speakers of different variants or dialects of English may submit varying or conflicting pronunciations for sets of words. For example, some transcriptions indicate that the users who input them had the *cot/caught* merger while others do not; in the training data "cot" is transcribed /k ɑ t/ and "caught" is transcribed /k ɔ t/, indicating a split, but "aughts" is transcribed as /ɑ t s/, indicating merger. There is also variation in the narrowness of transcription. For example, some transcriptions include aspiration on stressed-syllable-initial stops while others do not c.f. "kill" /kʰ ɪ l/ and "killer" /k ɪ l ɚ/.

Typically the set of English phonemes is taken to be somewhere between 38-45 depending on variant/dialect (McMahon, 2002). In exploring the training data, we found a total of 124 symbols in the training set transcriptions, many of which only appeared in a small set (1–5) of transcriptions. To reduce the effect of this long tail of infrequent symbols, we normalized the training set.

The main source of symbols in the long tail was the variation in the broadness of transcription—vowels were sometimes but not always transcribed with nasalization before a nasal consonant, aspiration on word-initial voiceless stops was inconsistently indicated, phonetic length was occasionally indicated, etc. There were also some cases of erroneous transcription that we uncovered by looking at the lowest frequency phones and the word-pronunciation pairs where they appeared. For instance, the IPA /j/ was transcribed as /y/ twice, the voiced alveolar approximant /ɹ/ was mistranscribed as the trill /r/ over 200 times, and we found a handful of issues where a phone was transcribed with a Unicode symbol not used in the IPA at all.

Most of these were cases where the rare variant was at least two orders of magnitude less frequent than the common variant of the symbol. There was, however, one class of sounds where the variation was less dramatically skewed; the consonants /m/, /n/, and /l/ appeared in unstressed syllables following schwa (/əm/, /ən/, /əl/) roughly one order of magnitude more frequently than their syllabic counterparts (/m̩/, /n̩/, /l̩/), and we opted not to normalize these. If we had normalized the syllabic variants, it would have resulted in more consistent g2p output but it would likely also have penalized our performance on the uncleaned test set.[7] In the end, our training data contained 47 phones (plus end-of-sequence and UNK symbols for some models).

# 3 Models

We trained and evaluated several models for this task, both publicly available, in-house, and custom developed, along with various ensembling permutations. In the end, we submitted three sets of baseline beating results. The organizers assigned sequential identifiers to multiple submissions (e.g. *Dialpad-N*); we include these in the discussion of our entries below, for ease of subsequent reference.

## 3.1 The Dialpad model (Dialpad-2)

Dialpad uses a g2p system internally for scalable generation of novel lexicon additions. We were motivated to enter this shared task as a means of assessing potential areas of improvement for our system; in order to do so we needed to assess our own performance as a baseline.

This model is a simple majority-vote ensemble of 3 existing publicly available g2p systems: *Phonetisaurus* (Novak et al., 2012), a WFST-based model, *Sequitur* (Bisani and Ney, 2008), a joint-sequence model trained via EM, and a neural sequence-to-sequence model developed at CMU as part of the CMUSphinx[8]

[6]E.g., the training data included the arguably French word-pronunciation pair: *embonpoint* /ɑ̃ b ɔ̃ p w ɛ̃/

[7]Although the possibility also exists that one or more of our models would have found and exploited contextual cues that weren't obvious to us by inspection.

[8]https://cmusphinx.github.io

toolkit (see subsection 3.2). As Dialpad uses a proprietary lexicon and phoneset internally, we retrained all three models on the cleaned version of the shared task training data, retaining default hyperparameters and architectures.

In the end, this ensemble achieved a test set WER of **41.72**, narrowly beating the baseline (results are discussed in more depth in Section 4).

### 3.2 A strong standalone model: CMUSphinx `g2p-seq2seq` (Dialpad-3)

CMUSphinx is a set of open systems and tools for speech science developed at Carnegie Mellon University, including a g2p system.[9] It is a neural sequence-to-sequence model (Sutskever et al., 2014) that is Transformer-based (Vaswani et al., 2017), written in Tensorflow (Abadi et al., 2015). A pre-trained 3-layer model is available for download, but it is trained on a dictionary that uses ARPABET, a substantially different phoneset from the IPA used in this challenge. For this reason we retrained a model from scratch on the cleaned version of the training data.

This model achieved a test set WER of **41.58**, again narrowly beating the baseline. Interestingly, this outperformed the Dialpad model which incorporates it, suggesting that Phonetisaurus and Sequitur add more noise than signal to predicted outputs, to say nothing of increased computational resources and training time. More generally, this points to the CMUSphinx seq2seq model as a simple and strong baseline against which future g2p research should be assessed.

### 3.3 A large ensemble (Dialpad-1)

In the interest of seeing what results could be achieved via further naive ensembling, our final submission was a large ensemble, comprising two variations on the baseline model, the Dialpad-2 ensemble discussed above, and two additional seq2seq models, one using LSTMs and the other Transformer-based. The latter additionally incorporated a sub-word extraction method designed to bias a model's input-output mapping toward "good" grapheme-phoneme correspondences.

The method of ensembling for this model is word level majority-vote ensembling. We select the most common prediction when there is a majority prediction (i.e. one prediction has more votes than all of the others). If there is a tie, we pick the prediction that was generated by the best standalone model with respect to each model's performance on the development set.

This collection of models achieved a test set WER of **37.43**, a 10.75% relative reduction in WER over the baseline model. As shown in Table 1, although a majority of the component models did not outperform the baseline, there was sufficient agreement across different examples that a simple majority voting scheme was able to leverage the models' varying strengths effectively. We discuss the components and their individual performance below and in Section 4.

#### 3.3.1 Baseline variations

The "foundation" of our ensemble was the default baseline model (Makarov and Clematide, 2018), which we trained using the raw data and default settings in order to reflect the baseline performance published by the organization. We included this in order to individually assess the effect of additional models on overall performance.

In addition to this default base, we added a larger version of the same model, for which we increased the number of encoder and decoder layers from 1 to 3, and increased the hidden dimensions 200 to 400.

#### 3.3.2 biLSTM+attention seq2seq

We conducted experiments with a RNN seq2seq model, comprising a biLSTM encoder, LSTM decoder, and dot-product attention.[10] We conducted several rounds of hyperparameter optimization over layer sizes, optimizer, and learning rate. Although none of these models outperformed the baseline, a small network (16-d embeddings, 128-d LSTM layers) proved to be efficiently trainable (2 CPU-hours) and improved the ensemble results, so it was included.

[9]https://github.com/cmusphinx/g2p-seq2seq

[10]We used the DyNet toolkit (Neubig et al., 2017) for these experiments.

#### 3.3.3 PAS2P: Pronunciation-assisted sub-words to phonemes

Sub-word segmentation is widely used in ASR and neural machine translation tasks, as it reduces the cardinality of the search space over word-based models, and mitigates the issue of OOVs. Use of sub-words for g2p tasks has been explore, e.g. Reddy and Goldsmith (2010) develop an MDL-based approach to extracting sub-word units for the task of g2p. Recently, a pronunciation-assisted sub-word model (PASM) (Xu et al., 2019) was shown to improve the performance of ASR models. We experimented with pronunciation-assisted sub-words to phonemes (PAS2P), leveraging the training data and a reparameterization of the IBM Model 2 aligner (Brown et al., 1993) dubbed *fast_align* (Dyer et al., 2013).[11]

The alignment model is used to find an alignment of sequences of graphemeres to their corresponding phonemes. We follow a similar process as Xu et al. (2019) to find the consistent grapheme-phoneme pairs and refinement of the pairs for the PASM model. We also collect grapheme sequence statistics and marginalize it by summing up the counts of each type of grapheme sequence over all possible types of phoneme sequences. These counts are the weights of each sub-word sequence.

Given a word and the weights for each sub-word, the segmentation process is a search problem over all possible sub-word segmentation of that word. We solve this search problem by building weighted FSTs[12] of a given word and the sub-word vocabulary, and finding the best path through this lattice. For example, the word "thoughtfulness" would be segmented by PASM as "th_ough_t_f_u_l_n_e_ss", and this would be used as the input in the PAS2P model rather than the full sequence of individual graphemes.

Finally, the PAS2P transducer is a Transformer-based sequence-to-sequence model trained using the ESPnet end-to-end speech processing toolkit (Watanabe et al., 2018), with pronunciation-assisted sub-words as inputs and phones as outputs. The model has 6 layers of encoder and decoder with 2048 units, and 4 attention heads with 256 units. We use dropout with a probability of 0.1 and label smoothing with a weight of 0.1 to regularize the model. This model achieved WERs of **44.84** and **43.40** on the development and test sets, respectively.

[11]https://github.com/clab/fast_align

[12]We use Pynini (Gorman, 2016) for this.

## 4 Results

Our main results are shown in Table 1, where we show both dev and test set WER for each individual model in addition to the submitted ensembles. In particular, we can see that many of the ensemble components do not beat the baseline WER, but nonetheless serve to improve the ensembled models.

| Model | dev | test |
|---|---|---|
| **Dialpad-3** | **43.30** | **41.58** |
| PAS2P | 44.84 | 43.40 |
| Baseline (large) | 44.99 | 41.65 |
| Baseline (organizer) | 45.13 | 41.94 |
| Phonetisaurus | 45.44 | 43.88 |
| Baseline (raw data) | 45.92 | 41.70 |
| Sequitur | 46.69 | 43.86 |
| biLSTM seq2seq | 47.89 | 44.05 |
| **Dialpad-2** | **43.83** | **41.72** |
| **Dialpad-1** | **40.12** | **37.43** |

Table 1: Results for components of ensembles, and submitted models/ensembles (bolded).

## 5 Additional experiments

We experimented with different ensembles and found that incorporating models with different architectures generally improves overall performance. In the standalone results, only the top three models beat the baseline WER, but adding additional models with higher WER than the baseline continues to reduce overall WER. Table 2 shows the effect of this progressive ensembling, from our top-3 models to our top-7 (i.e. the ensemble for the **Dialpad-1** model).

### 5.1 Edit distance-based voting

In addition to varying our ensemble sizes and components, we investigated a different ensemble voting scheme, in which ties are broken using edit distance when there is no 1-best majority option. That is, in the event of

| Model | dev | test |
|---|---|---|
| Ensemble-top3 | 41.10 | 39.71 |
| Ensemble-top4 | 40.74 | 38.89 |
| Ensemble-top5 | 40.50 | 38.12 |
| Ensemble-top6 | 40.31 | 37.69 |
| Ensemble-top7 (Dialpad-1) | 40.12 | 37.43 |

Table 2: Progressive ensembling results, with top-performing components

a tie, instead of selecting the prediction made by the best standalone model (our usual tie-breaking method), we select the prediction that minimizes edit distance to all other predictions that have the same number of votes. The idea of this method is to maximize sub-word level agreement. Although this method did not show clear improvements on the development set, we found after submission that it narrowly but consistently outperformed the top-N ensembles on the test set (see Table 3).

| Model | dev | test |
|---|---|---|
| ED-Dialpad-3 | 43.76 | 41.70 |
| ED-top3 | 41.24 | 39.40 |
| ED-top4 | 40.62 | 38.48 |
| ED-top5 | 40.50 | 37.69 |
| ED-top6 | 40.28 | 37.50 |
| ED-top7 | 40.21 | 37.31 |

Table 3: Results for ensembling with edit-distance tie-breaking

## 6 Error analysis

We conducted some basic analyses of the **Dialpad-1** submission's patterns of errors, to better understand its performance and identify potential areas of improvement.[13]

### 6.1 Oracle WER

We began by calculating the *oracle WER*, i.e. the theoretical best WER that the ensemble could have achieved if it had selected the correct/gold prediction every time it was present in the pool of component model predictions for a given input. The Dialpad-1 system's oracle WERs on the dev and test sets were **25.12** and **23.27**, respectively (c.f. 40.12 and 37.43 actual).

These represent massive performance improvements (approx. 15% absolute, or 37% relative, WER reduction), and suggest refinement of our output selection/voting method (perhaps via some kind of confidence weighting) could lead to much-improved results.

### 6.2 Data-related errors

We also investigated outputs for which none of our component models predicted the correct pronunciation, in hopes of finding some patterns of interest.

Many of the training data-related issues raised in section 2.1 appeared in the dev and test labels as well. In some cases this led to high cross-component agreement, even on incorrect predictions. Our hope that subtle contextual cues might reveal patterns in the distribution of syllabic versus schwa-following liquids and nasals was not borne out, e.g. our ensemble was led astray on words like "warble", which had a labelled pronunciation of /w ɔ ɹ b l̩/, while all 7 of our models predicted /w ɔ ɹ b ə l/, a functionally non-distinct pronunciation. In addition, the previously mentioned issue of /ɹ/ being mistranscribed as /r/ affected our performance, e.g. with the word "unilateral", whose labelled pronunciation was /j u n ɪ l æ t ə r ə l/, instead of /j u n ɪ l æ t ə ɹ ə l/, which was again the pronunciation predicted by all 7 models. Finally, narrowness of transcription was also an issue that affected our performance on the dev and test sets, e.g., for words like "cloudy" /k ɫ a ʊ d i/ and "cry" /k ɹ a ɪ̯/, for which we predicted /k l a ʊ d i/ and /k ɹ a ɪ/, respectively. In the end, it seems that noisiness in the data was a major source of errors for our submissions.[14]

Aside from issues arising due label noise, our systems also made some genuine errors that are typical of g2p models, mostly related to data distribution or sparsity. For example, our component models overwhelmingly predicted that "irreparate" (/ɪ ɹ ɛ p ə ɹ ə t/) should rhyme instead with "rate" (this "-ate-" /e ɪ t/ correspondence was overwhelmingly present in the training data), that "backache" (/b æ k e ɪ k/) must contain the affricate /t͡ʃ/, that

[13]We are grateful to an anonymous reviewer for suggesting that this would strengthen the paper.

[14]We nonetheless acknowledge the magnitude and challenge of the task of cleaning/normalizing a large quantity of user-generated data, and thank the organizers for the work that they did in this area.

"acres" (e ɪ k ɚ z/) rhymes with "degrees", and that "beret" has a /t/ sound in it. In each of these cases, there was either not enough samples in the training set to reliably learn the relevant grapheme-phoneme correspondence, or else a conflicting (but correct) correspondence was over-represented in the training data.

## 7 Conclusion

We presented and discussed three g2p systems submitted for the SIGMORPHON2021 English-only shared sub-task. In addition to finding a strong off-the-shelf contender, we show that naive ensembling remains a strong strategy in supervised learning, of which g2p is a sub-domain, and that simple majority-voting schemes in classification can often leverage the respective strengths of sub-optimal component models, especially when diverse architectures are combined. Additionally, we provided more evidence for the usefulness of linguistically-informed subword modeling as an input transformation on speech-related tasks.

We also discussed additional experiments whose results were not submitted, indicating the benefit of exploring top-N model vs ensemble trade-offs, and demonstrating the potential benefit of an edit-distance based tie-breaking method for ensemble voting.

Future work includes further search for the optimal trade-off between ensemble size and performance, as well as additional exploration of the edit-distance voting scheme, and more sophisticated ensembling/voting methods, e.g. majority voting at the phone level on aligned outputs.

## Acknowledgments

We are grateful to Dialpad Inc. for providing the resources, both temporal and computational, to work on this project.

## References

Martín Abadi, Ashish Agarwal, Paul Barham, Eugene Brevdo, Zhifeng Chen, Craig Citro, Greg S. Corrado, Andy Davis, Jeffrey Dean, Matthieu Devin, Sanjay Ghemawat, Ian Goodfellow, Andrew Harp, Geoffrey Irving, Michael Isard, Yangqing Jia, Rafal Jozefowicz, Lukasz Kaiser, Manjunath Kudlur, Josh Levenberg, Dan Mané, Rajat Monga, Sherry Moore, Derek Murray, Chris Olah, Mike Schuster, Jonathon Shlens, Benoit Steiner, Ilya Sutskever, Kunal Talwar, Paul Tucker, Vincent Vanhoucke, Vijay Vasudevan, Fernanda Viégas, Oriol Vinyals, Pete Warden, Martin Wattenberg, Martin Wicke, Yuan Yu, and Xiaoqiang Zheng. 2015. TensorFlow: Large-scale machine learning on heterogeneous systems. Software available from tensorflow.org.

Maximilian Bisani and Hermann Ney. 2008. Joint-sequence models for grapheme-to-phoneme conversion. *Speech Communication*, 50(5):434–451.

Peter F. Brown, Stephen A. Della Pietra, Vincent J. Della Pietra, and Robert L. Mercer. 1993. The mathematics of statistical machine translation: Parameter estimation. *Computational Linguistics*, 19(2):263–311.

Chris Dyer, Victor Chahuneau, and Noah A. Smith. 2013. A simple, fast, and effective reparameterization of IBM model 2. In *Proceedings of the 2013 Conference of the North American Chapter of the Association for Computational Linguistics: Human Language Technologies*, pages 644–648, Atlanta, Georgia. Association for Computational Linguistics.

Kyle Gorman. 2016. Pynini: A python library for weighted finite-state grammar compilation. In *Proceedings of the SIGFSM Workshop on Statistical NLP and Weighted Automata*, pages 75–80, Berlin, Germany. Association for Computational Linguistics.

Kyle Gorman, Lucas F.E. Ashby, Aaron Goyzueta, Arya McCarthy, Shijie Wu, and Daniel You. 2020. The SIGMORPHON 2020 shared task on multilingual grapheme-to-phoneme conversion. In *Proceedings of the 17th SIGMORPHON Workshop on Computational Research in Phonetics, Phonology, and Morphology*, pages 40–50, Online. Association for Computational Linguistics.

International Phonetic Association. 1999. *Handbook of the International Phonetic Association: A guide to the use of the International Phonetic Alphabet.* Cambridge University Press, Cambridge, U.K.

Jackson L. Lee, Lucas F.E. Ashby, M. Elizabeth Garza, Yeonju Lee-Sikka, Sean Miller, Arya D. McCarthy Alan Wong, and Kyle Gorman. 2020. Massively multilingual pronunciation mining with wikipron. In *Proceedings of the 12th Language Resources and Evaluation Conference*, pages 4216—4221, Marseille.

Peter Makarov and Simon Clematide. 2018. Imitation learning for neural morphological string transduction. In *Proceedings of the 2018 Conference on Empirical Methods in Natural Language Processing*, pages 2877–2882, Brussels, Belgium. Association for Computational Linguistics.

Peter Makarov and Simon Clematide. 2020. CLUZH at SIGMORPHON 2020 shared task on multilingual grapheme-to-phoneme conversion. In *Proceedings of the 17th SIGMORPHON Workshop on Computational Research in Phonetics, Phonology, and Morphology*, pages 171–176, Online. Association for Computational Linguistics.

April McMahon. 2002. *An Introduction to English Phonology*. Edinburgh University Press, Edinburgh, U.K.

Mehryar Mohri, Fernando Pereira, and Michael Riley. 2002. Weighted finite-state transducers in speech recognition. *Computer Speech & Language*, 16(1):69–88.

Graham Neubig, Chris Dyer, Yoav Goldberg, Austin Matthews, Waleed Ammar, Antonios Anastasopoulos, Miguel Ballesteros, David Chiang, Daniel Clothiaux, Trevor Cohn, Kevin Duh, Manaal Faruqui, Cynthia Gan, Dan Garrette, Yangfeng Ji, Lingpeng Kong, Adhiguna Kuncoro, Gaurav Kumar, Chaitanya Malaviya, Paul Michel, Yusuke Oda, Matthew Richardson, Naomi Saphra, Swabha Swayamdipta, and Pengcheng Yin. 2017. Dynet: The dynamic neural network toolkit.

Josef R. Novak, Nobuaki Minematsu, and Keikichi Hirose. 2012. WFST-based grapheme-to-phoneme conversion: Open source tools for alignment, model-building and decoding. In *Proceedings of the 10th International Workshop on Finite State Methods and Natural Language Processing*, pages 45–49, Donostia–San Sebastián. Association for Computational Linguistics.

Sravana Reddy and John Goldsmith. 2010. An MDL-based approach to extracting subword units for grapheme-to-phoneme conversion. In *Human Language Technologies: The 2010 Annual Conference of the North American Chapter of the Association for Computational Linguistics*, pages 713–716, Los Angeles, California. Association for Computational Linguistics.

Ilya Sutskever, Oriol Vinyals, and Quoc V Le. 2014. Sequence to sequence learning with neural networks. In *Advances in Neural Information Processing Systems*, volume 27. Curran Associates, Inc.

Ashish Vaswani, Noam Shazeer, Niki Parmar, Jakob Uszkoreit, Llion Jones, Aidan N Gomez, Ł ukasz Kaiser, and Illia Polosukhin. 2017. Attention is all you need. In *Advances in Neural Information Processing Systems*, volume 30. Curran Associates, Inc.

Shinji Watanabe, Takaaki Hori, Shigeki Karita, Tomoki Hayashi, Jiro Nishitoba, Yuya Unno, Nelson Enrique Yalta Soplin, Jahn Heymann, Matthew Wiesner, Nanxin Chen, Adithya Renduchintala, and Tsubasa Ochiai. 2018. Espnet: End-to-end speech processing toolkit. In *Proc. Interspeech 2018*, pages 2207–2211.

Hainan Xu, Shuoyang Ding, and Shinji Watanabe. 2019. Improving end-to-end speech recognition with pronunciation-assisted sub-word modeling. *ICASSP 2019 - 2019 IEEE International Conference on Acoustics, Speech and Signal Processing (ICASSP)*, pages 7110–7114.

# CLUZH at SIGMORPHON 2021 Shared Task on Multilingual Grapheme-to-Phoneme Conversion: Variations on a Baseline

**Simon Clematide** and **Peter Makarov**
Department of Computational Linguistics
University of Zurich, Switzerland
simon.clematide@cl.uzh.ch makarov@cl.uzh.ch

## Abstract

This paper describes the submission by the team from the Department of Computational Linguistics, Zurich University, to the Multilingual Grapheme-to-Phoneme Conversion (G2P) Task 1 of the SIGMORPHON 2021 challenge in the low and medium settings. The submission is a variation of our 2020 G2P system, which serves as the baseline for this year's challenge. The system is a neural transducer that operates over explicit edit actions and is trained with imitation learning. For this challenge, we experimented with the following changes: a) emitting phoneme segments instead of single character phonemes, b) input character dropout, c) a mogrifier LSTM decoder (Melis et al., 2019), d) enriching the decoder input with the currently attended input character, e) parallel BiLSTM encoders, and f) an adaptive batch size scheduler. In the low setting, our best ensemble improved over the baseline, however, in the medium setting, the baseline was stronger on average, although for certain languages improvements could be observed.

## 1 Introduction

The SIGMORPHON Grapheme-to-Phoneme Conversion task consists of mapping a sequence of characters in some language into a sequence of whitespace delimited International Phonetic Alphabet (IPA) symbols, which represent the pronunciation of this input character sequence (not necessarily a phonemic transcription, despite the name of the task) according to the language-specific conventions used in the English Wiktionary.[1] The data was collected and post-processed by the WikiPron project (Lee et al., 2020). Post-processing removes stress and syllable markers and applies IPA segmentation for combining and modifier diacritics as

| Lang. | Grapheme | Phoneme | Wiktionary |
|---|---|---|---|
| ice | persóna | pʰ ɛ r̥ s o u: n a | /ˈpʰɛr̥.sou:na/ |
| fra | williams | w i l j a m z | /wi.ljamz/ |
| bul | засичайки | z e s t͡ʃ ʃ ə j kʲ i | /zeˈsitʃəjkʲi/ |
| kor | 검출 | k ɘ: m t͡ɕʰ u ɭ | [ˈkʌ̹(:)mt͡ɕʰuɭ] |

Figure 1: Examples of the original G2P shared task data from four different languages and their pronunciation entries in Wiktionary.

well as contour information. See Figure 1 for the post-processed shared task entries and the original entries from the Wiktionary pronunciation section. For more information, we refer the reader to the shared task overview paper (Ashby et al., 2021).

In the low and medium data setting, the 2021 SIGMORPHON multilingual G2P challenge features ten different languages from various phylogenetic families and written in different scripts. The low setting comes with 800 training, 100 development and 100 test examples. In the medium setting, the data splits are 10 times larger. Although it is permitted to use external resources for the medium setting, all our models used exclusively the official training material.

Our system is a neural transducer with pointer network-like monotonic hard attention (Aharoni and Goldberg, 2017) that operates over explicit character edit actions and is trained with imitation learning (Daumé III et al., 2009; Ross et al., 2011; Chang et al., 2015). It is an adaptation of our type-level morphological inflection generation system that proved its data efficiency and performance in the SIGMORPHON 2018 shared task (Makarov and Clematide, 2018). G2P shares many similarities with traditional morphological string transduction: The changes are mostly local and often simple depending on how close the spelling of a language reflects pronunciation. For most languages, a substantial part of the work is actually

[1] https://en.wiktionary.org/



*Proceedings of the Seventeenth SIGMORPHON Workshop on Computational Research in Phonetics, Phonology, and Morphology*, pages 148–153

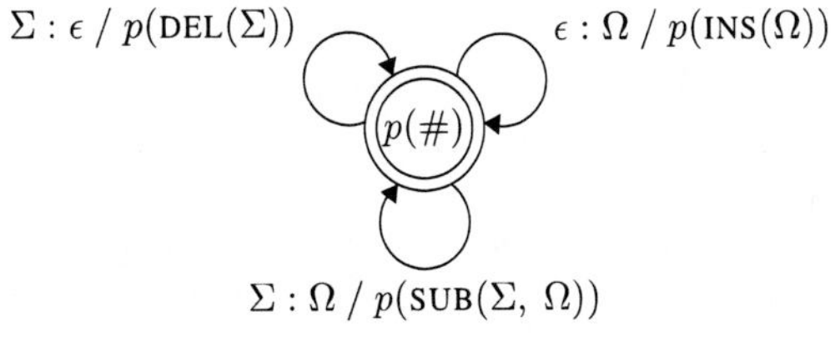


Figure 2: Stochastic edit distance (Ristad and Yianilos, 1998): A memoryless probabilistic FST. $\Sigma$ and $\Omega$ stand for any input and output symbol, respectively. Transition weights are to the right of the slash and $p(\#)$ is the final weight.

applying character-by-character substitutions. An extreme case is Georgian, which features an almost deterministic one-to-one mapping between graphemes and IPA segments that can be learned almost perfectly from little training data.[2]

The main goal of our submission was to test whether our last year's system, which is the baseline for this year's G2P challenge, already exhausts the potential of its architecture, or whether changes to the output representation (IPA segments vs. IPA Unicode codepoints; input character dropout), to the LSTM decoder (the mogrifier steps and the additional input of the attended character), to the BiLSTM encoder (parallel encoders), or to other hyper-parameter settings (adaptive batch size) can improve the results without replacing the LSTM-based encoder/decoder setup by a Transformer-based architecture (see e.g. Wu et al. (2021) for Transformer-based state-of-the-art results).

## 2 Model description

The model defines a conditional distribution over substitution, insertion and deletion edits $p_\theta(\mathbf{a} \mid \mathbf{x}) = \prod_{j=1}^{|\mathbf{a}|} p_\theta(a_j \mid a_{<j}, \mathbf{x})$, where $\mathbf{x} = x_1 \dots x_{|\mathbf{x}|}$ is an input sequence of graphemes and $\mathbf{a} = a_1 \dots a_{|\mathbf{a}|}$ is an edit action sequence. The output sequence of IPA symbols $\mathbf{y}$ is deterministically computed from $\mathbf{x}$ and $\mathbf{a}$. The model is equipped with an LSTM decoder and a bidirectional LSTM encoder (Graves and Schmidhuber, 2005). At each decoding step $j$, the model attends to a single grapheme $\mathbf{x}_i$. The attention steps monotonically through the input sequence, steered by the edits that consume input (e.g. a deletion shifts the attention to the next grapheme $\mathbf{x}_{i+1}$).

[2]Even a reduced training set of only 100 items allows a single model to achieve over 90% accuracy on the Georgian test set.

The imitation learning algorithm relies on an expert policy for suggesting intuitive and appropriate character substitution, insertion and deletion actions. For instance, for the data sample кит $\mapsto$ /kʲit/ (Russian: "whale"), we would like the following most natural edit sequence to attain the lowest cost: SUBS[k], INS[ʲ], SUBS[i], SUBS[t]. The cost function for these actions is estimated by fitting a Stochastic Edit Distance (SED) model (Ristad and Yianilos, 1998) on the training data, which is a memoryless weighted finite-state transducer shown in Figure 2. The resulting SED model is integrated into the expert policy, the SED policy, that uses Viterbi decoding to compute optimal edit action sequences for any point in the action search space: Given a transducer configuration of partially processed input, find the best edit actions to generate the remaining target sequence suffix. During training, an aggressive exploration schedule $p_{\text{sampling}}(i) = \frac{1}{1+\exp(i)}$ where $i$ is the training epoch number, exposes the model to configurations sampled by executing edit actions from the model. For an extended description of the SED policy and IL training, we refer the reader to the last year's system description paper (Makarov and Clematide, 2020).

### 2.1 Changes to the baseline model

This section describes the changes that we implemented in our submissions.

**IPA segments vs. IPA Unicode characters**: Emitting IPA segments in one action (including its whitespace delimiter), e.g., for the Russian example from above SUBS[kʲ•],[3] instead of producing the same output by three actions SUBS[k], INS[ʲ], INS[•] reduces the number of action predictions (and potential errors) considerably, which is beneficial. On the other hand, this might lead to larger action vocabularies and sparse training distributions. Therefore, we experimented with character (CHAR) and IPA segment (SEG) edit actions in our submission. Table 1 shows statistics on the resulting vocabulary sizes if CHAR or SEG actions are used. Some caution is needed though because some segments might only appear once in the training data, e.g. English has an IPA segment sː: that only appears in the word "psst".

**Input character dropout**: To prevent the model from memorizing the training set and to force it to learn about syllable contexts, we randomly replace

[3]• denotes whitespace symbol.

| S | Language | NFD$^{<}$ | SEG | C$^{NFC}$ | C$^{NFD}$ |
|---|---|---|---|---|---|
| L | ady | 0.5% | 67 | 37 | 37 |
| L | gre | 4.3% | 33 | 33 | 33 |
| L | ice | 30.3% | 60 | 36 | 36 |
| L | ita | 0.8% | 32 | 29 | 29 |
| L | khm | 0.5% | 47 | 36 | 34 |
| L | lav | 12.4% | 73 | 51 | 36 |
| L | mlt_latn | 9.0% | 41 | 29 | 29 |
| L | rum | 0.3% | 45 | 31 | 31 |
| L | slv | 4.3% | 48 | 38 | 30 |
| L | wel_sw | 2.4% | 43 | 37 | 37 |
| M | arm_e | 0.0% | 54 | 31 | 31 |
| M | bul | 3.5% | 46 | 34 | 34 |
| M | dut | 0.8% | 49 | 39 | 39 |
| M | fre | 0.1% | 39 | 36 | 36 |
| M | geo | 0.0% | 33 | 27 | 27 |
| M | hbs_latn | 3.7% | 63 | 43 | 33 |
| M | hun | 42.5% | 66 | 37 | 37 |
| M | jpn_hira | 36.1% | 64 | 42 | 39 |
| M | kor | 99.8% | 60 | 46 | 46 |
| M | vie_hanoi | 88.2% | 49 | 44 | 44 |
| H | eng_us | 0.0% | 124 | 83 | 80 |
| Average | | 16.2% | 54.1 | 39.0 | 37.0 |

Table 1: Statistics on Unicode normalization for low (L), medium (M), and high (H) settings (column S). Column NFD$^{<}$ specifies the percentage of training items where NFD normalized graphemes had smaller length difference to phonemes than in NFC normalization. Column SEG gives the vocabulary size of IPA segments (the counts are the same for NFC and NFD). Column C$^{NFC}$ reports the phoneme vocabulary size in NFC Unicode characters (CHAR) and C$^{NFD}$ in NFD.

an input character with the UNK symbol according to a linearly decaying schedule.[4]

**Mogrifier LSTM decoder**: Mogrifier LSTMs (Melis et al., 2019) iteratively and mutually update the hidden state of a previous time step with the current input before feeding the modified hidden state and input into a standard LSTM cell. On language modeling tasks with smaller corpora, this technique closed the gap between LSTM and Transformer models. We apply a standard mogrifier with 5 rounds of updates in our experiments. We expect the mogrifier decoder to profit from IPA segmentation because in this setup the decoder mogrifies neighboring IPA phoneme segments and not space and IPA characters.

**Enriching the decoder input with the currently attended input character**: The autoregressive decoder of the baseline system uses the LSTM decoder output of the previous time step and the BiLSTM encoded representation of the currently attended input character as input. Intuitively, by feeding the input character embedding directly into the decoder (as a kind of skip connection), we want to liberate the BiLSTM encoder from transporting the hard attention information to the decoder, thereby motivating the sequence encoder to focus more on the contextualization of the input character.

**Multiple parallel BiLSTM encoders**: Convolutional encoders typically use many convolutional filters for representation learning and Transformer encoders similarly feature multi-head attention. Using several LSTM encoders in parallel has been proposed by Zhu et al. (2017) for language modeling and translation and was e.g. also successfully used for named entity recognition (Žukov-Gregorič et al., 2018). Technically, the same input is fed though several smaller LSTMs, each with its own parameter set, and then their output is concatenated for each time step. The idea behind parallel LSTM encoders is to provide a more robust ensemble-style encoding with lower variance between models. For our submission, there was not enough time to systematically tune the input and hidden state sizes as well as the number of parallel LSTMs.

**Adaptive batch size scheduler**: We combine the ideas of "Don't Decay the Learning Rate, Increase the Batch Size" (Smith et al., 2017) and cyclical learning schedules by dynamically enlarging or reducing the batch size according to development set accuracy: Starting with a defined minimal batch size $m$ threshold, the batch size for the next epoch is set to $\lfloor m - 0.5 \rfloor$ if the development set performance improved, or $\lfloor m + 0.5 \rfloor$ otherwise.[5] If a predefined maximum batch size is reached, the batch size is reset in one step to the minimum threshold. The motivation for the reset comes from empirical observations that going back to a small batch size can help overcome local optima. With larger training sets, we subsample the training sets per epoch randomly in order to have a more dynamic behavior.[6]

[4] For all experiments, we start with a probability of 50% for UNKing a character in a word and reduce this rate over 10 epochs to a minimal probability of 1%. Light experimentation on a few languages led to this cautious setting, which might leave room for further improvement.

[5] See also the recent discussion on learning rates and batch sizes by Wu et al. (2021).

[6] The subsample size is set to 3,000 items per epoch in all our experiments.

## 2.2 Unicode normalization

For some writing systems, e.g. for Korean or Vietnamese, applying Unicode NFD normalization to the input has a great impact on the input sequence length and consequently on the G2P character correspondences. The decomposition of diacritics and other composing characters for all languages, as performed in the baseline, has the disadvantage of longer input sequences. We apply a simple heuristic to decide on NFD normalization based on a criterion for the minimum length distance between graphemes and phonemes: If more than 50% of the training grapheme sequences in NFD normalization have a smaller length difference compared to the phoneme sequence than their corresponding NFC variants, then NFD normalization is applied. See Table 1 for statistics, which indicate a preference for NFD for only 2 languages.

# 3 Submission details

Modifications such as mogrifier LSTMs, additional input character skip connections, or parallel encoders increase the number of model parameters and make it difficult to compare the baseline system directly with its variants. Additionally, we did not have enough time before the submission to systematically explore and fine-tune for the best combination of model modifications and hyper-parameters. In the end, after some light experimentation we had to stick to settings that might not be optimal.

We train separate models for each language on the official training data and use the development set exclusively for model selection. As beam decoding for mogrifier models sometimes suffered compared to greedy decoding, we built all ensembles from greedy model prediction. Like the baseline system (B), we train the SED model for 10 epochs, use one-layer LSTMs, hidden state dimension 200 for the decoder LSTMs and action embedding dimension 100. For the low (L) and medium (M) setting, we have the following specific hyper-parameters:

- patience: 12 (B), 24 (L), 18 (M)
- maximal epochs: 60 (B), 80 (L/M)
- minimal batch size:[7] 3 (L), 5 (M)
- maximal batch size: 10 (L/M)
- character embedding dimension:[8] 100 (B), 50(L/M)
- LSTM encoder hidden state dimension: 200 (B), 300 (L/M) divided by 6 parallel encoders.

We submit 3 ensemble runs for the low setting:

**CLUZH-1**: 15 models with CHAR input,
**CLUZH-2**: 15 models with SEG input,
**CLUZH-3**: 30 models with CHAR or SEG input.

We submit 4 ensemble runs for the medium setting:

**CLUZH-4**: 5 models with CHAR input,
**CLUZH-5**: 10 models with SEG input,
**CLUZH-6**: 5 models with SEG input,
**CLUZH-7**: 15 models with CHAR or SEG input.

Due to a configuration error, medium results were actually computed without two add-ons: mogrifier LSTMs and the additional input character. In post-submission experiments, we computed runs that enabled these features and report their results as well (CLUZH-4m/5m).

# 4 Results and discussion

Table 2 shows a comparison of results for the low setting. We report the development and test set average word error rate (WER) performance to illustrate the sometimes dramatic differences between these sets (e.g. Greek). Both runs containing CHAR action emitting models (CLUZH-1, CLUZH-3) have second best results (the best system reaches 24.1). The SEG models with IPA segmentation actions excel on some languages (Adyghe, Latvian), but fail badly on Slovene and Maltese. Only for Romanian and Italian, we see an improvement for the 30-strong mixed ensemble. The expectation that the size difference between the SEG and CHAR vocabulary correlates with language-specific performance differences cannot be confirmed given the numbers in Table 1. E.g. Latvian features 73 different IPA segments but only 51 IPA characters, still, the SEG variant shows only 49% WER.

Table 3 shows a comparison of results for the medium setting. We report selected development and test set average performance to illustrate that also in this larger setting, the expectation of a slightly higher development set performance does not always hold (e.g. Korean or Japanese). On the other hand, Bulgarian and Dutch have a sharp increase in errors on the test set compared to the development set. The comparison between runs with the mogrifier LSTM decoder and the attended character input (CLUZH-*N*m) or without (C-*N*) suggest that these changes are not beneficial. In the medium setting, C-4 (CHAR) and C-6 (SEG) can be directly

[7] The baseline system's batch size is 5.

[8] The motivation for lowering the character embedding size comes from adding the input character to the mogrifier decoder LSTM, which increases the parameter size for each of the 5 update weight matrices.

| LNG | CLUZH-1 (CHAR) AVERAGE dev | test | sd | E test | CLUZH-2 (SEG) AVERAGE dev | test | sd | E test | C-3 E test | OUR BASELINE AVERAGE dev | test | sd | E test | BSL E test | Other test |
|---|---|---|---|---|---|---|---|---|---|---|---|---|---|---|---|
| ady | 25.0 | 27.8 | 3.3 | 24 | 25.6 | 26.2 | 1.8 | **22** | **22** | 26 | 25.2 | 2.8 | 21 | **22** | **22** |
| gre | 6.5 | 22.2 | 2.3 | **20** | 5.1 | 22.8 | 2.8 | 22 | **20** | 5 | 26.0 | 3.3 | 25 | 21 | 21 |
| ice | 14.8 | 12.4 | 2.4 | **10** | 16.1 | 14.5 | 2.2 | 12 | **10** | 21 | 15.8 | 2.1 | 12 | 12 | 11 |
| ita | 24.5 | 27.0 | 2.2 | 23 | 24.4 | 26.3 | 3.2 | 24 | 21 | 25 | 22.7 | 3.5 | 19 | **19** | 20 |
| khm | 39.8 | 38.2 | 3.4 | 32 | 40.3 | 36.9 | 2.2 | 33 | 32 | 39 | 40.4 | 2.5 | 34 | 34 | **28** |
| lav | 47.2 | 53.7 | 2.8 | 53 | 46.9 | 55.3 | 3.7 | **49** | **49** | 44 | 56.5 | 2.2 | 54 | 55 | **49** |
| mlt | 17.0 | 18.0 | 2.4 | **12** | 19.7 | 21.2 | 2.9 | 16 | 14 | 23 | 21.8 | 5.1 | 17 | 19 | 18 |
| rum | 11.1 | 13.7 | 1.8 | 13 | 10.3 | 14.1 | 1.0 | 13 | 12 | 11 | 12.5 | 2.1 | 10 | **10** | **10** |
| slv | 46.4 | 56.4 | 2.7 | 50 | 48 | 60.2 | 3.4 | 59 | 55 | 44 | 54.2 | 2.1 | 51 | 49 | **47** |
| wel | 18.0 | 14.9 | 3.5 | **10** | 15.6 | 15.7 | 1.8 | 13 | 12 | 19 | 14.8 | 2.0 | 12 | **10** | 12 |
| AVG | 25.0 | 28.4 | 2.7 | 24.7 | 25.2 | 29.3 | 2.5 | 26.3 | 24.7 | 25.7 | 29.0 | 2.8 | 25.5 | 25.1 | 23.8 |

Table 2: Overview of the dev and test results in the low setting. C-3 is CLUZH-3 ensemble. OUR BASELINE shows the results for our own run of the baseline configuration. They are different from the official baseline results (BSL) due to different random seeds. Column sd always reports the test set standard deviation. E means ensemble results.

| LNG | C-4 $E_5$ test | CLUZH-4m (CHAR) AVERAGE dev | test | sd | $E_5$ test | C-5 $E_{10}$ test | CLUZH-5m (SEG) AVERAGE dev | test | sd | $E_{10}$ test | C-5l $E_{10}$ test | C-6 $E_5$ test | C-7 $E_{15}$ test | OUR BASELINE AVERAGE dev | test | sd | $E_{10}$ test | BSL $E_{10}$ test |
|---|---|---|---|---|---|---|---|---|---|---|---|---|---|---|---|---|---|---|
| arm | 7.1 | 5.4 | 7.9 | 0.7 | 6.4 | 6.6 | 5.1 | 7.2 | 0.5 | **6.2** | 7.1 | 6.6 | **6.4** | 5.8 | 7.8 | 0.7 | 6.5 | 7.0 |
| bul | 20.1 | 12.2 | 20.4 | 2.0 | 19.9 | 19.2 | 11.9 | 23.3 | 2.1 | 22.4 | 16.2 | 18.8 | 19.7 | 12.5 | 19.7 | 1.7 | 19.3 | **18.3** |
| dut | 15.0 | 13.1 | 18.3 | 1.2 | 14.8 | 14.9 | 12.4 | 16.8 | 0.6 | 14.6 | 14.5 | 15.6 | **14.7** | 13.1 | 17.7 | 1.3 | **14.3** | **14.7** |
| fre | **7.5** | 8.4 | 9.7 | 0.6 | 8.2 | **7.5** | 8.5 | 9.5 | 0.7 | 8.1 | 8.1 | **7.5** | 7.6 | 8.9 | 9.1 | 0.5 | 7.8 | 8.5 |
| geo | **.0** | .0 | .0 | .0 | .0 | **.0** | .0 | .0 | .0 | .0 | .0 | **.0** | **.0** | .0 | .0 | .0 | .0 | **.0** |
| hbs | 38.4 | 43.2 | 44.5 | 1.1 | 39.1 | 35.6 | 42.4 | 44.3 | 1.5 | 36.8 | 35.7 | 37.0 | 35.3 | 39.1 | 38.9 | 1.2 | 33.6 | **32.1** |
| hun | 1.5 | 1.8 | 1.8 | 0.1 | 1.6 | 1.2 | 1.7 | 1.5 | 0.3 | 1.0 | **0.9** | **1.0** | **1.0** | 1.7 | 2.0 | 0.3 | 1.8 | 1.8 |
| jpn | 5.9 | 6.9 | 6.8 | 0.2 | 5.5 | 5.3 | 6.8 | 6.5 | 0.3 | 5.4 | 5.2 | 5.5 | **5.0** | 6.8 | 6.4 | 0.5 | 5.5 | 5.2 |
| kor | **16.2** | 21.3 | 18.6 | 0.7 | 17.4 | 16.9 | 19.6 | 18.3 | 0.8 | 16.2 | **16.1** | 17.2 | 16.3 | 20.4 | 18.9 | 0.8 | 16.5 | 16.3 |
| vie | 2.3 | 1.2 | 2.4 | 0.1 | 2.3 | **2.0** | 1.2 | 2.1 | 0.1 | 2.1 | 2.2 | 2.1 | **2.0** | 1.4 | 2.5 | 0.2 | 2.4 | 2.5 |
| AVG | 11.4 | 11.4 | 13.0 | 0.7 | 11.5 | 10.9 | 11.0 | 12.9 | 0.7 | 11.3 | **10.6** | 11.1 | 10.8 | 11.0 | 12.3 | 0.7 | 10.8 | **10.6** |

Table 3: Overview of the development and test results in the medium setting. C-*N* is CLUZH-*N* ensemble. CLUZH-*N*m runs use the mogrifier decoder and additional input character in decoder (these are post-submisson runs). C-5l uses larger parameterization and reaches WER 10.60 (BSL: 10.64). OUR BASELINE shows the results for our own run of the baseline configuration. Boldface indicates best performance in official shared task runs; underline marks the best performance in post-submission configurations. Column sd always reports the test set standard deviation. $E_n$ means $n$-strong ensemble results.

compared because they feature the same ensemble size: The results suggest that IPA segmentation (SEG) for higher resource settings (and the specific medium languages) seems to be slightly better than CHAR. C-5l is a post-submission run with a larger parametrization.[9] This post-submission ensemble outperforms the baseline system by a small margin, but still struggles with Serbo-Croatian (hbs) compared to the official baseline results.

In a post-submission experiment on the high setting, we built a large[10] 5-strong SEG-based ensemble. It achieves an impressive low word error rate of 38.7 compared to the official baseline (41.94) and the best other submission (37.43).

**Future work:** Performance variance between different runs of our LSTM-based architecture makes it difficult to reliably assess the actual usefulness of the small architectural changes; extensive experimentation, e.g. in the spirit of Reimers and Gurevych (2017), is needed for that. One should also investigate the impact of the official data set splits: The observed differences between the development set and test set performance in the low

[9] Three parallel encoders with 200 hidden units each; character embedding dimension of 200; no mogrifier; no input character added to the decoder.

[10] Character embedding dimension: 200; action embedding dimension: 100; 10 parallel encoders with hidden state dimension 100; decoder hidden state dimension: 500; minimal batch size: 5; maximal batch size: 20; epochs: 200 (subsampled to 3,000 items); patience: 24; no mogrifier; no input character added to the decoder.

setting for Slovene or Greek are extreme. Cross-validation experiments might help assess the true difficulty of the WikiPron datasets.

## 5 Conclusion

This paper presents the approach taken by the CLUZH team to solving the SIGMORPHON 2021 Multilingual Grapheme-to-Phoneme Conversion challenge. Our submission for the low and medium settings is based on our successful SIGMORPHON 2020 system, which is a majority-vote ensemble of neural transducers trained with imitation learning. We add several modifications to the existing LSTM architecture and experiment with IPA segment vs. IPA character action predictions. For the low setting languages, our IPA character-based run outperforms the baseline and ranks second overall. The average performance of segment-based action edits suffers from performance outliers for certain languages. For the medium setting languages, we note small improvements on some languages, but the overall performance is lower than the baseline. Using a mogrifier LSTM decoder and enriching the encoder input with the currently attended input character did not improve performance in the medium setting. Post-submission experiments suggest that network capacity for the submitted systems was too small. A post-submission run for the high-setting shows considerable improvement over the baseline.

## References


Roee Aharoni and Yoav Goldberg. 2017. Morphological inflection generation with hard monotonic attention. In *ACL*.

Lucas F.E Ashby, Travis M. Bartley, Simon Clematide, Luca Del Signore, Cameron Gibson, Kyle Gorman, Yeonju Lee-Sikka, Peter Makarov, Aidan Malanoski, Sean Miller, Omar Ortiz, Reuben Raff, Arundhati Sengupta, Bora Seo, Yulia Spektor, and Winnie Yan. 2021. Results of the Second SIGMORPHON 2021 Shared Task on Multilingual Grapheme-to-Phoneme Conversion. In *Proceedings of 18th SIGMORPHON Workshop on Computational Research in Phonetics, Phonology, and Morphology*.

Kai-Wei Chang, Akshay Krishnamurthy, Hal Daumé, III, and John Langford. 2015. Learning to search better than your teacher. In *PMLR*, volume 37 of *Proceedings of Machine Learning Research*.

Hal Daumé III, John Langford, and Daniel Marcu. 2009. Search-based structured prediction. *Machine learning*, 75(3).

Alex Graves and Jürgen Schmidhuber. 2005. Framewise phoneme classification with bidirectional LSTM and other neural network architectures. *Neural Networks*, 18(5).

Jackson L. Lee, Lucas F.E. Ashby, M. Elizabeth Garza, Yeonju Lee-Sikka, Sean Miller, Alan Wong, Arya D. McCarthy, and Kyle Gorman. 2020. Massively multilingual pronunciation modeling with WikiPron. In *LREC*.

Peter Makarov and Simon Clematide. 2018. Imitation learning for neural morphological string transduction. In *EMNLP*.

Peter Makarov and Simon Clematide. 2020. CLUZH at SIGMORPHON 2020 shared task on multilingual grapheme-to-phoneme conversion. In *Proceedings of the 17th SIGMORPHON Workshop on Computational Research in Phonetics, Phonology, and Morphology*.

Gábor Melis, Tomás Kociský, and Phil Blunsom. 2019. Mogrifier LSTM. *CoRR*, abs/1909.01792.

Nils Reimers and Iryna Gurevych. 2017. Reporting score distributions makes a difference: Performance study of LSTM-networks for sequence tagging. In *EMNLP*.

Eric Sven Ristad and Peter N Yianilos. 1998. Learning string-edit distance. *IEEE Transactions on Pattern Analysis and Machine Intelligence*, 20(5).

Stephane Ross, Geoffrey Gordon, and Drew Bagnell. 2011. A reduction of imitation learning and structured prediction to no-regret online learning. In *PMLR*, volume 15 of *Proceedings of Machine Learning Research*.

Samuel L. Smith, Pieter-Jan Kindermans, and Quoc V. Le. 2017. Don't decay the learning rate, increase the batch size. *CoRR*, abs/1711.00489.

Shijie Wu, Ryan Cotterell, and Mans Hulden. 2021. Applying the transformer to character-level transduction. In *EACL*.

Danhao Zhu, Si Shen, Xin-Yu Dai, and Jiajun Chen. 2017. Going wider: Recurrent neural network with parallel cells. *CoRR*, abs/1705.01346.

Andrej Žukov-Gregorič, Yoram Bachrach, and Sam Coope. 2018. Named entity recognition with parallel recurrent neural networks. In *ACL*.

# What transfers in morphological inflection? Experiments with analogical models

**Micha Elsner**
Department of Linguistics
The Ohio State University
melsner0@gmail.com

## Abstract

This paper investigates how abstract processes like suffixation can be learned from morphological inflection task data using an analogical memory-based framework. In this framework, the inflection target form is specified by providing an example inflection of another word in the language. This model is capable of near-baseline performance on the SigMorphon 2020 inflection challenge. Such a model can make predictions for unseen languages, allowing one-shot inflection for natural languages and the investigation of morphological transfer with synthetic probes. Accuracy for one-shot transfer can be unexpectedly high for some target languages (88% in Shona) and language families (53% across Romance). Probe experiments show that the model learns partially generalizable representations of prefixation, suffixation and reduplication, aiding its ability to transfer. The paper argues that the degree of generality of these process representations also helps to explain transfer results from previous research.

## 1 Introduction

Morphological transfer learning has proven to be a powerful and effective technique for improving the performance of inflection models on under-resourced languages. The beneficial effects of transfer between source and target languages are known to be higher when the two are closely related (Anastasopoulos and Neubig, 2019) or typologically similar (Lin et al., 2019), mediated by the effect of script (Murikinati et al., 2020). But these effects are not always consistent; a variety of researchers report failure of transfer between closely related languages, or surprising successes with rather dissimilar ones (Sec 2). Pushing forward our understanding of these cases requires a more nuanced understanding of what is transferred by morphological transfer learning— that is, what abstract representational concepts do inflection networks acquire and how are these shared across languages?

This is a difficult question to address in the standard framework for inflection (Kann and Schütze, 2016), in which morphosyntactic properties are closely tied to their specific exponents in a particular language as well as to the more abstract processes by which these exponents are applied. In such a network, it is difficult to test whether a generic suffixation operation has been learned, without reference to a particular form/feature mapping, for instance between the Maori passive feature PASS and the spelling of a particular passive suffix *-tia*. Suffixing as a generic operation is much more likely to be useful in another language than the individual suffix. This work decouples these representational pieces by performing inflection in an analogical, memory-based framework.[1] In this framework, inflection instances do not have tags; rather, they include an instance of the desired mapping with respect to a different lemma (Figure 1). For example, to produce a passive Maori verb, the system takes an example verb with its passive and completes the four-part analogy: *lemma : target :: exemplar lemma : exemplar target.* The advantage of this redefinition of the task is that, in principle, the system does not need to learn anything about the individual affixes of a particular language, since these can be copied from the exemplar. Thus, it is possible to investigate how well such a system has learned a particular morphological process such as suffixation, which is expected to be present in a variety of languages.[2]

[1] "Memory-based" has been used in the literature to refer to models with dynamic read-write memory (Graves et al., 2016), as well as KNN-like exemplar models which store a large number of examples in a static memory (van den Bosch and Daelemans, 1999). The current work is of the latter type.

[2] Code available at: https://github.com/melsner/transformerbyexample.



*Proceedings of the Seventeenth SIGMORPHON Workshop on Computational Research in Phonetics, Phonology, and Morphology*, pages 154–166

Section 5 shows that this analogical framework for inflection can predict inflections across a variety of languages, demonstrating reasonable performance on the Sigmorphon 2020 multilingual benchmark (Vylomova et al., 2020). Section 6 describes one-shot learning experiments, performing language transfer without fine-tuning, and shows that for languages with concatenative affixes, one-shot transfer can be more effective than previously thought. Section 7 studies the system's ability to apply different types of morphological processes using constructed stimuli, showing that some configurations are capable of learning generic and transferable representations of processes including prefixing, suffixing and reduplication.

## 2 Related work

The overall positive effect of transfer learning is well established (McCarthy et al., 2019). Previous research has also evaluated how the choice of source language affects the performance in the target. While there is a robust trend for related languages to perform better, there are also many reports of exceptions. Kann (2020) finds that Hungarian is a better source for English than German and a better source for Spanish than Italian. She concludes that matching the target language's default affix placement (prefixing/suffixing) is important, and that agglutinative languages might be beneficial to transfer learning in general, but that genetic relatedness is not always a necessary or sufficient for effective transfer. Lin et al. (2019) also find that Hungarian and Turkish are good source languages for a surprising variety of unrelated targets. Rather than attribute this to agglutination, they propose that these languages lead to good transfer because of their large datasets and difficulty as tasks. Further puzzling results come from Anastasopoulos and Neubig (2019), who find that Italian data does not improve performance in closely related Ladin or Neapolitan[3] once monolingual hallucinated data is available, and that Latvian is as good a source for Scots Gaelic as its relative Irish.

Previous analyses of transfer learning have attempted to differentiate the contributions of various parts of the model through factored vocabularies or ciphering (Kann et al., 2017b; Jin and Kann, 2017). These methods give disjoint representations to characters and tags in the source and target languages, or disrupt the mapping between them. Low-level correspondence between character sets is the most important factor for successful transfer in very low-resource settings, but models with disjoint character representations still succeed at transfer once at least 200 target examples are available, indicating that higher-level information is also transferred and contributes to performance.

Kann et al. (2017b) also represents a prior one-shot morphological learning experiment. Their setting is not quite the same as the one here; they assume access to a single inflected form in half the paradigm cells in their target language (Spanish) which are used to fine-tune a pretrained system. Because their system uses the conventional tag-based framework, they are capable of filling cells for which no example is available (zero-shot learning), while the memory-based system presented here is not. On the other hand, the current work does not use fine-tuning or require target-language data at training time. They evaluate inflection on both seen and unseen cells as a function of five source languages, four of which are in the Romance family. The best one-shot transfer within Romance scores 44% exact match, the worst 13%. Transfer from unrelated Arabic scores 0%. One-shot learning experiments in this work use a much larger set of languages, and although performance in the typical case is similar, the best results are substantially better.

The memory-based design of the current work is rooted in cognitive theories of morphological processing. The widely accepted dual route model of morphological processing postulates that the mind retrieves familiar inflected forms from memory as well as synthesizing forms from scratch (Milin et al., 2017; Alegre and Gordon, 1998; Butterworth, 1983). It has often been claimed that memorized forms of specific words are central to the structure of inflection classes (Bybee and Moder, 1983; Bybee, 2006; Jackendoff and Audring, 2020). In such a theory, production of a form of a rare lemma is guided by the memory of the appropriate forms of common ones. Additional evidence for this view comes from historical changes in which one word's paradigm is analogically remodeled on another's (Krott et al., 2001; Hock and Joseph, 1996, ch.5). Liu and Hulden (2020) evaluate a model very similar to this one (a transformer in which target forms of other words, which they term "cross-table" examples, are provided as part of the input). They

[3]Regional Romance languages spoken in Northern and Southern Italy respectively.

| | Lemma | Target specification | → | Target |
|---|---|---|---|---|
| Standard inflection generation | waiata | V;PASS | | waiatatia |
| Memory-based | waiata | karanga : karangatia | | waiatatia |
| | waiata | kaukau : kaukauria | | waiatatia |

Figure 1: Differing inputs for inflection models, eliciting the passive of the Maori verb *waiata* "sing". The memory-based system relies on an exemplar verb as the target specifier; shown here are *karanga* "call", which takes a matching suffix, and *kaukau* "swim", which mismatches.

find that such examples are complementary to data hallucination and yield improved results in data-sparse settings. Some earlier non-neural models also rely on stored word forms (Skousen, 1989; Albright and Hayes, 2002).

## 3 Exemplar selection

The system uses instances generated as described in Figure 1, separating the lemma, exemplar lemma and exemplar form with punctuation characters. Each instance also contains two features indicating the language and language family of the example (e.g. LANG_MAO, FAM_AUSTRONESIAN).

The selection of the exemplar is critical to the model's performance. Ideally, the lemma and the exemplar inflect in the same way, reducing the inflection task to copying. But this is not always the case. For example, Maori verbs fall into inflection classes, as shown in Figure 1; when the exemplar comes from a different class than the lemma, copying will yield an invalid output, so the model has to guess which class the input belongs to.[4]

This paper presents experiments using two settings: In **random selection**, the exemplar lemma is chosen arbitrarily from the set of training lemma/form pairs for the appropriate language and cell. This makes the task difficult, but allows the model to learn to cope with the distribution of inputs it will face at test time. In **similarity-based selection**, each source lemma is paired with an exemplar for which the transductions are highly similar. This makes the task easy, but since it relies on access to the true target form, it can be used only for model training, not for testing.[5] All models are evaluated using instances generated using random selection.

To perform similarity-based selection, each lemma is aligned with its target form in the training data in order to extract an edit rule (Durrett and DeNero, 2013; Nicolai et al., 2016). (For the first memory-based example in Figure 1, both words have the same edit rule -+*tia*.) The selected exemplar/form pair uses the same edit rule, if possible. During training, a lemma is allowed to act as its own exemplar, so that there is always at least one candidate. However, words in the test set must be given exemplars from the training set. If a cell in the test set does not appear in the training set, no prediction can be made; in this case, the system outputs the lemma. Extending the model to cover this case is discussed below as future work.[6]

## 4 Model design

The system uses the character-based transformer (Wu et al., 2020) as its learning model; this is a sequence-to-sequence transformer (Vaswani et al., 2017) tuned for morphological tasks, and serves as a strong official baseline for the Sigmorphon 2020 task. Moreover, transformers are known to perform well in the few-shot setting (Brown et al., 2020). All default hyperparameters[7] match those of Wu et al. (2020).

As discussed in prior work (Anastasopoulos and Neubig, 2019; Kann and Schütze, 2017), it is important to pretrain the model to predispose it to copy strings. To ensure this, the system is trained on a synthetic dataset. Each synthetic instance is generated within a random character set. The instance consists of a random pseudo-lemma and pseudo-exemplar created by sampling word

[4] In cases of class-dependent syncretism, the model must also guess which cell is being specified. For instance, German feminine nouns do not inflect for case, but some masculine nouns do, so the combination of a masculine lemma and a feminine exemplar can yield an unsolvable prediction problem.

[5] Within the training set, the same lemma/inflected form pair can appear as both an exemplar and a target instance; a reviewer speculates that this might allow the model to memorize lexically-specific outputs within the training set even when using random selection. To avoid this issue, no training scores are reported in this paper.

[6] In the SigMorphon 2020 datasets, this rarely occurs in practice. $\geq 99\%$ of target cells are covered in all languages except Ingrian (98%), Evenki (96%), and notably Ludic (61%).

[7] Including 4 layers, batches of 64, and the learning rate schedule.

lengths from the training word length distribution and then filling each one with random characters. With probability 50% the example is given a prefix; independently with probability 50% a suffix; independently with probability 10% an infix at a random character position. Prefixes and suffixes are random strings between 2-5 characters long and infixes are 1-2 characters long. (This means that, in some cases, no affix is added and the transformation is the identity, as occurs in cases of morphological syncretism.) An example such instance is *mpieňjmel:rbeaikkea::**zlü**rbeaikkea**üe*** with output ***zlü**mpieňjmel**üe***. The language tags for these examples indicate the kinds of affixation operations which were performed, for example LANG_PREFIX_SUFFIX; the family tag identifies them as SYNTHETIC. While this synthetic dataset is inspired by hallucination techniques (Anastasopoulos and Neubig, 2019; Silfverberg et al., 2017), note that these synthetic instances are not presented to the model as part of any natural language.

The Sigmorphon 2020 data is divided into "development languages" (45 languages in 5 families: Austronesian, Germanic, Niger-Congo, Oto-Manguean and Uralic) and "surprise languages" (45 more languages, including some members of development families as well as unseen families). Data from all the "development languages", plus the synthetic examples from the previous stage, is used to train a multilingual model, which is fine-tuned family. Finally the family models are fine-tuned by language. During multilingual training and per-family tuning, the dataset is balanced to contain 20,000 instances per language; languages with more training instances than this are subsampled, while languages with fewer are upsampled by sampling multiple exemplars (with replacement) for each lemma/target pair. For the final language-specific fine-tuning stage, all instances from the specific language are used.

## 5 Fine-tuned results

This section shows the test results for fully fine-tuned models on the development languages. Table 1 shows the average exact match and standard deviation by language family. Full results are given in Appendix A. Tables also show the results of the official competition baseline which is closest to the current work, the character transformer (Wu et al., 2020) fine-tuned by language, TRM-SINGLE.

Because the results of exemplar-based models can vary based on the choice of exemplar, the system applies a simple post-process to compensate for unlucky choices: it runs each lemma with five randomly-selected exemplars and chooses the majority output.

| Family | Random | Similarity | Base |
|---|---|---|---|
| Austronesian (4) | 83 (13) | 67 (21) | 81 (18) |
| Germanic (10) | 87 (10) | 51 (16) | 90 (9) |
| Niger-Congo (9) | 98 (4) | 94 (9) | 97 (3) |
| Oto-Manguean (10) | 82 (16) | 39 (23) | 86 (12)3 |
| Uralic (11) | 92 (6) | 46 (14) | 93 (0.05) |
| Overall | 89 (12) | 57 (26) | 90 (11) |

Table 1: Fine-tuned accuracy scores for models trained with random and similarity-based selection, compared to the baseline. Num languages in family and score standard deviation across languages in parentheses.

Neither model achieves the same performance as the baseline (90%), although the random-exemplar model (89%) comes quite close. The similar-exemplar model (57%) is clearly inferior due to its severe mismatch between training and test settings. Performance varies across language families. All models perform well in Niger-Congo, although the conference organizers state that data from these languages may have been biased toward regular forms in an unrepresentative way.[8] The random-exemplar model is at or near baseline performance in Austronesian and Uralic, but falls further below baseline in Germanic and Oto-Manguean. Both of these families are characterized by complex inflection class structure in which randomly chosen exemplars are less likely to resemble the target for a given word.

The similar-exemplar model also performs poorly in Uralic. While some Uralic languages have inflection classes (Baerman, 2014), many (like Finnish) do not, but have complex systems of phonological alternations (Koskenniemi and Church, 1988). While the random-exemplar model can learn to compensate for these, the similar-exemplar model does not.

## 6 One-shot results

This section shows the results of one-shot learning. These experiments apply the multilingual and family models from the development languages to the surprise languages, without fine-tuning. For languages within development families, they use the appropriate family model; otherwise they use the

[8] A Swahili speaker confirms that some forms in the data appear artificially over-regularized (Martha Johnson p.c.).

multilingual model. Thus, the model's only access to information about the target language is via the provided exemplar.

Each experiment evaluates the results across five random exemplars per test instance (with replacement), but averages the results rather than applying majority selection. This computes the expected performance in the one-shot setting where only a single exemplar is available.

Results are shown in Table 2. One-shot learning is not competitive with the baseline fine-tuned system in any language family, but has some capacity to predict inflections in all families. Performance is generally better in families for which related languages were present in development.

The system trained with random exemplars achieves its best results on Tajik (Iranian: tgk, score 89%), Shona (Niger-Congo: sna, score 75%)[9], and Norwegian Nynorsk (Germanic: nno, score 42%). The system trained with similar exemplars achieves its best results on Shona (88%), Zarma (Songhay: dje, score 82%) and Tajik (79%). Notably, some of these high scores are achieved on languages that were difficult for the baseline systems; the score for Tajik beats the transformer baseline (56%), perhaps due to data sparsity, since baselines regularized using data hallucination perform better (93%).

Training with similar exemplars leads to clearly better results than random exemplars, a reversal of the trend observed with fine-tuning. This difference is particularly marked in Romance (53% average vs 5%). While the random-exemplar system is better at guessing what to do when the exemplar and target forms are divergent, this causes errors with unfamiliar languages. The system attempts to guess the correct inflection, rather than simply copying.

As an example, Table 3 shows an analysis of performance in Catalan (cat), selected because its results are fairly typical of the Romance family; the similar-exemplar system scores 53% while the random-exemplar system scores 12%. The table shows selected instances with different levels of exemplar match and mismatch. The first two, *arrissar* "curl" and *disputar* "discuss", match their exemplars well and are good cases for copying. The random-exemplar model gets these both wrong, segmenting incorrectly in the first and adding a spurious character in the second. The next two, *repetir* "repeat" and *engolir* "ingest", are mismatched with exemplars from a different inflection class; both systems make incorrect predictions, but the similar-exemplar system preserves the suffixes while the random-exemplar system does not. Finally, in the last example *llevar-se* "get up", the similar-exemplar model misinterprets the reflexive suffix *-se* as part of the verb stem, while the random-exemplar model fails to make any edit.

[9]As stated above, the Niger-Congo datasets are artificialized and probably does not represent the real difficulty of the inflection task.

| Family | Random | Similarity | Base |
|---|---|---|---|
| Germanic (3) | 29 (13) | 38 (22) | 80 (13) |
| Niger-Congo (1) | 75 (0) | 88 (0) | 100 (0) |
| Uralic (5) | 21 (9) | 28 (12) | 76 (26) |
| Afro-Asiatic (3) | 7 (3) | 26 (18) | 96 (3) |
| Algic (1) | 2 (0) | 14 (0) | 68 (0) |
| Dravidian (2) | 7 (7) | 13 (3) | 85 (9) |
| Indic (4) | 4 (5) | 4 (2) | 98 (3) |
| Iranian (3) | 35 (39) | 34 (32) | 82 (19) |
| Romance (8) | 6 (4) | 53 (19) | 99 (1) |
| Sino-Tibetan (1) | 21 (0) | 9 (0) | 84 (0) |
| Siouan (1) | 13 (0) | 13 (0) | 96 (0) |
| Songhay (1) | 21 (0) | 82 (0) | 88 (0) |
| Southern Daly | 4 (0) | 6 (0) | 90 (0) |
| Tungusic (1) | 28 (0) | 27 (0) | 57 (0) |
| Turkic (9) | 7 (8) | 19 (11) | 96 (7) |
| Uto-Aztecan (1) | 33 (0) | 30 (0) | 81 (0) |
| Overall | 14 (18) | 30 (25) | 90 (15) |

Table 2: One-shot accuracy scores for models trained with random and similarity-based selection, compared to the baseline. Num. languages in family and score standard deviation across languages in parentheses. Families represented in development above the line, surprise families below.

A more systematic analysis computes an alignment-based edit rule for each system prediction (King et al., 2020) and counts the unique rules used to form one-shot predictions in the Catalan development set. Over 37105 instances, the random-exemplar model applies 626 unique edit rules, 20 of which appear in correct predictions. The similar-exemplar model applies 3137 unique rules, 154 of them correctly. The greater variety of both correct and incorrect outputs from the similar-exemplar model demonstrates its preference for faithfulness to the exemplar rather than remodeling the output to fit language-specific constraints.

## 7 Synthetic transfer experiments

When transfer learning fails, it can be difficult to tell whether the system has failed to represent a general morphological process, or whether it misapplies what it has learned due to mismatched lexical/phonological triggers. Experiments on artificial data can probe what abstract processes the model

| Lemma | Exemplar | Rand. Sel. | Sim. Sel | Target |
|---|---|---|---|---|
| arrissar | posar : posarien | arrissaren | arrissarien | arrissarien |
| disputar | descriure : descriuria | disputarta | disputaria | disputaria |
| repetir | cremar : cremo | repetirer | repetio | repeteixo |
| engolir | forjar : forjava | engolire | engoliva | engolia |
| llevar-se | terminar : termino | llevar-se | llevor-se | llevo |

Table 3: Development data from Catalan (Romance: cat) showing the outputs of two one-shot systems.

has learned to apply, the links between these processes and language families, and the environments in which they can operate.

A probing dataset is synthesized to model several morphological operations (Figure 2), including prefix/suffix affixation, reduplication and gemination. Affixation is typologically widespread (Bickel and Nichols, 2013) and appears in every development language on which the model was trained. Suffixation is more common in Germanic and Uralic; Oto-Manguean tonal morphology is also often represented via word-final diacritics.[10] Prefixing is more common in the Niger-Congo family.

Reduplication appears in three of the four Austronesian development languages, Tagalog, Hiligaynon and Cebuano (WAL, 2013), but not in the Maori dataset provided. The probe language has partial reduplication of the first syllable, as found in Tagalog and Hiligaynon. Previous work with artificial data demonstrates that sequence-to-sequence learners can learn fully abstract representations of reduplication (Prickett et al., 2018; Nelson et al., 2020; Haley and Wilson, 2021), but it has not been previously shown that networks trained on real data do this in a transferable way. In one-shot language transfer, reduplication instances are actually ambiguous. Given an instance *modi : _ :: gobu : gogobu*, there are two plausible interpretations, reduplicative *momodi* and affixal *gomodi*. Thus, analysis of reduplicative instances can be informative about the model's learned linkage between language family and typology.

Gemination is a inflectional process whereby a segment is lengthened to mark some morphological feature (Samek-Lodovici, 1992). The probe language geminates the last non-final consonant. None of the development languages have morphological gemination.

The probe languages use two alphabets: the first is a common subset of characters which appear in at least half the languages of every development family.[11] The second is a subset of Cyrillic characters intended to test transfer to a less-familiar orthography; a few Uralic development languages are written in Cyrillic. Each language has 90 random lemmas, sampled with the frames *CVCV, CVCVC, CVCVCVC*; affixal languages have 30 affixes of types *VCV, CV, CVCV*, plus 7 single-letter affixes. No probe lemma coincides with any real lemma, and no probe affix has frequency $> 5\%$ as a string prefix or suffix in any real language. Affixal languages contain an instance for every lemma/affix pair. Reduplication and gemination languages have one instance per lemma.

The model is prompted to inflect the probes as if they are members of each language family, and as members of a comparatively well-resourced language selected from those families, specifically Tagalog (tgl), German (deu), Mezquital Otomi (ote), Swahili (swa) and Finnish (fin), as well as the synthetic suffixing language used in pretraining (suff). In addition to checking whether the output matches, the table shows whether reduplicated instances have been correctly reduplicated (using a regular expression).

Table 4 shows the results. A comparison between the random-exemplar and similar-exemplar models confirms the hypothesis from above that random-exemplar models have less generalizable representations of morphological processes, especially prefixation and suffixation. While both models are capable of attaching affixes in the synthetic language, the random-exemplar model learns very language- and suffix-specific rules for applying these operations, leading to very low accuracy for copying generic affixes. Both models show less language-specific remodeling of affixes in the family-only setting than when the probes are labeled as part of a particular language; this effect is again more pronounced for the random-exemplar model.

Both models learn to reduplicate arbitrary CV syllables, but this process is mostly restricted to

[10]No Unicode normalization was performed; Oto-Manguean tone diacritics are treated as characters (as are parts of the complex characters of the Indic scripts). The placement of these diacritics within the word varies from language to language.

[11]Consonants *mpbntdrlskgh*, vowels *aeiou*.

| Probe type | Lemma *semet* Exemplar | Target |
|---|---|---|
| Prefixing | kigu : igokigu | igosemet |
| Suffixing | kigu : kiguigo | semetigo |
| Reduplication | modi : momodi | sesemet |
| Gemination | bogu : boggu | semmet |

Figure 2: Probe tasks illustrated for a single lemma.

Tagalog,[12], with some generalization to Austronesian. Most other languages interpret reduplication instances as affixes.

Only the similar-exemplar model gets any gemination instances correct, and these primarily in Uralic.[13] This is unsurprising, since the model was never trained with morphological gemination. It demonstrates that the model's representations of morphological processes represent the input typology and are not simply artifacts of the transformer architecture. While Uralic does not have gemination as an independent morphological process, alternations involving geminates do occur in some paradigms; the NOM.PL of *tikka* "dart" is *tikat.*[14] The model seems to have learned a little about gemination from this morphophonological process, but not a fully generalized representation.

Affixation remains relatively successful when using Cyrillic characters (suffixes more than prefixes), but for the most part, less so than with Latin characters, although in the random-exemplar model, Cyrillic suffixes are somewhat *more* accurate, probably due to less interference from language-specific knowledge. This substantiates the general finding (Murikinati et al., 2020) that transfer across scripts is more difficult than within-script. Cyrillic reduplication sees a much larger drop in accuracy. The difference is probably that simple affixation is phonologically uncomplicated, while reduplication requires phonological information about vowels and consonants.

## 8 Discussion

These experiments with real and synthetic transfer suggest some useful insights into the problematic findings of earlier transfer experiments. Why is Hungarian so successful as a source language for unrelated targets? Kann (2020) suggests that it is its agglutinative nature. The results shown here offer some speculative support for this view—perhaps the relative segmentability of prototypically agglutinative languages (Plank, 1999) acts like the similar-exemplar setting in the memory-based model, giving the source model a general bias for concatenative affixation, unpolluted by too many lexical and phonological alternations. As reported here, such a model is a promising starting point for inflection in many non-agglutinative systems, such as Romance verbs, which nevertheless are strongly concatenative.

Where transfer between related languages fails, it is conjecturally possible that the source model representations of edit operations are too closely linked to particular phonological and lexical properties of the source. This is clearly shown in the synthetic transfer experiments, where generic suffixation fails in Germanic and Uralic despite these families being strongly suffixing, because the system has learned to remodel its outputs to conform too closely to source-language templates.

More broadly, the synthetic experiments show a link between language typology and learning of morphological processes, suggesting that language structure, not only language relatedness, is key to successful transfer— transfer of structural principles can lead to improvements even without cognate words or affixes. For instance, successful reduplication appears only in Austronesian and successful gemination only in Uralic. A promising direction for future work would be to replace the language family feature with a set of typological feature indicators such as WALs properties (WAL, 2013), which might help the model to learn faster in low-resource target languages.

Two other extensions might bring the memory-based model closer to the state of the art in supervised inflection prediction. First, although the SigMorphon 2020 datasets are balanced by paradigm cell, real datasets are Zipfian, with sparse coverage of cells (Blevins et al., 2017; Lignos and Yang, 2018). For languages with large paradigms, the model thus requires the capacity to fill cells for which no exemplar can be retrieved, perhaps using a variant of adaptive source selection (Erdmann et al., 2020; Kann et al., 2017a). Second, the similar-exemplar model performs better in one-shot transfer experiments, but is hampered in the su-

[12]The random-exemplar model has low accuracy for reduplication in Tagalog because it appends spurious Tagalog prefixes to the output, another example of a language-specific rule. However, the regular expression check confirms that reduplication is performed correctly.

[13]Because of this poor performance, Cyrillic gemination was not tested.

[14]See Silfverberg et al. (2021) for a fuller investigation of generalizable representations of gradation processes in Finnish noun paradigms.

| Model | Fam/Lg. | Pref | Pref (Cyrl) | Suff | Suff (Cyrl) | Redup. | Redup. (Cyrl) | Gem. |
|---|---|---|---|---|---|---|---|---|
| Rand. | austro | 62 | 36 | 26 | 38 | 0 (10) | 0 | 0 |
| | austro/tgl | 0 | 1 | 0 | 0 | 28 (90) | 3 (7) | 0 |
| | ger | 1 | 0 | 25 | 36 | 0 (3) | 0 | 0 |
| | ger/deu | 0 | 0 | 8 | 10 | 0 (3) | 0 | 0 |
| | n-congo | 92 | 55 | 40 | 41 | 0 (3) | 0 | 0 |
| | n-congo/swa | 100 | 76 | 36 | 25 | 0 (3) | 0 | 0 |
| | oto | 20 | 15 | 21 | 33 | 0 (3) | 0 | 0 |
| | oto/ote | 35 | 30 | 1 | 9 | 0 (3) | 0 | 0 |
| | uralic | 3 | 0 | 23 | 34 | 0 (3) | 0 | 0 |
| | uralic/fin | 0 | 0 | 7 | 22 | 0 (3) | 0 | 0 |
| | synth | 84 | 62 | 97 | 91 | 0 (3) | 0 | 0 |
| | synth/suff | 28 | 1 | 100 | 97 | 0 (3) | 0 | 0 |
| Sim. | austro | 86 | 75 | 94 | 85 | 30 (30) | 0 | 0 |
| | austro/tgl | 30 | 35 | 75 | 63 | 88 (88) | 8 (8) | 0 |
| | ger | 85 | 55 | 99 | 96 | 3 (3) | 0 | 8 |
| | ger/deu | 86 | 55 | 99 | 98 | 0 | 0 | 5 |
| | n-congo | 99 | 96 | 98 | 93 | 0 (3) | 0 | 3 |
| | n-congo/swa | 99 | 98 | 88 | 57 | 0 | 0 | 0 |
| | oto | 88 | 76 | 95 | 87 | 18 (18) | 0 | 0 |
| | oto/ote | 96 | 84 | 59 | 17 | 5 (5) | 0 | 0 |
| | uralic | 59 | 10 | 97 | 95 | 0 | 0 | 17 |
| | uralic/fin | 52 | 4 | 98 | 98 | 0 | 0 | 12 |
| | synth | 94 | 84 | 99 | 95 | 8 (10) | 0 | 2 |
| | synth/suff | 86 | 42 | 100 | 99 | 0 | 0 | 2 |

Table 4: Accuracy of synthetic probe tasks presented as different language and language family. (Cyrl) indicates Cyrillic alphabet. Parentheses in reduplication columns show frequency of correct CV reduplication.

pervised setting by train-test mismatch. Selecting training exemplars using a classifier which could also be used at inference time would reduce this mismatch. These experiments are left for future work.

Finally, since the memory-based architecture is cognitively inspired, it might be adapted as a cognitive model of language learning in contact situations. Work on this learning process suggests that speakers find it much easier to learn new exponents than to learn new morphological processes (Dorian, 1978; Mithun, 2020). Thus, the impact of source-language transfer may indeed be most significant in cases where the L1 and L2 (source and target) languages differ in the abstract mechanisms of inflection rather than the specifics. Historical contact-induced change provides evidence for this viewpoint in the form of systems which have changed to employ the same processes as a contact language. For example, Cappadocian Greek has become agglutinative through its extensive contact with Turkish (Janse, 2004). For other examples, see Green (1995); Thomason (2001).

## 9 Conclusion

The results of this paper demonstrate that the proposed cognitive mechanism of memory-based analogy provides a relatively strong basis for inflection prediction. Performance in a supervised setting is strongest in languages without large numbers of inflection classes, and requires training exemplars to be selected in the same way as test exemplars. Memory-based analogy also provides a foundation for one-shot transfer; in this case, training exemplars should closely match the elicited inflections, so that the model learns to copy rather than reconstruct the output form. One-shot transfer using this mechanism can achieve higher accuracy than previously thought, even when no genetically related languages are available in training. Scores vary widely, but can be over 80% for some languages.

Finally, this paper provides new evidence about what kinds of abstract information (beyond character correspondences) is transferred between languages when learning to inflect. The model learns general processes for prefixation and suffixation which apply (to some extent) across character sets, but its application of these can be disrupted by language-specific morpho-phonological rules. It also learns to reduplicate arbitrary CV sequences, but applies this process only when targeting a language with reduplication. Learning of morphological processes in general appears to be driven by the input typology. The discussion argues that the usefulness of general representations for prefixation and suffixation accounts for the puzzling effectiveness of agglutinative languages as transfer sources reported in previous research.

## Acknowledgments

This research is deeply indebted to ideas contributed by Andrea Sims. I am also grateful to members of LING 5802 in autumn 2020 at Ohio State, and to the three anonymous reviewers for their comments and suggestions. Parts of this work were run on the Ohio Supercomputer (OSC, 1987).

## References

2013. World atlas of language structures online. Available online at `https://wals.info/`, accessed 3 June 2020.

Adam Albright and Bruce Hayes. 2002. Modeling English past tense intuitions with minimal generalization. In *Proceedings of the Sixth Meeting of the Association for Computational Linguistics Special Interest Group in Computational Phonology in Philadelphia, July 2002*, pages 58–69.

Maria Alegre and Peter Gordon. 1998. Frequency effects and the representational status of regular inflections. *Journal of Memory and Language*, 40:41–61.

Antonios Anastasopoulos and Graham Neubig. 2019. Pushing the limits of low-resource morphological inflection. In *Proceedings of the 2019 Conference on Empirical Methods in Natural Language Processing and the 9th International Joint Conference on Natural Language Processing (EMNLP-IJCNLP)*, pages 984–996, Hong Kong, China. Association for Computational Linguistics.

Matthew Baerman. 2014. Covert systematicity in a distributionally complex system. *Journal of Linguistics*, pages 1–47.

Balthasar Bickel and Johanna Nichols. 2013. Fusion of selected inflectional formatives. In Matthew S. Dryer and Martin Haspelmath, editors, *The World Atlas of Language Structures Online*. Max Planck Institute for Evolutionary Anthropology, Leipzig.

James P. Blevins, Petar Milin, and Michael Ramscar. 2017. The Zipfian paradigm cell filling problem. In Ferenc Kiefer, James P. Blevins, and Huba Bartos, editors, *Perspectives on morphological organization: Data and analyses*, pages 141–158. Brill.

Antal van den Bosch and Walter Daelemans. 1999. Memory-based morphological analysis. In *Proceedings of the 37th Annual Meeting of the Association for Computational Linguistics*, pages 285–292, College Park, Maryland, USA. Association for Computational Linguistics.

Tom B Brown, Benjamin Mann, Nick Ryder, Melanie Subbiah, Jared Kaplan, Prafulla Dhariwal, Arvind Neelakantan, Pranav Shyam, Girish Sastry, Amanda Askell, et al. 2020. Language models are few-shot learners. *arXiv preprint arXiv:2005.14165*.

Brian Butterworth. 1983. Lexical representation. In Brian Butterworth, editor, *Language production, vol. 2: Development, writing and other language processes*, pages 257–294. Academic Press.

Joan Bybee. 2006. From usage to grammar: The mind's response to repetition. *Language*, 82(4):711–733.

Joan Bybee and Carol Moder. 1983. Morphological classes as natural categories. *Language*, 59(2):251–270.

Nancy C. Dorian. 1978. The fate of morphological complexity in language death: Evidence from East Sutherland Gaelic. *Language*, 54(3):590–609.

Greg Durrett and John DeNero. 2013. Supervised learning of complete morphological paradigms. In *Proceedings of the 2013 Conference of the North American Chapter of the Association for Computational Linguistics: Human Language Technologies*, pages 1185–1195, Atlanta, Georgia. Association for Computational Linguistics.

Alexander Erdmann, Tom Kenter, Markus Becker, and Christian Schallhart. 2020. Frugal paradigm completion. In *Proceedings of the 58th Annual Meeting of the Association for Computational Linguistics*, pages 8248–8273, Online. Association for Computational Linguistics.

Alex Graves, Greg Wayne, Malcolm Reynolds, Tim Harley, Ivo Danihelka, Agnieszka Grabska-Barwińska, Sergio Gómez Colmenarejo, Edward Grefenstette, Tiago Ramalho, John Agapiou, et al. 2016. Hybrid computing using a neural network with dynamic external memory. *Nature*, 538(7626):471–476.

Ian Green. 1995. The death of 'prefixing': contact induced typological change in northern australia. In *Annual Meeting of the Berkeley Linguistics Society*, volume 21, pages 414–425.

Coleman Haley and Colin Wilson. 2021. Deep neural networks easily learn unnatural infixation and reduplication patterns. *Proceedings of the Society for Computation in Linguistics*, 4(1):427–433.

Hans Henrich Hock and Brian D. Joseph. 1996. *Language history, language change and language relationship: An introduction to historical and comparative linguistics.* Mouton de Gruyter.

Ray Jackendoff and Jenny Audring. 2020. *The texture of the lexicon: Relational Morphology and the Parallel Architecture*. Oxford University Press.

Mark Janse. 2004. Animacy, definiteness, and case in Cappadocian and other Asia Minor Greek dialects. *Journal of Greek linguistics*, 5(1):3–26.

Huiming Jin and Katharina Kann. 2017. Exploring cross-lingual transfer of morphological knowledge in sequence-to-sequence models. In *Proceedings of the First Workshop on Subword and Character Level Models in NLP*, pages 70–75, Copenhagen, Denmark. Association for Computational Linguistics.

Katharina Kann. 2020. Acquisition of inflectional morphology in artificial neural networks with prior knowledge. In *Proceedings of the Society for Computation in Linguistics 2020*, pages 144–154, New York, New York. Association for Computational Linguistics.

Katharina Kann, Ryan Cotterell, and Hinrich Schütze. 2017a. Neural multi-source morphological reinflection. In *Proceedings of the 15th Conference of the European Chapter of the Association for Computational Linguistics: Volume 1, Long Papers*, pages 514–524, Valencia, Spain. Association for Computational Linguistics.

Katharina Kann, Ryan Cotterell, and Hinrich Schütze. 2017b. One-shot neural cross-lingual transfer for paradigm completion. In *Proceedings of the 55th Annual Meeting of the Association for Computational Linguistics (Volume 1: Long Papers)*, pages 1993–2003, Vancouver, Canada. Association for Computational Linguistics.

Katharina Kann and Hinrich Schütze. 2016. MED: The LMU system for the SIGMORPHON 2016 shared task on morphological reinflection. In *Proceedings of the 14th SIGMORPHON Workshop on Computational Research in Phonetics, Phonology, and Morphology*, pages 62–70, Berlin, Germany. Association for Computational Linguistics.

Katharina Kann and Hinrich Schütze. 2017. Unlabeled data for morphological generation with character-based sequence-to-sequence models. In *Proceedings of the First Workshop on Subword and Character Level Models in NLP*, pages 76–81, Copenhagen, Denmark. Association for Computational Linguistics.

David King, Andrea Sims, and Micha Elsner. 2020. Interpreting sequence-to-sequence models for Russian inflectional morphology. In *Proceedings of the Society for Computation in Linguistics 2020*, pages 481–490, New York, New York. Association for Computational Linguistics.

Kimmo Koskenniemi and Kenneth Ward Church. 1988. Complexity, two-level morphology and Finnish. In *Coling Budapest 1988 Volume 1: International Conference on Computational Linguistics*.

Andrea Krott, R Harald Baayen, and Robert Schreuder. 2001. Analogy in morphology: modeling the choice of linking morphemes in dutch.

Constantine Lignos and Charles Yang. 2018. Morphology and language acquisition. In Andrew Hippisley and Gregory T. Stump, editors, *Cambridge handbook of morphology*, pages 765–791. Cambridge University Press.

Yu-Hsiang Lin, Chian-Yu Chen, Jean Lee, Zirui Li, Yuyan Zhang, Mengzhou Xia, Shruti Rijhwani, Junxian He, Zhisong Zhang, Xuezhe Ma, Antonios Anastasopoulos, Patrick Littell, and Graham Neubig. 2019. Choosing transfer languages for cross-lingual learning. In *Proceedings of the 57th Annual Meeting of the Association for Computational Linguistics*, pages 3125–3135, Florence, Italy. Association for Computational Linguistics.

Ling Liu and Mans Hulden. 2020. Analogy models for neural word inflection. In *Proceedings of the 28th International Conference on Computational Linguistics*, pages 2861–2878, Barcelona, Spain (Online). International Committee on Computational Linguistics.

Arya D. McCarthy, Ekaterina Vylomova, Shijie Wu, Chaitanya Malaviya, Lawrence Wolf-Sonkin, Garrett Nicolai, Christo Kirov, Miikka Silfverberg, Sabrina J. Mielke, Jeffrey Heinz, Ryan Cotterell, and Mans Hulden. 2019. The SIGMORPHON 2019 shared task: Morphological analysis in context and cross-lingual transfer for inflection. In *Proceedings of the 16th Workshop on Computational Research in Phonetics, Phonology, and Morphology*, pages 229–244, Florence, Italy. Association for Computational Linguistics.

Petar Milin, Laurie Beth Feldman, Michael Ramscar, Roberta A. Hendrick, and R. Harald Baayen. 2017. Discrimination in lexical decision. *PLoS ONE*, 12(2):e0171935.

Marianne Mithun. 2020. Where is morphological complexity? In Peter Arkadiev and Francesco Gardani, editors, *The complexities of morphology*, pages 306–327. Oxford University Press.

Nikitha Murikinati, Antonios Anastasopoulos, and Graham Neubig. 2020. Transliteration for cross-lingual morphological inflection. In *Proceedings of the 17th SIGMORPHON Workshop on Computational Research in Phonetics, Phonology, and Morphology*, pages 189–197, Online. Association for Computational Linguistics.

Max Nelson, Hossep Dolatian, Jonathan Rawski, and Brandon Prickett. 2020. Probing RNN encoder-decoder generalization of subregular functions using reduplication. In *Proceedings of the Society for Computation in Linguistics 2020*, pages 167–178, New York, New York. Association for Computational Linguistics.

Garrett Nicolai, Bradley Hauer, Adam St Arnaud, and Grzegorz Kondrak. 2016. Morphological reinflection via discriminative string transduction. In *Proceedings of the 14th SIGMORPHON Workshop on Computational Research in Phonetics, Phonology, and Morphology*, pages 31–35, Berlin, Germany. Association for Computational Linguistics.

OSC. 1987. Ohio supercomputer center.

Frans Plank. 1999. Split morphology: How agglutination and flexion mix. *Linguistic Typology*, 3:279–340.

Brandon Prickett, Aaron Traylor, and Joe Pater. 2018. Seq2Seq models with dropout can learn generalizable reduplication. In *Proceedings of the Fifteenth Workshop on Computational Research in Phonetics, Phonology, and Morphology*, pages 93–100, Brussels, Belgium. Association for Computational Linguistics.

Vieri Samek-Lodovici. 1992. A unified analysis of crosslinguistic morphological gemination. In *Proceedings of CONSOLE*, volume 1, pages 265–283. Citeseer.

Miikka Silfverberg, Francis Tyers, Garrett Nicolai, and Mans Hulden. 2021. Do RNN states encode abstract phonological alternations? In *Proceedings of the 2021 Conference of the North American Chapter of the Association for Computational Linguistics: Human Language Technologies*, pages 5501–5513. Association for Computational Linguistics.

Miikka Silfverberg, Adam Wiemerslage, Ling Liu, and Lingshuang Jack Mao. 2017. Data augmentation for morphological reinflection. In *Proceedings of the CoNLL SIGMORPHON 2017 Shared Task: Universal Morphological Reinflection*, pages 90–99, Vancouver. Association for Computational Linguistics.

Royal Skousen. 1989. *Analogical modeling of language*. Springer Science & Business Media.

Sarah Grey Thomason. 2001. Contact-induced typological change. In *Language typology and language universals: An international handbook*, volume 2, pages 1640–1648.

Ashish Vaswani, Noam Shazeer, Niki Parmar, Jakob Uszkoreit, Llion Jones, Aidan N Gomez, Lukasz Kaiser, and Illia Polosukhin. 2017. Attention is all you need. In *NIPS*.

Ekaterina Vylomova, Jennifer White, Elizabeth Salesky, Sabrina J. Mielke, Shijie Wu, Edoardo Maria Ponti, Rowan Hall Maudslay, Ran Zmigrod, Josef Valvoda, Svetlana Toldova, Francis Tyers, Elena Klyachko, Ilya Yegorov, Natalia Krizhanovsky, Paula Czarnowska, Irene Nikkarinen, Andrew Krizhanovsky, Tiago Pimentel, Lucas Torroba Hennigen, Christo Kirov, Garrett Nicolai, Adina Williams, Antonios Anastasopoulos, Hilaria Cruz, Eleanor Chodroff, Ryan Cotterell, Miikka Silfverberg, and Mans Hulden. 2020. SIGMORPHON 2020 shared task 0: Typologically diverse morphological inflection. In *Proceedings of the 17th SIGMORPHON Workshop on Computational Research in Phonetics, Phonology, and Morphology*, pages 1–39, Online. Association for Computational Linguistics.

Shijie Wu, Ryan Cotterell, and Mans Hulden. 2020. Applying the transformer to character-level transduction. *arXiv preprint arXiv:2005.10213*.

## A Full results

For replicability, this appendix provides full results for all languages, as 0-1 accuracy on the official test datasets. The reported baseline is TRM-SINGLE, copied from `https://docs.google.com/spreadsheets/d/1ODFRnHuwN-mvGtzXA1sNdCi-jNqZjiE-i9jRxZCK0kg`. Scores for supervised systems on the development languages are shown in Table 5 and scores for one-shot systems on surprise languages are shown in Table 6. See Vylomova et al. (2020) for language abbreviation definitions.

| Lang | Fam | Rand | Sim | Base |
|---|---|---|---|---|
| ang | Indo-Eur: Germanic | 72 | 19 | 78 |
| azg | Oto-Manguean | 94 | 22 | 95 |
| ceb | Austronesian | 79 | 69 | 84 |
| cly | Oto-Manguean | 82 | 19 | 91 |
| cpa | Oto-Manguean | 74 | 33 | 91 |
| ctp | Oto-Manguean | 43 | 15 | 60 |
| czn | Oto-Manguean | 83 | 32 | 80 |
| dan | Indo-Eur: Germanic | 75 | 42 | 75 |
| deu | Indo-Eur: Germanic | 93 | 62 | 98 |
| eng | Indo-Eur: Germanic | 97 | 67 | 97 |
| est | Uralic | 94 | 47 | 95 |
| fin | Uralic | 100 | 39 | 100 |
| frr | Indo-Eur: Germanic | 81 | 39 | 87 |
| gaa | Niger-Congo | 100 | 100 | 98 |
| gmh | Indo-Eur: Germanic | 94 | 75 | 91 |
| hil | Austronesian | 97 | 74 | 98 |
| isl | Indo-Eur: Germanic | 88 | 37 | 97 |
| izh | Uralic | 85 | 33 | 87 |
| kon | Niger-Congo | 99 | 99 | 98 |
| krl | Uralic | 99 | 36 | 99 |
| lin | Niger-Congo | 100 | 100 | 100 |
| liv | Uralic | 93 | 54 | 96 |
| lug | Niger-Congo | 90 | 74 | 91 |
| mao | Austronesian | 71 | 57 | 52 |
| mdf | Uralic | 92 | 67 | 94 |
| mhr | Uralic | 91 | 67 | 93 |
| mlg | Austronesian | 100 | 100 | 100 |
| myv | Uralic | 93 | 61 | 94 |
| nld | Indo-Eur: Germanic | 99 | 61 | 99 |
| nob | Indo-Eur: Germanic | 75 | 47 | 76 |
| nya | Niger-Congo | 100 | 100 | 100 |
| ote | Oto-Manguean | 99 | 80 | 99 |
| otm | Oto-Manguean | 98 | 46 | 98 |
| pei | Oto-Manguean | 65 | 17 | 72 |
| sme | Uralic | 99 | 31 | 100 |
| sot | Niger-Congo | 100 | 100 | 98 |
| swa | Niger-Congo | 100 | 100 | 100 |
| swe | Indo-Eur: Germanic | 97 | 59 | 99 |
| tgl | Austronesian | 69 | 35 | 72 |
| vep | Uralic | 83 | 28 | 84 |
| vot | Uralic | 81 | 41 | 86 |
| xty | Oto-Manguean | 90 | 79 | 91 |
| zpv | Oto-Manguean | 87 | 46 | 85 |
| zul | Niger-Congo | 92 | 83 | 92 |
| Overall | | 89 | 57 | 90 |
| Stdev | | 12 | 26 | 11 |

Table 5: Zero-one test-set accuracy scores by language for SigMorphon 2020 development languages (supervised).

| Lang | Fam | Rand | Sim | Base |
|---|---|---|---|---|
| ast | Indo-Eur: Romance | 2 | 64 | 100 |
| aze | Turkic | 9 | 17 | 81 |
| bak | Turkic | 15 | 14 | 100 |
| ben | Indo-Aryan | 1 | 4 | 99 |
| bod | Sino-Tibetan | 21 | 9 | 84 |
| cat | Indo-Eur: Romance | 12 | 53 | 100 |
| cre | Algic | 2 | 14 | 68 |
| crh | Turkic | 24 | 45 | 99 |
| dak | Siouan | 13 | 13 | 96 |
| dje | Nilo-Saharan | 21 | 82 | 88 |
| evn | Tungusic | 28 | 27 | 57 |
| fas | Indo-Eur: Iranian | 2 | 13 | 100 |
| frm | Indo-Eur: Romance | 7 | 73 | 100 |
| fur | Indo-Eur: Romance | 11 | 19 | 100 |
| glg | Indo-Eur: Romance | 9 | 59 | 100 |
| gml | Indo-Eur: Germanic | 11 | 11 | 62 |
| gsw | Indo-Eur: Germanic | 33 | 64 | 93 |
| hin | Indo-Aryan | 0 | 1 | 100 |
| kan | Dravidian | 13 | 16 | 76 |
| kaz | Turkic | 0 | 7 | 98 |
| kir | Turkic | 2 | 6 | 98 |
| kjh | Turkic | 11 | 11 | 100 |
| kpv | Uralic | 17 | 47 | 97 |
| lld | Indo-Eur: Romance | 3 | 68 | 99 |
| lud | Uralic | 22 | 14 | 32 |
| mlt | Afro-Asiatic | 10 | 13 | 97 |
| mwf | Australian | 4 | 6 | 90 |
| nno | Indo-Eur: Germanic | 42 | 40 | 86 |
| olo | Uralic | 37 | 33 | 94 |
| ood | Uto-Aztecan | 33 | 30 | 81 |
| orm | Afro-Asiatic | 2 | 52 | 99 |
| pus | Indo-Eur: Iranian | 13 | 9 | 90 |
| san | Indo-Aryan | 13 | 5 | 93 |
| sna | Niger-Congo | 75 | 88 | 100 |
| syc | Afro-Asiatic | 8 | 13 | 91 |
| tel | Dravidian | 0 | 10 | 95 |
| tgk | Indo-Eur: Iranian | 89 | 79 | 56 |
| tuk | Turkic | 0 | 21 | 86 |
| udm | Uralic | 11 | 30 | 98 |
| uig | Turkic | 0 | 26 | 99 |
| urd | Indo-Aryan | 2 | 7 | 99 |
| uzb | Turkic | 0 | 21 | 100 |
| vec | Indo-Eur: Romance | 2 | 62 | 100 |
| vro | Uralic | 17 | 17 | 61 |
| xno | Indo-Eur: Romance | 2 | 22 | 96 |
| Overall | | 14 | 30 | 90 |
| Stdev | | 18 | 25 | 15 |

Table 6: Zero-one test-set accuracy scores by language for SigMorphon 2020 surprise languages (one-shot).

# Simple induction of (deterministic) probabilistic finite-state automata for phonotactics by stochastic gradient descent

**Huteng Dai**
Rutgers University
huteng.dai@rutgers.edu

**Richard Futrell**
University of California, Irvine
rfutrell@uci.edu

## Abstract

We introduce a simple and highly general phonotactic learner which induces a probabilistic finite-state automaton from word-form data. We describe the learner and show how to parameterize it to induce unrestricted regular languages, as well as how to restrict it to certain subregular classes such as Strictly $k$-Local and Strictly $k$-Piecewise languages. We evaluate the learner on its ability to learn phonotactic constraints in toy examples and in datasets of Quechua and Navajo. We find that an unrestricted learner is the most accurate overall when modeling attested forms not seen in training; however, only the learner restricted to the Strictly Piecewise language class successfully captures certain nonlocal phonotactic constraints. Our learner serves as a baseline for more sophisticated methods.

## 1 Introduction

Natural language phonotactics is argued to fall in the class of regular languages, or even in a smaller class of subregular languages (Rogers et al., 2013). This observation has motivated the study of probabilistic finite-state automata (PFAs) that generate these languages as models of phonotactics. Here we implement a simple method for the induction of PFAs for phonotactics from data, which can induce general regular languages in addition to languages in certain more restricted subclasses, for example, Strictly $k$-Local and Strictly $k$-Piecewise languages (Heinz, 2018; Heinz and Rogers, 2010). We evaluate our learner on corpus data from Quechua and Navajo, with a particular emphasis on the ability to learn nonlocal constraints.

We make both theoretical and empirical contributions. Theoretically, we present the differentiable linear-algebraic formulation of PFAs which enables learning of the structure of the automaton by gradient descent. In our framework, it is possible to induce an unrestricted automaton with a given number of states, or an automaton with hard-coded constraints representing various subregular languages. This work fills a gap in the formal linguistics literature, where learners have been developed within certain subregular classes (Shibata and Heinz, 2019; Heinz, 2010; Heinz and Rogers, 2010; Futrell et al., 2017), whereas our learner can in principle induce any (sub)regular language. In addition, we demonstrate how Strictly Local and Strictly Piecewise constraints can be encoded within our framework, and show how information-theoretic regularization can be applied to produce deterministic automata.

Empirically, our main result is to show that our approach gives reasonable and linguistically accurate results. We find that inducing an unrestricted PFA produces the best fit to held-out attested forms, while inducing an automaton for a Strictly 2-Piecewise language yields a model that successfully captures nonlocal constraints. We also analyze the nondeterminism of induced automata, and the extent to which induced automata overfit to their training data.

## 2 Model specification

### 2.1 Probabilistic Finite-state Automata

A **probabilistic finite-state automaton** (PFA) for generating sequences consists of a finite set of states $Q$, an inventory of symbols $\Sigma$, an **emission distribution** with probability mass function $p(x|q)$ which gives the probability of generating a symbol $x \in \Sigma$ given state $q \in Q$, and a **transition distribution** with probability mass function $p(q'|q, x)$ which gives the probability of transitioning into new state $q'$ from state $q$ after emission of symbol $x$.

We parameterize a PFA using a family of right-stochastic matrices. The **emission matrix E**, of



*Proceedings of the Seventeenth SIGMORPHON Workshop on Computational Research in Phonetics, Phonology, and Morphology*, pages 167–176

shape $|Q| \times |\Sigma|$, gives the probability of emitting a symbol $x$ given a state. Each row in the matrix represents a state, and each column represents an output symbol. Given a *distribution* on states represented as a stochastic vector $\mathbf{q}$, the probability mass function over symbols is:

$$p(\cdot|\mathbf{q}) = \mathbf{q}^\top \mathbf{E}. \tag{1}$$

Each symbol $x \in \Sigma$ is associated with a right-stochastic **transition matrix** $\mathbf{T}_x$ of shape $|Q| \times |Q|$, so that the probability distribution on following states given that the symbol $x$ was emitted from the distribution on states $\mathbf{q}$ is

$$p(\cdot|\mathbf{q}, x) = \mathbf{q}^\top \mathbf{T}_x. \tag{2}$$

Generation of a particular sequence $\mathbf{x} \in \Sigma^*$ works by starting in a distinguished **initial state** $q_0$, generating a symbol $x$, transitioning into the next state $q'$, and so on recursively until reaching a distinguished **final state** $q_f$. Given a PFA parameterized by matrices $\mathbf{E}$ and $\mathbf{T}$, the probability of a sequence $x_{t=1}^N$ marginalizing over all trajectories through states can be calculated according to the Forward algorithm (Baum et al., 1970; Vidal et al., 2005a, §3) as follows:

$$p(x_{t=1}^N|\mathbf{E}, \mathbf{T}) = f(x_{t=1}^N|\delta_{q_0}),$$

where $\delta_q$ is a one-hot coordinate vector on state $q$ and

$$f(\emptyset|\mathbf{q}) = \delta_{q_f}^\top \mathbf{q}$$
$$f(x_{t=1}^n|\mathbf{q}) = p(x_1|\mathbf{q}) \cdot f(x_{t=2}^n|\mathbf{q}^\top \mathbf{T}_{x_1}).$$

The important aspect of this formulation is that the probability of a sequence is a differentiable function of the matrices $\mathbf{E}$ and $\mathbf{T}$ that define the PFA. Because the probability function is differentiable, we can induce a PFA from a set of training sequences by using gradient descent to search for matrices that maximize the probability of the training sequences.

## 2.2 Learning by gradient descent

We describe a simple and highly general method for inducing a PFA from data by stochastic gradient descent. Although more specialized learning algorithms and heuristics exist for special cases (see for example Vidal et al., 2005b, §3), ours has the advantage of generality. Our goal is to see how effective this simple approach can be in practice.

Given a data distribution $X$ with support over $\Sigma^*$, we wish to learn a PFA by finding parameter matrices $\mathbf{E}$ and $\mathbf{T}$ to minimize an objective function of the form

$$J(\mathbf{E}, \mathbf{T}) = \langle -\log p(x|\mathbf{E}, \mathbf{T}) \rangle_{x \sim X} + C(\mathbf{E}, \mathbf{T}), \tag{3}$$

where $\langle \cdot \rangle_{x \sim X}$ indicates an average over values $x$ drawn from the data distribution $X$, and $-\log p(x|\mathbf{E}, \mathbf{T})$ is the **negative log likelihood** (NLL) of a sample $x$ under the model; the average negative log likelihood is equivalent to the **cross entropy** of the data distribution $X$ and the model. By minimizing cross-entropy, we maximize likelihood and thus fit to the data. The term $C(\mathbf{E}, \mathbf{T})$ represents additional complexity constraints on the $\mathbf{E}$ and $\mathbf{T}$ matrices, discussed in Section 2.4. When $C$ is interpreted as a log prior probability on automata, then minimizing Eq. 3 is equivalent to fitting the model by maximum a posteriori.

Given the formulation in Eq. 3, because the objective function is differentiable, we can search for the optimal matrices $\mathbf{E}$ and $\mathbf{T}$ by performing (stochastic) descent on the gradients of the objective. That is, for a parameter matrix $\mathbf{X}$, we can search for a minimum by performing updates of the form

$$\mathbf{X}' = \mathbf{X} - \eta \nabla J(\mathbf{X}), \tag{4}$$

where the scalar $\eta$ is the **learning rate**. In stochastic gradient descent, each update is performed using a random finite sample from the data distribution, called a **minibatch**, to approximate the average over the data distribution in Eq. 3.

However, we cannot apply these updates directly to the matrices $\mathbf{E}$ and $\mathbf{T}$ because they must be right-stochastic, meaning that the entries in each row must be positive and sum to 1. There is no guarantee that the output of Eq. 4 would satisfy these constraints. This issue was addressed by Dai (2021) by clipping the values of the matrix $\mathbf{E}$ to be between 0 and 1. A more general solution is that, instead of doing optimization on the $\mathbf{E}$ and $\mathbf{T}$ matrices directly, we instead do optimization over underlying real-valued matrices $\tilde{\mathbf{E}}$ and $\tilde{\mathbf{T}}$ such that

$$E_{ij} = \frac{\exp \tilde{E}_{ij}}{\sum_k \exp \tilde{E}_{ik}}, T_{ij} = \frac{\exp \tilde{T}_{ij}}{\sum_k \exp \tilde{T}_{ik}},$$

in other words we derive the matrices $\mathbf{E}$ and $\mathbf{T}$ by applying the **softmax** function to underlying matrices $\tilde{\mathbf{E}}$ and $\tilde{\mathbf{T}}$, whose entries are called logits. Gradient descent is then done on the objective as a function of the logit matrices $\tilde{\mathbf{E}}$ and $\tilde{\mathbf{T}}$. This approach to parameterizing probability distributions is standard in machine learning. Applied to induce a PFA with states $Q$ and symbol inventory $\Sigma$, our formulation yields a total of $|Q| \times (|Q| \times |\Sigma| - 1)$ meaningful trainable parameters.

We note that this procedure is not guaranteed to find an automaton that globally minimizes the objective when optimizing $\mathbf{T}$ (see Vidal et al., 2005b, §3). But in practice, stochastic gradient descent in high-dimensional spaces can avoid local minima, functioning as a kind of annealing (Bottou, 1991, §4); using these simple optimization techniques on non-convex objectives is now standard practice in machine learning.

### 2.3 Sequence representation and word boundaries

In order to model phonotactics, a PFA must be sensitive to the boundaries of words, because there are often constraints that apply only at word beginnings or endings (Hayes and Wilson, 2008; Chomsky and Halle, 1968). In order to account for this, we include in the symbol inventory $\Sigma$ a special word boundary delimiter $\#$, which occurs as the final symbol of each word, and which only occurs in that position. Furthermore, we constrain all matrices $\mathbf{T}$ to transition deterministically back into the initial state following the symbol $\#$, effectively reusing the initial state $q_0$ as the final state $q_f$.

By constructing the automata in this way, we ensure that their long-run behavior is well-behaved. If an automaton of this form is allowed to keep generating past the symbol $\#$, it will generate successive concatenated independent and identically distributed samples from its distribution over words, with boundary symbols $\#$ delineating them. This construction makes it possible to calculate stationary distributions over states and complexity measures related to them.

### 2.4 Regularization

The objective in Eq. 3 includes a regularization term $C$ representing complexity constraints. Any differentiable complexity measure could be used here. This regularization term can be viewed from a Bayesian perspective as defining a prior over automata, and providing an inductive bias. We propose to use this term to constrain the PFA induction process to produce deterministic automata.

Most formal work on probabilistic finite-state automata for phonology has focused on *deterministic* PFAs because of their nice theoretical properties (Heinz, 2010). A deterministic PFA is distinguished by having fully deterministic transition matrices $\mathbf{T}$. This condition can be expressed information-theoretically. Assuming $0 \log 0 = 0$, letting the entropy of a stochastic vector $\mathbf{p}$ be:

$$H[\mathbf{p}] = -\sum_i p_i \log p_i,$$

a PFA is deterministic when it satisfies the condition $H[\mathbf{q}^\top \mathbf{T}_x] = 0$ for all symbols $x$ and state distributions $\mathbf{q}$.

We can use this expression to monitor the degree of nondeterminism of a PFA during optimization, or to add a determinism constraint to the objective in Section 2.2. The average **nondeterminism** $N$ of a PFA is given by

$$N(\mathbf{E}, \mathbf{T}) = \sum_{ij} \hat{q}_i E_{ij} H[\delta_{q_i}^\top \mathbf{T}_j],$$

where $\hat{\mathbf{q}}$ is the **stationary distribution** over states, representing the long-run average occupancy distribution over states. The stationary distribution $\hat{\mathbf{q}}$ is calculated by finding the left eigenvector of the matrix $\mathbf{S}$ satisfying

$$\hat{\mathbf{q}}^\top \mathbf{S} = \hat{\mathbf{q}},$$

where $\mathbf{S}$ is a right stochastic matrix giving the probability that a PFA transitions from state $i$ to state $j$ marginalizing over symbols emitted:

$$S_{ij} = \sum_{x \in \Sigma} p(x|q_i) p(q_j|q_i, x).$$

For the Strictly Local and Strictly Piecewise automata, $N = 0$ by construction. For an automaton parameterized by $\mathbf{T} = \text{softmax}(\tilde{\mathbf{T}})$, it is not possible to attain $N = 0$, but nonetheless $N$ can be made arbitrarily small. There are alternative parameterizations where $N = 0$ is achievable, for example using the sparsemax function instead of softmax (Martins and Astudillo, 2016; Peters et al., 2019).

In order to constrain automata to be deterministic, we set the regularization term in Eq. 3 to be

$$C = \alpha N,$$

where $\alpha$ is a non-negative scalar determining the strength of the trade-off of cross entropy and nondeterminism in the optimization. With $\alpha = 0$ there is no constraint on the nondeterminism of the automaton, and minimizing the objective in Eq. 3 reduces to maximum likelihood estimation.

## 2.5 Implementing restricted automata

We define Strictly Local and Strictly Piecewise automata as automata that generate the respective languages. We implement Strictly Local and Strictly Piecewise automata by hard-coding the transition matrices $\mathbf{T}$. For these automata, we only do optimization over the emission matrices $\mathbf{E}$.

**Strictly Local** In a Strictly $k$-Local ($k$-SL) language, each symbol is conditioned only on *immediately preceding* $k-1$ symbol(s) (Heinz, 2018; Rogers and Pullum, 2011). We implement a 2-SL automaton by associating each state $q \in Q$ with a unique element $x$ in the symbol inventory $\Sigma$. Upon emitting symbol $x$, the automaton deterministically transitions into the corresponding state, denoted $q_x$. Thus the transition matrices have the form

$$\mathbf{T}_x = \begin{array}{c} \scriptstyle \cdots q_{\neq x} \cdots \quad q_x \quad \cdots q_{\neq x} \cdots \\ \begin{bmatrix} \vdots & \vdots & \vdots \\ \ldots 0 \ldots & 1 & \ldots 0 \ldots \\ \vdots & \vdots & \vdots \end{bmatrix} \end{array}.$$

This construction can be straightforwardly extended to $k$-SL, yielding $|\Sigma|^{k-1} \times (|\Sigma|-1)$ trainable parameters for a $k$-SL automaton.

**Strictly Piecewise** A Strictly $k$-Piecewise $k$-SP) language, each symbol depends on the presence of any preceding $k-1$ symbols at arbitrary distance (Heinz, 2007, 2018; Shibata and Heinz, 2019). For example, in a 2-SP language, in a string *abc*, *c* would be conditional on the presence of *a* and the presence of *b*, without regard to distance nor the relative order of *a* and *b*.

The implementation of an SP automaton is slightly more complex than the SL automaton, as the number of states required in a naïve implementation is exponential in the symbol inventory size, resulting in intractably large matrices. We circumvent this complexity by parameterizing a 2-SP automaton as a product of simpler automata. We associate each symbol $x \in \Sigma$ with a sub-automaton $A_x$ which has two states $q_0^x$ and $q_1^x$, with state $q_0^x$ indicating that the symbol $x$ has not been seen, and $q_1^x$ indicating that it has been seen. Each sub-automaton $A_x$ has an emission matrix $\mathbf{E}^{(x)}$ of size $2 \times |\Sigma|$ corresponding to the two states $q_0^x$ and $q_1^x$; the emission matrix for all states $q_0^x$ is constrained to be the uniform distribution over symbols. The transition matrices $\mathbf{T}^{(x)}$ are

$$\mathbf{T}_x^{(x)} = \begin{bmatrix} 0 & 1 \\ 0 & 1 \end{bmatrix}, \mathbf{T}_{y \neq x}^{(x)} = \begin{bmatrix} 1 & 0 \\ 0 & 1 \end{bmatrix}.$$

Then the probability of the $t$'th symbol in a sequence $x_t$ given a context of previous symbols $x_{i=1}^{t-1}$ is the geometric mixture of the probability of $x_t$ under each sub-automaton, also called the co-emission probability

$$p(x_t|x_{i=1}^{t-1}) \propto \prod_{y=1}^{|\Sigma|} p_{A_y}(x_t|x_{i=1}^{t-1}).$$

Because each sub-automaton $A_y$ is deterministic, its state after seeing the context $x_{i=1}^{t-1}$ is known, and the conditional probability $p_{A_y}(x_t|x_{i=1}^{t-1})$ can be computed using Eq. 1. For calculating the probability of a sequence, we assume an initial state of having seen the boundary symbol $\#$; that is, the sub-automaton $A_\#$ starts in state $q_1^\#$.

Using this parameterization, we can do optimization over the collection of emission matrices $\{\mathbf{E}^{(x)}\}_{x \in \Sigma}$. This construction yields $|\Sigma| \times (|\Sigma|-1)$ trainable parameters for the 2-SP automaton, the same number of parameters as the 2-SL automaton.

**SP + SL** It is also possible to create and train an automaton with the ability to condition on both 2-SL and 2-SP factors by taking the product of 2-SL and 2-SP automata, as proposed by Heinz and Rogers (2013). We refer to the language generated by such an automaton as 2-SL + 2-SP. We experiment with such product machines below.

## 2.6 Related work

PFA induction from data is a well-studied task which has been the subject of multiple competitions over the years (see Verwer et al., 2012, for a review). The most common approaches are variants of Baum-Welch and heuristic state-merging algorithms (see for example de la Higuera, 2010). Gibbs samplers and spectral methods have also been proposed (Gao and Johnson, 2008; Bailly, 2011; Shibata and Yoshinaka, 2012). Induction of restricted PDFAs, especially for SL and SP languages, is explored in Heinz and Rogers (2013, 2010)

Our work differs from previous approaches in its simplicity. Inspired by Shibata and Heinz (2019), we optimize the training objective directly via gradient descent, without approximations or heuristics other than the use of minibatches. The same algorithm is applied to learn both transition and emission structure, for learning of both general PFAs and restricted PDFAs. One of our contributions is to show that this very simple approach gives reasonable results for learning phonotactics.

## 3 Inducing toy languages

First, we test the ability of the model to recover automata for simple examples of subregular languages. We do so for the two subregular classes 2-SL and 2-SP described in Section 2.5. For each of these language classes, we implement a reference PFA which generates strings from a simple example language in that class, then generate $10,000$ sample sequences from the reference PFA. We then use these samples as training data, and study whether our learners can recover the relevant constraints from the data.

### 3.1 Evaluation

We evaluate the ability to induce appropriate automata in two ways. First, since we are studying very simple languages and automata, it is possible to directly inspect the $\mathbf{E}$ and $\mathbf{T}$ matrices and check that they implement the correct automaton by observing the transition and emission probabilities.

Second, we study the probabilities assigned to carefully selected strings which exemplify the constraints that define the languages. For each language, we define an **illegal test string** which violates the constraints of the language, and a minimally-different **legal test string**. Given an automaton, we can measure the **legal–illegal difference**: the log probability of the legal test string minus the log probability of the illegal test string. A larger legal–illegal difference indicates that the model is assigning a higher probability to the legal form compared to the illegal one and therefore is successfully learning the constraints represented by the testing data.

### 3.2 Languages

All languages are defined over the symbol inventory $\{a, b, c\}$ plus the boundary symbol #.

As an exemplar of 2-SL languages, we use the language characterized by the forbidden factor **ab*. A deterministic PFA for the language is given in Figure 1 (top). The language contains all strings that do not have an *a* followed immediately by a *b*. Our legal test string for this language is *bacccb#* and the illegal test string is *babccc#*.

As an exemplar of 2-SP languages, we use the language characterized by a forbidden factor $*a \ldots b$. This language contains all strings that do not have an *a* followed by a *b* at any distance. The reference automaton is given in Figure 1 (bottom). The legal test string is *baccca#* and the illegal test string is *bacccb#*.

### 3.3 Training parameters

The logit matrices $\tilde{\mathbf{E}}$ and $\tilde{\mathbf{T}}$ are initialized with random draws from a standard Normal distribution (Derrida, 1981). We perform stochastic gradient descent using the Adam algorithm, which adaptively sets the learning rate (Kingma and Ba, 2015). We perform $10,000$ update steps with starting learning rate $\eta = 0.001$ and minibatch size 5.

### 3.4 Results

Unrestricted PFA induction succeeds in recovering the reference automata for both toy languages. Learners restricted to the appropriate classes, as well as the automaton combining SL and SP factors, also succeed in inducing the appropriate automata, while learners restricted to the 'wrong' class fail.

Figure 1 shows the legal–illegal differences for test strings over the course of training. We can see that, when the learner is unrestricted or when the learner is in the appropriate class, it eventually picks up on the relevant constraint, with the legal–illegal difference increasing apparently without bound over training. Unrestricted learners take longer to reach this point, but they reach it reliably. On the other hand, looking at the legal–illegal differences for learners in the wrong class, we see that they asymptote to a small number and stop improving.

These results demonstrate that our simple method for PFA induction does succeed in inducing certain simple structures relevant for modeling phonotactics in a small, controlled setting. Next, we turn to induction of phonotactics from corpus data.

## 4 Corpus experiments

We evaluate our learner by training it on dictionary forms from Quechua and Navajo and then studying its ability to predict attested forms that were held out in training in addition to artificially constructed nonce forms which probe the ability of the model to represent nonlocal constraints.

### 4.1 Training parameters

All training parameters are as in Section 3.3, except that we train for $100,000$ steps, and control the

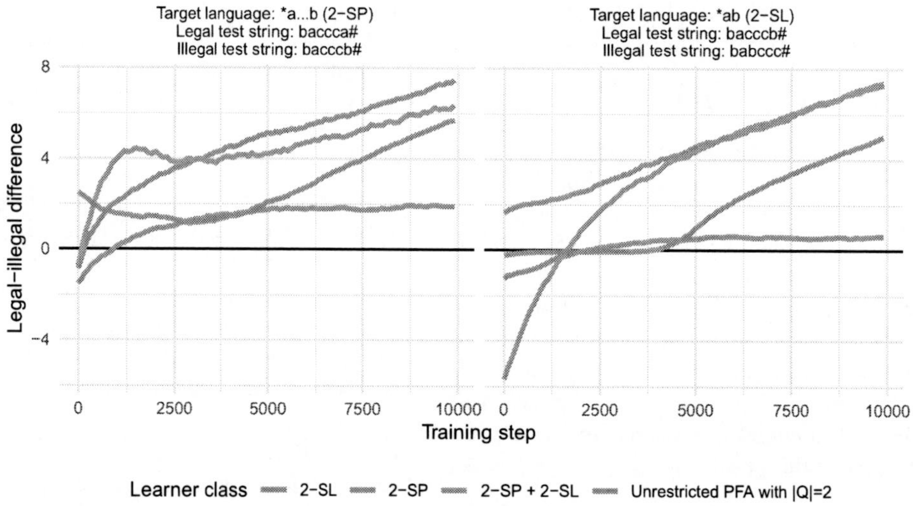


Figure 1: Difference in log probabilities for legal and illegal forms over the course of PFA induction for toy languages. A large positive value indicates that the relevant constraint has been learned.

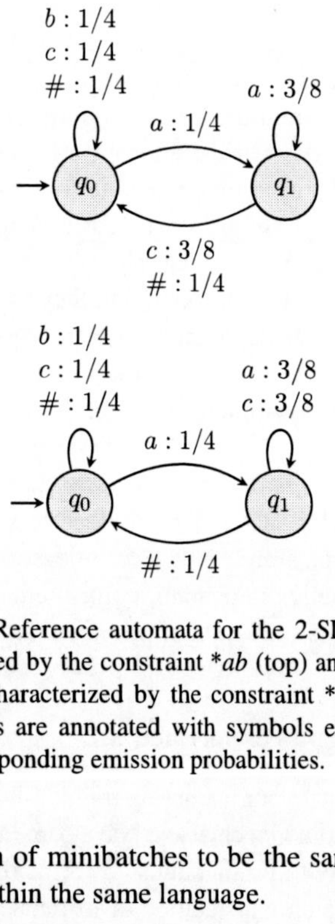

Figure 2: Reference automata for the 2-SL language characterized by the constraint **ab* (top) and the 2-SP language characterized by the constraint **a*. . . *b* (bottom). Arcs are annotated with symbols emitted and their corresponding emission probabilities.

succession of minibatches to be the same across models within the same language.

### 4.2 Dataset

The proposed learner is applied to the datasets of Navajo and Quechua (Gouskova and Gallagher, 2020), in which nonlocal phonotactics are attested.

In Navajo, the co-occurrence of alveolar and palatal strident is illegal. The learning data of Navajo includes $6,279$ Navajo phonological words; we divide this data into a training set of $5,023$ forms and a held-out set of $1,256$ forms. The nonce testing data of Navajo consists of $5,000$ generated nonce words, which were labelled as illegal ($N = 3,271$) and legal ($N = 1,729$) based on whether the nonlocal phonotactics are satisfied.

In Quechua, any stop cannot be followed by an ejective or aspirated stop at any distance. The learning data of Quechua includes $10,804$ phonological words, which we separate into $8,643$ training forms and $2,160$ held-out forms. The testing data of Quechua (Gouskova and Gallagher, 2020) consists of $24,352$ nonce forms which were manually classified as legal ($N = 18,502$) and illegal ($N = 5,810$, including stop-aspirate and stop-ejective pairs).

### 4.3 Dependent Variables

For the linguistic performance of the classifier, we study two main dependent variables. First, the average held-out negative log likelihood (NLL) indicates the ability of the model to assign high probabilities to unseen but attested forms—low NLL indicates higher probabilities. Second, using our nonce forms dataset, we measure the extent to which the model can differentiate the legal forms from the illegal forms using the *difference* in log likelihood for the legal forms minus the illegal forms. This is the same as the legal–illegal

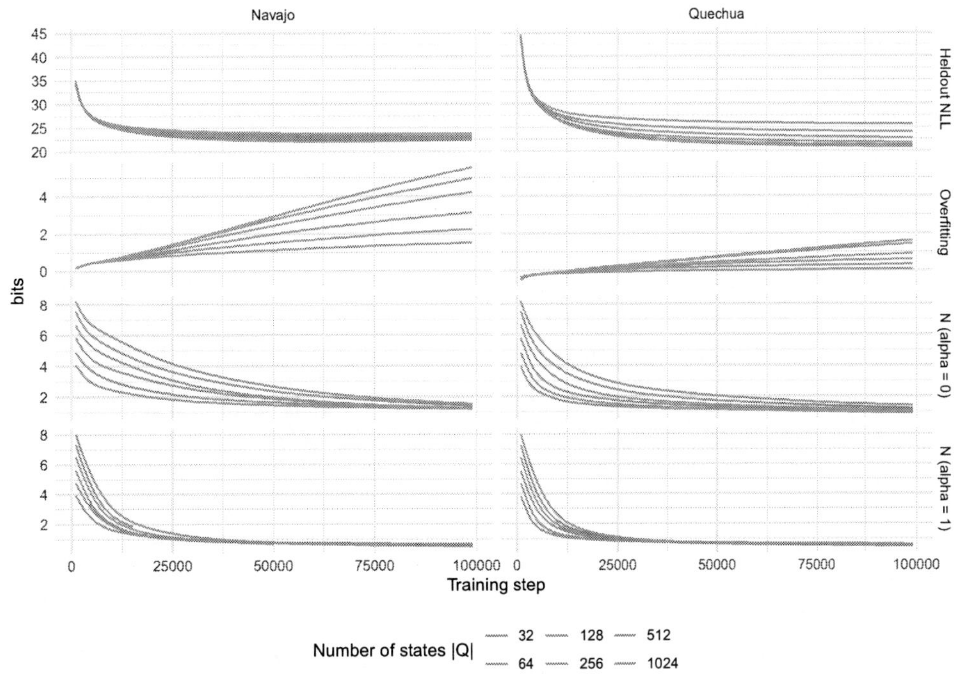


Figure 3: Accuracy and complexity metrics for unrestricted PFA induction. 'Overfitting' is the difference between held-out NLL and training set NLL. $N$ is nondeterminism and alpha is the regularization parameter $\alpha$ (see Section 2.4). Runs with $|Q| = 128, 256, 512$ and $\alpha = 1$ on Navajo data terminated early due to numerical underflow in the calculation of the stationary distribution.

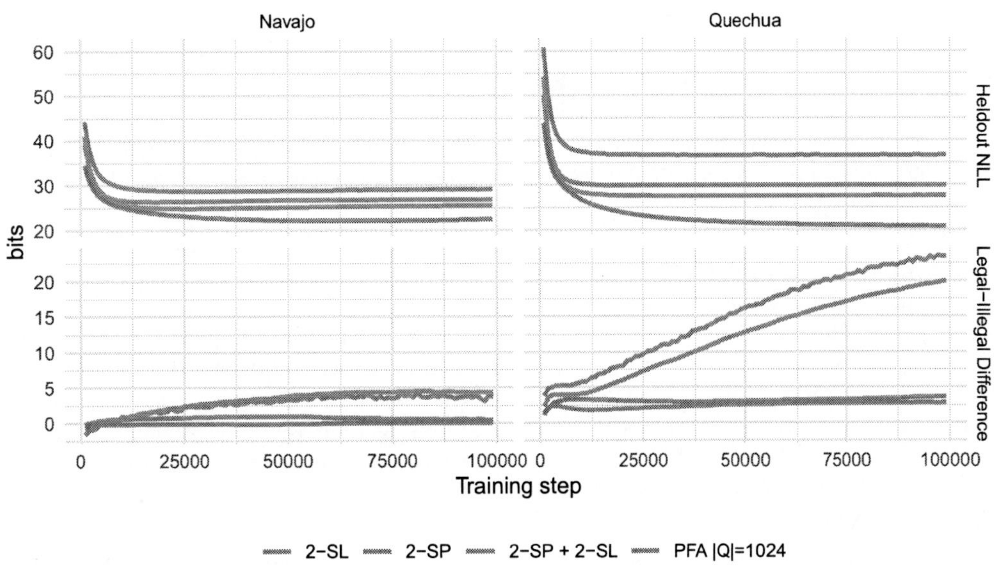


Figure 4: Performance of a 2-SP automaton, a 2-SL automaton, a 2-SP + 2-SL product automaton, and an unrestricted PFA with $1,024$ states and $\alpha = 0$. 'Heldout NLL' is the average NLL of a form in the set of attested forms never seen during training. 'Legal–illegal difference' is the difference in log likelihood between 'legal' and 'illegal' forms in the nonce test set.

difference described in Section 3.1, but now as an average over many legal–illegal nonce pairs instead of a difference for one pair.

### 4.4 Results

**Unrestricted PFA induction** Figure 3 shows results from induction of unrestricted PFAs with various numbers of states. We find that show the average NLL of forms in the heldout data, as well as 'overfitting', defined as the average held-out NLL minus the average training set NLL. This number shows the extent to which the model assigns higher probabilities to forms in the training set as opposed to the held-out set, an index of overfitting. We find that automata with more states fit the data better, but are also more prone to overfitting to the training set.

In Figure 3 (bottom two rows) we also show the measured nondeterminism $N$ of the induced automata throughout training, for different values of the regularization parameter $\alpha$ (see Section 2.4). We find that, even without an explicit constraint for determinism, the induced PFAs tend towards determinism over time, with $N$ reaching around $1.5$ bits by the final training step. Explicit regularization (with $\alpha = 1$) makes this process faster, with $N$ reaching around $0.5$ bits. Regularization for determinism has only a minimal effect on the NLL values.

**Linguistic performance and restricted models** Figure 4 shows held-out NLL and the legal–illegal difference for both languages, comparing the SL automaton, the SP automaton, the product SP + SL automaton, and a PFA with $1,024$ states and $\alpha = 0$.

In terms of the ability to predict attested held-out forms, the best model is consistently the unrestricted PFA, with the SP automaton performing the worst. However, in terms of predicting the ill-formedness of artificial forms violating nonlocal phonotactic constraints, the best model is either the SP automaton or the SP + SL product automaton. Both of these automata successfully induce the nonlocal constraint.

On the other hand, the unrestricted PFA learner shows no evidence at all of having learned the difference between legal and illegal forms in the artificial data, despite having the capacity to do so in theory, and despite succeeding in inducing a 2-SP language in Section 3.

### 4.5 Discussion

We find that an unrestricted PFA learner performs most accurately when predicting real held-out forms, while an SP learner is most effective in learning certain nonlocal constraints. In fact, in terms of its ability to model the nonlocal constraints, the PFA learner ends up comparable to an SL learner, which cannot learn the constraints at all. Meanwhile, the SP learner, which is unable to model *local* constraints, fares much worse than even the SL learner on predicting held-out forms. The product SP + SL learner combines the strengths of both restricted learners, but still does not assign as high probability to the real held-out forms as the unrestricted PFA learner.

This pattern of performance suggests that the PFA learner is using most of its states to model local constraints beyond those captured in a 2-SL language. These constraints are important for predicting real held-out forms. The SP automaton is unable to achieve strong performance on held-out forms without the ability to model these local constraints. On the other hand, the unrestricted PFA tends to overfit to its training data, perhaps explaining its failure to detect nonlocal constraints which are picked up by the appropriate restricted automata.

## 5 Conclusion

We introduced a framework for phonotactic learning based on simple induction of probabilistic finite-state automata by stochastic gradient descent. We showed how this framework can be used to learn unrestricted PFAs, in addition to PFAs restricted to certain formal language classes such as Strictly Local and Strictly Piecewise, via constraints on the transition matrices that define the automata. Furthermore, we showed that the framework is successful in learning some phonotactic phenomena, with unrestricted automata performing best in a wide-coverage evaluation on attested but held-out forms, and Strictly Piecewise automata performing best in a targeted evaluation using nonce forms focusing on nonlocal constraints.

Our results leave open the question of whether the unrestricted learner or one of the restricted learners is 'best' for learning phonotactics, since they perform differently on different metrics. A key question for future work is whether there might be some model that could do well in inducing *both* local and nonlocal constraints simultaneously, and performing well on both the held-out evaluation and the nonce form evaluation. Such a model could come in the form of another restricted language class such as Tier-Based Strictly Local languages (Heinz et al., 2011; Jardine and Heinz, 2016; McMullin, 2016; Jardine and McMullin, 2017), or perhaps in the form of a regularization term in the training objective which enforces an inductive bias that favors certain nonlocal interactions.

The code for this project is available at `http://github.com/hutengdai/PFA-learner`.

## Acknowledgments

This work was supported by a GPU Grant from the NVIDIA corporation. We thank the three anonymous reviewers and Adam Jardine, Jeff Heinz, and Dakotah Lambert for their comments.

## References

Raphael Bailly. 2011. Quadratic weighted automata: Spectral algorithm and likelihood maximization. In *Asian Conference on Machine Learning*, pages 147–163. PMLR.

Leonard E. Baum, Ted Petrie, George Soules, and Normal Weiss. 1970. A maximization technique occurring in the statistical analysis of probabilistic functions of Markov chains. *Annals of Mathematical Statistics*, 41:164–171.

Léon Bottou. 1991. Stochastic gradient learning in neural networks. *Proceedings of Neuro-Nımes*, 91(8):12.

Noam Chomsky and Morris Halle. 1968. *The Sound Pattern of English*. Harper & Row.

Huteng Dai. 2021. Learning nonlocal phonotactics in Strictly Piecewise phonotactic model. In *Proceedings of the 2020 Annual Meeting on Phonology*.

Colin de la Higuera. 2010. *Grammatical Inference: Learning Automata and Grammars*. Cambridge University Press.

Bernard Derrida. 1981. Random-energy model: An exactly solvable model of disordered systems. *Physical Review B*, 24(5):2613.

Richard Futrell, Adam Albright, Peter Graff, and Timothy J. O'Donnell. 2017. A generative model of phonotactics. *Transactions of the Association for Computational Linguistics*, 5:73–86.

Jianfeng Gao and Mark Johnson. 2008. A comparison of Bayesian estimators for unsupervised Hidden Markov Model POS taggers. In *Proceedings of the 2008 Conference on Empirical Methods in Natural Language Processing*, pages 344–352, Honolulu, Hawaii. Association for Computational Linguistics.

Maria Gouskova and Gillian Gallagher. 2020. Inducing nonlocal constraints from baseline phonotactics. *Natural Language & Linguistic Theory*, 38(1):77–116.

Bruce Hayes and Colin Wilson. 2008. A maximum entropy model of phonotactics and phonotactic learning. *Linguistic Inquiry*, 39(3):379–440.

Jeffrey Heinz. 2007. *The inductive learning of phonotactic patterns*. Ph.D. thesis, PhD dissertation, University of California, Los Angeles.

Jeffrey Heinz. 2010. Learning long-distance phonotactics. *Linguistic Inquiry*, 41(4):623–661.

Jeffrey Heinz. 2018. The computational nature of phonological generalizations. *Phonological Typology, Phonetics and Phonology*, pages 126–195.

Jeffrey Heinz, Chetan Rawal, and Herbert G. Tanner. 2011. Tier-based Strictly Local constraints for phonology. In *Proceedings of the 49th Annual Meeting of the Association for Computational Linguistics: Human Language Technologies*, pages 58–64, Portland, Oregon, USA. Association for Computational Linguistics.

Jeffrey Heinz and James Rogers. 2010. Estimating Strictly Piecewise distributions. In *Proceedings of the 48th Annual Meeting of the Association for Computational Linguistics*, pages 886–896, Uppsala, Sweden. Association for Computational Linguistics.

Jeffrey Heinz and James Rogers. 2013. Learning subregular classes of languages with factored deterministic automata. In *Proceedings of the 13th Meeting on the Mathematics of Language (MoL 13)*, pages 64–71, Sofia, Bulgaria. Association for Computational Linguistics.

Adam Jardine and Jeffrey Heinz. 2016. Learning Tier-based Strictly 2-Local languages. *Transactions of the Association for Computational Linguistics*, 4:87–98.

Adam Jardine and Kevin McMullin. 2017. Efficient learning of Tier-based Strictly $k$-Local languages. In *International Conference on Language and Automata Theory and Applications*, pages 64–76. Springer.

Diederik P. Kingma and Jimmy Ba. 2015. Adam: A method for stochastic optimization. In *3rd International Conference on Learning Representations, ICLR 2015, Conference Track Proceedings*, San Diego, CA.

Andre Martins and Ramon Astudillo. 2016. From softmax to sparsemax: A sparse model of attention and multi-label classification. In *International*

*Conference on Machine Learning*, pages 1614–1623. PMLR.

Kevin James McMullin. 2016. *Tier-based locality in long-distance phonotactics: learnability and typology*. Ph.D. thesis, University of British Columbia.

Ben Peters, Vlad Niculae, and André F. T. Martins. 2019. Sparse sequence-to-sequence models. In *Proceedings of the 57th Annual Meeting of the Association for Computational Linguistics*, pages 1504–1519, Florence, Italy. Association for Computational Linguistics.

James Rogers, Jeffrey Heinz, Margaret Fero, Jeremy Hurst, Dakotah Lambert, and Sean Wibel. 2013. Cognitive and sub-regular complexity. In *Formal Grammar*, pages 90–108. Springer.

James Rogers and Geoffrey K. Pullum. 2011. Aural pattern recognition experiments and the subregular hierarchy. *Journal of Logic, Language and Information*, 20(3):329–342.

Chihiro Shibata and Jeffrey Heinz. 2019. Maximum likelihood estimation of factored regular deterministic stochastic languages. In *Proceedings of the 16th Meeting on the Mathematics of Language*, pages 102–113, Toronto, Canada. Association for Computational Linguistics.

Chihiro Shibata and Ryo Yoshinaka. 2012. Marginalizing out transition probabilities for several subclasses of PFAs. *Journal of Machine Learning Research - Workshops and Conference Proceedings*, 21:259–263.

Sicco Verwer, Rémi Eyraud, and Colin de la Higuera. 2012. PAutomaC: A PFA/HMM learning competition. *Journal of Machine Learning Research - Workshops and Conference Proceedings*, 21.

Enrique Vidal, Franck Thollard, Colin de la Higuera, Francisco Casacuberta, and Rafael C. Carrasco. 2005a. Probabilistic finite-state machines – Part I. *IEEE Transactions on Pattern Analysis and Machine Intelligence*, 27(7):1013–1025.

Enrique Vidal, Franck Thollard, Colin de la Higuera, Francisco Casacuberta, and Rafael C. Carrasco. 2005b. Probabilistic finite-state machines – Part II. *IEEE Transactions on Pattern Analysis and Machine Intelligence*, 27(7):1026–1039.

# Recognizing Reduplicated Forms: Finite-State Buffered Machines

**Yang Wang**
Department of Linguistics
University of California, Los Angeles
Los Angeles, CA, USA
yangwangx@g.ucla.edu

## Abstract

Total reduplication is common in natural language phonology and morphology. However, formally as copying on reduplicants of unbounded size, unrestricted total reduplication requires computational power beyond context-free, while other phonological and morphological patterns are regular, or even sub-regular. Thus, existing language classes characterizing reduplicated strings inevitably include typologically unattested context-free patterns, such as reversals. This paper extends regular languages to incorporate reduplication by introducing a new computational device: finite state buffered machine (FSBMs). We give its mathematical definitions and discuss some closure properties of the corresponding set of languages. As a result, the class of regular languages and languages derived from them through a copying mechanism is characterized. Suggested by previous literature (Gazdar and Pullum, 1985), this class of languages should approach the characterization of natural language word sets.

## 1 The Puzzle of (Total) Reduplication

Formal language theory (FLT) provides computational mechanisms characterizing different classes of abstract languages based on their inherent structures. Following FLT in the study of human languages, in principle, researchers would expect a hierarchy of grammar formalisms that matches empirical findings: more complex languages in such a hierarchy are supposed to be 1) less common in natural language typology; and 2) harder for learners to learn.

The classical Chomsky Hierarchy (CH) puts formal languages into four levels with increasing complexity: regular, context-free, context-sensitive, recursively enumerable (Chomsky, 1956; Jäger and Rogers, 2012). Does the CH notion of formal complexity have the desired empirical correlates? Several findings suggest that those four levels do not align with natural languages precisely, some leading to major refinements on the CH. First, the unbounded crossing dependencies in Swiss-German case marking (Shieber, 1985) facilitated attempts to characterize mildly context-sensitive languages (MCS), which extend context-free languages (CFLs) but still preserve some useful properties of CFLs (e.g., Joshi, 1985; Seki et al., 1991; Stabler, 1997). Secondly, it is generally accepted that phonology is regular (e.g. Johnson, 1972; Kaplan and Kay, 1994). However, being regular is argued to be an unrestrictive property for phonological well-formed strings: for example, a language whose words are sensitive to an even or odd number of certain sounds is unattested (Heinz, 2018). With strong typological evidence, the sub-regular hierarchy was further developed, which continues to be an active area of research (e.g., McNaughton and Papert, 1971; Simon, 1975; Heinz, 2007; Heinz et al., 2011; Chandlee, 2014; Graf, 2017).

In this paper, we analyze another mismatch between existing well-known language classes and empirical findings: reduplication, which involves copying operations on certain base forms (Inkelas and Zoll, 2005). The reduplicated phonological strings are either of total identity (*total reduplication*) or of partial identity (*partial reduplication*) to the base forms. Table 1 provides examples showing the difference between total reduplication and partial reduplication: in Dyirbal, the pluralization of nominals is realized by fully copying the singular stems, while in Agta examples, plural forms only copy the first CVC sequence of the corresponding singular forms (Healey, 1960; Marantz, 1982).

Reduplication is common cross-linguistically. According to Rubino (2013) and Dolatian and Heinz (2020), 313 out of 368 natural languages exhibit productive reduplication, in which 35 languages only have total reduplication, but not partial



*Proceedings of the Seventeenth SIGMORPHON Workshop on Computational Research in Phonetics, Phonology, and Morphology*, pages 177–187

| Total reduplication: Dyirbal plurals (Dixon, 1972, 242) | | | |
|---|---|---|---|
| *Singular* | *Gloss* | *Plural* | *Gloss* |
| midi | 'little, small' | midi-midi | 'lots of little ones' |
| gulgiṛi | 'prettily painted men' | gulgiṛi-gulgiṛi | 'lots of prettily painted men' |

| Partial reduplication: Agta plurals (Healey, 1960,7) | | | |
|---|---|---|---|
| *Singular* | *Gloss* | *Plural* | *Gloss* |
| labáng | 'patch' | lab-labáng | 'patches' |
| takki | 'leg' | tak-takki | 'legs' |

Table 1: Total reduplication: Dyirbal plurals (top); partial reduplication: Agta plurals (bottom).

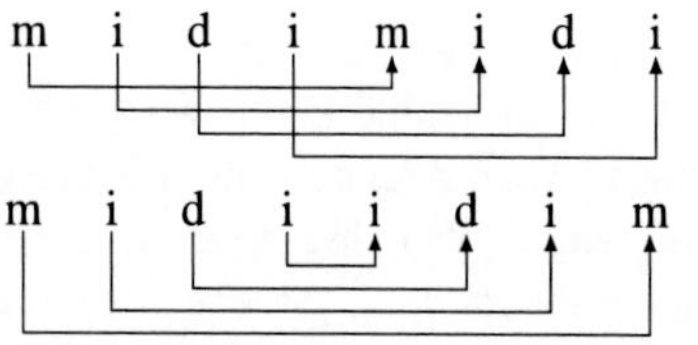


Figure 1: Crossing dependencies in Dyirbal total reduplication *'midi-midi'* (top) versus nesting dependencies in unattested string reversal *'midi-idim'* (bottom)

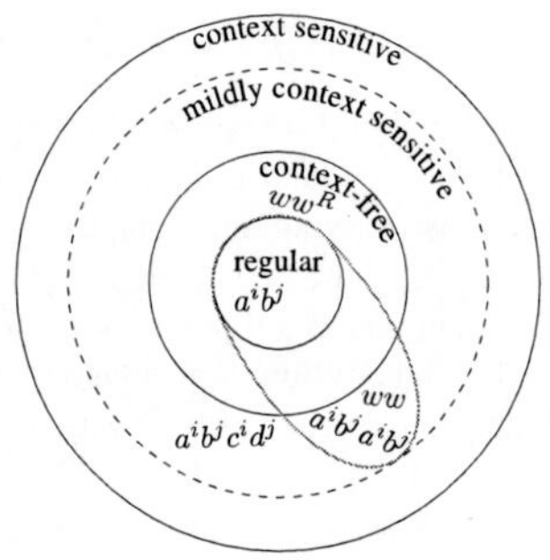


Figure 2: The class of regular with copying languages in CH

reduplication. As a comparison, it is widely recognized that context-free string reversals are rare in phonology and morphology (Marantz, 1982) and appear to be confined to language games (Bagemihl, 1989).

Unrestricted total reduplication, or unbounded copying, can be abstracted as $L_{ww} = \{ww \mid w \in \Sigma^*\}$, a well-known non-context free language (Culy, 1985; Hopcroft and Ullman, 1979).[1] Its non-context-freeness comes from the incurred crossing dependencies among symbols, similar to Swiss-German case marking constructions. However, the typologically-rare string reversals $ww^R$ demonstrate nesting dependencies, which are context-free (see Fig. 1 as an illustration).

Given most phonological and morphological patterns are regular, how can one fit in reduplicated strings without including reversals? Gazdar and Pullum (1985, 278) made the remark that

> We do not know whether there exists an independent characterization of the class of languages that includes the regular sets and languages derivable from them through reduplication, or what the time complexity of that class might be, but it currently looks as if this class might be relevant to the characterization of NL word-sets.

Motivated by Gazdar and Pullum (1985), this article aims to give a formal characterization of regular with copying languages. Specifically, it examines what minimal changes can be brought to regular languages to include stringsets with two adjacent copies, while excluding some typologically unattested context-free patterns, such as reversals, shown in Fig. 2. One possible way to probe such a language class is by adding copying to the set of operations whose closure defines regular languages. Instead, the approach we take in this paper is to add reduplication to finite state automata (FSAs), which compute regular languages.

[1] Total reduplication does not immediately guarantee *unboundedness*. When the set of bases is finite, i.e, $\{ww \mid w \in L\}$ when $L$ is finite, total reduplication *can* be squeezed in languages described by 1 way finite state machines (Chandlee, 2017), though doing so eventually leads to state explosion (Roark and Sproat, 2007; Dolatian and Heinz, 2020). Computationally, only total reduplication with infinite number of potential reduplicants is true *unbounded copying*. With careful treatment, unbounded copying, externalizing a primitive copying operation, can be justified as a model of reduplication in natural languages. More in-depth discussion of 1): *bounded* versus *unbounded* and 2): copying as a primitive operation can be found in Clark and Yoshinaka (2014); Chandlee (2017); Dolatian and Heinz (2020).

Various attempts followed this vein:[2] one example is finite state registered machine in Cohen-Sygal and Wintner (2006) (FSRAs) with finitely many registers as its memory, limited in the way that it only models *bounded copying*. The state-of-art finite state machinery that computes *unbounded copying* elegantly and adequately is 2-way finite state transducers (2-way FSTs), capturing reduplication as a string-to-string mapping ($w \to ww$) (Dolatian and Heinz, 2018a,b, 2019, 2020). To avoid the mirror image function ($w \to ww^R$), Dolatian and Heinz (2020) further developed subclasses of 2-way FSTs which cannot output anything during right-to-left passes over the input (cf. rotating transducers: Baschenis et al., 2017).

It should be noted that the issue addressed by 2-way FSTs is a different one: reduplication is modeled as a function ($w \to ww$), while this paper focuses on a set of languages containing identical substrings ($ww$). The stringset question is non-trivial and well-motivated for reasons of both formal aspects and its theoretical relevance. Firstly, since the studied 2-way FSTs are not readily invertible, how to get the inverse relation $ww \to w$ remains an open question, as acknowledged in Dolatian and Heinz (2020). Although this paper does not directly address this morphological analysis problem, recognizing which strings are reduplicated and belong to $L_{ww}$ or any other copying languages may be an important first step.[3]

As for the theoretical aspects, there are some attested forms of meaning-free reduplication in natural languages.Zuraw (2002) proposes *aggressive reduplication* in phonology: speakers are sensitive to phonological similarity between substrings within words and reduplication-like structures are attributed to those words. It is still arguable whether those meaning-free reduplicative patterns of unbounded strings are generated via a morphological function or not. Overall, it is desirable to have models that help to detect the substring identity within surface strings when those sub-strings are in the regular set.

This paper introduces a new computational device: finite state buffered machine (FSBMs). They are two-taped finite state automata, sensitive to copying activities within strings, hence able to detect identity between sub-strings. This paper is organized as follows: Section 2 provides a definition of FSBMs with examples. Then, to better understand the copying mechanism, complete-path FSBMs, which recognize exactly the same set of languages as general FSBMs, are highlighted. Section 3 examines the computational and mathematical properties of the set of languages recognized complete-path FSBMs. Section 4 concludes with discussion and directions for future research.

## 2 Finite State Buffered Machine

### 2.1 Definitions

FSBMs are two-taped automata with finite-state core control. One tape stores the input, as in normal FSAs; the other serves as an unbounded memory buffer, storing reduplicants temporarily for future identity checking. Intuitively, FSBMs is an extension to FSRAs but equipped with unbounded memory. In theory, FSBMs with a *bounded* buffer would be as expressive as an FSRA and therefore can be converted to an FSA.

The buffer interacts with the input in restricted ways: 1) the buffer is queue-like; 2) the buffer needs to work on the same alphabet as the input, unlike the stack in a pushdown automata (PDA), for example; 3) once one symbol is removed from the buffer, everything else must also be wiped off before the buffer is available for other symbol addition. These restrictions together ensure the machine does not generate string reversals or other non-reduplicative non-regular patterns.

There are three possible modes for an FSBM $M$ when processing an input: 1) in normal (N) mode, $M$ reads symbols and transits between states, functioning as a normal FSA; 2) in buffering (B) mode, besides consuming symbols from the input and taking transitions among states, it adds a copy of just-read symbols to the queue-like buffer, until it exits buffering (B) mode; 3) after exiting buffering (B) mode, $M$ enters emptying (E) mode, in which $M$ matches the stored symbols in the buffer against input symbols. When all buffered symbols have been matched, $M$ switches back to normal (N) mode for another round of computation. Under the current augmentation, FSBMs can only capture local reduplication with two adjacent, completely identical copies. It cannot handle non-local reduplication, nor multiple reduplication.

[2] Some other examples, pursuing more linguistically sound and computationally efficient finite state techniques, are Walther (2000), Beesley and Karttunen (2000) and Hulden (2009). However, they fail to model unbounded copying. Roark and Sproat (2007), Cohen-Sygal and Wintner (2006) and Dolatian and Heinz (2020) provide more comprehensive reviews.

[3] Thanks to the reviewer for bringing this point up.

**Definition 1.** A **Finite-State Buffered Machine (FSBM)** is a 7-tuple $\langle \Sigma, Q, I, F, G, H, \delta \rangle$ where

- Q: a finite set of states
- I $\subseteq Q$: initial states
- F $\subseteq Q$: final states
- $G \subseteq Q$: states where the machine must enter buffering (B) mode
- $H \subseteq Q$: states visited while the machine is emptying the buffer
- $G \cap H = \emptyset$
- $\delta$: $Q \times (\Sigma \cup \{\epsilon\}) \times Q$: the state transitions according to a specific symbol

Specifying $G$ and $H$ states allows an FSBM to control what portions of a string are copied. To avoid complications, $G$ and $H$ are defined to be disjoint. In addition, states in $H$ identify certain special transitions. Transitions between two $H$ states check input-memory identity and consume symbols in both the input and the buffer. By contrast, transitions with at least one state not in $H$ can be viewed as normal FSA transitions. In all, there are effectively two types of transitions in $\delta$.

**Definition 2.** A configuration of an FSBM $D = (u, q, v, t) \in \Sigma^* \times Q \times \Sigma^* \times \{\text{N}, \text{B}, \text{E}\}$, where $u$ is the input string; $v$ is the string in the buffer; $q$ is the current state and $t$ is the current mode the machine is in.

**Definition 3.** Given an FSBM M and $x \in (\Sigma \cup \{\epsilon\})$, $u, w, v \in \Sigma^*$, we define that a configuration $D_1$ yields a configuration $D_2$ in $M$ ($D_1 \vdash_M D_2$) as the smallest relation such that: [4]

- For every transition $(q_1, x, q_2)$ with at least one state of $q_1, q_2 \notin H$
  $(xu, q_1, \epsilon, \text{N}) \vdash_M (u, q_2, \epsilon, \text{N})$ with $q_1 \notin G$
  $(xu, q_1, v, \text{B}) \vdash_M (u, q_2, vx, \text{B})$ with $q_2 \notin G$
- For every transition $(q_1, x, q_2)$ and $q_1, q_2 \in H$
  $(xu, q_1, xv, \text{E}) \vdash_M (u, q_2, v, \text{E})$
- For every $q \in G$
  $(u, q, \epsilon, \text{N}) \vdash_M (u, q, \epsilon, \text{B})$
- For every $q \in H$
  $(u, q, v, \text{B}) \vdash_M (u, q, v, \text{E})$
  $(u, q, \epsilon, \text{E}) \vdash_M (u, q, \epsilon, \text{N})$

[4]Note that a machine cannot do both symbol consumption and mode changing at the same time.

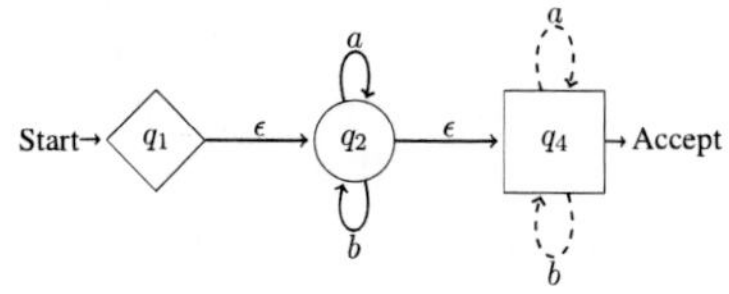


Figure 3: An FSBM $M_1$ with G = $\{q_1\}$ (diamond) and H = $\{q_3\}$ (square); dashed arcs are used only for the emptying process. L($M_1$) = $\{ww \mid w \in \{a, b\}^*\}$

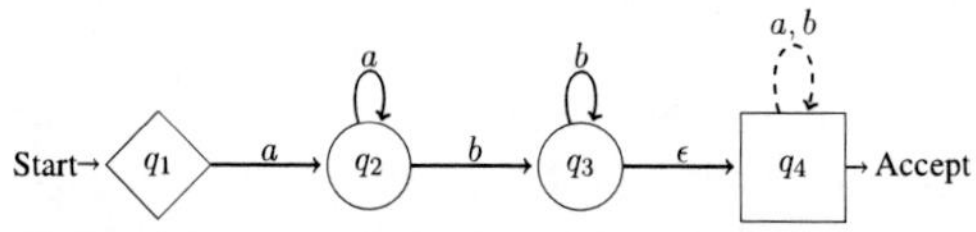


Figure 4: An FSBM $M_2$ with G = $\{q_1\}$ and H = $\{q_4\}$. L($M_2$) = $\{a^i b^j a^i b^j \mid i, j \geq 1\}$

**Definition 4.** A run of FSBM $M$ on $w$ is a sequence of configurations $D_0, D_1, D_2 \ldots D_m$ such that 1): $\exists\, q_0 \in I$, $D_0 = (w, q_0, \epsilon, \text{N})$; 2): $\exists\, q_f \in F$, $D_m = (\epsilon, q_f, \epsilon, \text{N})$; 3): $\forall 0 \leq i < m$, $D_i \vdash_M D_{i+1}$. The language recognized by an FSBM M is denoted by $L(M)$. $w \in L(M)$ iff there's a run of $M$ on $w$.

### 2.2 Examples

In all illustrations, $G$ states are drawn with diamonds and $H$ states are drawn with squares. The special transitions between $H$ states are dashed.

**Example 1. Total reduplication** Figure 3 offers an FSBM $M_1$ for $L_{ww}$, with any arbitrary strings made out of an alphabet $\Sigma = \{a, b\}$ as candidates of bases.

$L_{ww}$ is the simplest representation of unbounded copying, but this language is somewhat structurally dull. For the rest of the illustration, we focus on the FSBM $M_2$ in Figure 4. $M_2$ recognizes the non-context free $\{a^i b^j a^i b^j \mid i, j \geq 1\}$. This language can be viewed as total reduplication added to the regular language $\{a^i b^j \mid i, j \geq 1\}$ (recognized by the FSA $M_0$ in Figure 5).

State $q_1$ is an initial state and more importantly a $G$ state, forcing $M_2$ to enter B mode before it takes any arcs and transits to other states. Then, $M_2$ in B mode always keeps a copy of consumed input

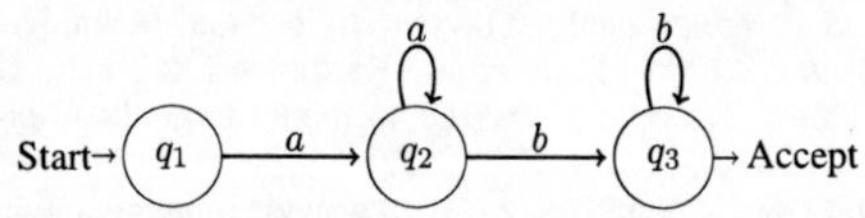


Figure 5: An FSA $M_0$ with $L(M_0)$= $\{a^i b^j \mid i, j \geq 1\}$

symbols until it proceeds to $q_4$, an $H$ state. State $q_4$ requires $M_2$ to stop buffering and switch to E mode in order to check for string identity. Using the special transitions between $H$ states (in this case, $a$ and $b$ loops on State $q_4$), $M_2$ checks whether the stored symbols in the buffer matches the remaining input. If so, after emitting out all symbols in the buffer, $M_2$ with a blank buffer can switch to N mode. It eventually ends at State $q_4$, a legal final state. Figure 6 gives a complete run of $M_2$ on the string "*abbabb*". Figure 7 shows $M_2$ rejects the non-total reduplicated string "*ababb*" since a final configuration cannot be reached.

**Example 3. Partial reduplication** Assume $\Sigma = \{b, t, k, ng, l, i, a\}$, the FSBM $M_3$ in Figure 8 serves as a model of two Agta CVC reduplicated plurals in Table 1.

Given the initial state $q_1$ is in $G$, $M_3$ has to enter B mode before it takes any transitions. In B mode, $M_3$ transits to a plain state $q_2$, consuming an input consonant and keeping it in the buffer. Similarly, $M_3$ transits to a plain state $q_3$ and then to $q_4$. When $M_3$ first reaches $q_4$, the buffer would contain a CVC sequence. $q_4$, an $H$ state, urges $M_3$ to stop buffering and enter E mode. Using the special transitions between $H$ states (in this case, loops on $q_4$), $M_3$ matches the CVC in the buffer with the remaining input. Then, $M_3$ with a blank buffer can switch to N mode at $q_4$. $M_3$ in N mode loses the access to loops on $q_4$, as they are available only in E mode. It transits to $q_5$ to process the rest of the input by the normal transitions between $q_5$. A successful run should end at $q_5$, the only final state. Figure 9 gives a complete run of $M_3$ on the string "*taktakki*".

### 2.3 Complete-path FSBMs

As shown in the definitions and the examples above, an FSBM is supposed to end in N mode to process an input. There are two possible scenarios for a run to meet this requirement: either never entering B mode or undergoing full cycles of N, B, E, N mode changes. The corresponding languages reflect either no copying (functioning as plain FSAs) or full copying, respectively.

In any specific run, it is the states that inform an FSBM $M$ of its modality. The first time $M$ reaches a $G$ state, it has to enter B mode and keeps buffering when it transits between plain states. The first time when it reaches an $H$ state, $M$ is supposed to enter E mode and transit only between $H$ states in E mode. Hence, to go through full cycles of mode changes, once $M$ reaches a $G$ state and switches to B mode, it has to encounter some $H$ states later to be put in E mode. To allow us to only reason about only the "useful" arrangements of $G$ and $H$ states, we impose an ordering requirement on $G$ and $H$ states along a path in a machine and define a complete path.

**Definition 5.** A path $s$ from an initial state to a final state in a machine is said to be complete if

1. for one $H$ state in $s$, there is always a preceding $G$ state;
2. once one $G$ state is in $s$, $s$ must contain must contain at least one $H$ following that $G$ state
3. in between $G$ and the first $H$ are only plain states.

Schematically, with $P$ representing those non-$G$, non-$H$ plain states and $I, F$ representing initial, final states respectively, the regular expression denoting the state information in a path $s$ should be of the form: $I(P^*GP^*HH^*P^* \mid P^*)^*F$.

**Definition 6.** A **complete-path** finite state buffered machine is an FSBM in which all possible paths are complete.

Example FSBMs we provide so far (Figure 3, Figure 4 and in Figure 8) are complete-path FSBMs. For the rest of this section, we describe several cases of an incomplete path in a machine $M$.

**No $H$ states** When a $G$ state does not have any reachable $H$ state following it, there is no complete run, since $M$ always stays in B mode.

**No $H$ states in between two $G$ states** When a $G$ state $q_0$ has to transit to another $G$ state $q_0'$ before any $H$ states, $M$ cannot go to $q_0'$, for $M$ would enter B mode at $q_0$ while transiting to another $G$ state in B mode is ill-defined.

***H* states first** When $M$ has to follow a path containing two consecutive $H$ states before any $G$ state, it would clash in the end, because the transitions among two $H$ states can only be used in E mode. However, it is impossible to enter E mode without entering B mode enforced by some $G$ states.

It should be emphasized that $M$ in N mode can pass through one (and only one) $H$ state to another plain state. For instance, the language of the FSBM

|  | *Used Arc* | *State Info* | *Configuration* |  |
|---|---|---|---|---|
| 1. | *N/A* | $q_1 \in I$ | (*abbabb*, $q_1$, $\epsilon$, N) |  |
| 2. | *N/A* | $q_1 \in G$ | (*abbabb*, $q_1$, $\epsilon$, B) | Buffering triggered by $q_1$ and empty buffer |
| 3. | ($q_1$, a, $q_2$) | $q_2 \notin G$ | (*bbabb*, $q_2$, *a*, B) |  |
| 4. | ($q_2$, b, $q_3$) |  | (*babb*, $q_3$, *ab*, B) |  |
| 5. | ($q_3$, b, $q_3$) |  | (*abb*, $q_3$, *abb*, B) |  |
| 6. | ($q_3$, $\epsilon$, $q_4$) |  | (*abb*, $q_4$, *abb*, B) | Emptying triggered by $q_4$ |
| 7. | *N/A* |  | (*abb*, $q_4$, *abb*, E) |  |
| 8. | ($q_4$, a, $q_4$) |  | (*bb*, $q_4$, *bb*, E) |  |
| 9. | ($q_4$, b, $q_4$) |  | (*b*, $q_4$, *b*, E) |  |
| 10. | ($q_4$, b, $q_4$) | $q_4 \in H$ | ($\epsilon$, $q_4$, $\epsilon$, E) | Normal triggered by $q_4$ and empty buffer |
| 11. | *N/A* | $q_4 \in F$ | ($\epsilon$, $q_4$, $\epsilon$, N) |  |

Figure 6: $M_2$ in Figure 4 accepts *abbabb*

|  | *Used Arc* | *State Info* | *Configuration* |  |
|---|---|---|---|---|
| 1. | *N/A* | $q_1 \in I$ | (*ababb*, $q_1$, $\epsilon$, N) |  |
| 2. | *N/A* | $q_1 \in G$ | (*ababb*, $q_1$, $\epsilon$, B) | Buffering triggered by $q_1$ and empty buffer |
| 3. | ($q_1$, a, $q_2$) | $q_2 \notin G$ | (*babb*, $q_2$, *a*, B) |  |
| 4. | ($q_2$, b, $q_3$) | $q_3 \in H$ | (*abb*, $q_3$, *ab*, B) |  |
| 6. | ($q_3$, $\epsilon$, $q_4$) |  | (*abb*, $q_4$, *ab*, B) | Emptying triggered by $q_4$ |
| 5. | *N/A* |  | (*abb*, $q_4$, *ab*, E) |  |
| 6. | ($q_4$, a, $q_4$) |  | (*bb*, $q_4$, *b*, E) |  |
| 7. | ($q_4$, b, $q_4$) | $q_4 \in H$ | (*b*, $q_4$, $\epsilon$, E) | Normal triggered by $q_4$ and empty buffer |
| 8. | *N/A* |  | (*b*, $q_4$, $\epsilon$, N) |  |
|  |  |  | Clash |  |

Figure 7: $M_2$ in Figure 4 rejects *ababb*

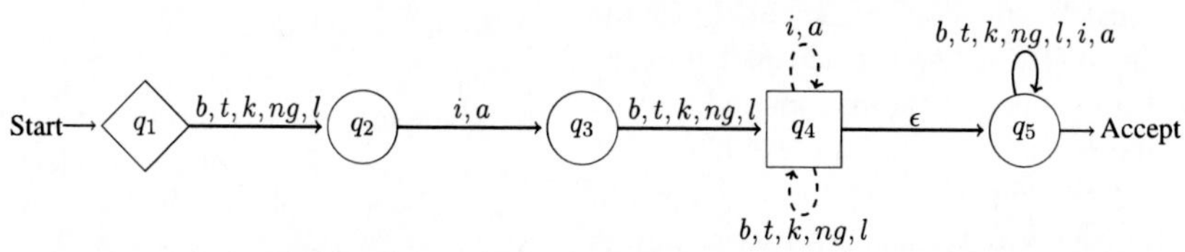


Figure 8: An FSBM $M_3$ for Agta CVC-reduplicated plurals: G = $\{q_1\}$ and H = $\{q_4\}$

|  | *Used Arc* | *State Info* | *Configuration* |  |
|---|---|---|---|---|
| 1. | *N/A* | $q_1 \in G$ | (*taktakki*, $q_1$, $\epsilon$, N) | Buffering triggered by $q_1$ and empty buffer |
| 2. | *N/A* |  | (*taktakki*, $q_1$, $\epsilon$, B) |  |
| 3. | ($q_1$, t, $q_2$) | $q_2 \notin G$ | (*aktakki*, $q_2$, *t*, B) |  |
| 4. | ($q_2$, a, $q_3$) |  | (*ktakki*, $q_3$, *ta*, B) |  |
| 5. | ($q_3$, k, $q_4$) | $q_4 \in H$ | (*takki*, $q_4$, *tak*, B) | Emptying triggered by $q_4$ |
| 6. | *N/A* |  | (*takki*, $q_4$, *tak*, E) |  |
| 7. | ($q_4$, t, $q_4$) |  | (*akki*, $q_4$, *ak*, E) |  |
| 8. | ($q_4$, a, $q_4$) |  | (*kki*, $q_4$, *k*, E) |  |
| 9. | ($q_4$, k, $q_4$) | $q_4 \in H$ | (*ki*, $q_4$, $\epsilon$, E) | Normal triggered by $q_4$ and empty buffer |
| 10. | *N/A* |  | (*ki*, $q_4$, $\epsilon$, N) |  |
| 11. | ($q_4$, $\epsilon$, $q_5$) |  | (*ki*, $q_5$, $\epsilon$, N) |  |
| 12. | ($q_5$, $k$, $q_5$) |  | ($i$, $q_5$, $\epsilon$, N) |  |
| 13. | ($q_5$, $i$, $q_5$) | $q_5 \in F$ | ($\epsilon$, $q_5$, $\epsilon$, N) |  |

Figure 9: $M_3$ in Figure 8 accepts *taktakki*

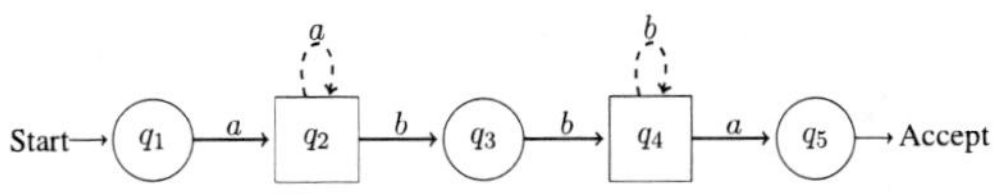


Figure 10: An incomplete FSBM $M_4$ with G = $\emptyset$ and H = $\{q_2, q_4\}$; $L(M_4) = \{abba\}$

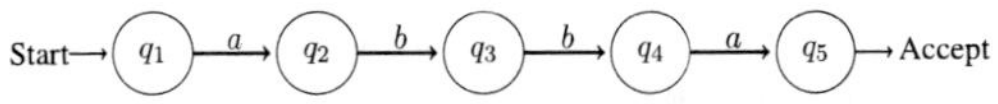


Figure 11: An FSA (or an FSBM with $G = \emptyset$ and $H = \emptyset$) whose language is equivalent as $M_4$ in Figure 10

$M_4$ in Figure 10 is equivalent to the language recognized by the FSA in Figure 11. $M_4$ remains to be an incomplete FSBM because it doesn't have any G state preceding the H states $q_2$ and $q_4$.

The languages recognized by complete-path FSBMs are precisely the languages recognized by general FSBMs. One key observation is the language recognized by the new machine is the union of the languages along all possible paths. Then, the validity of such a statement builds on different incomplete cases of $G$ and $H$ states along a path: they either recognize the empty-set language or show equivalence to finite state machines. Therefore, the language along an incomplete path of the machine is still in the regular set. Only a complete path containing at least one well-arranged $G \dots HH^*$ sequence uses the copying power and extends the regular languages. Therefore, in the next section, we focus on complete-path FSBMs.

## 3 Some closure properties of FSBMs

In this section, we show some closure properties of complete-path FSBM-recognizable languages and their linguistic relevance. Section 3.1 discusses its closure under intersection with regular languages; Section 3.2 shows it is closed under homomorphism; Section 3.3 briefly mentions union, concatenation, Kleene star. These operations are of special interests because they are regular operations defining regular expressions (Sipser, 2013, 64). That complete-path FSBMs are closed under regular operations leads to a conjecture that the set of languages recognized by the new automata is equivalent to the set of languages denoted by a version of regular expression with copying added.

Noticeably, given FSBMs are FSAs with a copying mechanism, the proof ideas in this section are similar to the corresponding proofs for FSAs, which can be found in Hopcroft and Ullman (1979) and Sipser (2013).

### 3.1 Intersection with FSAs

**Theorem 1.** *If $L_1$ is a complete-path FSBM-recognizable language and $L_2$ is a regular language, then $L_1 \cap L_2$ is a complete-path FSBM-recognizable language.*

In other words, if $L_1$ is a language recognized by a complete-path FSBM $M_1 = \langle Q_1, \Sigma, I_1, F_1, G_1, H_1, \delta_1 \rangle$, and $L_2$ is a language recognized by an FSA $M_2 = \langle Q_2, \Sigma, I_2, F_2, \delta_2 \rangle$, then $L_1 \cap L_2$ is a language recognizable by another complete-path FSBM. It is easy to construct an intersection machine $M$ where $M = \langle Q, \Sigma, I, F, G, H, \delta \rangle$ with 1) $Q = Q_1 \times Q_2$; 2) $I = I_1 \times I_2$; 3) $F = F_1 \times F_2$; 4) $G = G_1 \times Q_2$; 5) $H = H_1 \times Q_2$; 6) $((q_1, q_1'), x, (q_2, q_2')) \in \delta$ iff $(q_1, x, q_2) \in \delta_1$ and $(q_1', x, q_2') \in \delta_2$. Paths in $M$ would inherit the completeness from $M_1$ given the current construction. Then, $L(M) = L_1 \cap L_2$, as $M$ simulates $L_1 \cap L_2$ by running $M_1$ and $M_2$ simultaneously. $M$ accepts $w$ if and only if both $M_1$ and $M_2$ accept $w$.

In nature, FSAs can be viewed as FSBMs without copying: they can be converted to an FSBM with an empty $G$ set, an empty $H$ set and trivially no special transitions between $H$ states.

That FSBM-recognizable languages are closed under intersection with regular languages is of great relevance to phonological theory: assume a natural language $X$ imposes backness vowel harmony, which can be modeled by an FSA $M_{VH}$. In addition, this language also requires phonological strings of certain forms to be reduplicated, which can be modeled by an FSBM $M_{RED}$. One hereby can construct another FSBM $M_{RED+VH}$ to enforce both backness vowel harmony and the total identity of sub-strings in those forms. Not limited to harmony systems, phonotactics other than identity of sub-strings are regular (Heinz, 2018), indicating almost all phonological markedness constraints can be modeled by FSAs. When FSBMs intersect with FSAs computing those phonotactic restrictions, the resulting formalism is still an FSBM but not other grammar with higher computational power. Thus, FSBMs can model natural language phonotactics once including recognizing surface sub-string identity.

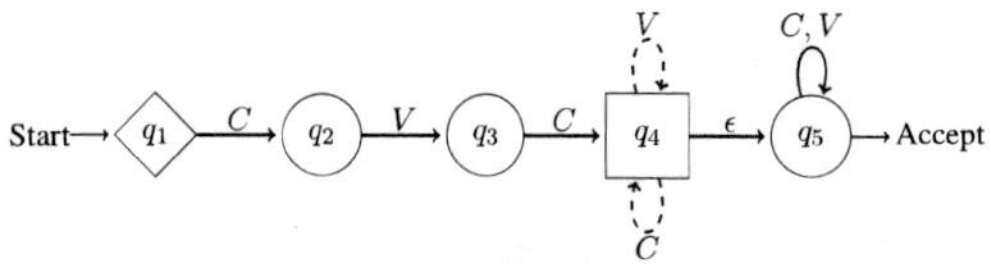

Figure 12: An FSBM $M_5$ on the alphabet $\{C, V\}$ such that $L(M_5) = h(L(M_3))$ with $M_3$ in Figure 8

### 3.2 Homomorphism and inverse alphabetic homomorphism

**Definition 7.** A (string) homomorphism is a function mapping one alphabet to strings of another alphabet, written $h : \Sigma \to \Delta^*$. We can extend $h$ to operate on strings over $\Sigma^*$ such that 1) $h(\epsilon_\Sigma) = \epsilon_\Delta$; 2) $\forall a \in \Sigma$, $h(a) \in \Delta^*$; 3) for $w = a_1 a_2 \dots a_n \in \Sigma^*$, $h(w) = h(a_1)h(a_2)\dots h(a_n)$ where each $a_i \in \Sigma$. An alphabetic homomorphism $h_0$ is a special homomorphism with $h_0$: $\Sigma \to \Delta$.

**Definition 8.** Given a homomorphism $h$: $\Sigma \to \Delta^*$ and $L_1 \subseteq \Sigma^*$, $L_2 \subseteq \Delta^*$, define $h(L_1) = \{h(w) \mid w \in L_1\} \subseteq \Delta^*$ and $h^{-1}(L_2) = \{w \mid h(w) = v \in L_2\} \subseteq \Sigma^*$.

**Theorem 2.** *The set of complete-path FSBM-recognizable languages is closed under homomorphisms.*

Theorem 2. can be proved by constructing a new machine $M_h$ based on $M$. The informal intuition goes as follows: relabel the odd arcs to mapped strings and add states to split the arcs so that there is only one symbol or $\epsilon$ on each arc in $M_h$. When there are multiple symbols on normal arcs, the newly added states can only be plain non-$G$, non-$H$ states. For multiple symbols on the special arcs between two $H$ states, the newly added states must be $H$ states. Again, under this construction, complete paths in $M$ lead to newly constructed complete paths in $M_h$.

The fact that complete-path FSBMs guarantee the closure under homomoprhism allows theorists to perform analyses at certain levels of abstraction of certain symbol representations. Consider two alphabets $\Sigma = \{b, t, k, ng, l, i, a\}$ and $\Delta = \{C, V\}$ with a homomorphism $h$ mapping every consonant $(b, t, k, ng, l)$ to $C$ and mapping every vowel $(i, a)$ to $V$. As illustrated by $M_3$ on alphabet $\Sigma$ (Figure 8) and $M_5$ on alphabet $\Delta$ (Figure 12), FSBM-definable patterns on $\Sigma$ would be another FSBM-definable patterns on $\Delta$.

We conjecture that the set of languages recognized by complete-path FSBMs is not closed under inverse alphabetic homomorphisms and thus inverse homomorphism. Consider a complete-path FSBM-recognizable language $L = \{a^i b^j a^i b^j \mid i, j \geq 1\}$ (cf. Figure 4). Consider an alphabetic homomorphism $h : \{0, 1, 2\} \to \{a, b\}^*$ such that $h(0) = a$, $h(1) = a$ and $h(2) = b$. Then, $h^{-1}(L) = \{(0|1)^i 2^j (0|1)^i 2^j \mid i, j \geq 1\}$ seems to be challenging for FSBMs. Finite state machines cannot handle the incurred crossing dependencies while the augmented copying mechanism only contributes to recognizing *identical* copies, but not general cases of symbol correspondence. [5]

### 3.3 Other closure properties

**Union** Assume there are complete-path FSBMs $M_1$ and $M_2$ such that $L(M_1) = L_1$ and $L(M_2) = L_2$, then $L_1 \cup L_2$ is a complete-path FSBM-recognizable language. One can construct a new machine $M$ that accepts an input $w$ if either $M_1$ or $M_2$ accepts $w$. The construction of $M$ keeps $M_1$ and $M_2$ unchanged, but adds a new plain state $q_0$. Now, $q_0$ becomes the only initial state, branching into those previous initial states in $M_1$ and $M_2$ with $\epsilon$-arcs. In this way, the new machine would guess on either $M_1$ or $M_2$ accepts the input. If one accepts $w$, $M$ will accept $w$, too.

**Concatenation** Assume there are complete-path FSBMs $M_1$ and $M_2$ such that $L(M_1) = L_1$ and $L(M_2) = L_2$, then there is a complete-path FSBM $M$ that can recognize $L_1 \circ L_2$ by normal concatenation of two automata. The new machine adds a new plain state $q_0$ and makes $q_0$ the only initial state, branching into those previous initial states in $M_1$ with $\epsilon$-arcs. All final states in $M_2$ are the only final states in $M$. Besides, the new machine adds $\epsilon$-arcs from any old final states in $M_1$ to any possible initial states in $M_2$. A path in the resulting machine is guaranteed to be complete because it is essentially the concatenation of two complete paths.

**Kleene Star** Assume there is a complete-path FSBM $M_1$ such that $L(M_1) = L_1$, $L_1^*$ is a complete-path FSBM-recognizable language. A new automaton $M$ is similar to $M_1$ with a new initial state $q_0$. $q_0$ is also a final state, branching into

[5]The statement on the inverse homomorphism closure is left as a conjecture. We admit that a more formal and rigorous mathematical proof proving $h^{-1}(L)$ is not complete-path FSBM-recognizable should be conducted. To achieve this goal, a more formal tool, such as a developed pumping lemma for the corresponding set of languages, is important.

old initial states in $M_1$. In this way, $M$ accepts the empty string $\epsilon$. $q_0$ is never a G state nor an H state. Moreover, to make sure $M$ can jump back to an initial state after it hits a final state, $\epsilon$-arcs from any final state to any old initial states are added.

## 4 Discussion and conclusion

In summary, this paper provides a new computational device to compute unrestricted total reduplication on any regular languages, including the simplest copying language $L_{ww}$ where $w$ can be any arbitrary string of an alphabet. As a result, it introduces a new class of languages incomparable to CFLs. This class of languages allows *unbounded* copying without generating non-reduplicative non-regular patterns: we hypothesize context-free string reversals are excluded since the buffer is queue-like. Meanwhile, the MCS Swiss-German cross-serial dependencies, abstracted as $\{a^ib^jc^id^j \mid i, j \geq 1\}$, is also excluded, since the buffer works on the same alphabet as the input tape and only matches *identical* sub-strings.

Following the sub-classes of 2-way FSTs in Dolatian and Heinz (2018a,b, 2019, 2020), which successfully capture unbounded copying as *functions* while exclude the mirror image mapping, complete-path FSBMs successfully capture the total-reduplicated stringsets while exclude string reversals. Comparison between the characterized languages in this paper and the image of functions in Dolatian and Heinz (2020) should be further carried out to build the connection. Moreover, one natural next step is to extend FSBMs as acceptors to finite state buffered transducers (FSBT). Our intuition is FSBTs would be helpful in handling the morphological analysis question ($ww \to w$), a not-yet solved problem in the 2-way FSTs that Dolatian and Heinz (2020) study. After reading the first $w$ in input and buffering this chunk of string in the memory, the transducer can output $\epsilon$ for each matched symbol when transiting among $H$ states.

Another potential area of research is applying this new machinery to Primitive Optimality Theory (Eisner, 1997; Albro, 1998). Albro (2000, 2005) used weighted finite state machine to model constraints while represented the set of candidates by Multiple Context Free Grammars to enforce base-reduplicant correspondence (McCarthy and Prince, 1995). Parallel to Albro's way, given complete-path FSBMs are intersectable with FSAs, it is possible to computationally implement the reduplicative identity requirement by complete-path FSBMs without using the full power of mildly context sensitive formalisms. To achieve this goal, future work should consider developing an efficient algorithm that intersects complete-path FSBMs with *weighted* FSAs.

The present paper is the first step to recognize reduplicated forms in adequate yet more restrictive models and techniques compared to MCS formalisms. There are some limitations of the current approach on the whole typology of reduplication. Complete-path FSBMs can only capture local reduplication with *two* adjacent identical copies. As for non-local reduplication, the modification should be straightforward: the machines need to allow the filled buffer in N mode (or in another newly-defined memory holding mode) and match strings only when needed. As for multiple reduplication, complete-path FSBMs can easily be modified to include multiple copies of the same base form ($\{w^n \mid w \in \Sigma^*, n \in \mathbb{N}\}$) but cannot be easily modified to recognize the non-semilinear language containing copies of the copy ($\{w^{2^n} \mid w \in \Sigma^*, n \in \mathbb{N}\}$). It remains to be an open question on the computational nature of multiple reduplication. Last but not the least, as a reviewer points out, recognizing non-identical copies can be achieved by either storing or emptying not exactly the same input symbols, but mapped symbols according to some function $f$. Under this modification, the new automata would recognize $\{a^nb^n \mid n \in \mathbb{N}\}$ with $f(a) = b$ but still exclude string reversals. In all, detailed investigations on how to modify complete-path FSBMs should be the next step to complete the typology.


## Acknowledgments

The author would like to thank Tim Hunter, Bruce Hayes, Dylan Bumford, Kie Zuraw, and the members of the UCLA Phonology Seminar for their feedback and suggestions. Special thanks to the anonymous reviewers for their constructive comments and discussions. All errors remain my own.


## References


Daniel M Albro. 1998. Evaluation, implementation, and extension of primitive optimality theory. Master's thesis, UCLA.

Daniel M. Albro. 2000. Taking primitive Optimality Theory beyond the finite state. In *Proceedings of the Fifth Workshop of the ACL Special Interest Group in Computational Phonology*, pages 57–67, Centre Universitaire, Luxembourg. International Committee on Computational Linguistics.

Daniel M Albro. 2005. *Studies in computational optimality theory, with special reference to the phonological system of Malagasy*. Ph.D. thesis, University of California, Los Angeles, Los Angeles.

Bruce Bagemihl. 1989. The crossing constraint and 'backwards languages'. *Natural language & linguistic Theory*, 7(4):481–549.

Félix Baschenis, Olivier Gauwin, Anca Muscholl, and Gabriele Puppis. 2017. Untwisting two-way transducers in elementary time. In *2017 32nd Annual ACM/IEEE Symposium on Logic in Computer Science (LICS)*, pages 1–12.

Kenneth R. Beesley and Lauri Karttunen. 2000. Finite-state non-concatenative morphotactics. In *Proceedings of the 38th Annual Meeting of the Association for Computational Linguistics*, pages 191–198, Hong Kong. Association for Computational Linguistics.

Jane Chandlee. 2014. *Strictly local phonological processes*. Ph.D. thesis, University of Delaware.

Jane Chandlee. 2017. Computational locality in morphological maps. *Morphology*, 27:599–641.

Noam Chomsky. 1956. Three models for the description of language. *IRE Trans. Inf. Theory*, 2:113–124.

Alexander Clark and Ryo Yoshinaka. 2014. Distributional learning of parallel multiple context-free grammars. *Mach. Learn.*, 96(1–2):5–31.

Yael Cohen-Sygal and Shuly Wintner. 2006. Finite-state registered automata for non-concatenative morphology. *Computational Linguistics*, 32(1):49–82.

Christopher Culy. 1985. The complexity of the vocabulary of bambara. *Linguistics and philosophy*, 8(3):345–351.

Robert M. W. Dixon. 1972. *The Dyirbal Language of North Queensland*, volume 9 of *Cambridge Studies in Linguistics*. Cambridge University Press, Cambridge.

Hossep Dolatian and Jeffrey Heinz. 2018a. Learning reduplication with 2-way finite-state transducers. In *Proceedings of the 14th International Conference on Grammatical Inference*, volume 93 of *Proceedings of Machine Learning Research*, pages 67–80. PMLR.

Hossep Dolatian and Jeffrey Heinz. 2018b. Modeling reduplication with 2-way finite-state transducers. In *Proceedings of the Fifteenth Workshop on Computational Research in Phonetics, Phonology, and Morphology*, pages 66–77, Brussels, Belgium. Association for Computational Linguistics.

Hossep Dolatian and Jeffrey Heinz. 2019. RedTyp: A database of reduplication with computational models. In *Proceedings of the Society for Computation in Linguistics (SCiL) 2019*, pages 8–18.

Hossep Dolatian and Jeffrey Heinz. 2020. Computing and classifying reduplication with 2-way finite-state transducers. *Journal of Language Modelling*, 8(1):179–250.

Jason Eisner. 1997. Efficient generation in primitive Optimality Theory. In *35th Annual Meeting of the Association for Computational Linguistics and 8th Conference of the European Chapter of the Association for Computational Linguistics*, pages 313–320, Madrid, Spain. Association for Computational Linguistics.

Gerald Gazdar and Geoffrey K Pullum. 1985. Computationally relevant properties of natural languages and their grammars. *New generation computing*, 3(3):273–306.

Thomas Graf. 2017. The power of locality domains in phonology. *Phonology*, 34(2):385–405.

Phyllis M. Healey. 1960. *An Agta Grammar*. Bureau of Printing, Manila.

Jeffrey Heinz. 2007. *The Inductive Learning of Phonotactic Patterns*. Ph.D. thesis, University of California, Los Angeles.

Jeffrey Heinz. 2018. The computational nature of phonological generalizations. In Larry Hyman and Frans Plank, editors, *Phonological Typology*, Phonetics and Phonology, chapter 5, pages 126–195. De Gruyter Mouton.

Jeffrey Heinz, Chetan Rawal, and Herbert G Tanner. 2011. Tier-based strictly local constraints for phonology. In *Proceedings of the 49th Annual Meeting of the Association for Computational Linguistics: Human language technologies*, pages 58–64.

John E Hopcroft and Jeffrey D Ullman. 1979. Introduction to automata theory, languages, and computation. *Addison-Welsey, NY.*

Mans Hulden. 2009. *Finite-state Machine Construction Methods and Algorithms for Phonology and Morphology*. Ph.D. thesis, University of Arizona, Tucson, USA.

Sharon Inkelas and Cheryl Zoll. 2005. *Reduplication: Doubling in morphology*, volume 106. Cambridge University Press.

Gerhard Jäger and James Rogers. 2012. Formal language theory: refining the chomsky hierarchy. *Philosophical Transactions of the Royal Society B: Biological Sciences*, 367(1598):1956–1970.

C. Douglas Johnson. 1972. *Formal Aspects of Phonological Description*. Monographs on linguistic analysis. Mouton, The Hague.

Aravind K. Joshi. 1985. *Tree adjoining grammars: How much context-sensitivity is required to provide reasonable structural descriptions?*, Studies in Natural Language Processing, page 206–250. Cambridge University Press.

Ronald M. Kaplan and Martin Kay. 1994. Regular models of phonological rule systems. *Comput. Linguist.*, 20(3):331–378.

Alec Marantz. 1982. Re reduplication. *Linguistic inquiry*, 13(3):435–482.

John J. McCarthy and Alan S. Prince. 1995. Faithfulness and reduplicative identity. In Jill N. Beckman, Laura Walsh Dickey, and Suzanne Urbanczyk, editors, *Papers in Optimality Theory.* GLSA (Graduate Linguistic Student Association), Dept. of Linguistics, University of Massachusetts, Amherst, MA.

Robert McNaughton and Seymour A Papert. 1971. *Counter-Free Automata (MIT research monograph no. 65).* The MIT Press.

Brian Roark and Richard Sproat. 2007. *Computational approaches to morphology and syntax*, volume 4. Oxford University Press.

Carl Rubino. 2013. Reduplication. In Matthew S. Dryer and Martin Haspelmath, editors, *The World Atlas of Language Structures Online*. Max Planck Institute for Evolutionary Anthropology, Leipzig.

Hiroyuki Seki, Takashi Matsumura, Mamoru Fujii, and Tadao Kasami. 1991. On multiple context-free grammars. *Theoretical Computer Science*, 88(2):191–229.

Stuart M Shieber. 1985. Evidence against the context-freeness of natural language. In *Philosophy, Language, and Artificial Intelligence*, pages 79–89. Springer.

Imre Simon. 1975. Piecewise testable events. In *Automata Theory and Formal Languages*, pages 214–222, Berlin, Heidelberg. Springer Berlin Heidelberg.

Michael Sipser. 2013. *Introduction to the Theory of Computation*, third edition. Course Technology, Boston, MA.

Edward Stabler. 1997. Derivational minimalism. In *Logical Aspects of Computational Linguistics*, pages 68–95, Berlin, Heidelberg. Springer Berlin Heidelberg.

Markus Walther. 2000. Finite-state reduplication in one-level prosodic morphology. In *1st Meeting of the North American Chapter of the Association for Computational Linguistics*.

Kie Zuraw. 2002. Aggressive reduplication. *Phonology*, 19(3):395–439.

# An FST morphological analyzer for the Gitksan language

**Clarissa Forbes**[α] **Garrett Nicolai**[β] **Miikka Silfverberg**[β]
[α]University of Arizona [β]University of British Columbia
forbesc@email.arizona.edu first.last@ubc.ca

**Abstract**

This paper presents a finite-state morphological analyzer for the Gitksan language. The analyzer draws from a 1250-token Eastern dialect wordlist. It is based on finite-state technology and additionally includes two extensions which can provide analyses for out-of-vocabulary words: rules for generating predictable dialect variants, and a neural guesser component. The pre-neural analyzer, tested against interlinear-annotated texts from multiple dialects, achieves coverage of (75-81%), and maintains high precision (95-100%). The neural extension improves coverage at the cost of lowered precision.

## 1 Introduction

Endangered languages of the Americas are typically underdocumented and underresourced. Computational tools like morphological analyzers present the opportunity to speed up ongoing documentation efforts by enabling automatic and semi-automatic data analysis. This paper describes the development of a morphological analyzer for Gitksan, an endangered Indigenous language of Western Canada. The analyzer is capable of providing the base form and morphosyntactic description of inflected word forms: a word *gupdiit* 'they ate' is annotated `gup-TR-3PL`.

Our Gitksan analyzer is based on two core documentary resources: a wordlist spanning approximately 1250 tokens, and an 18,000 token interlinear-annotated text collection. Due to the scarcity of available lexical and corpus resources, we take a rule-based approach to modeling of morphology which is less dependent on large datasets than machine learning methods. Our analyzer is based on finite-state technology (Beesley and Karttunen, 2003) using the *foma* finite-state toolkit (Hulden, 2009b).

Our work has three central goals: (1) We want to build a flexible morphological analyzer to supplement lexical and textual resources in support of language learning. Such an analyzer can support learners in identifying the base-form of inflected words where the morpheme-to-word ratio might be particularly high, in a way not addressed by a traditional dictionary. It may also productively generate inflected forms of words. (2) We want to facilitate ongoing efforts to expand the aforementioned 1250 token wordlist into a broad-coverage dictionary of the Gitksan language. Running our analyzer on Gitksan texts, we can rapidly identify word forms whose base-form has not yet been documented. An analyzer can also help automate the process of identifying sample sentences for dictionary words, the addition of which substantially increases the value of the dictionary. (3) We want to use the model to further our understanding of Gitksan morphology. Unanalyzeable and erroneously analyzed forms can help us identify shortcomings in our description of the morphological system and can thus feed back into the documentation effort of the language.

The Gitksan-speaking community recognizes two dialects: Eastern (Upriver) and Western (Downriver). Our analyzer is based on resources which mainly represent the Eastern dialect. Consequently, our base analyzer achieves higher coverage of 71% for the Eastern dialect as measured on a manually annotated test set. For the Western dialect, coverage is lower at 53%. In order to improve coverage on the Western variety, we explore two extensions to our analyzer. First, we implement a number of dialectal relaxation rules which model the orthographic variation between Eastern and Western dialects. This leads to sizable improvements in coverage for the Western dialect (around 9%-points on types and 6%-points on tokens). Moreover, the precision of our analyzer remains high both for the Eastern and West-



*Proceedings of the Seventeenth SIGMORPHON Workshop on Computational Research in Phonetics, Phonology, and Morphology*, pages 188–197

ern dialects even after applying dialect rules. Secondly, we extend our FST morphological analyzer by adding a data-driven neural guesser which further improves coverage both for the Eastern and Western varieties.

## 2 The Gitksan Language

The Gitxsan are one of the indigenous peoples of British Columbia, Canada. Their traditional territories consist of upwards of 50,000 square kilometers of land along the Skeena River in the BC northern interior. The Gitksan language is the easternmost member of the Tsimshianic family, which spans the entirety of the Skeena and Nass River watersheds to the Pacific Coast. Today, Gitksan is the most vital Tsimshianic language, but is still critically endangered with an estimated 300-850 speakers (Dunlop et al., 2018).

The Tsimshianic family can be broadly understood as a dialect continuum, with each village along these rivers speaking somewhat differently from its neighbors up- or downstream, and the two endpoints being mutually unintelligible. The six Gitxsan villages are commonly divided into two dialects: East/Upriver and West/Downriver. The dialects have some lexical and phonological differences, with the most prominent being a vowel shift. Consider the name of the Skeena River: *Xsan, Ksan* (Eastern) vs *Ksen* (Western).

### 2.1 Morphological description

The Gitksan language has strict VSO word order and multifunctional, fusional morphology (Rigsby, 1986). It utilizes prefixation, suffixation, and both pro- and en-cliticization. Category derivation and number marking are prefixal, while markers of argument structure, transitivity, and person/number agreement are suffixal.

The Tsimshianic languages have been described as having word-complexity similar to German (Tarpent, 1987). The general structure of a noun or verb stem is presented in the template in Figure 1. A stem consists of minimally a root (typically CVC); an example is monomorphemic *gup* 'eat'. Stems may also include derivational prefixes or transitivity-related suffixes; compare *gupxw* 'be eaten; be edible'.

In sentential context, stems are inflected for features like transitivity and person/number. Our analyzer is concerned primarily with stem-external inflection and cliticization. The structure of stem-external morphology for the most complex word type, a transitive verb, is schematized in the template in Figure 2; an example word with all these slots filled would be *'naag̱asḵ'otsdiitg̱athl* 'apparently they cut.PL open (common noun)'

On the left edge of the stem can appear any number of modifying 'proclitics'. These contribute locative, adjectival, and manner-related information to a noun or verb, often producing semi- or non-compositional idioms in a similar fashion to Germanic particle verbs.[1] It is often unclear whether these proclitics constitute part of the root or stem, or if they are distinct words entirely. The orthographic boundaries on this edge are consequently sometimes fuzzy. Sometimes clear contrasts are presented, as with the sequence *lax̱-yip* 'on-earth': we see compositional *lax̱ yip* 'on the ground' versus lexicalized *lax̱yip* 'land, territory'. However, the boundary between compositional and idiomatic is not always so obvious, as in examples like (1).

(1)
a. *saa-'witxw* (away-come, 'come from')
b. *ḵ'ali-aks* (upstream-water, 'upriver')
c. *xsi-ga'a* (out-see, 'choose')
d. *luu-no'o* (in-hole, 'annihilate')

Inflectional morphology largely appears on the right edge of the stem. The main complexity of Gitksan inflection involves homophony and opacity: a similar or identical wordform often has multiple possible analyses. For example, a word like *gubin* transparently involves a stem *gup* 'eat' and a 2SG suffix *-n*, but the intervening vowel *i* might be analyzed as epenthetic, as transitive inflection (TR), or as a specially-induced transitivizing suffix (T), resulting in three possible analyses in (2). Similarly, a word *gupdiit* involves the same stem *gup* 'eat' and a 3PL suffix *-diit*, but this suffix is able to delete preceding transitive suffixes, resulting in four possible analyses as in (3).

(2) *gubin*
a. gup-2SG
b. gup-TR-2SG
c. gup-T-2SG

(3) *gupdiit*
a. gup-3PL
b. gup-TR-3PL
c. gup-T-3PL
d. gup-T-TR-3PL

[1] E.g. ***nach**slagen* 'look up' in German.

| Derivation– | Proclitics– | Plural– | **Root** | –Argument Structure |
|---|---|---|---|---|

Figure 1: Morphological template of a complex nominal or verbal stem

| Proclitics– | **Stem** | –Transitive | –Person/Number | =Epistemic | =Next Noun Class |
|---|---|---|---|---|---|

Figure 2: Morphological template of modification, inflection, and cliticization for a transitive verbal predicate

Running speech in Gitksan is additionally rife with clitics, which pose a more complex problem for morphological modeling. First, there are a set of ergative 'flexiclitics', which are able to either procliticize or encliticize onto a subordinator or auxiliary, or stand independently. The same combination of host and clitic might result in sequences like *n=ii* (1SG=and), *ii=n* (and=1SG), or *ii na* (and 1SG) (Stebbins, 2003; Forbes, 2018).

Second, all nouns are introduced with a noun-class clitic that attaches to the preceding word, as illustrated by the VSO sentence in (4). Here, the proper noun clitic *=s* attaches to the verb but is syntactically associated with *Mary*, and the common noun clitic *=hl* attaches to *Mary* but is associated with *g̲ayt* 'hat'.

(4) Giigwis Maryhl g̲ayt.
giikw-i-t =s Mary =hl g̲ayt
buy-TR-3.II =PN Mary =CN hat
'Mary bought a hat.'

Any word able to precede a noun phrase is a possible host for one of these clitics (hence their appearance on transitive verbs in Figure 2).

Finally, there are several sentence-final and second-position clitics. whose distribution is based on prosodic rather than strictly categorial properties; these attach on the right edge of subordinators/auxiliaries, predicates, and argument phrases, depending on the structure of the sentence.

A large part of Gitksan's unique morphological complexity therefore arises not in nominal or verbal inflection, but in the flexibility of multiple types of clitics used in connected speech, and the logic of which possible sequences can appear with which wordforms.

## 2.2 Resources

The Gitksan community orthography was designed and documented in the Hindle and Rigsby (1973) wordlist (H&R). Though it originally reflected only the single dialect of one of the authors (Git-an'maaxs, Eastern), this orthography is in broad use today across the Gitxsan community for all dialects, as well as neighboring Nisg̲a'a, with some variations. Given the relatively short period that this orthography has been in use, orthographic conventions can vary widely across dialects and writers. In producing this initial analyzer, we attempt to mitigate the issue by working with a small number of more-standardized sources: the original H&R and an annotated, multidialectal text collection.

We worked with a digitized version of the H&R wordlist (Mother Tongues Dictionaries, 2020). The original wordlist documents only the Git-an'maaxs Eastern dialect; our version adds a small number of additional dialect variants, and fifteen common verbs and subordinators. In total, the list contains approximately 1250 lexemes and phrases, plus noted variants and plural forms.

The analyzer was informed by descriptive work on both Gitksan and its mutually intelligible neighbor Nisg̲a'a. This work details many aspects of Gitksan inflection, including morphological opacity and the complex interactions of certain suffixes and clitics (Rigsby, 1986; Tarpent, 1987; Hunt, 1993; Davis, 2018; Brown et al., 2020).

A text collection of approximately 18,000 words was also used in the development and evaluation of the analyzer. This collection consists of oral narratives given by three speakers from different villages: Ansbayaxw (Eastern), Gijigyukwhla'a (Western), and Git-anyaaw (Western) (cf. Forbes et al., 2017). It includes multiple genres: personal anecdotes, traditional tales (*ant'imahlasxw*), histories of ownership (*adaawk̲*), recipes, and explanations of cultural practice. The collection is fully annotated in the 'interlinear gloss' format with free translation, exemplified in (5).

(5) Ii al'algaltgathl get,
ii CVC-alg̲al-t=gat=hl get
CCNJ PL-watch-3.II=REPORT=CN people
'And they stood by and watched,'

The analyzed corpus provides insight into the use of clitics in running speech, and is the dataset against which we test the results of the analyzer.

## 3 Related Work

While considering different approaches to computational modeling of Gitksan morphology, finite-state morphology arose as a natural choice. At the present time, finite-state methods are quite widely applied for Indigenous languages of the Americas. Chen and Schwartz (2018) present a morphological analyzer for St. Lawrence Island / Central Siberian Yupik for aid in language preservation and revitalization work. Strunk (2020) present another analyzer for Central Alaskan Yupik. Snoek et al. (2014) present a morphological analyzer for Plains Cree nouns and Harrigan et al. (2017) present one for Plains Cree verbs. Littell (2018) build a finite-state analyzer for Kwak'wala. All of the above are languages which present similar challenges to the ones encountered in the case of Gitksan: word forms consisting of a large number of morphemes, both prefixing and suffixing morphology and morphophonological alternations. Finite-state morphology is well-suited for dealing with these challenges. It is noteworthy that similarly to Gitksan, a number of the aforementioned languages are also undergoing active documentation efforts.

While we present the first morphological analyzer for Gitksan which is capable of productive inflection, this is not the first electronic lexical resource for the Gitksan language. Littell et al. (2017) present an electronic dictionary interface Waldayu for endangered languages and apply it to Gitksan. The model is capable of performing fuzzy dictionary search which is an important extension in the presence of orthographic variation which widely occurs in Gitksan. While this represents an important development for computational lexicography for Gitksan, the method cannot model productive inflection which is important particularly for language learners who might not be able to easily deduce the base-form of an inflected word (Hunt et al., 2019). As mentioned earlier, our model can analyze inflected forms of lexemes.

We extend the coverage of our finite-state analyzers by incorporating a neural morphological guesser which can be used to analyze word forms which are rejected by the finite-state analyzer. Similar mechanisms have been explored for other American Indigenous languages. Micher (2017) use segmental recurrent neural networks (Kong et al., 2015) to augment a finite-state morphological analyzer for Inuktitut.[2] These jointly segment the input word into morphemes and label each morpheme with one or more grammatical tags. Very silmilarly to the approach that we adopt, Schwartz et al. (2019) and Moeller et al. (2018) use attentional LSTM encoder-decoder models to augment morphological analyzers for extending morphological analyzers for St. Lawrence Island / Central Siberian Yupik and Arapaho, respectively.

## 4 The Model

Our morphological analyzer was designed with several considerations in mind. First, given the small amount of data at our disposal, we chose to construct a rule-based finite state transducer, built from a predefined lexicon and morphological description. The dependence of this type of analyzer on a lexicon supports one of the major goals of this project: lexical discovery from texts. Words which cannot be analyzed will likely be novel lemmas that have yet to be documented. Furthermore, the process of constructing a morphological description allows for the refinement of our understanding of Gitksan morphology and orthographic standards. For example, there is a common post-stem rounding effect that generates variants such as *jog̲at, jog̲ot* 'those who live'; the project helps us identify where this effect occurs. Our analyzer can also later serve as a tool to explore of the behavior of less-documented constructions (e.g. distributive, partitive), as grammatical and pedagogical resources continue to be developed.

Our general philosophy was to take a maximal-segmentation approach to inflection and cliticization: morphemes were added individually, and interactions between morphemes (e.g. deletion) were derived through transformational rules based on morphological and phonological context. Most interactions of this kind are strictly local; there are few long-distance dependencies between morphemes. The only exception to the minimal chunking rule is a specific interaction between noun-class clitics and verbal agreement: when these clitics append to verbal agreement suffixes, they either agglutinate with (6-a) or delete them (6-b) depending on whether the agreement and noun-class morpheme are associated with the same noun (Tarpent, 1987; Davis, 2018). That is, the conditioning factor for this alternation is syntactic, not morphophonological.

[2] The Uquailaut morphological analyzer: `http://www.inuktitutcomputing.ca/Uqailaut`

(6) Realizations of *gup-i-t=hl* (eat-TR-3=CN)

  a. *gubithl* 'he/she ate (common noun)'

  b. *gubihl* '(common noun) ate'

The available set of resources further constrained our options for the analyzer's design and our means of evaluating it. The H&R wordlist is quite small, and of only a single dialect, while the corpus for testing was multidialectal. We therefore aimed to produce a flexible analyzer able to recognize orthographic variation, to maximize the value of its small lexicon.

### 4.1 FST implementation

Our finite-state analyzer was written in *lexc* and *xfst* format and compiled using *foma* (Hulden, 2009b). Finite-state analyzers like this one are constructed from a dictionary of stems, with affixes added left-to-right, and morpho-phonological rewrite rules applied to produce allomorphs and contextual variation. The necessary components of the analyzer are therefore a lexicon, a morphotactic description, and a set of morphophonological transformations, as illustrated in Figure 3.

Our analyzer's lexicon is drawn from the H&R wordlist. As a first step, each stem from that list was assigned a lexical category to determine its inflectional possibilities. The resulting 1506 word + category pairs were imported to category-specific groups in the morphotactic description.

Any of the major stem categories could be used to start a word; modifiers, preverbs, and prenouns could also be used as verb/noun prefixes. Each categorized group flowed to a series of category-specific sections which appended the appropriate part of speech, and then listed various derivational or inflectional affixes that could be appended. A morphological group would terminate either with a hard stop (#) or by flowing to a final group 'Word', where clitics were appended.

Finally, forms were subject to a sequence of orthographic transformations reflecting morphophonological rules. Some examples included the deletion of adjacent morphemes which could not co-occur, processes of vowel epenthesis or deletion, vowel coloring by rounded and back consonants, and prevocalic stop voicing.

A sample form produced by the FST for the word *saabisbisdiithl* 'they tore off (pl. common noun)' is in example (7). This form involves a preverb *saa* being affixed directly to a transitive verb *bisbis*, a reduplicated plural form of the verb which was listed directly in the H&R wordlist (the symbol ^ marks morpheme boundaries).[3] After the verb, we find two inflectional suffixes and one clitic. Ultimately, rewrite rules are used to delete the transitive suffix and segmentation boundaries (8).

(7) `saa^bisbis^i^diit^hl`
  `saa+PVB-bisbis+VT-TR-3PL=CN`

(8) `saabisbisdiithl`

### 4.2 Analyzer iterations

We built and evaluated four iterations of the Gitksan morphological analyzer based upon the foundation presented in Section 4.1: the v1. **Lexical FST**, v2. **Complete FST**, v3. **Dialectal FST** and v4. **FST+Neural**. Each iteration cumulatively expands the previous one by incorporating additional vocabulary items, rules or modeling components.

The first analyzer (v1: **Lexical FST**) included only the open-class categories of verbs, nouns, modifiers, and adverbs which made up the bulk of the H&R wordlist. The main focus of the morphotactic description was transitive inflection, person/number-agreement, and cliticization for these categories. Some semi-productive argument structural morphemes (e.g. the passive *-xw* or antipassive *-asxw*) were also included.

The second analyzer (v2: **Complete FST**) incorporated functional and closed-class morphemes such as subordinators, pronouns, prepositions, quotatives, demonstratives, and aspectual particles, including additional types of clitics.

The third analyzer (v3: **Dialectal FST**) further incorporated predictable stem-internal variation, such as the vowel shift and dorsal stop lenition/-fortition seen across dialects. In order to apply the vowel shift in a targeted way, all items in the lexicon were marked for stress using the notation `$`. Parses prior to rule application now appear as in (9) (compare to (7)).

(9) `s$aa^bisb$is^i^diit^hl`

Finally, we seek to expand the coverage of the analyzer through machine learning, namely neural architectures (v4: **FST+Neural**). Our FST architecture allows for the automatic extraction of surface-analysis pairs; this enables us to create

[3]The FST has no component to productively handle reduplication but this would be possible to implement given a closed lexicon Hulden (2009a, Ch. 4).

```
LEXICON RootN
maa'y         N ;
smax          N ;
LEXICON RootVI
yee           VI ;
t'aa          VI ;
LEXICON RootPrenoun
lax_          Prenoun ;
```

(a) Lexicon

```
LEXICON N
+N:           NInfl ;
LEXICON NInfl
-ATTR:^m      # ;
-SX:^it       Word ;
              Agr_II ;
              Word ;
LEXICON Prenoun
+PNN:         # ;
+PNN:         RootN ;
```

(b) Morphotactic description

**Deletion before -3PL:**
ˆi → 0 / _ ˆdiit

**Vowel insertion:**
0 → i / C ˆ _ Sonorant #

**Prevocalic voicing:**
p,t,ts,k,<u>k</u> → b,d,j,g,<u>g</u> / _ V

(c) Rewrite rules

Figure 3: Three main components of the FST (simplified)

a training set for the neural models. We experiment with two alternative neural architectures - the Hard-Attentional model over edit actions (**HA**) described by Makarov and Clematide (2018), and the transformer model (Vaswani et al., 2017), as implemented in Fairseq (**Fairseq**) (Ott et al., 2019). Unlike the FST, the neural models can extend morphological patterns beyond a defined series of stems, analyzing forms that the FST cannot recognize.

For both models, we extract 10,000 random analysis pairs, with replacement; early stopping for both models uses a 10% validation set extracted from the training, with no overlap between training and validation sets (although stem overlap is allowed). The best checkpoint is chosen based on validation accuracy. The HA model uses a Chinese Restaurant Process alignment model, and is trained for 60 epochs, with 10 epochs patience; the encoder and decoder both have hidden dimension 200, and are trained with 50% dropout on recurrent connections. The Transformer model is a 3-layer, 4-head transformer trained for 50 epochs. The encoders and decoders each have an embedding size of 512, and feed-forward size of 1024, with 50% dropout and 30% attentional dropout. We optimize using Adam (0.9, 0.98), and cross-entropy with 20% label-smoothing as our objective.

Any wordform which received no analysis from the FST was provided a set of five possible analyses each from the HA and Fairseq models.

## 5 Evaluation

### 5.1 FST Coverage

The analyzers were run on two 2000-token datasets drawn from the multidialectal corpus: an Eastern Gitksan dataset (1 speaker), and a Western Gitksan dataset (2 speakers and dialects). Token and type coverage for the three FSTs is provided in Table 1, representing the percentage of wordforms for which each analyzer was able to provide one or more possible parses.

| | | Types | Tokens |
|---|---|---|---|
| East | Lexical | 63.12% | 54.17% |
| | Complete | 71.10% | 81.48% |
| | Dialectal | 71.10% | 81.48% |
| West | Lexical | 45.49% | 38.09% |
| | Complete | 53.20% | 70.12% |
| | Dialectal | 62.35% | 75.98% |

Table 1: Analyzer coverage on 2000-token datasets

The effect of adding function-word coverage to the second 'Complete' analyzer was broadly similar across dialects, increasing type coverage by about 8% and token coverage by 27-32%, demonstrating the relative importance of function words to lexical coverage.

The first two analyzers performed substantially better on the Eastern dataset which more closely matched the dialect of the wordlist/lexicon. The third 'Dialectal' analyzer incorporated four types of predictable stem-internal allomorphy to generate Western-style variants. These transformations had no effect on coverage for the Eastern dataset, but increased type and token coverage for the Western dataset by 9% and 6% respectively.

### 5.2 FST precision

While our analyzer manipulates vocabulary items at the level of the stem seen in the lexicon, the corpus used for evaluation is annotated to the level of the root and was not always comparable (e.g. *ihlee'etxw* 'red' vs *ihlee'e-xw* 'blood-VAL'). Accuracy evaluation therefore had to be done manually by comparing the annotated analysis in the corpus to the parse options produced by the FST (10).

(10) *japhl*

a. `make[-3.II]=CN` (Corpus)

b. `j$ap+N=CN`
`j$ap+N-3=CN`
`j$ap+VT-3=CN` (FSTv3)

We evaluated the accuracy of the Dialectal FST on two smaller datasets: 150 tokens Eastern, and 250 tokens Western. These datasets included 85 and 180 unique wordform/annotation pairs respectively. The same wordform might have multiple attested analyses, depending on its usage. The performance of the Dialectal analyzer on each dataset is summarized in Table 2. Precision is calculated as the percentage of word/annotation pairs for which the analyzer produced a parse matching the context-sensitive annotation in the corpus.[4] Other analyses produced by the FST were ignored. For example in (10), the token would be evaluated as correct given the final parse, which uses the appropriate stem (*jap* 'make') and matching morphology; the other parses using a different stem (*jap* 'box trap') and/or different morphology could not qualify the token as correctly parsed. Only parsable wordforms were considered (i.e. English words and names are excluded).

| | East | West |
|---|---|---|
| Coverage | 71.76% (61/85) | 68.89% (124/180) |
| Correct parse | 71.76% (61) | 64.44% (116) |
| Incorrect parse | 0.00% (0) | 2.78% (5) |
| Name, English | 2.5% (2) | 3.33% (6) |
| No parse | 27.5% (22) | 29.44% (53) |
| Precision | 100.00% (61/61) | 95.87% (116/121) |

Table 2: Accuracy evaluation for dialectal analyzer (v3) on small datasets

The Western dataset was larger, and consisted of two distinct dialects, in contrast to the smaller and more homogeneous Eastern dataset. Regardless, analyzer coverage between the two datasets was comparable (68-72%) and precision was very high (95-100%). When this analyzer was able to provide a possible parse, one was almost always correct.

[4]Note that precision is computed only on word forms which received at least one analysis from the FST.

To further understand the analyzer's limitations, we categorized the reasons for erroneous and missing analyses, listed in Table 3. In addition to the small datasets, for which all words were checked, we also evaluated the 100 most-frequent word/analysis pairs in the larger datasets.

The majority of erroneous and absent analyses were due to the use of new lemmas not in the lexicon, or novel variants not captured by productive stem-alternation rules. Novel lemmas made up about 18% each of the small datasets, and 4-8% of the top-100 most frequent types. Some functional items had specific dialectal realizations; for example, all three speakers used a different locative preposition (*g̲oo-*, *g̲o'o-*, *g̲a'a-*), only one of which was recognized.

There were also a few errors attributable to the morphotactic rules encoded in the parser. For example, there were several instances in the dataset of supposed 'preverb' modifiers combining with nouns (e.g. *t'ip-no'o=si*, sharply.down-hole=PROX, 'this steep-sided hole'), which the parser could not recognize. This category combination flags the need for further documentation of certain 'preverbs'. As a second example, numbers attested without agreement were not recognized because the analyzer expected that they would always agree. This could be fixed by updating the morphotactic description for numbers (e.g. to more closely match intransitive verbs).

### 5.3 FST + Neural performance

The addition of the neural component significantly increased the analyzer's coverage (mean HA: +21%, Fairseq: +17%), but at the expense of precision (mean -15% for both). The results of the manual accuracy evaluation are presented in Figure 4. There remained several forms for which the neural analyzers produced no analyses.

Both analyzers performed better on the 100-most-frequent types datasets, where they tended to accurately identify dialectal variants of common words (e.g. *t'ihlxw* from *tk'ihlxw* 'child', *diye* from *diya* '3=QUOT (third person quotative)'). In the small datasets of running text, these models were occasionally able to correctly identify unknown noun and verb stems that had minimal inflection. However, they struggled with identifying categories, and often failed to identify correct inflection. These difficulties stem from category-flexibility and homophony in Gitksan. Nouns and

| | East | | West | |
|---|---|---|---|---|
| | 150 tokens (22) | Top-100 (17) | 250 tokens (58) | Top-100 (23) |
| New lemma | 15 | 2 | 30 | 2 |
| New function word | 1 | 2 | 4 | 6 |
| Lexical variant | 3 | 8 | 6 | 5 |
| Functional variant | 2 | 3 | 9 | 9 |
| Morphotactic error | 1 | 2 | 9 | 1 |

Table 3: Categorization of erroneous and absent analyses for dialectal analyzer (FSTv3)

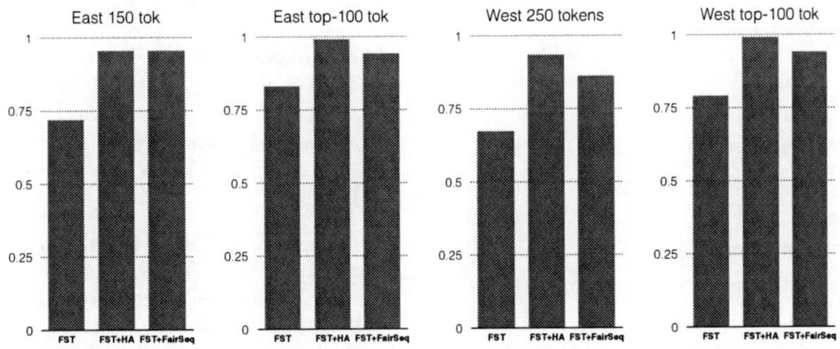


Figure 4: Proportion of forms which receive the correct analysis from each of our models (indicated in blue) and the number of forms which receive only incorrect analyses from our models (indicated in red). The remaining forms received no analyses.

verbs use the exact same inflection and clitics, making the category itself difficult to infer. Short inflectional sequences have a large number of homophonous parses, and even more differ only by a character or two.

Qualitatively, the HA model tended to produce more plausible predictions, often producing the correct stem or else a mostly-plausible analysis that could map to the same surface form, but with incorrect categories or inflection. In contrast, the Fairseq model often introduced stem changes or inflectional sequences which could not ultimately map to the surface form. Example (11) provides a sample set of incorrect predictions (surface-plausible analyses are starred).

(11) *ksimaasdiit* `ksi+PVB-m$aas+VT-TR-3PL`

a. HA model
`xsim$aas+N-3PL` (*)
`xsim$aas+N-T-3PL` (*)
`xsim$aas+NUM-3PL` (*?)
`xsim$aast+N-T-3PL`

b. Fairseq model
`xsim$aast+N-3PL`
`xsim$aast+N=RESEM`
`xsim$aast+N-SX=PN`
`xsim$as+N-3PL`

Further work can be done to improve the performance of the neural addition, such as training the model on attested tokens instead of, or in addition to, tokens randomly generated from the FST analyzer.

## 6 Discussion and Conclusions

The grammatically-informed FST is able to handle many of Gitksan's morphological complexities with a high degree of precision, including homophony, contextual deletion, and position-flexible clitics. The FST analyzer's patchy coverage can be attributed to its small lexicon. Unknown lexical items and variants comprised roughly 18% of each small dataset. Notably, errors and unidentified forms in the FST analyzer signal the current limits of morphotactic descriptions and lexical documentation. The analyzer can therefore serve as a useful part of a documentary linguistic workflow to quickly and systematically identify novel lexical items and grammatical rules from texts, facilitating the expansion of lexical resources. It can also be used as a pedagogical tool to identify word stems in running text, or to generate morphological exercises for language learners.

The neural system, with its expanded coverage, can serve as part of a feedback system with a human in the loop, informing future iterations of the annotation process. While its precision is lower than the FST, it can still inform annotators on words that the FST does not analyze. Newly-annotated data can then be used to enlarge the FST coverage.

## Acknowledgments

*'Wii t'isim ha'miyaa nuu'm aloohl* the fluent speakers who continue to share their knowledge with me (Barbara Sennott, Vincent Gogag, Hector Hill, Jeanne Harris), as well as the UBC Gitksan Research Lab. This research was supported by funding from the National Endowment for the Humanities (Documenting Endangered Languages Fellowship) and the Social Sciences and Humanities Research Council of Canada (Grant 430-2020-00793). Any views/findings/conclusions expressed in this publication do not necessarily reflect those of the NEH, NSF or SSHRC.

## References

Kenneth R Beesley and Lauri Karttunen. 2003. Finite-state morphology: Xerox tools and techniques. *CSLI, Stanford*.

Colin Brown, Clarissa Forbes, and Michael David Schwan. 2020. Clause-type, transitivity, and the transitive vowel in Tsimshianic. In *Papers of the International Conference on Salish and Neighbouring Languages 55*. UBCWPL.

Emily Chen and Lane Schwartz. 2018. A morphological analyzer for st. lawrence island/central siberian yupik. In *Proceedings of the Eleventh International Conference on Language Resources and Evaluation (LREC 2018)*.

Henry Davis. 2018. Only connect! a unified analysis of the Tsimshianic connective system. *International Journal of American Linguistics*, 84(4):471–511.

Britt Dunlop, Suzanne Gessner, Tracey Herbert, and Aliana Parker. 2018. Report on the status of BC First Nations languages. Report of the First People's Cultural Council. Retrieved March 24, 2019.

Clarissa Forbes. 2018. *Persistent ergativity: Agreement and splits in Tsimshianic*. Ph.D. thesis, University of Toronto.

Clarissa Forbes, Henry Davis, Michael Schwan, and the UBC Gitksan Research Laboratory. 2017. Three Gitksan texts. In *Papers for the 52nd International Conference on Salish and Neighbouring Languages*, pages 47–89. UBC Working Papers in Linguistics.

Atticus G Harrigan, Katherine Schmirler, Antti Arppe, Lene Antonsen, Trond Trosterud, and Arok Wolvengrey. 2017. Learning from the computational modelling of plains cree verbs. *Morphology*, 27(4):565–598.

Lonnie Hindle and Bruce Rigsby. 1973. A short practical dictionary of the Gitksan language. *Northwest Anthropological Research Notes*, 7(1).

Mans Hulden. 2009a. *Finite-state machine construction methods and algorithms for phonology and morphology*. Ph.D. thesis, The University of Arizona.

Mans Hulden. 2009b. Foma: a finite-state compiler and library. In *Proceedings of the 12th Conference of the European Chapter of the Association for Computational Linguistics: Demonstrations Session*, pages 29–32. Association for Computational Linguistics.

Benjamin Hunt, Emily Chen, Sylvia L.R. Schreiner, and Lane Schwartz. 2019. Community lexical access for an endangered polysynthetic language: An electronic dictionary for St. Lawrence Island Yupik. In *Proceedings of the 2019 Conference of the North American Chapter of the Association for Computational Linguistics (Demonstrations)*, pages 122–126, Minneapolis, Minnesota. Association for Computational Linguistics.

Katharine Hunt. 1993. *Clause Structure, Agreement and Case in Gitksan*. Ph.D. thesis, University of British Columbia.

Lingpeng Kong, Chris Dyer, and Noah A Smith. 2015. Segmental recurrent neural networks. *arXiv preprint arXiv:1511.06018*.

Patrick Littell. 2018. Finite-state morphology for kwak'wala: A phonological approach. In *Proceedings of the Workshop on Computational Modeling of Polysynthetic Languages*, pages 21–30, Santa Fe, New Mexico, USA. Association for Computational Linguistics.

Patrick Littell, Aidan Pine, and Henry Davis. 2017. Waldayu and waldayu mobile: Modern digital dictionary interfaces for endangered languages. In *Proceedings of the 2nd Workshop on the Use of Computational Methods in the Study of Endangered Languages*, pages 141–150.

Peter Makarov and Simon Clematide. 2018. Neural transition-based string transduction for limited-resource setting in morphology. In *Proceedings of the 27th International Conference on Computational Linguistics*, pages 83–93, Santa Fe, New Mexico, USA. Association for Computational Linguistics.

Jeffrey Micher. 2017. Improving coverage of an Inuktitut morphological analyzer using a segmental recurrent neural network. In *Proceedings of the 2nd Workshop on the Use of Computational Methods in the Study of Endangered Languages*, pages 101–106, Honolulu. Association for Computational Linguistics.

Sarah Moeller, Ghazaleh Kazeminejad, Andrew Cowell, and Mans Hulden. 2018. A neural morphological analyzer for arapaho verbs learned from a finite state transducer. In *Proceedings of the Workshop on Computational Modeling of Polysynthetic Languages*, pages 12–20.

Mother Tongues Dictionaries. 2020. Gitksan. Edited by the UBC Gitksan Research Lab. Accessed June 4, 2020. (https://mothertongues.org/gitksan).

Myle Ott, Sergey Edunov, Alexei Baevski, Angela Fan, Sam Gross, Nathan Ng, David Grangier, and Michael Auli. 2019. fairseq: A fast, extensible toolkit for sequence modeling. In *Proceedings of the 2019 Conference of the North American Chapter of the Association for Computational Linguistics (Demonstrations)*, pages 48–53, Minneapolis, Minnesota. Association for Computational Linguistics.

Bruce Rigsby. 1986. Gitxsan grammar. Master's thesis, University of Queensland, Australia.

Lane Schwartz, Emily Chen, Benjamin Hunt, and Sylvia LR Schreiner. 2019. Bootstrapping a neural morphological analyzer for st. lawrence island yupik from a finite-state transducer. In *Proceedings of the Workshop on Computational Methods for Endangered Languages*, volume 1.

Conor Snoek, Dorothy Thunder, Kaidi Loo, Antti Arppe, Jordan Lachler, Sjur Moshagen, and Trond Trosterud. 2014. Modeling the noun morphology of plains cree. In *Proceedings of the 2014 Workshop on the Use of Computational Methods in the Study of Endangered Languages*, pages 34–42.

Tonya Stebbins. 2003. On the status of intermediate form-classes: Words, clitics, and affixes in Coast Tsimshian (Sm'algyax). *Linguistic Typology*, 7(3):383–415.

Lonny Strunk. 2020. *A Finite-State Morphological Analyzer for Central Alaskan Yup'Ik*. Ph.D. thesis, University of Washington.

Marie-Lucie Tarpent. 1987. *A Grammar of the Nisgha Language*. Ph.D. thesis, University of Victoria.

Ashish Vaswani, Noam Shazeer, Niki Parmar, Jakob Uszkoreit, Llion Jones, Aidan N Gomez, Lukasz Kaiser, and Illia Polosukhin. 2017. Attention is all you need. *arXiv preprint arXiv:1706.03762*.

# Comparative Error Analysis in Neural and Finite-state Models for Unsupervised Character-level Transduction

**Maria Ryskina**[1] **Eduard Hovy**[1] **Taylor Berg-Kirkpatrick**[2] **Matthew R. Gormley**[3]
[1]Language Technologies Institute, Carnegie Mellon University
[2]Computer Science and Engineering, University of California, San Diego
[3]Machine Learning Department, Carnegie Mellon University
mryskina@cs.cmu.edu hovy@cmu.edu
tberg@eng.ucsd.edu mgormley@cs.cmu.edu

**Abstract**

Traditionally, character-level transduction problems have been solved with finite-state models designed to encode structural and linguistic knowledge of the underlying process, whereas recent approaches rely on the power and flexibility of sequence-to-sequence models with attention. Focusing on the less explored unsupervised learning scenario, we compare the two model classes side by side and find that they tend to make different types of errors even when achieving comparable performance. We analyze the distributions of different error classes using two unsupervised tasks as testbeds: converting informally romanized text into the native script of its language (for Russian, Arabic, and Kannada) and translating between a pair of closely related languages (Serbian and Bosnian). Finally, we investigate how combining finite-state and sequence-to-sequence models at decoding time affects the output quantitatively and qualitatively.[1]

## 1 Introduction and prior work

Many natural language sequence transduction tasks, such as transliteration or grapheme-to-phoneme conversion, call for a character-level parameterization that reflects the linguistic knowledge of the underlying generative process. Character-level transduction approaches have even been shown to perform well for tasks that are not entirely character-level in nature, such as translating between related languages (Pourdamghani and Knight, 2017).

Weighted finite-state transducers (WFSTs) have traditionally been used for such character-level tasks (Knight and Graehl, 1998; Knight et al., 2006). Their structured formalization makes it easier to encode additional constraints, imposed either

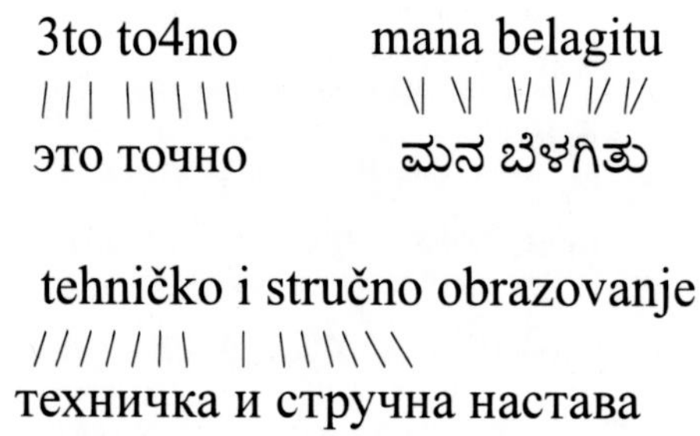


Figure 1: Parallel examples from our test sets for two character-level transduction tasks: converting informally romanized text to its original script (top; examples in Russian and Kannada) and translating between closely related languages (bottom; Bosnian–Serbian). Informal romanization is idiosyncratic and relies on both visual (ч → 4) and phonetic (т → t) character similarity, while translation is more standardized but not fully character-level due to grammatical and lexical differences ('настава' → 'obrazovanje') between the languages. The lines show character alignment between the source and target side where possible.

by the underlying linguistic process (e.g. monotonic character alignment) or by the probabilistic generative model (Markov assumption; Eisner, 2002). Their interpretability also facilitates the introduction of useful inductive bias, which is crucial for unsupervised training (Ravi and Knight, 2009; Ryskina et al., 2020).

Unsupervised neural sequence-to-sequence (seq2seq) architectures have also shown impressive performance on tasks like machine translation (Lample et al., 2018) and style transfer (Yang et al., 2018; He et al., 2020). These models are substantially more powerful than WFSTs, and they successfully learn the underlying patterns from

[1]Code will be published at https://github.com/ryskina/error-analysis-sigmorphon2021



*Proceedings of the Seventeenth SIGMORPHON Workshop on Computational Research in Phonetics, Phonology, and Morphology*, pages 198–211

monolingual data without any explicit information about the underlying generative process.

As the strengths of the two model classes differ, so do their weaknesses: the WFSTs and the seq2seq models are prone to different kinds of errors. On a higher level, it is explained by the structure–power trade-off: while the seq2seq models are better at recovering long-range dependencies and their outputs look less noisy, they also tend to insert and delete words arbitrarily because their alignments are unconstrained. We attribute the errors to the following aspects of the trade-off:

**Language modeling capacity:** the statistical character-level n-gram language models (LMs) utilized by finite-state approaches are much weaker than the RNN language models with unlimited left context. While a word-level LM can improve the performance of a WFST, it would also restrict the model's ability to handle out-of-vocabulary words.

**Controllability of learning:** more structured models allow us to ensure that the model does not attempt to learn patterns orthogonal to the underlying process. For example, domain imbalance between the monolingual corpora can cause the seq2seq models to exhibit unwanted style transfer effects like inserting frequent target side words arbitrarily.

**Search procedure:** WFSTs make it easy to perform exact maximum likelihood decoding via shortest-distance algorithm (Mohri, 2009). For the neural models trained using conventional methods, decoding strategies that optimize for the output likelihood (e.g. beam search with a large beam size) have been shown to be susceptible to favoring empty outputs (Stahlberg and Byrne, 2019) and generating repetitions (Holtzman et al., 2020).

Prior work on leveraging the strength of the two approaches proposes complex joint parameterizations, such as neural weighting of WFST arcs or paths (Rastogi et al., 2016; Lin et al., 2019) or encoding alignment constraints into the attention layer of seq2seq models (Aharoni and Goldberg, 2017; Wu et al., 2018; Wu and Cotterell, 2019; Makarov et al., 2017). We study whether performance can be improved with simpler decoding-time model combinations, reranking and product of experts, which have been used effectively for other model classes (Charniak and Johnson, 2005; Hieber and Riezler, 2015), evaluating on two unsupervised tasks: decipherment of informal romanization (Ryskina et al., 2020) and related language translation (Pourdamghani and Knight, 2017).

While there has been much error analysis for the WFST and seq2seq approaches separately, it largely focuses on the more common supervised case. We perform detailed side-by-side error analysis to draw high-level comparisons between finite-state and seq2seq models and investigate if the intuitions from prior work would transfer to the unsupervised transduction scenario.

## 2 Tasks

We compare the errors made by the finite-state and the seq2seq approaches by analyzing their performance on two unsupervised character-level transduction tasks: translating between closely related languages written in different alphabets and converting informally romanized text into its native script. Both tasks are illustrated in Figure 1.

### 2.1 Informal romanization

Informal romanization is an idiosyncratic transformation that renders a non-Latin-script language in Latin alphabet, extensively used online by speakers of Arabic (Darwish, 2014), Russian (Paulsen, 2014), and many Indic languages (Sowmya et al., 2010). Figure 1 shows examples of romanized Russian (top left) and Kannada (top right) sentences along with their "canonicalized" representations in Cyrillic and Kannada scripts respectively. Unlike official romanization systems such as pinyin, this type of transliteration is not standardized: character substitution choices vary between users and are based on the specific user's perception of how similar characters in different scripts are. Although the substitutions are primarily phonetic (e.g. Russian н /n/ $\rightarrow$ n), i.e. based on the pronunciation of a specific character in or out of context, users might also rely on visual similarity between glyphs (e.g. Russian ч /t͡ʃʲ/ $\rightarrow$ 4), especially when the associated phoneme cannot be easily mapped to a Latin-script grapheme (e.g. Arabic ع /ʕ/ $\rightarrow$ 3). To capture this variation, we view the task of decoding informal romanization as a many-to-many character-level decipherment problem.

The difficulty of deciphering romanization also depends on the type of the writing system the language traditionally uses. In alphabetic scripts, where grapheme-to-phoneme correspondence is mostly one-to-one, there tends to be a one-to-one monotonic alignment between characters in the romanized and native script sequences (Figure 1, top left). *Abjads* and *abugidas*, where graphemes correspond to consonants or consonant-vowel syllables, increasingly use many-to-one alignment in their romanization (Figure 1, top right), which makes learning the latent alignments, and therefore decoding, more challenging. In this work, we experiment with three languages spanning over three major types of writing systems—Russian (alphabetic), Arabic (abjad), and Kannada (abugida)—and compare how well-suited character-level models are for learning these varying alignment patterns.

### 2.2 Related language translation

As shown by Pourdamghani and Knight (2017) and Hauer et al. (2014), character-level models can be used effectively to translate between languages that are closely enough related to have only small lexical and grammatical differences, such as Serbian and Bosnian (Ljubešić and Klubička, 2014). We focus on this specific language pair and tie the languages to specific orthographies (Cyrillic for Serbian and Latin for Bosnian), approaching the task as an unsupervised orthography conversion problem. However, the transliteration framing of the translation problem is inherently limited since the task is not truly character-level in nature, as shown by the alignment lines in Figure 1 (bottom). Even the most accurate transliteration model will not be able to capture non-cognate word translations (Serbian 'настава' [nastava, 'education, teaching'] → Bosnian 'obrazovanje' ['education']) and the resulting discrepancies in morphological inflection (Serbian -а endings in adjectives agreeing with feminine 'настава' map to Bosnian -o representing agreement with neuter 'obrazovanje').

One major difference with the informal romanization task is the lack of the idiosyncratic orthography: the word spellings are now consistent across the data. However, since the character-level approach does not fully reflect the nature of the transformation, the model will still have to learn a many-to-many cipher with highly context-dependent character substitutions.

## 3 Data

Table 1 details the statistics of the splits used for all languages and tasks. Below we describe each dataset in detail, explaining the differences in data split sizes between languages. Additional preprocessing steps applied to all datasets are described in §3.4.[2]

### 3.1 Informal romanization

| | |
|---|---|
| **Source:** | de el menu:) |
| **Filtered:** | de el menu<...> |
| **Target:** | دي ألمنه<...> |
| **Gloss:** | 'This is the menu' |

Figure 2: A parallel example from the LDC BOLT Arabizi dataset, written in Latin script (source) and converted to Arabic (target) semi-manually. Some source-side segments (in red) are removed by annotators; we use the version without such segments (filtered) for our task. The annotators also standardize spacing on the target side, which results in difference with the source (in blue).

**Arabic** We use the LDC BOLT Phase 2 corpus (Bies et al., 2014; Song et al., 2014) for training and testing the Arabic transliteration models (Figure 2). The corpus consists of short SMS and chat in Egyptian Arabic represented using Latin script (*Arabizi*). The corpus is fully parallel: each message is automatically converted into the standardized dialectal Arabic orthography (CODA; Habash et al., 2012) and then manually corrected by human annotators. We split and preprocess the data according to Ryskina et al. (2020), discarding the target (native script) and source (romanized) parallel sentences to create the source and target monolingual training splits respectively.

**Russian** We use the romanized Russian dataset collected by Ryskina et al. (2020), augmented with the monolingual Cyrillic data from the Taiga corpus of Shavrina and Shapovalova (2017) (Figure 3). The romanized data is split into training, validation, and test portions, and all validation and test sentences are converted to Cyrillic by native speaker annotators. Both the romanized and the native-script sequences are collected from public posts and comments on a Russian social network vk.com, and they are on average 3 times longer than the messages in the Arabic dataset (Table 1). However, although both sides were scraped from the same online platform, the relevant Taiga data is collected primarily from political discussion groups, so there is still a substantial domain mismatch between the source and target sides of the data.

[2] Links to download the corpora and other data sources discussed in this section can be found in Appendix A.

| | Train (source) | | Train (target) | | Validation | | Test | |
|---|---|---|---|---|---|---|---|---|
| | Sent. | Char. | Sent. | Char. | Sent. | Char. | Sent. | Char. |
| Romanized Arabic | 5K | 104K | 49K | 935K | 301 | 8K | 1K | 20K |
| Romanized Russian | 5K | 319K | 307K | 111M | 227 | 15K | 1K | 72K |
| Romanized Kannada | 10K | 1M | 679K | 64M | 100 | 11K | 100 | 10K |
| Serbian→Bosnian | 160K | 9M | 136K | 9M | 16K | 923K | 100 | 9K |
| Bosnian→Serbian | 136K | 9M | 160K | 9M | 16K | 908K | 100 | 10K |

Table 1: Dataset splits for each task and language. The source and target train data are monolingual, and the validation and test sentences are parallel. For the informal romanization task, the source and target sides correspond to the Latin and the original script respectively. For the translation task, the source and target sides correspond to source and target languages. The validation and test character statistics are reported for the source side.

| | Annotated |
|---|---|
| **Source:** | proishodit s prirodoy 4to to very very bad |
| **Filtered:** | proishodit s prirodoy 4to to <...> |
| **Target:** | происходит с природой что-то <...> |
| **Gloss:** | 'Something very very bad is happening to the environment' |
| | **Monolingual** |
| **Source:** | — |
| **Target:** | это видеоролики со съезда партии "Единая Россия" |
| **Gloss:** | 'These are the videos from the "United Russia" party congress' |

Figure 3: **Top:** A parallel example from the romanized Russian dataset. We use the filtered version of the romanized (source) sequences, removing the segments the annotators were unable to convert to Cyrillic, e.g. code-switched phrases (in red). The annotators also standardize minor spelling variation such as hyphenation (in blue). **Bottom:** a monolingual Cyrillic example from the `vk.com` portion of the Taiga corpus, which mostly consists of comments in political discussion groups.

| | |
|---|---|
| **Target:** | ಮೂಲ ಸಾಕೆಟ್‌ನಲ್ಲಿ DDR3ಯನ್ನು ಬಳಸಲು |
| **Source:** | moola saaketnalli ddr3yannu balasalu |
| **Gloss:** | 'to use DDR3 in the source circuit' |

Figure 4: A parallel example from the Kannada portion of the Dakshina dataset. The Kannada script data (target) is scraped from Wikipedia and manually converted to Latin (source) by human annotators. Foreign target-side characters (in red) get preserved in the annotation but our preprocessing replaces them with UNK on the target side.

| | |
|---|---|
| **Serbian:** | свако има право на живот, слободу и безбедност личности. |
| **Bosnian:** | svako ima pravo na život, slobodu i osobnu sigurnost. |
| **Gloss:** | 'Everyone has the right to life, liberty and security of person.' |

Figure 5: A parallel example from the Serbian–Cyrillic and Bosnian–Latin UDHR. The sequences are not entirely parallel on character level due to paraphrases and non-cognate translations (in blue).

**Kannada** Our Kannada data (Figure 4) is taken from the Dakshina dataset (Roark et al., 2020), a large collection of native-script text from Wikipedia for 12 South Asian languages. Unlike the Russian and Arabic data, the romanized portion of Dakshina is not scraped directly from the users' online communication, but instead elicited from native speakers given the native-script sequences. Because of this, all romanized sentences in the data are parallel: we allocate most of them to the source side training data, discarding their original script counterparts, and split the remaining annotated ones between validation and test.

### 3.2 Related language translation

Following prior work (Pourdamghani and Knight, 2017; Yang et al., 2018; He et al., 2020), we train our unsupervised models on the monolingual data from the Leipzig corpora (Goldhahn et al., 2012). We reuse the non-parallel training and synthetic parallel validation splits of Yang et al. (2018), who generated their parallel data using the Google Translation API. Rather than using their synthetic test set, we opt to test on natural parallel data from the Universal Declaration of Human Rights (UDHR), following Pourdamghani and Knight (2017).

We manually sentence-align the Serbian–

Cyrillic and Bosnian–Latin declaration texts and follow the preprocessing guidelines of Pourdamghani and Knight (2017). Although we strive to approximate the training and evaluation setup of their work for fair comparison, there are some discrepancies: for example, our manual alignment of UDHR yields 100 sentence pairs compared to 104 of Pourdamghani and Knight (2017). We use the data to train the translation models in both directions, simply switching the source and target sides from Serbian to Bosnian and vice versa.

### 3.3 Inductive bias

As discussed in §1, the WFST models are less powerful than the seq2seq models; however, they are also more structured, which we can use to introduce inductive bias to aid unsupervised training. Following Ryskina et al. (2020), we introduce informative priors on character substitution operations (for a description of the WFST parameterization, see §4.1). The priors reflect the visual and phonetic similarity between characters in different alphabets and are sourced from human-curated resources built with the same concepts of similarity in mind. For all tasks and languages, we collect phonetically similar character pairs from the phonetic keyboard layouts (or, in case of the translation task, from the default Serbian keyboard layout, which is phonetic in nature due to the dual orthography standard of the language). We also add some visually similar character pairs by automatically pairing all symbols that occur in both source and target alphabets (same Unicode codepoints). For Russian, which exhibits a greater degree of visual similarity than Arabic or Kannada, we also make use of the Unicode confusables list (different Unicode codepoints but same or similar glyphs).[3]

It should be noted that these automatically generated informative priors also contain noise: keyboard layouts have spurious mappings because each symbol must be assigned to exactly one key in the QWERTY layout, and Unicode-constrained visual mappings might prevent the model from learning correspondences between punctuation symbols (e.g. Arabic question mark ؟ → ?).

### 3.4 Preprocessing

We lowercase and segment all sequences into characters as defined by Unicode codepoints, so diacritics and non-printing characters like ZWJ are also treated as separate vocabulary items. To filter out foreign or archaic characters and rare diacritics, we restrict the alphabets to characters that cover 99% of the monolingual training data. After that, we add any standard alphabetical characters and numerals that have been filtered out back into the source and target alphabets. All remaining filtered characters are replaced with a special UNK symbol in all splits except for the target-side test.

## 4 Methods

We perform our analysis using the finite-state and seq2seq models from prior work and experiment with two joint decoding strategies, reranking and product of experts. Implementation details and hyperparameters are described in Appendix B.

### 4.1 Base models

Our finite-state model is the WFST cascade introduced by Ryskina et al. (2020). The model is composed of a character-level n-gram language model and a script conversion transducer (emission model), which supports one-to-one character substitutions, insertions, and deletions. Character operation weights in the emission model are parameterized with multinomial distributions, and similar character mappings (§3.3) are used to create Dirichlet priors on the emission parameters. To avoid marginalizing over sequences of infinite length, a fixed limit is set on the delay of any path (the difference between the cumulative number of insertions and deletions at any timestep). Ryskina et al. (2020) train the WFST using stochastic stepwise EM (Liang and Klein, 2009), marginalizing over all possible target sequences and their alignments with the given source sequence. To speed up training, we modify their training procedure towards 'hard EM': given a source sequence, we predict the most probable target sequence under the model, marginalize over alignments and then update the parameters. Although the unsupervised WFST training is still slow, the stepwise training procedure is designed to converge using fewer data points, so we choose to train the WFST model only on the 1,000 shortest source-side training sequences (500 for Kannada).

Our default seq2seq model is the unsupervised neural machine translation (UNMT) model of Lample et al. (2018, 2019) in the parameterization of He et al. (2020). The model consists of an

[3]Links to the keyboard layouts and the confusables list can be found in Appendix A.

| | Arabic | | | Russian | | | Kannada | | |
|---|---|---|---|---|---|---|---|---|---|
| | CER | WER | BLEU | CER | WER | BLEU | CER | WER | BLEU |
| WFST | .405 | .86 | 2.3 | .202 | .58 | 14.8 | .359 | **.71** | 12.5 |
| Seq2Seq | .571 | .85 | 4.0 | .229 | **.38** | **48.3** | .559 | .79 | 11.3 |
| Reranked WFST | **.398** | .85 | 2.8 | .195 | .57 | 16.1 | **.358** | **.71** | 12.5 |
| Reranked Seq2Seq | .538 | **.82** | **4.6** | .216 | .39 | 45.6 | .545 | .78 | **12.6** |
| Product of experts | .470 | .88 | 2.5 | **.178** | .50 | 22.9 | .543 | .93 | 7.0 |

Table 2: Character and word error rates (lower is better) and BLEU scores (higher is better) for the romanization decipherment task. **Bold** indicates best per column. Model combinations mostly interpolate between the base models' scores, although reranking yields minor improvements in character-level and word-level metrics for the WFST and seq2seq respectively. **Note:** base model results are not intended as a direct comparison between the WFST and seq2seq, since they are trained on different amounts of data.

| | srp→bos | | | bos→srp | | |
|---|---|---|---|---|---|---|
| | CER | WER | BLEU | CER | WER | BLEU |
| WFST | **.314** | .50 | 25.3 | .319 | .52 | 25.5 |
| Seq2Seq | .375 | .49 | 34.5 | .395 | .49 | 36.3 |
| Reranked WFST | **.314** | .49 | 26.3 | **.317** | .50 | 28.1 |
| Reranked Seq2Seq | .376 | **.48** | 35.1 | .401 | **.47** | 37.0 |
| Product of experts | .329 | .54 | 24.4 | .352 | .66 | 20.6 |
| (Pourdamghani and Knight, 2017) | — | — | **42.3** | — | — | **39.2** |
| (He et al., 2020) | .657 | .81 | 5.6 | .693 | .83 | 4.7 |

Table 3: Character and word error rates (lower is better) and BLEU scores (higher is better) for the related language translation task. **Bold** indicates best per column. The WFST and the seq2seq have comparable CER and WER despite the WFST being trained on up to 160x less source-side data (§4.1). While none of our models achieve the scores reported by Pourdamghani and Knight (2017), they all substantially outperform the subword-level model of He et al. (2020). **Note:** base model results are not intended as a direct comparison between the WFST and seq2seq, since they are trained on different amounts of data.

LSTM (Hochreiter and Schmidhuber, 1997) encoder and decoder with attention, trained to map sentences from each domain into a shared latent space. Using a combined objective, the UNMT model is trained to denoise, translate in both directions, and discriminate between the latent representation of sequences from different domains. Since the sufficient amount of balanced data is crucial for the UNMT performance, we train the seq2seq model on all available data on both source and target sides. Additionally, the seq2seq model decides on early stopping by evaluating on a small parallel validation set, which our WFST model does not have access to.

The WFST model treats the target and source training data differently, using the former to train the language model and the latter for learning the emission parameters, while the UNMT model is trained to translate in both directions simultaneously. Therefore, we reuse the same seq2seq model for both directions of the translation task, but train a separate finite-state model for each direction.

### 4.2 Model combinations

The simplest way to combine two independently trained models is reranking: using one model to produce a list of candidates and rescoring them according to another model. To generate candidates with a WFST, we apply the $n$–shortest paths algorithm (Mohri and Riley, 2002). It should be noted that the $n$–best list might contain duplicates since each path represents a specific source–target character alignment. The length constraints encoded in the WFST also restrict its capacity as a reranker: beam search in the UNMT model may produce hypotheses too short or long to have a non-zero

| Input | свако има право да слободно учествује у културном животу заједнице, да ужива у уметности и да учествује у научном напретку и у добробити која отуда проистиче. |
|---|---|
| Ground truth | svako ima pravo da slobodno sudjeluje u kulturnom životu zajednice, da uživa u umjetnosti i da učestvuje u znanstvenom napretku i u njegovim koristima. |
| WFST | svako ima pravo da slobodno učestvuje u kulturnom životu sjednice , da uživa u metnosti i da učestvuje u naučnom napretku i u dobrobiti koja otuda pr ističe . |
| Reranked WFST | svako ima pravo da slobodno učestvuje u kulturnom životu sjednice , da uživa u metnosti i da učestvuje u naučnom napretku i u dobrobiti koja otuda pr ističe . |
| Seq2Seq | svako ima pravo da slobodno učestvuje u kulturnom životu zajednice , da učestvuje u naučnom napretku i u dobrobiti koja otuda proističe . |
| Reranked Seq2Seq | svako ima pravo da slobodno učestvuje u kulturnom životu zajednice , da uživa u umjetnosti i da učestvuje u naučnom napretku i u dobrobiti koja otuda proističe |
| Product of experts | svako ima pravo da slobodno učestvuje u kulturnom za u sajednice , da živa u umjetnosti i da učestvuje u naučnom napretku i u dobroj i koja otuda proisti |
| Subword Seq2Seq | sami ima pravo da slobodno utiče na srpskom nivou vlasti da razgovaraju u bosne i da djeluje u međunarodnom turizmu i na buducnosti koja muža decisno . |

Table 4: Different model outputs for a srp→bos translation example. Prediction errors are highlighted in red. Correctly transliterated segments that do not match the ground truth (e.g. due to paraphrasing) are shown in yellow. Here the WFST errors are substitutions or deletions of individual characters, while the seq2seq drops entire words from the input (§5 #4). The latter problem is solved by reranking with a WFST for this example. The seq2seq model with subword tokenization (He et al., 2020) produces mostly hallucinated output (§5 #2). Example outputs for all other datasets can be found in the Appendix.

probability under the WFST.

Our second approach is a product-of-experts-style joint decoding strategy (Hinton, 2002): we perform beam search on the WFST lattice, reweighting the arcs with the output distribution of the seq2seq decoder at the corresponding timestep. For each partial hypothesis, we keep track of the WFST state $s$ and the partial input and output sequences $x_{1:k}$ and $y_{1:t}$.[4] When traversing an arc with input label $i \in \{x_{k+1}, \epsilon\}$ and output label $o$, we multiply the arc weight by the probability of the neural model outputting $o$ as the next character: $p_{\text{seq2seq}}(y_{t+1} = o | x, y_{1:t})$. Transitions with $o = \epsilon$ (i.e. deletions) are not rescored by the seq2seq. We group hypotheses by their consumed input length $k$ and select $n$ best extensions at each timestep.

### 4.3 Additional baselines

For the translation task, we also compare to prior unsupervised approaches of different granularity: the deep generative style transfer model of He et al. (2020) and the character- and word-level WFST decipherment model of Pourdamghani and Knight (2017). The former is trained on the same training set tokenized into subword units (Sennrich et al., 2016), and we evaluate it on our UDHR test set for fair comparison. While the train and test data of Pourdamghani and Knight (2017) also use the same respective sources, we cannot account for tokenization differences that could affect the scores reported by the authors.

[4]Due to insertions and deletions in the emission model, $k$ and $t$ might differ; epsilon symbols are not counted.

## 5 Results and analysis

Tables 2 and 3 present our evaluation of the two base models and three decoding-time model combinations on the romanization decipherment and related language translation tasks respectively. For each experiment, we report character error rate, word error rate, and BLEU (see Appendix C). The results for the base models support what we show later in this section: the seq2seq model is more likely to recover words correctly (higher BLEU, lower WER), while the WFST is more faithful on character level and avoids word-level substitution errors (lower CER). Example predictions can be found in Table 4 and in the Appendix.

Our further qualitative and quantitative findings are summarized in the following high-level take-aways:

**#1: Model combinations still suffer from search issues.** We would expect the combined decoding to discourage all errors common under one model but not the other, improving the performance by leveraging the strengths of both model classes. However, as Tables 2 and 3 show, they instead

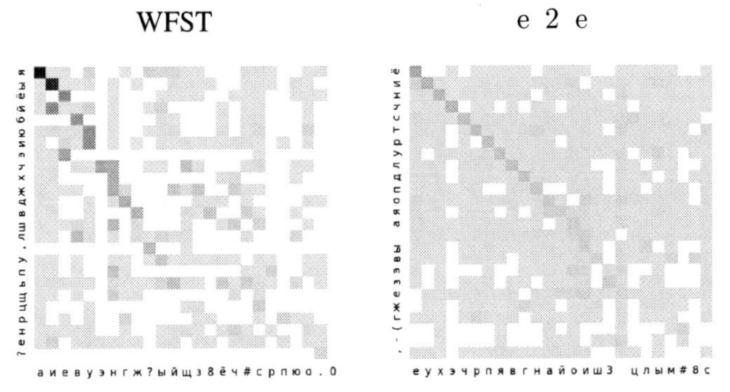


Figure 6: Highest-density submatrices of the two base models' character confusion matrices, computed in the Russian romanization task. White cells represent zero elements. The WFST confusion matrix (left) is noticeably sparser than the seq2seq one (right), indicating more repetitive errors. # symbol stands for UNK.

mostly interpolate between the scores of the two base models. In the reranking experiments, we find that this is often due to the same base model error (e.g. the seq2seq model hallucinating a word mid-sentence) repeating across all the hypotheses in the final beam. This suggests that successful reranking would require a much larger beam size or a diversity-promoting search mechanism.

Interestingly, we observe that although adding a reranker on top of a decoder does improve performance slightly, the gain is only in terms of the metrics that the base decoder is already strong at—character-level for reranked WFST and word-level for reranked seq2seq—at the expense of the other scores. Overall, none of our decoding strategies achieves best results across the board, and no model combination substantially outperforms both base models in any metric.

**#2: Character tokenization boosts performance of the neural model.** In the past, UNMT-style models have been applied to various unsupervised sequence transduction problems. However, since these models were designed to operate on word or subword level, prior work assumes the same tokenization is necessary. We show that for the tasks allowing character-level framing, such models in fact respond extremely well to character input.

Table 3 compares the UNMT model trained on characters with the seq2seq style transfer model of He et al. (2020) trained on subword units. The original paper shows improvement over the UNMT baseline in the same setting, but simply switching to character-level tokenization without any other changes results in a 30 BLEU points gain for either direction. This suggests that the tokenization choice could act as an inductive bias for seq2seq models, and character-level framing could be useful even for tasks that are not truly character-level.

This observation also aligns with the findings of the recent work on language modeling complexity (Park et al., 2021; Mielke et al., 2019). For many languages, including several Slavic ones related to the Serbian–Bosnian pair, a character-level language model yields lower surprisal than the one trained on BPE units, suggesting that the effect might also be explained by the character tokenization making the language easier to language-model.

**#3: WFST model makes more repetitive errors.** Although two of our evaluation metrics, CER and WER, are based on edit distance, they do not distinguish between the different types of edits (substitutions, insertions and deletions). Breaking them down by the edit operation, we find that while both models favor substitutions on both word and character levels, insertions and deletions are more frequent under the neural model (43% vs. 30% of all edits on the Russian romanization task). We also find that the character substitution choices of the neural model are more context-dependent: while the total counts of substitution errors for the two models are comparable, the WFST is more likely to repeat the same few substitutions per character type. This is illustrated by Figure 6, which visualizes the most populated submatrices of the confusion matrices for the same task as heatmaps. The WFST confusion matrix is noticeably more sparse, with the same few substitutions occurring much more frequently than others: for example, WFST often mistakes я for a and rarely for other characters, while the neural model's substitutions of я are distributed closer to uniform. This suggests that the WFST errors might be easier to correct with rule-based postprocessing. Interestingly, we did not observe the same effect for the translation task, likely due to a more constrained nature of the orthography conversion.

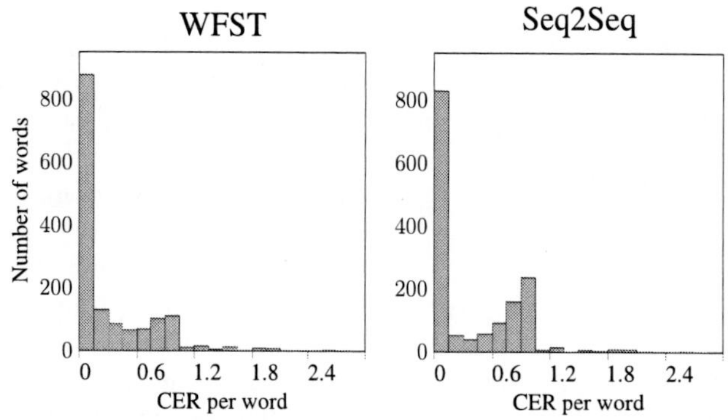


Figure 7: Character error rate per word for the WFST (left) and seq2seq (right) bos→srp translation outputs. The predictions are segmented using Moses tokenizer (Koehn et al., 2007) and aligned to ground truth with word-level edit distance. The increased frequency of CER=1 for the seq2seq model as compared to the WFST indicates that it replaces entire words more often.

**#4: Neural model is more sensitive to data distribution shifts.** The language model aiming to replicate its training data distribution could cause the output to deviate from the input significantly. This could be an artifact of a domain shift, such as in Russian, where the LM training data came from a political discussion forum: the seq2seq model frequently predicts unrelated domain-specific proper names in place of very common Russian words, e.g. жизнь [žizn, 'life'] → Зюганов [Zjuganov, 'Zyuganov (politician's last name)'] or это [èto, 'this'] → Единая Россия [Edinaja Rossija, 'United Russia (political party)'], presumably distracted by the shared first character in the romanized version. To quantify the effect of a mismatch between the train and test data distributions in this case, we inspect the most common word-level substitutions under each decoding strategy, looking at all substitution errors covered by the 1,000 most frequent substitution 'types' (ground truth–prediction word pairs) under the respective decoder. We find that 25% of the seq2seq substitution errors fall into this category, as compared to merely 3% for the WFST—notable given the relative proportion of in-vocabulary words in the models' outputs (89% for UNMT vs. 65% for WFST).

Comparing the error rate distribution across output words for the translation task also supports this observation. As can be seen from Figure 7, the seq2seq model is likely to either predict the word correctly (CER of 0) or entirely wrong (CER of 1), while the the WFST more often predicts the word partially correctly—examples in Table 4 illustrate this as well. We also see this in the Kannada outputs: WFST typically gets all the consonants right but makes mistakes in the vowels, while the seq2seq tends to replace the entire word.

## 6 Conclusion

We perform comparative error analysis in finite-state and seq2seq models and their combinations for two unsupervised character-level tasks, informal romanization decipherment and related language translation. We find that the two model types tend towards different errors: seq2seq models are more prone to word-level errors caused by distributional shifts while WFSTs produce more character-level noise despite the hard alignment constraints.

Despite none of our simple decoding-time combinations substantially outperforming the base models, we believe that combining neural and finite-state models to harness their complementary advantages is a promising research direction. Such combinations might involve biasing seq2seq models towards WFST-like behavior via pretraining or directly encoding constraints such as hard alignment or monotonicity into their parameterization (Wu et al., 2018; Wu and Cotterell, 2019). Although recent work has shown that the Transformer can learn to perform character-level transduction without such biases in a supervised setting (Wu et al., 2021), exploiting the structured nature of the task could be crucial for making up for the lack of large parallel corpora in low-data and/or unsupervised scenarios. We hope that our analysis provides insight into leveraging the strengths of the two approaches for modeling character-level phenomena in the absence of parallel data.

## Acknowledgments

The authors thank Badr Abdullah, Deepak Gopinath, Junxian He, Shruti Rijhwani, and Stas Kashepava for helpful discussion, and the anonymous reviewers for their valuable feedback.

## References


Roee Aharoni and Yoav Goldberg. 2017. Morphological inflection generation with hard monotonic attention. In *Proceedings of the 55th Annual Meeting of the Association for Computational Linguistics (Volume 1: Long Papers)*, pages 2004–2015, Vancouver, Canada. Association for Computational Linguistics.

Cyril Allauzen, Michael Riley, Johan Schalkwyk, Wojciech Skut, and Mehryar Mohri. 2007. OpenFst: A general and efficient weighted finite-state transducer library. In *Proceedings of the Ninth International Conference on Implementation and Application of Automata, (CIAA 2007)*, volume 4783 of *Lecture Notes in Computer Science*, pages 11–23. Springer. `http://www.openfst.org`.

Sowmya V. B., Monojit Choudhury, Kalika Bali, Tirthankar Dasgupta, and Anupam Basu. 2010. Resource creation for training and testing of transliteration systems for Indian languages. In *Proceedings of the Seventh International Conference on Language Resources and Evaluation (LREC'10)*, Valletta, Malta. European Language Resources Association (ELRA).

Ann Bies, Zhiyi Song, Mohamed Maamouri, Stephen Grimes, Haejoong Lee, Jonathan Wright, Stephanie Strassel, Nizar Habash, Ramy Eskander, and Owen Rambow. 2014. Transliteration of Arabizi into Arabic orthography: Developing a parallel annotated Arabizi-Arabic script SMS/chat corpus. In *Proceedings of the EMNLP 2014 Workshop on Arabic Natural Language Processing (ANLP)*, pages 93–103, Doha, Qatar. Association for Computational Linguistics.

Eugene Charniak and Mark Johnson. 2005. Coarse-to-fine n-best parsing and MaxEnt discriminative reranking. In *Proceedings of the 43rd Annual Meeting of the Association for Computational Linguistics (ACL'05)*, pages 173–180, Ann Arbor, Michigan. Association for Computational Linguistics.

Kareem Darwish. 2014. Arabizi detection and conversion to Arabic. In *Proceedings of the EMNLP 2014 Workshop on Arabic Natural Language Processing (ANLP)*, pages 217–224, Doha, Qatar. Association for Computational Linguistics.

Jason Eisner. 2002. Parameter estimation for probabilistic finite-state transducers. In *Proceedings of the 40th Annual Meeting of the Association for Computational Linguistics*, pages 1–8, Philadelphia, Pennsylvania, USA. Association for Computational Linguistics.

Dirk Goldhahn, Thomas Eckart, and Uwe Quasthoff. 2012. Building large monolingual dictionaries at the Leipzig corpora collection: From 100 to 200 languages. In *Proceedings of the Eighth International Conference on Language Resources and Evaluation (LREC'12)*, pages 759–765, Istanbul, Turkey. European Language Resources Association (ELRA).

Kyle Gorman. 2016. Pynini: A Python library for weighted finite-state grammar compilation. In *Proceedings of the SIGFSM Workshop on Statistical NLP and Weighted Automata*, pages 75–80, Berlin, Germany. Association for Computational Linguistics.

Nizar Habash, Mona Diab, and Owen Rambow. 2012. Conventional orthography for dialectal Arabic. In *Proceedings of the Eighth International Conference on Language Resources and Evaluation (LREC'12)*, pages 711–718, Istanbul, Turkey. European Language Resources Association (ELRA).

Bradley Hauer, Ryan Hayward, and Grzegorz Kondrak. 2014. Solving substitution ciphers with combined language models. In *Proceedings of COLING 2014, the 25th International Conference on Computational Linguistics: Technical Papers*, pages 2314–2325, Dublin, Ireland. Dublin City University and Association for Computational Linguistics.

Junxian He, Xinyi Wang, Graham Neubig, and Taylor Berg-Kirkpatrick. 2020. A probabilistic formulation of unsupervised text style transfer. In *International Conference on Learning Representations*.

Felix Hieber and Stefan Riezler. 2015. Bag-of-words forced decoding for cross-lingual information retrieval. In *Proceedings of the 2015 Conference of the North American Chapter of the Association for Computational Linguistics: Human Language Technologies*, pages 1172–1182, Denver, Colorado. Association for Computational Linguistics.

G. E. Hinton. 2002. Training products of experts by minimizing contrastive divergence. *Neural Computation*, 14(8):1771–1800.

Sepp Hochreiter and Jürgen Schmidhuber. 1997. Long short-term memory. *Neural computation*, 9(8):1735–1780.

Ari Holtzman, Jan Buys, Li Du, Maxwell Forbes, and Yejin Choi. 2020. The curious case of neural text degeneration. In *International Conference on Learning Representations*.

Cibu Johny, Lawrence Wolf-Sonkin, Alexander Gutkin, and Brian Roark. 2021. Finite-state script normalization and processing utilities: The Nisaba Brahmic library. In *Proceedings of the 16th Conference of the European Chapter of the Association for Computational Linguistics: System Demonstrations*, pages 14–23, Online. Association for Computational Linguistics.

Kevin Knight and Jonathan Graehl. 1998. Machine transliteration. *Computational Linguistics*, 24(4):599–612.

Kevin Knight, Anish Nair, Nishit Rathod, and Kenji Yamada. 2006. Unsupervised analysis for decipherment problems. In *Proceedings of the COLING/ACL 2006 Main Conference Poster Sessions*, pages 499–506, Sydney, Australia. Association for Computational Linguistics.

Philipp Koehn, Hieu Hoang, Alexandra Birch, Chris Callison-Burch, Marcello Federico, Nicola Bertoldi, Brooke Cowan, Wade Shen, Christine Moran, Richard Zens, Chris Dyer, Ondřej Bojar, Alexandra Constantin, and Evan Herbst. 2007. Moses: Open source toolkit for statistical machine translation. In *Proceedings of the 45th Annual Meeting of the Association for Computational Linguistics Companion Volume Proceedings of the Demo and Poster Sessions*, pages 177–180, Prague, Czech Republic. Association for Computational Linguistics.

Guillaume Lample, Alexis Conneau, Ludovic Denoyer, and Marc'Aurelio Ranzato. 2018. Unsupervised machine translation using monolingual corpora only. In *International Conference on Learning Representations*.

Guillaume Lample, Sandeep Subramanian, Eric Smith, Ludovic Denoyer, Marc'Aurelio Ranzato, and Y-Lan Boureau. 2019. Multiple-attribute text rewriting. In *International Conference on Learning Representations*.

Percy Liang and Dan Klein. 2009. Online EM for unsupervised models. In *Proceedings of Human Language Technologies: The 2009 Annual Conference of the North American Chapter of the Association for Computational Linguistics*, pages 611–619, Boulder, Colorado. Association for Computational Linguistics.

Chu-Cheng Lin, Hao Zhu, Matthew R. Gormley, and Jason Eisner. 2019. Neural finite-state transducers: Beyond rational relations. In *Proceedings of the 2019 Conference of the North American Chapter of the Association for Computational Linguistics: Human Language Technologies, Volume 1 (Long and Short Papers)*, pages 272–283, Minneapolis, Minnesota. Association for Computational Linguistics.

Nikola Ljubešić and Filip Klubička. 2014. {bs,hr,sr}WaC - web corpora of Bosnian, Croatian and Serbian. In *Proceedings of the 9th Web as Corpus Workshop (WaC-9)*, pages 29–35, Gothenburg, Sweden. Association for Computational Linguistics.

Peter Makarov, Tatiana Ruzsics, and Simon Clematide. 2017. Align and copy: UZH at SIGMORPHON 2017 shared task for morphological reinflection. In *Proceedings of the CoNLL SIGMORPHON 2017 Shared Task: Universal Morphological Reinflection*, pages 49–57, Vancouver. Association for Computational Linguistics.

Sabrina J. Mielke, Ryan Cotterell, Kyle Gorman, Brian Roark, and Jason Eisner. 2019. What kind of language is hard to language-model? In *Proceedings of the 57th Annual Meeting of the Association for Computational Linguistics*, pages 4975–4989, Florence, Italy. Association for Computational Linguistics.

Mehryar Mohri. 2009. Weighted automata algorithms. In *Handbook of weighted automata*, pages 213–254. Springer.

Mehryar Mohri and Michael Riley. 2002. An efficient algorithm for the n-best-strings problem. In *Seventh International Conference on Spoken Language Processing*.

Kishore Papineni, Salim Roukos, Todd Ward, and Wei-Jing Zhu. 2002. BLEU: A method for automatic evaluation of machine translation. In *Proceedings of the 40th Annual Meeting of the Association for Computational Linguistics*, pages 311–318, Philadelphia, Pennsylvania, USA. Association for Computational Linguistics.

Hyunji Hayley Park, Katherine J. Zhang, Coleman Haley, Kenneth Steimel, Han Liu, and Lane Schwartz. 2021. Morphology matters: A multilingual language modeling analysis. *Transactions of the Association for Computational Linguistics*, 9:261–276.

Martin Paulsen. 2014. Translit: Computer-mediated digraphia on the Runet. *Digital Russia: The Language, Culture and Politics of New Media Communication*.

Nima Pourdamghani and Kevin Knight. 2017. Deciphering related languages. In *Proceedings of the 2017 Conference on Empirical Methods in Natural Language Processing*, pages 2513–2518, Copenhagen, Denmark. Association for Computational Linguistics.

Pushpendre Rastogi, Ryan Cotterell, and Jason Eisner. 2016. Weighting finite-state transductions with neural context. In *Proceedings of the 2016 Conference of the North American Chapter of the Association for Computational Linguistics: Human Language Technologies*, pages 623–633, San Diego, California. Association for Computational Linguistics.

Sujith Ravi and Kevin Knight. 2009. Learning phoneme mappings for transliteration without parallel data. In *Proceedings of Human Language Technologies: The 2009 Annual Conference of the North American Chapter of the Association for Computational Linguistics*, pages 37–45, Boulder, Colorado. Association for Computational Linguistics.

Brian Roark, Richard Sproat, Cyril Allauzen, Michael Riley, Jeffrey Sorensen, and Terry Tai. 2012. The OpenGrm open-source finite-state grammar software libraries. In *Proceedings of the ACL 2012 System Demonstrations*, pages 61–66, Jeju Island, Korea. Association for Computational Linguistics.

Brian Roark, Lawrence Wolf-Sonkin, Christo Kirov, Sabrina J. Mielke, Cibu Johny, Isin Demirsahin, and Keith Hall. 2020. Processing South Asian languages written in the Latin script: The Dakshina dataset. In *Proceedings of the 12th Language Resources and Evaluation Conference*, pages 2413–2423, Marseille, France. European Language Resources Association.

Maria Ryskina, Matthew R. Gormley, and Taylor Berg-Kirkpatrick. 2020. Phonetic and visual priors for decipherment of informal Romanization. In *Proceedings of the 58th Annual Meeting of the Association for Computational Linguistics*, pages 8308–8319, Online. Association for Computational Linguistics.

Rico Sennrich, Barry Haddow, and Alexandra Birch. 2016. Neural machine translation of rare words with subword units. In *Proceedings of the 54th Annual Meeting of the Association for Computational Linguistics (Volume 1: Long Papers)*, pages 1715–1725, Berlin, Germany. Association for Computational Linguistics.

Tatiana Shavrina and Olga Shapovalova. 2017. To the methodology of corpus construction for machine learning: Taiga syntax tree corpus and parser. In *Proc. CORPORA 2017 International Conference*, pages 78–84, St. Petersburg.

Zhiyi Song, Stephanie Strassel, Haejoong Lee, Kevin Walker, Jonathan Wright, Jennifer Garland, Dana Fore, Brian Gainor, Preston Cabe, Thomas Thomas, Brendan Callahan, and Ann Sawyer. 2014. Collecting natural SMS and chat conversations in multiple languages: The BOLT phase 2 corpus. In *Proceedings of the Ninth International Conference on Language Resources and Evaluation (LREC'14)*, pages 1699–1704, Reykjavik, Iceland. European Language Resources Association (ELRA).

Felix Stahlberg and Bill Byrne. 2019. On NMT search errors and model errors: Cat got your tongue? In *Proceedings of the 2019 Conference on Empirical Methods in Natural Language Processing and the 9th International Joint Conference on Natural Language Processing (EMNLP-IJCNLP)*, pages 3356–3362, Hong Kong, China. Association for Computational Linguistics.

Shijie Wu and Ryan Cotterell. 2019. Exact hard monotonic attention for character-level transduction. In *Proceedings of the 57th Annual Meeting of the Association for Computational Linguistics*, pages 1530–1537, Florence, Italy. Association for Computational Linguistics.

Shijie Wu, Ryan Cotterell, and Mans Hulden. 2021. Applying the transformer to character-level transduction. In *Proceedings of the 16th Conference of the European Chapter of the Association for Computational Linguistics: Main Volume*, pages 1901–1907, Online. Association for Computational Linguistics.

Shijie Wu, Pamela Shapiro, and Ryan Cotterell. 2018. Hard non-monotonic attention for character-level transduction. In *Proceedings of the 2018 Conference on Empirical Methods in Natural Language Processing*, pages 4425–4438, Brussels, Belgium. Association for Computational Linguistics.

Zichao Yang, Zhiting Hu, Chris Dyer, Eric P. Xing, and Taylor Berg-Kirkpatrick. 2018. Unsupervised text style transfer using language models as discriminators. In *NeurIPS*, pages 7298–7309.

## A Data download links

The romanized Russian and Arabic data and preprocessing scripts can be downloaded here. This repository also contains the relevant portion of the Taiga dataset, which can be downloaded in full at this link. The romanized Kannada data was downloaded from the Dakshina dataset.

The scripts to download the Serbian and Bosnian Leipzig corpora data can be found here. The UDHR texts were collected from the corresponding pages: Serbian, Bosnian.

The keyboard layouts used to construct the phonetic priors are collected from the following sources: Arabic 1, Arabic 2, Russian, Kannada, Serbian. The Unicode confusables list used for the Russian visual prior can be found here.

## B Implementation

**WFST** We reuse the unsupervised WFST implementation of Ryskina et al. (2020),[5] which utilizes the OpenFst (Allauzen et al., 2007) and OpenGrm (Roark et al., 2012) libraries. We use the default hyperparameter settings described by the authors (see Appendix B in the original paper). We keep the hyperparameters unchanged for the translation experiment and set the maximum delay value to 2 for both translation directions.

**UNMT** We use the PyTorch UNMT implementation of He et al. (2020)[6] which incorporates improvements introduced by Lample et al. (2019) such as the addition of a max-pooling layer. We use a single-layer LSTM (Hochreiter and Schmidhuber, 1997) with hidden state size 512 for both the encoder and the decoder and embedding dimension 128. For the denoising autoencoding loss, we adopt the default noise model and hyperparameters as described by Lample et al. (2018). The autoencoding loss is annealed over the first 3 epochs. We predict the output using greedy decoding and set the maximum output length equal to the length of the input sequence. Patience for early stopping is set to 10.

**Model combinations** Our joint decoding implementations rely on PyTorch and the Pynini finite-state library (Gorman, 2016). In reranking, we rescore $n = 5$ best hypotheses produced using beam search and $n$–shortest path algorithm for the UNMT and WFST respectively. Product of experts decoding is also performed with beam size 5.

## C Metrics

The character error rate (CER) and word error rate (WER) as measured as the Levenshtein distance between the hypothesis and reference divided by reference length:

$$\mathrm{ER}(h, r) = \frac{dist(h, r)}{len(r)}$$

with both the numerator and the denominator measured in characters and words respectively.

We report BLEU-4 score (Papineni et al., 2002), measured using the Moses toolkit script.[7] For both BLEU and WER, we split sentences into words using the Moses tokenizer (Koehn et al., 2007).

[5] https://github.com/ryskina/romanization-decipherment

[6] https://github.com/cindyxinyiwang/deep-latent-sequence-model

[7] https://github.com/moses-smt/mosesdecoder/blob/master/scripts/generic/multi-bleu.perl

| Input | kongress ne odobril biudjet dlya osuchestvleniye "bor'bi s kommunizmom" v yuzhniy amerike. | |
|---|---|---|
| Ground truth | конгресс не одобрил бюджет для осуществления "борьбы с коммунизмом" в южной америке. | kongress ne odobril bjudžet dlja osuščestvlenija "bor'by s kommunizmom" v južnoj amerike. |
| WFST | конгресс не одобрил виудет дла осусчествлениые "бор#би с коммунизмом" в уузнани америке. | kongress ne odobril viudet dla osusčestvleniye "bor#bi s kommunizmom" v uuznani amerike. |
| Reranked WFST | конгресс не одобрил видет дела осусчествлениые "бор#би с коммунизмом" в уузнани америке. | kongress ne odobril videt dela osusčestvleniye "bor#bi s kommunizmom" v uuznani amerike. |
| Seq2Seq | конгресс не одобрил бы удивительно с коммунизмом" в южный америке. | kongress ne odobril by udivitel'no s kommunizmom" v južnyj amerike. |
| Reranked Seq2Seq | конгресс не одобрил бюджет для осуществление "борьбы с коммунизмом" в южный америке. | kongress ne odobril bjudžet dlja osuščestvlenie "bor'by s kommunizmom" v južnyj amerike. |
| Product of experts | конгресс не одобрил бидет для а осуществлениые "борьбы с коммунизмом" в уузнник амери | kongress ne odobril bidet dlja a osuščestvleniye "bor'by s kommunizmom" v uuznnik ameri |

Table 5: Different model outputs for a Russian transliteration example (left column—Cyrillic, right—scientific transliteration). Prediction errors are shown in red. Correctly transliterated segments that do not match the ground truth because of spelling standardization in annotation are in yellow. # stands for UNK.

| Input | ana h3dyy 3lek bokra 3la 8 kda | |
|---|---|---|
| Ground truth | انا حأعدي عليك بكرة على 8كده | AnA H>Edy Elyk bkrp ElY 8 kdh |
| WFST | انا حد يي لك بكر لأ 8كده | AnA Hd yy lk bkr l> 8 kdh |
| Reranked WFST | انا حد يي لك بكر لأ 8كده | AnA Hd yy lk bkr l> 8 kdh |
| Seq2Seq | انا بأدي أخلك حر أول 1كده | AnA b>dy >xlk Hr >wl 1 kdh |
| Reranked Seq2Seq | انا بأدي أخلك حر أول 1كده | AnA b>dy >xlk Hr >wl 1 kdh |
| Product of experts | انا دي لك ب كرا ألا 8كده | AnA dy lk b krA >lA 8 kdh |

Table 6: Different model outputs for an Arabizi transliteration example (left column—Arabic, right—Buckwalter transliteration). Prediction errors are highlighted in red in the romanized versions. Correctly transliterated segments that do not match the ground truth because of spelling standardization during annotation are highlighted in yellow.

| Input | kshullaka baalina avala horaatavannu adu vivarisuttade. | |
|---|---|---|
| Ground truth | ಕ್ಷುಲ್ಲಕ ಬಾಳಿನ ಅವಳ ಹೋರಾಟವನ್ನು ಅದು ವಿವರಿಸುತ್ತದೆ. | kṣullaka bāḷina avaḷa hōrāṭavannu adu vivarisuttade. |
| WFST | ಕುಹೂಲ್ಲಾಖೆ ಬಾಲಿನು ವಾಳ ಹೊರತಾವನ್ನು ಆದು ವಿವರಿಸುತ್ತದೆ. | kuhūllākhe bālinu vāḷa horatāvannu ādu vivarisuttade. |
| Reranked WFST | ಕುಹೂಲ್ಲಾಖೆ ಬಾಲಿನ ವಾಳು ಹೊರತಾವನ್ನು ಆದು ವಿವರಿಸುತ್ತದೆ. | kuhūllākhe bālina vāḷu horatāvannu ādu vivarisuttade. |
| Seq2Seq | ಕಳುಹುಳ್ಳ ಬಾವಿಂಗ್ ಇಲ್ಲವೇ ಹೋರಾಟವನ್ನು ಇದು ವಿವರಿಸುತ್ತದೆ. | kaḷuhuḷḷa bāviṁg illavē hōrāṭavannu idu vivarisuttade. |
| Reranked Seq2Seq | ಕಳುಹುಳ್ಳ ಬಾವಿಂತ ಇಲ್ಲವೇ ಹೋರಾಟವನ್ನು ಇದು ವಿವರಿಸುತ್ತದೆ. | kaḷuhuḷḷa bāviṁta illavē hōrāṭavannu idu vivarisuttade. |
| Product of experts | ಕಳ್ಳ ಬಾಕಲಿನ್ನ ವಾಲಾ ಹೋರಾಟತ್ವಾನ್ನು ದು ವಿವಾರಿಸುತ್ತದ | kaḷḷa bākalinna vālā hōrāṭatvānnu du vivārisuttada |

Table 7: Different model outputs for a Kannada transliteration example (left column—Kannada, right—ISO 15919 transliterations). The ISO romanization is generated using the Nisaba library (Johny et al., 2021). Prediction errors are highlighted in red in the romanized versions.

# Finite-state Model of Shupamem Reduplication

**Magdalena Markowska, Jeffrey Heinz, and Owen Rambow**
Stony Brook University
Department of Linguistics &
Institute for Advanced Computational Science
{magdalena.markowska, jeffrey.heinz, owen.rambow}@stonybrook.edu

## Abstract

Shupamem, a language of Western Cameroon, is a tonal language which also exhibits the morpho-phonological process of full reduplication. This creates two challenges for a finite-state model of its morpho-syntax and morphophonology: how to manage the full reduplication, as well as the autosegmental nature of lexical tone. Dolatian and Heinz (2020) explain how 2-way finite-state transducers can model full reduplication without an exponential increase in states, and finite-state transducers with multiple tapes have been used to model autosegmental tiers, including tone (Wiebe, 1992; Dolatian and Rawski, 2020a; Rawski and Dolatian, 2020). Here we synthesize 2-way finite-state transducers and multitape transducers, resulting in a finite-state formalism that subsumes both, to account for the full reduplicative processes in Shupamem which also affect tone.

## 1 Introduction

Reduplication is a very common morphological process cross-linguistically. Approximately 75% of world languages exhibit partial or total reduplication (Rubino, 2013). This morphological process is particularly interesting from the computational point of view because it introduces challenges for 1-way finite-state transducers (FSTs). Even though partial reduplication can be modelled with 1-way FSTs (Roark and Sproat, 2007; Chandlee and Heinz, 2012), there is typically an explosion in the number of states. Total reduplication, on the other hand, is the only known morphophonological process that cannot be modelled with 1-way FSTs because the number of copied elements, in principle, has no upper bound. Dolatian and Heinz (2020) address this challenge with 2-way FSTs, which can move back and forth on the input tape, producing a faithful copy of a string. Deterministic 2-way FSTs can model both partial and full segmental reduplication in a compact way.

However, many languages that exhibit reduplicative processes also are tonal, which often means that tones and segments act independently from one another in their morpho-phonology. For instance, in Shupamem, a tonal language of Western Cameroon, *ndáp* 'house' → *ndâp ndàp* 'houses' (Markowska, 2020).

| | | |
|---|---|---|
| *tones* | H | HL L |
| *segments* | ndap | ndap ndap |

Pioneering work in autosegmental phonology (Leben, 1973; Williams, 1976; Goldsmith, 1976) shows tones may act independently from their tone-bearing units (TBUs). Moreover, tones may exhibit behavior that is not typical for segments (Hyman, 2014; Jardine, 2016), which brings yet another strong argument for separating them from segments in their linguistic representations. Such autosegmental representations can be mimicked using finite-state machines, in particular, Multi-Tape Finite-State Transducers (MT FSTs) (Wiebe, 1992; Dolatian and Rawski, 2020a; Rawski and Dolatian, 2020). We note that McCarthy (1981) uses the same autosegmental representations in the linguistic representation to model templatic morphology, and this approach has been modeled for Semitic morphological processing using multitape automata (Kiraz, 2000; Habash and Rambow, 2006).

This paper investigates what finite-state machinery is needed for languages which have both reduplication and tones. We first argue that we need a synthesis of the aforementioned transducers, i.e. 1-way, 2-way and MT FSTs, to model morphology in the general case. The necessity for such a formal device will be supported by the morpho-phonological processes present in Shupamem nominal and verbal reduplication. We then discuss an



*Proceedings of the Seventeenth SIGMORPHON Workshop on Computational Research in Phonetics, Phonology, and Morphology*, pages 212–221

alternative, in which we use the MT FST to handle both reduplication and tones. It is important to emphasize that all of the machines we discuss are deterministic, which serves as another piece of evidence that even such complex processes like full reduplication can be modelled with deterministic finite-state technology (Chandlee and Heinz, 2012; Heinz, 2018).

This paper is structured as follows. First, we will briefly summarize the linguistic phenomena observed in Shupamem reduplication (Section 2). We then provide a formal description of the 2-way (Section 3) and MT FSTs (Section 4). We propose a synthesis of the 1-way, 2-way and MT FSTs in Section 5 and further illustrate them using relevant examples from Shupamem in Section 6. In Section 7 we discuss a possible alternative to the model which uses only MT FSTs. Finally, in Section 8 we show that the proposed model works for other tonal languages as well, and we conclude our contributions.

## 2 Shupamem nominal and verbal reduplication

Shupamem is an understudied Grassfields Bantu language of Cameroon spoken by approximately 420,000 speakers (Eberhard et al., 2021). It exhibits four contrastive surface tones (Nchare, 2012): high (H; we use diacritic V́ on a vowel as an orthographic representation), low (L; diacritic V̀), rising (LH; diacritic V̌), and falling (HL; diacritic V̂). Nouns and verbs in the language reduplicate to create plurals and introduce semantic contrast, respectively. Out of 13 nouns classes, only one exhibits reduplication. Nouns that belong to that class are monosyllabic and carry either H or L lexical tones. Shupamem verbs are underlyingly H or rising (LH). Table 1 summarizes the data adapted from Markowska (2020).

In both nouns and verbs, the first item of the reduplicated phrase is the base, while the reduplicant is the suffix. We follow the analysis in Markowska (2020) and summarize it here. The nominal reduplicant is toneless underlyingly, while the verbal reduplicant has an H tone. Furthermore, the rule of Opposite Tone Insertion explains the tonal alternation in the base of reduplicated nouns, and Default L-Insertion accounts for the L tone on the suffix. Interestingly, more tonal alternations are observed when the tones present in the reduplicated phrase interact with other phrasal/grammatical tones. For the purpose of this paper, we provide only a summary of those tonal alternations in Table 2.

| | Transl. | Lemma | Red form |
|---|---|---|---|
| **Nouns** | | H | HL L |
| | 'crab' | *kám* | *kâm kàm* |
| | | L | LH L |
| | 'game' | *kàm* | *kǎm kàm* |
| **Verbs** | | H | $H^{\downarrow}H$ |
| | 'fry' | *ká* | *ká k*$^{\downarrow}$*á* |
| | | LH | $LH^{\downarrow}H$ |
| | 'peel' | *kǎ* | *kǎ k*$^{\downarrow}$*á* |

Table 1: Nominal and verbal reduplication in Shupamem

| | Red. tones | Output |
|---|---|---|
| **Nouns** | HL L | HL $\underline{\text{H}}$ |
| | LH L | LH $\underline{\text{H}}$ |
| **Verbs** | $H^{\downarrow}H$ | $H^{\downarrow}H$ |
| | $LH^{\downarrow}H$ | $\underline{\text{HL LH}}$ |

Table 2: Tonal alternations: interaction of tones for reduplicated forms ("Red. tones") with grammatical H tones

The underlined tones indicate changes triggered by the H grammatical/phrasal tone. In the observance of H tone associated with the right edge of the subject position in Shupamem, the L tone that is present on the surface in the suffix of reduplicated nouns (recall Table 1), now is represented with an H tone. Now it should be clear that the noun reduplicant should, in fact, be toneless in the underlying representation (UR). While the presence of H tone directly preceding the reduplicated verb does not affect H-tone verbs, such as *ká* 'fry', it causes major tonal alternations in rising reduplicated verbs. Let us look at a particular example representing the final row in Table 2:

*pə́* 'PASTIII' + *kǎ ká* 'peel.CONTR' → *pə́ kâ kǎ*

The H tone associated with the tense marker introduces two tonal changes to the reduplicated verb: it causes tonal reversal on the morphological base, and it triggers L-tone insertion to the left edge of the reduplicant.

The data in both Table 1 and 2 show that 1) verbs and nouns in Shupamem reduplicate fully at the segmental level, and 2) tones are affected by phonological rules that function solely at the suprasegmental level. Consequently, a finite-state model of the language must be able to account for

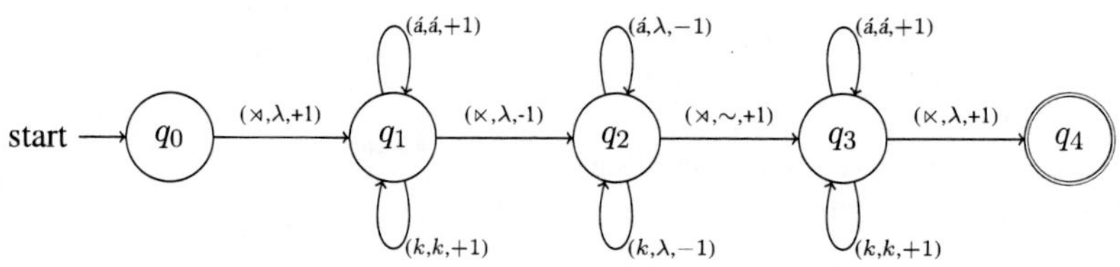


Figure 1: 2-way FST for total reduplication of *ká* 'fry.IMP → *ká ká* 'fry.IMP as opposed to boiling'

those factors. In the next two sections, we will provide a brief formal introduction to 2-way FSTs and MT-FSTs, and explain how they correctly model full reduplication and autosegmental representation, respectively.

In this paper, we use an orthographic representation for Shupamem which uses diacritics to indicate tone. Shupamem does not actually use this orthography; however, we are interested in modeling the entire morpho-phonology of the language, independently of choices made for the orthography. Furthermore, many languages do use diacritics to indicate tone, including the Volta-Niger languages Yoruba and Igbo, as well as Dschang, a Grassfields language closely related to Shupamem. (For a discussion of the orthography of Cameroonian languages, with a special consideration of tone, see (Bird, 2001).) Diacritics are also used to write tone in non-African languages, such as Vietnamese. Therefore, this paper is also relevant to NLP applications for morphological analysis and generation in languages whose orthography marks tones with diacritics: the automata we propose could be used to directly model morpho-phonological computational problems for the orthography of such languages.

## 3 2-way FSTs

As Roark and Sproat (2007) point out, almost all morpho-pholnological processes can be modelled with 1-way FSTs with the exception of full reduplication, whose output is not a regular language. One way to increase the expressivity of 1-way FST is to allow the read head of the machine to move back and forth on the input tape. This is exactly what 2-way FST does (Rabin and Scott, 1959), and Dolatian and Heinz (2020) explain how these transducers model full reduplication not only effectively, but more faithfully to linguistic generalizations.

Similarly to a 1-way FST, when a 2-way FST reads an input, it writes something on the output tape. If the desired output is a fully reduplicated string, then the FST faithfully 'copies' the input string while scanning it from left to right. In contrast, while scanning the string from right to left, it outputs nothing ($\lambda$), and it then copies the string again from left to right.

Figure 1 illustrates a deterministic 2-way FST that reduplicates *ká* 'fry.IMP'; readers are referred to Dolatian and Heinz (2020) for formal definitions. The key difference between deterministic 1-way FSTs and deterministic 2-way FSTs are the addition of the 'direction' parameters $\{+1, 0, -1\}$ on the transitions which tell the FST to advance to the next symbol on the input tape (+1), stay on the same symbol (0), or return to the previous symbol (-1). Deterministic 1-way FSTs can be thought of as deterministic 2-way FSTs where transitions are all (+1).

The input to this machine is $\rtimes$*ká*$\ltimes$. The $\rtimes$ and $\ltimes$ symbols mark beginning and end of a string, and $\sim$ indicates the boundary between the first and the second copy. None of those symbols are essential for the model, nevertheless they facilitate the transitions. For example, when the machine reads $\ltimes$, it transitions from state $q_1$ to $q_2$ and reverses the direction of the read head. After outputting the first copy (state $q_1$) and rewinding (state $q_2$), the machine changes to state $q_3$ when it scans the left boundary symbol $\rtimes$ and outputs $\sim$ to indicate that another copy will be created. In this particular example, not marking morpheme boundary would not affect the outcome. However, in Section 5, where we propose the fully-fledged model, it will be crucial to somehow separate the first from second copy.

## 4 Multitape FSTs

Multiple-tape FSTs are machines which operate in the exact same was as 1-way FST, with one key difference: they can read the input and/or write the output on multiple tapes. Such a transducer can operate in an either synchronous or asynchronous manner, such that the input will be read on all tapes and an output produced simultaneously, or the machine will operate on the input tapes one by one. MT-FST can take a single ('linear') string as an input and output multiple strings on multiple tapes or it can do the reverse (Rabin and Scott, 1959; Fischer, 1965).

To illustrate this idea, let us look at Shupamem noun *màpàm* 'coat'. It has been argued that Shupamem nouns with only L surface tones will have the L tone present in the UR (Markowska, 2019, 2020). Moreover, in order to avoid violating the Obligatory Contour Principle (OCP) (Leben, 1973), which prohibits two identical consecutive elements (tones) in the UR of a morpheme, we will assume that only one L tone is present in the input. Consequently, the derivation will look as shown in Table 3.

| **Input:** | T-tape | L |
|---|---|---|
| **Input:** | S-tape | mapam |
| **Output:** | Single tape | màpàm |

Table 3: Representation of MT-FST for *màpàm* 'coat'

Separating tones from segments in this manner, i.e. by representing tones on the T(one)-tape and segments on the S(segmental)-tape, faithfully resembles linguistic understanding of the UR of a word. The surface form *màpàm* has only one L tone present in the UR, which then spreads to all TBUs, which happen to be vowels in Shupamem, if no other tone is present.

An example of a multi-tape machine is presented in Figure 2. For better readability, we introduce a generalized symbols for vowels (V) and consonants (C), so that the input alphabet is $\Sigma_{\rtimes} = \{(C, V), (L, H)\} \cup \{\rtimes, \ltimes\}$, and the output alphabet is $\Gamma = \{C, \acute{V}, \grave{V}\}$. The machine operates on 2 input tapes and writes the output on a single tape. Therefore, we could think of such machine as a *linearizer*. The two input tapes represent the Tonal and Segmental tiers and so we label them T and S, respectively. We illustrate the functioning of the machine using the example (mapam, L) $\rightarrow$ màpàm 'coat'. While transitioning from state $q_0$ to $q_1$, the output is an empty string since the left edge marker is being read on both tapes simultaneously. In state $q_1$, when a consonant is being read, the machine outputs the exact same consonant on the output tape. However, when the machine reaches a vowel, it outputs a vowel with a tone that is being read at the same time on the T-tape (in our example, (L, V) $\rightarrow$ V̀) and transitions to state $q_2$ (if the symbol on the T-tape is H) or $q_3$ (for L, as in our example). In states $q_2$ and $q_3$, consonants are simply output as in state $q_1$, but for vowels, one of three conditions may occur: the read head on the Tonal tape may be H or L, in which case the automaton transitions (if not already there) to $q_2$ (for H) or $q_3$ (for L), and outputs the appropriate orthographic symbol. But if on the Tonal tape the read head is on the right boundary marker $\ltimes$, we are in a case where there are more vowels in the Segmental tape than tones in the Tonal tape. This is when the OCP determines the interpretation: all vowels get the tone of the last symbol on the Tone tier (which we remember as states $q_2$ and $q_3$). In our example, this is an L. Finally, when the Segmental tape also reaches the right boundary marker $\ltimes$, the machine transitions to the final state $q_4$. This ('linearizing') MT-FST consists of 4 states and shows how OCP effects can be handled with asynchronous multitape FSTs. Note that when there are more tones on the Tonal tier than vowels on the Segmental tier, they are simply ignored. We refer readers to Dolatian and Rawski (2020b) for formal definitions of these MT transducers.

We are also interested in the *inverse* process – that is, a finite-state machine that in the example above would take a single input string [màpàm] and produce two output strings [L] and [mapam]. While multitape FSTs are generally conceived as relations over n-ary relations over strings, Dolatian and Rawski (2020b) define their machines deterministically with $n$ input tapes and a single output tape. We generalize their definition below.

Similarly to spreading processes described above, separating tones from segments give us a lot of benefits while accounting for tonal alternations taking place in nominal and verbal reduplication in Shupamem. First of all, functions such as Opposite Tone Insertion (OTI) will apply solely at the tonal level, while segments can be undergoing other operations at the same time (recall that MT-FSTs can operate on some or all tapes simultaneously). Secondly, representing tones separately from segments make tonal processes local, and therefore all the alternations can be expresses with less powerful functions (Chandlee, 2017).

Now that we presented the advantages of MT-FSTs, and the need for utilizing 2-way FSTs to model full reduplication, we combine those machines to account for all morphophonological pro-

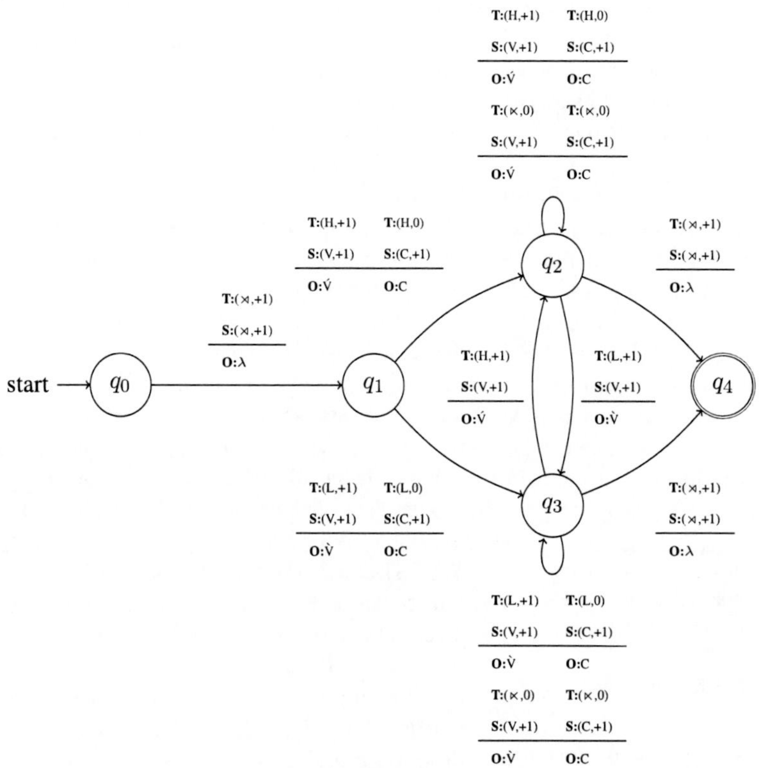


Figure 2: MT-FST: linearize
C and V are notational meta-symbols for consonants and vowels, resp.; T indicates the tone tape, S, the segmental tape, and O the output tape.

cesses described in Section 2.

## 5 Deterministic 2-Way Multi-tape FST

Before we define Deterministic 2-Way Multi-tape FST (or 2-way MT FST for short) we introduce some notation. An alphabet $\Sigma$ is a finite set of symbols and $\Sigma^*$ denotes the set of all strings of finite length whose elements belong to $\Sigma$. We use $\lambda$ to denote the empty string. For each $n \in \mathbb{N}$, an $n$-string is a tuple $\langle w_1, \dots w_n \rangle$ where each $w_i$ is a string belonging to $\Sigma_i^*(1 \leq i \leq n)$. These $n$ alphabets may contain distinct symbols or not. We write $\vec{w}$ to indicate a $n$-string and $\vec{\lambda}$ to indicate the $n$-string where each $w_i = \lambda$. We also write $\vec{\Sigma}$ to denote a tuple of $n$ alphabets: $\vec{\Sigma} = \Sigma_1 \times \cdots \Sigma_n$. Elements of $\vec{\Sigma}$ are denoted $\vec{\sigma}$.

If $\vec{w}$ and $\vec{v}$ belong to $\vec{\Sigma}^*$ then the pointwise concatenation of $\vec{w}$ and $\vec{v}$ is denoted $\vec{w}\vec{v}$ and equals $\langle w_1, \dots w_n \rangle \langle v_1, \dots v_n \rangle = \langle w_1 v_1, \dots w_n v_n \rangle$. We are interested in functions that map $n$-strings to $m$-strings with $n, m \in \mathbb{N}$. In what follows we generally use the index $i$ to range from 1 to $n$ and the index $j$ to range from 1 to $m$.

We define Deterministic 2-Way $n, m$ Multitape FST (2-way $(n, m)$ MT FST for short) for $n, m \in \mathbb{N}$ by synthesizing the definitions of Dolatian and Heinz (2020) and Dolatian and Rawski (2020b); $n, m$ refer to the number of input tapes and output tapes, respectively. A Deterministic 2-Way $n, m$ Multitape FST is a six-tuple $(Q, \vec{\Sigma}, \vec{\Gamma}, q_0, F, \delta)$, where

- $\vec{\Sigma} = \langle \Sigma_1 \dots \Sigma_n \rangle$ is a tuple of $n$ input alphabets that include the boundary symbols, i.e., $\{\rtimes, \ltimes\} \subset \Sigma_i,\ 1 \leq i \leq n$,
- $\vec{\Gamma}$ is a tuple of $m$ output alphabets $\Gamma_j$ $(1 \leq j \leq m)$,
- $\delta : Q \times \vec{\Sigma} \rightarrow Q \times \vec{\Gamma}^* \times \vec{D}$ is the transition function. $D$ is an alphabet of directions equal to $\{-1, 0, +1\}$ and $\vec{D}$ is an $n$-tuple. $\vec{\Gamma}^*$ is a $m$-tuple of strings written to each output tape.

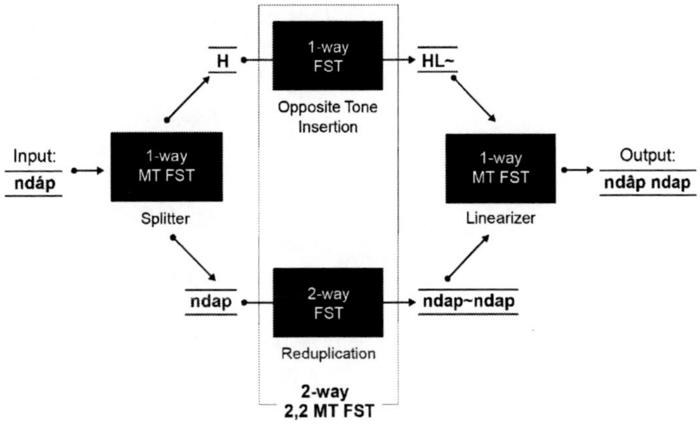


Figure 3: Synthesis of 2-way FST and MT-FST

We understand $\delta(q, \vec{\sigma}) = (r, \vec{v}, \vec{d})$ as follows. It means that if the transducer is in state $q$ and the $n$ read heads on the input tapes are on symbols $\langle \sigma_1, \ldots \sigma_n \rangle = \vec{\sigma}$, then several actions ensue. The transducer changes to state $r$ and pointwise concatenates $\vec{v}$ to the $m$ output tapes. The $n$ read heads then move according to the instructions $\vec{d} \in \vec{D}$. For each read head on input tape $i$, it moves back one symbol iff $d_i = -1$, stays where it is iff $d_i = 0$, and advances one symbol iff $d_i = +1$. (If the read head on an input tape "falls off" the beginning or end of the string, the computation halts.)

The function recognized by a 2-way $(n, m)$ MT FST is defined as follows. A *configuration* of a $n, m$-MT-FST $T$ is a 4-tuple $\langle \vec{\Sigma}^*, q, \vec{\Sigma}^*, \vec{\Gamma}^* \rangle$. The meaning of the configuration $(\vec{w}, q, \vec{x}, u)$ is that the input to $T$ is $\vec{w}\vec{x}$ and the machine is currently in state $q$ with the $n$ read heads on the first symbol of each $x_i$ (or has fallen off the right edge of the $i$-th input tape if $x_i = \lambda$) and that $\vec{u}$ is currently written on the $m$ output tapes.

If the current configuration is $(\vec{w}, q, \vec{x}, \vec{u})$ and $\delta(q, \vec{\sigma}) = (r, \vec{v}, \vec{d})$ then the next configuration is $(\vec{w}', r, \vec{x}', \vec{u}\vec{v})$, where for each $i$, $1 \leq i \leq n$:

- $\vec{w}' = \langle w'_1 \ldots w'_n \rangle$ and $\vec{x}' = \langle x'_1 \ldots x'_n \rangle$ $(1 \leq i \leq n)$;
- $w'_i = w_i$ and $x'_i = x_i$ iff $d_i = 0$;
- $w'_i = w_i\sigma$ and $x'_i = x''_i$ iff $d_i = +1$ and there exists $\sigma \in \Sigma_i, x''_i \in \Sigma^*_i$ such that $x_i = \sigma x''_i$;
- $w'_i = w''_i$ and $x'_i = \sigma x_i$ iff $d_i = -1$ and there exists $\sigma \in \Sigma_i, w''_i \in \Sigma^*_i$ such that $w_i = \sigma w''_i$.

We write $(\vec{w}, q, \vec{x}, \vec{u}) \rightarrow (\vec{w}', r, \vec{x}', \vec{u}\vec{v})$. Observe that since $\delta$ is a function, there is at most one next configuration (i.e., the system is deterministic). Note there are some circumstances where there is no next configuration. For instance if $d_i = +1$ and $x_i = \lambda$ then there is no place for the read head to advance. In such cases, the computation halts.

The transitive closure of $\rightarrow$ is denoted with $\rightarrow^+$. Thus, if $c \rightarrow^+ c'$ then there exists a finite sequence of configurations $c_1, c_2 \ldots c_n$ with $n > 1$ such that $c = c_1 \rightarrow c_2 \rightarrow \ldots \rightarrow c_n = c'$.

At last we define the function that a 2-way $(n, m)$ MT FST $T$ computes. The input strings are augmented with word boundaries on each tape. Let $\overrightarrow{\rtimes w \ltimes} = \langle \rtimes w_1 \ltimes, \ldots \rtimes w_n \ltimes \rangle$. For each $n$-string $\vec{w} \in \vec{\Sigma}^*$, $f_T(\vec{w}) = \vec{u} \in \vec{\Gamma}^*$ provided there exists $q_f \in F$ such that $(\vec{\lambda}, q_0, \overrightarrow{\rtimes w \ltimes}, \vec{\lambda}) \rightarrow^+ (\overrightarrow{\rtimes w \ltimes}, q_f, \vec{\lambda}, \vec{u})$.

If $f_T(\vec{w}) = \vec{u}$ then $\vec{u}$ is unique because the sequence of configurations is determined deterministically. If the computation of a 2-way MT-FST $T$ halts on some input $\vec{w}$ (perhaps because a subsequent configuration does not exist), then we say $T$ is undefined on $\vec{w}$.

The 2-way FSTs studied by Dolatian and Heinz (2020) are 2-way 1,1 MT FST. The $n$-MT-FSTs studied by Dolatian and Rawski (2020b) are 2-way $n$,1 MT FST where none of the transitions contain the $-1$ direction. In this way, the definition presented here properly subsumes both.

Figure 4 shows an example of a 1,2 MT FST that "splits" a phonetic (or orthographic) transcription of a Shupamem word into a linguistic representation with a tonal and segmental tier by outputting two output strings, one for each tier.

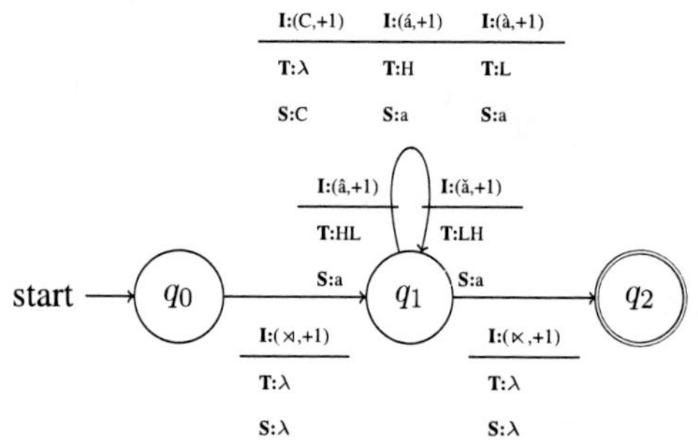


Figure 4: MT-FST: split ndáp → (ndap, H) 'house', C and V are notational meta-symbols for consonants and vowels, resp.; T indicates the output tone tape, S – the segmental output tape, and I – the input.

## 6 Proposed model

As presented in Figure 3, our proposed model, i.e. 2-way 2,2 MT FST, consists of 1-way and 2-way deterministic transducers, which together operate on two tapes. Both input and output are represented on two separate tapes: Tonal and Segmental Tape. Such representation is desired as it correctly mimics linguistic representations of tonal languages, where segments and tones act independently from each other. On the T-tape, a 1-way FST takes the *H* tone associated with the lexical representation of *ndáp* 'house' and outputs *HL*∼ by implementing the Opposite Tone Insertion function. On the S-tape, a 2-way FST takes *ndap* as an input, and outputs a faithful copy of that string (*ndap ndap).* The ∼ symbol significantly indicates the morpheme boundary and facilitates further output linearization. A detailed derivation of *ndáp* ↦ *ndâp ndap* is shown in Table 4.

Figure 3 also represents two additional 'transformations': splitting and linearizing. First, the phonetic transcription of a string (*ndáp)* is split into tones and segments with a 1,2 MT FST. The output (H, ndap) serves as an input to the 2-way 2,2 MT FST. After the two processes discussed above apply, together acting on both tapes, the output is then linearized with an 2,1 MT FST. The composition of those three machines, i.e. 1,2 MT, 2-way 2,2 MT FST, and 2,1 MT FSTs is particularly useful in applications where a phonetic or orthographic representations needs to be processed.

As was discussed in Section 2, the tone on the second copy is dependent on whether there was an H tone preceding the reduplicated phrase. If there was one, the tone on the reduplicant will be H. Otherwise, the L-Default Insertion rule will insert L tone onto the toneless TBU of the second copy. Because those tonal changes are not part of the reduplicative process *per se*, we do not represent them either in our model in Figure 3, or in the derivation in Table 4. Those alternations could be accounted for with 1-way FST by simply inserting H or L tone to the output of the composed machine represented in Figure 3.

Modelling verbal reduplication and the tonal processes revolving around it (see Table 2) works in the exact same way as described above for nominal reduplication. The only difference are the functions applied to the T-tape.

## 7 An Alternative to 2-Way Automata

2-way $n$,$m$ MT FST generalize regular functions (Filiot and Reynier, 2016) to functions from $n$-strings to $m$-strings. It is worth asking however, what each of these mechanisms brings, especially in light of fundamental operations such as functional composition.

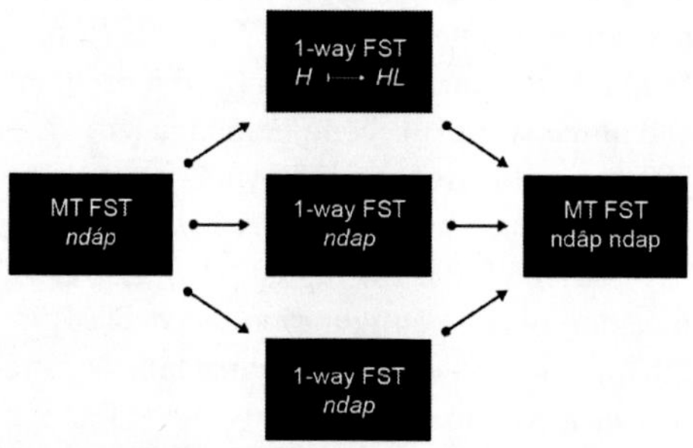


Figure 5: An alternative model for Shupamem reduplication

For instance, it is clear that 2-way 1, 1 MT FSTs can handle full reduplication in contrast to 1-way 1, 1 MT FSTs which cannot. However, full reduplication can also be obtained via the composition of a 1-way 1,2 MT FST with a 1-way 2, 1 MT FST. To illustrate, the former takes a single string as an input, e.g. *ndap*, and 'splits' it into two identical copies represented on two separate output tapes. Then the 2-string output by this machines becomes the input to the next 1-way 2,1 MT FST. Since this machine is asynchronous, it can linearize the

| State | Segment-tape | Tone-tape | S-output | T-output |
|---|---|---|---|---|
| $q_0$ | $\rtimes ndap \ltimes$ | $\rtimes H \ltimes$ | $\lambda$ | $\lambda$ |
| $q_1$ | $\rtimes ndap \ltimes$ **S**:$\rtimes$:+1 | $\rtimes H \ltimes$ **T**:$\rtimes$:+1 | n | HL |
| $q_1$ | $\rtimes ndap \ltimes$ **S**:n:+1 | $\rtimes H \ltimes$ **T**:H:+1 | nd | HL∼ |
| $q_1$ | $\rtimes ndap \ltimes$ **S**:d:+1 | $\rtimes H \ltimes$ **T**:$\ltimes$:0 | nda | HL∼ |
| $q_1$ | $\rtimes ndap \ltimes$ **S**:a:+1 | $\rtimes H \ltimes$ **T**:$\ltimes$:0 | ndap | HL∼ |
| $q_1$ | $\rtimes ndap \ltimes$ **S**:p:+1 | $\rtimes H \ltimes$ **T**:$\ltimes$:0 | ndap∼ | HL∼ |
| $q_2$ | $\rtimes ndap \ltimes$ **S**:$\ltimes$:-1 | $\rtimes H \ltimes$ **T**:$\ltimes$:0 | ndap∼ | HL∼ |
| $q_2$ | $\rtimes ndap \ltimes$ **S**:p:-1 | $\rtimes H \ltimes$ **T**:$\ltimes$:0 | ndap∼ | HL∼ |
| $q_2$ | $\rtimes ndap \ltimes$ **S**:a:-1 | $\rtimes H \ltimes$ **T**:$\ltimes$:0 | ndap∼ | HL∼ |
| $q_2$ | $\rtimes ndap \ltimes$ **S**:d:-1 | $\rtimes H \ltimes$ **T**:$\ltimes$:0 | ndap∼ | HL∼ |
| $q_2$ | $\rtimes ndap \ltimes$ **S**:n:-1 | $\rtimes H \ltimes$ **T**:$\ltimes$:0 | ndap∼ | HL∼ |
| $q_3$ | $\rtimes ndap \ltimes$ **S**:$\rtimes$:+1 | $\rtimes H \ltimes$ **T**:$\ltimes$:0 | ndap∼n | HL∼ |
| $q_3$ | $\rtimes ndap \ltimes$ **S**:n:+1 | $\rtimes H \ltimes$ **T**:$\ltimes$:0 | ndap∼nd | HL∼ |
| $q_3$ | $\rtimes ndap \ltimes$ **S**:d:+1 | $\rtimes H \ltimes$ **T**:$\ltimes$:0 | ndap∼nda | HL∼ |
| $q_3$ | $\rtimes ndap \ltimes$ **S**:a:+1 | $\rtimes H \ltimes$ **T**:$\ltimes$:0 | ndap∼ndap | HL∼ |
| $q_3$ | $\rtimes ndap \ltimes$ **S**:p:+1 | $\rtimes H \ltimes$ **T**:$\ltimes$:0 | ndap∼ndap | HL∼ |

Table 4: Derivation of *ndáp* ↦ *ndâp ndap* 'houses'

This derivation happens in the two automata in the center of Figure 3. The FST for the Segmental tier is the one shown in Figure 1, and the states in the table above refer to this FST.

2-string (e.g. *(ndap, ndap))* to a 1-string (*ndap ndap*) by reading along one of these input tapes (and writing it) and reading the other one (and writing it) only when the read head on the first input tape reaches the end. Consequently, an alternative way to model full reduplication is to write the exact same output on two separate tapes, and then linearize it. Therefore, instead of implementing Shupamem tonal reduplication with 2-way 2,2 MT FST, we could use the composition of two 1-way MT-FST: 1,3 MT-FST and 3,1 MT-FST as shown in Figure 5. (We need three tapes, two Segmental tapes to allow reduplication as just explained, and one Tonal tape as discussed before.)

This example shows that additional tapes can be understood as serving a similar role to registers in register automata (Alur and Černý, 2011; Alur et al., 2014). Alur and his colleagues have shown that deterministic 1-way transducers with registers are equivalent in expressivity to 2-way deterministic transducers (without registers).

## 8 Beyond Shupamem

The proposed model is not limited to modeling full reduplication in Shupamem. It can be used for other tonal languages exhibiting this morphological process. We provide examples of the applicability of this model for the three following languages: Adhola, Kikerewe, and Shona. And we predict that other languages could also be accounted for.

All three languages undergo full reduplication at the segmental level. What differs is the tonal pattern governing this process. In Adhola (Kaplan, 2006), the second copy is always represented with a fixed tonal pattern H.HL, where '.' indicates syllable boundary, irregardless of the lexical tone on the non-reduplicated form. In the following examples, unaccented vowels indicate low tone. For instance, *tiju* 'work' ↦ *tija tíjâ* 'work too much', *tʃemó* 'eat' ↦ *tʃemá tʃ'ꜜémâ* 'eat too much'. In Kikerewe (Odden, 1996), if the first (two) syllable(s) of the verb are marked with an H tone, the H tone would also be present in the first two syllables of the reduplicated phrase. On the other hand, if the last two syllables of the non-reduplicated verb are marked with an H tone, the H tone will be present on the last two syllables of the reduplicated phrase. For instance, *bíba* 'plant' ↦ *bíba biba* 'plant carelessly, here and there', *bibílé* 'planted (yesterday)' ↦ *bibile bibílé* 'planted (yesterday) carelessly, here and there'. Finally, in KiHehe (Odden and Odden, 1985), if an H tone appears in the first syllable of the verb, the H tone will also be present in the first syllable of the second copy, for example *dóongoleesa* 'roll' ↦ *dongolesa dóongoleesa* 'roll a bit'.

The above discussed examples can be modelled in a similar to Shupamem way, such that, first, the input will be output on two tapes: Tonal and Segmental, then some (morpho-)phonological processes will apply on both level. The final step is the 'linearization', which will be independent of the case. For example, in Kikerewe, if the first tone that is read on the Tonal tape is H, and a vowel is read on the Segmental tape, the output will be a vowel with an acute accent. If the second tone is L, as in *bíba*, this L tone will be 'attached' to every remaining vowel in the reduplicated phrase. While Kikerewe provides an example where there are more TBUs than tones, Adhola presents the reverse situation, where there are more tones than TBU (contour tones). Consequently, it is crucial to mark syllable boundaries, such that only when '.' or the right edge marker (⋊) is read, the FST will output the 'linearized' element.

## 9 Conclusion

In this paper we proposed a deterministic finite-state model of total reduplication in Shupamem. As it is typical for Bantu languages, Shupamem is a tonal language in which phonological processes operating on a segmental level differ from those on suprasegmental (tonal) level. Consequently, Shupamem introduces two challenges for 1-way FSTs: language copying and autosegmental representation. We addressed those challenges by proposing a synthesis of a deterministic 2-way FST, which correctly models total reduplication, and a MT FST, which enables autosegmental representation. Such a machine operates on two tapes (Tonal and Segmental), which faithfully replicate the linguistic analysis of Shupamem reduplication discussed in Markowska (2020). Finally, the outputs of the 2-way 2,2 MT FST is linearized with a separate 2,1 MT FST outputting the desired surface representation of a reduplicated word. The proposed model is based on previously studied finite-state models for reduplication (Dolatian and Heinz, 2020) and tonal processes (Dolatian and Rawski, 2020b,a).

There are some areas of future research that we plan to pursue. First, we have suggested that we can handle reduplication using the composition of 1-way deterministic MT FSTs, dispensing with the need for 2-way automata altogether. Further formal comparison of these two approaches is warranted. More generally, we plan to investigate the closure properties of classes of 2-way MT FSTs. A third line of research is to collect more examples of full reduplication in tonal languages and to include them in the RedTyp database (Dolatian and Heinz, 2019) so a broader empirical typology can be studied with respect to the formal properties of these machines.

## References


Rajeev Alur, Adam Freilich, and Mukund Raghothaman. 2014. Regular combinators for string transformations. In *Proceedings of the Joint Meeting of the Twenty-Third EACSL Annual Conference on Computer Science Logic (CSL) and the Twenty-Ninth Annual ACM/IEEE Symposium on Logic in Computer Science (LICS)*, CSL-LICS '14, pages 9:1–9:10, New York, NY, USA. ACM.

Rajeev Alur and Pavol Černý. 2011. Streaming transducers for algorithmic verification of single-pass list-processing programs. In *Proceedings of the 38th Annual ACM SIGPLAN-SIGACT Symposium on Principles of Programming Languages*, POPL '11, page 599–610, New York, NY, USA. Association for Computing Machinery.

Steven Bird. 2001. Orthography and identity in Cameroon. *Written Language & Literacy*, 4(2):131–162.

Jane Chandlee. 2017. Computational locality in morphological maps. *Morphology*, pages 1–43.

Jane Chandlee and Jeffrey Heinz. 2012. Bounded copying is subsequential: Implications for metathesis and reduplication. In *Proceedings of the Twelfth Meeting of the Special Interest Group on Computational Morphology and Phonology*, pages 42–51, Montréal, Canada. Association for Computational Linguistics.

Hossep Dolatian and Jeffrey Heinz. 2019. Redtyp: A database of reduplication with computational models. In *Proceedings of the Society for Computation in Linguistics*, volume 2. Article 3.

Hossep Dolatian and Jeffrey Heinz. 2020. Computing and classifying reduplication with 2-way finite-state transducers. *Journal of Language Modelling*, 8(1):179–250.

Hossep Dolatian and Jonathan Rawski. 2020a. Computational locality in nonlinear morphophonology. Ms., Stony Brook University.

Hossep Dolatian and Jonathan Rawski. 2020b. Multi input strictly local functions for templatic morphology. In *In Proceedings of the Society for Computation in Linguistics*, volume 3.

David M. Eberhard, Gary F. Simmons, and Charles D. Fenning. 2021. *Enthologue: Languages of the World*. 24th edition. Dallas, Texas: SIL International.

Emmanuel Filiot and Pierre-Alain Reynier. 2016. Transducers, logic and algebra for functions of finite words. *ACM SIGLOG News*, 3(3):4–19.

Patric C. Fischer. 1965. Multi-tape and infinite-state automata-a survey. *Communications of the ACM*, pages 799–805.

John Goldsmith. 1976. *Autosegmental Phonology*. Ph.D. thesis, Massachusetts Institute of Technology.

Nizar Habash and Owen Rambow. 2006. Magead: A morphological analyzer for Arabic and its dialects. In *Proceedings of the 21st International Conference on Computational Linguistics and 44th Annual Meeting of the Association for Computational Linguistics (Coling-ACL'06)*, Sydney, Australia.

Jeffrey Heinz. 2018. The computational nature of phonological generalizations. In Larry Hyman and Frans Plank, editors, *Phonological Typology*, Phonetics and Phonology, chapter 5, pages 126–195. De Gruyter Mouton.

Larry Hyman. 2014. How autosegmental is phonology? *The Linguistic Review*, 31(2):363–400.

Adam Jardine. 2016. Computationally, tone is different. *Phonology*, 33:247–283.

Aaron F. Kaplan. 2006. Tonal and morphological identity in reduplication. In *Proceedings of the Annual Meeting of the Berkeley Linguistics Society*, volume 31.

George Anton Kiraz. 2000. Multi-tiered nonlinear morphology using multi-tape finite automata: A case study on Syriac and Arabic. *Computational Linguistics*, 26(1):77–105.

William R. Leben. 1973. *Suprasegmental Phonology*. Ph.D. thesis, Massachusetts Institute of Technology.

Magdalena Markowska. 2019. Tones in Shuapmem possessives. Ms., Graduate Center, City University of New York.

Magdalena Markowska. 2020. Tones in Shupamem reduplication. *CUNY Academic Works*.

John McCarthy. 1981. A prosodic theory of nonconcatenative morphology. *Linguistic Inquiry*, 12:373–418.

Abdoulaye L. Nchare. 2012. *The Grammar of Shupamem*. Ph.D. thesis, New York University.

David Odden. 1996. Patterns of reduplication in kikerewe. *OSU WPL*, 48:111–148.

David Odden and Mary Odden. 1985. Ordered reduplication in KiHehe. *Linguistic Inquiry*, 16:497–503.

Michael O Rabin and Dana Scott. 1959. Finite automata and their decision problems. *IBM journal of research and development*, 3:114–125.

Jonathan Rawski and Hossep Dolatian. 2020. Multi-input strict local functions for tonal phonology. *Proceedings of the Society for Computation in Linguistics*, 3(1):245–260.

Brian Roark and Richard Sproat. 2007. *Computational Approaches to Morphology and Syntax*. Oxford University Press, Oxford.

Carl Rubino. 2013. *Reduplication*. Max Planck Institute for Evolutionary Anthropology, Leipzig.

Bruce Wiebe. 1992. Modelling autosegmental phonology with multi-tape finite state transducers.

Edwin S. Williams. 1976. Underlying tone in Margi and Igbo. *Linguistic Inquiry*, 7:463–484.

# Improved pronunciation prediction accuracy using morphology

**Dravyansh Sharma, Saumya Yashmohini Sahai, Neha Chaudhari[†], Antoine Bruguier**
[†]Google LLC[*]
dravyans@andrew.cmu.edu, sahai.17@osu.edu,
neha7.chaudhari@gmail.com, bruguier@almuni.caltech.edu

## Abstract

Pronunciation lexicons and prediction models are a key component in several speech synthesis and recognition systems. We know that morphologically related words typically follow a fixed pattern of pronunciation which can be described by language-specific paradigms. In this work we explore how deep recurrent neural networks can be used to automatically learn and exploit this pattern to improve the pronunciation prediction quality of words related by morphological inflection. We propose two novel approaches for supplying morphological information, using the word's morphological class and its lemma, which are typically annotated in standard lexicons. We report improvements across a number of European languages with varying degrees of phonological and morphological complexity, and two language families, with greater improvements for languages where the pronunciation prediction task is inherently more challenging. We also observe that combining bidirectional LSTM networks with attention mechanisms is an effective neural approach for the computational problem considered, across languages. Our approach seems particularly beneficial in the low resource setting, both by itself and in conjunction with transfer learning.

## 1 Introduction

Morphophonology is the study of interaction between morphological and phonological processes and mostly involves description of sound changes that take place in morphemes (minimal meaningful units) when they combine to form words. For example, the plural morpheme in English appears as '-s' or '-es' in orthography and as [s], [z], and [ɪz] in phonology, e.g. in *cops*, *cogs* and *courses*. The different forms can be thought to be derived from a common plural morphophoneme which undergoes context dependent transformations to produce the correct phones.

A *pronunciation model*, also known as a grapheme to phoneme (G2P) converter, is a system that produces a phonemic representation of a word from its written form. The word is converted from the sequence of letters in the orthographic script to a sequence of phonemes (sound symbols) in a pre-determined transcription, such as IPA or X-SAMPA. It is expensive and possibly, say in morphologically rich languages with productive compounding, infeasible to list the pronunciations for all the words. So one uses rules or learned models for this task. Pronunciation models are important components of both speech recognition (ASR) and synthesis (text-to-speech, TTS) systems. Even though end-to-end models have been gathering recent attention (Graves and Jaitly, 2014; Sotelo et al., 2017), often state-of-the-art models in industrial production systems involve conversion to and from an intermediate phoneme layer.

A single system of morphophonological rules which connects morphology with phonology is well-known (Chomsky and Halle, 1968). In fact computational models for morphology such as the two-level morphology of Koskenniemi (1983); Kaplan and Kay (1994) have the bulk of the machinery designed to handle phonological rules. However, the approach involves encoding language-specific rules as a finite-state transducer, a tedious and expensive process requiring linguistic expertise. Linguistic rules are augmented computationally for small corpora in Ermolaeva (2018), although scalability and applicability of the approach across languages is not tested.

We focus on using deep neural models to improve the quality of pronunciation prediction using

[*]Part of the work was done when D.S., N.C. and A.B. were at Google.



*Proceedings of the Seventeenth SIGMORPHON Workshop on Computational Research in Phonetics, Phonology, and Morphology*, pages 222–228

morphology. G2P fits nicely in the well-studied sequence to sequence learning paradigms (Sutskever et al., 2014), here we use extensions that can handle supplementary inputs in order to inject the morphological information. Our techniques are similar to Sharma et al. (2019), although the goal there is to lemmatize or inflect more accurately using pronunciations. Taylor and Richmond (2020) consider improving neural G2P quality using morphology, our work differs in two respects. First, we use morphology class and lemma entries instead of morpheme boundaries for which annotations may not be as readily available. Secondly, they consider BiLSTMs and Transformer models, but we additionally consider architectures which combine BiLSTMs with attention and outperform both. We also show significant gains by morphology injection in the context of transfer learning for low resource languages where sufficient annotations are unavailable.

## 2 Background and related work

Pronunciation prediction is often studied in settings of speech recognition and synthesis. Some recent work explores new representations (Livescu et al., 2016; Sofroniev and Çöltekin, 2018; Jacobs and Mailhot, 2019), but in this work, *a pronunciation is a sequence of phonemes, syllable boundaries and stress symbols* (van Esch et al., 2016). A lot of work has been devoted to the G2P problem (e.g. see Nicolai et al. (2020)), ranging from those focused on accuracy and model size to those discussing approaches for data-efficient scaling to low resource languages or multilingual modeling (Rao et al., 2015; Sharma, 2018; Gorman et al., 2020).

Morphology prediction is of independent interest and has applications in natural language generation as well as understanding. The problems of lemmatization and morphological inflection have been studied in both contextual (in a sentence, which involves morphosyntactics) and isolated settings (Cohen and Smith, 2007; Faruqui et al., 2015; Cotterell et al., 2016; Sharma et al., 2019).

*Morphophonological prediction*, by which we mean viewing morphology and pronunciation prediction as a single task with several related inputs and outputs, has received relatively less attention as a language-independent computational task, even though the significance for G2P has been argued (Coker et al., 1991). Sharma et al. (2019) show improved morphology prediction using phonology, and Taylor and Richmond (2020) show the reverse. The present work aligns with the latter, but instead of requiring full morphological segmentation of words we work with weaker and more easily annotated morphological information like word lemmas and morphological categories.

## 3 Improved pronunciation prediction

We consider the G2P problem, i.e. prediction of the sequence of phonemes (pronunciation) from the sequence of graphemes in a single word. The G2P problem forms a clean, simple application of seq2seq learning, which can also be used to create models that achieve state-of-the-art accuracies in pronunciation prediction. Morphology can aid this prediction in several ways. One, we could use morphological category as a non-sequential side input. Two, we could use the knowledge of the morphemes of the words and their pronunciations which may be possible with lower amounts of annotation. For example, the lemma (and its pronunciation) may already be annotated for an out-of-vocabulary word. Often standard lexicons list the lemmata of derived/inflected words, lemmatizer models can be used as a fallback. Learning from the exact morphological segmentation (Taylor and Richmond, 2020) would need more precise models and annotation (Demberg et al., 2007).

Given the spelling, language specific models can predict the pronunciation by using knowledge of typical grapheme to phoneme mappings in the language. Some errors of these models may be fixed with help from morphological information as argued above. For instance, homograph pronunciations can be predicted using morphology but it is impossible to deduce correctly using just orthography.[1] The pronunciation of 'read' (/ɹiːd/ for present tense and noun, /ɹɛd/ for past and participle) can be determined by the part of speech and tense; the stress shifts from first to second syllable between 'project' noun and verb.

### 3.1 Dataset

We train and evaluate our models for five languages to cover some morphophonological diversity: (American) English, French, Russian, Spanish and Hungarian. For training our models, we use pronunciation lexicons (word-pronunciation pairs) and morphological lexicons (containing *lex-*

[1]Homographs are words which are spelt identically but have different meanings and pronunciations.

*ical form*, i.e. lemma and morphology class) of only inflected words of size of the order of $10^4$ for each language (see Table 5 in Appendix A). For the languages discussed, these lexicons are obtained by scraping[2] Wiktionary data and filtering for words that have annotations (including pronunciations available in the IPA format) for both the *surface form* and the *lexical form*. While this order of data is often available for high-resource languages, in Section 3.3 we discuss extension of our work to low-resource settings using Finnish and Portuguese for illustration where the Wiktionary data is about an order of magnitude smaller.

| Word (language) | Morph. Class | Pron. | LS | LP |
|---|---|---|---|---|
| masseuses (fr) | n-f-pl | /ma.søz/ | masseur | /ma.sœʁ/ |
| fagylaltozom (hu) | v-fp-s-in-pr-id | /ˈfɒɟlɒltozom/ | fagylaltozik | /ˈfɒɟlɒltozik/ |

Table 1: Example annotated entries. (v-fp-s-in-pr-id: Verb, first-person singular indicative present indefinite)

We keep 20% of the pronunciation lexicons aside for evaluation using word error rate (WER) metric. WER measures an output as correct if the entire output pronunciation sequence matches the ground truth annotation for the test example.

#### 3.1.1 Morphological category

The morphological category of the word is appended as an ordinal encoding to the spelling, separated by a special character. That is, the categories of a given language are appended as unique integers, as opposed to one-hot vectors which may be too large in morphologically rich languages.

#### 3.1.2 Lemma spelling and pronounciation

Information about the lemma is given to the models by appending both, the lemma pronounciation ⟨LP⟩ and lemma spelling ⟨LS⟩ to the word spelling ⟨WS⟩, all separated by special characters, like, ⟨WS⟩§⟨LP⟩¶⟨LS⟩. Lemma spelling can potentially help in irregular cases, for example 'be' has past forms 'gone' and 'were', so the model can reject the lemma pronunciation in this case by noting that the lemma spellings are different (but potentially still use it for 'been').

### 3.2 Model details

The models described below are implemented in OpenNMT (Klein et al., 2017).

[2]kaikki.org/dictionary/

#### 3.2.1 Bidirectional LSTM networks

LSTM (Hochreiter and Schmidhuber, 1997) allows learning of fixed length sequences, which is not a major problem for pronunciation prediction since grapheme and phoneme sequences (represented as one-hot vectors) are often of comparable length, and in fact state-of-the-art accuracies can be obtained using bidirectional LSTM (Rao et al., 2015). We use single layer BiLSTM encoder - decoder with 256 units and 0.2 dropout to build a character level RNN. Each character is represented by a trainable embedding of dimension 30.

#### 3.2.2 LSTM based encoder-decoder networks with attention (BiLSTM+Attn)

Attention-based models (Vaswani et al., 2017; Chan et al., 2016; Luong et al., 2015; Xu et al., 2015) are capable of taking a weighted sample of input, allowing the network to focus on different possibly distant relevant segments of the input effectively to predict the output. We use the model defined in Section 3.2.1 with Luong attention (Luong et al., 2015).

#### 3.2.3 Transformer networks

Transformer (Vaswani et al., 2017) uses self-attention in both encoder and decoder to learn rich text representaions. We use a similar architecture but with fewer parameters, by using 3 layers, 256 hidden units, 4 attention heads and 1024 dimensional feed forward layers with relu activation. Both the attention and feedforward dropout is 0.1. The input character embedding dimension is 30.

### 3.3 Transfer learning for low resource G2P

Both non-neural and neural approaches have been studied for transfer learning (Weiss et al., 2016) from a high-resource language for low resource language G2P setting using a variety of strategies including semi-automated bootstrapping, using acoustic data, designing representations suitable for neural learning, active learning, data augmentation and multilingual modeling (Maskey et al., 2004; Davel and Martirosian, 2009; Jyothi and Hasegawa-Johnson, 2017; Sharma, 2018; Ryan and Hulden, 2020; Peters et al., 2017; Gorman et al., 2020). Recently, transformer-based architectures have also been used for this task (Engelhart et al., 2021). Here we apply a similar approach of using representations learned from the high-resource languages as an additional input for low-resource models but for our BiLSTM+Attn architecture. We

| **Model** | Inputs | *en* | *fr* | *ru* | *es* | *hu* |
|---|---|---|---|---|---|---|
| **BiLSTM** | (b/+c/+l) | (39.7/39.4/37.1) | (8.69/8.94/7.94) | (5.26/4.87/5.60) | (1.13/1.44/1.30) | (6.96/5.85/7.21) |
| **BiLSTM+Attn** | (b/+c/+l) | (36.9/36.1/**31.0**) | (4.45/4.20/**4.12**) | (5.06/**3.80**/4.04) | (0.32/0.32/**0.29**) | (1.78/1.31/**1.12**) |
| **Transformer** | (b/+c/+l) | (40.2/39.3/37.7) | (8.19/7.11/10.6) | (6.57/6.38/5.36) | (2.29/1.62/2.20) | (8.20/4.93/8.11) |

Table 2: Models and their Word Error Rates (WERs). 'b' corresponds to baseline (vanilla G2P), '+c' refers to morphology class injection (Sec. 3.1.1) and '+l' to addition of lemma spelling and pronunciation (Sec. 3.1.2).

evaluate our model for two language pairs — *hu* (high) - *fi* (low) and *es* (high) and *pt* (low) (results in Table 3). We perform morphology injection using lemma spelling and pronunciation (Sec. 3.1.2) since it can be easier to annotate and potentially more effective (per Table 2). *fi* and *pt* are not really low-resource, but have relatively fewer Wiktionary annotations for the lexical forms (Table 5).

| **Model** | *fi* | *fi+hu* | *pt* | *pt+es* |
|---|---|---|---|---|
| **BiLSTM+Attn** (base) | 18.53 | 9.81 | 62.65 | 58.87 |
| **BiLSTM+Attn** (+lem) | 9.27 | **8.45** | 59.63 | **55.48** |

Table 3: Transfer learning for vanilla G2P (base) and morphology augmented G2P (+lem, Sec. 3.1.2).

## 4 Discussion

We discuss our results under two themes — the efficacy of the different neural models we have implemented, and the effect of the different ways of injecting morphology that were considered.

We consider three neural models as described above. To compare the neural models, we first note the approximate number of parameters of each model that we trained:

- BiLSTM: ~1.7M parameters,
- BiLSTM+Attn: ~3.5M parameters,
- Transformer: ~5.2M parameters.

For BiLSTM and BiLSTM+Attn, the parameter size is based on neural architecture search i.e. we estimated sizes at which accuracies (nearly) peaked. For transformer, we believe even larger models can be more effective and the current size was chosen due to computational restrictions and for "fairer" comparison of model effectiveness. Under this setting, BiLSTM+Attn models seem to clearly outperform both the other models, even without morphology injection (cf. Gorman et al. (2020), albeit it is in the multilingual modeling context). Transformer can beat BiLSTM in some cases even with the suboptimal model size restriction, but is consistently worse when the sequence lengths are larger which is the case when we inject lemma spellings and pronunciations.

We also look at how adding lexical form information, i.e. morphological class and lemma, helps with pronunciation prediction. We notice that the improvements are particularly prominent when the G2P task itself is more complex, for example in English. In particular, ambiguous or exceptional grapheme subsequence (e.g. `ough` in English) to phoneme subsequence mappings, may be resolved with help from lemma pronunciations. Also morphological category seems to help for example in Russian where it can contain a lot of information due to the inherent morphological complexity (about 25% relative error reduction). See Appendix B for more detailed comparison and error analysis for the models.

Our transfer learning experiments indicate that morphology injection gives even more gains in low resource setting. In fact for both the languages considered, adding morphology gives almost as much gain as adding a high resource language to the BiLSTM+Attn model. This could be useful for low resource languages like Georgian where a high resource language from the same language family is unavailable. Even with the high resource augmentation, using morphology can give a significant further boost to the prediction accuracy.

## 5 Conclusion

We note that combining BiLSTM with attention seems to be the most attractive alternative in getting improvements in pronunciation prediction by leveraging morphology, and hence correspond to the most appropriate 'model bias' for the problem from among the alternatives considered. We also note that all the neural network paradigms discussed are capable of improving the G2P prediction quality when augmented with morphological information. Since our approach can potentially support partial/incomplete data (using appropriate ⟨`MISSING`⟩ or ⟨`N/A`⟩ tokens), one can use a single model which injects morphology class and/or lemma pronunciation as available. For languages where neither is available, our results suggest building word-lemma lists or utilizing effective lemmatizers (Faruqui et al., 2015; Cotterell et al., 2016).

## 6 Future work

Our work only leverages the inflectional morphology paradigms for better pronunciation prediction. However in addition to inflection, morphology also results in word formation via derivation and compounding. Unlike inflection, derivation and compounding could involve multiple root words, so an extension would need a generalization of the above approach along with appropriate data. An alternative would be to learn these in an unsupervised way using a dictionary augmented neural network which can efficiently refer to pronunciations in a dictionary and use them to predict pronunciations of polymorphemic words using pronunciations of the base words (Bruguier et al., 2018). It would be interesting to see if using a combination of morphological side information and dictionary-augmentation results in a further accuracy boost. Developing non-neural approaches for the morphology injection could be interesting, although as noted before, the neural approaches are the state-of-the-art (Rao et al., 2015; Gorman et al., 2020).

One interesting application of the present work would be to use the more accurate pronunciation prediction for morphologically related forms for efficient pronunciation lexicon development (useful for low resource languages where high-coverage lexicons currently don't exist), for example annotating the lemma pronunciation should be enough and the pronunciation of all the related forms can be predicted with high accuracy. This is hugely beneficial for languages where there are hundreds or even thousands of surface forms associated with the same lemma. Another concern for reliably using the neural approaches is explainability (Molnar, 2019). Some recent research looks at explaining neural models with orthographic and phonological features (Sahai and Sharma, 2021), an extension for morphological features should be useful.

## References


Antoine Bruguier, Anton Bakhtin, and Dravyansh Sharma. 2018. Dictionary Augmented Sequence-to-Sequence Neural Network for Grapheme to Phoneme prediction. *Proc. Interspeech 2018*, pages 3733–3737.

William Chan, Navdeep Jaitly, Quoc Le, and Oriol Vinyals. 2016. Listen, attend and spell: A neural network for large vocabulary conversational speech recognition. In *Acoustics, Speech and Signal Processing (ICASSP), 2016 IEEE International Conference on*, pages 4960–4964. IEEE.

Noam Chomsky and Morris Halle. 1968. The sound pattern of English.

Shay B Cohen and Noah A Smith. 2007. Joint morphological and syntactic disambiguation. In *Proceedings of the 2007 Joint Conference on Empirical Methods in Natural Language Processing and Computational Natural Language Learning (EMNLP-CoNLL)*.

Cecil H Coker, Kenneth W Church, and Maik Y Liberman. 1991. Morphology and rhyming: Two powerful alternatives to letter-to-sound rules for speech synthesis. In *The ESCA Workshop on Speech Synthesis*.

Ryan Cotterell, Christo Kirov, John Sylak-Glassman, David Yarowsky, Jason Eisner, and Mans Hulden. 2016. The SIGMORPHON 2016 shared task—morphological reinflection. In *Proceedings of the 14th SIGMORPHON Workshop on Computational Research in Phonetics, Phonology, and Morphology*, pages 10–22.

Marelie Davel and Olga Martirosian. 2009. Pronunciation dictionary development in resource-scarce environments.

Vera Demberg, Helmut Schmid, and Gregor Möhler. 2007. Phonological constraints and morphological preprocessing for grapheme-to-phoneme conversion. In *Proceedings of the 45th Annual Meeting of the Association of Computational Linguistics*, pages 96–103.

Eric Engelhart, Mahsa Elyasi, and Gaurav Bharaj. 2021. Grapheme-to-Phoneme Transformer Model for Transfer Learning Dialects. *arXiv preprint arXiv:2104.04091*.

Marina Ermolaeva. 2018. Extracting morphophonology from small corpora. In *Proceedings of the Fifteenth Workshop on Computational Research in Phonetics, Phonology, and Morphology*, pages 167–175.

Daan van Esch, Mason Chua, and Kanishka Rao. 2016. Predicting Pronunciations with Syllabification and Stress with Recurrent Neural Networks. In *INTERSPEECH*, pages 2841–2845.

Manaal Faruqui, Yulia Tsvetkov, Graham Neubig, and Chris Dyer. 2015. Morphological inflection generation using character sequence to sequence learning. *arXiv preprint arXiv:1512.06110*.

Kyle Gorman, Lucas FE Ashby, Aaron Goyzueta, Arya D McCarthy, Shijie Wu, and Daniel You. 2020. The SIGMORPHON 2020 shared task on multilingual grapheme-to-phoneme conversion. In *Proceedings of the 17th SIGMORPHON Workshop on Computational Research in Phonetics, Phonology, and Morphology*, pages 40–50.

Alex Graves and Navdeep Jaitly. 2014. Towards end-to-end speech recognition with recurrent neural networks. In *International Conference on Machine Learning*, pages 1764–1772.

Sepp Hochreiter and Jürgen Schmidhuber. 1997. Long short-term memory. *Neural computation*, 9(8):1735–1780.

Cassandra L Jacobs and Fred Mailhot. 2019. Encoder-decoder models for latent phonological representations of words. In *Proceedings of the 16th Workshop on Computational Research in Phonetics, Phonology, and Morphology*, pages 206–217.

Preethi Jyothi and Mark Hasegawa-Johnson. 2017. Low-resource grapheme-to-phoneme conversion using recurrent neural networks. In *2017 IEEE International Conference on Acoustics, Speech and Signal Processing (ICASSP)*, pages 5030–5034. IEEE.

Ronald M Kaplan and Martin Kay. 1994. Regular models of phonological rule systems. *Computational linguistics*, 20(3):331–378.

Guillaume Klein, Yoon Kim, Yuntian Deng, Jean Senellart, and Alexander Rush. 2017. OpenNMT: Open-source toolkit for neural machine translation. In *Proceedings of ACL 2017, System Demonstrations*, pages 67–72, Vancouver, Canada. Association for Computational Linguistics.

Kimmo Koskenniemi. 1983. Two-Level Model for Morphological Analysis. In *IJCAI*, volume 83, pages 683–685.

Karen Livescu, Preethi Jyothi, and Eric Fosler-Lussier. 2016. Articulatory feature-based pronunciation modeling. *Computer Speech & Language*, 36:212–232.

Minh-Thang Luong, Hieu Pham, and Christopher D Manning. 2015. Effective Approaches to Attention-based Neural Machine Translation. In *Proceedings of the 2015 Conference on Empirical Methods in Natural Language Processing*, pages 1412–1421.

Sameer Maskey, Alan Black, and Laura Tomokiya. 2004. Boostrapping phonetic lexicons for new languages. In *Eighth International Conference on Spoken Language Processing*.

Christoph Molnar. 2019. *Interpretable Machine Learning*. `https://christophm.github.io/interpretable-ml-book/`.

Garrett Nicolai, Kyle Gorman, and Ryan Cotterell. 2020. Proceedings of the 17th SIGMORPHON Workshop on Computational Research in Phonetics, Phonology, and Morphology. In *Proceedings of the 17th SIGMORPHON Workshop on Computational Research in Phonetics, Phonology, and Morphology*.

Ben Peters, Jon Dehdari, and Josef van Genabith. 2017. Massively Multilingual Neural Grapheme-to-Phoneme Conversion. *EMNLP 2017*, page 19.

Kanishka Rao, Fuchun Peng, Haşim Sak, and Françoise Beaufays. 2015. Grapheme-to-phoneme conversion using long short-term memory recurrent neural networks. In *Acoustics, Speech and Signal Processing (ICASSP), 2015 IEEE International Conference on*, pages 4225–4229. IEEE.

Zach Ryan and Mans Hulden. 2020. Data augmentation for transformer-based G2P. In *Proceedings of the 17th SIGMORPHON Workshop on Computational Research in Phonetics, Phonology, and Morphology*, pages 184–188.

Saumya Sahai and Dravyansh Sharma. 2021. Predicting and explaining french grammatical gender. In *Proceedings of the Third Workshop on Computational Typology and Multilingual NLP*, pages 90–96.

Dravyansh Sharma. 2018. On Training and Evaluation of Grapheme-to-Phoneme Mappings with Limited Data. *Proc. Interspeech 2018*, pages 2858–2862.

Dravyansh Sharma, Melissa Wilson, and Antoine Bruguier. 2019. Better Morphology Prediction for Better Speech Systems. In *INTERSPEECH*, pages 3535–3539.

Pavel Sofroniev and Çağrı Çöltekin. 2018. Phonetic vector representations for sound sequence alignment. In *Proceedings of the Fifteenth Workshop on Computational Research in Phonetics, Phonology, and Morphology*, pages 111–116.

Jose Sotelo, Soroush Mehri, Kundan Kumar, Joao Felipe Santos, Kyle Kastner, Aaron Courville, and Yoshua Bengio. 2017. Char2wav: End-to-end speech synthesis.

Ilya Sutskever, Oriol Vinyals, and Quoc V Le. 2014. Sequence to sequence learning with neural networks. *arXiv preprint arXiv:1409.3215*.

Jason Taylor and Korin Richmond. 2020. Enhancing Sequence-to-Sequence Text-to-Speech with Morphology. *Submitted to IEEE ICASSP*.

Ashish Vaswani, Noam Shazeer, Niki Parmar, Jakob Uszkoreit, Llion Jones, Aidan N Gomez, Łukasz Kaiser, and Illia Polosukhin. 2017. Attention is all you need. In *Proceedings of the 31st International Conference on Neural Information Processing Systems*, pages 6000–6010.

Karl Weiss, Taghi M Khoshgoftaar, and DingDing Wang. 2016. A survey of transfer learning. *Journal of Big data*, 3(1):1–40.

Kelvin Xu, Jimmy Ba, Ryan Kiros, Kyunghyun Cho, Aaron Courville, Ruslan Salakhudinov, Rich Zemel, and Yoshua Bengio. 2015. Show, attend and tell: Neural image caption generation with visual attention. In *International conference on machine learning*, pages 2048–2057.

| **Model** | Inputs | en | de | es | ru | avg. rel. gain |
|---|---|---|---|---|---|---|
| **BiLSTM** | (b/+c/+l) | (31.0/30.5/25.2) | (17.7/15.5/12.3) | (8.1/7.9/6.7) | (18.4/15.6/15.9) | (-/+7.9%/+20.0%) |
| **BiLSTM+Attn** | (b/+c/+l) | (29.0/27.1/21.3) | (12.0/11.6/11.6) | (4.9/2.6/2.4) | (14.1/13.6/13.1) | (-/+15.1%/+22.0%) |

Table 4: Number of total Wiktionary entries, and inflected entries with pronunciation and morphology annotations, for the languages considered.

# Appendix

## A On size of data

We record the size of data scraped from Wiktionary in Table 5. There is marked inconsistency in the number of annotated inflected words where the pronunciation transcription is available, as a fraction of the total vocabulary, for the languages considered.

In the main paper, we have discussed results on the publicly available Wiktionary dataset. We perform more experiments on a larger dataset ($10^5$-$10^6$ examples of annotated inflections per language) using the same data format and methodology for (American) English, German, Spanish and Russian (Table 4). We get very similar observations in this regime as well in terms of relative gains in model performances using our techniques, but these results are likely more representative of word error rates for the whole languages.

| Language | Total senses | Annotated inflections |
|---|---|---|
| en | 1.25M | 7543 |
| es | 0.93M | 28495 |
| fi | 0.24M | 3663 |
| fr | 0.46M | 24062 |
| hu | 77.7K | 31486 |
| pt | 0.39M | 2647 |
| ru | 0.47M | 20558 |

Table 5: Number of total Wiktionary entries, and inflected entries with pronunciation and morphology annotations, for the languages considered.

## B Error analysis

Neural sequence to sequence models, while highly accurate on average, make "silly" mistakes like omitting or inserting a phoneme which are hard to explain. With that caveat in place, there are still reasonable patterns to be gleaned when comparing the outputs of the various neural models discussed here. BiLSTM+Attn model seems to not only be making fewer of these "silly" mistakes, but also appears to be better at learning the genuinely more challenging predictions. For example, the French word *pédagogiques* ('pedagogical', plural) /pe.da.gɔ.ʒik/ is pronounced correctly by BiLSTM+Attn, but as /pe.da.ʒɔ.ʒik/ by BiLSTM. Similarly BiLSTM+Attn predicts /ˈdʒæmɪŋ/, while Transformer network says /ˈdʒamɪŋ/ for *jamming* (en). We note that errors for Spanish often involve incorrect stress assignment since the grapheme-to-phoneme mapping is highly consistent.

Adding morphological class information seems to reduce the error in endings for morphologically rich languages, which can be an important source of error if there is relative scarcity of transcriptions available for the inflected words. For example, for our BiLSTM+Attn model, the pronunciation for фуррем (ru, 'furry' instrumental singular noun) is fixed from /ˈfurʲːem/ to /ˈfurʲːɪm/, and *koronavírusról* (hu, 'coronavirus' delative singular) gets corrected from /ˈkoronɒviːruʃoːl/ to /ˈkoronɒviːruʃroːl/. On the other hand, adding lemma pronunciation usually helps with pronouncing the root morpheme correctly. Without the lemma injection, our BiLSTM+Attn model mispronounces *debriefing* (en) as /dɪˈbɹiːfɪŋ/ and *sentences* (en) as /sɛnˈtɛnsɪz/. Based on these observations, it sounds interesting to try to inject both categorical and lemma information simultaneously.

# Author Index

**Association for Computational Linguistics**
209 N. Eighth Street
Stroudsburg, Pennsylvania 18360

ISBN 978-1-7138-3385-7

CURRAN ASSOCIATES INC.
proceedings.com